LANDSCAPE PLANTS
FOR
EASTERN NORTH
AMERICA

LANDSCAPE PLANTS
FOR
EASTERN NORTH
AMERICA

Exclusive of Florida
and the
Immediate Gulf Coast

HARRISON L. FLINT
Purdue University

Drawings by

Jenny M. Lyverse

A Wiley-Interscience Publication
JOHN WILEY & SONS
New York • Chichester • Brisbane • Toronto • Singapore

Library of Congress Cataloging in Publication Data

Flint, Harrison L. (Harrison Leigh), 1929–
    Landscape plants for eastern North America.

    "A Wiley-Interscience publication."
    Includes indexes.
    1. Ornamental woody plants—United States. 2. Ground
cover plants—United States. 3. Landscape gardening—
United States. 4. Ornamental woody plants—Canada.
5. Ground cover plants—Canada. 6. Landscape gardening
—Canada. I. Lyverse, Jenny M. II. Title. III. Title:
Eastern North America.

SB435.5.F55 1982   635.9′7   82-16068
ISBN 0-471-86905-8

Printed in the United States of America

10 9 8 7 6 5

To my students

PREFACE

It is my intention that this book serve two primary functions. First, it is a source of selection-related information about landscape plants useful within the stated geographical limits, for landscape designers and others having responsibility for the selection of landscape plants. Second, it is a text and reference book for students of horticulture and landscape architecture who are building their knowledge of landscape plant materials. Its distinctiveness lies in its orientation to the design-related selection process, its broad geographical coverage, and the distinctiveness of its illustrations.

Since identification and selection of landscape plants are largely separate functions, information on plant identification has been omitted deliberately, although some of the photographs will be of incidental use for this purpose. Moreover, little or no attempt has been made to deal with botanical systematics other than when interrelatedness of plants impinges on the selection process or when it is necessary for nomenclatural clarity.

Botanical nomenclature follows that of *Hortus Third* (New York: Macmillan, 1976) in most instances, with rare departures to acknowledge different authorities or more recent treatment. The same has been done with family names; even though this is not always consistent with most recent phylogenetic treatment, it is presently the path of least confusion for most readers. This book has been written for professional landscape architects and plantsmen, but at the same time a serious attempt has been made to minimize specialized botanical terms and other technical jargon so that serious amateurs might find it useful as well.

I have worked in the northeastern and midwestern United States and have studied and photographed landscape plants throughout most of the geographical area covered by this book. But I also rely heavily on the expertise and local and regional experience of many knowledgeable amateur and professional plantsmen throughout the region.

A complete acknowledgment of help received would be most difficult, since a great many colleagues, teachers, and former students have had a hand in this book. But there is a smaller, special group of people who have tolerated my incessant questioning over a substantial number of years and whose patient answers have contributed in a major way to my education and to the content of this book. They include Fred M. Abbey, North Ferrisburgh, Vermont; Jack W. Caddick, Kingston, Rhode Island; Eugene Cline, Canton, Georgia; John F. Cornman, Ithaca, New York; W. A. Cumming, Morden, Manitoba; Tom Dodd, Jr., Semmes, Alabama; Alfred J. Fordham, Westwood, Massachusetts; Edward R. Hasselkus, Madison, Wisconsin; Case Hoogendoorn, Middletown, Rhode Island; E. J. Horder, Mobile, Alabama; the late Alfred Johnson, St. Paul, Minnesota; Clarence E. Lewis, East Lansing, Michigan; J. C. McDaniel, Urbana, Illinois; and Robert G. Mower, Ithaca, New York.

I am indebted to others for ideas gained by reading their writings and in most instances through personal conversation as well: A. R. Buckley, Ottawa, Canada; Michael A. Dirr, Athens, Georgia; Fred Galle, Pine Mountain, Georgia; the late Donald Hoag, Fargo, North Dakota; Richard Jaynes, New Haven, Connecticut; Neil G. Odenwald, Baton Rouge, Louisiana; Lawrence Sherk, Etobicoke, Ontario; the late F. L. Skinner, Dropmore, Manitoba; Brooks Wigginton, Wheeling, West Virginia; Donald Wyman, Weston, Massachusetts; and others.

Special appreciation goes to Ruth V. Kvaalen, who reviewed the manuscript in great detail and contributed many suggestions, especially concerning nomenclature. Additional suggestions on the text were made by Jenny M. (Lyverse) Smith, whose illustrations have also given this book distinctive character. The manuscript was thoroughly reviewed at completion by Edward R. Hasselkus, Henry P. Orr, Harry Ponder, Lawrence G. Sherk, and Brooks Wigginton, whose efforts I greatly appreciate.

Assistance with unappealing tasks such as proofreading of typescript and general encouragement were given by Elsie S. Flint, John H. Flint, and Sarah B. Lowe.

Photographs on pages 32 and 343 were furnished, respectively, by Sarah B. Lowe and Theodore D. Walker. Other photographs are my own.

Finally, the encouragement of my colleagues at Purdue University and that of the University administration in providing a climate conducive to activities such as this is greatly appreciated.

It may be true that no book is ever finished. Revised editions regularly contain information and insights not included in first writings. I welcome suggestions and criticisms toward this end.

HARRISON L. FLINT

West Lafayette, Indiana
December 1982

CONTENTS

INTRODUCTION

Purpose of the Book

The selection of landscape plants is a two-part process involving development of a bank of information on site requirements and landscape characteristics of prospective plant choices together with a creative process of matching plant traits with design needs. Some designers meticulously follow an orderly sequence of steps leading to selection, whereas others work more informally and intuitively. Whether the process is orderly and stepwise or seemingly random, planting designers all need a basic fund of information with which to begin the design process. This book is intended to fill that need.

Content of the Book

SCOPE

This book is useful in most of eastern North America, southward to about 30° north latitude (Baton Rouge, Louisiana; Mobile, Alabama; Tallahassee, Florida) and westward to central Manitoba and the western boundaries of Minnesota, Iowa, Missouri, Arkansas, and Louisiana, or approximately 96−98° west longitude. Species included are mostly trees, shrubs, and woody vines and groundcovers, but some herbaceous groundcover plants are included since they are functional landscape plants.

Inclusion of information on 500 primary species and twice that number of related species in a single book precludes comprehensive treatment. And relating that information to a land area of more than a million square miles precludes a high degree of geographical resolution. But the outlines on specific plants that follow will serve as a reminder of many important characteristics and site requirements, as well as a starting place for more detailed study. Additional information can be obtained from local and regional publications on landscape plants and native flora as well as from nurserymen, landscape designers, contractors, and other professionals with local experience.

PRIMARY AND SECONDARY SPECIES

Decisions as to primary and secondary, or "related species," status are based on several considerations.

1. As a general rule, in spite of the following exceptions, the primary species is closely related to the related species listed under it and generally preferred over them, more commonly used, or more easily available.

2. When several species are similar in most of their characteristics and requirements, usually only one has been given primary status, even though those relegated to related species status sometimes are more important landscape plants than other species that have received primary status. For example, *Betula papyrifera* (paper birch) and *B. pendula* (European white birch) are so similar in general effect and requirements that it would be repetitious to give both primary status. Because of this, *B. pendula* is treated as a related species even though it is more important in our area than *Betula lenta* (sweet birch), which is given primary status because of its distinctness.

3. When there is little to recommend either of two similar species, one native and the other exotic (nonnative), over the other, the native species usually is given primary status and the exotic treated as a related species, (illustrated by the case of *Betula papyrifera* and *B. pendula*).

4. Included in the related species category are species of different genera related within a family to the primary species. For example, inclusion of *Broussonetia papyrifera* (paper mulberry) under *Morus alba* (white mulberry).

In some instances, species treated as related species are not very closely related botanically. For example, *Euphorbia cyparissias* is listed under *Sedum*, a member of the Crassulaceae, only because of similarity in site requirements and landscape function. In another instance, *Cliftonia* and *Cyrilla*, members of the Cyrillaceae, are treated as related species under

Clethra even though they belong not only to different families but even different taxonomic orders. The relationship here is one of function and landscape character rather than botanical

relationship. It should not be assumed that related species are invariably closely related botanically to the primary species under which they are listed, even though that usually is the case.

Nomenclature

SCIENTIFIC NAMES

Botanical or scientific names are called *binomials* because they consist of two names. The first name, always initially capitalized, is the *genus* (plural *genera*) name, describing the kind of plant, for instance, maple (*Acer*), dogwood (*Cornus*), or yew (*Taxus*). The second name, never capitalized in most modern usage, is the *species* (plural also *species*) name, describing the individual type within the kind, for instance, red maple (*Acer rubrum*), flowering dogwood (*Cornus florida*), or Japanese yew (*Taxus cuspidata*). In technical writings, a third name or abbreviation designating the author of the binomial is added to it. In the context of this book, the usefulness of author designations is deemed insufficient to justify their inclusion.

Plant species sometimes are subdivided into lesser categories of *subspecies* (ssp.), *variety* (var.), and *forma* (f.). These names, when applicable, are appended to the binomial following the appropriate abbreviation: for instance, *Acer saccharum* ssp. *floridanum* (Florida sugar maple), *Rhododendron catawbiense* var. *album* (white-flowered Catawba rhododendron), and *Cercis canadensis* f. *alba* (white-flowered redbud). Subspecies and varieties (not to be confused with horticultural varieties or cultivars) occur as natural subpopulations within species populations, having their own geographic ranges and tending to breed true to type, whereas forms are more or less individual occurrences, sometimes repeated, appearing randomly rather than in a geographical pattern, and usually not breeding true. Since many forms tend to be reproduced in cultivation more than in nature, they are often given cultivar names, sometimes identical with old form names except for the notation used (see Cultivars). For instance, *Cercis canadensis* f. *alba* is often listed as *Cercis canadensis* 'Alba.' This practice is confusing, and not recommended, but it does occur.

SYNONYMS

In botanical nomenclature, a synonym is an illegitimate botanical name, incorrect either in form or application. Therefore it is not acceptable to interchange it with the correct name, as is true for synonyms outside of scientific context. Legitimacy of botanical names is determined by application of the International Code of Botanical Nomenclature (ICBN), an agreement among botanists around the world. Since plant classification and nomenclature is an ongoing field of scientific inquiry, names that previously have been considered correct sometimes must be discarded in the face of new evidence and replaced by different names. When this happens, the previously accepted name becomes a synonym. Since there usually is a great time lag between such name changes and their commercial acceptance, many synonyms are still in use in nursery catalogs. To reduce the resulting confusion, such commonly used synonyms are listed here following the corresponding correct name.

CULTIVARS

The *cultivar*, derived from "cultivated variety," is the taxonomic unit of cultivated plant nomenclature. Cultivated plants are subject to the same rules of botanical nomenclature that wild plants are, and additionally to a separate set of regulations governing the naming of cultivars, the International Code of Nomenclature for Cultivated Plants (ICNCP). Cultivars, unlike botanical categories, are not italicized in printed text and are either enclosed in single quotation marks or preceded by the abbreviation cv. For example, compact winged euonymus can be written either *Euonymus alata* 'Compacta' or *Euonymus alata* cv. Compacta. Cultivar names are always initially capitalized, and those named since January 1, 1959 must be written in the vernacular of the country of origin, although Latinized cultivar names may be accepted as correct if they were applied before that date.

Occasionally two or more cultivar names are applied to the same clone or to plants too similar to justify their separation. There are ways of determining which cultivar name should receive priority, but they are sometimes uncertain and usually tedious. In part because of the difficulty in dealing with cultivated plant nomenclature, cultivars have received relatively little attention from plant taxonomists. Consequently, when synonymous cultivar names are listed here, no implication of priority or legitimacy is intended, even though the cultivar name used by the author usually appears first.

COMMON NAMES

Common names are simply colloquial names in more or less common usage, but there is a tendency in some writings to coin appropriate vernacular names in cases where a common name is not known to be in use. This causes confusion, so an attempt has been made here to resist the impulse to coin new common names

and as much as possible to use names that are known or thought to be in common usage.

It should be emphasized that, in general, common names are not arbitrated by either national or international bodies, and so there are no "correct" or "incorrect" common names in the same sense as scientific names. An exception is that the forestry profession in the United States has agreed to specific common names for a few important forest species.

PLANT PATENTS

New cultivars can be patented in much the same way as devices and processes, and for the same time period: 17 years. A considerable number of the plants included here have been under patents that have since expired. Others still under patent at this writing are indicated by patent number and year assigned. Plants under patent cannot be propagated legally except under license from the patent holder, but patents impose no restrictions on landscape use of plants obtained from legitimate sources.

Plant Size Groups

Several decades ago a size-group numbering system was devised by the late Professor Ralph W. Curtis of Cornell University. This system has been adopted by a generation of Curtis' former students, some of whom are now teachers in the area of landscape plant materials, and at least one additional generation, including the present author. For the purposes of this book, the Curtis

system has been modified by (a) converting to the metric system, (b) eliminating gaps between numbers, and (c) adding a category to classify tree sizes more closely. The modified version used here is outlined in Table 1. These numbers, appended to the scientific name of the species listed, give a quick reference to functional size.

Geographic Ranges

NATIVE RANGE

Natural plant species grow wild in well-defined areas. These may coincide closely with the areas where the species are adapted to landscape use, as with *Cornus florida* (flowering dogwood). But native range limits depend on other factors that do not limit landscape use such as the ability to reproduce naturally without human help. Because of this, many species can be used far outside their native ranges. An extreme example is *Taxodium distichum* (bald cypress), confined

by its reproductive needs to areas near watercourses in the Deep South and northward on the Atlantic Coast to southern Delaware and in the Mississippi basin to southwestern Indiana, but successfully used in landscape plantings in many upland areas, some at least 400 miles north of its northernmost native stands. In spite of such discrepancies between natural and useful ranges, knowledge of the natural range of a native species can be useful in predicting its adaptability to landscape use. Sensitive designers and plantsmen

Table 1. Plant Size Group Designations

| Size Group Number | Height | | Human Scale | Description |
	Meters	Approximate Equivalent (ft)		
1		Depends partially on support provided		Climber
2	to. 0.5	to 1½	Ankle height	Groundcover
3	0.5−1	1½−3	Knee height	Dwarf shrub
4	1−2	3−6½	Chest height	Small shrub
5	2−4	6½−13	Overhead	Medium shrub
6	4−8	13−26	Overhead	Large shrub or small tree
7	8−16	26−52	Overhead	Medium tree
8	16+	52+	Overhead	Large tree

will look closely at native habitats, observing their extent and character, in predicting performance of landscape plants.

Native ranges of species from other parts of the world often are not known with as much resolution as those from eastern North America, but they can be useful in predicting the success of those species in our area if the native range is known to have a climate that is more or less analogous to that of the area in which the landscape site is located. For example, the climate of Manchuria is similar enough to that of much of the northeastern United States and adjacent Canada that many Manchurian species are well adapted to this area.

Some landscape plants have no native range because they have arisen by hybridization of other species. Such hybrid species are given a collective name, indicated as a species name preceded by "×," as in *Berberis* ×*mentorensis* (Mentor barberry), which is not a species but rather a collection of all hybrids of *B. julianae* (wintergreen barberry) × *B. thunbergii* (Japanese barberry).

USEFUL RANGE

The area in which a particular plant species is adapted to landscape use is defined primarily by

plant hardiness zones, which are based on average annual minimum temperatures. Several different hardiness zone maps have been published. Since they differ in numbering systems, it is essential to use plant hardiness zone ratings only with the map that was used in assigning the ratings. The map used in assigning plant ratings in this book is that prepared at the U.S. National Arboretum and published by the U.S. Department of Agriculture* (Figure I-1).

To define useful range only by hardiness zones is convenient but a great oversimplification. Even though temperature may be the dominant factor determining useful range, other components of climate and soils play important roles in limiting the useful ranges of many species. Often more detailed information on soil and climate is available from state, provincial, or federal agricultural research stations or extension services. Such information, as well as the advice of experienced local plantsmen, can add greatly to a designer's confidence in specifying plant material.

Plant Hardiness Zone Map, Misc. Pub. No. 814, Agr. Res. Service, U.S. Dept. of Agriculture, 1965.

Plant Function

The first consideration in selecting landscape plants is to know the purpose for which a plant is being selected. Plants function in many ways.

The functions listed under individual species are not intended to be all-inclusive but represent most common usage. Since they are described in a single word or a few words at most, they are intended to serve only as reminders. Much more information will be found in books on planting design.

Size and Habit

Plant size groups are useful for classifying plants by functional height, but size and shape are ever-changing characteristics of most landscape plants. Because of this, two form drawings are included for most of the primary species, one at an early functional size, the second at mature or ordinary maximum size for the species. It is not intended that the two drawings represent the same individual plant at different ages, in the same season, or pruned alike. In some instances, two different seasonal aspects are deliberately included. For instance, the young plant of *Chionanthus virginicus* (fringetree) is represented in flower in late spring, while the mature plant is shown in summer condition. Or, a tree that can be trained to a single or multiple trunks or a shrub that can also function as a small tree may be shown in both ways. The addition of time notations gives information about early growth

rate and at least suggests something about longevity. Oversimplification once more is necessary. Inherent variation among individuals within most woody plant species is considerable. Not all plants will look like the examples shown, and site variables can also greatly affect both growth rate and longevity. For example, street trees planted in relatively small soil pockets seldom even approach the maximum size that the same trees would reach in a lawn planting, and their useful life sometimes is shortened greatly by their environment.

Maximum sizes shown are related to plant performance in eastern North America. Trees introduced to our area from the Pacific Northwest such as *Sequoiadendron giganteum* (giant sequoia) and *Thuja plicata* (giant arborvitae) never assume the proportions that they would in their native habitats.

Adaptability

Information on site requirements is summarized in the bar graphs under each primary species. Tolerance is indicated by the blackened portion of each bar. For example, the hypothetical plant described in Figure I-2 will do well in any light condition except full shade and perhaps full sun in summer, but needs at least half shade in winter. The shaded (stippled) area in the first bar indicates qualified tolerance, and the nature of the qualification in each case is explained in the text following the bar graphs. In this case, the tolerance of full sun might hold only for part of the useful range, with light shade necessary in the South and perhaps in the Midwest. The full range of light conditions that exists in landscape sites cannot be represented adequately by a single bar graph. The difference between the full shade cast by mature tree canopies far overhead and that under the low, dense canopy of *Acer platanoides* (Norway maple), for example, is profound, and many other variations exist in landscape sites. The bar notation is useful for developing pools of plants from which to make choices for specific situations, but final selection

should be based on firsthand observation and local experience.

Our hypothetical plant tolerates little wind. The reason for this and the degree of wind tolerated in each instance is stated or implied in the accompanying text. Possible reasons include soft-wooded branches that are prone to storm damage, fragile leaves such as those of *Acer palmatum* (Japanese maple) or *Magnolia macrophylla* (bigleaf magnolia) that may be damaged by strong summer winds, or evergreen foliage that is prone to winter dehydration. Plants that are more susceptible to diseases in humid or poorly circulated air may be shown as having a requirement for wind rather than merely tolerating it.

Soil moisture tolerances also require further explanation. A bar blackened all the way to the wet end indicates a plant such as *Cephalanthus occidentalis* (buttonbush) or *Taxodium distichum* (bald cypress) that will grow in standing water for at least part of the year, and a bar blackened to about halfway between the wet end and the center, as shown in our hypothetical example,

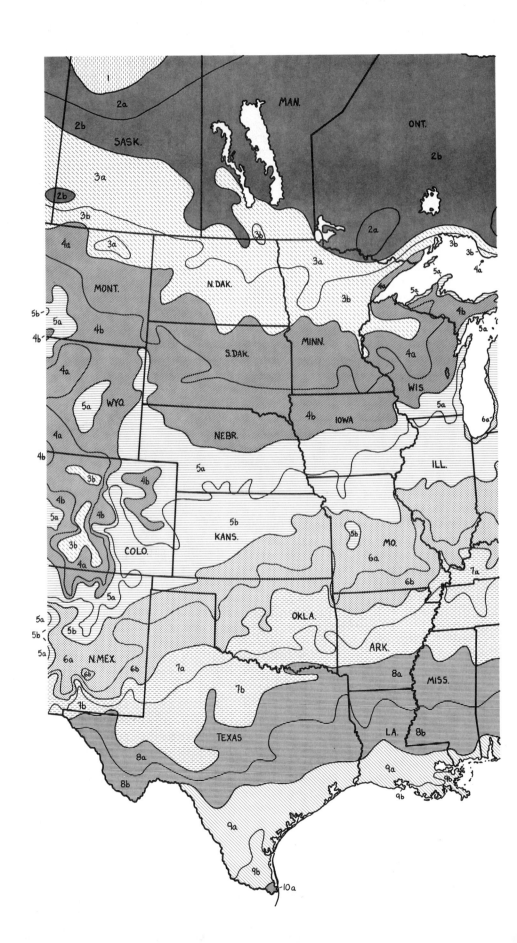

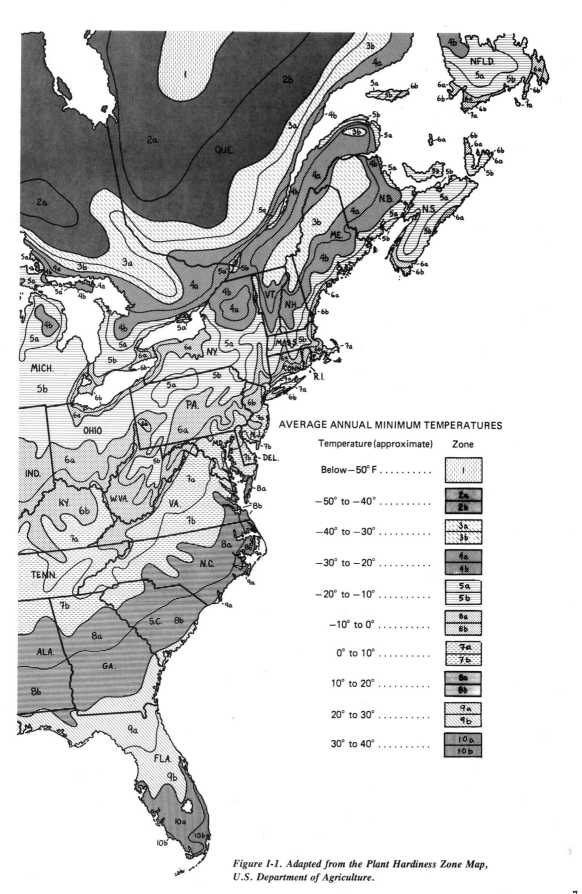

AVERAGE ANNUAL MINIMUM TEMPERATURES

Temperature (approximate)		Zone
Below −50° F		1
−50° to −40°		2a / 2b
−40° to −30°		3a / 3b
−30° to −20°		4a / 4b
−20° to −10°		5a / 5b
−10° to 0°		6a / 6b
0° to 10°		7a / 7b
10° to 20°		8a / 8b
20° to 30°		9a / 9b
30° to 40°		10a / 10b

Figure I-1. Adapted from the Plant Hardiness Zone Map,
U.S. Department of Agriculture.

can be considered to represent an "average" landscape plant, requiring good soil drainage but perhaps tolerating brief periods of flooding. A bar blackened to halfway between the center and dry end represents a plant that would tolerate occasional brief drought but not prolonged dry periods, and a bar blackened to the dry end represents a highly drought-tolerant plant. But soil moisture tolerances are seen to be even more complex than this when the differences between wet soil in a peat bog and that in a heavy clay soil are considered. As with light conditions, the bar notation is useful for initial sorting, but final selection should be based on more sophisticated appraisal of the site and prospective choices.

The final bar in Figure I-2 indicates the range of soil acidity in which our hypothetical plant can be expected to grow well. Our plant is clearly an "acid-soil" plant, performing best below pH 5.5. The largest number of such species included are members of the Ericaceae (Heath Family), but other acid-soil plants are also included. Some plants perform poorly in very acidic soil, and those that are known to have a requirement for higher soil pH are indicated. Currently available information on soil acidity requirements of landscape plants is not complete, and careful designers will rely on their own observations and other local experience rather than a simplistic comparison of a soil test with the bar notation. Soil pH is a common limiting factor in selection with only a relatively small number of species in most parts of our area, since the great majority of plants show wide tolerance of soil acidity. But for those

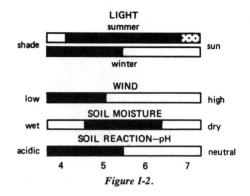

Figure I-2.

species with narrower requirements, proper soil acidity makes the difference between success and failure.

In summary, it can be seen from the bar graphs that our hypothetical species performs well in any light conditions in summer except full shade and perhaps full sun (more explanation in the text). But in winter it must be at least half shaded for protection against dehydration. It needs acidic soil (pH not exceeding 5.5) that is reasonably well drained yet not excessively dry. From this much information alone, it is apparent that this plant would be a poor choice for a windswept site or a calcareous (high limestone content) soil unless major modification of microclimate or soil were practicable.

In many instances, more detailed information or qualification about environmental tolerances will be included in the text. But the designer's accumulated experience will provide the ultimate confidence in selection of plants.

Seasonal Interest

Colorful flowers, foliage, and fruits provide obvious seasonal interest. The more subtle attractions of colorful or corky winter twigs, patterned or bicolored bark, conspicuous winter buds, and unusual form, texture, or branching patterns all contribute to a plant's character in the landscape. The creative designer will come to know plants in all seasons and will learn to combine them skillfully into a year-round, interesting landscape. This can be done without introducing strong color at any one season, if that is the objective. In any case, seasonal color perhaps should be biased by the time factor. How does one rate *Syringa vulgaris* (common lilac), for

example, with a week or two of fragrant, colorful flowers and little other seasonal interest, against a shrub such as *Cornus racemosa* (gray dogwood), which is quietly colorful over the greater part of the year?

The seasonal "clock" accompanying each primary species is intended for quick reference to duration and intensity of seasonal color. The hypothetical species represented in Figure I-3 is shown by the blackened sectors to be highly colorful or otherwise interesting in late spring and late autumn, perhaps in the form of flowers and either fruits or autumn foliage. It is mildly interesting during summer and early autumn, as

Figure 1-3.

shown by the stippled area, perhaps because its foliage has character. The absence of any shading during winter and early spring suggests that this species is not an evergreen and has no other winter interest. If it were an evergreen with undistinguished foliage it would be represented by a stipple, or if the evergreen foliage were colorful or richly textured, the entire clock face would be blackened.

Timing of the seasons obviously varies over our area, and how a season is defined is arbitrary at best. For example, *Cornus florida* (flowering dogwood) may reach its flowering peak by mid-March in the southern extremes of our area (Zone 9a), whereas trees in the northern extremes of the useful range for that species (Zone 5b) flower nearly two months later. There is a rule of thumb that spring advances about one degree of latitude every five to seven days, but this also depends upon longitude and elevation, closeness to water, and weather variations in individual years. It is probably more meaningful to delineate the seasons according to plant developmental events than by the calendar. For example, *Cornus mas* (cornelian-cherry dogwood) flowers close to April 1 in most years in Lafayette, Indiana. One could consider this the beginning of spring or instead could use the flowering of *Viburnum farreri* (fragrant viburnum), which usually comes closer to the vernal equinox at this location. Any attempt to refine the boundaries of the seasons beyond observation of phenological (developmental) events probably will result in frustration. As constant as the seasons are in the long run, they are notably fickle on an annual basis.

Problems and Maintenance

Without question, the need for maintenance is an important criterion in selecting landscape plants, and it appears to be growing in importance. But willingness and ability to provide maintenance is a highly variable characteristic of people, which any serious grower of hybrid tea roses knows. It seems that there is a place for both low-maintenance and high-maintenance landscape plants. The important thing is to know which is which and to select according to the situation. Maintenance is dealt with here only as it is related to plant selection. Detailed information on maintenance is included in other books, and can be obtained from state, provincial, or local extension service offices. It is especially important to obtain reliable, up-to-date information on the use of pesticides because of the potential hazards involved and the fact that pesticides and their regulation are subject to change.

One of the most serious limitations to plant selection is that of commercial availability. Most landscape nurseries offer a limited array of landscaped plants, and these vary from year to year. Many plants are available only from a few nurseries specializing in unusual plants or in select groups such as rhododendrons, heaths, or groundcovers. Moreover, some plants that were once unavailable are being reintroduced into commerce, and some formerly available are no longer.

Commercial availability is an ever-changing picture. Because of this and the continuous proliferation of new cultivars, planting designers who want to make effective use of the rich body of landscape plants that are available in eastern North America have no choice but to maintain a library of at least a few nursery catalogs and a ready hand on the telephone to update their information on sources as necessary.

ALPHABETICAL LIST OF PLANTS

Abelia ×grandiflora 4−5

Glossy abelia
Evergreen or semievergreen shrub
Caprifoliaceae (Honeysuckle Family)

Hybrid origin. *A. chinensis* × *A. uniflora.*

Size and Habit. Height is limited by winterkill of stems in Zones 6a−7a.

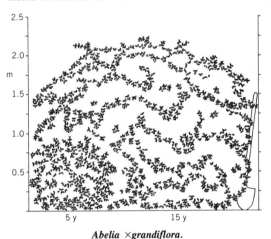

Abelia ×grandiflora.

Adaptability

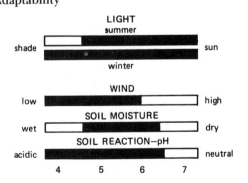

Useful Range. USDA Zones 6a−9a+.

Function. Border, facing, foundation, hedge, massing, specimen, screen (Zones 7b−9a+).

Seasonal Interest. *Flowers:* Pale pink to white, 2 cm/0.8 in. long, numerous, in leafy clusters (panicles), opening gradually through middle and late summer. *Foliage:* Glossy, evergreen

(semievergreen in Zones 6a−7a), 2.5 cm/1 in. long, fine-textured, bright to dark green, bronzing in winter.

Problems and Maintenance. Annual pruning is required to remove deadwood in Zones 6a−7a.

Cultivars. 'Edward Goucher' (hybrid of A. ×grandiflora × A. schumanii) is similar to A. ×grandiflora except with larger, deeper rose-purple flowers, slightly lower stature, and slightly less cold hardiness. It is inferior to A. ×grandiflora in landscape effect in spite of its larger flowers. 'Sherwoodii' is an excellent semidwarf selection of A. ×grandiflora, not exceeding 1 m/3.3 ft in height with slightly finer foliage texture.

Abies concolor 8

White fir
Evergreen tree
Pinaceae (Pine Family)

Native Range. Southwestern United States and adjacent Mexico.

Useful Range. USDA Zones 4a−8b.

Function. Specimen, hedge, massing, screen.

Size and Habit

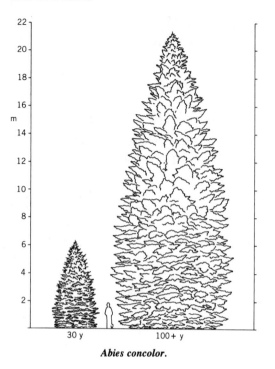

Abies concolor.

Adaptability. Better adapted to hot, dry summers than most *Abies* species.

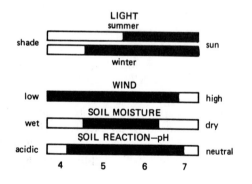

Seasonal Interest. *Foliage:* Evergreen, highly glaucous on both sides. The flat, curved needles, about 5 cm/2 in. long, give a pleasing texture. Color and form are reminiscent of the bluer

forms of Colorado spruce but less positive in effect and more versatile in design.

Problems and Maintenance. Little or no maintenance normally is required.

Cultivars. 'Candicans' has striking, silvery blue foliage. 'Compacta' is slower growing than the species type. 'Conica' is also slower growing, with more compact pyramidal form. 'Pyramidalis' is very narrowly pyramidal and compact in form, making a striking vertical accent. 'Violacea' has stronger silvery blue foliage and seldom is commercially available.

Related Species

Abies balsamea 8 (balsam fir). Usually a sparse-growing tree, but attractive and useful in extreme northern zones (2a–5a), this tree is poorly adapted to cultivation except in areas close to its native range from Labrador to Minnesota and south to West Virginia.

Abies fraseri 8 (Fraser fir). This is the southern counterpart of A. *balsamea*, sometimes referred to as southern balsam fir. It is subject to the same limitations as A. *balsamea*, but useful in somewhat warmer zones (5a–7a) in areas close to its native range. Inferior to A. *concolor* and the better Asian and European firs in landscape effect in most of the useful range.

Abies lasiocarpa 8 (Rocky Mountain fir). This large tree, native from Alaska to New Mexico, has needles shorter than those of A. *concolor* but equally glaucous. The species type, like some other conifers from the Pacific Northwest, has not performed well in most of eastern North America, but var. *arizonica* (cork or Arizona fir) has done somewhat better in our area, making a compact, small tree with strong bluish foliage. The semidwarf form 'Compacta' is even more compact and is useful as a specimen in Zones 5a–7b, and perhaps in colder and warmer zones as well.

Abies procera 8 (synonym: A. *nobilis*; noble fir). This large tree from the Pacific Northwest grows more slowly in our area but is better adapted to warm climates than most firs, useful in Zones 6a–7b. The selection 'Glauca' has silvery blue-green foliage.

Abies homolepis 8

Nikko fir
Evergreen tree
Pinaceae (Pine Family)

Native Range. Japan.

Useful Range. USDA Zones 5a−6b.

Function. Massing, screen, specimen.

Size and Habit

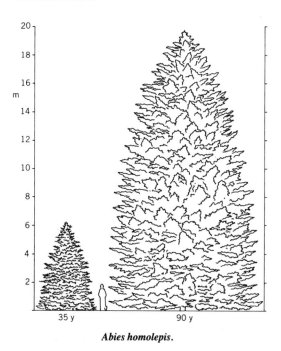

Abies homolepis.

Adaptability. Light shade helps in establishment in the Midwest and South.

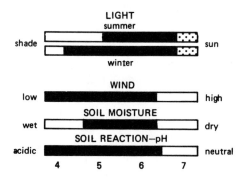

Seasonal Interest. *Foliage:* Evergreen, dark green needles, about 2.5 cm/1 in. long, with broad white stomatal bands underneath. Foliage is denser than that of many firs. *Cones:* Purplish to 10 cm/4 in. long, borne erectly on branches, add interest early in the growing season, then turn brown at maturity.

Problems and Maintenance. Little or no maintenance is required in areas where this tree is adapted.

Related Species

Abies firma 8 (Momi fir). Another handsome Japanese species, better than most firs in the South (Zones 6b−9a), but seldom available.

Abies holophylla 8 (needle fir). A seemingly widely adapted fir from Manchuria and Korea (Zones 5a−7a) with bright green foliage, it needs wider trial to assess adaptability more accurately.

Keteleeria davidiana 8 (David keteleeria). This evergreen tree from China is closely related to *Abies* and resembles a fir while young, eventually becoming rounded or flat-topped and open in habit. It is so seldom used in our area that its limitations are not well known, but it is worth trying more widely in Zones 8b−9a+ and perhaps even to Zone 7b.

Keteleeria fortunei 8 (Fortune keteleeria). This close relative of *K. davidiana* is similar in all respects but probably less cold-hardy and rarer in cultivation in our area. It is worthy of trial at least in Zone 9a and southward.

Abies koreana 7

Korean fir
Evergreen tree
Pinaceae (Pine Family)

Native Range. Korea.

Useful Range. USDA Zones 5a–7a, perhaps also Zone 4b.

Function. Specimen, screen.

Size and Habit

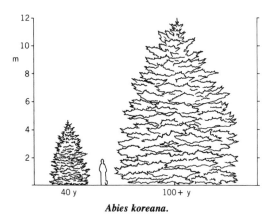

Abies koreana.

Adaptability

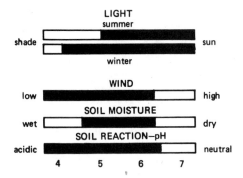

Seasonal Interest. *Foliage:* Evergreen, dark green needles, to 2 cm/0.8 in. long, with broad white

stomatal bands underneath. Foliage appears dense, in part because of compact growth. *Cones:* Violet-purple, about 5 cm/2 in. long, borne erectly on branches, beginning when the tree is young, 1–2 m/3.3–6.6 ft tall.

Problems and Maintenance. Little or no maintenance is required in areas where this tree is adapted.

Cultivars. 'Prostrate Beauty' also known as f. *prostrata* and 'Compact Dwarf,' probably is nothing more than the result of propagation by cuttings from lower branches of trees of the species. It is an excellent, hardy, dense shrub, grows to at least 2 to 3 times wide as high, and is useful for massing and foundation planting over at least as wide an area as the species (Zones 4b–7b). Commercial availability is limited, but ease of cutting propagation and growing popularity of the plant suggests greater availability in the future.

Abies koreana 'Prostrate Beauty.'

Related Species

Abies veitchii 8 (Veitch fir). A handsome fir from Japan for northern climates, this does not do well in even marginally southern areas, presumably because of less drought resistance than some other Asian firs. This graceful tree with handsome dark green foliage, white underneath, and bluish purple cones, is useful in Zones 3b–5b and relatively cool, moist sites in Zone 6.

Abies nordmanniana 8

Nordmann fir
Evergreen tree
Pinaceae (Pine Family)

Native Range. Caucasus Mountains.

Useful Range. USDA Zones 5b–7b.

Function. Specimen, screen.

Size and Habit

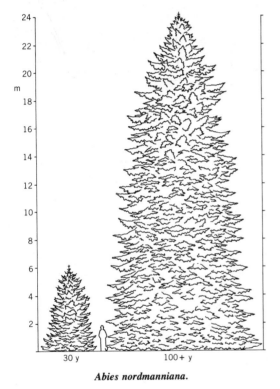

Abies nordmanniana.

Adaptability

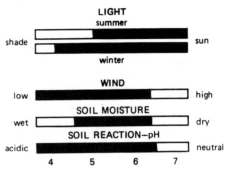

Seasonal Interest. *Foliage:* Evergreen, dark green needles, 2.5 cm/1 in. or longer, with prominent stomatal lines underneath, among the most handsome of any fir under good conditions.

Problems and Maintenance. Little or no maintenance is required in areas where this tree is adapted.

Related Species

Abies cephalonica 8 (Greek fir). A widely adapted fir with deep green, pointed needles, white underneath, it tolerates extremes of heat and drought better than most firs (Zones 5a–8a).

Abies pinsapo 8 (Spanish fir). This distinctive tree with short, blunt needles is one of the better firs for southern areas (Zones 6b–8a). The selection 'Glauca,' with blue-green foliage, is fairly well known on the East Coast.

Acanthopanax sieboldianus 5

Synonym: A. *pentaphyllus*
Fiveleaf aralia
Deciduous shrub
Araliaceae (Aralia Family)

Native Range. Japan.

Useful Range. USDA Zones 4a–8a.

Function. Border, barrier hedge or mass, screen.

Size and Habit

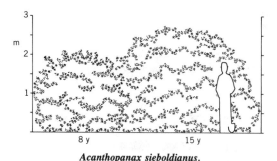

Acanthopanax sieboldianus.

Adaptability. Well-adapted to dry, city conditions and heavy shade.

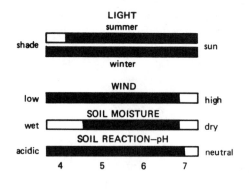

Seasonal Interest. *Flowers:* Small, pale green, not conspicuous but interesting at close range. *Foliage:* Attractive, dark green, palmately compound leaves, the leaflets, 2.5 cm/1 in. or more

in length, give a rich effect with distinctive texture when the form of the plant is properly maintained. Prickles are small and inconspicuous yet wickedly sharp, making the plant an effective barrier.

Acanthopanax sieboldianus.

Problems and Maintenance. Little maintenance is usually required, but pruning by selective thinning of old branches and light heading-back is necessary on almost an annual basis to maintain the form of the plant. Under poor growing conditions, where this plant nevertheless might well be used, pruning can be done less frequently. Under such conditions, the alternative of renewal pruning to a few inches from the ground can be considered, but under good growing conditions this may promote excessive vigor and soft, sprawling growth.

Cultivars. 'Variegatus,' with white-margined leaves, is striking but rarely cultivated.

Acer buergeranum 6

Trident maple
Deciduous tree
Aceraceae (Maple Family)

Native Range. Japan.

Useful Range. USDA Zones 6a−8a, and at least marginally in Zone 5b.

Function. Street or patio tree, specimen.

Size and Habit

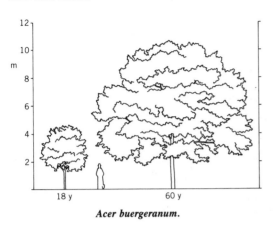

Acer buergeranum.

Adaptability. Individual trees may be adapted to colder zones than indicated. Further testing is needed to determine limits of hardiness more accurately.

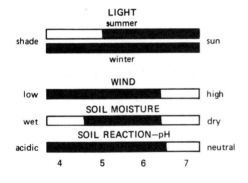

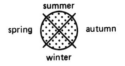

Seasonal Interest. *Foliage:* Bright green leaves, 3–8 cm/1–3 in. long, have distinctive shape and texture. *Bark:* Multicolored flaking lends mild interest at all seasons.

Acer buergeranum.

Problems and Maintenance. Little or no maintenance is required in areas where this tree is adapted.

Acer campestre 7

Hedge maple
Deciduous tree
Aceraceae (Maple Family)

Native Range. Europe and western Asia.

Useful Range. USDA Zones 5a–8b.

Function. Shade or patio tree, tall hedge or screen.

Size and Habit

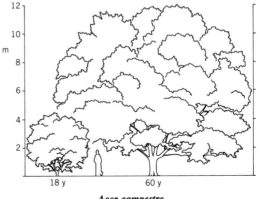

Acer campestre.

Adaptability. Its extensive natural range in Europe suggests a wide variation in adaptation. When possible, use material that has been grown successfully in the local area for some time. Selection of superior cultivars from this highly variable species should be worthwhile.

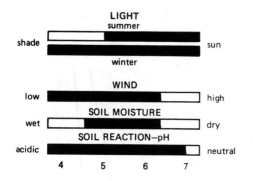

Seasonal Interest. *Foliage:* Dark green leaves, 5–10 cm/2–4 in. across with characteristic rounded lobes, give a clean, crisp texture during summer and remain green late, occasionally turning a clear gold color before falling.

Problems and Maintenance. This tree is relatively maintenance-free.

Cultivars. Although little or nothing has yet been done, useful cultivars probably could be selected from the range of variation that exists in this species. Selection for form, foliage retention or autumn color, and adaptation would enhance the value of the species.

Acer ginnala 6

Amur maple
Deciduous shrub or tree
Aceraceae (Maple Family)

Native Range. Central and northern Manchuria, Japan.

Size and Habit

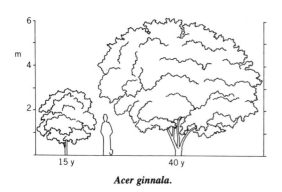

Acer ginnala.

Useful Range. USDA Zones 3a–6b.

Function. Patio shade tree, hedge, screen, specimen.

Adaptability. This species seems to be best adapted to northern areas with relatively cool summers.

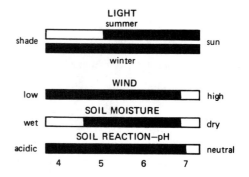

Seasonal Interest. *Flowers:* Pale yellow, in clusters (panicles) to 5 cm/2 in. across, fragrant, with the young foliage. *Foliage:* Clean, dark green in summer, to 8 cm/3 in. long but narrow, with elongated central lobes, deep red to fiery scarlet in early autumn. *Fruits:* Reddish to varying degrees, in summer.

Acer ginnala.

Acer ginnala.

Problems and Maintenance. Relatively trouble-free and requiring little maintenance, but weed seedlings may be a minor problem in some areas.

Cultivars. Because of wide variation in form, foliage, and fruit color, selection of desirable clones seems appropriate, but little has yet been done. One form with outstanding summer fruit color has been selected at the University of Minnesota Landscape Arboretum. 'Compactum' and 'Durand Dwarf' have been selected for compact form, but the latter is not widely available.

Acer griseum 6

Paperbark maple
Deciduous tree
Aceraceae (Maple Family)

Native Range. China.

Useful Range. USDA Zones 5a−7b+.

Function. Patio tree, specimen.

Size and Habit

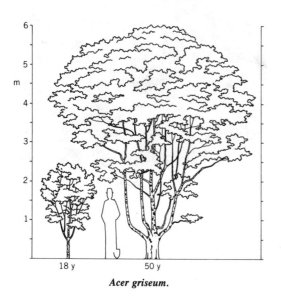

Acer griseum.

polished on old trunks, by far the outstanding landscape feature of this tree, accentuated by the relatively open branching habit of mature trees.

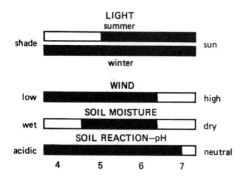

Acer griseum, mature tree.

Adaptability. Once thought not hardy north of Zone 6a, but with further trial at least some genetic material has been found hardy in southern Wisconsin (Zone 5a). Southern limits are not clearly established.

Seasonal Interest. *Foliage:* Trifoliolate leaves of interesting texture, soft green, changing little in autumn before falling in most years and locations, but sometimes turn a good red color. *Bark:* Cinnamon-brown bark, exfoliating or smoothly

Problems and Maintenance. Relatively maintenance-free; some careful pruning may be desirable on some specimens to open the branching and display the bark to better advantage in summer. Availability is limited by propagation problems, but should improve with better techniques and the considerable attention this tree is now receiving.

Cultivars. Little or no selection of cultivars has been carried out because of problems in vegetative propagation. Virtually all trees from seedling lots have significant bark interest, another reason that little attention has been given to the selection of superior types.

Acer maximowiczianum 7

Synonym: A. *nikoense*
Nikko maple
Deciduous tree
Aceraceae (Maple Family)

Native Range. Japan, China.

Useful Range. USDA Zones 5a–7a.

Function. Shade tree, specimen.

Size and Habit

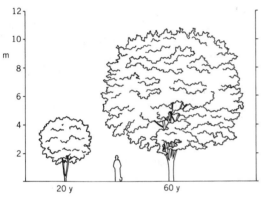

Acer maximowiczianum.

Adaptability

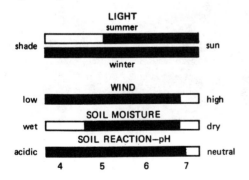

Seasonal Interest. *Flowers:* Yellow with unfolding foliage, not conspicuous. *Foliage:* Trifoliolate, with leaflets 5–10 cm/2–4 in. long,

medium green, fuzzy underneath, turning bright to deep red in autumn.

Problems and Maintenance. This tree is trouble-free and needs little maintenance.

Related Species

Acer diabolicum 6 (devil or horned maple). This Japanese maple seems better adapted to the South than many other maples and becomes a graceful and attractive small tree. It is seldom available and then only as the var. *purpurascens*, which has red flowers and fruits and foliage that is reddish on emergence. It is useful, on a trial basis, in Zones 5a–8b and perhaps also Zone 4b.

Acer mandshuricum 6 (Manchurian maple). Another cold-hardy (Zones 4b–6b), round-topped, small shade tree with trifoliolate, dark green leaves, whitish underneath and with red petioles, turning bright red in autumn.

Acer triflorum 6 (three-flower maple). Another small, trifoliolate maple, distinguished by attractive striped and flaking bark, similar in most other respects, including hardiness, to A. *maximowicziana*.

Acer negundo 7

Box elder, Manitoba maple
Deciduous tree
Aceraceae (Maple Family)

Native Range. Eastern United States and adjacent Canada.

Useful Range. USDA Zones 2a – 8a.

Function. Shade tree.

Size and Habit

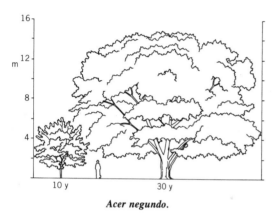

Acer negundo.

Adaptability. This is one of the most cold-hardy of all shade trees, thus valued in cold regions where few other trees will grow. It is surprisingly widely adapted in the South but is not a high-priority tree in any but cold regions, because of weak wood and short life.

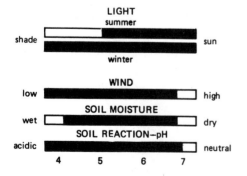

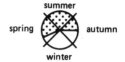

Seasonal Interest. *Flowers:* Pale yellow, in early spring; not showy but with fleeting landscape interest. *Foliage:* Strikingly white variegated in the cultivar listed, but with little or no landscape value in the species. In fact somewhat ragged looking.

Problems and Maintenance. The most serious maintenance problem is pruning to remove storm damaged wood, sufficient reason for not growing the tree when alternatives are available. This seems to be less of a problem in the northern prairies, where the tree has specific value because of its adaptability, but box-elder bug remains a problem in many areas.

Cultivars. Several cultivars have been selected, but only 'Variegatum,' with handsome, white-margined leaflets, is commonly used.

Acer negundo 'Variegatum.'

Acer palmatum 6

Japanese maple
Deciduous tree
Aceraceae (Maple Family)

Native Range. Korea, Japan.

Useful Range. USDA Zones 5b−9a, with selection of appropriate genetic material.

Function. Specimen, patio tree, accent in border.

Size and Habit

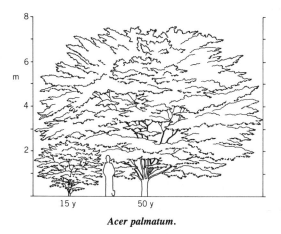

Acer palmatum.

Adaptability. Cold hardiness varies with the cultivar. Most are cold-hardy to Zone 6b, only a few to Zone 5b. Young foliage is susceptible to drying in full sun and strong wind. Plant in protected sites.

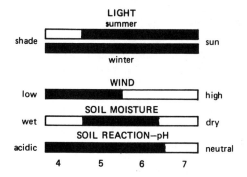

Seasonal Interest. *Foliage:* Handsomely textured, 5−10 cm/2−4 in. across, regularly palmately lobed in the species and some cultivars, incised to the petiole (effectively compound) in other cul-

tivars, with many intermediates; medium green in summer (in the species) to pale green, yellow, or red-purple, that of most cultivars turns red in autumn. *Twigs:* Green to full or deep red in most cultivars; smooth, with a polished appearance. One cultivar has brilliant scarlet twigs, especially in late winter and early spring.

Problems and Maintenance. This tree is relatively trouble-free and needs little maintenance.

Cultivars. More than 50 cultivars are usually available from nurseries in the United States. These vary in foliage color and degree of leaf dissection, with at least one selection for twig color. Their nomenclature is somewhat confused. Whenever possible, it is a good idea to become acquainted with local sources of supply and to specify by local designation as well as correct cultivar name to avoid confusion. Hardiness of cultivars varies, another reason for observing local performance, at least in Zones 5 and 6. A few of the more common varieties and cultivars are listed here:

'Atropurpureum' (bloodleaf Japanese maple) is similar to the species type except that it has dark red foliage all season. One of the most common cultivars.

'Aureum' (golden Japanese maple) leaves are clear yellow at first, later turning golden yellow.

'Bloodgood' has rosy red foliage in early summer, turning deep red later, and is probably the best red-leaved selection.

'Burgundy Lace' has dark red, deeply incised foliage.

Var. *dissectum* (threadleaf Japanese maple) actually is a group of variants with deeply incised foliage, almost threadlike in texture, and dark red to yellow-green. Several cultivars have been selected, mostly under Japanese names, but including 'Ornatum,' reputedly the hardiest of the group (to Zone 5b).

'Osakazuki' has relatively large, yellow to yellow-green leaves, turning brilliant red in autumn.

'Sangokaku' (= 'Senkaki;' red-twig Japanese

maple), with light green foliage and brilliant red twigs, especially in late winter and spring.

Related Species

Acer circinatum 6 (vine maple). This small tree, native to the Pacific Northwest, is similar to A. *palmatum* except in having more showy flowers, greater shade tolerance, and twisted growth habit. Useful in Zones 6a−8b.

Acer japonicum 6 (fullmoon maple). This small tree is similar in effect to A. *palmatum*, but with nearly circular leaves having many lobes. Useful in Zones 5b−8b. Several cultivars have been selected, including 'Aconitifolium,' with deeply incised leaves, 'Aureum', with yellow foliage, and 'Macrophyllum' and 'Microphyllum,' with unusually large and small leaves, respectively.

Acer pensylvanicum 7

Striped maple, moosewood
Deciduous tree
Aceraceae (Maple Family)

Native Range. Eastern United States and adjacent Canada.

Useful Range. USDA Zones 3b−7a.

Function. Specimen (in shade), woodland borders, naturalizing.

Size and Habit

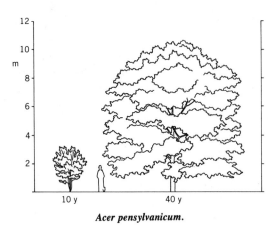

Acer pensylvanicum.

Adaptability. Grows best with at least partial shade.

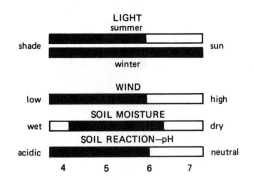

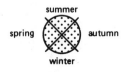

Seasonal Interest. *Flowers:* Small, yellow, in pendulous, chainlike clusters (racemes) to 15 cm/6 in. long, in late spring. *Foliage:* Coarse, dull green, turning yellow in autumn. *Bark:* Young branches are longitudinally striped whitish and green, the outstanding landscape feature of this tree.

Problems and Maintenance. This tree is relatively trouble-free, given a proper site, and needs little or no maintenance.

Cultivars. 'Erythrocladum' has bright red twigs in winter but seldom is available.

Acer tegmentosum.

Related Species

Acer capillipes 7 (Japanese striped maple).   This tree is similar to A. *pensylvanicum*, but with finer-textured, red-petioled foliage, more tolerant of full sun, and less cold-tolerant (Zone 5b−7b+).

Acer davidii 7 (David maple).   Similar to the above species, with even more striking green and white striped bark and foliage that turns yellow to purple in autumn, this Chinese species is better adapted to southern conditions than A. *pensyl-* *vanicum* (Zones 7a−9a+), but not tolerant of full sun.

Acer grosseri 6 (snake-skin maple).   This small tree from China is little known and probably not commercially available in our area at present, but it is worthy of reintroduction for its interesting bark alone. Not greatly different from the other striped maples; A. *capillipes*, A. *davidii*, A. *pensylvanicum*, A. *rufinerve*, and A. *tegmentosum*, it typically holds its bark color to a greater age than any of these. But it is no more cold-hardy or heat-resistant than A. *davidii*.

Acer rufinerve 7 (redvein maple).   Another Japanese counterpart of A. *pensylvanicum*, this tree has somewhat finer-textured, darker green foliage, turning deep red in autumn. It is less cold-hardy (Zones 6a−8a+) than A. *pensyl-vanicum* but somewhat more satisfactory in sun.

Acer tegmentosum 6 (Manchurian striped maple).   This small tree has the same striped bark that characterizes all the maples in this group. It is almost as cold-hardy (Zones 5a−7a) as A. *pensylvanicum*, is more tolerant of sun, and has finer-textured foliage.

Acer platanoides 8

Norway maple
Deciduous tree
Aceraceae (Maple Family)

Native Range. Europe, Caucasus Mountains.

Useful Range. USDA Zones 4a−7b with selection of appropriate genetic material.

Function. Shade, street tree.

Size and Habit

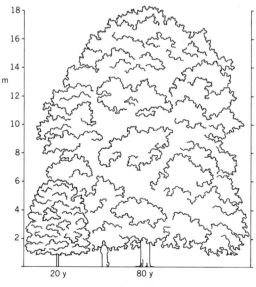

Acer platanoides.

Adaptability. Better adapted to city conditions than most maples.

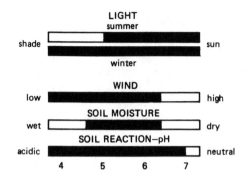

LIGHT
summer

shade ▭▬▬▬ sun
▬▬▬▬▬

winter

WIND
low ▬▬▬▭ high

SOIL MOISTURE
wet ▭▬▬▭ dry

SOIL REACTION–pH
acidic ▬▬▬▬▭ neutral

4   5   6   7

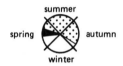

summer

spring ✴ autumn

winter

Seasonal Interest. *Flowers:* Yellow-green to bright yellow in early spring, in loose, rounded clusters, 5 cm/2 in. across, among the most colorful of any of the maples. *Foliage:* Dark green (white-variegated or deep red in cultivars), and coarse-textured, individually 10−18 cm/4−7 in. across, turning dull yellow in late autumn in some years.

Problems and Maintenance. Little or no maintenance is required except for removal or pruning of diseased or storm damaged trees. Verticillium wilt has been a problem in some areas, requiring removal and substitution. This tree's shallow roots and dense canopy make it impossible to maintain turfgrass or groundcovers underneath, and mulches are the best solution. Frost-cracking of trunks is sometimes a problem in Zone 4.

Cultivars. 'Albo-variegatum' and 'Drummondii' (harlequin maple) both have white variegated foliage and are striking in the landscape but slow-growing, cold-hardy to Zone 5a or perhaps 4b. Reversions to green foliage sometimes occur, and such branches must be removed to preserve the cultivar.

'Cleveland' is an excellent, upright street tree with oval form not requiring as much lateral space as the species.

'Columnare' has columnar form with a width about half the height, excellent for use where lateral space is restricted.

'Crimson King,' 'Faasen's Black,' and 'Royal Red' all have dark red foliage during the entire growing season. These differ in hardiness, 'Crimson King' and 'Royal Red' to Zone 4b, and 'Faasen's Black' to Zone 5b.

'Emerald Queen' is vigorous, upright, and oval in form, with rich green foliage.

'Erectum' is a tightly columnar form, with a width one-third to one-half the height, even less in young trees.

'Globosum' is low-growing and broad-spreading, with globose form, especially when young. It seldom exceeds 5m/16 ft in height and is useful for planting under low utility wires.

'Greenlace' (Plant Patent No. 2759, 1967), has deeply cut foliage, giving a finer texture than the species.

'Schwedleri' is an old cultivar with deep red foliage in early summer, gradually fading to bronze and then green in late summer. It is at least as cold-hardy as the hardiest of the other red-leaved cultivars, to Zone 4b, perhaps 4a.

'Summershade' has unusually leathery, dark green foliage and fast, upright growth. In limited trials it has seemed unusually drought-tolerant and cold-hardy, at least to Zone 4b.

Related Species

Acer miyabei 7 (Miyabe maple). This low-branching tree, to 10 m/33 ft tall, is open in habit and useful in Zones 5a−7b+.

Acer mono 7 (mono maple). This handsome, intermediate-size tree, to 15 m/50 ft, resembles an oversize Japanese maple with foliage and form vaguely reminiscent of A. *palmatum.* Foliage is bright, light green when first expanding, later darker green, trunks lightly striped. Useful in Zones 5b−7b+.

Acer pseudoplatanus 8 (sycamore maple). One of the relatively few native European trees useful in our area, this makes a fine shade tree, similar in habit to A. *platanoides,* but with more leathery foliage and irregularly scaly, orange-brown bark.

Acer pseudoplatanus.

It is less cold-hardy than A. *platanoides*, but useful in Zones 5b−7b. In the northern parts of its range, trunks of young trees should be wrapped to reduce trunk scald during establishment. Several foliage variants have been named in Europe, where this is a popular shade tree. They include 'Brilliantissimum,' with leaves emerging pink, then turning yellow and finally green, 'Leopoldii' and 'Nizetii,' with yellow variegated leaves, 'Purpureum,' with leaves deep purple underneath (leaves of the species type are often purple tinged), 'Variegatum,' with white variegated foliage, and 'Worleei,' with golden yellow leaves on red petioles. None of these variants are commonly available, and A. *pseudoplatanus* is not a common tree in any form in our area.

Acer truncatum 6 (Shantung maple). This native of northern China is closely related to A. *mono* but smaller. Seldom if ever commercially available, this tree could be a worthwhile addition to the list of small trees for northern areas. Useful in Zones 4a−6b with selection of appropriate genetic material.

Acer rubrum 8

Red or swamp maple
Deciduous tree
Aceraceae (Maple Family)

Native Range. Eastern United States and adjacent Canada, from the Gulf Coast and most of peninsular Florida to 49° north latitude in Canada.

Useful Range. USDA Zones 3b−9a with selection of appropriate genetic material.

Function. Shade, street tree.

Size and Habit

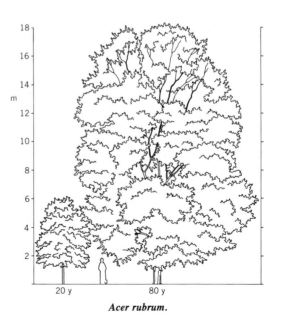

Acer rubrum.

Adaptability. Especially valued for its tolerance of poorly drained soil and even soil that is alternately wet and dry.

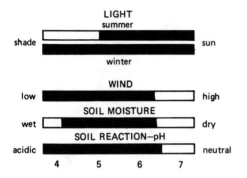

Seasonal Interest. *Flowers:* Dull to bright red in early spring, especially showy on some female trees, in clusters 5 cm/2 in. or more across, with color continued by the developing fruits. In general, flower color is more showy in the South than in the North. *Foliage:* Medium texture, whitish beneath with red petioles, 5−10 cm/2−4

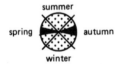

in. long, turning bright scarlet to yellow in autumn. *Trunks and branches:* Silvery gray branches add winter color and are interesting in contrast with flowers in spring.

Problems and Maintenance. Little maintenance is required except for pruning following storm damage, since this tree is weaker-wooded than A. *platanoides* and A. *saccharum* (but less prone to such damage than A. *saccharinum*).

Varieties and Cultivars. Because of the wide adaptability and seasonal interest of this species, there is a continuing selection of outstanding cultivars. At any time there probably will be several incompletely evaluated cultivars on the market.

'Armstrong' and 'Columnare' are narrow, more or less columnar forms. It has been speculated that 'Armstrong' is really a hybrid of A. *saccharinum*, which might account for graft failures that have occurred on rootstocks of A. *rubrum*. In spite of its rapid growth and very narrow form, it has little or no fall foliage color, and in any case it should be used with caution until the graft problem is solved.

'Autumn Flame' was selected for excellent, relatively early but persistent fall color and compact, rounded form.

'Bowhall' (= 'Scanlon,' = 'Pyramidale') is upright with oval to pyramidal form. It is a relatively compact but full-size tree, with very good autumn foliage color.

Var. *drummondii* is a native to lowlands along the southeast Atlantic Coast and Mississippi River basin and favored over the species type for landscape use in the coastal areas of the Deep South. It has unusually colorful red flowers and large red fruits (on females), is very tolerant of wet soil, and is useful in Zones 7a−9a+.

'Gerling' is a broadly pyramidal form, to 10m/33 ft tall.

'Globosum' and 'Tilford' are relatively low, globose forms, not exceeding 8 m/25 ft in height.

'October Glory,' 'Morgan,' and 'Red Sunset' are selections for outstanding late fall foliage color. 'October Glory' is especially late in coloring, an indication of late acclimation for winter that is confirmed by winter damage in Zones 3b−4. It may prove to be a superior selection for southern areas, however. 'Red Sunset' is not as late in coloring as 'October Glory' and somewhat more cold-hardy, but perhaps not to Zone 3b.

'Schlesingeri' was selected for unusually early autumn foliage color, some two weeks or more earlier than the average for the species.

Acer saccharinum 8

Silver maple
Deciduous tree
Aceraceae (Maple Family)

Native Range. Eastern United States and adjacent Canada, extending westward into the Central Plains, but rarely to the Gulf or southeastern Atlantic coasts.

Useful Range. USDA Zones 3a–9a with selection of appropriate genetic material.

Function. Shade tree, especially for quick, temporary effect.

Size and Habit

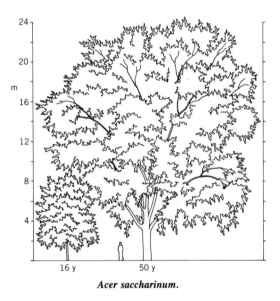

Acer saccharinum.

Adaptability. Especially valued for its tolerance of both dry and relatively wet soil and for its fast growth.

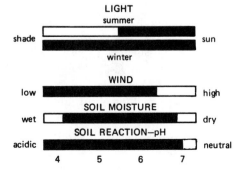

Seasonal Interest. *Flowers:* Dull reddish orange, not as showy as those of A. *platanoides* or A. *rubrum*, in early spring. *Foliage:* Medium- to fine-textured (in cutleaved forms), silvery gray underneath, 10–12 cm/4–5 in. across, some-

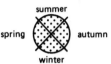

times turning clear yellow in autumn but more often falling with little color change. *Trunk and branches:* Silvery gray branches add winter color, along with orange inner bark displayed as bark flakes from trunks.

Problems and Maintenance. This is a high-maintenance tree because of several unfortunate characteristics. Its fast growth results in relatively soft wood, making it unusually susceptible to storm damage. This is often aggravated in street trees by severe pruning, allegedly done to reduce storm breakage. Unusually soft growth follows severe pruning, making the tree more susceptible to storm injury than if no pruning had been done. Furthermore, the silver maple is shallow-rooted, causing lawn maintenance problems, and seeds freely, giving rise to weed seedlings.

Cultivars. 'Beebe Cutleaf Weeping' has pendulous branches and deeply incised leaves. 'Silver Queen' has only staminate (male) flowers, and so is seedless and does not give rise to weed seedlings. Otherwise it is fast-growing. 'Wieri' (=var. *laciniatum*) has incised leaves and upright growth habit.

Acer saccharum 8

Sugar, hard, or rock maple
Deciduous tree
Aceraceae (Maple Family)

Native Range. Northeastern and north-central United States and adjacent Canada, as far south as 35 degrees north latitude.

Useful Range. USDA Zones 3b−7b with selection of appropriate genetic material.

Function. Shade tree.

Size and Habit

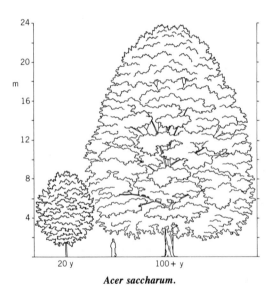

Acer saccharum.

Adaptability. This tree is not as tolerant of difficult sites as many other trees are, and it is especially intolerant of compacted soil, road salts, and urban stresses. But its performance is reward-

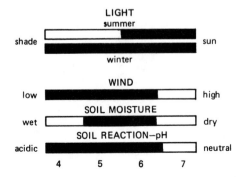

ing on good sites, where its growth rate is moderate and potentially faster with careful maintenance.

Seasonal Interest. *Flowers:* Pale yellow in early spring, in clusters that usually are less showy than those of *A. platanoides* but significant against blue sky. *Foliage:* Dark green in summer, turning bright red or golden-orange in autumn, 8−14 cm/3−5.5 in. across, giving a medium-coarse texture.

Problems and Maintenance. This low-maintenance tree has few problems on well-drained, fertile soils and is hard-wooded, seldom suffering storm damage. Problems can result, however, from planting too close to roads and highways where soil is dry, poorly drained, or compacted, and where de-icing salts are used.

Cultivars. 'Globosum' is a shrubby, globose tree, useful only in special situations that require this form.

'Green Mountain' is an excellent upright, oval form with thick, leathery, scorch-resistant leaves, remaining dark green late, then turning golden-yellow, occasionally red tinged. Probably the best cultivar for the Midwest and other localities with dry summers.

'Newton Sentry' (= 'Columnare,' = 'Erectum') is an excellent columnar selection (height about four times width at maturity) with a strong central leader.

'Sweet Shadow' has deeply cut, dark green foliage, giving a finer texture than the species type, comparable to that of *A. platanoides* 'Greenlace.'

'Temple's Upright' (= f. *monumentale*) is strikingly vertical, with fastigiate form, very narrow when young, but several main trunks develop with age, pulling apart until the tree assumes a narrow vase shape. For long-term columnar effect, use 'Newton Sentry' in preference.

Related Species and Subspecies

Acer barbatum 7 (synonym: A. *floridanum;* Florida maple, southern sugar maple). This southern counterpart of the sugar maple has smaller, pubescent leaves and is presumably much less cold-hardy than A. *saccharum* but better adapted in Zones 8 and 9.

Acer saccharum ssp. *leucoderme* 6 (synonym: A. *leucoderme;* chalk maple). This tree has smaller leaves than ssp. *saccharum* and is much smaller in stature, comparable with the flowering dogwood (*Cornus florida*). It has smooth, whitish bark and scarlet fall foliage color; it is useful in Zones 6a−8b.

Acer saccharum ssp. *nigrum* 8 (synonym: A. *nigrum,* black maple). This tree is very similar to the species type but easily distinguishable in summer by pubescent leaf undersides and conspicuous foliated stipules in early summer. The two are generally interchangeable in landscape use, but ssp. *nigrum* has dull, golden-yellow autumn foliage color, occasionally red tinged, and may be more adaptable to calcareous soils and drier climates.

Acer tataricum 6

Tatarian maple
Deciduous tree
Aceraceae (Maple Family)

Native Range. Southeastern Europe, western Asia.

Useful Range. USDA Zones 3a−6b.

Function. Patio shade tree, specimen. This species reaches functional size more rapidly than many other small maples.

Size and Habit

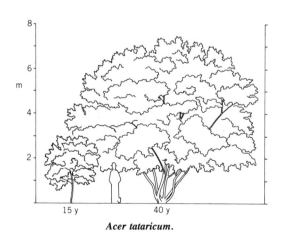

Acer tataricum.

Adaptability

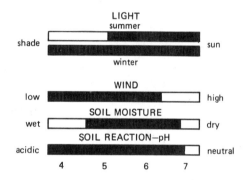

Seasonal Interest. *Foliage:* Dark green, slightly wrinkled leaves, 5−10 cm/2−4 in. long, that turn yellowish in autumn. *Fruits:* Bright red from midsummer to early autumn.

Problems and Maintenance. This tree is generally trouble-free except that it can be damaged severely by ice storms, requiring corrective pruning or replacement.

Cultivars. None are available.

Related Species

Acer spicatum 6 (mountain maple). This shrubby tree is native to northern parts of the eastern United States and in Canada from Labrador to the northern plains. It grows best in partial shade and has functional value only in the coldest climates (Zones 2−4), with fruiting and foliage interest similar to that of A. *tataricum*.

Acer spicatum.

Actinidia arguta 1

Bower actinidia
Deciduous vine
Actinidiaceae (Actinidia Family)

Native Range. Manchuria, Korea, Japan.

Useful Range. USDA Zones 4b−8a.

Function. Screen (with support).

Size and Habit. Grows and climbs very rapidly by twining, reaching massive size and heights of 8−10 m/25−30 ft. This is not a vine for small properties.

Adaptability

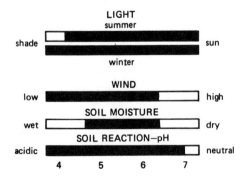

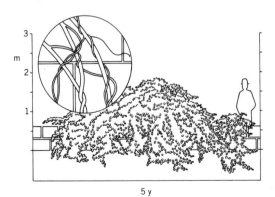

Actinidia arguta.

Seasonal Interest. *Foliage:* Lustrous, dark green, moderately coarse leaves, 8–12 cm/3–5 in. long with bright red petioles, forming a handsome, dense mass that remains green late.

Actinidia arguta.

Problems and Maintenance. This vine is relatively trouble-free and needs no maintenance other than pruning in situations where the rapid growth cannot be accommodated.

Cultivars. None are available.

Related Species

Actinidia chinensis 1 (Chinese actinidia, Chinese gooseberry, kiwi fruit). This vine is much less cold-hardy than A. *arguta*, useful in Zones 7b–9a+, but it is an equally fast-growing screen in the South, with the added interest of showy white to pale yellow flowers, a velvety coat of reddish hairs on young stems and petioles, and hairy, edible fruits (sold in produce markets as "kiwi fruit"), on female plants (*Actinidia* spp. are dioecious).

Actinidia kolomikta 1 (Kolomikta actinidia). Similar in hardiness to A. *arguta*, but much less vigorous. It is grown primarily for its variegated foliage blotched with pink and white, more noticeable in male plants than in females.

Actinidia polygama 1 (silver vine). Similar in hardiness and vigor to A. *kolomikta* but with bright green foliage, silvery yellow when young. This weak-climbing vine is subject to damage by cats, which are strongly attracted to it.

Aegopodium podagraria 2

Bishop's weed, gout weed
Herbaceous groundcover
Umbelliferae (Parsley Family)

Native Range. Europe; naturalized in North America.

Useful Range. USDA Zones 3b–9a+.

Function. Groundcover.

Size and Habit

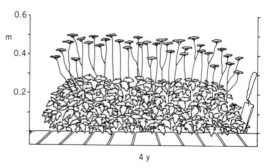

Aegopodium podagraria.

Adaptability. This is one of the toughest and most widely adaptable of all ground-covers, one of the few that will tolerate deep shade and rather dry soil simultaneously.

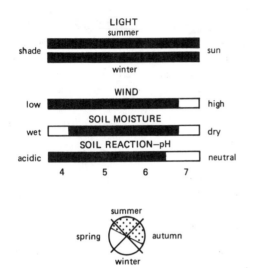

Seasonal Interest. *Flowers:* Small, white, in flat-topped clusters (umbels), resembling those of carrot, in early summer, not showy. *Foliage:* Compound, light to medium green leaves produce medium-fine texture and die to the ground in autumn without color change.

Problems and Maintenance. This plant is trouble-free but can be weedy itself, and it always should be bounded by pavement, buildings, or steel edging to contain it and prevent it from becoming a serious weed problem.

Cultivars. 'Variegatum' has irregularly white-margined leaves, is slightly less aggressive than the green-leaved species type, and is used much more commonly.

Aesculus ×carnea 8

Red horse chestnut
Deciduous tree
Hippocastanaceae (Horse Chestnut Family)

Hybrid Origin. A. *hippocastanum* × A. *pavia*.

Size and Habit

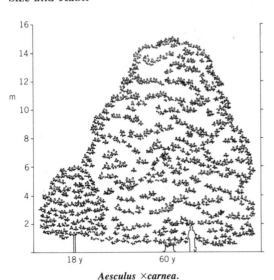

Aesculus ×carnea.

Useful Range. USDA Zones 5a−8b.

Function. Specimen, shade tree.

Adaptability. This hybrid is somewhat more drought-tolerant than A. *hippocastanum*.

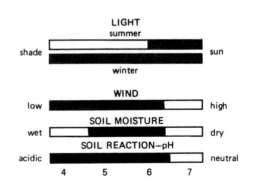

Aesculus hippocastanum 'Baumannii.'

Seasonal Interest. *Flowers:* Pink to red flowers in erect pyramidal clusters, 12–20 cm/5–8 in. long, in late spring. *Foliage:* Dark green, coarse, palmately compound with leaflets to 25 cm/10 in. long. *Fruits:* Glossy brown nuts in large husks.

Problems and Maintenance. Leaf, twig, and fruit litter makes this tree a poor choice for street or urban use. Leaf scorch disease is less serious than with A. *hippocastanum*, but it can be a problem in some areas. Sun-scald of trunks also can be a problem in Zone 5a.

Cultivars. 'Briotii' (ruby horse chestnut) is slightly lower in stature (to 13 m/42 ft) than average for this species. With its large, bright red flowers, it is by far the most popular cultivar.

Related Species

Aesculus hippocastanum 8 (common horse chestnut). This Balkan tree is similar to A. ×*carnea*, except that it is slightly larger at maturity, to 25 m/82 ft tall, somewhat more susceptible to drought injury and leaf-scorch disease, and it has white flowers, red-marked inside. There is little reason to use this species in preference to A. ×*carnea* except for slightly greater hardiness (Zone 4a) and for the double-flowered form 'Baumannii' (Baumann horse chestnut) which, because it is not pollinated, holds its flowers for a longer time than the species and is free from fruit litter.

Aesculus pavia 6 (red buckeye). This small, shrubby tree, to 6–8 m/20–26 ft tall, native to the southeastern United States, has red flowers that are less showy than those of A. ×*carnea* 'Briotii' and is poorer in form. It is susceptible to a serious leaf-spot disease, even in the wild. Otherwise it is useful in Zones 6a–9a, and perhaps also Zone 5.

Aesculus splendens 5 (flame buckeye). This is an irregularly growing shrub native to the south-central United States, from Alabama to Louisiana, useful in Zones 6a–9a, with red flowers as showy as those of A. ×*carnea* 'Briotii.' It is seldom available but worthy of wider trial where it can be found. According to some authorities, it should not be considered a species but rather a variant of A. *pavia*. Whichever name may be correct, it is recognized in landscape use for its smaller stature and red flowers.

Aesculus glabra 7

Ohio buckeye
Deciduous tree
Hippocastanaceae (Horse Chestnut Family)

Native Range. Central midwestern United States
and southwestward to Texas.

Useful Range. USDA Zones 3a−8b.

Function. Specimen, shade tree.

Size and Habit

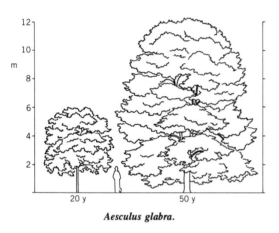

Aesculus glabra.

Adaptability. This tree is more drought-resistant
than the horse chestnuts and better adapted to the
Midwest.

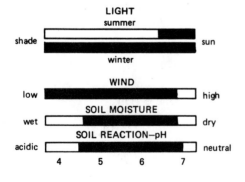

Seasonal Interest. *Flowers.* Small, pale yellow
flowers in erect, pyramidal clusters, 10−15
cm/4−6 in. long, in middle spring. *Foliage:*
Medium green, palmately compound, not as
coarse as that of the horse chestnuts, with leaflets
8−12 cm/3−5 in. long, turning yellow or
orange-red in autumn. *Fruits:* Smooth brown
nuts in husks.

Problems and Maintenance. Leaf, twig, and
fruit litter is messy, but this is not as great a
problem as it is with the horse chestnuts because
all plant parts are smaller. This tree is considered
difficult to transplant.

Varieties. Var. *arguta* is a shrub or small shrubby
tree, to 3 m/10 ft, native to the southwestern part
of its natural range from Arkansas to Texas, and
presumably better adapted to cultivation than the
species would be in that region, but not functional as a shade tree.

Related Species

Aesculus octandra 8 (yellow or sweet buckeye).
This large tree is native to central Appalachia and
westward through the Ohio River valley. Like the
smaller A. *glabra*, which it resembles, it seems
better adapted and more trouble-free in the central United States (USDA Zones 5a−8a) than A.
hippocastanum, which has been more widely
used in the past. The pink-flowered variety *virginica* probably is not commercially available at
present.

Aesculus parviflora 5

Bottlebrush buckeye
Deciduous shrub
Hippocastanaceae (Horse Chestnut Family)

Size and Habit

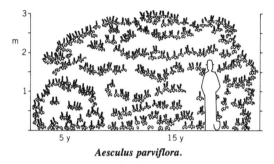

Aesculus parviflora.

Adaptability

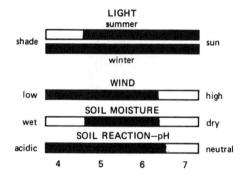

Native Range. Southeastern United States.

Useful Range. USDA Zones 5a–9a.

Function. Specimen, massing. Because of its tendency to spread to a great width, this plant should be reserved for relatively large-scale situations.

Seasonal Interest. *Flowers:* White flowers in cylindrical clusters to 25 cm/10 in., in midsummer. *Foliage:* Dark green, palmately compound, with leaflets 10–20 cm/4–8 in. long, producing a distinctively coarse texture and falling with little color change in autumn. *Fruits:* Smooth brown nuts in husks.

Problems and Maintenance. This plant is relatively maintenance-free, since the fruit and foliage litter remains hidden beneath the mound-like form, and leaf-scorch is not usually a serious problem. In all but very large-scale situations, pruning and digging out sucker shoots may be necessary to control size.

Ailanthus altissima 7−8

Synonym: *A. glandulosa*
Tree of heaven
Deciduous tree
Simaroubaceae (Quassia Family)

Native Range. Northern China; naturalized in the eastern United States.

Useful Range. USDA Zones 5a−9a.

Function. Fast-growing shade tree in situations where other trees will not grow.

Size and Habit

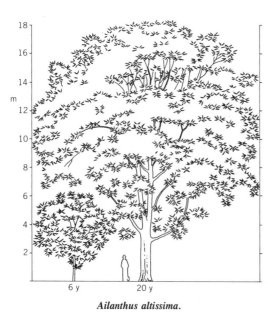

Ailanthus altissima.

Adaptability. This is among the most widely adaptable of all trees, growing rapidly even in poor soil, in warm and moderately cold climates,

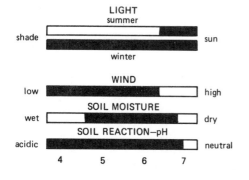

and in proximity to salt at the seashore or near salted roads in the North. Its adaptability has made it both a noxious weed in good soils and a useful shade tree in many inner city environments. Individual trees are short lived.

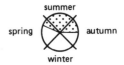

Seasonal Interest. *Flowers:* Dioecious plant, relatively inconspicuous in bloom, but staminate (male) flowers give off a disagreeable odor. *Foliage:* Handsome, dark green, pinnately compound leaves, to 0.8 m/2.6 ft long, give this tree a coarse, "tropical" appearance. *Fruits:* Dull yellow to bright red on individual female trees, ornamental in late summer and early autumn.

Problems and Maintenance. When both male and female trees are present, seedlings will germinate and grow in any available space, becoming a serious weed problem. This tree is short-lived with soft wood easily damaged by wind and ice, and produces considerable foliage and twig litter.

Varieties. Var. *erythrocarpa* has dark green foliage, whitened underneath, and bright red fruits in late summer and early autumn.

Related Species

Cedrela sinensis 6−7 (Chinese toon). This Chinese tree is reminiscent of *Ailanthus* in form, even though it is not in the same family but rather in the Meliaceae (mahogany family), with very large (to 60 cm/2 ft), pinnately compound leaves and fairly conspicuous clusters of whitish flowers in early summer. It is hardy in Zones 6b−9a+.

Melia azedarach 6 (chinaberry tree). This fast-growing but short-lived tree in the Meliaceae is adapted to poor growing conditions, but only in the Deep South (Zones 8b−9a+). It is native to the Himalayas but naturalized throughout the tropics and subtropics, including the far southern United States. Seasonal interest includes fragrant, pale purple flowers in middle spring, dense, dark green foliage all summer, and, in autumn, small, pale yellow fruits, which are toxic to animals, including humans.

Picrasma quassioides 7 (Korean bitternut). This small tree (to 10 m/33 ft) is similar in form and foliage to A. *altissima* and belongs to the same family but is slower growing, with reddish brown bark and red to yellow autumn foliage color. It is hardy in Zones 6b−9a+ but probably not commercially available.

Ajuga reptans 2

Carpet bugle, bugleweed
Evergreen or semievergreen groundcover
Labiatae (Mint Family)

Native Range. Europe, naturalized locally in North America.

Useful Range. USDA Zones 3b−9a.

Function. Groundcover.

Size and Habit

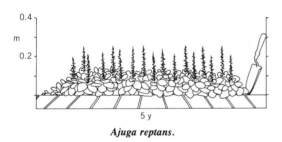

Ajuga reptans.

Adaptability. Protection from full sun is necessary for best results in the Midwest and South.

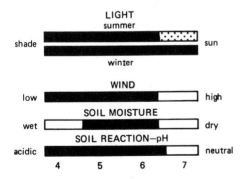

Seasonal Interest. *Flowers:* Blue, rose-pink, or white, small but borne in large numbers in spikelike clusters to 15 cm/6 in. tall, very showy in late spring. *Foliage:* Nearly evergreen, lustrous leaves make a solid mat of interesting texture, but in the North become dull and dingy by late winter.

Problems and Maintenance. This excellent groundcover is unusually trouble-free and requires little maintenance after establishment, or even during establishment, since it grows rapidly. Its rapid growth can be a problem, however, and planting beds sometimes are best enclosed in edging to prevent encroachment into turf areas.

Cultivars. 'Alba' has creamy white flowers and light green foliage. 'Bronze Beauty' has bronze foliage and deep blue flowers. 'Emerald Green' is notable for its clump-forming growth habit, making it easier to control. 'Pink Beauty' and 'Rosy Spires' have rosy pink flowers and bright green foliage. 'Variegata' has white variegated leaves and is less vigorous than other selections.

Related Species

Ajuga genevensis 2 (Geneva or Alpine bugleweed). This Eurasian species differs little from the closely related A. *reptans*, is less commonly available, and probably is less effective as a groundcover.

Ajuga pyramidalis 2 (pyramidal bugleweed). This European species has larger leaves and flowering spikes than those of A. *reptans* and is best known for the selection 'Metallica Crispa,' which has deeply bronzed leaves and rich blue flowers.

Akebia quinata 1 and 2

Fiveleaf akebia
Deciduous or semievergreen vine or groundcover
Lardizabalaceae (Lardizabala Family)

Native Range. China, Korea, and Japan.

Useful Range. USDA Zones 4b–9a.

Function. Screen (with support), groundcover.

Size and Habit. This fine-textured vine climbs rapidly by twining and makes an effective screen on a trellis, chain-link fence, or similar support. Its neat texture makes it a good choice for small-scale situations, provided its growth can be kept within bounds.

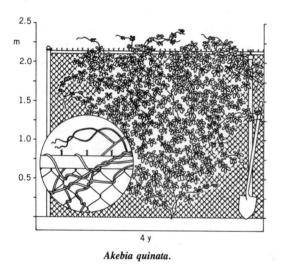

Akebia quinata.

Adaptability. Grows rapidly on good soil.

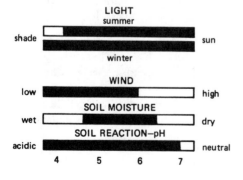

Seasonal Interest. *Flowers:* Small, fragrant, but inconspicuous, deep red-purple flowers in early spring. *Foliage:* Dark green, fine-textured, palmately compound foliage gives neat textural interest and persists well into winter. *Fruits:* Interesting purplish pods that open to show black seeds. Fruits seldom are formed in cultivation without hand cross-pollination between clones.

Problems and Maintenance. This vine requires little or no maintenance except when it is necessary to prune it to prevent it from overgrowing the planting site. When it is used as a groundcover, initial mulching or weeding is necessary, but in good soil it covers rapidly and little further weed control is necessary. At times it may be overly aggressive, climbing over adjacent shrubs.

Cultivars. None are available.

Related Species

Akebia trifoliata 1 and 2 and *Akebia* ×*pentaphylla* 1 and 2 (A. *quinata* × A. *trifoliata*) are similar to A. *quinata* in adaptability and landscape effect, but they are slightly less handsome and probably not available.

Albizia julibrissin 6

Silk tree, mimosa
Deciduous tree
Leguminosae (Legume Family)

Native Range. Central Asia: Iran to China.

Useful Range. USDA Zones 6a−9a+ with selection of appropriate genetic material (see Cultivars).

Function. Specimen, patio tree, border accent. Used primarily for its seasonal color and texture, secondarily for function.

Size and Habit

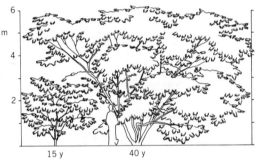

15 y   40 y

Albizia julibrissin.

Adaptability. This tree is unusually well adapted to hot, dry summers.

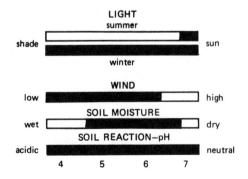

Seasonal Interest. *Flowers:* Pale to rosy pink flowers in fluffy round clusters from early to midsummer in the South and mid- to late summer in the North, remaining colorful for a month or more. *Foliage:* Extremely fine-textured, bright green, doubly compound leaves give striking contrast to most other foliage and add to the gracefulness of the plant. *Fruits:* Flat pods add interest in late summer and early autumn.

Albizia julibrissin.

Albizia julibrissin.

Problems and Maintenance. This tree is subject to mimosa webworm and requires a spray program to avoid disfiguring of foliage in some areas. Many trees are susceptible to a serious disease, mimosa wilt, but there are resistant clones (see Cultivars). It is subject to topkill in some winters in the northern part of its useful range and to wind damage, but it returns to good form in a few years with corrective pruning. As a result of these problems, this tree is a short-lived, high-maintenance plant. But in spite of this, it is widely used for its unique interest.

Cultivars. 'Charlotte' and 'Tryon' have been selected by the U.S. Department of Agriculture as resistant to mimosa wilt disease. They are useful in Zones 7b–9a+.

'Ernest Wilson' is an unusually hardy and low-growing form selected from seed collected by E. H. Wilson in Korea in 1918 and released as a cultivar by the Arnold Arboretum 50 years later. It is useful in Zones 6a–9a+ and can be propagated easily by juvenile softwood cuttings forced from root pieces.

F. rosea is a collective name without current botanical standing that includes individual trees having unusual hardiness and deep pink flower color, among them 'Ernest Wilson.'

Alnus glutinosa 7–8

European or black alder
Deciduous tree
Betulaceae (Birch Family)

Native Range. Northern Eurasia and southward to Caucasus.

Useful Range. USDA Zones 4a–8b.

Function. Fast-growing shade tree, specimen, naturalizing.

Size and Habit

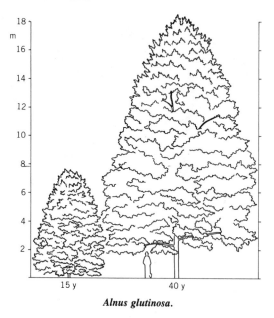

Alnus glutinosa.

Adaptability. Alders are unusual in that they combine a tolerance of wet soils and the ability to use atmospheric nitrogen with the help of nitrogen-fixing bacteria. In this way, they grow quickly in soils that are both infertile and poorly drained, as well as in drier sites, making them useful for urban planting.

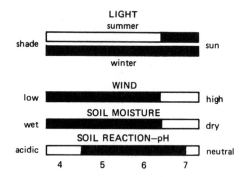

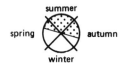

Seasonal Interest. *Flowers:* Dormant flower catkins of two distinct types (male and female) add quiet interest in winter, especially when the male catkins expand and open in late winter and spring. *Foliage:* Leaves, rounded and 5–10 cm/2–4 in. long, remain dark green all summer (when not infested with leaf miners or tent caterpillars) and into autumn, when they fall with little color change.

Problems and Maintenance. Alders are relatively short-lived in most situations, and their foliage may be disfigured by leaf miners, tent caterpillars, and woolly alder aphids if a spray program is not provided. Their broad adaptability makes them useful in some situations in spite of their problems.

Cultivars. 'Laciniata' has deeply cut foliage, giving much finer texture than the species, but is seldom available. 'Pyramidalis' has a narrowly pyramidal form and is somewhat denser and lower branching than the species. Several additional cultivars have been selected in Europe but are seldom if ever used in North America.

Related Species

Alnus incana 6–7 (speckled alder). Similar to A. *glutinosa* in most respects, but slower-growing and extremely hardy, at least as far north as Zone 3a. It is native to Eurasia as well as North America. The North American form (var. *glauca*) is shrubby or a very small tree at best, and the Eurasian type (var. *vulgaris*) is a small tree, similar in general growth to A. *glutinosa*.

Alnus oregona 7 (synonym: A. *rubra*; red alder). This native of the Pacific Northwest is comparable in size and function to A. *incana* var. *vulgaris* and A. *glutinosa*. It is alleged to be more susceptible to tent caterpillar than some other alders, and, regardless of this, probably is of little interest as a landscape tree in eastern North America.

Alnus rugosa 6 (synonym: A. *serrulata*; smooth or hazel alder). This native of eastern North America is similar in size to the North American A. *incana* var. *glauca*, but more southern in distribution and adaptability (Zones 3b–9a), depending on the geographical origin of the genetic material.

Amelanchier arborea 6–7

Synonym: often called A. *canadensis*, a name properly given to a relatively obscure species that seldom is cultivated
Shadblow, downy serviceberry or servicetree, juneberry
Rosaceae (Rose Family)

Native Range. Eastern United States and adjacent Canada, west to Iowa, south to northern Georgia and Lousiana.

Useful Range. USDA Zones 3b–8a.

Function. Specimen or patio tree or shrub, border, naturalizing.

Size and Habit

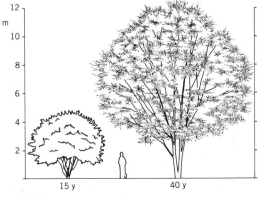

Amelanchier arborea.

Adaptability. Even though the species as a whole is widely adapted, it is probably a good idea to select plants grown from material native to the same region where they will be used for best adaptation and performance.

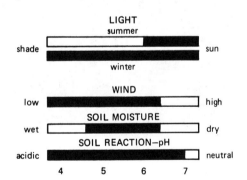

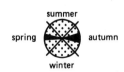

Seasonal Interest. *Flowers:* Small but numerous in early spring, giving a lacy, billowy appearance to the plant, but lasting for only a few days. *Foliage:* Downy and silvery green when young, enhancing and extending the graceful, billowy appearance of the flowers in early spring, becoming neutral green, the leaves 3−8 cm/1−3 in. long when fully expanded, turning red-orange or russet-gold in autumn and falling early. *Fruits:* Turn from red to deep blue-purple, and usually taken by birds as soon as they are ripe. Valued for preserves when they can be picked before the birds take them. *Bark:* Silvery gray with subtle darker striping on main branches and trunks.

Amelanchier arborea.

Amelanchier arborea.

Problems and Maintenance. This tree is subject to several troubles common to members of the rose family and the pome-fruit subfamily in particular, especially fire blight and mites. These can be controlled in most situations without difficulty. Scale insects also can be a problem, especially in the warmer areas, yet this is not usually considered a high-maintenance tree, especially in naturalized plantings.

Cultivars. None are available.

Related Species

Amelanchier alnifolia 4−5 (saskatoon, juneberry, serviceberry), *Amelanchier florida* 4−6, *Amelan-*

Amelanchier arborea.

chier spicata 3−4 (synonym: A. *humilis;* low serviceberry). These species all are relatively low, thicket-forming shrubs with upright branches. They offer similar hardiness and seasonal interest to the larger serviceberries, but with little of their gracefulness. Since they do not function as trees, they are considerably less useful in the landscape than A. *arborea,* A. ×*grandiflora* and A. *laevis,* but A. *alnifolia* is outstanding for its large fruits, which are valued for preserves.

Amelanchier ×*grandiflora* 6 (apple serviceberry). Hybrid between two tall-growing species (A. *arborea* × A. *laevis*) and similar to them. The foliage is not as downy as that of A. *arborea* nor as red at emergence as A. *laevis,* and the flowers are larger and more showy than those of either parent. Useful in Zones 3b−8a.

Amelanchier laevis 6 (Allegheny serviceberry). Very similar to A. *arborea* except the largest forms of the latter, and functionally interchangeable in most landscape situations. Its new foliage is smooth rather than downy and reddish at first unfolding, quickly turning green. Useful in Zones 3b−8a.

Amorpha canescens 3

Leadplant
Deciduous shrub
Leguminosae (Pea Family)

Native Range. Central North America: Manitoba and Saskatchewan to Louisiana and northern Mexico.

Useful Range. USDA Zones 3a−9a.

Function. Border, specimen.

Size and Habit. A. *canescens* is a subshrub, killing to the ground each winter over most of its useful range and returning to flower in a single growing season.

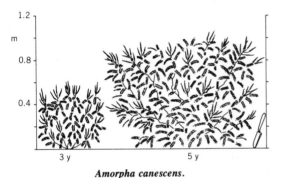

Amorpha canescens.

Adaptability. This shrub is unusually well adapted to hot climates and dry, infertile soils, probably the principal reason to consider it for landscape use.

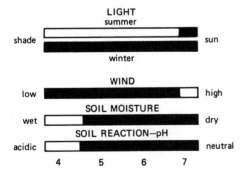

Seasonal Interest. *Flowers:* Small, blue in fairly colorful spikes to 15 cm/6 in. long, from early to middle summer. *Foliage:* Gray, hairy, compound with many small leaflets, producing fine texture. *Fruits:* Small pods, not conspicuous.

Problems and Maintenance. Leadplant is one of the most trouble-free of shrubs, requiring little or no maintenance other than annual removal of the winterkilled top when necessary.

Related Species

Amorpha fruticosa 6 (false indigo). Unlike A. *canescens*, this large shrub, native to much of our area, does not regularly winterkill to the ground except from Zone 4 northward. Since it becomes too large and ungainly to be useful, it should be given radical renewal pruning every year or two. Even then it lacks the interest of A. *canescens*, and in most situations other shrubs perform more effectively. Still, it does tolerate difficult site conditions and it is widely adapted as a native plant from New England to Saskatchewan and southward to Florida and Mexico in Zones 3b−9a.

Amorpha nana 3 (dwarf false indigo). This tidy dwarf shrub with very fine-textured green foliage, native from Manitoba and Saskatchewan to northern Mexico, is useful as a border shrub for its foliage and purple flowers, in spikes to 10 cm/4 in. long in late spring, in Zones 3a−9a.

Ampelopsis brevipedunculata 1

Porcelain or Amur ampelopsis
Deciduous vine
Vitaceae (Grape Family)

Native Range. Northeastern Asia.

Useful Range. USDA Zones 5a−9a.

Function. Screen (with support), specimen.

Size and Habit. Grows vigorously and climbs by tendrils to heights of 5 m/16 ft or greater.

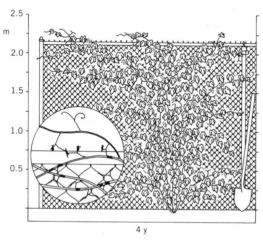

Ampelopsis brevipedunculata.

Adaptability. This widely adapted vine grows well in most soil, but it can be slow in establishment.

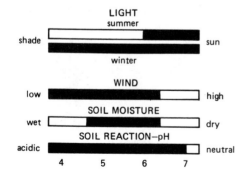

Seasonal Interest. *Foliage:* Bright green, lobed, handsomely textured. *Fruits:* Small berries that appear to be made of porcelain, progressing through pastel shades of yellow, lilac, green, and blue, all colors sometimes appearing in a single cluster.

Problems and Maintenance. This vine is relatively troublefree, but the foliage may be chewed by insects such as the Japanese beetle.

Varieties and Cultivars. 'Elegans' has smaller, white and pink variegated leaves and slower growth, is less useful for screening, but is interesting for specimen use. Var. *maximowiczii* has more finely dissected foliage than the species type.

Related Species

Ampelopsis arborea 1 (peppervine). This vigorous vine is graceful but not dense enough to be very functional as a screen. The foliage is doubly compound and semievergreen, the flowers are fairly large but not conspicuous, and the fruits are about the same size as those of A. *brevipedunculata* but dark purple. It may need to be pruned for restraint in warmer areas. Hardy in Zones 7b−9a+.

Several other species of *Ampelopsis* have been cultivated, most with no advantage over those listed here. *Ampelopsis humulifolia* may have advantages for screening and handsome foliage, but lacks the strong fruiting interest of A. *brevipedunculata* and probably is not commercially available.

Aralia elata 6–7

Japanese angelica tree, devil's walking stick
Deciduous shrub or tree
Araliaceae (Aralia Family)

Native Range. Japan, Korea, Manchuria.

Useful Range. USDA Zones 4a–9a.

Function. Distinctive specimen shrub or tree, of umbrellalike form and coarse texture, branching sparsely.

Size and Habit

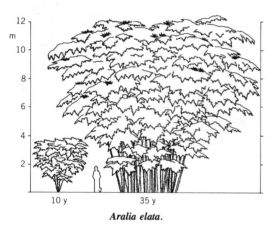

Aralia elata.

Adaptability. Unusually tolerant of widely varying soil and environmental conditions, including dry city sites.

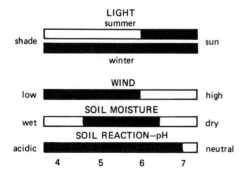

Seasonal Interest. *Flowers:* Small, creamy white, in huge clusters (compound umbels) to 45 cm/18 in. across, in midsummer. *Foliage:* Huge, coarse-textured, doubly compound leaves, to 1 m/3.3 ft long, turning dull reddish in autumn.

Problems and Maintenance. Fast-growing sucker shoots must be removed if this plant is to be used in tree form; otherwise it becomes a thicket. Branches. petioles, and even leaf surfaces have sharp prickles, a problem around small children. There are few other problems.

Cultivars. 'Aureovariegata' has yellow variegated leaf margins. 'Variegata' has white variegated leaf margins.

Relates Species

Aralia spinosa 6–7 (Hercules' club, angelica tree, devil's walking stick). This is the American counterpart of A. *elata*, native from Pennsylvania to Florida, Texas, and Iowa. Similar in landscape use to, and interchangeable with, A. *elata*, except in Zone 4, where it is not fully hardy.

Arctostaphylos uva-ursi 2

Bearberry, kinnikinick
Evergreen groundcover
Ericaceae (Heath Family)

Native Range. Circumpolar: northern parts of Asia, Europe, and North America, farther south at high elevations.

Useful Range. USDA Zones 3a–7a with selection of appropriate genetic material, and with snow cover in Zones 3–5.

Function. Excellent evergreen groundcover.

Size and Habit

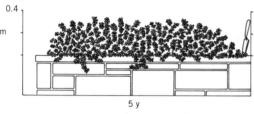

Arctostaphylos uva-ursi.

Adaptability. This groundcover is unusually well adapted to very infertile, sandy, acidic soils and cold climates, but is best in areas with fairly cool summers. It is subject to desiccation in winter sun and wind.

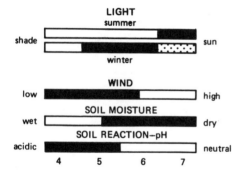

Seasonal Interest. *Flowers:* Small, pink, in midspring. *Foliage:* Evergreen, neatly fine-textured, lustrous, turning bronze-purple in winter. *Fruits:* Bright red berries in summer.

Arctostaphylos uva-ursi.

Problems and Maintenance. This plant is trouble-free, requiring little maintenance once established. Transplanting can be a problem unless pot-grown plants are specified, but large sods also can be moved successfully.

Cultivars. None are available.

Related Species

Arctostaphylos manzanita 5 (Parry manzanita). This large shrub bears little resemblance to *A. uva-ursi*. It has regular form, handsome evergreen foliage, white or pink flowers in spring, and ornamental red fruits that are useful for preserves. It is one of several species of *Arctostaphylos* native to the West Coast of the United States and valued for landscape planting there. Worthy of wider trial in the Southeast in localities with moderate summer temperatures and acid soil in Zones 7b–9a+.

Ardisia crenata 3—4

Coral ardisia, coralberry, spiceberry, Christmas berry
Evergreen shrub
Myrsinaceae (Myrsine Family)

Native Range. India to Japan.

Useful Range. USDA Zone 9a+.

Function. Specimen, mass planting, naturalizing.

Size and Habit. Upright in form, spreading by underground shoots but not making a dense mass.

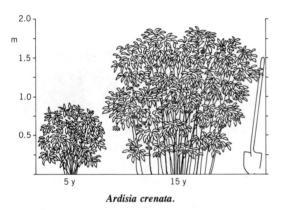

Ardisia crenata.

Adaptability

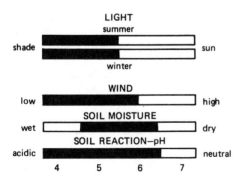

Seasonal Interest. *Flowers:* Small, pink or white, in terminal clusters on branches, not highly conspicuous. *Foliage:* Leathery, evergreen leaves, to 8 cm/3 in. long, lustrous with

glandular-crisped margins. *Fruits:* Long-lasting bright red (or white) berries, about 1.2 cm/0.5 in. across.

Problems and Maintenance. This plant is generally trouble-free and requires little or no maintenance when used in good sites.

Cultivars. 'Alba' has white berries.

Related Species

Ardisia crispa 3—4 (Chinese ardisia). Very similar to A. *crenata*, often confused with it, and equivalent in landscape use. Differs from A. *crenata* in having slightly pubescent young growth.

Ardisia japonica 2 (Japanese ardisia, marlberry). This low-growing plant is useful as a woodland groundcover. Like A. *crenata* and A. *crispa*, it grows best mulched in reasonably fertile, well-drained soil in partial shade. Its seasonal interest is similar, consisting primarily of bright red fruits and evergreen foliage. Considerably lower-growing and hardier than the other two species, useful in Zones 7a—9a+.

Aristolochia durior 1

Synonyms: A. *macrophylla*, A. *sipho*
Dutchman's pipe
Deciduous vine
Aristolochiaceae (Birthwort Family)

Size and Habit. Grows vigorously and climbs by twining to heights of 8 m/25 ft.

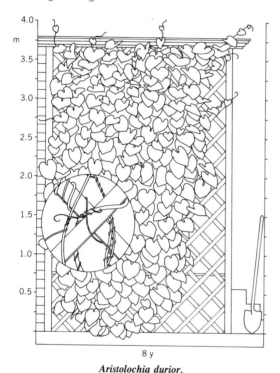

Aristolochia durior.

Adaptability

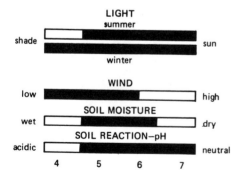

Native Range. East-central to midwestern United States.

Useful Range. USDA Zones 4b–7b.

Function. Screen (with support).

Seasonal Interest. *Flowers:* Inconspicuous but interesting pipelike greenish flowers. *Foliage:* Dark green, heart-shaped or kidney-shaped leaves to 30 cm/12 in. long and broad, giving very coarse texture.

Aristolochia durior.

Problems and Maintenance. This vine is relatively trouble-free and needs practically no maintenance.

Aronia arbutifolia 5

Red chokeberry
Deciduous shrub
Rosaceae (Rose Family)

Native Range. Most of eastern United States.

Useful Range. USDA Zones 4b−9a.

Function. Specimen, shrub border, naturalizing. Most useful in mass plantings, except for the cultivar 'Brilliantissima.'

Size and Habit

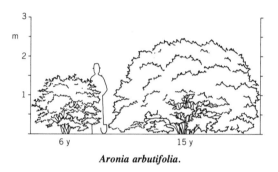

Aronia arbutifolia.

Adaptability. This shrub is unusually versatile with respect to soil and climatic adaptation, including dry, infertile soils.

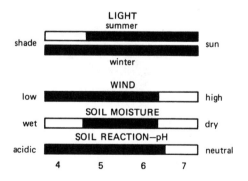

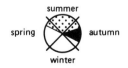

Seasonal Interest. *Flowers:* Small, white (or pinkish), in clusters, only moderately showy, in late spring. *Foliage:* Medium or gray-green leaves, 3−5 cm/1−2 in. long, fuzzy underneath, lustrous above, turning reddish in autumn. *Fruits:* Bright red berries in clusters, showy in autumn.

Aronia arbutifolia.

Problems and Maintenance. Chokeberries are subject to some of the problems of the rose family in general and pome fruits in particular, but less so than many others in that group and generally require little maintenance.

Cultivars. 'Brilliantissima' has unusually showy, shiny red berries.

Related Species

Aronia melanocarpa 3−4 (black chokeberry). This shrub is similar to A. *arbutifolia*, except that is has more upright branching, tending to form low thickets, and black berries. It is useful in Zones 3b−7b.

Aronia prunifolia 5 (purple chokeberry). This is similar to A. *arbutifolia*, but with less showy, purple berries.

Artemisia abrotanum 4

Southernwood, oldman wormwood
Deciduous subshrub
Compositae (Composite Family)

Native Range. Southern Europe, escaped from cultivation in the United States.

Useful Range. USDA Zones 3b—8b.

Function. Border, mass planting (in dry or alkaline soil), special effects (foliage).

Size and Habit

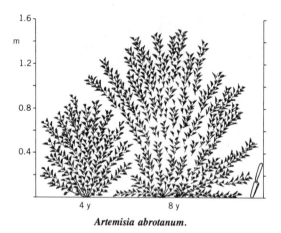

Artemisia abrotanum.

Adaptability. This plant is unusually tolerant of dry and alkaline soils, hot summers, and salt spray.

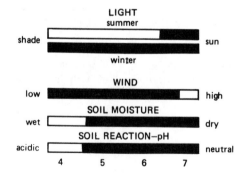

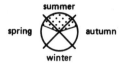

Seasonal Interest. *Foliage:* Finely dissected, fine-textured, grayish foliage is strongly pungent when crushed or brushed against.

Problems and Maintenance. A relatively trouble-free plant, the top kills to the ground each winter in northern areas, returning vigorously the following growing season.

Cultivars. 'Nana' is a dwarf form that usually remains below 50 cm/20 in. high, spreading widely to 2 m/6.6 ft or more. Foliage color is not particularly good, and this cultivar is not as hardy as the species, but it is useful in Zones 4b—8b.

Related Species

Artemisia schmidtiana 3 (satin wormwood). This perennial herb from Japan has finely dissected silvery gray foliage, aromatic when crushed. The low-growing selections 'Nana' and 'Silver Mound,' remaining lower than 15 cm/6 in. and 30 cm/12 in. respectively, are functional groundcovers during the growing season, useful in Zones 3b—9a+.

Artemisia stellerana 3 (dusty miller, beach wormwood). This groundcover or low massing plant is grown for the white, felty, dissected foliage, coarser than that of A. *abrotanum*. Like other *Artemisia* species, it is relatively salt tolerant.

Artemisia tridentata 5 (sagebrush). This somewhat ragged shrub is useful only in extremely dry, alkaline soils, seldom encountered in eastern North America.

Asarum caudatum 2

British Columbia wild ginger
Evergreen groundcover
Aristolochiaceae (Birthwort Family)

Native Range. Northwestern North America: British Columbia to California.

Useful Range. USDA Zones 6a−8a, probably also Zones 4 and 5 where snow cover is reliable, or with other protection from full winter sun and wind.

Function. Groundcover.

Size and Habit

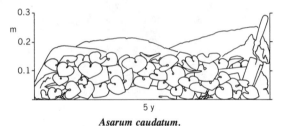

Asarum caudatum.

Adaptability. The requirement for shade is greater in the South and Midwest than in northern and mountain areas.

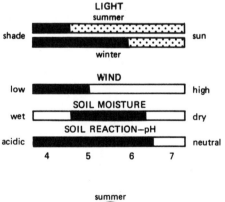

Seasonal Interest. *Flowers:* Brownish crimson, distinctive and interesting, but borne under the leaves and seldom fully visible, in late spring.

Foliage: Evergreen, lustrous, heart-shaped, 10−15 cm/4−6 in. long, providing exceptional year-round textural interest.

Problems and Maintenance. Wild gingers usually are trouble-free, given a proper site initially.

Related Species

Asarum canadense 2 (American wild ginger, Canada snakeroot).   This native of northeastern North America, from New Brunswick to North Carolina and Missouri, differs from A. *caudatum* in that it is deciduous or semievergreen at best. It is useful in Zones 4a−7a and parts of warmer zones with moderate summers.

Asarum canadense.

Asarum europeaeum 2 (European wild ginger). This impressive evergreen from Europe has more glossy and rounded leaves than A. *caudatum*, seldom more than 8 cm/3 in. across, making it one of the most handsome of all groundcovers, useful in Zones 5a−8b. Like A. *caudatum*, it requires protection from full sun.

Asarum shuttleworthii 2 (Shuttleworth wild ginger).   This native of the southeastern United States from North Carolina to Alabama, has evergreen, elongated, heart-shaped leaves, 5−8 cm/2−3 in. long, sometimes beautifully mottled with light and dark green. Useful in Zones 6b−8b, perhaps also Zone 5, and is best in sites that are fully or at least half shaded.

Asimina triloba 6–7

Pawpaw
Deciduous tree
Annonaceae (Custard Apple Family)

Native Range. Eastern United States.

Useful Range. USDA Zones 5b–8a.

Function. Specimen, screen, mass planting, edible fruit.

Size and Habit. Form stiffly upright and pyramidal, spreading by suckers.

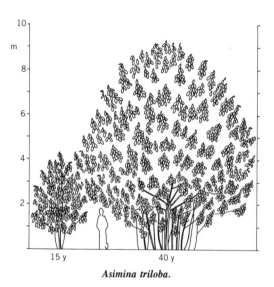

Asimina triloba.

Adaptability

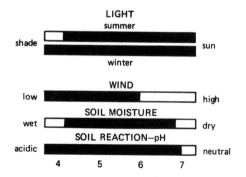

Seasonal Interest. *Flowers:* Dark red, inconspicuous but interesting, in midspring. *Foliage:* Dark green, drooping, giving distinctive texture,

Asimina triloba.

turning bright yellow in autumn. *Fruits:* Green to yellow-brown, somewhat bananalike, edible, in early autumn. Two fruiting forms exist, one with palatable yellow flesh, the other with greenish white flesh of inferior flavor. At least two clones (cultivars or seedlings) must be present for cross-pollination and good fruiting.

Problems and Maintenance. This shrub has wide-ranging roots, making it difficult to transplant, and it tends to grow suckers that must be removed from specimen trees. But it is relatively pest-free. A small number of people show skin sensitivity to this plant.

Cultivars. 'Overleese' has been selected for large fruits, 'Taylor' and 'Taytwo' for superior flavor. There is considerable interest in this plant as a fruit crop in the east-central United States, and additional selections are likely to be named and released.

Aspidistra elatior 3

Aspidistra, cast iron plant
Evergreen groundcover
Liliaceae (Lily Family)

Native Range. Japan.

Useful Range. USDA Zones 8b−9a+.

Function. Groundcover, accent.

Size and Habit

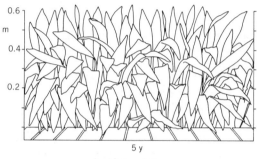

Aspidistra elatior.

Adaptability

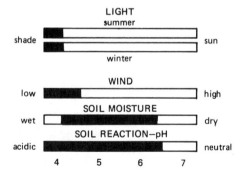

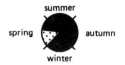

Seasonal Interest. *Foliage:* Dark green, parallel-veined, evergreen, the leaves stiff and swordlike, narrowing to a petiole at the ground. Numerous leaves make a tight mass in time.

Problems and Maintenance. In spite of its general durability, the leaves will scorch in full sun, and occasionally will be frozen back in Zones 8 and 9a, but they return rather quickly. Otherwise, this is a low-maintenance groundcover, since the tight foliage mass resists weed invasion.

Cultivars. 'Variegata' has white and green striped leaves. It is somewhat less vigorous and more prone to foliage scorch than the green-leaved form, but striking for landscape accent. The white variegation tends to disappear in very fertile soils, so heavy fertilization should be avoided.

Related Species

Rohdea japonica 3 (lily of China). This relative of *Aspidistra* from China and Japan is an equally useful groundcover in Zones 8a−9a+. Several cultivars with variegated leaves have been selected, but their availability is limited.

Aucuba japonica 5

Japanese aucuba, Japanese laurel
Evergreen shrub
Cornaceae (Dogwood Family)

Native Range. Japan to Himalayas.

Useful Range. USDA Zones 7b–9a+.

Function. Screen, specimen, mass or foundation planting.

Size and Habit

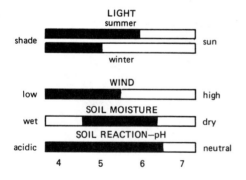

Aucuba japonica.

Adaptability. Given reasonably moist soil and shade from full winter sun, this plant is widely adaptable, even to city conditions.

LIGHT
summer
shade ████████████░░░░░ sun
winter
shade ██████████░░░░░░░ sun

WIND
low ████████░░░░░░░ high

SOIL MOISTURE
wet ░░░░░░░░░░░░░░░ dry

SOIL REACTION–pH
acidic ███████████░░░░░ neutral
    4   5   6   7

Seasonal Interest. *Flowers:* Small, reddish brown, inconspicuous in early spring, dioecious. *Foliage:* Evergreen, dark olive green, leathery leaves, 8–18 cm/3–7 in. long and half as wide, giving a coarse texture. Some cultivars have variegated foliage. *Fruits:* Red fruits, to 1.5 cm/0.6 in. across, in clusters 3–8 cm/1–3 in. long on female plants, colorful in winter. For maximum fruiting interest, plant mostly females with an occasional male for pollination.

Problems and Maintenance. Foliage burns in full sun, so shade should always be provided, especially in winter and especially for cultivars with variegated foliage. A leaf-spot disease is occasionally troublesome in warmer zones. Otherwise, this shrub is relatively trouble-free. Occasional pruning may be desirable to restrain height growth and maintain fullness.

Cultivars. 'Crotonifolia' and 'Fructu Albo' have white variegated foliage; 'Fructu albo' also has whitish pink fruits. 'Dentata' and 'Serratifolia' have more distinctly toothed leaves than the species type. 'Goldieana' has mostly yellow foliage. 'Longifolia' (='Angustifolia,' ='Salicifolia') has narrow green leaves. 'Macrophylla' has unusually large, broad leaves. 'Nana' is dwarf in growth habit. 'Picturata' (= 'Aureo-maculata') has dark green leaves with a large gold blotch in the center of each. 'Variegata' (= 'Maculata,' gold dust plant) has dark green leaves with bright gold flecks and blotches over the surfaces.'Viridis' is a vigorous, green-leaved selection.

Baccharis halimifolia 5

Groundsel bush, eastern baccharis
Deciduous or evergreen shrub
Compositae (Composite Family)

Native Range. Atlantic Coast marshes, Massachusetts to Texas.

Useful Range. USDA Zones 4a–9a.

Function. Specimen, mass plantings (in wet or salty sites).

Size and Habit

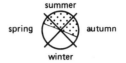

Seasonal Interest. *Flowers:* Whitish, in small heads, noticeable but not showy, in late summer. *Foliage:* Deciduous in the North to evergreen in the South, the leaves medium green, 2.5–7 cm/1–2.8 in. long, fine-textured, and making a loosely open mass. *Fruit:* Seed heads carry the whitish appearance of the flowers into autumn.

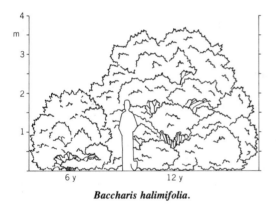

Baccharis halimifolia.

Baccharis halimifolia.

Adaptability. This loose shrub is remarkably well adapted to sites subject to salt spray as well as to wet soil, and it is used primarily for this reason but also grows well in "normal" planting sites.

Problems and Maintenance. This shrub is relatively trouble-free, but pruning may occasionally be needed to maintain vigor and fullness.

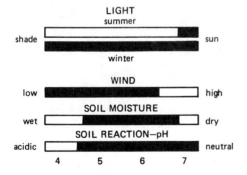

Bambusa glaucescens 5−6

Synonyms: *B. argentea, B. multiplex*
Evergreen shrub
Hedge bamboo
Gramineae (Grass Family)

Native Range. China.

Useful Range. USDA Zone 9a+, and protected sites in Zone 8b, but suffers some winterburn even in Zone 9a.

Function. Hedge, screen, specimen.

Size and Habit

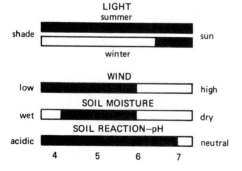

Bambusa glaucescens.

Adaptability. Protection from full winter sun and wind will reduce winterburn of foliage.

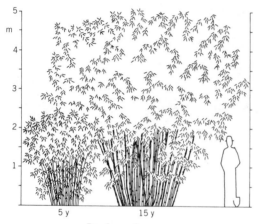

Seasonal Interest. *Foliage:* Evergreen leaves, up to 15 cm/6 in. long, are medium green, whitened underneath. *Stems:* Green at first, becoming dull

yellow when mature, to 3 cm/1.2 in. across, making a dense mass adequate for screening.

Problems and Maintenance. Bamboos are generally free of pest problems in our area. Some may become a problem themselves by spreading aggressively, but *B. glaucescens* is not one of the worst offenders.

Varieties and Cultivars. 'Alphonse Karr' has stems emerging pinkish, maturing golden yellow, with longitudinal green stripes. It grows to heights of 8−10 m/26−33 ft under ideal conditions, but usually remains lower in our area.
  'Fernleaf' has finer-textured foliage than the species type and rarely exceeds 5−6 m/16−20 ft in height.
  Var. *riviereorum* (Chinese goddess bamboo) is dwarf, growing to 2−3 m/6.6−10 ft under ideal conditions, often lower in our area, with arching branches and fine-textured foliage, useful only as a specimen for accent.
  'Silverstripe' has some white striped leaves, others normal yellow-green, with narrow yellow stripes on some stems, growing to 8−10 m/26−33 ft or taller under ideal growing conditions.
  'Stripestem Fernleaf' is a lower-growing selection, 2−3 m/6.6−10 ft tall, with green striped yellow stems.

Related Species

Arundinaria disticha 3 (synonyms: *Bambusa disticha, B. nana, Sasa disticha;* dwarf fernleaf bamboo). This Japanese native with bright green leaves makes an effective groundcover in Zones 8a−9a+.

Arundinaria pygmaea 2 (synonyms: *Bambusa pygmaea, Pleioblastus pygmaea, Sasa pygmaea;* pigmy bamboo). This low, mat-forming bamboo from Japan with bright green leaves and purplish stems is useful as a groundcover, especially on wet soils, in Zones 8a−9a+. It may spread beyond bounds if not restricted with edging or pavement. The selection 'Variegata' has white-margined leaves.

Arundinaria simonii 6 (synonym: *Pleioblastus simonii*; Simon bamboo). This Japanese native reaches about the same size as *B. glaucescens*, but it is somewhat less aggressive and more cold hardy. Useful in Zones 8a–9a+.

Arundinaria variegata 3 (dwarf whitestripe bamboo). This native of Japan with white striped foliage makes an effective but rather tall groundcover. It is useful in Zones 6b–9a+.

Arundinaria variegata.

Phyllostachys aurea 6 (synonym: *Bambusa aurea*; golden or fishpole bamboo). This Chinese species is another of the taller bamboos that are useful for screening, in this case in Zones 8a–9a+. The stems are distinctly golden yellow and of good wood quality.

Phyllostachys aureosulcata 6 (yellowgroove bamboo). This Chinese species is similar in general effect to *P. aurea*, but it spreads more aggressively. Its dull green stems, striped yellow, are not as strong as those of *P. aurea*. It is useful at least in Zones 7b–9a+.

Phyllostachys bambusoides 7 (timber bamboo). This Chinese species is widely cultivated in Japan and elsewhere in eastern Asia for construction purposes. It is useful for special effects in Zones 8a–9a+.

Phyllostachys nigra 6 (black bamboo). Another Chinese species, this is distincitve in that the stems mature to a brownish or purplish black. It is useful for special effects and screening in Zones

8a–9a+. The selection 'Henon' is more vigorous and taller, to 10–15 m/33–49 ft where hardy, in Zones 8a–9a.

Sasa palmata 4 (synonym: *Bambusa palmata*; palmate bamboo). This species from Japan and Sakhalin is one of the hardiest of all bamboos, useful in Zones 6a–8a. It is not as functional as many, however, since it is too tall to be effective as a groundcover and not reliably tall enough for screening, and it is aggressive and difficult to control.

Sasa palmata.

Sasa palmata.

Sasa veitchii 3 (Kuma bamboo grass). This fast-spreading bamboo from Japan makes an effective, large-scale groundcover but is too aggressive for many situations. It is useful, with this limitation, in Zones 8a–9a+ and perhaps also in Zone 7.

Berberis julianae 4

Wintergreen barberry
Evergreen shrub
Berberidaceae (Barberry Family)

Native Range. China.

Useful Range. USDA Zones 6b−9a.

Function. Border, hedge, barrier, specimen.

Size and Habit

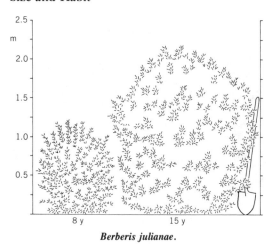

Berberis julianae.

Adaptability. This handsome shrub grows best in full sun in Zones 7a−8a, but it will benefit from light shade and protection from wind in winter in Zone 6b and in summer in Zones 8b and 9a.

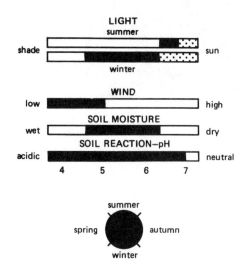

Seasonal Interest. *Flowers:* Yellow, small but fairly showy, in midspring. *Foliage:* Evergreen,

dark green, lustrous, 5−10 cm/2−4 in. long, on spiny or thorny branches. *Fruits:* Inconspicuous blue-black berries in autumn.

Problems and Maintenance. Certain species of *Berberis* serve as alternate hosts for black stem rust of wheat, an economically serious disease. Except for the highly susceptible *B. vulgaris*, those mentioned here are listed as resistant to this disease by the U.S. Department of Agriculture. These barberries are relatively free of troubles and need for maintenance. Their thorniness makes them difficult to handle in landscape construction, and they are best avoided in children's play areas.

Cultivars. 'Compactum' remains more compact and lower than the species type, not exceeding 1.5 m/5 ft for many years.

Related Species

Berberis gagnepainii 4 (black barberry).   Like *B. julianae*, widely adapted (Zones 6b−9a) and requiring fairly good soil conditions and some protection from wind for best performance. Leaves are somewhat longer and narrower than that of *B. julianae*.

Berberis panlanensis 4 (synonym: *B. sanguinea*; red-flowered barberry).   Differs little from *B. gagnepainii* except in having still narrower leaves, flowers red on the outside, and somewhat less cold hardiness, useful in Zones 7a−9a.

Berberis sargentiana 4 (Sargent barberry).   Differs little from *B. gagnepainii* except in hardiness (Zones 7a−9a).

Berberis wisleyensis.

Berberis wisleyensis 4 (synonym: *B. triacan-thophora;* threespine barberry). Slightly lower in stature than the above species and somewhat hardier, useful in Zones 6b–9a, with unusually handsome foliage, dark green above and chalky white underneath.

The above species all are evergreen and of Chinese origin. Except for differences in hardiness and small variations in landscape character, they can be considered equivalent to *B. julianae* in landscape function and requirements.

Berberis koreana 4

Korean barberry
Deciduous shrub
Berberidaceae (Barberry Family)

Native Range. Korea.

Useful Range. USDA Zones 3b–8a.

Function. Border, hedge, specimen. Neither full nor tall enough to be an effective visual screen.

Seasonal Interest. *Flowers:* Small, golden-yellow, in fairly showy hanging clusters, in midspring. *Foliage:* Relatively large leaves (for a barberry), rounded and finely spined on thorny branches, turning bright red in autumn. *Fruits:* Bright red berries in showy hanging clusters in autumn.

Size and Habit

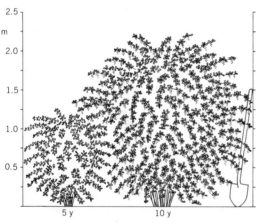

Berberis koreana.

Berberis koreana.

Adaptability

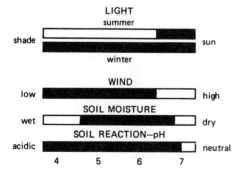

Problems and Maintenance. This shrub is relatively trouble-free but requires occasional light pruning to maintain fullness. It should only be pruned heavily for renewal, since this destroys its form and fruiting display for a time. Use of all deciduous barberries is barred in Canada as a control measure for black stem rust of wheat.

Related Species

Berberis gilgiana 4 (wildfire barberry). Similar to *B. koreana* in appearance and landscape function and useful in Zones 5b–8a, but probably not available.

Berberis vulgaris 5 (common barberry). Similar to *B. koreana*, this European species, naturalized in North America, is commonly seen in many areas of eastern North America. Unlike the other species included here, it is susceptible to black stem rust of wheat, so it has been largely eradicated in wheat-growing areas and must, by law, be removed when found in Canada. It obviously should not be planted in these areas.

Berberis ×mentorensis 4

Mentor barberry
Semievergreen shrub
Berberidaceae (Barberry Family)

Hybrid Origin. *B. julianae* × *B. thunbergii*.

Useful Range. USDA Zones 5b−9a.

Function. Hedge, border, specimen.

Size and Habit

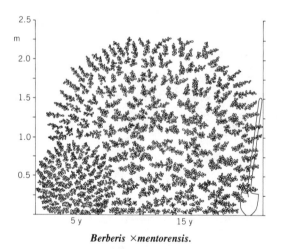

Berberis ×mentorensis.

This, with cold hardiness, makes it a valued plant in the Midwest.

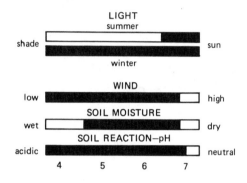

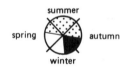

Seasonal Interest. *Flowers:* Small, yellow, noticeable but not showy, in midspring. *Foliage:* Fine-textured, leathery, blue-green, and slightly spiny; semievergreen, finally turning red-orange before falling in early winter.

Problems and Maintenance. This is one of the most maintenance-free shrubs, seldom requiring more than occasional pruning, and that only where it is used as a formal hedge.

Adaptability. This shrub is unusually well adapted to hot, dry summers, retaining good foliage character even in substantial drought.

Berberis thunbergii 4

Japanese barberry
Deciduous shrub
Berberidaceae (Barberry Family)

Native Range. Japan.

Useful Range. USDA Zones 4b(a)−9a, depending on cultivar.

Function. Hedge, border, specimen.

Size and Habit

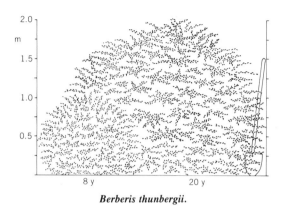

Berberis thunbergii.

Adaptability

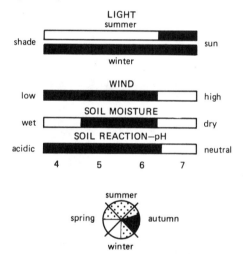

Seasonal Interest. *Flowers:* Small, yellow, interesting with expanding foliage but not showy. *Foliage:* Neatly fine-textured, bright green, turning scarlet in autumn. *Fruits:* Numerous, small, elongated, red berries are noticeable with green foliage, and add striking interest as the leaves change to red and remain after leaf fall.

Problems and Maintenance. This species is relatively durable and trouble-free, requiring little maintenance in good sites. Even though in the past it has been thought to be resistant to black stem rust of wheat, new races of the disease-causing fungus have infected certain cultivars of *B. thunbergii* f. *atropurpurea* in Canada, and the use of all deciduous barberries is now banned by the Canadian government.

Forms and Cultivars. F. *atropurpurea* differs from the species type in that its foliage turns deep red-purple in direct sun. Several cultivars selected for intensity of red color, for instance, 'Cardinal,' 'Humber Red,' 'Redbird,' and 'Sheridan Red,' are useful in Zones 4b–8b but now are barred from use in Canada, where most of them originated.

'Atropurpurea Nana' (= 'Crimson Pygmy') is a fine dwarf selection from f. *atropurpurea* that grows to about 1 m/3.3 ft in height and becomes broader than high.

'Aurea' has bright yellow foliage in direct sun, and slower growth than the species.

'Erecta' has an upright growth habit, useful for narrow hedges. Unless it is kept vigorous it may not remain upright, but branches may fall into prostrate or ascending positions.

'Minor' is at least as dwarf as 'Crimson Pygmy,' but it has green foliage.

'Kobold' (Plant Patent No. 3038, 1971) is a low-growing, dense selection with unusually heavy foliage.

'Sparkle' has unusually glossy, leathery, rich green foliage and slightly more compact growth than the species type.

Berberis verruculosa 3

Warty barberry
Evergreen shrub
Berberidaceae (Barberry Family)

Native Range. China.

Useful Range. USDA Zones 6a–9a.

Function. Border, hedge, specimen.

Size and Habit. Lower in relation to height than most other barberries; moundlike and compact.

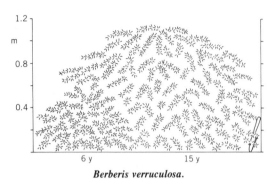

Berberis verruculosa.

Adaptability. Best in full sun in Zones 6b–8a, it benefits from light shade and protection from wind in winter in Zone 6a and from light shade in summer in Zones 8b–9a.

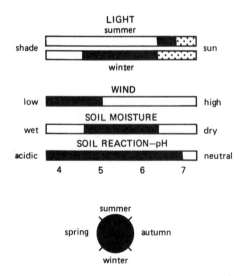

Seasonal Interest. *Flowers.* Yellow, small but fairly showy, in midspring. *Foliage:* Evergreen, dark green and lustrous above, chalky white underneath, fine-textured and spiny on thorny branches, bronzing in winter. *Fruits:* Inconspicuous blue-black berries in autumn.

Problems and Maintenance. Certain species of *Berberis* serve as alternate hosts for black stem rust of wheat, an economically serious disease (see Problems and Maintenance, *B. julianae*).

Related Species

Berberis buxifolia 5 (Magellan barberry). This relatively large shrub is not particularly functional except for the dwarf selection 'Nana,' a low, moundlike plant to 0.5 m/1.6 ft in height, useful in Zones 6a–8a.

Berberis candidula 3 (paleleaf barberry). Similar to *B. verruculosa* and equivalent in hardiness, landscape function, and interest but rarely available.

Berberis candidula.

Berberis ×chenaultii 4 (Chenault barberry). This hybrid of *B. verruculosa* × *B. gagnepainii*, intermediate in size between the parents, appears as a larger edition of *B. verruculosa* with similar foliage and hardiness.

Betula lenta 7–8

Sweet birch, cherry birch
Deciduous tree
Betulaceae (Birch Family)

Native Range. Northeastern United States and southward in the Appalachian Mountains to northern Alabama.

Useful Range. USDA Zones 4a–7b.

Function. Shade tree, naturalizing.

Size and Habit

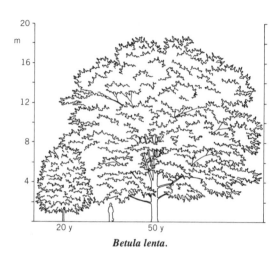

Betula lenta.

Adaptability

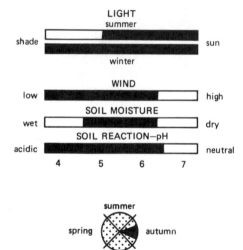

Seasonal Interest. *Foliage:* Clean, dark green, turning bright golden yellow in autumn. *Trunk and branches:* Red-brown, lustrous and lenticular, cherrylike. *Twigs:* Inner bark of young twigs has a wintergreen flavor and is a commercial source of this flavoring.

Problems and Maintenance. Two insects, the bronze birch borer and leaf miner, are potential problems, but limited experience suggests that *B. lenta* is not nearly as susceptible as the white-barked birches. It is susceptible to stem canker disease, but less so in naturalized settings or where adequate moisture is available.

Related Species

Betula alleghaniensis 7–8 (synonym: *B. lutea; yellow birch*).   This tree is generally similar in size, form, and growth rate to *B. lenta*, and it grows wild in about the same area and also in the Great Lakes region and westward to Minnesota. This tree is less tolerant of dry soil and other stresses than *B. lenta* and is equally susceptible to stem cankers. It is even less common in landscape use than *B. lenta*, but it makes a handsome shade tree in areas where it is adapted, with unusual, amber to silvery gray, peeling bark. It grows best in Zones 3b–6b in areas with moderate summer temperatures and adequate moisture.

Betula alleghaniensis.

Betula nigra 8

River birch
Deciduous tree
Betulaceae (Birch Family)

Native Range. Eastern United States: south to
Florida, north to Minnesota, west to Kansas.

Useful Range. USDA Zones 4a−9a with selection of appropriate genetic material.

Function. Shade tree, specimen, naturalizing.

Size and Habit

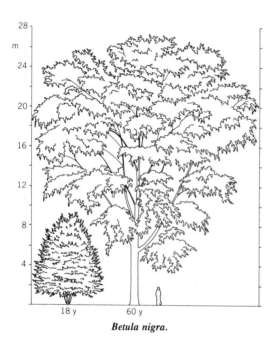

Betula nigra.

Adaptability. This is probably the most widely
adaptable of all the birches, but it occasionally
shows iron chlorosis in soil of neutral and higher
pH. It is far superior to other birches in the South
and Midwest.

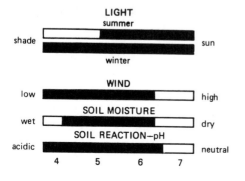

Seasonal Interest. *Foliage:* Clean, medium green
foliage, turning yellowish in autumn. *Trunk and
branches:* Reddish brown to pale tan bark peels
and curls, giving young trunks and branches a
handsome, bicolored appearance.

Betula nigra.

Problems and Maintenance. This tree is widely
used and seldom troubled by bronze birch borer.
Leaf miner can be a minor problem, especially in
the Northeast.

Related Species

Betula albo-sinensis 8 (Chinese paper birch).
Uncommon but similar in many respects to *B.
nigra.* The curling, pink to orange-red bark is
even more striking than that of *B. nigra* and
suggests using this tree primarily as a specimen
for accent and color. It is native to China and
useful in Zones 5b−8a.

Betula davurica 7 (Dahurian birch).   This uncommon tree from northeastern Asia and Japan is
being tried increasingly in the northern states. It
is similar to *B. nigra* in landscape use.

Betula papyrifera 8

Paper birch, canoe birch
Deciduous tree
Betulaceae (Birch Family)

Native Range. Northern North America: Labrador to Alaska and southward into the northern United States and in the Appalachian and Rocky Mountains.

Useful Range. USDA Zones 2b–7a with selection of appropriate genetic material, but not fully satisfactory in warmer areas than Zone 5a.

Function. Shade tree, specimen.

Size and Habit

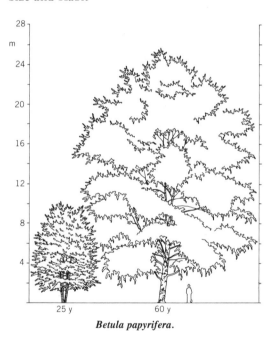

Betula papyrifera.

Adaptability. *B. papyrifera* performs best in areas having mild summers and adequate moisture.

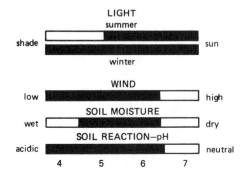

Seasonal Interest. *Foliage:* Rich green leaves, 5–10 cm/2–4 in. long, turn clear yellow before falling in autumn. *Trunk and branches:* smooth bark, marked with horizontal lenticels, is reddish brown at first, becoming papery white on the trunk as the tree ages, striking in all seasons.

Betula papyrifera.

Problems and Maintenance. This handsome tree is very susceptible to bronze birch borer, especially when growing under moisture stress, which is usually the case in the Midwest and South. It is best reserved for northern, mountain, and coastal areas having cool summers, but it can be functional for short life spans in other parts of its useful range with careful maintenance: irrigation and spraying for bronze birch borer. Planting on shaded north sides of buildings has been helpful in some areas, suggesting that soil temperature is a critical factor in this tree's success, although shade has also been said to discourage egg deposition by borers. In the northeastern United States and adjacent Canada, leaf miners are also troublesome, disfiguring the foliage annually unless a carefully timed spray program is adhered to.

Varieties. Several natural varieties exist over the native range, from tall trees to shrubby mountain forms, but there has not been enough interest in selecting distinctive forms to lead to the naming of cultivars, which has been done with *B. pendula*. In general, it is best to use seed sources as close as possible to the areas where the resulting trees will be used.

Related Species

Betula maximowicziana 8 (monarch birch). This vigorous Japanese tree is similar in size and landscape use to *B. papyrifera*, but has larger leaves, 8−14 cm/3−5.5 in. long, and is much less cold-hardy, only to Zone 5b or 6a. There has been much interest in this tree recently because of its alleged resistance to bronze birch borer, but this has not been well established, and any resistance may vary among individual trees. Regardless of this, it is a handsome tree, with trunks ranging from tawny pink to white.

Betula pendula 7−8 (synonyms: *B. alba, B. verrucosa*; European white birch). This handsome shade and specimen tree from northern Europe is widely used in our area, frequently where it is poorly adapted. Its requirements and its susceptibility to attack by borers are similar to those of *B. papyrifera*, and the species type can be considered equivalent in landscape use, even though it is smaller at maturity, seldom exceeding 20 m/66 ft in height, and slightly less cold-hardy, useful in Zones 3a−5b. This species is planted primarily for its distinctive cultivars, which include the following. 'Dalecarlica' has deeply cut leaves. 'Fastigiata' is fastigiate (narrow branching angles) and has a columnar form when young, broadening to oval with age, if it survives that long. 'Gracilis' has a gracefully pendulous growth habit and deeply cut leaves. 'Purpurea'

and 'Purple Splendor' have deep purple foliage, contrasting with the white bark in summer, but they are not vigorous trees. 'Tristis' has a gracefully pendulous growth habit but lacks the cut leaves of 'Gracilis.' 'Youngii' is a relatively small tree, so strongly pendulous that it must be grafted on an upright seedling trunk to keep its branches off the ground.

Betula platyphylla 7 (synonym: *B. mandshurica*; Manchurian or Japanese white birch). This white-barked birch is similar in most respects to *B. papyrifera* and equally cold-hardy in the Manchurian form. The var. *japonica*, a somewhat larger tree from Japan, may not be as well adapted to very cold climates, but it is useful at least in Zones 5a−7b. Plantings of this variety have given some indication of resistance to borers, and this probably will result in wider availability of this tree, perhaps selection of superior forms, and possibly even the use of this species in breeding programs.

Betula populifolia 6−7 (gray birch). This small tree, native to the northeastern United States and adjacent Canada, has slender, usually multiple, trunks. The grayish white bark is more distinctly black-marked than that of the other white-barked species listed here, and its foliage is badly disfigured by leaf miners in much of the Northeast. In spite of these problems, it is widely adaptable to wet and dry soils, and it is commonly used in clump form for accent in and near its native range in Zones 4a−7a.

Buddleia alternifolia 5

Fountain buddleia
Deciduous subshrub
Loganiaceae (Logania Family)

Native Range. China.

Useful Range. USDA Zones 4b−7b.

Function. Border, specimen, cutting.

Size and Habit

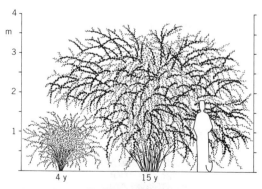

Buddleia alternifolia.

Adaptability. This graceful shrub is well adapted to poor soils but not to wet or excessively dry soils.

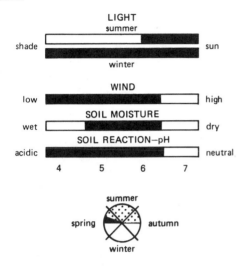

Seasonal Interest. *Flowers:* Small lilac or lavender flowers in clusters all along the past year's stem growth, giving the appearance of long spikes, on pendulous main branches in midspring. *Foliage:* Gray-green, narrow leaves present a graceful, airy appearance.

Buddleia alternifolia.

Problems and Maintenance. This shrub is relatively trouble-free, requiring little or no maintenance other than pruning every few years after flowering, for thinning and removal of winterkilled twig tips (in northern zones).

Cultivars. 'Argentea' has more silvery gray foliage than is typical.

Related Species

Buddleia davidii 4 (orange-eye butterfly bush). This plant is more tender than *B. alternifolia,* and very different functionally. The top kills back

to the ground each winter in Zones 5a−6b, and even where topkilling is not so drastic (Zone 7) best results can be obtained by pruning off the entire top in spring. After new growth starts in late spring, the plant grows rapidly to 1−2 m/3.3−6.6 ft) and bears large spikes of pink, red, purple, or white flowers in late summer. Many showy cultivars have been selected, and these are primarily useful as specimens for late summer color.

Buddleia davidii.

Vitex agnus-castus 4−5 (chaste tree). This member of the Verbenaceae (verbena family) is native to southern Europe and has become naturalized in parts of the South, where it grows into a large, rangy shrub, useful only for its interesting, aromatic, compound, gray-green leaves and loose panicles, 10−20 cm/4−8 in. long, of fragrant, violet flowers in late summer. It is useful in Zones 6b−9a+, but north of Zone 7b it usually is winterkilled to the ground, quickly returning to flower at a height of about 1−1.5 m/3.3−5 ft the following summer. It requires annual removal of deadwood, as does *Buddleia davidii.* The selection 'Alba' has white flowers, and 'Rosea' has pink flowers.

Vitex negundo 4−6 (negundo chaste tree). This tall shrub, occasionally a small tree, is native to southeastern Africa and southern and eastern Asia. It is similar to V. *agnus-castus* except that it has finer-textured foliage and its flowers are less showy and effective for a shorter time in late summer. Yet it is more cold-hardy, useful in Zones 5b−9a+ but remaining below 2 m/6.6 ft because of winterkill in Zones 5b−6b. Var. *heterophylla* (synonym: var. *incisa;* cut-leaved chaste tree) is interesting for the fine texture of its dissected leaves.

Buxus sempervirens 4

Common box
Evergreen shrub
Buxaceae (Box Family)

Native Range. Mediterranean region (Africa, Asia, and Europe), and Asia Minor.

Useful Range. USDA Zones 6a−8b, some cultivars to Zone 5a.

Function. Hedge, specimen, rock garden, edging.

Size and Habit

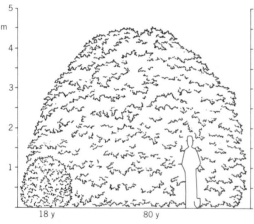

Buxus sempervirens.

Adaptability. Some shade from winter sun is desirable at the northern extremities of the useful range of any specific cultivar (see Cultivars). This plant is very susceptible to salt damage.

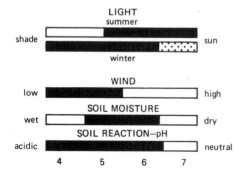

Seasonal Interest. *Foliage:* Fine-textured, evergreen, dark green to dull bluish green, depending on cultivar.

Buxus sempervirens, as background for *Iberis sempervirens*.

Problems and Maintenance. Relatively trouble-free and maintenance-free. Even light pruning is seldom necessary except when it is used as a formal hedge. Insects and mites may necessitate periodic control measures. Leaves, and especially clippings, of box are toxic to livestock, so this plant should not be used within reach of foraging animals.

Cultivars. There are many cultivars of *B. sempervirens*, and they are often confused in commerce. For northern range extremes, a few cultivars have proved unusually hardy among 60 tested at Purdue University, including 'Northland,' 'Inglis,' 'Vardar Valley,' and 'Welleri.' Of these, 'Vardar Valley' is a low, slow-growing plant with dull, blue-green foliage. The others are similar in having somewhat more upright growth and darker green foliage.

   In the southern part of the range, many additional cultivars, including the following, can be grown. 'Albo-Marginata,' 'Argentea,'

'Argenteo-Variegata,' 'Elegans,' 'Elegantissima,' and 'Variegata' all have more or less white variegated foliage. 'Aureo-Variegata' and 'Marginata' have yellow variegated foliage. 'Angustifolia,' 'Longifolia,' and 'Salicifolia' all have narrowly elongated leaves. 'Arborescens' is very upright, treelike in habit, not well suited for hedges or mass plantings. This probably is the type of the species. 'Bullata' has large, puckered leaves. 'Columnaris,' 'Conica,' 'Fastigiata,' 'Navicularis,' and 'Pyramidata' all have upright forms. 'Glauca' is pyramidal, with blue-green foliage. 'Suffruticosa' is the most dwarf selection of box, used widely in the southeastern states as an edging plant, remaining below 0.5 m/1.6 ft for many years.

Buxus microphylla, hedge.

Related Species

Buxus harlandii 4 (Harland box).   This compact species from China has glossy bright green leaves, to 3 cm/1.2 in. long and conspicuously notched at the apex. Less hardy than other *Buxus* species listed, it is nevertheless useful in Zones 8b−9a+, with occasional winterburn in Zone 8b.

Buxus microphylla 3 (littleleaf box).   This highly variable species from China, Japan, and Korea differs from *B. sempervirens* primarily in its size, but its leaves usually are paler green than those of *B. sempervirens*, usually bronzing in winter.

The var. *japonica* has relatively large leaves, to 3 cm/1.2 in. long, and is useful in Zones 6b−9a+. It includes such cultivars as 'Richardii' and 'Rotundifolia.'

The var. *koreana* (Korean box) has smaller, duller green leaves, turning brownish green in winter, and is one of the hardiest of all boxwoods, useful in Zones 5a−8a.

'Sunnyside' is a fast-growing, unusually hardy selection of *B. microphylla* that is not nearly as widely used as it might be. It proved among the hardiest of more than 60 *Buxus* selections in short-term tests at Purdue University, where it suffered no injury whereas only a few other selections escaped severe injury. It is useful in Zones 5b−8b.

'Wintergreen,' with bright green leaves that hold their color well in winter, is useful in Zones 5a−8b.

Sheridan hybrids.   The following cultivars have been selected from a cross between *Buxus microphylla* and *B. sempervirens* made at Sheridan Nurseries, Etobicoke, Ontario: 'Green Gem' is a slow-growing, globose form with deep green foliage that needs little or no pruning. 'Green Mountain' is upright and pyramidal in form with deep green foliage that needs little or no pruning. 'Green Velvet' is vigorous, with a full, rounded form, especially useful for low hedges. It has unusually good winter color. 'Winter Beauty,' actually a selection from *Buxus microphylla* var. *koreana* at Sheridan Nurseries, is globose in outline with little or no pruning and has a particularly attractive bronze winter color.

Several other cultivars are available. Because cultivars vary greatly in adaptation to northern and southern range extremes, and because considerable confusion exists about *Buxus* cultivars, the best guide to success is to use material propagated from plants that have been growing in the local area for some time.

Callicarpa dichotoma 4

Chinese beautyberry
Deciduous shrub
Verbenaceae (Vervain Family)

Native Range. China, Korea, occasionally escaped in the United States.

Useful Range. USDA Zones 5b–8b.

Function. Border, specimen.

Size and Habit

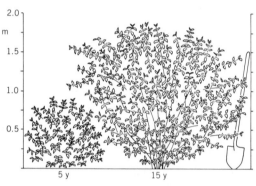

Callicarpa dichotoma.

Adaptability

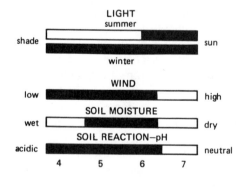

Seasonal Interest. *Flowers:* Pale pink in early summer, more or less obscured by foliage. *Foliage:* medium green, turning purplish or yellowish in late autumn. *Fruits:* Light purple berries in axillary clusters, small but striking because of their unusual color, in autumn.

Problems and Maintenance. Because of winter dieback in some locations and years and a tendency toward rank growth, it is difficult to keep this plant in attractive form without regular pruning. When it is used in a mixed shrub border for fruiting interest, this may not be a serious problem, since it will be partly hidden by other plants. Some pruning, however, will almost certainly be needed in any case.

Related Species

Callicarpa americana 4 (American beautyberry, French mulberry). This native of the south-central United States is similar to *C. dichotoma* except that it is slightly larger and much less hardy, useful in Zones 7a–9a. The var. *lactea* has white fruits.

Callicarpa americana.

Callicarpa japonica 4 (Japanese beautyberry). This shrub is similar to *C. dichotoma* in general effect, size, and useful range, differing in having deeper purple fruits and yellow autumn foliage. The var. *leucocarpa* has white fruits.

Callistemon citrinus 5

Synonym: *C. lanceolatus*
Crimson bottlebrush
Evergreen shrub
Myrtaceae (Myrtle Family)

Native Range. Australia.

Useful Range. USDA Zones 9a+.

Function. Massing, specimen (for its open branching pattern and flowering interest), partial screen.

Size and Habit

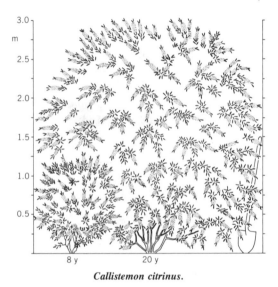

Callistemon citrinus.

Adaptability. This plant should be grown on the dry side, in full sun or nearly so, with low soil fertility to avoid excessive growth. Good for seashore planting.

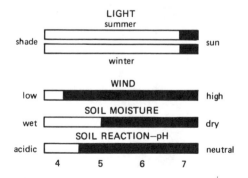

Seasonal Interest. *Flowers:* Bright red flowers in dense spikes resembling bottlebrushes, in greatest numbers in spring, but intermittently year-round. *Foliage:* Evergreen leaves, linear or broader, to 8 cm/3 in. long, stiff and leathery.

Problems and Maintenance. If the soil is too moist, root- and crown-attacking fungus diseases can be a problem. Maintain it on the dry side with low fertility and good air circulation. This will also promote a more compact and attractive plant form.

Cultivars. 'Splendens' has very narrowly linear leaves and unusually showy flowers.

Related Species

Several other species of *Callistemon* are in limited use. Probably none are hardier than *C. citrinus*, nor more ornamental or useful.

Myrtus communis.

Myrtus communis 4−5 (myrtle). This ever-green shrub, native to the Mediterranean region, has been used more widely in Europe than in North America, but it is useful in Zone 9a+ in our area. With dark green, aromatic leaves to 5 cm/2 in. long and small white flowers in late spring, it makes an elegant, compact mass when young and vigorous, and it takes on a more open, tufted habit with age. Myrtle is especially noted for growing well in hot, dry sites, but it performs better with a regular supply of moisture, remaining fuller and less leggy. Cultivars include the following.

'Compacta' is slow growing and compact with small leaves, remaining below 1 m/3.3 ft for an extended period of time. It is barely cold-hardy in Zone 9a.

'Variegata' has small, white-edged leaves and is about as slow-growing and tender as 'Compacta,' barely useful in our area.

All true myrtles are difficult to transplant unless grown in containers and should be specified as potted plants.

Calocedrus decurrens 7

Synonym: *Libocedrus decurrens*
Incense cedar
Evergreen tree
Cupressaceae (Cypress Family)

Native Range. Western United States and adjacent Mexico.

Useful Range. USDA Zones 6b−9a and Zone 6a in protected sites.

Function. Specimen, screen.

Size and Habit. In our area, this tree does not attain the full size that can be seen in its moist native habitats on the West Coast.

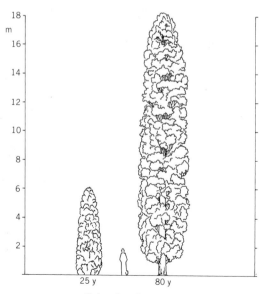

Calocedrus decurrens.

Adaptability. Regular supply of soil moisture favors maximum growth and development.

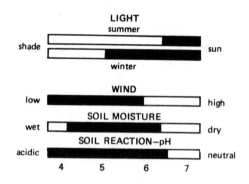

Seasonal Interest. *Foliage:* Evergreen, lustrous, dark green, scalelike, in vertical planes, pleasantly aromatic when crushed. *Trunk and branches:* Cinnamon-brown to reddish brown bark tends to shred, adding minor landscape interest to larger trees.

Problems and Maintenance. This tree is relatively trouble-free once established in a good site.

Calycanthus floridus 4−5

Sweetshrub, Carolina allspice
Deciduous shrub
Calycanthaceae (Calycanthus Family)

Native Range. Southern United States, coastal plain.

Useful Range. USDA Zones 5b−9a+.

Function. Specimen, border, foundation.

Size and Habit

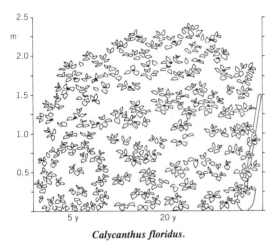

Calycanthus floridus.

Adaptability

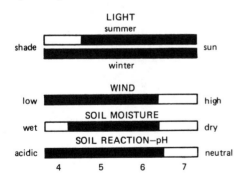

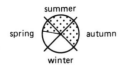

Seasonal Interest. *Flowers:* Deep red or reddish brown, pleasantly fragrant but not showy, opening with newly expanding leaves in late spring.

Foliage: Lustrous, dark green, fragrant when crushed, turning yellowish in autumn, never striking but always clean looking.

Calycanthus floridus.

Problems and Maintenance. This shrub is unusual in its freedom from problems and maintenance. It may require renewal pruning after several years to avoid a leggy appearance, but even this will seldom be needed.

Related Species

Calycanthus fertilis 5 (mountain spicewood, sweetshrub). Similar in landscape usage to *C. floridus*, but native to the Appalachian region instead of the Coastal Plain and much less fragrant. Useful in Zones 5b−9a.

Calycanthus mohrii 4 (Mohr sweetshrub). Similar to *C. floridus* but native to the southern Appalachians. Slightly lower and more compact in habit with reddish purple flowers.

All three species of *Calycanthus* can be considered equivalent in landscape use except for fragrance and availability, where the choice usually is *C. floridus*.

Camellia sasanqua 6

Sasanqua camellia
Evergreen shrub
Theaceae (Tea Family)

Native Range. China and Japan.

Useful Range. USDA Zones 7b−9a+.

Function. Screen, border, specimen. This plant is more useful in the landscape than *C. japonica* because it is denser yet less formal in appearance.

Seasonal Interest. *Flowers:* Large (4−6 cm/ 1½−2½ in.), white or pink, single (double in a few cases), opening over a two- to three-month period in autumn. *Foliage:* Evergreen, lustrous, and dark green, of medium texture (leaves to 5 cm/2 in. long).

Size and Habit

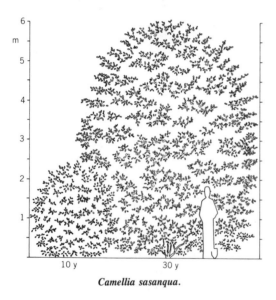

Camellia sasanqua.

Camellia sasanqua.

Problems and Maintenance. Mulching is necessary for best performance, since camellias are shallow-rooted. Occasional irrigation may be needed during prolonged dry periods. Scale insects can be troublesome and spraying may be necessary. A twig dieback disease is also a problem in some areas.

Adaptability. Camellias grow and flower best with full sun during the growing season, but they require light shade and protection from wind during winter in Zone 7 to prevent foliage scorch.

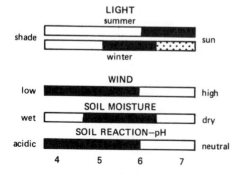

Cultivars. Many cultivars exist, but only a few are usually available in a particular locality. Select cultivars in local use in consultation with local nurserymen and other specialists. Cultivars vary primarily in flower characteristics but also in growth habit, an important consideration in selecting for functional use.

Related Species

Camellia japonica 6 (common camellia). Differs from *C. sasanqua* in having larger leaves and usually larger and more showy flowers, opening from late autumn until spring. Since the growth habit usually is looser and more open, *C. japonica* is not as functional a landscape plant as

C. sasanqua and, in fact, is usually grown as a garden specimen or for cut flowers in much the same way as garden roses are. It has about the same useful range as *C. sasanqua*.

Camellia japonica.

Camellia reticulata 6 (net-veined camellia). This shrub or small tree has larger flowers than *C. japonica*, to 15 cm/6 in. across, and persistent, leathery, dull green leaves. Useful in Zone 9a+, this species is of interest primarily as a parent of large-flowering hybrids.

Campsis radicans 1

Synonym: *Bignonia radicans*
Common trumpet creeper, trumpetvine
Deciduous vine
Bignoniaceae (Bignonia Family)

Native Range. East-central to south-central United States.

Useful Range. USDA Zones 4b–9a.

Function. Specimen, screen (with support).

Size and Habit. Grows very rapidly and climbs by aerial rootlets to heights of 8–10 m/26–33 ft or greater.

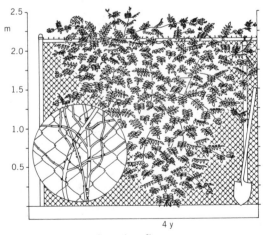

Campsis radicans.

Adaptability. Unusually widely adapted to different soil and environmental conditions but will not perform well in shade.

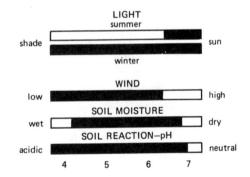

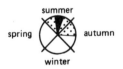

Seasonal Interest. *Flowers:* Large (5 cm/2 in.), bright red-orange or yellow, trumpet shaped, in midsummer. *Foliage:* Doubly compound, dark green, of crisp texture, unfolding late and with little autumn interest.

Problems and Maintenance. This vine is relatively trouble-free, but its great vigor presents a problem in any but large-scale situations. It requires strong support because of its mass. Regu-

Campsis radicans.

lar pruning to control size and maintain fullness close to the ground is essential when using this vine as a screen.

Cultivars. 'Flava' has yellow flowers.

Related Species and Hybrids

Campsis grandiflora 1 (Chinese trumpet-vine). Weakly climbing but vigorous vine with very large (8 cm/3 in.), scarlet to orange-pink flowers in loose clusters in late summer. Much less cold-hardy than *C. radicans* (Zones 7b —9a+).

Campsis ×*tagliabuana* 'Madame Galen' 1 (Madame Galen trumpetvine) This vigorous hybrid (*C. grandiflora* × *C. radicans*) combines much of the hardiness of *C. radicans* with flowers about as large and showy as those of *C. grandiflora*. This is a larger-flowering substitute for *C. radicans* in Zones 5b—9a.

Bignonia capreolata 1 (crossvine). This close relative of *Campsis* differs in having evergreen

foliage and a relatively short flowering period in spring, and it is much less cold-hardy, useful in Zones 8a—9a+. Its flowers are similar to those of *Campsis radicans*, except that they are lighter-colored inside, giving a bicolored effect. It has the same disadvantages as *C. radicans*: excessively vigorous growth and greater size than can be accommodated by small-scale landscape situations. It is equally free of insect and disease problems, and climbs by tendrils with adhesive discs, making a large evergreen mass on wall supports very quickly.

Clytostoma callistegioides 1 (synonyms: *Bignonia speciosa*, *B. violacea*; violet or lavender trumpet-vine, Argentine trumpetvine). Another relative of *Bignonia* and *Campsis* in the Bignoniaceae (Bignonia Family), this vigorous, high-climbing vine has large (to 8 cm/3 in. long and wide), pale lavender and purple-streaked, trumpetlike flowers, appearing in great numbers in spring. The evergreen, compound leaves add year-round interest. This plant is inevitably sparse at the base, a consideration in its use. Useful only in the mildest climates of the South (Zone 9a+) in full sun or partial shade.

Macfadyena unguis-cati 1 (synonyms: *Bignonia chamberlayni*, *B. tweediana*, *Doxantha unguis-cati*; catclaw creeper). This vigorous, high climbing vine from the southeastern United States holds to its support by hooked tendrils, hence the common name. It has evergreen, pale green leaves with two narrow leaflets and a central tendril, and great numbers of bright, golden-yellow, funnel-shaped flowers, to 10 cm/4 in. long, in midspring. Hardy in Zones 9a+, partly hardy in Zone 8.

Caragana arborescens 6

Siberian peatree
Deciduous shrub
Leguminosae (Pea Family)

Native Range. Manchuria and Siberia.

Useful Range. USDA Zones 2a—6b, but of questionable value in Zones 5 and 6.

Function. Shelter belt, windbreak, screen border, specimen.

Size and Habit

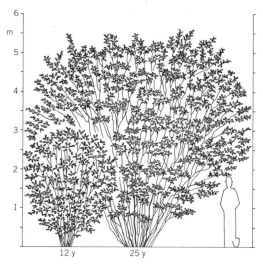

Caragana arborescens.

Adaptability. This shrub's landscape value rests primarily on its ability to withstand the extreme cold and dryness of the northern areas of the United States and Canada.

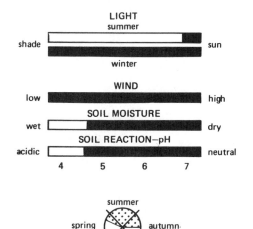

Seasonal Interest. *Flowers:* Small, yellow and pealike in late spring or early summer. *Foliage:* Small, compound leaves make a sparse mass. *Fruits:* Small, inconspicuous pods turn brown on ripening.

Problems and Maintenance. Mites and insects frequently defoliate this plant in late summer. Even though it grows reasonably well in spite of this, its appearance is impaired. Because of this

problem and its general sparseness, this shrub is seldom useful in small-scale plantings but is reserved primarily for shelter-belt planting in exposed northern areas, where it requires no maintenance.

Varieties and Forms. F. *lorbergii* is a graceful plant, to 2.5 m/8 ft, with linear leaves, giving it a very fine texture. Not widely available, but a possibility for textural accent in a mixed border or as a specimen.

Var. *nana* includes variable plants of unpredictable growth rate. Some individuals remain dwarf, below 1 m/3.3 ft, for several years; others grow rapidly to above eye level. In any case, these plants usually are more ornamental than the species type because of their greater fullness and concentration of flowers and foliage. Plants that reach heights of 2.5 m/8 ft or greater are superior to the species type for visual screening. Further selection for desirable clones may make this plant more useful in the future.

Var. *pendula* has a strongly weeping growth habit and usually is grafted on a standard (high on an upright seedling) and used as a specimen for accent in formal landscapes.

Related Species

Caragana aurantiaca 3 (orange peashrub), *Caragana brevifolia* 4 (short-leaved peashrub), and *Caragana pygmaea* 3 (pigmy peashrub). These low-growing, relatively compact shrubs from Siberia and adjacent areas are useful in the same areas as *C. arborescens* as corner and foundation plantings, facing shrubs for the front of mixed shrub borders, or divider plantings below eye level. *C. brevifolia* is especially valuable, where available, for its apparent resistance to mites and tolerance of dry soil.

Caragana frutex 5 (Russian peashrub). This shrub is intermediate in height between the dwarf species (above) and *C. arborescens*, and it usually makes a more dense foliage mass than *C. arborescens*, with dark green, fine-textured foliage. Its only problem is a tendency to sucker freely. The selection 'Globosa,' selected at the Skinner Nursery, Dropmore, Manitoba, is compact, maturing at about 1 m/3.3 ft, dark green, and apparently mite resistant.

Caragana microphylla 5 (little-leaved peashrub). This shrub is similar to *C. arborescens* except in its slightly finer-textured foliage and more spreading growth habit.

Cassia corymbosa 5 (flowery senna). This native of South America is the only woody species of *Cassia* fully hardy in our area. Not dense enough or permanent enough for screening, this shrub is planted for its yellow flowers, which are showy from late summer well into autumn. It is useful in Zones 8b−9a+. Many other woody species of *Cassia* are valued as landscape plants for tropical and subtropical climates. A few are marginally hardy in Zone 9a and planted there for their autumn flowering interest.

Colutea arborescens 5 (bladder senna). This undistinguished shrub from the Mediterranean region is similar to *Caragana arborescens* except that it is less cold hardy. It is useful in Zones

6a−9a, and perhaps also Zone 5. Its yellow flowers have red markings and appear with those of *Caragana* in late spring, then continue through midsummer. The low-growing cultivar 'Bullata,' 1.5 m/5 ft tall, is of some interest as a dwarf plant and is useful in Zones 6a−9a.

Halimodendron halodendron 4 (salt tree). This native of central Asia is similar to its close relative, *Caragana arborescens*, in general effect, except that it has lilac-purple flowers, less than 2 cm/0.8 in. across in small clusters opening in early summer. This shrub's principal value is its ability to tolerate difficult conditions, including alkaline and even saline soils. It is useful in Zones 3a−6b but of questionable value other than for its salt tolerance.

Carpinus betulus 7

European hornbeam
Deciduous tree
Betulaceae (Birch Family)

Native Range. Europe and Asia Minor.

Useful Range. USDA Zones 5a−7a.

Function. Shade and street tree, specimen, screen.

Size and Habit

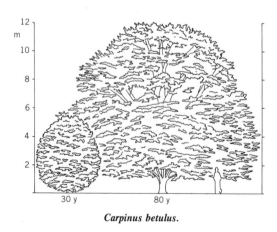

Carpinus betulus.

Adaptability

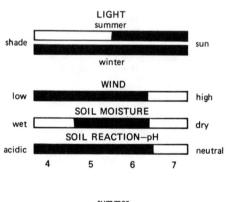

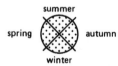

Seasonal Interest. *Foliage:* Dark green, crisply textured, remaining green late in autumn, occasionally turning yellowish before falling. *Fruits:* Pendulous clusters of small nutlets partly enclosed by green, leafy bracts, inconspicuous. *Trunk and branches:* Smooth gray bark is darker than that of beeches, otherwise similar.

Problems and Maintenance. This tree is relatively trouble-free and long-lived, but may be damaged in areas subjected to frequent ice storms.

Cultivars. 'Columnaris' is narrowly oval and compact in habit, maintaining a central trunk, sometimes mistakenly sold under the name 'Fastigiata.' It is useful primarily as a specimen or large-scale screen.

'Fastigiata' is fastigiate (with narrow branching angles, broomlike), in outline oval to vase-shaped with age, not maintaining a single central trunk. Somewhat broader and more open than 'Columnaris,' it is seldom available. Seedlings of C. *betulus* show considerable variation in growth rate, branching angles, and width, and a large number of variants could be selected and named if one wanted to add to the considerable confusion that exists over the few existing cultivars.

Carpinus betulus 'Fastigiata.'

Carpinus caroliniana 7

American hornbeam, blue beech, ironwood
Deciduous tree
Betulaceae (Birch Family)

Native Range. Eastern North America.

Useful Range. USDA Zones 3b–9a.

Function. Shade, patio, or street tree; specimen; naturalizing.

Size and Habit

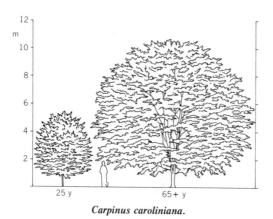

Carpinus caroliniana.

Adaptability

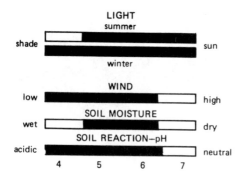

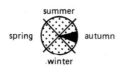

Seasonal Interest. *Foliage:* Lacy, light green in spring, turning deep green by midsummer, then to red-orange in autumn. *Fruits:* Pendulous clusters of small nutlets partly enclosed by green leafy bracts, inconspicuous. *Trunk and branches:* Sinewy appearing main branches with smooth, light gray bark add distinct winter interest

Problems and Maintenance. This tree is relatively trouble-free and needs little maintenance, but it may be damaged in areas subjected to frequent ice storms.

Related Species

Carpinus cordata 7. This small tree from eastern Asia is very similar to *C. japonica* and

Carpinus caroliniana.

functionally equivalent. Neither of these two species is commonly available, but both show promise as small shade trees.

Carpinus cordata.

Carpinus japonica 7 (Japanese hornbeam). This species is similar to *C. caroliniana* in landscape use and general appearance but differs in having somewhat larger leaves, turning dull red in autumn, and red-tinged fruiting clusters in late summer. It is also less hardy, useful in Zones 5b−8b, and seldom commercially available.

Carya illinoinensis 8

Synonym: *Carya pecan, Hicoria pecan*
Pecan
Deciduous tree
Juglandaceae (Walnut Family)

Native Range. Central North America from the Mississippi Basin westward to Kansas and Texas and southward to high elevations in Mexico.

Useful Range. USDA Zones 6a−9a+. For good results in Zones 6 and 7a, use only the hardiest cultivars, originating from the northern parts of the natural range.

Function. Shade tree, specimen, naturalizing, preservation of wild stands, edible nut production.

Adaptability

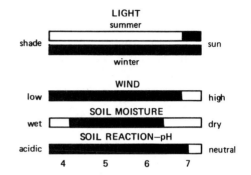

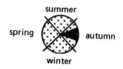

Size and Habit

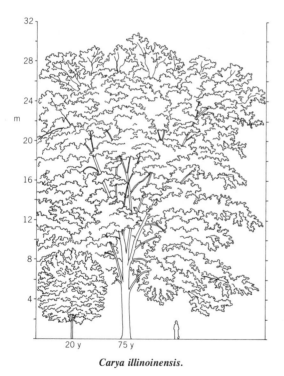

Carya illinoinensis.

Seasonal Interest. *Foliage:* Medium green, compound leaves allow filtered sunlight to pass, and turn clear yellow in autumn. *Fruits:* Edible nuts are highly valued, the most important commercially of any *Carya* species. Husks open on the tree and the nuts fall, leaving the husks attached to the branches for a time. *Trunk and branches:* Light gray or tan bark has landscape interest in winter sun.

Problems and Maintenance. This tree is not easily transplanted, but it is considerably less difficult than most other *Carya* species. Where nut production is secondary to use, it needs little maintenance.

Cultivars. Selections of *Carya illinoinensis* have been made for nut production and for hardiness. For landscape use, cultivars are of less specific value except for northern areas, where selection of hardy cultivars may prove the easiest way of ensuring adapted trees. Trees grown from nuts collected from wild trees in the northern parts of the range may be as well adapted as hardy cultivars, however. When nut production is of interest, follow the advice of local nut growers concerning cultivars wherever possible.

Carya ovata 8

Shagbark hickory
Deciduous tree
Juglandaceae (Walnut Family)

Native Range. Eastern United States and parts of adjacent Canada, scattered in high elevations in Mexico.

Useful Range. USDA Zones 4b–8b.

Function. Shade tree, specimen, naturalizing, edible nut production.

Size and Habit

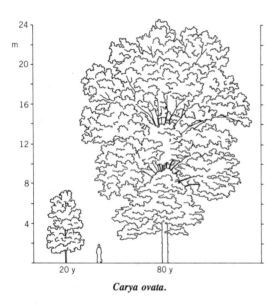

Carya ovata.

Adaptability

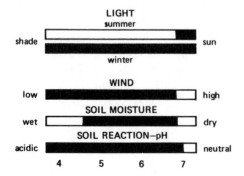

Seasonal Interest. *Foliage:* Rich green, compound leaves turn golden-bronze in autumn. *Fruits:* Edible nuts in small husks, the sweetest and thinnest-shelled among the hickories, except the pecan (*C. illinoinensis*). *Trunks and branches:* Shaggy bark comes off in large plates, adds considerable landscape interest year-round.

Problems and Maintenance. Hickories as a group are difficult to transplant in large sizes because they have a deep tap root and feeding roots so extensive that few can be recovered in digging. Young trees that have been root pruned regularly or container grown are less difficult to establish. Foliage and husks make considerable ground litter.

Cultivars. Cultivars of *Carya ovata* have been selected for nut production. For landscape use, it is not necessary to use cultivars. In situations where nut production also is a consideration, consult local nut growers about suitable cultivars for the area where the trees are to be planted.

Related Species

Carya cordiformis 8 (bitternut hickory). This large tree, to 20–30 m/66–98 ft, native to the eastern United States and adjacent Canada, has inedible nuts and less landscape character than several other *Carya* species, but it is worth preserving in site development in Zones 4b–8b.

Carya glabra 8 (pignut hickory). This very large tree, to 30–40 m/98–131 ft tall in time, native to the eastern United States and parts of adjacent Canada, has nuts of little value, but it is better adapted to dry soil and temperature extremes than most hickories. It is useful in Zones 5b–9a+ but difficult to transplant, and it more often will be preserved in site development than planted.

Carya laciniosa 8 (shellbark hickory). This very large tree, to 30–40 m/98–131 ft tall in time, native to east-central North America from New York to Iowa and south to Tennessee and Texas, is very similar to *C. ovata* and just as useful for planting or preservation in development in Zones 5b−8b.

Carya tomentosa 8 (mockernut hickory). Another large tree, to 20−30 m/66−98 ft, this native of the eastern United States and parts of adjacent Canada is similar in landscape effect and usefulness to *C. cordiformis*. Its usefulness is largely limited to preservation in site development in Zones 5a−9a.

Caryopteris ×clandonensis 3

Bluebeard
Deciduous subshrub
Verbenaceae (Vervain Family)

Hybrid origin. *C. incana* × *C. mongholica*.

Useful Range. USDA Zones 4a−8b. Tops are winterkilled regularly in Zones 4−6 and in some winters in Zones 7−8, but the plant returns to bloom in a single season.

Function. Specimen, border.

Size and Habit

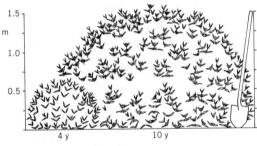

Caryopteris ×clandonensis.

Adaptability

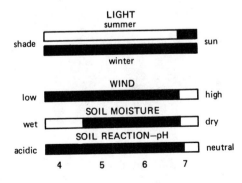

Seasonal Interest. *Flowers*: Blue, in flat, lateral clusters in late summer and into early autumn. *Foliage*: Grayish green, medium fine in texture.

Problems and Maintenance. Since the tops are often winterkilled, they should be pruned to within a few inches of the ground each spring. The plant then will return quickly to flower in the same year. Even when the tops are not winterkilled, successive seasons' growth can become straggly, so drastic spring renewal pruning is recommended even in the South to maintain plant form. Otherwise, little or no maintenance is needed.

Cultivars. Several selections have been made, and new ones probably will appear in the future. 'Blue Mist,' with light blue flowers, and 'Azure Blue' and 'Heavenly Blue,' with deeper blue flowers, have been in use for several years.

Related Species

Caryopteris incana 4 (synonym: *C. tangutica*; blue spirea, bluebeard). This shrub from China and Japan is taller and less cold-hardy than *C. ×clandonensis* (to Zone 7a) and largely replaced by the hybrid in landscape use.

Caryopteris mongholica 3 (Mongolian bluebeard). This shrub is unusually cold-hardy (to Zone 3b) but less showy than *C. clandonensis* and largely replaced by it in landscape use.

Castanea mollissima 7

Chinese chestnut
Deciduous tree
Fagaceae (Beech Family)

Native Range. China and Korea.

Useful Range. USDA Zones 5b–7b.

Function. Shade tree, specimen, edible nut production.

Size and Habit

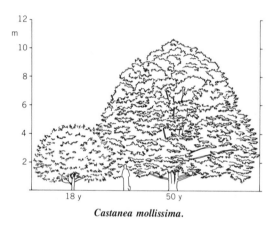

Castanea mollissima.

Adaptability

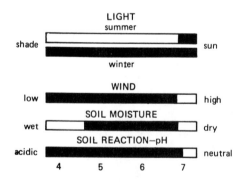

Seasonal Interest. *Flowers:* Creamy white, cylindrical male catkins, to 12 cm/5 in. long, in late spring or early summer. *Foliage:* Leathery, dark green, and lustrous above, soft-downy underneath, remaining green late, finally turning yellow-bronze in late autumn. *Fruits:* Edible nuts in large, sharply prickly husks, a nuisance when they litter the ground.

Castanea mollissima.

Castanea mollissima.

Problems and Maintenance. For good nut production, it is necessary to provide for cross-pollination between two or more cultivars or seedlings and to follow a spray program as necessary. The troublesome prickly husks form whether or not pollination occurs. Otherwise, *C. mollissima* is relatively trouble-free. Even though the tree is cold-hardy in Zone 5b and perhaps in sheltered areas in Zone 5a, summers may be too cool and too short in these zones for the nuts to ripen fully.

The most serious problem of *Castanea* species is the chestnut blight disease, which has nearly eradicated the native North American chestnut, *Castanea dentata*. Different species of *Castanea* differ widely in susceptibility to this disease, *C. mollissima* being highly resistant.

Cultivars. Several cultivars and hybrids of *C. mollissima* have been selected for nut production by the U.S. Department of Agriculture and the Connecticut Agricultural Experiment Station. When selecting trees for nut production in a specific locality, it is best to consult the closest cooperative extension service office for information on appropriate cultivars and culture.

Related Species

Castanea crenata 7 (Japanese chestnut). This blight-resistant species is being used in hybridization to obtain blight-resistant cultivars with superior nut production. It is useful in Zones 6a–7b and perhaps more widely.

Castanea dentata 8 (American chestnut). This handsome, large tree has superior nuts, timber, and landscape value, and is hardy in Zones 4b–8a, but unfortunately it has been nearly decimated by chestnut blight. A few trees growing outside the principal range of the species prior to the outbreak of this disease have managed to escape it for long periods, but they presumably would be susceptible if the disease were introduced into their locality. In spite of great public interest in finding resistant trees, no truly resistant forms have been found. *C. dentata* has been crossed with blight-resistant species (e.g., *C. crenata*) in attempts to develop superior cultivars. Evaluation is still going on.

Castanea pumila 6 (Alleghany chinquapin). This small, shrubby tree, native to the eastern and South-central United States, is useful as a specimen or for naturalizing in sandy soil in Zones 5a–9a. Its leaves are green above and whitened underneath, turning yellow in autumn.

Castanea sativa 8 (Spanish chestnut). This large tree, native to the Mediterranean region, is the source of most edible chestnuts marketed in North America. It is less hardy than *C. dentata* and *C. mollissima* (to Zone 6b) and blight-susceptible as well, so it is no better a prospect for landscape use than *C. dentata*.

Catalpa bignonioides 7

Southern catalpa, Indian bean
Deciduous tree
Bignoniaceae (Bignonia Family)

Native Range. Southeastern United States: Mississippi to Florida, and naturalized in many areas farther north.

Useful Range. USDA Zones 5a–9a.

Function. Shade, specimen.

Size and Habit

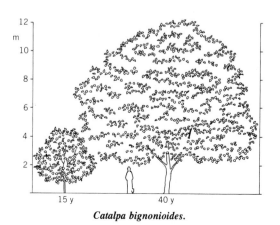

Catalpa bignonioides.

Adaptability. One of the most widely adaptable of all trees to heat and cold, wetness and dryness, and varying light and soil conditions.

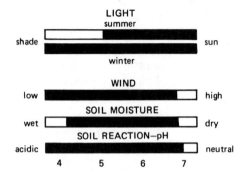

Seasonal Interest. *Flowers:* White with brown or yellowish markings in throat, very showy in early summer. *Foliage:* Large, bright green leaves give the tree a coarse texture. *Fruits:* Long, hanging seed pods are conspicuous after the leaves have fallen, but a litter problem later.

Problems and Maintenance. The long, leathery seed pods of this tree create a serious litter problem when they fall at different times during fall and winter. Catalpas are often infested with large worms that are valued as bait by fishermen, but they are objectionable in small-scale situations and can defoliate trees when present in large numbers.

Cultivars. 'Aurea' has bright golden foliage in early summer, soon turning green but making the tree a striking landscape accent for a short time. 'Nana' is a dwarf form, usually grafted on a standard (high on an upright seedling), making a rather strong landscape accent, and grown solely for its unusual form.

Related Species

Catalpa ovata 7 (Chinese or yellow catalpa). This Chinese species is similar to *C. bignonioides* in size, with poorer form and with yellowish flowers marked orange and purple in late spring. It is useful in Zones 4b–9a.

Catalpa speciosa 8 (northern or western catalpa). This tall, rather narrow tree to 20–30 m/66–99 ft, is native from southern Indiana to Arkansas and western Tennessee and is even coarser than *C. bignonioides* because of its larger leaves and pods. Useful in large-scale, parklike plantings in Zones 4a–9a.

Catalpa speciosa.

Ceanothus ovatus 3

Inland ceanothus
Deciduous shrub
Rhamnaceae (Buckthorn Family)

Native Range. Northeastern United States to Nebraska, Colorado, and Texas.

Useful Range. USDA Zones 3b–8a.

Function. Massing, border, foundation, specimen.

Size and Habit

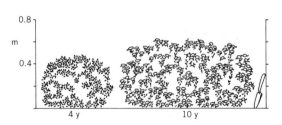

Ceanothus ovatus.

Adaptability. This is one of the most adaptable low shrubs to temperature extremes, dryness, wind, and poor soil.

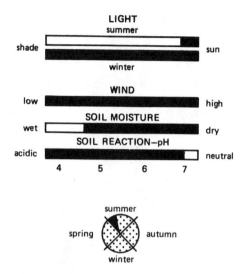

Seasonal Interest. *Flowers:* Small, white, in flattened clusters in early summer. *Foliage:* Medium green leaves, 2.5−5 cm/1−2 in. long, neutral in effect.

Ceanothus ovatus.

Problems and Maintenance. This shrub is trouble-free and requires no maintenance—not even pruning, since its growth habit is dense and compact, but it tends to be short lived.

Related Species

Ceanothus americanus 3 (New Jersey tea). Similar to *C. ovatus* but slightly taller and more open. Native from Ontario and Manitoba in Canada to South Carolina, Texas, and Nebraska. Slightly larger flower clusters are offset by less compact habit.

Many additional species of *Ceanothus* and their hybrids native to western North America are in landscape use on the West Coast. These are evergreen and far more handsome than the above species, but they are not cold-hardy in the northeastern and midwestern United States and are apparently poorly adapted to the southeastern states as well. They might be tried experimentally in Zones 8a−9a+.

Cedrus libani 8

Cedar of Lebanon
Evergreen tree
Pinaceae (Pine Family)

Native Range. Asia Minor.

Useful Range. USDA Zones 5b−9a. Only the var. *stenocoma* is cold-hardy in areas colder than Zone 7.

Function. Specimen, screen, massing.

Size and Habit

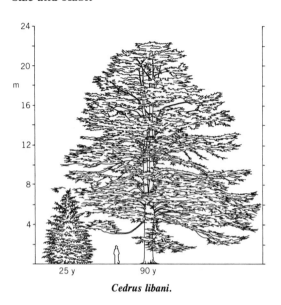

Cedrus libani.

Adaptability

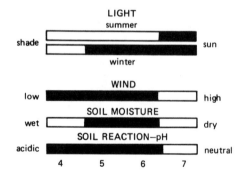

Seasonal Interest. *Foliage:* Dark green, evergreen, needlelike, solitary or in rosettes. *Cones:* Male cones numerous, small, on low branches; female cones large, to 10 cm/4 in. long, few, on short branches in top of tree, erect, requiring two years to develop, ripening purplish and then disintegrating on the tree.

Cedrus libani.

Problems and Maintenance. Cedars occasionally are subject to damage by borers, especially in the South. Otherwise they are trouble-free.

Varieties and Cultivars. Var. *stenocoma* is similar to the species type except that it is cold-hardy. Native to the highest elevations in the natural range of this species, trees of this variety are useful in Zones 5b–9a. 'Pendula' has an interesting weeping form but seldom is available commercially.

Related Species

Cedrus atlantica 7 (Atlas cedar). This native of the Atlas Mountains of northwestern Africa is potentially a large tree, but seldom exceeds 18 m/60 ft in height in landscape use. Generally similar to *C. libani*, this tree is somewhat more open and sparsely branching, with distinctive form and texture, and is useful in Zones 7a–9a. The selection 'Glauca' with striking blue foliage is widely grown for accent in color and form. The weeping and narrow forms, 'Pendula' and 'Fastigiata,' are known but are seldom available commercially.

Cedrus atlantica 'Glauca.'

Cedrus deodara 7 (Deodar cedar). This native of central Asia is potentially a large tree but usually does not exceed 15 m/50 ft in height in landscape use. It is picturesque, with gracefully sweeping, plumose branches and medium to light green foliage. This is a popular specimen tree in Zones 7b−9a+, but the cultivars 'Kashmir' and 'Kingsville,' selected from plants grown from seeds collected at high elevations in the natural range, are probably cold-hardy to Zone 6b.

Celastrus scandens 1 and 2

American bittersweet
Deciduous vine
Celastraceae (Staff Tree Family)

Native Range. Eastern United States and adjacent Canada, southwesterly to New Mexico.

Size and Habit. Grows rapidly and scrambles over ground or climbs by twining to heights of 4−6 m/13−19 ft.

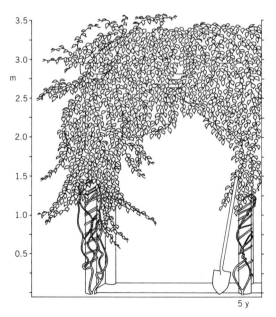

Celastrus scandens.

Useful Range. USDA Zones 3b−8b.

Function. Screen (with strong support), specimen, large-scale groundcover.

Adaptability

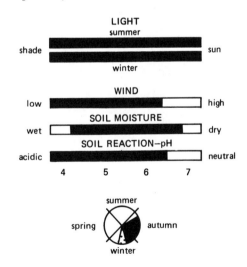

Seasonal Interest. *Foliage:* Lustrous, bright green, turning clear yellow in autumn. *Fruits:* Deep yellow in terminal clusters with red-orange arils covering the seeds and appearing as the fruit splits, showy in autumn and well into winter. Usually dioecious; plant females with an occasional male in the same planting to ensure maximum fruiting.

Problems and Maintenance. Generally trouble-free, but very vigorous, best in large-scale situations.

Varieties. Named varieties and cultivars are not available, but plants of known sex are available in some nurseries. Plants with flowers of both sexes on the same plant are known but seldom available commercially.

Related Species

Celastrus rosthornianus 1 and 2 (synonym: *C. loeseneri*; Loesener bittersweet). This species from China is available in North America and is a possible substitute for *C. scandens* in Zones 4b−8b, with fruiting interest similar to that of *C. scandens* but in lateral rather than terminal clusters. It is reputed to be less fully dioecious than other species, with most plants bearing fruits.

Celastrus orbiculatus 1 and 2 (oriental bittersweet). From China and Japan, this species is about as common in landscape use as the native *C. scandens* but is slightly less cold-hardy (Zones 5a−8b), with fruits in lateral rather than terminal clusters, and somewhat higher climbing, to 10−12 m/33−40 ft.

Tripterygium regelii 1 and 5 (tripterygium). This native of Japan, Korea, and Manchuria forms a large, sprawling shrub growing to 2 m/6.6 ft or higher and at least as wide, but with support it will function as a loosely scrambling vine. It is effective as a visual screen and barrier where enough ground space can be given to its spread. Its small, creamy white flowers are borne in showy terminals clusters, to 20 cm/8 in. long, in midsummer, and its pale green, three-winged fruits add mild interest in autumn, but the lustrous bright green leaves, 8−15 cm/3−6 in. long, and the dense mass that they form are the most important landscape feature of this plant. It is tolerant of a wide range of soils and exposures and is useful in Zones 5b−8b and perhaps colder zones as well.

Celtis occidentalis 8

Common hackberry
Deciduous tree
Ulmaceae (Elm Family)

Native Range. Northeastern and north-central United States and adjacent Canada.

Useful Range. USDA Zones 3b−8b.

Function. Shade, street, or avenue tree. Perhaps the best substitute in form and adaptability for the American elm in the Midwest.

Size and Habit

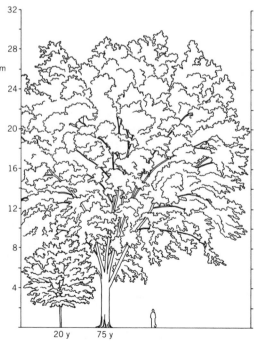

Celtis occidentalis.

Adaptability. Unusually well adapted to cold, heat, dryness, wind, and alkaline soils, therefore a valuable tree in the Midwest and plains states.

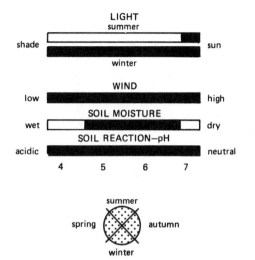

Seasonal Interest. *Foliage:* Medium green, of medium to coarse texture, the leaves 5−12 cm/2−5 in. long, turning dull yellow in autumn. *Fruits:* Small, inconspicuous, purple-black berries in late summer and autumn. *Trunk and branches:* Medium gray bark, sometimes smooth to warty, sometimes vertically ridged.

Problems and Maintenance. This tree is susceptible to a witch's broom condition, caused by a mite, in which many small twigs proliferate from a single point on a branch and then die. The condition seldom damages trees seriously, but it can become unsightly. On the other hand, large numbers of witch's brooms can add winter branching interest. When this tree is selected, it should be in spite of this problem rather than with the expectation of controlling it. The same is true for nipple gall of the foliage, caused by an insect, which disfigures the leaves but usually does little permanent damage.

Related Species

Celtis bungeana 7 (Bunge hackberry). This tree from northeastern Asia is smaller than *C. laevigata,* to 15 m/50 ft, with smooth, light gray bark and lustrous, bright green foliage. It is not susceptible to the witch's broom condition that affects most *Celtis* species and is a handsome, functional tree, useful in Zones 6a−9a, perhaps also in colder zones, but very seldom commercially available.

Celtis laevigata 8 (sugar hackberry). This slender-branched tree from the southeastern and south-central United States is slightly smaller than *C. occidentalis,* to 20−25 m/66−82 ft tall, and unusually well adapted to hot, dry climates and alkaline soils. Its light green leaves, smaller than those of *C. occidentalis,* turn dull yellow in autumn, and its light gray, smooth bark is roughened by corky, warty growths, giving mild winter interest. It is useful in Zones 6a−9a+.

Cephalanthus occidentalis 5

Buttonbush
Deciduous shrub
Rubiaceae (Madder Family)

Native Range. Eastern North America and southwestward to Texas and California.

Useful Range. USDA Zones 4b−9a, with selection of appropriate genetic material.

Function. Shrub border, naturalizing in wet sites.

Size and Habit

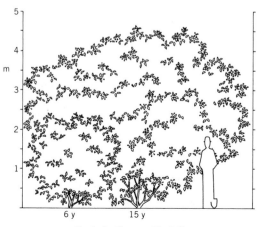

Cephalanthus occidentalis.

Adaptability. Valued for its extremely wide adaptability, this shrub is planted for its tolerance of wet soil more than for any other reason.

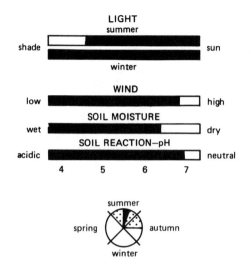

Seasonal Interest. *Flowers:* Creamy white, in globular heads 2–3 cm/1 in. across in midsummer, attractive to bees. *Foliage:* Dark green, lustrous in summer through early autumn. *Fruits:* Globular, similar to flower heads, but greenish or red tinged in early autumn, then disintegrating.

Problems and Maintenance. This shrub is coarse and short-lived and loses its form after a few years. At that point, it is best to cut it down close to the ground in spring for renewal. Otherwise it is trouble-free.

Related Species

Adina rubella 5 (glossy adina).   This graceful relative of *Cephalanthus* has deep green, glossy foliage similar in texture to that of *Abelia* ×*grandiflora*, not nearly as evergreen but persisting late into autumn. The leaves, only 2.5 cm/1 in. long, are reddish bronze when young, adding more interest than the small heads of the flowers, which are whitish or tinted red-purple, appearing in middle to late summer. This shrub is probably not commercially available at present but is potentially useful in Zones 6b–9a. Winter damage tends to restrict its height to less than 1.5 m/5 ft north of Zone 7, similar to *Abelia* ×*grandiflora*.

Leptodermis oblonga 3 (Chinese leptodermis).   This delicate shrub has medium green, fine-textured foliage with individual leaves only 2 cm/0.8 in. long and small clusters of violet-purple flowers opening from midsummer to early autumn. Even though it probably is not commercially available at present, it is potentially useful as a low border shrub or for massing in Zones 6b–9a.

Pinckneya pubens 6 (fevertree, Georgia bark).   This small, narrow tree with distinctly horizontal branching is native to the extreme southeastern United States. It is colorful in flower in midsummer, primarily because of the rosy pink calyx lobes, one of which in each flower is enlarged and petal-like, to 8 cm/3 in. long. The true petals are fused into a pale yellow, trumpet-shaped corolla about 2.5 cm/1 in. long. *Pinckneya* is soft-wooded, short-lived, and seldom commercially available, but it is highly distinctive and potentially useful in Zones 8a–9a+.

Cercidiphyllum japonicum 8

Katsura tree
Deciduous tree
Cercidiphyllaceae (Cercidiphyllum Family)

Native Range. Japan and China.

Useful Range. USDA Zones 5a–9a, but in Zones 8 and 9 it is useful only in good soil with ample moisture and in partial shade.

Function. Shade tree, specimen. Form depends on method of training and age (see Problems and Maintenance).

Size and Habit

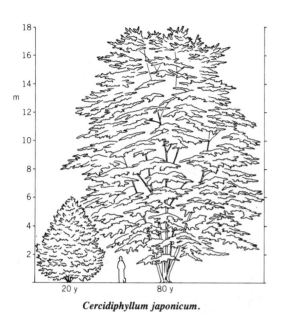

Cercidiphyllum japonicum.

Seasonal Interest. *Foliage:* Bright red when first unfolding in some trees, medium green and of distinctive texture in summer, the leaves rounded, 5–10 cm/2–4 in. long, turning yellowish, pink, or deep red in autumn, depending on moisture and soil fertility. *Trunk and branches:* Bark on older trees is grayish brown and slightly shaggy, adding mild year-round interest.

Problems and Maintenance. Left alone, this tree tends to form several trunks and an interesting habit. When a single trunk is wanted, competing trunks must be removed from the young tree.

Varieties. Var. *sinense* from China does not differ appreciably from the Japanese species type except that it is probably considerably less cold-hardy and seldom is commercially available.

Adaptability. Best in full sun in soil with adequate moisture, except in Zones 8 and 9, where some shade is necessary.

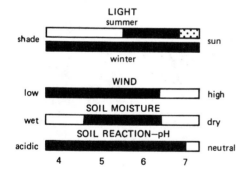

Cercis canadensis 6–7

Eastern redbud
Deciduous tree
Leguminosae (Pea Family)

Native Range. Eastern and south-central United States, southward into Texas.

Useful Range. USDA Zones 5b(a)–9a+ with selection of appropriate genetic material. Hardiness in Zone 5a depends on selection from most northern wild material.

Function. Patio tree, specimen, naturalizing.

Size and Habit. Form varies from low (to 6 m/20 ft), compact, and rounded in full sun to loose, open, and taller (to 12 m/40 ft) in shaded sites.

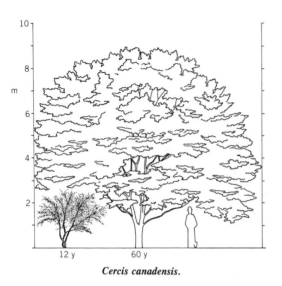

Cercis canadensis.

Adaptability. Even though the family Leguminosae includes many plants that can use atmospheric nitrogen, *Cercis* species apparently lack this ability. Nevertheless, these trees succeed in soil of relatively low fertility.

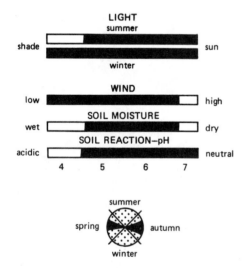

Seasonal Interest. *Flowers:* Purplish pink, clear pink or white, small clusters appearing before foliage in early to midspring, sometimes developing in large clusters directly on trunks and large branches. *Foliage:* Light green as it emerges during the last days of flowering, dark green in summer, turning bright yellow in autumn in most years. *Fruits:* Flat pods to about 8 cm/3 in. long, from late summer into winter, conspicuous when borne in large numbers after the leaves have fallen. *Trunk and branches:* Dark gray-brown bark sloughs off on trunks and branches of older trees to expose reddish inner bark.

Cercis canadensis.

Cercis canadensis.

Problems and Maintenance. Several insects can disfigure the foliage mildly but are not usually serious problems. Stem canker and verticillium wilt occasionally can be serious. Otherwise, this tree has few problems and requires little maintenance.

Forms and Cultivars. 'Alba,' selected from the wild in Missouri, has white flowers. 'Forest Pansy' (Plant Patent No. 2556, 1965) has foliage opening bright crimson, turning to deep red-purple as it matures, and becoming greenish bronze by early autumn. This makes a striking specimen in early summer, but it is disease susceptible and sometimes short lived. 'Pinkbud' and 'Wither's Pink Charm' have clear pink flowers, more versatile in combination with certain other colors than the typical purplish pink flowers of the species. 'Royal,' a white-flowered selection from western Illinois, may prove to be more cold-hardy than 'Alba,' and has slightly larger flowers.

Related Species

Cercis chinensis 6 (Chinese redbud). This small tree from China is more shrubby than *C. canadensis*, offering little shade. It is usually planted for the showy, bright, rosy-purple flowers, larger than those of *C. canadensis* and opening about two weeks later. It is useful in Zones 6b−9a+.

Cercis reniformis 6 (synonym: *Cercis texensis*; Texas redbud). Similar to *C. canadensis* but with leathery, rounded foliage more like that of *C. siliquastrum*. Much less cold-hardy than *C. canadensis* (Zones 8a−9a+), but the selection

'Oklahoma,' which probably belongs to this species, is more cold-hardy than the species type and useful at least to Zone 6b.

Cercis reniformis 'Oklahoma.'

Cercis siliquastrum 6 (Judas tree). This native of southern Europe and adjacent Asia Minor is probably useful only in Zone 9a+ and less useful than the other species listed here, with an irregular growth habit and no flowering advantage. In fact it is less showy than *C. chinensis*.

Chaenomeles speciosa 4

Synonyms: *Chaenomeles lagenaria, Cydonia lagenaria*
Flowering quince
Deciduous shrub
Rosaceae (Rose Family)

Native Range. China, long cultivated in Japan.

Useful Range. USDA Zones 4b−9a. May flower poorly following severe winters in Zones 4b and 5 and mild winters in Zones 8b and 9a.

Function. Specimen, border, barrier, hedge. When used as a hedge, it is best pruned informally to preserve flowering and character of form. Density and thorny branches make it an effective barrier.

Size and Habit

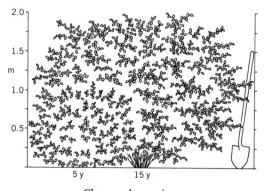

Chaenomeles speciosa.

Adaptability. This shrub is widely adapted to soil and moisture variations but performs best in full sun.

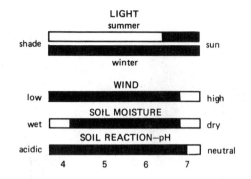

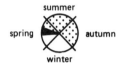

Seasonal Interest. *Flowers:* Showy, red, pink, or white, single or double, in early spring to mid-spring. *Foliage:* New foliage emerges red-bronze in late spring, then turns glossy dark green, remaining green until it falls in late autumn. *Fruits:* Applelike, pale green to yellow, interesting but not showy, useful in making preserves when fully ripe (yellow) in autumn.

Problems and Maintenance. This shrub is subject to occasional gall and mite infestations, apple scab, and fire blight, but differs in susceptibility among cultivars. It requires minimal pruning to maintain form and vigor. Overwinter rabbit damage can be severe in the North in some years and areas.

Cultivars. Well over 100 cultivars exist. In practice, selection will be limited by the relatively small number of cultivars available at a given time and place. Select those that have performed well in the locality in question.

A few of the most popular currently are listed. 'Appleblossom' has pale pink flowers, red in bud, borne in large numbers on a semierect plant. 'Cameo' has double, apricot-pink flowers on a thornless, low-spreading plant. 'Nivalis' has white flowers on an upright and vigorous but full plant. 'Pink Lady' is low and slow-growing with clear, rose-pink flowers. 'Texas Scarlet' is low and compact with large red flowers. 'Toyonishiki' is vigorous and more trouble-free than some other cultivars, with white, pink, and red flowers on the same plant.

Related Species

Chaenomeles japonica 3 (Japanese or lesser flowering quince). This species is much lower-growing than *C. speciosa*, seldom exceeding 1 m/3.3 ft, and is useful for its low stature in Zones 4b–9a. The range of flower colors is similar to that of *C. speciosa* except that there are few if any good reds. Apple scab is often serious enough to defoliate plants by late summer.

Chaenomeles ×*superba* 4 (hybrid Japanese flowering quince). This hybrid group is similar to its parents (*C. japonica* × *C. speciosa*) but intermediate in size, to 1.5 m/5 ft, with many good cultivars. It is useful in Zones 5a–9a.

Chaenomeles ×*californica* 4 (California hybrid flowering quince). This is a mixed hybrid group involving at least three parent species (*C.* ×*superba* 'Corallina' × *C. cathayensis*) developed by W. B. Clarke, San Jose, California. It includes many showy cultivars, mostly less cold-hardy than the others listed above but useful in Zones 6b–9a, some also in Zones 5b and 6a.

Chamaecyparis lawsoniana 3–7

Lawson false cypress, Port Orford cedar
Evergreen tree or shrub
Cupressaceae (Cypress Family)

Native Range. Northwestern United States.

Useful Range. USDA Zones 5b–8a. Hardiness north of Zone 6b depends on cultivar and selection of planting site away from afternoon sun and wind in winter.

Function. Specimen tree, screen (species type and taller cultivars), foundation (intermediate cultivars), and rock garden (dwarf cultivars).

Size and Habit

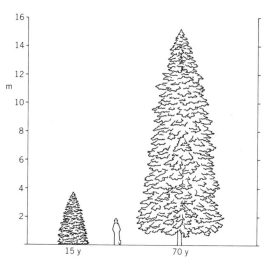

Chamaecyparis lawsoniana.

Chamaecyparis lawsoniana.

Adaptability. This species performs best in relatively moist soil and high humidity, especially in coastal areas.

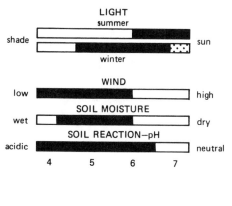

Seasonal Interest. *Foliage:* Evergreen, dense, scalelike (needlelike when juvenile) in flat sprays arranged in more-or-less vertical planes, strikingly so in some cultivars, medium green to steely blue-green, golden in certain cultivars. *Trunk and branches:* Shredding, reddish brown bark adds interest to larger specimens at all seasons.

Problems and Maintenance. This evergreen is relatively free of problems and maintenance when used in the proper climate, but in areas with hot, dry summers it is susceptible to serious mite infestations.

Cultivars. 'Allumii' (scarab false cypress) is a columnar form with steely blue-green foliage, striking in its vertical layering. It is an excellent narrow screen, reaching 2−4 m/6.6−13 ft in height fairly quickly, eventually 6−10 m/20−33 ft if left unpruned.

'Ellwoodii' (Ellwood false cypress) is upright, compact, and relatively slow-growing with soft, blue-green juvenile foliage. It reaches screening height (2 m/6.6 ft) only after 10 or more years, so it is used primarily as a specimen for accent.

'Fletcheri' (Fletcher false cypress) is similar to 'Ellwoodii' in general form and growth rate but has deep blue-green, partly juvenile foliage and an unusually interesting texture for this species.

'Forsteckensis' (Forsteck false cypress) is a dwarf, globose form, not exceeding 1 m/3.3 ft in height and spread for many years, with dense, blue-green foliage on twisted branchlets.

Many other cultivars are used on the West Coast, varying from very dwarf to full-size forms and including bright to bluish green, golden-yellow, and variegated foliage variants. Most are planted in eastern North America only by collectors.

Related Species

Chamaecyparis nootkatensis 6−8 (Alaska or Nootka false cypress). This tall tree, to 40 m/130 ft in native habitat from Alaska to Oregon but seldom over 15 m/49 ft in our area, is useful in Zones 5b–7b, in areas with relatively cool, moist summers. The cultivar 'Compacta' is much slower growing, remaining low for years, and 'Pendula' is a handsome, fast-growing accent plant with strongly pendent branchlets.

Chamaecyparis thyoides.

Chamaecyparis thyoides 5–7 (swamp or Atlantic white cedar).   This tree, native from Maine to northern Florida and coastal Alabama and Mississippi, is useful, depending on geographic origin of genetic material, in Zones 5a–9a+. It is similar in general appearance to *Juniperus virginiana.* The cultivars 'Andelyensis,' an excellent, tightly columnar, semidwarf form growing slowly to 3 m/10 ft, and 'Ericoides,' a semidwarf, low-pyramidal form, growing to 1.5 m/5 ft with heathlike foliage texture, are fairly commonly used as specimens.

Chamaecyparis nootkatensis 'Pendula.'

Chamaecyparis obtusa 3–7

Hinoki false cypress
Evergreen tree or shrub
Cupressaceae (Cypress Family)

Native Range. Japan and Taiwan.

Useful Range. USDA Zones 5a–8a.

Function. Specimen tree, screen (species type and taller cultivars), foundation (intermediate varieties), rock garden (dwarf cultivars), and bonsai.

Size and Habit

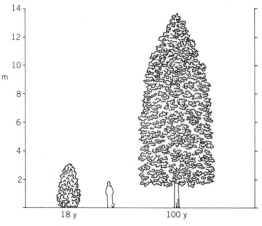

Chamaecyparis obtusa.

Adaptability. This species performs best in relatively moist soil and high humidity but tolerates more average conditions as well.

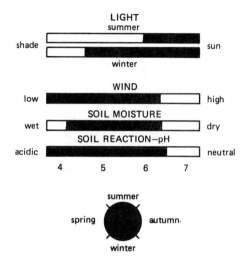

Seasonal Interest. *Foliage:* Evergreen, glossy, dark green, scalelike leaves, white-marked underneath, give outstanding color and texture at all seasons. *Trunk and branches:* Shredding, reddish brown bark adds interest to older specimens at all seasons.

Problems and Maintenance. This plant is relatively free of problems and maintenance when used in the proper climate, but in areas with hot, dry summers it is susceptible to mite infestations.

Cultivars. There is a continuous range of slow-growing variants, much confused and frequently misnamed. The more common ones often can be obtained under the following cultivar names.

'Compacta' has compact branching habit, eventually reaching at least 2 m/6.6 ft in height and spread. It may even reach screening height, but too slowly to consider this a normal function.

'Nana Gracilis' is similar to 'Compacta' except that it has more obviously twisted branchlets and is somewhat more vigorous and less compact, eventually reaching at least 3 m/10 ft in height.

'Nana' is similar to 'Nana Gracilis,' but much slower-growing, varying greatly in growth rate but usually remaining below 1 m/3.3 ft for many years. The extreme dwarfs are even smaller.

Many other variants in foliage color, texture, and growth rate have been named. A few of the more common are listed here.

'Coralliformis' is a dwarf with twisted twigs (foliage), a coral-like texture, and dark green color.

'Crippsii' is slow-growing, to 3 m/10 ft or taller in time, with handsomely textured foliage that is bright golden-yellow where it is exposed to direct sun.

'Filicoides' is slow-growing, to 3 m/10 ft or taller in time, with loosely arranged, dark green, fernlike foliage giving a picturesque appearance to the plant. Useful only as a specimen, but an excellent choice for this purpose in intensive landscapes where moisture can be supplied.

'Lycopodioides' is a dwarf with tufted and flattened branches.

'Spiralis' is a dwarf with spirally twisted small branches.

'Tetragona' is a dwarf with tufted branches, tending to be four-sided in cross section.

'Tetragona Aurea' is similar to 'Tetragona' except that it has golden-yellow foliage in direct sun.

Chamaecyparis pisifera 3–8

Sawara false cypress, retinospora
Evergreen tree or shrub
Cupressaceae (Cypress Family)

Native Range. Japan.

Useful Range. USDA Zones 5a–8a.

Function. Screen, specimen tree, rock garden (dwarf cultivars), bonsai. The species and full-size cultivars are sometimes used as foundation plantings but soon outgrow such sites and must be replaced. Such cultivars should be grown as trees, and slow-growing forms of this and other species should be used for small-scale plantings.

Size and Habit

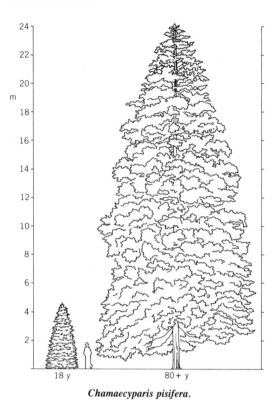

Chamaecyparis pisifera.

Adaptability. This species of *Chamaecyparis* performs best in relatively moist soil and high humidity, but it grows well in average sites in the central Midwest.

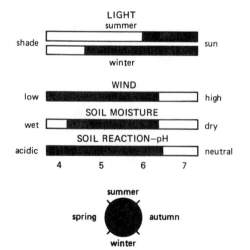

Seasonal Interest. *Foliage*: Evergreen, bright, dark or bluish green, of three distinct types (see Cultivars). *Trunk and branches*: Shredding, red-

dish brown bark adds interest to larger specimens at all seasons.

Problems and Maintenance. This plant is relatively free of problems and maintenance when used in the proper climate.

Cultivars. Cultivars belong to three foliage groups. Those in the "filifera" group (thread Sawara false cypress) have pendent, threadlike branches giving an unusual, fine, stringy texture. Individual leaves are scalelike and appressed tightly to the stem. Those in the "plumosa" group (plume Sawara false cypress) have foliage similar to the species type except that it is more plumose. Individual leaves are scalelike but spread away from the stem more than those of the "filifera" group. The "squarrosa" group (moss Sarawa false cypress) has soft, needlelike leaves spreading widely from the stem, giving a mosslike appearance.

Within these groups, many variants in growth rate, form, and color have been selected and named. A few of the more common are:

'Boulevard' (= 'Cyano-viridis') is a slow-growing, densely pyramidal form in the "squarrosa" group, with steely blue-green foliage, soft to the touch.

'Filifera' is typical of the "filifera" group, not a dwarf but remaining below 3 m/10 ft for years.

'Filifera Aurea' is similar to 'Filifera' except for its golden-yellow foliage in full sun, especially bright as it first emerges.

'Filifera Aurea Nana' and 'Golden Mop' are dwarfs in the "filifera" group with golden-yellow foliage, remaining below 1 m/3.3 ft for 10 years or more.

'Plumosa' is typical of the "plumosa" group, growing to full size.

'Plumosa Aurea' is similar to 'Plumosa' except that the foliage on the outside of the plant exposed to direct sun is golden-yellow, especially in early summer.

'Plumosa Compressa' is a dwarf, moundlike form in the "plumosa" group, not exceeding 1 m/3.3 ft in height and spread in 10 years or more. Its upright, nearly mosslike branches are tipped with pale yellow.

'Plumosa Nana' is a dwarf, flattened and globe to pillowlike in form. It seldom exceeds 1.5 m/5 ft in height but will double that in spread after several years.

Chimonanthus praecox 5

Wintersweet
Deciduous shrub
Calycanthaceae (Calycanthus Family)

Size and Habit

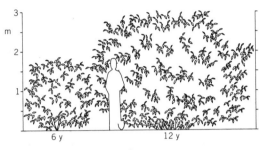

Chimonanthus praecox.

Adaptability. In areas having hot summers, this shrub performs best with at least light shade. It is widely adapted to soil conditions, including fairly wet soil.

LIGHT

Native Range. China.

Useful Range. USDA Zones 7b−9a+.

Function. Screen, border, specimen. Functions well as a screen when suckers are allowed to develop at base, but requires much space.

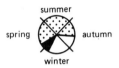

Seasonal Interest. *Flowers:* Pale yellow with deep red-brown centers, very fragrant, opening very early in spring, long before the leaves unfold, or even in warm periods in late winter. *Foliage:* Rich green, relatively coarse, the leaves 8−15 cm/3−6 in. long, making a dense mass and remaining green until frost.

Problems and Maintenance. This shrub is virtually trouble-free, requiring no maintenance except occasional pruning to rejuvenate the plant by removing old wood.

Varieties. Var. *grandiflorus* has larger leaves and larger but less fragrant flowers.

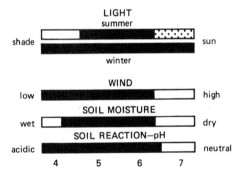

Chionanthus virginicus 6

White fringetree, old man's beard
Deciduous shrub
Oleaceae (Olive Family)

Native Range. Southeastern and south-central United States.

Useful Range. USDA Zones 5a−9a.

Function. Specimen, border.

Size and Habit

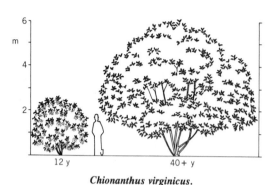

Chionanthus virginicus.

Chionanthus virginicus.

Adaptability. Performs best in reasonably moist sites in full sun.

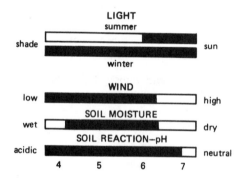

Seasonal Interest. *Flowers:* White, fringelike, dioecious, in loose clusters, 10–20 cm/4–8 in. long, the largest on male plants, very showy in late spring. *Foliage:* Coarsely textured, elliptical leaves, 8–20 cm/3–8 in. long, expanding very late in spring, turning yellow in autumn. *Fruits:* Blue-black fruits on female plants resemble small olives, to 2 cm/0.8 in. long. Male plants must be in the vicinity for pollination and fruit set.

Chionanthus virginicus.

Problems and Maintenance. Little maintenance is needed other than pruning out old branches every few years.

Cultivars. None are available, nor are plants of known sex unless they are selected when old enough to flower, since this species is usually propagated by seeds.

Related Species

Chionanthus retusus 6 (oriental fringetree). This Asian counterpart of C. *virginicus* from China

Chionanthus retusus.

Chionanthus retusus var. *serrulatus.*

Chionanthus retusus var. *serrulatus.*

and Taiwan flowers later than C. *virginicus* and is seldom available commercially. The species type becomes a small, ascending tree, to 6 m/20 ft, resembling a miniature American elm in form, with lightly striped bark. The var. *serrulatus* from Taiwan has a very different form, branching close to the ground and assuming a broad vase shape. It has handsome, exfoliating, cinnamon-brown bark. *C. retusus* is hardy in Zones 6a–9a, but var. *serrulatus* may not be hardy in colder areas than zones 6b or 7a.

Cinnamomum camphora 7

Camphor tree
Evergreen tree
Lauraceae (Laurel Family)

Native Range. China, Japan, Taiwan.

Useful Range. USDA Zone 9a+.

Function. Shade tree, specimen, screen, windbreak. Well adapted to city street use except for fruit litter.

Size and Habit

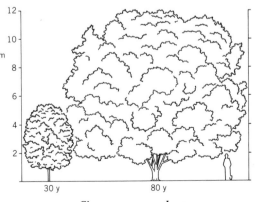

Cinnamomum camphora.

Adaptability

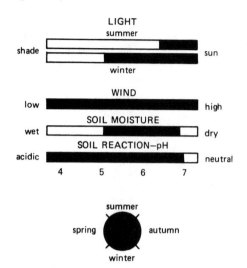

Seasonal Interest. *Flowers:* Inconspicuous, in spring. *Foliage:* Evergreen, glossy, bright to olive green, giving off a camphor odor when crushed. *Fruits:* Small, round, black fruits add minor landscape interest but litter the ground when they fall.

Problems and Maintenance. This tree is very shallow-rooted and casts dense shade, discouraging the use of turf or groundcover plants underneath it. Probably best handled in a mulched bed, but it also grows well close to paved areas when good drainage is provided. In Zone 9a, the top occasionally freezes back and pruning is necessary to remove deadwood. This has the effect of maintaining the size of the tree under 10 m/33 ft. In warmer climates, this tree reaches heights of 25–30 m/82–98 ft.

Related Species

Laurus nobilis 6 (laurel, sweet bay). This is the true laurel from the Mediterranean, the foliage of which was used in wreaths in early times and is the bay leaf seasoning used in cooking. Even though it forms a tree to 10 m/33 ft or taller in its native habitat, it seldom becomes more than a shrubby tree to 5 m/16 ft in the southeastern United States but is effective as a very small shade or patio tree. It is best grown in full sun in open, breezy sites on well-drained soil. Flowering and fruiting interest are insignificant compared with the crisp, olive green foliage. Useful in Zones 8a–9a+ and in protected sites in Zone 7.

Persea borbonia 6 (red bay persea). This evergreen tree in the Lauraceae (Laurel Family), native to the southeastern United States, grows to heights of 10 m/33 ft and occasionally nearly twice that in native habitat. Its flowers in middle spring are not conspicuous, but the berries that follow add landscape interest in late summer and early autumn. They are lustrous, blue-black, 1 cm/0.4 in. across, borne in loose clusters on red pedicels that remain colorful after the berries have fallen. This tree is considered difficult to establish and is seldom used. If the problem of establishment is solved by producing the tree in containers, it will be a most useful landscape tree for Zones 8a–9a+, tolerating wet soils but also performing well in soils of average moisture content.

Persea palustris 6 (swamp bay persea). This tree is similar to *P. borbonia* in just about every respect. The two species can be considered equivalent in landscape use but neither is often available. *P. palustris* may be even more tolerant of wet soil than *P. borbonia*.

Umbellularia californica 7–8 (California laurel, Oregon myrtle). This large tree is similar in general landscape effect while young to *Laurus nobilis* and, except for its dense foliage canopy, to *Persea* species, but eventually may reach heights of 20 m/66 ft or greater in good sites. This is a popular shade tree on the West Coast but probably is not commercially available in our area except from West Coast sources. No doubt some attempts have been made to use it in the southeastern United States, and it deserves further trial in Zones 8 and 9a.

Cistus ×purpureus 4

Purple rockrose
Evergreen shrub
Cistaceae (Rockrose Family)

Hybrid origin. *C. incanus* × *C. ladanifer.*

Useful Range. USDA Zones 8b−9a+.

Function. Specimen, border, massing.

Size and Habit

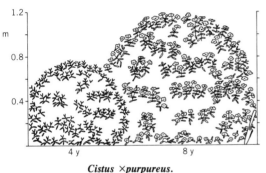

Cistus ×purpureus.

Adaptability. *Cistus* species perform best on well-drained limestone soil in full sun.

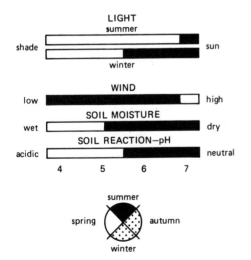

Seasonal Interest. *Flowers:* Purple with yellow and deep red center blotches and yellow stamens, to 8 cm/3 in. in diameter, early summer and intermittently until autumn. *Foliage:* Evergreen, rather fine-textured, narrow (6−8 cm/2−3 in. long), gray-green and thickly pubescent underneath.

Problems and Maintenance. *Cistus* species are maintenance-free once established except for occasional pruning for rejuvenation. All are considered difficult to transplant; use pot-grown plants.

Related Species and Hybrids

More than 20 species and hybrids are presently in cultivation, but few are available in our area. A few of the most common are listed here.

Cistus ×*cyprius* 5 (spotted rockrose). Flowers 6−8 cm/2.4−3 in. across with white, purple, and yellow blotches, yellow stamens, and glandular-sticky foliage. Hybrid origin: *C. laurifolius* × *C. ladanifer.* Hardy in Zones 8a−9a+.

Cistus ×*hybridus* 3 (synonym: *C. corbariensis;* white rockrose). This hybrid of *C. populifolius* × *C. salviifolius* has white flowers with yellow throats, resembling single roses, 3.5 cm/1.4 in. across, in early summer. It is useful in Zone 9a+.

Cistus incanus 3 (synonym: *C. villosus;* hairy rockrose). Rose to purple, yellow-centered flowers, 5 cm/2 in. across, foliage roughened and scaly-pubescent with longer gray hairs underneath. From southwestern Europe. Useful in Zones 7b−9a+, one of the hardiest species of *Cistus.* The hybrid (probably *C. incanus* × *C. laurifolius*) 'Silver Pink' is a low shrub, to 0.5 m/1.6 ft, with clear, light pink flowers and silvery gray foliage.

Cistus ladanifer 4 (laudanum, gum rockrose). White flowers, yellow in center, 8−10 cm/3−4 in. across, and glandular-sticky foliage. From the western Mediterranean. Hardy in Zone 9a+.

Cistus laurifolius 4 (laurel rockrose). White flowers, yellow in center, 5−8 cm/2−3 in. across, foliage dark green and smooth above, glandular-sticky below. From the Mediterranean region. Hardy in Zones 7b−9a+; one of the hardiest species of *Cistus.* Its hybrid (with *C. monspeliensis*), *C.* ×*glaucus* 3, bears flowers in larger numbers.

Cistus salviifolius 3 (sage rockrose). This rockrose has sage-green, net-veined leaves and flowers

Cistus ×glaucus.

Helianthemum nummularium 2 (sunrose). This low-growing relative of *Cistus* has evergreen or semievergreen leaves to 2.5 cm/1 in. long, and flowers similar to those of the rockrose except that they are only 2.5 cm/1 in. across, borne in clusters in midsummer. Useful as a groundcover in hot, dry sites, especially in full sun and high-limestone soil, in Zones 6b–9a+ and northward to Zone 6a with protection from winter sun and wind and to Zone 5a with reliable winter snow cover. Several cultivars are available, with pink, white, or different shades of yellow and orange flowers.

similar to those of *C. ×hybridus*, but larger, in late spring. Useful in Zone 9a+.

Cladrastis lutea 7

American yellowwood
Deciduous tree
Leguminosae (Pea Family)

Native Range. Southeastern United States, in Appalachians and as far west as Missouri and Arkansas.

Useful Range. USDA Zones 4b–8a.

Function. Shade tree, specimen.

Size and Habit

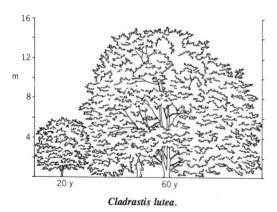

Cladrastis lutea.

Adaptability

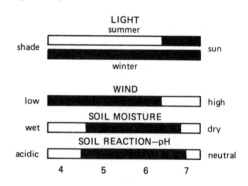

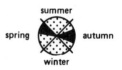

Seasonal Interest. *Flowers:* Fragrant, white, pealike, in hanging clusters, 25–40 cm/10–16 in. long, resembling those of wisteria, in late spring. *Foliage:* Dark green, compound, casting very heavy shade and turning delicate shades of gold and orange in autumn. *Fruits:* Small, inconspicuous pods. *Trunk and branches:* Smooth, silvery gray bark, similar in color and texture to that of Asiatic magnolias and beech, maintains the tree's interest in winter.

Problems and Maintenance. This tree is generally trouble-free but is occasionally subject to a vascular disease that originates in the narrow crotches of the main limbs where moisture can collect and eventually kills the tree. A dense canopy of large trees is less troublesome to turf grass underneath than might be expected, probably because of deep rooting, but alternatives to turf such as groundcover or mulch may still be preferable for low maintenance. Care should be taken not to break or prune branches in spring, since they will bleed sap heavily at that season, weakening the tree if excessive.

Related Species

Cladrastis platycarpa 8 (Japanese yellowwood). The Asian counterpart of *C. lutea,* this tree is similar in general landscape effect but differs in its upright clusters of flowers that are somewhat later and less showy than those of *C. lutea.* The useful range of *C. platycarpa* is not well known, but it includes at least Zones 5b−7b. It is seldom available commercially.

Maackia amurensis 7 (Amur maackia). Similar in general form to *Cladrastis,* with somewhat finer-textured compound leaves, yellowish white flowers in upright clusters in midsummer, and smooth bark of an unusual olive-brown color. Its overall usefulness is no greater than that of *Cladrastis,* and it has less showy flowers and little or no autumn foliage color. It is well adapted to northern climates, however, with a useful range of Zones 4b−6b or perhaps wider, but is seldom

available commercially. The related *M. chinensis,* slightly more showy in flower and probably less cold-hardy, is even rarer than *M. amurensis.*

Maackia amurensis.

Clematis armandii 1

Armand clematis
Evergreen vine
Ranunculaceae (Buttercup Family)

Native Range. China.

Useful Range. USDA Zones 7b−9a+.

Function. Specimen, screen (with support). Like most *Clematis* species, this requires a wire or trellis support to accommodate twining petioles. Its effectiveness as a screen is limited by narrow leaves and a tendency to become leafless at the base (see Problems and Maintenance).

Size and Habit

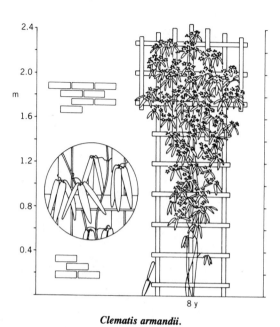

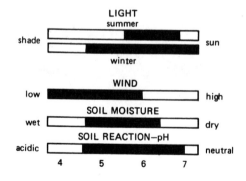

Clematis armandii.

Adaptability

Seasonal Interest. *Flowers:* Fragrant, white, and starlike against dark green foliage, in axillary clusters in late spring. *Foliage:* Evergreen, leathery, narrow leaves make a dense mass because of their numbers. *Fruits:* Plumy styles give added interest in late summer.

Problems and Maintenance. To maintain fullness at the base of the plant and its effectiveness as a screen some top pruning may be necessary immediately after flowering, every two to three years. Aphids may be a problem in many areas but can be controlled by an appropriate spray if necessary.

Cultivars. 'Farquhariana' (='Apple Blossom') has light pink flowers but is less cold-hardy (Zone 9a+).

Related Species

Clematis delavayi 4 (Delavay clematis). Shrubby, upright plant from China with small (2–3 cm/1 in.) white flowers in terminal clusters in late summer, unlike any other *Clematis* species. Hardy in Zones 7a–9a.

Clematis ×jackmanii 1

Jackman clematis
Deciduous vine
Ranunculaceae (Buttercup Family)

Hybrid origin. C. *lanuginosa* × C. *viticella*.

Useful Range. USDA Zones 4a–8a. Certain hybrids are somewhat less cold-hardy, some only to Zone 6a.

Function. Specimen. Vining *Clematis* species and cultivars climb by twining petioles, so wire or trellis support must be provided. Most of the large-flowered types do not grow vigorously enough to function as effective screens, but C. ×*jackmanii* is more vigorous than most.

Size and Habit

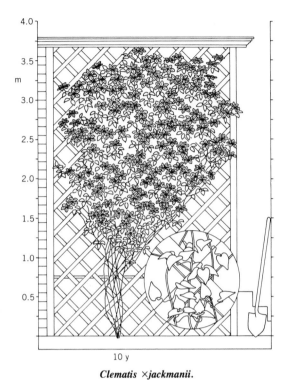

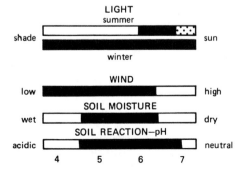

Clematis ×*jackmanii.*

Adaptability. Large-flowered *Clematis* species and cultivars require rather precise site conditions, including relatively cool soil (deep preparation of planting holes and use of a mulch, groundcover, or low shrub cover to shade the soil surface). Incorporation of lime in acidic soils is also standard practice. The less vigorous cultivars should receive partial shade in summer, especially in hot areas.

LIGHT
summer
shade [ ] sun
winter

WIND
low high

SOIL MOISTURE
wet dry

SOIL REACTION—pH
acidic neutral
4　5　6　7

Seasonal Interest. *Flowers:* Large (to 10−15 cm/4−6 in.), rich, velvety purple (rich deep red, violet, pale blue or white in certain cultivars) on new growth in midsummer. *Foliage:* Medium green. *Fruits:* Plumy styles are fairly showy in late summer and early autumn.

Problems and Maintenance. The large-flowered *Clematis* species and cultivars commonly are winterkilled to the ground in the North. Even when this does not occur, those that flower on current season's growth, including *C.* ×*jackmanii* and its cultivars, should be pruned back heavily in spring to encourage low branching, vigor, and flowering.

Cultivars and Hybrids

Jackman hybrids. Many cultivars have been selected from *C.* ×*jackmanii* populations and hybrids with other species. These are collectively called the Jackman Group of hybrids. All flower in summer on the current year's growth. Few usually are available at a given time and place, and most are offered for sale only by specialists. A few of the best known are listed here.

'Alba' has large white flowers with pale blue edges, including a few double flowers early in the season from the previous year's wood if not winterkilled. 'Comtesse de Bouchaud' has large, rose-colored flowers with six sepals (appearing as petals). 'Mme Baron Veillard' has large, lilac-rose flowers in early summer, then occasionally until autumn. 'Mme Edouard Andre' has velvety, deep red-purple flowers in midsummer. 'Rubra' has deep red-purple flowers in midsummer, including a few double flowers early in the season from the previous year's wood if not winterkilled. 'Superba' has unusually large, deep purple flowers, constituting an improved form of *C.* ×*jackmanii.*

Lanuginosa hybrids. This group of hybrids is derived from the *C. lanuginosa* parent of *C.* ×*jackmanii.* Its members are similar to the Jackman Group but tend to be less hardy (Zones 6a−8a, colder zones in a few cases). Some of the best known are listed here.

'Crimson King' has large, deep red flowers in late summer, but is weak-growing. 'Elsa Spaeth' has very large, lavender-blue flowers in late summer. 'Lady Caroline Neville' has very large, pale mauve flowers in midsummer and occasionally until autumn. 'Mrs. Cholmondeley' has very large, light blue flowers in early summer and occasionally until autumn and is more cold-hardy than most in this group (to Zone 4b). 'Ramona' has very large, lavender-blue flowers in midsummer. 'William Kennett' has double lavender flowers having eight overlapping sepals with wavy margins in early summer to midsummer.

Viticella hybrids. This group of hybrids, flowering on the current year's growth like the Jackman and Lanuginosa hybrids, is derived from *C. viticella*. A few of the most common cultivars that are hardy northward at least to Zone 4b are listed here.

'Ascotiensis' has large (to 15 cm/6 in.) sky-blue flowers in late summer. 'Huldine' has near-white (pale purple) flowers in great numbers from midsummer to autumn. This has been found to be the most vigorous and free-flowering of all white *Clematis* grown at the University of Minnesota Landscape Arboretum. 'Kermesina' has bright, wine-red flowers in summer and is actually a selection from *C. viticella* rather than a hybrid. 'Ville de Lyon' has large, red-purple flowers in midsummer and occasionally during late summer.

Clematis 'Ville de Lyon.'

Related Species

Clematis alpina 1 (alpine clematis). This Eurasian species is notable for its bell-shaped, blue-violet flowers and low habit, climbing only a few feet. Since it flowers on the previous season's wood in early spring, its floral display is vulnerable to winter damage in spite of its name. It is rare in commerce in North America but widely planted in England and potentially useful in Zones 6b–8a in areas having moderate summers and perhaps farther north as well.

Clematis florida 1 (cream clematis). This Chinese species with creamy white sepals and showy purple stamens, flowering in early summer on the previous season's wood, is useful in Zones 6b–9a and is best known for its hybrids: 'Belle of Woking,' with large, double, pale mauve to silvery gray flowers, and 'Duchess of Edinburgh,' with large, fragrant, double, pure white flowers, both flowering in spring on the previous season's wood.

Clematis lanuginosa 1 (Ningpo clematis). Another Chinese native, this species has large white to pale lilac flowers. It is little used other than as a parent of the Lanuginosa hybrids (see Cultivars and Hybrids).

Clematis ×*lawsoniana* 1 (Lawson clematis). This hybrid species (*C. lanuginosa* × *C. patens*) has large, rosy purple to pale blue flowers, noteworthy among the *C. lanuginosa* hybrids only for the selection 'Henryi,' which has large white flowers (brownish stamens) appearing in late summer.

Clematis macropetala 1 (big-petal clematis). This native of northern China and Siberia is useful in Zones 3b–7a, perhaps also in colder zones. It has large, bell-shaped, nodding, blue-violet flowers, the centers filled with staminodes (modified stamens resembling petals) of paler color. Several cultivars have been selected, including 'Markham's Pink,' with rose-pink flowers and 'White Moth,' with white flowers.

Clematis occidentalis 1 (synonym: *C. verticillaris;* mountain clematis). This native of northeastern North America is one of the most cold-hardy of all *Clematis* species, useful in Zones 3a–5b and farther south at high elevations, but it seldom is available or used, even in cold climates.

Clematis patens 1 (lilac clematis).   Like *C. florida*, this species and most of its hybrids flower on the previous season's wood but usually somewhat earlier than *C. florida*, in late spring. Some members of this group often fail to flower in northern climates because of winterkilling of tops, including dormant flower buds, and most are best used in Zones 6b−8a or farther south in areas with relatively cool summers. *C. patens* has very large, lilac-colored flowers with purple stamens. A few of the more common hybrids are listed here.

'Lasurstern' has very large, deep blue-purple flowers in spring, followed by a second flowering from the current season's growth in late summer in some years. 'Miss Bateman' has large, creamy white flowers (red-brown stamens) in late spring. 'Nelly Moser' has large, pale lavender-pink flowers with rosy pink stripes, somewhat double, in late spring, sometimes with a few flowers on new growth in late summer. 'The President' has large, dark blue-purple flowers in early summer, usually continuing intermittently from new growth until autumn, consequently better adapted to cold climates (Zones 4b−8a).

Clematis viticella 1 (Italian clematis).   This Eurasian species is involved in many hybrids, including the Jackman hybrids and Viticella hybrids. The parent species has blue or purple flowers, to 5 cm/2 in. across, in middle to late summer, is best known in the form of its hybrids, and is adapted to use in Zones 5a−7b. The recent selection, 'Betty Corning,' released in the early 1970s by the U.S. National Arboretum, flowers more freely and over a longer period than typical *C. viticella*.

Clematis maximowicziana 1

Synonyms: *C. dioscoreifolia* var. *robusta*, and *C. paniculata*, as it is most commonly known in commerce. The true *C. paniculata* is an entirely different species from New Zealand.
Sweet autumn clematis
Deciduous vine
Ranunculaceae (Buttercup Family)

Native Range. Japan.

Useful Range. USDA Zones 4a−9a.

Function. Screen (with support), specimen. This is clearly the most effective *Clematis* species for functional use in the North, and probably the best for the South also. Since *Clematis* species climb and hold by twining petioles, they require wire or fine lattice trellis support and are especially well adapted to cover chainlink fences.

Size and Habit

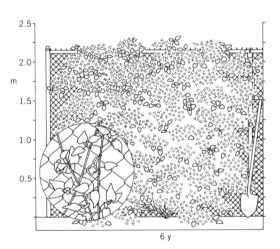

Clematis maximowicziana.

Adaptability. This species is more widely tolerant of site conditions than many *Clematis* species but performs best in full sun and well-drained soil that is not too acidic.

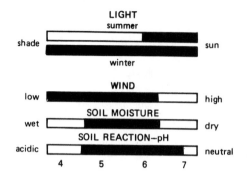

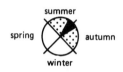

Seasonal Interest. *Flowers:* Fragrant, white, small but in great numbers in late summer and early autumn, very showy against dark green foliage. *Foliage:* Dark green, leathery, making a dense mass that remains green late into autumn. *Fruits:* Plumy styles give a silvery, shimmering appearance to the plant after flowering until frost.

Problems and Maintenance. Once established, this plant is usually trouble-free. In the coldest part of its useful range the top may winterkill, requiring pruning to remove the dead wood. In such situations, the vine returns vigorously to function and flower in the following growing season.

Related Species

Clematis apiifolia 1 (October clematis).   This Chinese species is similar to *C. maximowicziana*

in hardiness, flower color, and lateness of bloom, but inferior in vigor and foliage quality and seldom available commercially.

Clematis drummondii 1 (Drummond clematis). This native of the southwestern United States has small white flowers and showy, plumy styles. It is of interest in Zones 6a–8a, primarily for its usefulness in hot, dry climates in the southwestern parts of our area.

Clematis flammula 1 (plume clematis).   This Mediterranean species is less cold-hardy (Zones 6a–9a) than *C. maximowicziana* but similar in vigor, long-persistent foliage, and general flowering effect. It flowers over a long period in autumn and the plumy styles are showy after flowering.

Clematis ×*jouiniana* 1 (Jouin clematis). Shrubby, weakly climbing hybrid (*C. heracleifolia* × *C. vitalba*), with white flowers in late summer, turning purplish and lasting well into autumn.

Clematis virginiana 1 (virgin's bower).   This North American species is similar in general effect to *C. maximowicziana* but less vigorous and more delicate, flowering a few weeks earlier, and slightly more cold-hardy (Zones 3b–7b). Less functional, less used, and less available than *C. maximowicziana.*

Clematis vitalba 1 (traveler's joy).   This Eurasian and North African counterpart of *C. virginiana* is similar in vigor and general effect to *C. maximowicziana*, but less functional, flowering a few weeks earlier, and with less effective foliage, not persisting as late in autumn.

Clematis montana 1

Anemone clematis
Deciduous vine
Ranunculaceae (Buttercup Family)

Native Range. Central China to Himalayas.

Useful Range. USDA Zones 6b–8a.

Function. Specimen, screen. This species is more vigorous than many *Clematis* species, functioning well as a screen (to 5–6 m/16–20 ft) with good growing conditions from Zone 6b southward.

Size and Habit

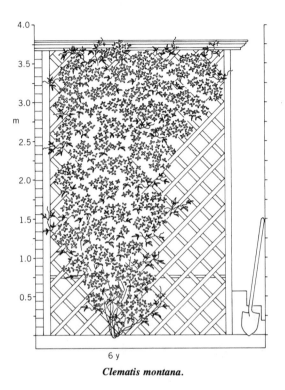

Clematis montana.

Adaptability. This species is adaptable to the same conditions as *C. ×jackmanii* and most of the large-flowered hybrids.

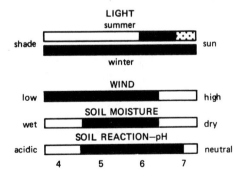

Seasonal Interest. *Flowers*: Medium in size (about 5 cm/2 in.), white or pink, in late spring, initiated on previous season's growth. *Foliage*:

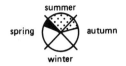

Medium green. *Fruits*: Plumy styles add interest in summer and early autumn.

Clematis montana.

Problems and Maintenance. Since flowers of *C. montana* are initiated in the previous growing season like those of *C. florida* and *C. patens* hybrids (see under *C. ×jackmanii*), the dormant flower buds must survive winter before they can flower in any number. So when plants are killed to the ground in colder climates, they may return with luxuriant vegetation but with no flowers. Because of this, the species and hybrids in this group are usually not recommended in areas colder than Zone 6a, and some are marginally useful even there.

Varieties and Cultivars. 'Alba' has white flowers. Var. *grandiflora* has pink flowers, somewhat larger (to 8 cm/3 in.) than those of the species type, but is seldom available. 'Lilacina' has bluish pink flowers, usually less attractive than those of the species, and is seldom available commercially. Var. *rubens* (pink anemone clematis) is the most common form of this species, with rosy pink flowers and reddish young foliage. It is reputedly slightly hardier than the species type and is useful in Zones 6a–8a. 'Tetrarose' is a vigorous tetraploid form with large (to 8 cm/3 in.) pink-purple flowers. Its hardiness limits are not well known in North America. Var. *wilsonii* has relatively large (to 8 cm/3 in.) white flowers.

Clematis tangutica 1

Golden clematis
Deciduous vine
Ranunculaceae (Buttercup Family)

Native Range. Mongolia and northern China.

Useful Range. USDA Zones 2b−8a.

Function. Specimen.

Size and Habit

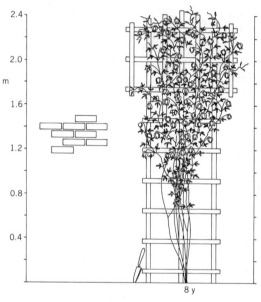

Clematis tangutica.

Seasonal Interest. *Flowers:* Soft yellow, bell-shaped, with sepals spreading somewhat to 5−10 cm/2−4 in. across, flowering heavily in June, intermittently during the summer, and again heavily in late summer or early autumn. *Foliage:* Finer textured than that of many *Clematis* species, seldom full enough for effective screening. *Fruits:* Long, plumy styles add interest from midsummer through autumn along with the flowers.

Clematis tangutica.

Adaptability. This species is similar in requirements to most other *Clematis* species but is less tolerant of shade than most, performing best in full sun.

Problems and Maintenance. The top kills to the ground in cold climates, but the plant returns vigorously to bloom in the same growing season.

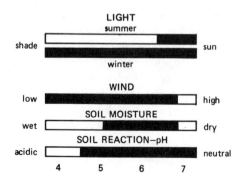

Clematis texensis 1

Scarlet or Texas clematis
Deciduous vine
Ranunculaceae (Buttercup Family)

Native Range. Texas.

Useful Range. USDA Zones 4b—8b.

Function. Specimen, screening (under good conditions).

Size and Habit

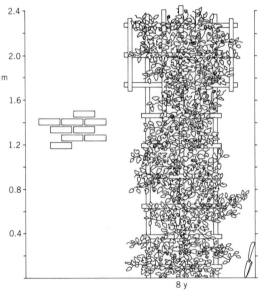

Clematis texensis.

Adaptability. This species is similar in requirements to most *Clematis* species but is more tolerant of hot, dry sites than most.

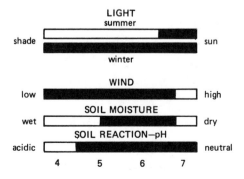

Seasonal Interest. *Flowers:* Scarlet, bell-shaped, narrowed at the mouth, 2.5 cm/1 in. long, borne singly but in great numbers under good conditions. *Foliage:* Medium green, finer textured than that of most *Clematis* species, neat and dense enough for screening when growth is vigorous. *Fruits:* Plumy styles add interest after flowering and into early autumn.

Clematis texensis.

Problems and Maintenance. This species is top-killed over most of its useful range, but the plant returns vigorously the next spring and flowers heavily in a single growing season.

Cultivars. 'Duchess of Albany', a vigorous vine, actually is a hybrid (probably *C. texensis* × *C. ×jackmanii*), with large (to 6 cm/2.5 in.), pink-purple flowers, dark brown in the center, with creamy white streaks on the outside of the sepals. Flowers are borne in early summer and continue intermittently during the remainder of the summer.

Related Species

Clematis viorna 1 (leather flower). This native of the eastern United States has red-purple, bell- or urn-shaped flowers similar in size to those of *C. texensis* over a long period in late spring and summer. It is useful in Zones 6a—8b.

Clerodendrum trichotomum 5−6

Harlequin glory bower
Deciduous shrub
Verbenaceae (Vervain Family)

Native Range. China, Japan.

Useful Range. USDA Zones 6b−8b.

Function. Screen, specimen, shrub or tree, or cutting for decorations. As a screen it requires considerable space because of its tendency to spread widely.

Size and Habit

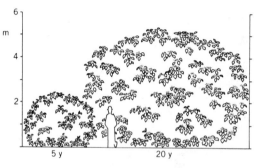

Clerodendrum trichotomum.

Adaptability

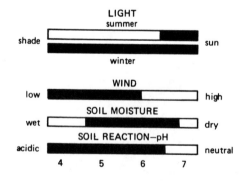

Seasonal Interest. *Flowers:* Fragrant, white, small but numerous, in red calyces in late summer. *Foliage:* Coarse, light green, 10−20 cm/4−8 in. long, superficially resembling that of *Catalpa*, remaining green until frost, and giving off an unpleasant odor when crushed. *Fruits:* Small, bright blue berries displayed in the persistent, star-shaped red calyces.

Problems and Maintenance. Hardiness is marginal in Zone 6, and the entire top may be killed to the ground in some winters. When this happens, the plant returns quickly during the following growing season and usually flowers and fruits in the same summer and autumn. The screening function may be lost temporarily but soon returns. When pruned into a low tree form, however, winterkilling may destroy the character of the plant, so this usage is inappropriate in areas colder than Zone 7a or 7b.

Related Species

Clerodendrum bungei 4 (Bunge glory bower). Somewhat lower-growing and less cold-hardy (Zones 7b−8b) than *C. trichotomum*, but returns equally easily following topkilling in winter. Flowers are rosy red in headlike clusters with less conspicuous calyces than those of *C. trichotomum*.

Clethra alnifolia 5

Summersweet
Deciduous shrub
Clethraceae (Clethra Family)

Native Range. Eastern United States.

Useful Range. USDA Zones 4b − 9a +.

Function. Screen, specimen, massing, border. Spreads slowly into large clumps by underground stems but can be controlled easily.

Size and Habit

Clethra alnifolia.

Clethra alnifolia.

Adaptability. Unusually well adapted to wet or moist soils and not well suited to dry soils (see Problems and Maintenance). Tolerant of seaside conditions.

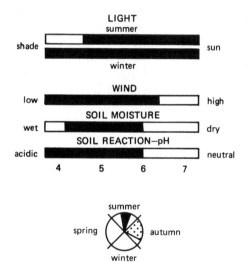

Seasonal Interest. *Flowers:* Fragrant, white (or pink), in small, tight spikes from midsummer to late summer. *Foliage:* Dark green, crisp in summer, turning yellowish to orange in autumn, showy in some years and situations. *Fruits:* Inconspicuous, dry capsules.

Problems and Maintenance. This plant's greatest problem is infestation by mites. They seldom are troublesome on moist soils, but they almost invariably become a problem on dry soils. This species tolerates moderately dry soils except for the aggravation of the mite problem.

Cultivars. 'Rosea' has light pink flowers; otherwise it is similar to the species type.

Related Species

Clethra acuminata 6 (cinnamon clethra, white alder). This native of the southeastern United States is larger, coarser, less cold-hardy (Zones 6a−9a+), and less showy in flower than *C. alnifolia* but is useful as a large shrub specimen because of the polished-looking, cinnamon-brown bark on its branches.

Clethra barbinervis 6 (Japanese clethra). This Asian counterpart of *C. acuminata* has more character as a specimen than any other species of *Clethra* with its graceful growth habit, horizontally nodding flower clusters, and cinnamon-brown, shredding bark. It seems to be less susceptible to mite infestation than *C. alnifolia*, but it is less hardy (Zones 6b−9a+) and its flowers have little fragrance.

Clethra barbinervis.

Clethra barbinervis.

The following species of other genera are included here, not because they are very closely related to *Clethra*, but because they have certain functional, esthetic, geographic, and ecological characteristics in common with *Clethra*. Both *Cliftonia* and *Cyrilla* belong to the *Cyrillaceae* (Cyrilla Family), which is closely allied to the Ericaceae (Heath Family).

Cliftonia monophylla 5 (buckwheat tree). This large shrub is native to the southeastern United States and grows well in moist to wet acid soil with maximum sun. It has upright spikes of fragrant white or pinkish flowers in early to midspring. The dry capsules that follow resemble buckwheat and suggest the common name. It is useful in naturalizing or in mixed borders in Zones 7b−9a+.

Cyrilla racemiflora 6 (leatherwood, titi, American or swamp cyrilla).   This large shrub or small tree, native to the southeastern United States, is useful in Zones 6a−9a+ and grows well in wet or dry acid soil in full sun. Its small spikes of white flowers, resembling small bottlebrushes, encircle

Cyrilla racemiflora.

the base of the new growth at odd angles, giving a distinctive appearance to the rather open plant. Like *Cliftonia*, this shrub is useful primarily for naturalizing.

Convallaria majalis 2

Lily of the valley
Herbaceous groundcover
Liliaceae (Lily Family)

Native Range. Europe; naturalized in eastern North America.

Useful Range. USDA Zones 3a−7b and perhaps even colder areas.

Function. Groundcover.

Size and Habit

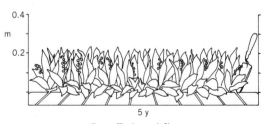

Convallaria majalis.

Adaptability. Lily of the valley performs best in at least partial shade. More shade and occasional irrigation are necessary for best results in areas with hot summers.

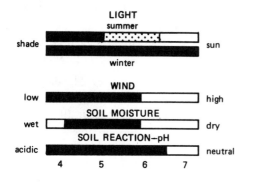

Seasonal Interest. *Flowers:* Highly fragrant, waxy white, bell-shaped, about 1 cm/0.4 in. long, nodding in upright racemes in late spring. *Foliage:* Rich green, oval leaves form a dense mat during the growing season, but they may become dingy and tattered by autumn, and they die back in winter. *Fruits:* Orange-red, not borne in large numbers.

Problems and Maintenance. This is one of the most trouble-free groundcovers, needing only thinning and fertilization when crowded by growing in one place for a long time. The fruits are toxic, may be attractive to small children.

Cultivars. 'Aureo-variegata' has yellow striped leaves. A novelty, it is seldom commercially available. 'Prolificans' has double, white flowers. 'Rosea' has delicately pale pink flowers.

Cornus alba 5

Tatarian dogwood
Deciduous shrub
Cornaceae (Dogwood Family)

Native Range. Siberia, Manchuria, northern China, North Korea.

Useful Range. USDA Zones 3a–8a.

Function. Screen, border, specimen.

Size and Habit

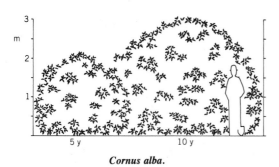

Cornus alba.

Adaptability. Broadly adapted to soil type, acidity, moisture, and light conditions.

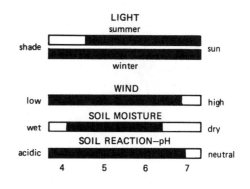

Seasonal Interest. *Flowers:* Small, white, in flattened clusters in late spring and early summer. *Foliage:* Medium green, making a dense mass suitable for screening, turning dull to rich red in autumn. *Fruits:* White to pale blue in late summer and autumn. *Twigs:* Reddish from late summer until late autumn, becoming progressively brighter red until early spring, then reverting to green as new growth begins.

Problems and Maintenance. This shrub may be seriously infested with scale insects, but these can be controlled without difficulty by timely spraying.

Cultivars. 'Argenteo-marginata' (= 'Elegantissima') is less vigorous than the species type, with leaves somewhat narrower and with white variegated margins. 'Sibirica' and 'Westonbirt' are very similar—perhaps the same clone—with unusually brilliant stem color, especially in late winter and early spring. Because of low vigor, these selections are not useful for screening. 'Spaethii' is less vigorous than the species type, with yellow-margined leaves.

Related Species

Cornus hessei 3 (Hesse dogwood). This dwarf species, probably from northeastern Asia, seldom exceeds 0.5 m/1.6 ft in height and has very dark green foliage, pink tinted flowers, and bluish white fruits. It is useful in small-scale situations in Zones 5a–8a, perhaps also Zone 4, but may not be commercially available at present.

Cornus sanguinea 5 (red or bloodtwig dogwood). This European native has been used as a landscape plant for more than 200 years because of its blood red autumn foliage and winter twigs. It is useful in Zones 4a–8a, but has no advantage over *C. alba*, *C. amomum*, and *C. sericea*, and in fact usually is inferior to the better selections of *C. alba* and *C. sericea* for winter color. The selection 'Wisley Form' is more colorful than the species type but is not commonly available in our area.

Cornus alternifolia 6

Pagoda dogwood
Deciduous shrub or small tree
Cornaceae (Dogwood Family)

Native Range. Northeast United States and adjacent Canada, southward to northern Georgia, westward to eastern Missouri.

Useful Range. USDA Zones 4a–7a.

Function. Specimen, patio tree, border accent, naturalizing. Strongly layered, open branching suggests the name "pagoda dogwood."

Size and Habit

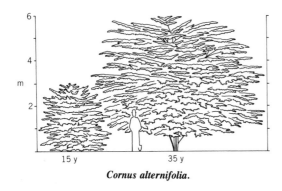

Cornus alternifolia.

Adaptability. Comparable in requirements to *Cornus florida* except for useful range. Best with relatively cool summers and with some shade in the southern parts of its useful range. A possible substitute in form, although not in flowering interest, for *Cornus florida* in Zones 4 and 5.

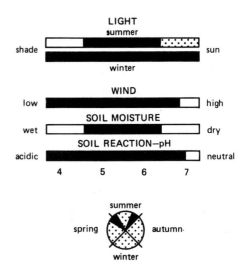

Seasonal Interest. *Flowers:* Small, white, in large flattened clusters in late spring. *Foliage:* Handsome, dark to light green, displayed well with alternate placement and strong planar positioning, giving a layered effect unequalled even by *Cornus florida*. *Fruits:* Black-blue when ripe, following green and purplish stages, in large flat clusters on showy red stalks. *Twigs:* Smooth and greenish, the layered branching providing quiet winter interest.

Cornus alternifolia.

Problems and Maintenance. This species has been troubled by a twig blight disease in some localities and seems to be most successful when used in or near its natural range where it usually has been relatively trouble-free.

Cultivars. 'Argentea' has creamy, white variegated leaves but is not widely used or available.

Related Species

Cornus controversa 7 (giant dogwood). This east Asian counterpart of *C. alternifolia* is similar in its alternate leaf arrangement and strongly layered branching and seasonal interest, but it becomes a much larger tree than *C. alternifolia*, 10−15 m/33−50 ft or more in height and often wider than tall. It is less cold-hardy (Zones 6a−8a) but better adapted to areas with warm summers than *C. alternifolia* and seems not to be troubled by the twig blight that sometimes infects *C. alternifolia*. It is seldom available commercially, but it may be more commonly grown in the future. This is not a tree for a small property because of its great horizontal spread (to 15−20 m/50−65 ft in time).

Cornus coreana 7−8 (Korean dogwood). This may be the largest tree of all dogwoods, eventually reaching heights of 15−20 m/50−65 ft. It has lustrous, dark green foliage, flowering interest similar to that of *C. alternifolia* except slightly later, and plated bark similar to that of *C. florida* except coarser in texture. This tree is not well known and probably is not available at present, but it is a potentially useful tree in Zones 6a−8a and perhaps colder zones as well.

Cornus amomum 5

Silky dogwood
Deciduous shrub
Cornaceae (Dogwood Family)

Native Range. Eastern and north-central United States and adjacent Canada.

Useful Range. USDA Zones 4b−9a+; one of the few shrub dogwoods that is well adapted to the far South.

Function. Naturalizing, screen, border.

Size and Habit

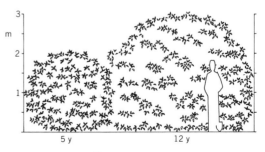

Cornus amomum.

Adaptability. Broadly adapted to soil type, acidity, and moisture conditions, and to considerable shade as well as full sun. Commonly found on old strip-mined sites in the Midwest.

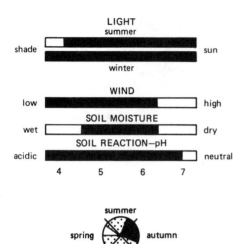

Seasonal Interest. *Flowers:* Small, yellowish white, in early summer in flattened clusters covered with silky hairs. *Foliage:* Medium green, making a fairly dense mass suitable for screening when grown in full sun, turning dull to rich red

in autumn. *Fruits:* Blue berries in late summer and autumn. *Twigs:* Reddish from autumn until early spring, adding landscape color in winter, but less so than stems of C. *alba* and C. *sericea.*

Problems and Maintenance. This shrub occasionally may be infested with scale insects, but these can be controlled without difficulty in the few cases where it is necessary.

Related Species

Cornus drummondii 5–6 (roughleaf dogwood). This plant is similar to C. *amomum* except that it is more upright in form, does not form thickets as freely, and has whitish berries. It is useful for naturalizing or preserved in native stands throughout its range, from Ontario and the midwestern states to Texas in Zones 4b–8b. It may be obtained inadvertently from nurseries as C. *racemosa.*

Cornus purpusii 5 (synonym: C. *obliqua*; pale dogwood). This shrub is similar to C. *amomum* but is more northern in native habitat and in useful range (Zones 3b–8a). It is less useful for screening than C. *amomum* because of its more open branching, but occasionally it is used for naturalizing or preserved in its natural range.

Cornus florida 6–7

Flowering dogwood
Deciduous tree
Cornaceae (Dogwood Family)

Native Range. Eastern United States from New England to Florida, westward to Michigan and Texas, and a small part of adjacent Ontario.

Useful Range. USDA Zones 5b–8b (5a and 9a with selection of appropriate genetic material).

Function. Specimen, patio tree, naturalizing, border accent.

Size and Habit

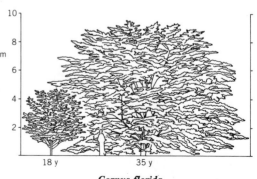

Cornus florida.

Adaptability. Performs best in full sun in the North but with some shade in the South.

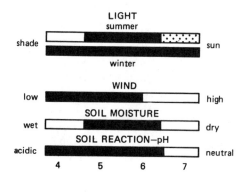

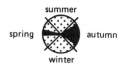

Seasonal Interest. *Flowers:* Small terminal clusters surrounded by snow white (or pink to red) bracts in midspring. *Foliage:* Medium green, not noteworthy in summer but turning deep to bright red in autumn. *Fruits:* Bright red and shiny in tight terminal clusters in autumn. *Twigs:* Smooth, gray-green, the layered branching providing quiet winter interest. *Trunks:* Coarsely plated bark on all but very young trees.

Cornus florida.

Problems and Maintenance. This tree is susceptible to borers but less so with a good maintenance program, including fertilization and irrigation in times of severe drought. Good soil drainage is essential. Transplanting is sometimes difficult and must be done carefully.

Cultivars. 'Alba Plena' (= 'Pluribracteata') has multiple bracts, up to twice the normal number. 'Cherokee Princess,' 'Cloud 9,' 'Springtime,' and others are selections for precocious flowering, large, pure white bracts, and good form. 'Cherokee Chief' and 'Sweetwater Red' are selections from *f. rubra* for deep rose or red bracts and are of southern origin (hardy in Zones 6a–8b). 'Fastigiata' has a narrow form when young, which is less noticeable as the tree approaches maturity. 'Fragrant Cloud' (Plant Patent No. 2819, 1969) is erect in growth habit and has white bracts and a gardenialike fragrance when the flowers open fully. It has not been tested enough for its useful range to be known. 'Pendula' has a strongly weeping growth habit and is of value only as a novelty. 'Rainbow' (Plant Patent No. 2743, 1967) and 'Welchii' have tricolored (green, white, pink) leaves and are very

Cornus florida 'Welchii.'

striking plants but not as functional as most cultivars. F. *rubra* includes all naturally occurring forms with pink or red bracts. 'Welch's Junior Miss' has multicolored (white or red) bracts and good fall foliage color. Its chief value may be its adaptability to southern areas (through Zone 9a) because of a low chilling requirement for breaking winter bud dormancy. Cold-hardiness in the North is not well known but probably is less than that of other cultivars listed.

Plants grown from extreme northern seed sources probably are more cold-hardy than most plants in commerce (to Zone 5a). Such plants have been grown by nurseries located near the northern extremes of the natural range.

Related Species

Cornus canadensis 2 (bunchberry).   This herbaceous groundcover plant, growing only to about 20 cm/8 in. tall, covers large expanses of deciduous forest floor from Greenland through northern North America to northeastern Asia. In our area it grows wild as far south as the mountains of West Virginia. Its white-bracted flowers in late spring or early summer and tight clusters of red berries in late summer and autumn bear a startling resemblance to those of *C. florida*. Bunchberry is not easy to establish, and it grows best in mountain and seashore areas where summers are relatively cool and moist. It requires acidic, well-drained soil that is not excessively dry and at least partial sun. Useful, under these conditions, in Zones 2–5b, perhaps to Zone 6b or 7a in some coastal areas in the Northeast where the predominantly sandy soils would need to be supplemented with organic matter such as peat.

Cornus nuttallii 6 (Pacific dogwood).   A magnificent tree, to 25 m/80 ft tall in native habitat in the Pacific Northwest, but not well adapted in the eastern half of North America. It is of interest here primarily for the cultivar 'Eddie's White Wonder' (Plant Patent No. 2413, 1964), believed to be a hybrid of *C. florida*, with as many as six large bracts surrounding flower clusters. Early trials suggest that it is hardy at least in Zones 7a–8b, but it is not yet fully proven as a landscape plant for the eastern United States.

Cornus kousa 6

Japanese or Chinese dogwood
Deciduous tree
Cornaceae (Dogwood Family)

Native Range. Japan, Korea, China.

Useful Range. USDA Zones 5a–7b.

Function. Specimen, patio tree, border accent.

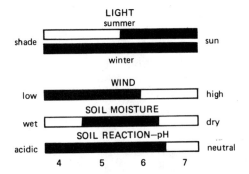

Size and Habit

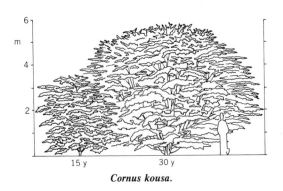

Cornus kousa.

Adaptability. Similar to *C. florida* in requirements except that it is less tolerant of shade and slightly more tolerant of heat and drought in the Midwest and Upper South.

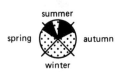

Seasonal Interest. *Flowers:* Small terminal clusters surrounded by white, pointed bracts in early summer. Bracts may become tinged with pink if the nights are very cool during flowering. *Foliage:* Medium green leaves are slightly smaller than those of *C. florida*, not noteworthy in summer but turning dull to bright red in autumn. *Fruits:* Dull red, dangling, aggregate fruits, superficially resembling oversize raspberries, add interest in late summer. For heavy fruiting, and especially for development of viable seeds, more than one individual plant or clone must be present. *Twigs:* Light gray-brown, offering less winter interest than those of *C. florida* even though they show similar horizontally layered branching.

Cornus kousa.

Problems and Maintenance. This tree is relatively trouble-free if planted in well-drained soil, given some protection from strong winds, and maintained well (i.e., fertilized every year or two and irrigated in times of severe drought).

Varieties and Cultivars. Var. *chinensis* includes all plants having their origin in China rather than Japan or Korea, differing from the species type in only minor details of pubescence. Some writers have claimed greater hardiness for var. *chinensis,* but there is little clear evidence of this, and trees are frequently mislabeled in commerce. It is likely that different seed sources in China, and probably Japan and Korea as well, vary in hardiness, but too small a sample of native Chinese material has been introduced to give any assurance that the hardiest existing material has ever come to North America. 'Milky Way' has been selected for unusually heavy flowering. 'Summer Stars' (= 'Summerstar,' Plant Patent No. 3090, 1972) is a recent selection for retention of bracts until late summer. Inflorescences are not large but are borne in large numbers.

Cornus kousa is receiving increasing attention by horticulturists, and additional superior cultivars can be expected to appear in the future.

Cornus mas 6

Synonym: *C. mascula*
Cornelian cherry
Deciduous shrub or small tree
Cornaceae (Dogwood Family)

Native Range. Southeastern Europe and western Asia.

Useful Range. USDA Zones 5a−8a, but flower buds are sometimes winter killed in Zone 5a.

Function. Screen, hedge, border, specimen.

Size and Habit

Cornus mas.

Adaptability. One of the most widely adapted of the dogwoods but not as tolerant of wet soil as most of the shrub dogwoods.

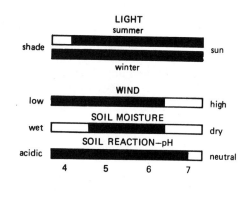

Seasonal Interest. *Flowers:* Small, yellow, in large numbers in rounded clusters (umbels) before foliage appears in early spring, best displayed against a dark background of shadow or evergreen trees. *Foliage:* Dark green, lustrous, crisp-appearing, as handsome as that of any dogwood, making a dense mass that functions as a most effective screen. May or may not turn red in autumn, apparently depending on soil, climate, and perhaps genetic material. If it does not color well, it at least holds good green color until it falls in late autumn. *Fruits:* Bright red, or yellow in a cultivar, cherrylike, to 1.5 cm/0.6 in. long, ripening in late summer, the effect short-lived because of birds and early drop. *Trunk and branches:* Flaking, bicolored bark in muted gray and tan adds quiet winter interest to older plants.

Cornus mas.

Problems and Maintenance. This is one of the most trouble-free landscape plants in good sites.

Cultivars. 'Flava,' with yellow fruits, may not be available in our area. Considerable additional variation probably exists in natural populations in western Asia, and the location of material of extreme cold-hardiness there may extend the useful range of this species northward in the future.

Related Species

Cornus officinalis 6 (Japanese cornel). This Asian shrub or small tree is very similar to *C. mas* but more open in growth habit, making it less useful as a screen or hedge but more valuable as a specimen shrub or small patio tree. Its flowering interest is similar, and the bicolored, flaking winter bark is somewhat more conspicuous than that of *C. mas.*

Cornus officinalis.

Cornus racemosa 5

Synonym: *C. paniculata*
Gray dogwood
Deciduous shrub
Cornaceae (Dogwood Family)

Native Range. Northeastern United States and adjacent Canada to Nebraska, southward to northern Georgia.

Useful Range. USDA Zones 3b–7b.

Function. Naturalizing, massing, screen, border.

Size and Habit

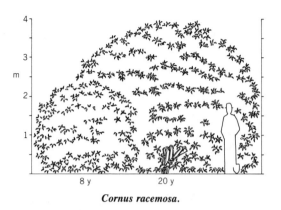

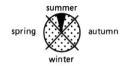

Cornus racemosa.

Adaptability. Widely adapted to difficult site conditions including dry, gravelly soil often found at roadsides.

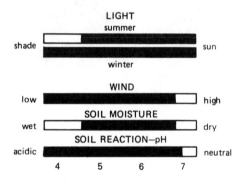

Seasonal Interest. *Flowers*: Small, creamy white, not as showy as some of the other shrub dog-

woods, in early summer. *Foliage*: Light green, medium fine texture, turning purplish to deep purple in autumn. *Fruits*: White berries on bright red pedicels are colorful in midsummer but usually are taken by birds rather quickly. The red pedicels remain colorful for most of the summer. *Twigs*: Older branches gray, very young twigs red tinged, offering subtle winter interest, most noticeable in late winter.

Problems and Maintenance. This shrub needs little maintenance in naturalized settings except to control occasional insect infestations, especially scale insects, which are troublesome in some areas. When used for massing, pruning to within a few inches of the ground every few years will promote fullness. Such drastic pruning should be done no later than the begining of summer to allow time for new growth and acclimation in preparation for the next winter.

Related Species

Cornus stricta 5 (synonym: *C. foemina*; stiff dogwood). Like C. *racemosa*, this shrub is stiffly upright in growth habit, but it is less tolerant of dry soil and much more southern in distribution and useful range (Zones 5b–9a). Like *C. racemosa*, it is a neutral plant, useful for massing or naturalizing.

Cornus sericea 5

Synonym: *C. stolonifera*
Red osier dogwood
Deciduous shrub
Cornaceae (Dogwood Family)

Native Range. Newfoundland to Manitoba, south to Virginia and Nebraska, and extending westward to the Pacific Northwest and New Mexico.

Useful Range. USDA Zones 3a–8a.

Function. Screen, massing, bank cover, border, specimen. Spreads rapidly by creeping stems (stolons) into large masses.

Size and Habit

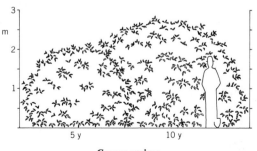

Cornus sericea.

Adaptability

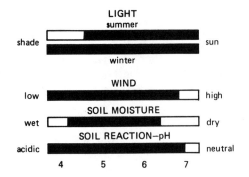

Seasonal Interest. *Flowers:* Small, white, in flattened clusters in late spring and early summer. *Foliage:* Medium green, making a dense mass suitable for screening, turning dull to rich red in autumn. *Fruits:* White to pale blue in late summer and autumn. *Twigs:* Reddish (or yellow-green) from late summer until late autumn, becoming progressively brighter red (or yellow) until early spring, then reverting to green as new growth begins.

Problems and Maintenance. This shrub may be seriously infested with scale insects in some areas, but control is not difficult for knowledgeable landscape maintenance specialists.

Cultivars. 'Flaviramea' (= 'Aurea,' = 'Lutea'; goldentwig dogwood) differs from the species type only in lacking red pigmentation. Fall foliage and

winter stem color is yellow rather than red. The twigs are such a bright yellow that they make this plant an excellent choice for winter color. 'Kelseyi' (Kelsey dwarf dogwood) is a miniature version of *C. sericea*, reaching a maximum height of about 0.6 m/2 ft, with compact form and attractive foliage, useful as a large-scale groundcover. It does not flower or fruit and is disappointing in winter because the stems do not color well. It is less cold-hardy than the species type (Zones 5a–8a).

Cornus sericea 'Kelseyi.'

Related Species

Cornus rugosa 5 (synonym: *C. circinata*; round-leaved dogwood). This upright shrub is useful for naturalizing or preserving stands in its native range, from Nova Scotia to Manitoba and southward to Iowa and Pennsylvania (Zones 3a–7a). It is generally similar to *C. sericea* except that it has less colorful purplish twigs and pale bluish berries.

Coronilla varia 2

Crown vetch
Herbaceous groundcover
Leguminosae (Pea Family)

Native Range. Europe; naturalized in northeastern North America.

Useful Range. USDA Zones 4b–9a, to Zone 3b with reliable snow cover.

Function. Large-scale groundcover, roadside bank cover.

Size and Habit

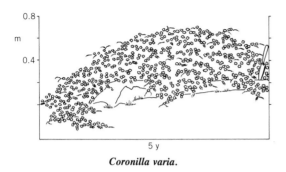

Coronilla varia.

Adaptability. Highly acidic soils should be limed at least to pH 6.0, preferably to pH 6.5.

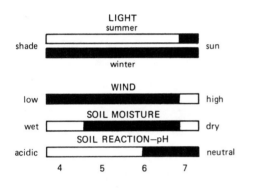

Seasonal Interest. *Flowers:* Light pink or white, individually only 1.2 cm/0.5 in. long but borne in great numbers in crown-shaped clusters to 4 cm/1.6 in. across, starting to flower in early summer and continuing intermittently until early autumn. *Foliage:* Compound leaves with many small leaflets give a vaguely fernlike appearance and form a dense máss, killing to the ground in late autumn.

Problems and Maintenance. Relatively trouble-free, crown vetch requires little or no maintenance after establishment, which usually is rapid if the soil is adequately limed before planting. Old plantings may benefit from cutting and removing the tops in spring.

Cultivars. Several cultivars have been selected for rapid establishment and vigor. 'Penngift' is perhaps the most widely available.

Related Species

Lotus corniculatus 2 (birdsfoot trefoil). This Eurasian legume with deep green leaves and golden-yellow flowers during summer and intermittently into autumn is useful in the same ways that crown vetch is. It is not as vigorous and tall-growing as crown vetch but it is more tolerant of wet and acidic soils. For best results, the soil should be limed to at least pH 6.0 if necessary. This plant is useful in Zones 3b–9a and perhaps colder zones as well.

Trifolium incarnatum 3 (crimson clover). This vigorous legume from southern Europe, naturalized in areas of the southern United States, is actually an annual plant, perpetuating itself by natural reseeding in the South. Even when it is used for temporary revegetation, it often persists as a large-scale groundcover. It is useful in Zones 6a–9a and farther north but with less reliable reseeding. Mowing can be done, but it must be delayed past seed ripening if the cover is to be perpetuated for another year. The spikes of crimson flowers, to 6 cm/2.4 in. long, add color from late spring to midsummer.

Corylopsis glabrescens 5

Fragrant winter hazel
Deciduous shrub
Hamamelidaceae (Witch Hazel Family)

Native Range. Japan.

Useful Range. USDA Zones 5b–9a.

Function. Screen, border, specimen; requires much ground space.

Size and Habit

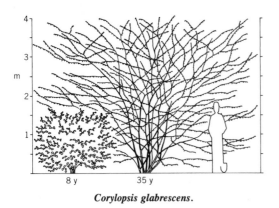

Corylopsis glabrescens.

Adaptability. Avoid dry or windy locations or sites prone to late spring frosts to protect the early flowers.

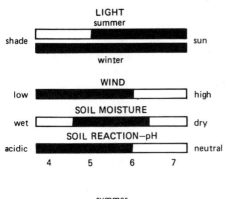

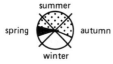

Seasonal Interest. *Flowers:* Fragrant, pale yellow, in drooping clusters, 2−4 cm/0.8−1.6 in. long, before the new foliage appears. *Foliage:* Medium or bluish green with interesting texture caused by venation and leaf shape, borne on gracefully slender branches and sometimes turning clear yellow in autumn.

Problems and Maintenance. This shrub is relatively trouble-free in good soil and a protected location except for the susceptibility of the early flowers to late spring frosts.

Related Species

Corylopsis pauciflora 4 (buttercup winter hazel). Smaller than *C. glabrescens*, slightly less colorful in flower, and slightly less cold-hardy (Zones 6a−9a).

Corylopsis sinensis 5 (Chinese winter hazel). Similar to *C. glabrescens* but more showy in flower and slightly less cold-hardy (Zones 6a−9a).

Corylopsis sinensis.

Corylopsis spicata 4 (spike winter hazel). Similar in size to *C. pauciflora*, but its flowers are more showy. Brighter yellow than those of *C. sinensis*. Useful in Zones 6a−9a.

Corylopsis veitchiana 4 (Veitch winter hazel). This Chinese species is similar to *C. spicata*, but its paler yellow flowers are intermediate in showiness between *C. pauciflora* and *C. spicata*, and it is useful in Zones 6a−9a.

Corylus avellana 5

European hazel or filbert
Deciduous shrub
Betulaceae (Birch Family)

Native Range. Europe.

Useful Range. USDA Zones 4b−8b.

Function. Specimen, border accent. Nuts are edible.

Size and Habit

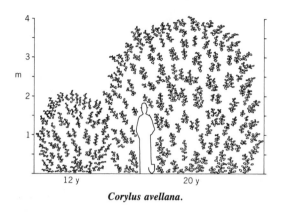

Corylus avellana.

Adaptability. This is one of the best adapted large shrubs to poor, dry soil over a wide climatic range.

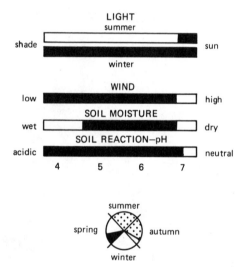

Seasonal Interest. *Flowers:* Large, pendulous male catkins in late winter or early spring. The female flowers are inconspicuous. *Foliage:* Crisp, dark to medium green, of interesting texture. *Fruits:* Nuts with distinctive husks add quiet summer and autumn interest. *Twigs:* Of distinctive, year-round interest in the case of the cultivar 'Contorta' only (see Cultivars).

Problems and Maintenance. Relatively trouble-free, this plant seldom requires maintenance, but rootstocks of grafted cultivars may produce root suckers that must be removed to prevent their overgrowing the cultivar scion.

Cultivars. 'Aurea' (golden hazelnut) has bright yellow foliage in spring and early summer, turning dull green by midsummer. 'Contorta' (contorted hazelnut, Harry Lauder's walking stick) has curled and contorted twigs and branches, making it a popular specimen for accent, especially in formal landscaping settings, reaching heights of about 2 m/6.6 ft. 'Pendula' (weeping hazelnut) is strongly pendulous and rounded in form, making an interesting specimen, but it is not very functional. Usually grafted on a seedling of *C. avellana*, 1–1.5 m/3.3–5 ft above ground level, the grafted plant ultimately reaches about 2 m/6.6 ft in height.

Related Species

Corylus americana 5 (American hazelnut). This thicket-forming shrub, native to much of the eastern United States and Canada, occasionally reaches 3 m/10 ft in height but usually remains lower, especially in poor, gravelly soils in which it nevertheless grows well. Useful primarily for naturalizing in poor soil in Zones 3a–8b.

Corylus cornuta 5 (beaked hazelnut). Native to approximately the same range as *C. americana*, this species is generally similar to and inter-changeable with it in landscape use in Zones 2b–8b.

Corylus maxima 6 (filbert). This large shrub or small tree from southeastern Europe and adjacent Asia is valued for its nuts. In landscape use it is most valued for the selection 'Purpurea,' with deep purple foliage. It is useful in Zones 5b–8b.

Corylus colurna 7–8

Turkish filbert
Deciduous tree
Betulaceae (Birch Family)

Native Range. Southeastern Europe and adjacent Asia.

Useful Range. USDA Zones 5a–8b.

Function. Shade tree, specimen, edible nuts.

Size and Habit

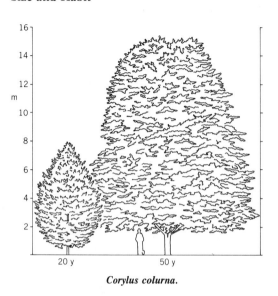

Corylus colurna.

Female flowers are inconspicuous. *Foliage:* Crisp, dark to medium green, of interesting texture. *Fruits:* Nuts, with distinctive husks, are edible. *Twigs and bark:* Roughly corky, gray, mildly interesting in winter.

Corylus colurna.

Adaptability. This is an unusually drought-resistant shade tree, worth planting for this and for its ease of maintenance.

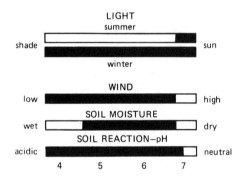

Seasonal Interest. *Flowers:* Large, pendulous male catkins in early spring or late winter.

Problems and Maintenance. Relatively trouble-free but damaged by sapsuckers in some areas, otherwise requiring little or no attention.

Cotinus coggygria 6

Smoke tree, smoke bush
Deciduous shrub or small tree
Anacardiaceae (Cashew Family)

Native Range. Southern Europe to Himalayas and China.

Useful Range. USDA Zones 5a−7b.

Function. Specimen, border, massing. Usually not full enough for effective screening.

Size and Habit

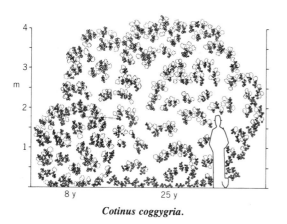

Cotinus coggygria.

Cotinus coggygria.

Adaptability

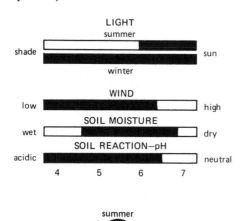

Seasonal Interest. *Flowers:* Small, individually inconspicuous but borne in loose, fuzzy panicles to 20 cm/8 in. across. *Foliage:* Leaves bluish green (except in red- and purple-leaved cultivars) and rounded, making a loose foliage mass, turning yellowish to orange in autumn in some years. *Fruits:* Small and individually inconspicuous, but by fruiting time the large loose panicles are showy because of the plumose hairs borne by sterile flowers in the cluster. The effect is to give the plant a "smoky" appearance in middle to late summer.

Problems and Maintenance. Relatively trouble-free, this plant requires little maintenance except when pruning to enhance foliage color (see Forms and Cultivars).

Forms and Cultivars. F. *purpureus* (= var. *purpureus*) has purple fruiting panicles and young leaves. Color varies among individual plants or clones and with plant vigor, and purple-leaved cultivars tend to be less cold-hardy than the species type. 'Royal Purple' is a clone selected from f. *purpureus* for deep purple foliage color. Heavy pruning in spring will promote vigor and intense purple foliage color while keeping plant size below eye level, but at the expense of fruiting interest.

When plants are grown from seed of f. *purpureus*, many variants in foliage color from nearly green to pale reddish to purple can be obtained. Several additional variants obtained in this way have been named and introduced but as yet are seldom available.

Related Species

Cotinus obovatus 7 (synonym: *C. americanus*; American smoke tree). Native to the south-central United States, this tree, to 10 m/33 ft or taller, is much less showy in fruit than *C. coggygria* but has fine bronze to red-orange fall foliage in some years. Unfortunately, it is weak-wooded, and trees may be devastated by ice storms that do only minor damage to many other trees.

Cotoneaster apiculatus 3

Cranberry cotoneaster
Deciduous shrub
Rosaceae (Rose Family)

Native Range. Western China.

Useful Range. USDA Zones 5a−8b, but may be impractical south of Zone 7b because of insect problems.

Function. Border (front), rock garden, groundcover (with mulch), espalier.

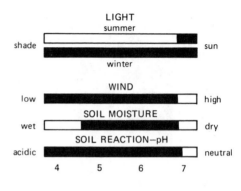

Size and Habit

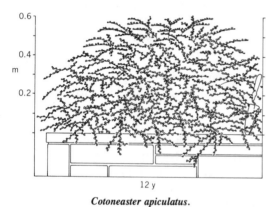

Cotoneaster apiculatus.

Adaptability. This species is more resistant to extremes of soil and climate than most of the other low-growing cotoneasters and for this reason is favored in the Midwest.

Seasonal Interest. *Flowers:* Small, rosy pink with the unfolding leaves in late spring. *Foliage:* Lustrous, dark green, to 1.5 cm/0.6 in. long, refined in texture and pattern, turning deep reddish in autumn. *Fruits:* Bright red, larger (to 1 cm/0.4 in.) than those of other low-growing cotoneasters, in late summer and autumn.

Problems and Maintenance. Cotoneasters in general, like other members of the pome-fruit subfamily of the rose family, are susceptible to a variety of insect pests and diseases, but this is not a serious enough problem to eliminate them as landscape plants except in the South. Some maintenance is required in some years to control lacebugs, mites, scale insects, and fire blight. *C. apiculatus* is less troubled than average among cotoneasters in the Midwest.

Cotoneaster dammeri 2

Bearberry cotoneaster
Evergreen to semievergreen groundcover
Rosaceae (Rose Family)

Native Range. Central China.

Useful Range. USDA Zones 6a−9a+, but may be impractical in some far southern areas because of insect problems. May persist for several years in zones colder than 6a under reliable winter snow cover.

Function. Rock garden, groundcover.

Size and Habit

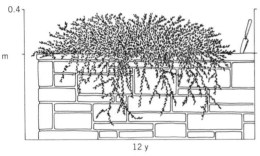

Cotoneaster dammeri.

Adaptability

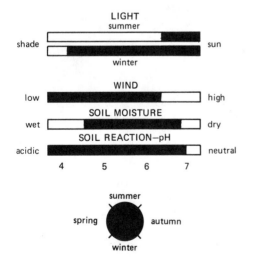

Seasonal Interest. *Flowers:* White with deep red anthers, only 1 cm/0.4 in. across, contrasting with the dark foliage in late spring. *Foliage:*

Evergreen (Zones 8a−9a+) or semievergreen (Zones 6a−7b), lustrous medium to dark green leaves, 1.5−3 cm/0.6−1.2 in. long, in a loose branching pattern. *Fruits:* Bright red, 0.6 cm/0.25 in. across, colorful in autumn.

Cotoneaster dammeri.

Problems and Maintenance. Like all cotoneasters, this species is susceptible to a variety of insect pests and diseases (see *C. apiculatus,* Problems and Maintenance), but it is less troubled than many other cotoneasters, one of the reasons that it is useful in the South as well as farther north.

Cultivars. 'Coral Beauty' and 'Skogsholmen' show promise of slightly greater cold hardiness than the species type and are vigorous, covering large areas relatively rapidly. 'Skogsholmen' is rather sparse in fruiting, however, perhaps because of self-incompatibility, but 'Coral Beauty' bears heavy crops of bright red berries. A few other selections have been made in Europe and imported into North America. They generally bear fruit more freely and may be important additions when fully evaluated.

Related Species

Cotoneaster congestus 3 (Pyrenees cotoneaster). This relatively low, compact shrub has evergreen leaves smaller than those of *C. dammeri* and none of its trailing habit. It is useful primarily as a rock garden specimen in Zones 6b−9a.

Cotoneaster conspicuus 3 (wintergreen cotoneaster). This relatively low, spreading shrub from western China has fine-textured evergreen foliage and is useful as a specimen or for massing in Zones 6b–9a. The variety *decorus* (necklace cotoneaster) is prostrate with ascending branches.

Cotoneaster microphyllus 3 (little-leaved cotoneaster). This handsome, low shrub with fine-textured, evergreen foliage and spreading growth habit is similar generally to *C. congestus* and *C. conspicuus*, but slightly more cold-hardy, useful in Zones 6a–9a.

Cotoneaster divaricatus 4

Spreading cotoneaster
Deciduous shrub
Rosaceae (Rose Family)

Native Range. China.

Useful Range. USDA Zones 5a–8b, but may be impractical south of Zone 7b because of insect problems: lacebugs, mites, scale insects.

Function. Border, informal hedge, massing, specimen, espalier.

Seasonal Interest. *Flowers:* Small, pale pink, with the young leaves in late spring. *Foliage:* Lustrous, dark green, to 2 cm/0.8 in. long, spaced along stems to produce a loose but regular pattern, remaining green late but turning reddish before falling in autumn in some years. *Fruits:* Small (0.6 cm/0.25 in.), red, in late summer and autumn.

Size and Habit

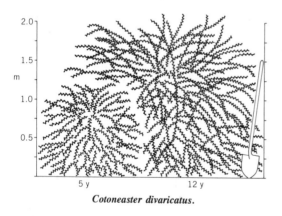

Cotoneaster divaricatus.

Cotoneaster divaricatus.

Adaptability. This is among the best adapted cotoneasters for the Midwest.

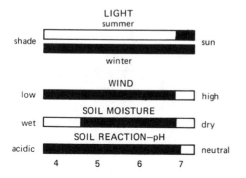

Problems and Maintenance. Like all cotoneasters, this species is susceptible to a variety of insect pests and diseases, few serious enough to eliminate it as a landscape plant except in the South and in areas where fire blight is severe. Some maintenance may be necessary in some years to control lacebugs, mites, scale insects, and fire blight, but less than for many other *Cotoneaster* species.

Related Species

Cotoneaster dielsianus 4 (Diel's cotoneaster). This close relative of *C. divaricatus*, also from China, is similar in its arching branches and small leaves, but its branches are more pendulous and its fruits brighter red. It is useful in Zones 6a–8b.

Cotoneaster franchetii 5 (Franchet cotoneaster). This larger Chinese shrub has medium-small leaves like *C. dielsianus* and *C. divaricatus* and bright, red-orange fruits. It is hardy in Zones 6a–8a.

Cotoneaster zabelii 4 (Zabel or cherryberry cotoneaster). The young leaves and stems of this Chinese species are covered with whitish gray pubescence, and it has relatively large (to 0.7 cm/0.3 in.), bright red fruits, borne on slender, graceful branches. It is useful in Zones 5a–7b.

Cotoneaster horizontalis 3

Rockspray cotoneaster
Deciduous shrub
Rosaceae (Rose Family)

Native Range. Western China.

Useful Range. USDA Zones 5b–8b, but may be impractical south of Zone 7b because of insect problems: lace bugs, mites, scale insects.

Function. Border (front), rock garden, groundcover (with mulch), espalier.

Seasonal Interest. *Flowers:* Small, pink, with the young leaves in late spring. *Foliage:* Lustrous, dark green, refined in texture and regularly spaced along stems branching in a "fishbone" pattern, remaining green late in autumn, sometimes turning reddish before falling. *Fruits:* Small (0.5 cm/0.2 in.), bright red, held tightly against the stems in late summer and autumn.

Size and Habit

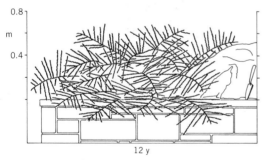

Cotoneaster horizontalis.

Cotoneaster horizontalis.

Adaptability

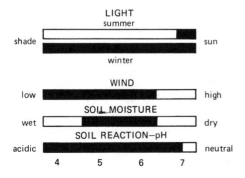

Problems and Maintenance. Like all cotoneasters, this species is susceptible to a variety of insect pests and diseases (see *C. divaricatus*, Problems and Maintenance), few serious enough to eliminate it as a landscape plant except in the South and in areas where fire blight is severe.

Varieties and Cultivars. Var. *perpusillus* is lower-growing than the species type and has smaller leaves. It is useful only as a specimen in small-scale plantings. 'Robustus' is somewhat taller and more vigorous than the species type. 'Tom Thumb' is a dwarf, compact selection, useful in rock gardens or small-scale, formal situations.

Related Species

Cotoneaster adpressus 2 (creeping cotoneaster). This excellent creeping plant forms a denser mat of foliage than most low-growing cotoneasters and is slower-growing than *C. apiculatus* and *C. horizontalis*, valuable for rock gardens and other small-scale sites where adherence to modest size is important. Hardy in Zones 5b–8b. The variety *praecox* (early creeping cotoneaster) is taller and more vigorous, nearly as tall as *C. apiculatus*,

with fruits of about the same size. It is comparable in general effect to that species but less cold-hardy, useful in Zones 6a–8b. The cultivar 'Little Gem' is a dwarf edition of the species comparable with *C. horizontalis* 'Tom Thumb.'

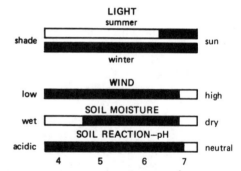

Cotoneaster adpressus.

Cotoneaster lucidus 5

Hedge cotoneaster
Deciduous shrub
Rosaceae (Rose Family)

Native Range. Central Asia: Altai Mountains.

Useful Range. USDA Zones 2b–6b, possibly even colder zones.

Function. Hedge, screen, windbreak.

Size and Habit

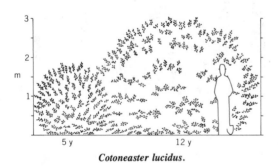

Cotoneaster lucidus.

Adaptability. This is one of the most cold-hardy of cotoneasters and among the hardiest of all shrubs. Valued as a screen and small-scale windbreak in the northern prairies of Canada and the United States, it is adaptable farther south but

not widely used, since alternatives are more attractive.

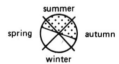

Seasonal Interest. *Flowers:* Small, pink, in late spring and early summer. *Foliage:* Glossy leaves, 2.5–5.0 cm/1–2 in. long, turn orange before falling in autumn. *Fruits:* Small, black, and inconspicuous.

Problems and Maintenance. This species is susceptible to the usual insect and disease problems of cotoneasters and other members of the pome-fruit subfamily of the rose family, and maintenance may be necessary in some years to control mites, scale insects, and fire blight.

Related Species

Cotoneaster acutifolius 5 (Peking cotoneaster). Similar in most respects to *C. lucidus*, but with foliage turning red-orange shortly before falling. This species and *C. lucidus* are confused in commerce, many plants of *C. lucidus* being sold as *C. acutifolius*. The two are similar in hardiness.

Cotoneaster foveolatus 5 (glossy cotoneaster). This shrub is similar to *C. lucidus* in its Chinese origin and in general effect but has red-orange autumn foliage briefly. It is not as dense or cold-hardy as *C. lucidus*, but it is useful in Zones 5a–7a.

Cotoneaster multiflorus 5

Many-flowered cotoneaster
Deciduous shrub
Rosaceae (Rose Family)

Native Range. Western China.

Useful Range. USDA Zones 4b–7a.

Function. Border, screen, specimen, espalier.

Size and Habit

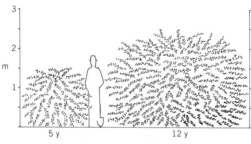

Cotoneaster multiflorus.

Adaptability

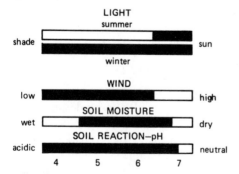

Seasonal Interest. *Flowers:* White, small but making a great show in numbers in midspring. *Foliage:* Dull green, forming a good neutral background for the flowers and fruits. Falls with little or no color change in autumn. *Fruits:* Bright red berries are fairly showy in autumn.

Isolated plants may not fruit well, possibly because of a need for cross-pollination.

Problems and Maintenance. This shrub is subject to the usual insect and disease problems of cotoneasters and other members of the pome-fruit subfamily of the rose family, but less so than many cotoneasters. Some maintenance may still be needed in some years to control fire blight, mites, and scale insects.

Varieties. Var. *calocarpus* has larger, more showy fruits borne in great numbers and is usually used in preference to the species type.

Related Species

Cotoneaster racemiflorus 5 (redbead cotoneaster). This shrub is similar in size and habit to *C. multiflorus* but with slightly smaller, dull gray-green leaves and greater cold hardiness (Zones 3b–7a). It is most commonly used in the form of the variety *soongoricus* (Sungari cotoneaster), which gives a magnificent display of pink fruits in late summer and autumn.

Cotoneaster racemiflorus var. *soongoricus.*

Cotoneaster salicifolius 5

Willowleaf cotoneaster
Evergreen or semievergreen shrub
Rosaceae (Rose Family)

Native Range. Western China.

Useful Range. USDA Zones 6b–9a+, but hardiness in Zones 6b and 7a is restricted to the variety *floccosus*.

Function. Informal hedge or screen, specimen, espalier.

Size and Habit. Var. *floccosus* is illustrated.

Cotoneaster salicifolius var. *floccosus*.

Adaptability

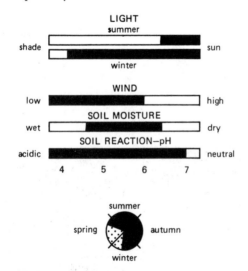

Seasonal Interest. *Flowers:* Small, white, inconspicuous, early summer. *Foliage:* Handsome, narrow, leathery leaves, to 8 cm/3 in. long, are

dark green above, whitish underneath, and evergreen (Zones 8a–9a+) to semievergreen (Zones 6b–7b), turning reddish in autumn. *Fruits:* Small but numerous and bright red, making a striking display in autumn and early winter.

Cotoneaster salicifolius.

Problems and Maintenance. Subject to the usual insect and disease problems of cotoneasters, this species succeeds better in the South than most cotoneasters in spite of this. It may require maintenance in some years to control lacebug, scale, and fire blight and, since it grows rapidly and becomes large quickly, it may require pruning to keep it in scale in some situations, but a better solution is to use it only where there is ample space for it.

Varieties. Var. *floccosus* has glossy foliage, woolly underneath, and is more cold-hardy (to Zone 6b) than the species type.

Related Species and Hybrids

Cotoneaster frigidus 6 (Himalayan cotoneaster). This large, vigorous, deciduous shrub from the Himalayas is limited to the South (Zones 7b–8b) and has an outstanding display of red fruits in late summer and autumn. It is not as functional as some other cotoneasters because its great vigor and ultimate size are difficult to accommodate in many sites.

Cotoneaster henryanus 5 (Henry cotoneaster). Another large shrub from China for the South (Zones 7b–9a) with semievergreen foliage, this is similar to *C. salicifolius* in general appearance but has larger leaves, 5−12 cm/2−5 in. long.

Cotoneaster lacteus 5 (synonym: *C. parneyi*; milky cotoneaster). This handsome, semievergreen shrub from China is useful in the South (Zones 7b−9a). It is distinctive for its white, downy, young leaves and stems, contrasting with the olive green color of older foliage, and for its showy red fruits that persist well into winter.

Cotoneaster pannosus 4 (silverleaf cotoneaster). Still another semievergreen Chinese cotoneaster, this is useful in the South (Zones 7b−9a), and distinctive for the white, woolly undersides of the foliage.

Cotoneaster ×*watereri* 6 (Waterer cotoneaster). A hybrid of *C. frigidus* × *C. henryanus*,

Cotoneaster lacteus.

this large shrub has dark green, narrow leaves and red fruits and is useful only in the South (Zones 7b−9a).

Crataegus crus-galli 7

Cockspur hawthorn
Deciduous tree
Rosaceae (Rose Family)

Native Range. Northeastern North America, south to North Carolina, west to Kansas.

Useful Range. USDA Zones 4a−6b.

Function. Specimen, screen, barrier, patio (with pruning to eliminate the hazard of thorns on the lower part of the plant).

Size and Habit

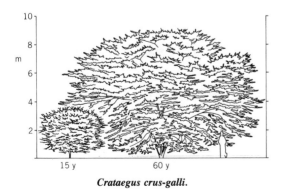

Crataegus crus-galli.

Adaptability. This tree is well adapted to environmental stresses, including urban environments, but its thorns preclude some urban uses.

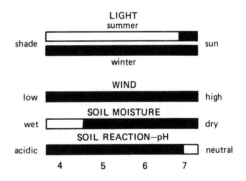

Seasonal Interest. *Flowers:* Small, white, in clusters in late spring. *Foliage:* Glossy, dark green leaves, 2.5−8 cm/1−3 in. long, making a dense mass and persisting with little color change until they fall in late autumn. *Fruits:* Bright red, to about 1 cm/0.4 in. across, persisting well into winter (when not diseased). *Twigs and branches:* Strongly horizontal branching is conspicuous at all seasons and bears very large thorns.

Problems and Maintenance. *C. crus-galli* is moderately susceptible to infection by the cedar apple rust fungus, especially the fruits, which take on the pink color of the fungus fruiting bodies but lose their autumn show. Plant away from native eastern red cedar *(Juniperus virginiana)* and its varieties, which are alternate hosts of the causal fungus, or be prepared to tolerate a certain amount of disease. Transplanting problems have been encountered but do not seem serious with proper handling. Dormant trees should be planted after a few days' activation in a warm, moist atmosphere, with care to prevent drying during handling.

Cultivars. 'Inermis' is a recent thornless selection.

Related Species

Crataegus ×*lavallei* 6 (Lavalle hawthorn). This hybrid (probably *C. crus-galli* × *C. pubescens*) is stiffly upright in habit when young, later becoming ovoid in form, and usually thornless. Its dark green, lustrous leaves, to 10 cm/4 in. long, turn bronze in autumn and the large (1.5 cm/0.6 in.), orange-red fruits persist well into winter. Unfortunately, leaves and fruits are often disfigured by rust. Also, this tree is slow to become anchored after transplanting, requiring longer initial staking. It is useful in Zones 4b−7a.

Crataegus ×*prunifolia* 6 (synonym: *C. crus-galli* 'Splendens'). This hybrid, probably of *C.*

Crataegus ×*lavallei.*

crus-galli × *C. succulenta* var. *macracantha*, is not greatly different from *C. crus-galli* and can be considered interchangeable in landscape use.

Crataegus succulenta 6 (fleshy hawthorn)   This wide-ranging species from the northeastern to southwestern United States is similar in landscape effect to *C. crus-galli*. The variety *macracantha* (synonym: *Crataegus macracantha*) is somewhat denser and more vigorous and is valued in the north-central United States as a hedge, screen, or specimen.

Crataegus marshallii 6

Marshall or parsley hawthorn
Deciduous tree
Rosaceae (Rose Family)

Native Range. Southeastern and south-central United States.

Useful Range. USDA Zones 6b−9a.

Function. Specimen, patio tree.

Size and Habit

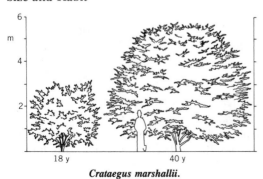

Crataegus marshallii.

Adaptability. This species is unusual among the hawthorns for its ability to tolerate wet soil, but it performs best with good drainage.

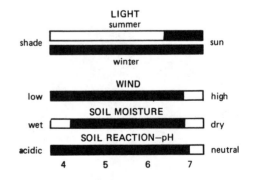

Seasonal Interest. *Flowers:* Small, white or pinkish, in numerous clusters in late spring. *Foliage:* Medium green, finely cut, giving a "parsley" appearance from which the common name is taken, turning yellowish in autumn. *Fruits:*

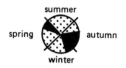

Bright red, to 0.8 cm/0.3 in. across, colorful from midautumn into winter. *Trunks and branches:* Flaking, gray-brown outer bark reveals red-brown inner bark that adds winter interest.

Problems and Maintenance. This species is subject to problems of hawthorns in general but is more trouble-free than most in the South.

Related Species

Crataegus aprica 6 (sunny hawthorn). This small, open tree, native to the southeastern United States, has a distinctive, zigzag branching habit, small leaves, relatively large white flowers in late spring, and dull orange-red fruits, 1.2 cm/0.5 in. across, that are colorful in late autumn. It is useful in Zones 6b–9a.

Other *Crataegus* species native to the South may be of value locally, at least worth preserving in development even though seldom available for planting.

Crataegus mollis 6

Downy hawthorn
Deciduous tree
Rosaceae (Rose Family)

Native Range. Eastern and central North America: Ontario to Virginia, westward to South Dakota and Kansas.

Useful Range. USDA Zones 3a–6b.

Function. Patio tree, specimen, naturalizing. More often preserved in natural sites than planted.

Size and Habit

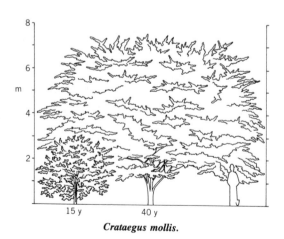

Crataegus mollis.

Adaptability

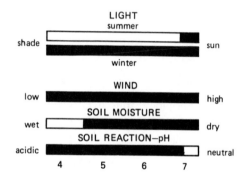

Seasonal Interest. *Flowers:* White, to 2.5 cm/1 in., not persisting for long. *Foliage:* Dull medium green, coarser than that of the better hawthorns and disfigured by rust where the disease is present, turning yellowish in autumn. *Fruits:* Bright red, to 2 cm/0.8 in., sweet and edible.

Problems and Maintenance. This species is more susceptible to cedar apple rust fungus than most hawthorns and is best used where the eastern red cedar (*Juniperus virginiana*) is not present in quantity. Aphids also can be troublesome. Transplanting difficulties have been reported but usually are not serious with proper handling (see *C. crus-galli*, Problems and Maintenance).

Related Species

Crataegus chrysocarpa 5 (roundleaf hawthorn). This large shrub or small tree from the northern plains of Canada and the United States as far south as New Mexico is extremely cold-hardy (Zones 3a–6a) with glossy, dark green foliage, many large thorns, and a good show of orange-red fruits, to 1 cm/0.4 in. across, in early autumn.

Crataegus punctata 6 (dotted hawthorn). This North American native exhibits in the extreme the horizontal branching that is typical of many

hawthorns, spreading in time to a width of as much as 12 m/40 ft, and it is highly susceptible to cedar apple rust. Its fruits are similar in size to those of *C. mollis*, but duller red with dots over the surface. The variety *aurea* has yellow fruits and seldom is commercially planted, but it can be preserved in the wild where native to developed sites.

Other *Crataegus* species native to the North may be of value locally and are at least worth preserving in development even when not available for planting.

Crataegus monogyna 6

Singleseed hawthorn, English hawthorn
Deciduous tree
Rosaceae (Rose Family)

Native Range. Mediterranean Region: southern Europe, North Africa, Asia Minor.

Useful Range. USDA Zones 5a–7b.

Function. Specimen, patio tree, screen, hedge.

Size and Habit

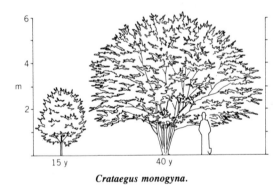

Crataegus monogyna.

Adaptability

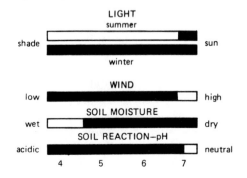

Seasonal Interest. *Flowers:* Small, white, in clusters in very late spring. *Foliage:* Medium green, strongly lobed and finer in texture than most hawthorns, remaining green and falling early in autumn. *Fruits:* Red, to about 1 cm/0.4 in. across, but not as showy as those of some other hawthorns. *Trunk and branches:* Smooth bark is olive green to yellow-orange, often striking in color at close range.

Problems and Maintenance. Like all hawthorns, this tree is susceptible to cedar apple rust and is best used where the eastern red cedar (*Juniperus virginiana*) is not present in great quantity. Aphids also can be troublesome. Transplanting difficulties have been experienced but usually are not serious with proper handling (see *C. crus-galli*, Problems and Maintenance). A trunk canker disease, perhaps initiated or aggravated by sun-scald in winter, can be a serious problem in some areas, especially on the columnar selection 'Stricta.' Consult local plantsmen about the seriousness of this problem in specific areas.

Cultivars. 'Compacta' is a selection for compact, thornless growth, making a miniature specimen usually not over 3 m/10 ft. tall. 'Inermis' is thornless and more vigorous than 'Compacta' but slower to reach full size than the species type. 'Stricta' is very narrow when young, broadening with age to an oval form, and thornless. It seldom bears fruit.

Related Species

Crataegus laevigata 6 (synonym: *C. oxyacantha*; English hawthorn, May tree). This native of Europe and North Africa has been grown as a specimen, hedge, and screen for hundreds of years in Europe, and its cultivars are the most showy in flower of all the hawthorns and colorful when the bright red fruits ripen in early autumn

Crataegus laevigata.

Crataegus laevigata.

as well. Unfortunately, it is more prone to disease problems and aphids than many hawthorns, and there are better choices for most functional purposes. The species type is hardy in Zones 5a−7b, but some cultivars probably are not reliably hardy north of Zone 6b. The cultivars 'Paul's Scarlet,' 'Plena,' and 'Rosea-plena' have, respectively, double rose, double white, and double pink flowers. 'Crimson Cloud' (Plant Patent No. 2679, 1966) has been selected for single, bright red flowers, but its broad adaptability in eastern North America has yet to be fully evaluated.

Crataegus ×*mordenensis* 6 (Morden hawthorn). This is actually a group of hybrids of *C. laevigata* 'Paul's Scarlet' × *C. succulenta*. The first and best known selection is 'Toba,' a small tree (to 5 m/16 ft), with double pink flowers, darkening with age, followed by only a few red fruits and glossy, lobed leaves. This cultivar resembles *C. laevigata* 'Paul's Scarlet' and 'Rosea-plena' and is equally susceptible to fire blight but is much more cold-hardy, to Zone 3b. A more recent selection of *C.* ×*mordenensis*, 'Snowbird,' has pure white flowers and relatively few bright crimson fruits and is said to be even more cold-hardy than 'Toba.'

Crataegus pinnatifida 6 (Chinese hawthorn). This very hardy tree (Zones 3b−7a) from northeastern Asia has been found to grow well in North Dakota. It has lustrous, dark green, finely cut leaves, snowy white flowers in late spring, and bright red fruits to 2.5 cm/1 in. across in autumn. It is round-headed and compact in form, making an excellent specimen or patio tree with relatively few small thorns.

Crataegus phaenopyrum 6

Washington hawthorn
Deciduous tree
Rosaceae (Rose Family)

Native Range. Southeastern United States, west to Missouri.

Useful Range. USDA Zones 4b−8b.

Function. Specimen, patio tree, screen, hedge.

Size and Habit

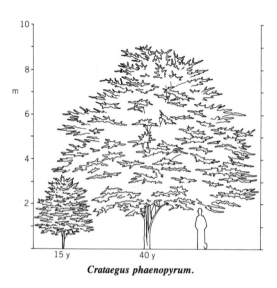

Crataegus phaenopyrum.

Crataegus phaenopyrum.

Adaptability

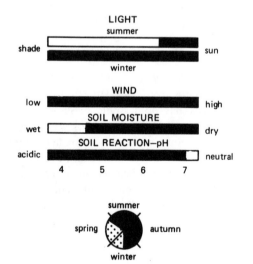

Problems and Maintenance. This species is less susceptible to insect and disease problems than most hawthorns, only occasionally requiring control measures. Because of this and its outstanding seasonal interest, *C. phaenopyrum* is one of the most versatile and valuable of all the hawthorns for landscape use. Transplanting difficulties have been reported but usually are not serious with proper handling (see *C. crus-galli,* Problems and Maintenance).

Cultivars. 'Fastigiata' is columnar to narrowly pyramidal in form, with smaller flowers and fruits than the species type. 'Vaughn,' a recent selection, is believed to be a hybrid (*C. phaenopyrum* × *C. crus-galli*). It is outstanding for autumn and winter fruiting interest and unusually fast growing but exceptionally thorny and highly susceptible to cedar apple rust.

Seasonal Interest. *Flowers:* Small, white, in clusters in late spring or early summer. *Foliage:* Dark green, lustrous, 2.5−8 cm/1−3 in. long, turning orange-red in autumn in some locations in some years. *Fruits:* Shiny, bright red, only 0.6 cm/0.25 in. across but large numbers are borne in showy clusters in autumn and part or all of winter. *Twigs and branches:* Horizontally layered branching, but less striking than some other hawthorns.

Crataegus viridis 7

Green hawthorn
Deciduous tree
Rosaceae (Rose Family)

Native Range. Southeastern and south-central United States.

Useful Range. USDA Zones 5a–9a and perhaps colder zones as well.

Function. Specimen, patio tree, screen, hedge.

Size and Habit

Seasonal Interest. *Flowers:* Small, white, in loose clusters in late spring. *Foliage:* Bright green, lustrous, with little autumn color change. *Fruits:* Bright orange-red but not lustrous, 0.6–0.8 cm/0.25–0.3 in. across, in clusters persisting through part or all of winter. *Trunk and branches:* Silvery gray, adding winter interest, along with the persistent fruits. Bark on older trunks flakes off, exposing the orange-brown inner bark in interesting patterns.

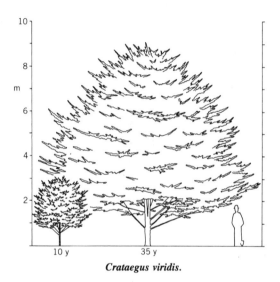

Crataegus viridis.

Adaptability. This species is unusual among hawthorns for its ability to grow well in both wet and dry sites.

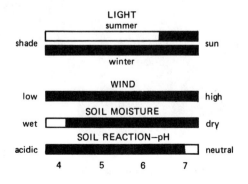

Crataegus viridis 'Winter King'.

Problems and Maintenance. This species is less susceptible to insect and disease problems than most hawthorns, seldom requiring maintenance.

Cultivars. 'Winter King,' a selection for outstanding fruit size and retention, was introduced in 1955 by Simpson Orchard Co., Vincennes, Indiana. It has grown rapidly in popularity, rivalling C. *phaenopyrum* in the Midwest.

Related Species

Crataegus nitida 6 (glossy hawthorn). This midwestern native has flower, foliage, and fruiting interest similar to that of C. *phaenopyrum*.

Cryptomeria japonica 8

Cryptomeria, Japanese cedar
Evergreen tree
Taxodiaceae (Taxodium Family)

Native Range. Japan.

Useful Range. USDA Zones 6b–9a+.

Function. Specimen, screen.

Size and Habit

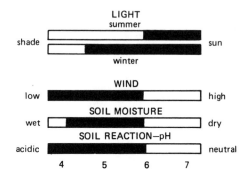

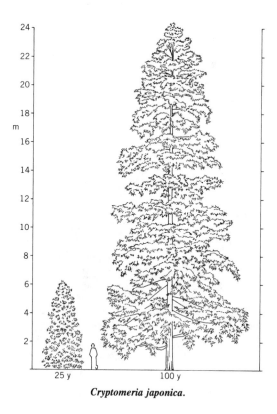

Cryptomeria japonica.

Seasonal Interest. *Foliage:* Short, glossy needles, attached spirally to long, whiplike twigs in plumy clusters, give an elegant and distinctive texture to the plant throughout the year. Foliage bronzes in winter. *Trunk:* Rich reddish-brown bark shreds in long strips like that of *Chamaecyparis* species and *Sequoiadendron.*

Cryptomeria japonica.

Adaptability. This tree performs best with light shade, at least in winter, in northern inland areas. In coastal areas, where this tree is at its best, exposure to full sun gives best results.

Problems and Maintenance. This tree is relatively trouble-free in good sites. Dead foliage sometimes clings rather than falling and must be removed manually to bring out the plant's best appearance. Relatively windy coastal sites in mild climates promote sweeping away of dried foliage by wind and rain.

Cultivars. More than a dozen variants have been named, but few are widely available.

'Lobbii' is usually thought to be more compact and more elegantly sculptured than the species type, but observers of mature specimens see little difference between the two. The supposed distinctness of 'Lobbii' may be really just the contrast between the foliage of mature specimens and that of juvenile seedlings. 'Lobbii' is commercially grafted on seedlings and as such may be simply a means of obtaining the mature plant character in a shorter time.

'Nana' is a dwarf selection, moundlike and seldom over 0.5—1 m/1.6—3.3 ft in height, useful only in rock gardens and other small-scale situations.

Related Species

Taiwania cryptomerioides 8 (taiwania). This large, evergreen tree from the mountains of Taiwan is closely related to *Cryptomeria*. It has not been tried in much of our area but has been growing successfully for years in at least one site in Zone 9a. If it were available, this tree could be used more widely as an evergreen screen in the mildest parts of our area.

Cunninghamia lanceolata 8

Common China fir
Evergreen tree
Taxodiaceae (Taxodium Family)

Native Range. China.

Useful Range. USDA Zones 7a−9a+.

Function. Specimen, screen.

Size and Habit

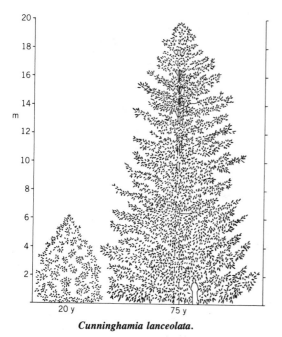

Cunninghamia lanceolata.

Adaptability. Best in full sun except at northern edges of the useful range, where light shade, especially in winter, reduces winter desiccation.

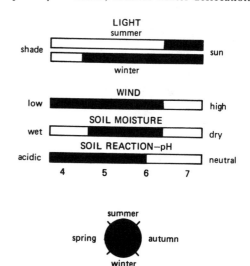

Seasonal Interest. *Foliage:* Glossy, acicular needles are prickly to the touch and give the plant a distinctive texture. The foliage turns bronze in winter. *Trunk and branches:* The bark is fibrous and rich red-brown, similar to that of *Chamaecyparis* and *Sequoiadendron*. When cut back or killed by cold, lower parts of branches regenerate many shoots that eventually replace those lost. Even trees killed nearly to the ground will regenerate sprouts from the trunk and roots.

Cunninghamia lanceolata.

Problems and Maintenance. This tree is relatively trouble-free except for winter desiccation of
foliage or killback of branches in northern areas
and occasional mite infestation.

Cultivars. 'Glauca' has more-or-less blue-green
foliage.

Related Species

Araucaria araucana 8 (monkey-puzzle tree, Chilean pine). This large, evergreen tree has sharply pointed needles on closely spaced, conspicuously whorled, ropelike branches and is useful in
Zones 8a–9a+. Other *Araucaria* species, A.
bidwillii 8 (bunya-bunya) and A. *heterophylla* 8
(synonym: A. *excelsa*; Norfolk Island pine), are
considered subtropical, although A. *bidwillii* has
survived limited trial in Zone 9a.

Araucaria araucana.

Araucaria araucana.

×*Cupressocyparis leylandii* 8

Cupressocyparis, Leyland cypress
Evergreen tree
Cupressaceae (Cypress Family)

Hybrid origin. *Chamaecyparis nootkatensis* ×
Cupressus macrocarpa.

Useful Range. USDA Zones 7a−9a+.

Function. Screen, hedge, specimen.

Size and Habit

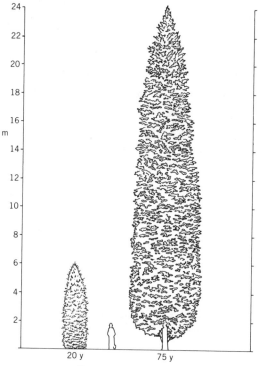

×*Cupressocyparis leylandii.*

Adaptability

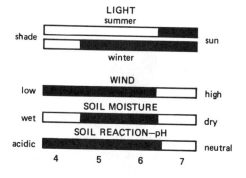

Seasonal Interest. *Foliage:* Dark green or
blue-green, scalelike, resembling that of
Chamaecyparis nootkatensis.

Problems and Maintenance. This tree has been
relatively trouble-free to date but occasionally
may be infested with mites. This species was not
widely used in North America during the first 70
years after its discovery in 1888, but it is rapidly
becoming a popular choice for screening.
Further growth in popularity may uncover other
problems.

Cultivars. In Great Britain, several color and
form variants have been selected, but such cultivars are seldom available in North America at
present. Once well known, their popularity could
grow rapidly. A few of the most distinctive
selections are 'Leighton Green,' which is narrowly columnar, 'Naylor's Blue,' which has
blue-green foliage, and 'Silver Dust,' which is a
white variegated mutant of 'Leighton Green' that
was selected at the U.S. National Arboretum in
1960.

Related Species

Cupressus arizonica 7 (Arizona cypress). This
more-or-less columnar tree has blue-green,
scalelike foliage and reddish brown, peeling bark.
It does best in full sun and very well-drained,
even dry, soil and probably is not widely useful in
the eastern United States but should be hardy in
Zones 7b−9a.

Cupressus bakeri 7 (Modoc cypress). Large,
dense shrub or small tree with blue-green,
scalelike foliage and reddish brown, peeling bark.
This is the hardiest *Cupressus* species (Zones
6b−9a), yet not widely used.

Cupressus macrocarpa 8 (Monterey cypress).
This large, long-lived tree is native to California
and valued for seaside planting there. In spite of
its involvement in ×*Cupressocyparis leylandii,*
C. macrocarpa itself seems poorly adapted to the
eastern United States, except possibly in seashore

sites, where it should be planted only experimentally in Zones 8a–9a+.

Cupressus sempervirens 7 (Italian cypress). This rather tall tree with dark-green scalelike foliage is best known in the form of the selection 'Stricta' (columnar Italian cypress), familiar in photographs of Mediterranean gardens as an extremely narrow specimen, often six to ten times as tall as it is broad. It grows well in southern coastal gardens in Zones 9a+, but it usually is short-lived because the moist climate encourages foliage diseases that can become serious.

Cupressus arizonica.

Cycas revoluta 3–4

Sago palm, Japanese fern palm
Evergreen shrub
Cycadaceae (Cycad Family)

Native Range. Southern Japan.

Useful Range. USDA Zones 8b–9a+.

Function. Specimen, massing, foundation.

Size and Habit

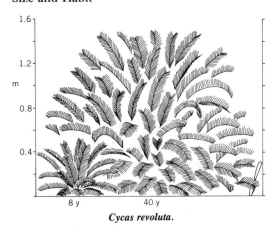

Cycas revoluta.

Adaptability. Within its useful range, this plant is broadly tolerant of different soil conditions.

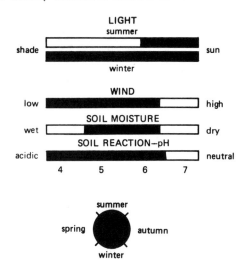

Seasonal Interest. *Flowers and seeds:* Cycads are dioecious. The male inflorescence or strobilus (bearing spore cases) is conelike, erect in the center of the plant, and up to 0.5 m/1.6 ft long.

The corresponding structures on female plants are flat and spreading, eventually bearing large numbers of orange-red seeds, 4 cm/1.6 in. across. *Foliage:* The rich, dark green, compound leaves, 0.5–1 m/1.6–3.3 ft long on young plants to 2 m/6.6 ft on old plants, are similar to those of ferns or palms, arising fountainlike out of the center of the plant, each new set of leaves unfolding in spring.

Problems and Maintenance. This plant is practically trouble-free and requires no maintenance other than cleaning: removing dust from the leaves and any debris from the center of the plant. Foliage and seeds are reported to be poisonous to animals.

Related Species

Zamia floridana 3 (coontie, Seminole bread). This lower growing relative of *Cycas revoluta* belongs to another family of cycads, the Zamiaceae (Zamia Family). Native to Florida, it is less cold-hardy than *Cycas revoluta* but useful in Zones 9a+. In general appearance it is similar to *Cycas* but slightly less regular, and it has smaller and less interesting male strobili and less colorful seeds.

Cydonia sinensis 6

Chinese quince
Deciduous shrub or small tree
Rosaceae (Rose Family)

Native Range. China.

Useful Range. USDA Zones 6b–9a.

Function. Specimen or patio tree. Grown primarily for bark interest.

Size and Habit

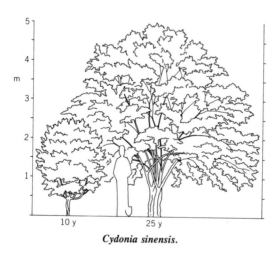

Cydonia sinensis.

Adaptability. This plant is widely adapted to soil and moisture variations but grows best in full sun or light shade.

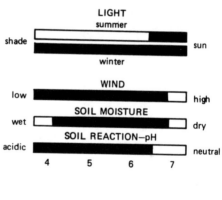

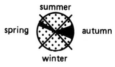

Seasonal Interest. *Flowers:* Pale pink in late spring, partly obscured by the leaves and not showy. *Foliage:* Gray-green, rather sparse, turning red in autumn. *Fruits:* Large, aromatic, yellow when ripe, useful for preserves. *Trunk and branches:* Multicolored flaking bark and sinewy form of trunk and main branches of old specimens add landscape interest year-round.

Cydonia sinensis.

Problems and Maintenance. This plant is subject to occasional mite infestation and fire blight in some areas, and it needs minimal pruning to maintain form.

Related Species

Cydonia oblonga 6 (quince).   This central Asian tree is the quince from which preserves are made commercially, seldom used solely for its landscape character. Its form and flowering are less impressive than those of several other small trees, and it has several insect and disease problems. It is useful in Zones 6a—9a.

Cyrtomium falcatum 3

Holly fern
Evergreen groundcover
Polypodiaceae (Polypody Family)

Native Range. Asia, Polynesia, South Africa.

Useful Range. USDA Zones 8b—9a+.

Function. Groundcover, specimen. Spreads slowly, so it is particularly useful in small areas for contrast with finer-textured groundcovers.

Size and Habit

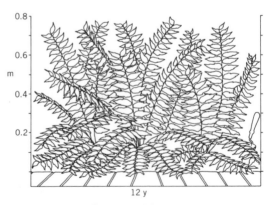

Cyrtomium falcatum.

Adaptability. Best with a reliable supply of moisture, but can tolerate occasional periods of drought.

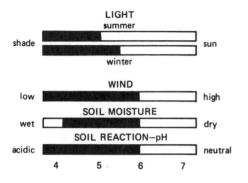

Seasonal Interest. *Foliage:* Evergreen, leathery, glossy, yellow-green to dark green, superficially resembling holly leaves.

Problems and Maintenance. Relatively trouble-free, requiring little or no maintenance once established.

Cultivars. A few named foliage variants are available commercially, including the following. 'Butterfieldii' and 'Rochfordianum' have deeply incised leaf margins. 'Rochfordianum' is the most common cultivar in landscape use. 'Compactum' is lower in stature, compact in growth.

Cytisus ×kewensis 2

Kew broom
Deciduous shrub
Leguminosae (Pea Family)

Hybrid origin. *Cytisus ardoini × C. multiflorus.*

Useful Range. USDA Zones 6b−9a+.

Function. Specimen, groundcover, rock garden.

Size and Habit

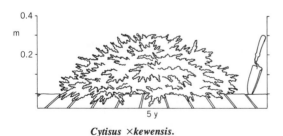

Cytisus ×kewensis.

Adaptability. Full sun and well-drained soil are essential to the success of *Cytisus* species. They are tolerant of wind except during winter cold extremes in the northern parts of their useful ranges, and their ability to use atmospheric nitrogen enables them to tolerate infertile soils.

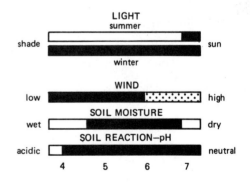

Seasonal Interest. *Flowers:* Pale yellow, pealike, borne on ascending tips of creeping stems before the small leaves emerge in midspring. *Foliage:*

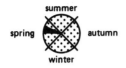

Very small leaves are inconspicuous. *Twigs and branches:* Green twigs are fairly conspicuous in winter.

Problems and Maintenance. *Cytisus* species are relatively free of insect and disease problems but difficult to transplant except as container-grown plants. They may need to be pruned occasionally to remove deadwood in the North or to control the size of the plant in the South. Light pruning to remove old flowering branches will stimulate new stem growth and enhance flowering in the following year.

Related Species

Cytisus albus 2 (Portuguese broom). A low-growing broom with paler yellow flowers than those of *C. ×kewensis*, not to be confused with the taller white Spanish broom (*C. multiflorus*), which has been misnamed *C. albus.* Useful in Zones 6a−9a+.

Cytisus ardoini 2 (Ardoin broom). A low-growing Mediterranean broom with bright yellow flowers and very tiny leaves. Useful in Zones 6b−9a+.

Cytisus ×beanii 2 (Bean's broom). Relatively low, to 0.5 m/1.6 ft in height, with deep yellow flowers, resulting from the cross *C. ardoini* × *C. purgans.* Useful in Zones 6a−9a+.

Cytisus decumbens 2 (prostrate broom). A Mediterranean native, one of the finest low groundcovers (0.2 m/0.7 ft) among the brooms, with brilliant yellow flowers in late spring. Useful in Zones 6a−9a+.

Cytisus procumbens 3 (ground broom). Similar to *C. decumbens* except taller (to 0.8 m/2.6 ft) and useful in Zones 6a−9a+.

Cytisus purpureus 3 (purple broom). More distinctive than most of the above species, with purple flowers at the same time as *C. ×kewensis.* In fact, the two make an excellent companion planting, since their flower colors are complementary and harmonious. Useful in Zones 6a−9a+.

Cytisus ×praecox 4

Warminster broom
Deciduous shrub
Leguminosae (Pea Family)

Hybrid origin. *Cytisus multiflorus* × *C. purgans.*

Useful Range. USDA Zones 6a−9a+.

Function. Specimen, rock garden.

Size and Habit

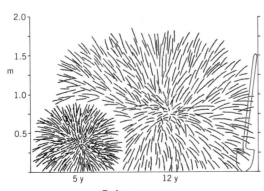

Cytisus ×praecox.

Adaptability. See *C. ×kewensis,* Adaptibility.

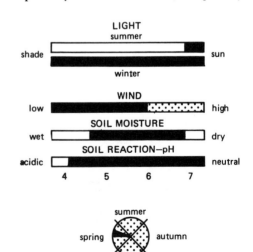

Seasonal Interest. *Flowers:* Pale yellow, pealike, with an unpleasant odor, borne on twigs before the small leaves emerge in midspring. *Foliage:* Very small leaves are inconspicuous. *Twigs and*

branches: Green twigs are conspicuous in winter and evident in all seasons because of the sparse foliage.

Cytisus ×praecox.

Problems and Maintenance. See *C. ×kewensis,* Problems and Maintenance.

Cultivars. Several cultivars have been selected in Europe, but few of these are available at any given time in North America. Some of the more popular ones are listed here. 'Albus' is lower growing (to 1 m/3.3 ft in height) with white flowers. 'Allgold' is similar in growth to the typical form but with golden-yellow flowers. 'Goldspear' and 'Luteus' are slower growing (to 1 m/3.3 ft in height) with golden-yellow flowers. 'Zeelandia' is at least as vigorous as the species, with pale yellow and red flowers, giving an overall effect of pink.

Related Species

Cytisus multiflorus 4 (white Spanish broom). This tall-growing species, to 2m/6.6 ft or occasionally taller, makes a striking display of white flowers at about the same time as its hybrid, *C. ×praecox* or slightly later, and is slightly less cold-hardy, useful in Zones 6b−9a+.

Cytisus nigricans 3 (spike broom). Hardier than most brooms, useful in Zones 5a−9a, and later-flowering, with lemon-yellow flowers in terminal spikes in early summer.

Cytisus purgans 3 (Provence broom). Similar in effect to *C. nigricans,* with yellow flowers borne toward the ends of stiffly upright branches, but flowers in late spring and is less hardy, useful in Zones 6a−9a+.

Cytisus scoparius 4

Scotch Broom
Deciduous shrub
Leguminosae (Pea Family)

Native Range. Central and southern Europe.

Useful Range. USDA Zones 6b−9a+, marginally hardy in Zones 6a, the hybrids hardy northward only to Zone 7a or 7b.

Function. Specimen, border, large-scale rock garden. Too tall to be useful as a groundcover.

Size and Habit

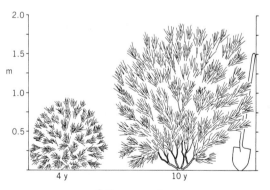

Cytisus scoparius.

Adaptability. See *C.* ×*kewensis*, Adaptability.

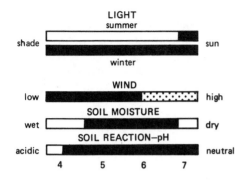

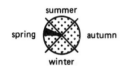

Seasonal Interest. *Flowers:* Yellow (many other colors in hybrids—see Cultivars), pealike, borne on upright stems before leaves emerge. *Foliage:* Small, relatively inconspicuous leaves. *Twigs and branches:* Green twigs are fairly conspicuous in winter and noticeable at other seasons.

Problems and Maintenance. This shrub is relatively free of insect and disease problems but difficult to transplant except as container-grown plants. It may need pruning to remove deadwood following extreme winters in the North or for renewal in the South.

Cultivars. More than 50 cultivars, mostly hybrids with unknown male parents are in commerce, but very few of these are available in eastern North America. A few of the most common, and those most likely to be available at any given time, are listed here.

'Andreanus' is an upright selection with flowers yellow except for wing petals marked with deep red, the first plant of the species to be found with other than yellow flowers.

'Burkwoodii' is also upright in form with rich red-brown flowers.

'Golden Sunlight' is spreading in habit with bright golden-yellow flowers.

'Moonlight' is upright in habit with pale yellow flowers, similar in effect to *C.* ×*praecox*.

'Pink Beauty' is one of the best pink-flowered selections.

'Prostratus' is prostrate in habit, sometimes grafted on an upright seedling, or "standard," resulting in an umbrella or weeping form.

'Red Wings' and 'San Francisco' have deep velvety red flowers. 'Stanford' has multicolored flowers with the general effect of orange from a distance.

Related Species

Cytisus battandieri 6 (Morocco broom). This tall shrub, to 4 m/13 ft, is unusual among the brooms for its large, silvery, hairy leaves, to 9 cm/3.5 in. long, and golden-yellow flowers in dense, upright spikes, to 13 cm/5 in. long. Useful only in Zone 9a+.

Daphne ×*burkwoodii* 3−4

Burkwood daphne
Semievergreen shrub
Thymelaeaceae (Mezereum Family)

Hybrid origin. *D. caucasica* × *D. cneorum*.

Useful Range. USDA Zones 4b−7b, perhaps colder zones with reliable winter snow cover and areas with mild summers and cool soils in Zone 8.

Function. Specimen, foundation, border, rock garden.

Size and Habit

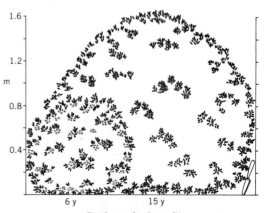

Daphne ×*burkwoodii*.

Adaptability. This plant is more easily grown than most *Daphne* species, but it must have perfect soil drainage and a relatively cool root zone, and it seems to perform best in sandy soils of low fertility but with a reasonably reliable moisture supply. It has been written that limestone soil is necessary for *Daphne* species, but this probably is not true.

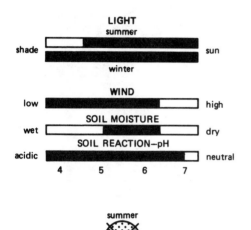

Seasonal Interest. *Flowers:* Small, white, but pink in bud, fragrant, mid to late spring. *Foliage:* Small, rounded, dull blue-green leaves offer neat texture in summer through autumn, and part of winter in the South, with little color change. *Fruits:* Small red berries in early summer are poisonous to animals, including humans.

Problems and Maintenance. This shrub is difficult to transplant except as container-grown plants. *Daphne* species have been known to die suddenly and mysteriously, but at least some such cases can be explained by temporary raising of water tables during unusually wet seasons. Both foliage and fruits of *Daphne* species are strongly poisonous, so these plants should not be used where they are accessible to animals and small children.

Cultivars. 'Carol Mackie' has uniformly creamy, white-margined leaves, contrasting with the normal dark green in a strikingly crisp texture pattern. 'Somerset' is probably no better than some plants now carried in commerce simply as

D. ×burkwoodii, but this clone probably is more floriferous and compact than average for the species.

Daphne ×burkwoodii 'Carol Mackie.'

Related Species

Daphne cneorum 2 (rose daphne).   This low, moundlike plant from Europe has neat, fine-textured, more or less evergreen foliage and rosy pink, delightfully fragrant flowers. It has been highly popular for rock garden or groundcover use, and probably would have even greater use if it were not for its tendency to die suddenly without any explanation. Plantings have performed well for many years on light, sandy soils having perfect drainage, lending support to the idea that perfect soil aeration may be the key to longevity of *Daphne* species. It is hardy in Zones 4b−7b and in colder zones where winter snow cover is reliable. The selection 'Ruby Glow' has deeper pink flowers.

Daphne giraldii 3

Giraldi daphne
Deciduous shrub
Thymelaeaceae (Mezereum Family)

Native Range. Northwestern China.

Useful Range. USDA Zones 2b—7a, perhaps somewhat farther south as well.

Function. Specimen, border, rock garden.

Size and Habit

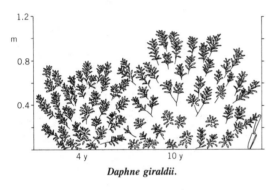

Daphne giraldii.

Adaptability. As with other *Daphne* species, cool, perfectly drained soil of low fertility seems to give the best performance.

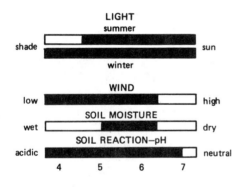

Seasonal Interest. *Flowers:* Small, yellow, lightly fragrant, in clusters in late spring. *Foliage:* Simi-

lar in texture to that of *D. mezereum*, whitish underneath but not conspicuously so. *Fruits:* Small, bright scarlet in midsummer, poisonous (see *Daphne ×burkwoodii*).

Daphne giraldii.

Problems and Maintenance. This shrub seems relatively trouble-free but is not used widely enough to predict potential problems with certainty. Its cold-hardiness and yellow flowers distinguish it from other *Daphne* species. Plant parts are poisonous (see *Daphne ×burkwoodii*).

Related Species

Daphne alpina 2 (alpine daphne).   This dwarf plant from the European Alps is seldom used but is a good rock garden specimen where and when available. It appears as a smaller version of *D. altaica* and is useful in Zones 5a—7a and probably colder zones as well with snow cover.

Daphne altaica 4 (Altai daphne).   This little-used deciduous daphne from the Altai mountains of central Asia is similar in general effect to *D. giraldii* except for its fragrant, white flowers and yellowish red fruits. Its hardiness is not well tested, but it is useful at least in Zones 5a—7a and probably in at least parts of Zone 4 as well.

Daphne mezereum 3

February daphne
Deciduous shrub
Thymelaeaceae (Mezereum Family)

Native Range. Europe and western Asia, naturalized in the northeastern United States.

Useful Range. USDA Zones 3b–7b.

Function. Border, specimen, foundation.

Size and Habit

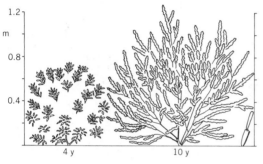

Daphne mezereum.

Adaptability. This shrub performs best in sandy soil, high in organic matter but low in fertility, with reliable moisture supply but perfect drainage. Contrary to a common belief, limestone soil is probably of no specific benefit.

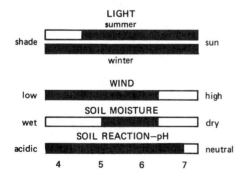

Seasonal Interest. *Flowers:* Small, fragrant, rosy purple (or creamy white), conspicuous because they appear before leaves begin to expand, in early spring. *Foliage:* Rather small (3–8 cm/1–3 in.), elongated leaves, rounded on the ends, dull green and inconspicuous. *Fruits:* Bright scarlet

(yellow in the white flowering cultivar), to 0.8 cm/0.3 in., borne close to the stems in late summer, and poisonous (see *Daphne ×burkwoodii*).

Problems and Maintenance. This shrub is relatively trouble-free but difficult to transplant except as container-grown plants. It is usually more reliable than some *Daphne* species once it is established in a suitable site. In fact, it has become naturalized in the northeastern United States. Plant parts are poisonous (see *Daphne ×burkwoodii*).

Cultivars. 'Alba' is identical with the species type except that it has creamy white flowers and yellow fruits.

Related Species

Daphne genkwa 3 (lilac daphne).   This low shrub has fragrant, lilac-colored flowers in large clusters that superficially resemble those of lilac and appear before the new leaves in early spring. It is not widely used or available, but it is a good selection for variety and early spring color. Useful in Zones 6b–9a.

Daphne odora 4

Winter daphne
Evergreen shrub
Thymelaeaceae (Mezereum Family)

Native Range. China.

Useful Range. USDA Zones 7a–8b.

Function. Border, specimen, foundation.

Size and Habit

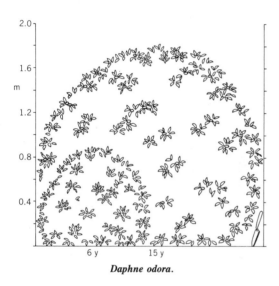

Daphne odora.

Adaptability. Like other *Daphne* species, this shrub is best grown in perfectly drained soil of low fertility. Unlike other *Daphne* species, it grows best with at least partial shade and in soil that is never excessively dry.

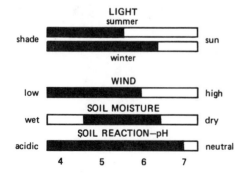

Seasonal Interest. *Flowers:* Small, highly fragrant, rosy purple outside, near white inside, from early through middle spring. *Foliage:* Evergreen,

leathery, dark green, 5–8 cm/2–3 in. long, and narrow, making a compact, fine-textured mass year-round.

Daphne odora.

Problems and Maintenance. This shrub reputedly is difficult to transplant and unreliable in establishment, but specialists do not fully agree on this. It apparently performs reasonably well in the South but is not long-lived. Plant parts are poisonous (see *Daphne* ×*burkwoodii*).

Cultivars. 'Alba' has pure white flowers. 'Aureomarginata' and 'Marginata,' probably identical, have a narrow leaf margin of pale yellow.

Related Species

Daphne collina 3. This compact, rounded shrub from the Mediterranean region is smaller than *D. odora*, with lustrous evergreen foliage and rosy purple flowers in late spring. Useful in the rock garden in Zones 7b–9a.

Daphne ×*mantensiana* 3 (Manten's daphne). This low evergreen hybrid (*D.* ×*burkwoodii* × *D. retusa*) is represented commercially by the selection 'Manten,' with fragrant and showy orchid-purple flowers, opening intermittently from late spring to early autumn. Its useful range is not well established but includes at least Zones 7a–8b.

Daphne retusa 3 and *Daphne tangutica* 4. These related species from western China are both evergreen with fragrant flowers, rosy purple outside, near white inside, in late and early spring, respectively. They have not been tried widely enough for their useful ranges to be known and probably are not commercially available.

Davidia involucrata 6−7

Dove tree
Deciduous tree
Nyssaceae (Tupelo Family)

Native Range. Western China.

Useful Range. USDA Zones 6b−8b, var. *vilmoriniana* also in Zone 6a.

Function. Specimen, border, patio tree (with pruning for form). Usually used more for its unique flowering interest than for specific function.

Size and Habit

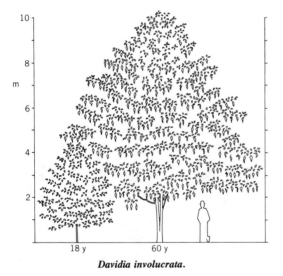

Davidia involucrata.

Seasonal Interest. *Flowers:* Small, yellow, in crowded globose heads, surrounded at the base by two large, white, papery, pointed bracts, the lower 15 cm/6 in. long, the upper one much smaller, showy in late spring. Usually does not flower annually, but the creamy white bracts give it a truly unique appearance when it does. *Foliage:* Coarsely toothed, dull green, giving textural contrast.

Problems and Maintenance. This tree, although introduced in 1904 with much publicity, still is not widely enough used to suggest that all its potential problems are known. To date it has proved trouble-free except for the poorly understood unreliability of flowering, perhaps variable among different plants.

Varieties. Var. *vilmoriniana* differs little from the species type except in having slightly duller foliage and slightly greater cold-hardiness, at least to Zone 6a.

Adaptability

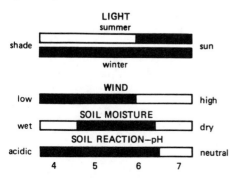

Deutzia gracilis 3

Slender deutzia
Deciduous shrub
Saxifragaceae (Saxifrage Family)

Native Range. Japan.

Useful Range. USDA Zones 5b–8b.

Function. Border, low informal hedge.

Size and Habit

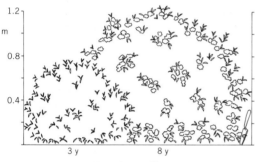

Deutzia gracilis.

Adaptability

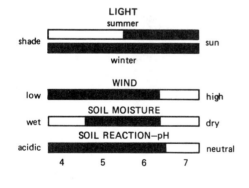

Seasonal Interest. *Flowers:* White, in upright clusters, 5–8 cm/2–3 in. long, in late spring. *Foliage:* Dull green, somewhat finer-textured, falling in autumn without much color change.

Problems and Maintenance. This shrub is relatively free of insect and disease problems but requires fairly regular pruning (every 2–3 years) to remove old stems and maintain plant form and vigor.

Cultivars. 'Aurea' has yellow foliage but is not one of the better yellow-leaved shrubs.

Related Species and Hybrids

Deutzia ×candelabrum 4 (candle deutzia). This hybrid *(D. gracilis × D. scabra)* has white flowers, slightly later than those of *D. gracilis*, in upright, candlelike clusters, to 10 cm/4 in. long, and is useful in Zones 6a–8b.

Deutzia ×lemoinei 4 (Lemoine deutzia). This hybrid *(D. parviflora × D. gracilis)* has showy flowers in clusters similar to but slightly later than those of *D. gracilis* in late spring and is more cold-hardy than *D. gracilis* (Zones 5a–8b). The selection 'Compacta' differs in its compact growth to a maximum height of about 1.5 m/5 ft and slightly greater cold hardiness (to Zone 4b).

Deutzia ×lemoinei.

Deutzia parviflora 4 (Mongolian deutzia). This plant differs from *D. ×lemoinei* primarily in its flattened clusters of white flowers and slightly greater cold hardiness (Zones 4b–8a).

Deutzia scabra 5

Fuzzy deutzia
Deciduous shrub
Saxifragaceae (Saxifrage Family)

Native Range. China, Japan.

Useful Range. USDA Zones 6a–8b.

Function. Specimen, border, screen (with careful pruning in Zones 6b and southward).

Size and Habit

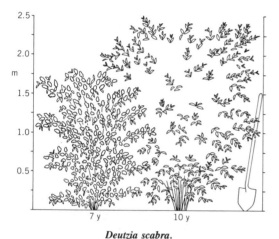

Deutzia scabra.

Adaptability

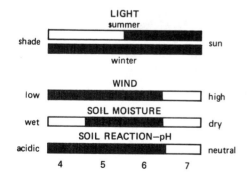

Seasonal Interest. *Flowers:* White or pink outside, in upright clusters, 6–12 cm/2.5–5 in. long, in late spring and early summer. *Foliage:*

Dull green, neutral in summer with rough pubescence and little or no autumnal color change.

Problems and Maintenance. This shrub is relatively free of insect and disease problems but requires annual pruning in the North to maintain good form and condition, since some winter twig and branch dieback occurs regularly in Zone 6 and sometimes in Zone 7. Deutzias generally do not flower on current season's growth but initiate flower buds that become dormant before opening and must survive the winter in a dormant condition to flower the following spring or summer.

Cultivars. 'Candidissima' is late flowering (very early summer) with pure white, double flowers in large upright clusters. Because of the double-flowered condition, usually associated with sterility, petal drop is not triggered by pollination and flowers remain showy for a relatively long time. But this is still a short time in the full annual cycle, and the plant remains uninteresting for most of the year.

'Pride of Rochester' is the best known cultivar of *D. scabra* with double white flowers, purple on the outside. 'Flore Pleno' and 'Plena' are similar to 'Pride of Rochester' and to each other (probably identical).

Related Species and Hybrids

Deutzia discolor 4.   This Chinese species is seldom if ever available, but impressive in bloom with its white flowers and useful in Zones 6b–8b.

Deutzia ×elegantissima 5.   This tall hybrid of *D. purpurascens* × *D. scabra* has rosy pink flowers and is useful in Zones 6b–8a but is seldom available.

Deutzia grandiflora 4 (early deutzia).   This shrub from northern China has very large clusters of white flowers in middle to late spring, at least a month earlier than those of *D. scabra* and two weeks earlier than those of *D. gracilis*. It is useful in Zones 6a–8b.

Deutzia ×hybrida 4 (hybrid deutzia).   This hybrid of *D. longifolia* × *D. discolor* has large pink flowers in late spring. The cultivars 'Contraste' and 'Mont Rose' are sometimes available and useful in Zones 6b–8b.

Deutzia longifolia 4 (longleaf deutzia). This shrub from western China has purple flowers and long, coarse leaves, but probably is not available, even though it is useful in Zones 6b–8b.

Deutzia ×*magnifica* 4 (showy deutzia). This hybrid of *D. scabra* × *D. vilmoriniae* is an outstandingly showy plant with double flowers in clusters to 6 cm/2.5 in. across in very late spring or early summer. Flower clusters are more compact in the selection 'Erecta.' It is useful in Zones 6b–8b.

Deutzia purpurascens 4 (purple deutzia). This Chinese species with showy purple flowers in late spring is seldom available but best known through its parentage of hybrid cultivars. Useful, when available, in Zones 6b–8b.

Deutzia ×*rosea* 4 (rose deutzia). This hybrid of *D. gracilis* × *D. purpurascens* has pink and white flowers at about the same time as its parents in late spring and is useful in Zones 6a–8b. The cultivar 'Eximia' is outstanding with large pink flowers.

Deutzia vilmoriniae 4 (Vilmorin deutzia). This Chinese species, known primarily as a parent of hybrid cultivars, has showy white flowers in very late spring or early summer and is useful in Zones 6b–8b.

Diervilla sessilifolia 4

Southern bush honeysuckle
Deciduous shrub
Caprifoliaceae (Honeysuckle Family)

Native Range. Southeastern United States.

Useful Range. USDA Zones 4b–8a.

Function. Large-scale groundcover, bank cover. Spreads by underground stems to make a dense mass.

Size and Habit

Diervilla sessilifolia.

Adaptability. Unusually widely adapted to soils, light, and moisture conditions.

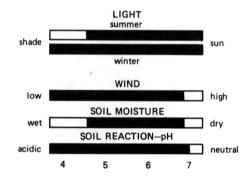

Seasonal Interest. *Flowers:* Yellow, similar to those of the honeysuckles, in early summer; interesting but not showy. *Foliage:* Smooth, dark green, turning reddish before falling in autumn.

Problems and Maintenance. This shrub is unusually free of insects and diseases but requires pruning every three years or so to maintain form and density. This can be accomplished most easily by drastic renewal pruning: cutting off tops a short distance above ground level in spring, allowing ample time for regrowth and acclimation before the onset of winter.

Related Species

Diervilla lonicera 3 (synonym: *D. trifida*; northern bush honeysuckle).   This shrub is very similar to *D. sessilifolia* except that it is lower in stature with smaller leaves and inflorescences, and considerably more cold-hardy. It is useful in Zones 2b−7b.

Diervilla rivularis 4.   This shrub is very similar to *D. sessilifolia* and completely interchangeable in landscape function and appearance. Seldom available for planting, it grows wild in the cooler parts of the southeastern United States.

Diospyros virginiana 7

Common persimmon
Deciduous tree
Ebenaceae (Ebony Family)

Native Range. Southeastern and south-central United States.

Useful Range. USDA Zones 5b−9a+.

Function. Shade tree, naturalizing, edible fruit. Well adapted to city use, but not as a street tree because of the fruit litter.

Size and Habit

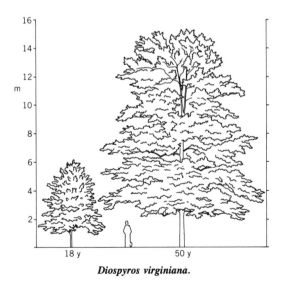

Diospyros virginiana.

Adaptability

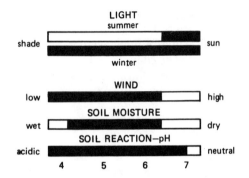

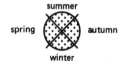

Seasonal Interest. *Flowers:* Small, whitish, inconspicuous, mostly dioecious, but sometimes with a few perfect flowers on male or female trees. *Foliage:* Dark green, making a dense

Diospyros virginiana.

canopy, turning dull yellow or orange in autumn. *Fruits:* Relatively large, to 3.5 cm/1.4 in., borne close to branches, dull green at first, then dull yellow-orange and edible when fully ripe, falling to the ground and causing a litter problem. *Trunk:* Bark is regularly fissured, exposing cracks of red-orange inner bark that is interesting at close range in all seasons.

Problems and Maintenance. This tree is unusually trouble-free except for a leaf-spot disease that limits its use in the South. Maintenance consists largely of cleaning up fallen fruits in autumn. Transplanting is difficult; when possible, specify young, container-grown trees.

Cultivars. Several cultivars have been selected for outstanding fruits. For most landscape use, especially as a city tree, it would be more appropriate to select and name cultivars for being nonfruiting along with desirable foliage and form, and such cultivars may eventually be available commercially.

Related Species

Diospyros kaki 7 (Japanese persimmon). Like *D. virginiana*, this is a medium-height tree, to 10−15 m/33−49 ft, that functions as a good shade tree as well as having edible fruit. The fruits are considerably larger than those of *D. virginiana*, to 8 cm/3 in. across, and are borne on most plants, since the dioecious tendency is weak in this species. Usually grown primarily for fruit, incidentally for landscape effect, and useful only in Zone 9a+.

Diospyros lotus 7 (date plum). This is an Asian counterpart of *D. virginiana* and very similar in landscape effect but perhaps slightly less cold-hardy. It is seldom used or available.

Bumelia lanuginosa 6 (woolly buckthorn, gum-elastic, chittimwood). This spiny shrub or small tree, native to the southeastern and south-central United States from Virginia to Missouri and southward to Florida and Texas, is in the Sapotaceae (Sapodilla Family), which is closely allied to the Ebenaceae. *Bumelia* has no outstanding seasonal interest, but its rounded leaves, 3−8 cm/1−3 in. long, dark green and lustrous above and woolly underneath, remain green very late into autumn. The feature that gives it landscape value is its freedom from problems and outstanding tolerance of heat and dryness, and it finds occasional use in Zones 6b−9a in the southwestern parts of our area.

Dirca palustris 4

Leatherwood
Deciduous shrub
Thymelaeaceae (Mezereum Family)

Native Range. Much of eastern North America.

Useful Range. USDA Zones 4a−8b.

Function. Specimen, border, naturalizing, massing.

Size and Habit

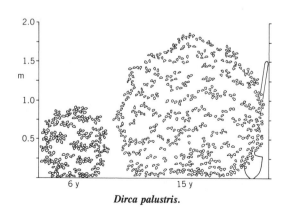

Dirca palustris.

Adaptability. Especially useful in wet soil in cold climates, but unusually wide in its adaptation to soil and climate.

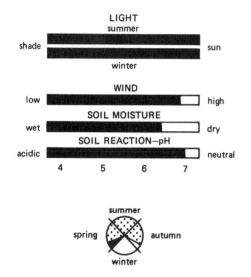

Edgeworthia papyrifera.

Seasonal Interest. *Flowers:* Small, pale yellow before foliage in early spring; not showy, but conspicuous at short range at that season. *Foliage:* Medium to light green, rounded. Inconspicuous but distinctive. *Fruits:* Small, pale green or reddish. *Twigs:* Exceptionally flexible and tough, giving rise to the common name.

Problems and Maintenance. This shrub is trouble-free once it is established.

Related Species

Edgeworthia papyrifera 4 (paperbush). This deciduous shrub from China is similar in growth habit to *Daphne* and *Dirca*, its relatives in the Mezereum Family, except for its more open growth and ternate branching. Its fragrant yellow flowers, covered with silky hairs in bud, are borne

in pendulous clusters in early spring before the new foliage emerges. The common name, paperbush, comes from the use of this plant in making fine quality paper in Japan. This is an interesting specimen for early spring flowers in parts of the Deep South (Zones 8b−9a+) where summer heat is moderate (high elevations or coastal areas).

Elaeagnus angustifolia 6

Russian olive, oleaster
Deciduous shrub or small tree
Elaeagnaceae (Oleaster Family)

Native Range. Southern Europe to central Asia.

Useful Range. USDA Zones 3a−7b.

Function. Hedge, screen, windbreak, specimen tree.

Size and Habit

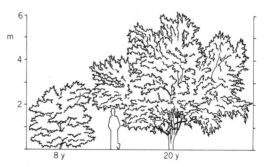

Elaeagnus angustifolia.

Adaptability. Well adapted to the cold, drought, and wind of the northern prairies of Canada and the United States, and frequently included in shelter-belt plantings there. Well adapted also to the seashore and other high-salt areas.

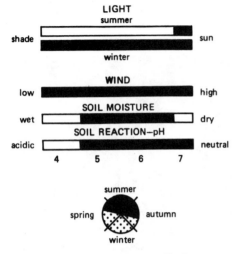

Seasonal Interest. *Flowers:* Small, fragrant, yellow, effective only at close range, in very late spring. *Foliage:* fine-textured and silvery gray-green as it first emerges in late spring, and it holds most of this color until late autumn. *Fruits:* Green to yellowish when ripe, covered with silvery scales. Interesting and conspicuous when borne in large numbers. *Trunk and branches:* Rich brown, shredding bark adds quiet year-round interest.

Problems and Maintenance. This shrub is fairly trouble-free except for a canker disease that occasionally kills a tree within a year after first symptoms appear. For this reason and the fact that it is prone to damage from ice storms, this plant is losing popularity in Zones 5−6. When planted in beds with plants other than turf, it will be necessary to remove root suckers occasionally.

Related Species

Elaeagnus commutata 5 (silverberry elaeagnus). This native of much of northern Canada and the Rocky Mountain region is an irregularly growing, strongly suckering shrub with the most intensely silvered foliage of all *Elaeagnus* species that can be grown in the North. It is useful for screening, with some pruning to promote fullness, or for a silvery gray accent in shrub borders in Zones 2a−6b, possibly even in Zone 1.

Elaeagnus pungens 5

Thorny elaeagnus
Evergreen shrub
Elaeagnaceae (Oleaster Family)

Native Range. Japan.

Useful Range. USDA Zones 7a−9a+.

Function. Hedge, screen, border.

Size and Habit

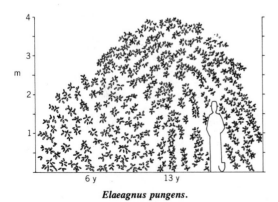

Elaeagnus pungens.

Adaptability. Unusually well adapted to soil and climatic extremes within the South, including seashore conditions.

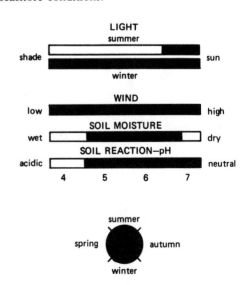

Seasonal Interest. *Flowers:* Small, fragrant, silvery white in midautumn. *Foliage:* Evergreen, dark green with a few silvery scales on the upper surface and covered with silvery and brown scales underneath, borne on spiny branches. *Fruits:* Brown, then red when fully ripe in spring, to 1.5 cm/0.6 in. with scattered silvery or brown scales.

Elaeagnus pungens.

Problems and Maintenance. This shrub is trouble-free, requiring little maintenance beyond pruning when treated as a hedge, a major reason for its great popularity in the South.

Cultivars. Several foliage and form variants have been selected. Some of the most common are listed here. 'Aurea' has golden-yellow leaf margins. 'Fruitlandii' has unusually handsome, dark green leaves and rapid, dense growth. 'Maculata' (= 'Aureo-maculata') has an irregular golden blotch in the center of each leaf. 'Variegata' has pale yellow leaf margins.

Related Species and Hybrids

Elaeagnus ×*ebbingei* 5.　This hybrid (*E. macrophylla* × *E. pungens*), originating in Holland, is similar in most respects to *E. pungens*, including its useful range, but it is not spiny and has slightly larger leaves.

Elaeagnus macrophylla 5.　This species from Japan and Korea is similar to *E. pungens* except that it has larger leaves and is not spiny, but it is seldom available.

Elaeagnus umbellata 5

Autumn elaeagnus, autumn olive
Deciduous shrub
Elaeagnaceae (Oleaster Family)

Native Range. China, Japan, Korea.

Useful Range. USDA Zones 5a−9a.

Function. Hedge, screen, border, naturalizing, wildlife cover.

Size and Habit

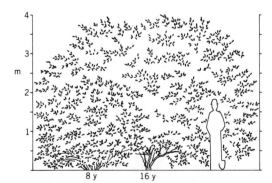

Elaeagnus umbellata.

Adaptability. Widely tolerant of soil and climatic conditions, including exposure to salt.

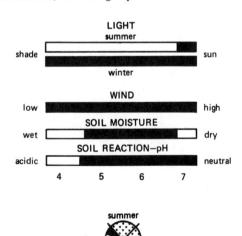

Seasonal Interest. *Flowers:* Small, fragrant, pale yellow with silvery scales in late spring. *Foliage:* Medium green, flecked with silvery scales, especially underneath. *Fruits:* Silvery brown, then red with flecks of silver when ripe in autumn, attractive to birds.

Problems and Maintenance. This shrub is trouble-free, requiring no maintenance other than pruning to develop fullness and to control size when necessary.

Cultivars. The so-called Cardinal Strain is a seedline developed by the U.S. Soil Conservation Service. It is recommended by that agency as superior to the species type for conservation use and is superior also for landscape interest and vigor.

Related Species

Elaeagnus multiflora 5 (cherry elaeagnus). This shrub from China and Japan functions as a smaller version of *E. umbellata*, reaching heights of 2−3 m/6.6−10 ft, with a relatively wide-spreading habit. It is otherwise similar to *E.*

Elaeagnus multiflora.

umbellata except in having larger red fruits, ripening in late summer. It is somewhat less cold-hardy than *E. umbellata*, but useful in Zones 5b−9a.

Elsholtzia stauntonii 3

Staunton elsholtzia
Deciduous subshrub
Labiatae (Mint Family)

Native Range. Northern China.

Useful Range. USDA Zones 5a−7a.

Function. Border (front).

Size and Habit

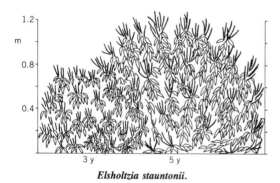

Elsholtzia stauntonii.

Seasonal Interest. *Flowers:* Lilac-purple, in terminal spikes in late summer and beginning of

autumn. *Foliage:* Aromatic when crushed but of little other interest.

Adaptability

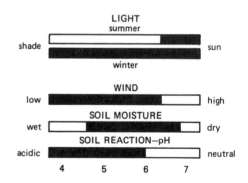

Elsholtzia stauntonii.

Problems and Maintenance. Elsholtzia is one of many subshrubs that have the ability, when winterkilled to the ground, to return quickly and flower heavily in late summer of the same year. When this happens, it is only necessary to re- move the dead stems in spring, but any live stems are best pruned away at the same time to main- tain good form. Otherwise, elsholtzia is relatively free of maintenance, since it is seldom troubled by insects or diseases.

Empetrum nigrum 2

Crowberry
Evergreen groundcover
Empetraceae (Crowberry Family)

Native Range. Arctic (Asia, Europe, North America) and coastal areas and high elevations in temperate North America, southward to New York and northern California.

Useful Range. USDA Zones 2–6b (in areas having moderate summers).

Function. Groundcover, rock garden.

Size and Habit

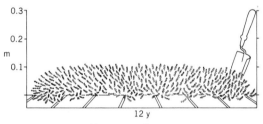

Empetrum nigrum.

Adaptability. This plant is best adapted to north- ern bogs and mountaintop sites where it grows wild, but it can be used equally well in rock gardens and other landscape situations if soil moisture is provided with excellent drainage.

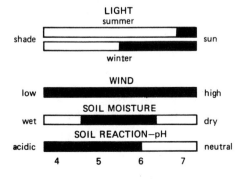

Seasonal Interest. *Flowers:* Very small, purple, inconspicuous, in midspring. *Foliage:* Evergreen, very fine-textured, needlelike, dark green, lus- trous, making a thick mass that is handsome at all seasons. *Fruits:* Round, black, as wide as the needlelike leaves are long (0.5 cm/0.2in.), not showy.

Problems and Maintenance. Given a proper site and adequate time for establishment, this plant is relatively maintenance-free. It does not compete well with weeds, so it should be heavily mulched, especially during establishment.

Related Species

Empetrum eamesii 2 (rockberry). This creeping plant from Newfoundland, Labrador and adja- cent Quebec is slightly finer textured than *E. nigrum* but similar enough to be interchangeable in landscape use. It is seldom available but useful in Zones 2–6b in areas with cool summers.

Ceratiola ericoides 4 (ceratiola, rosemary). This evergreen shrub native to the Coastal Plain of the southeastern United States has needlelike foliage similar to that of *Empetrum* and green or reddish fruits. It is useful in Zone 9a+ but is seldom available for planting.

Corema conradii 2 (poverty grass, broom crow- berry). This low shrub native to the northern Atlantic Coast is useful as a groundcover on sandy soil, and has evergreen, needlelike foliage with purple flowers, fairly colorful on male plants, in spring. It is useful in Zones 5b–7a, perhaps in more southern zones as well. It is seldom available for planting, but with care it can be preserved in its native habitat.

Enkianthus campanulatus 5−6

Redvein enkianthus
Deciduous shrub
Ericaceae (Heath Family)

Native Range. Japan.

Useful Range. USDA Zones 5b−8a.

Function. Specimen, border. Adds variety to mixed ericaceous plantings.

Size and Habit

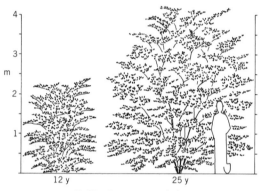

Enkianthus campanulatus.

Adaptability

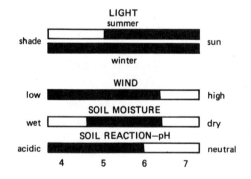

Seasonal Interest. *Flowers:* Small, bell-shaped, yellowish with red markings, in middle to late spring. *Foliage:* Dark green with red petioles, giving distinctive color and texture, turning dull to brilliant red in autumn.

Enkianthus campanulatus.

Problems and Maintenance. Once established in proper site and soil, this plant requires little or no maintenance other than to control occasional mite infestations. Even this is seldom a problem in good soils.

Varieties and Cultivars. 'Albiflorus' has pale, nearly white flowers. Var. *palibinii* has flowers more intensely red-marked and more showy than those of the species type.

Related Species

Enkianthus perulatus 4 (white enkianthus). This is a smaller shrub, to about 2 m/6.6 ft, with pure white flowers, slightly earlier and smaller than those of *E. campanulatus* but conspicuous because of their contrast with the dark green foliage. It is slightly less cold-hardy than *E. campanulatus* but useful in Zones 6a−8b.

Elliottia racemosa 5−6 (southern plume, Georgia plume). This large shrub or very small specimen tree, to 3 m/10 ft or occasionally taller, has clusters of lightly fragrant white flowers in midsummer. It grows best in sandy, acid soils and withstands some drought. It is seldom available as yet, but may become more widely available in the future. Useful in Zones 7b−9a, perhaps also Zones 6a−7a.

Tripetaleia paniculata 4. This Japanese member of the Heath Family is similar to *Enkianthus perulatus* in size but resembles *Elliottia* more in habit and flowering, with white or pink tinged flowers in late summer. It probably is not commercially available, but it is a potentially useful addition to landscapes in Zones 7a−9a and perhaps also Zone 6.

Zenobia pulverulenta 4 (dusty zenobia).   Similar to *Enkianthus perulatus* in size and flowers, this shrub is much less regular in outline, with foliage strongly whitened by a waxy bloom. Its fragrant white flowers appear in late spring or early summer. It grows wild on the coastal plain of the southeastern United States and requires acid, well drained soil. Like *Elliottia* and *Tripetaleia*, it belongs to the Heath Family and is seldom available for planting.

Epigaea repens 2

Trailing arbutus, Mayflower
Evergreen groundcover
Ericaceae (Heath Family)

Native Range. Eastern North America, Newfoundland to northern Florida.

Useful Range. USDA Zones 3a−8b.

Function. Groundcover (small-scale), naturalizing.

Size and Habit

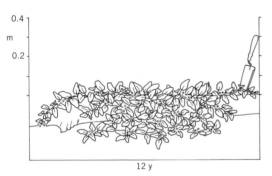

12 y

Epigaea repens.

Adaptability. This plant requires acid, sandy soil with good surface drainage, a light mulch, and watering to prevent excessive drying during estab-

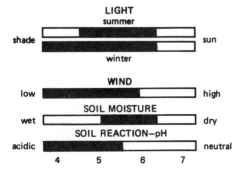

lishment. Protect it from wind and full sun. Use only nursery-grown plants, preferably potted, to ease transplanting. There is little chance of success in moving wild plants, and it is illegal in most areas because this species is becoming endangered in the wild.

Seasonal Interest. *Flowers:* Small, to 0.8 cm/0.3 in., but very fragrant, pink or white, appearing in early spring. This is the state or provincial flower of Massachusetts and Nova Scotia. *Foliage:* Evergreen, leathery, forming a loose mat on the ground.

Problems and Maintenance. This plant is trouble-free once established, but its slow growth and difficulty in establishment in any but the required site conditions has limited its use.

Related Species

Chimaphila umbellata 2 (pipsissewa, wintergreen).   This creeping plant has evergreen foliage and flowering stems ascending to 25 cm/10 in. tall. Small (1.5 cm/0.6 in.) pink flowers are borne in small, flat clusters in late summer. This plant is similar in site requirements to *Epigaea repens* but is not a member of the Heath Family (Ericaceae)—rather the closely related Shinleaf Family (Pyrolaceae). It is no more difficult to establish than *Epigaea* but is available in very few specialized nurseries.

Epimedium grandiflorum 2

Bishop's hat, barrenwort
Herbaceous groundcover
Berberidaceae (Barberry Family)

Native Range. Northeastern Asia.

Useful Range. USDA Zones 3b–8a.

Function. Groundcover.

Size and Habit

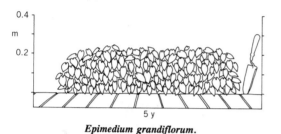

Epimedium grandiflorum.

Adaptability

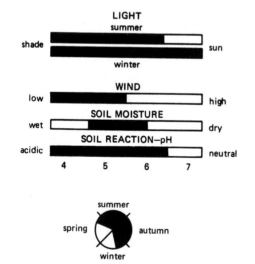

Seasonal Interest. *Flowers:* Distinctively shaped, like a Bishop's hat, 2.5–5 cm/1–2 in. across, the sepals deep red and violet, the petals white, opening in late spring. *Foliage:* Light green, heart-shaped, thin, leathery leaflets, to 8 cm/3 in. long, borne in clusters of three on wiry petioles, are red-bronze as they unfold and again in autumn, making an impressive mass of foliage.

Problems and Maintenance. *Epimedium* species are generally trouble-free and require little maintenance other than cutting off the dead foliage before new growth begins in spring.

Cultivars. Several cultivars have been selected, but those belonging to the different species are confused in commerce (see Related Species). The selection 'Violaceum' (synonym: *E. violaceum*) has more dominantly violet flower parts.

Related Species and Hybrids

Epimedium alpinum 2 (alpine barrenwort). This native of southern Europe has small red and yellow flowers, 1.5 cm/0.6 in. across, but otherwise is similar to *E. grandiflorum.*

Epimedium pinnatum 2 (yellow barrenwort). This central Asian plant has bright yellow flowers, about 2 cm/0.8 in. across, with red spurs.

Epimedium ×*rubrum* 2 (synonym: *E. alpinum* var. *rubrum*; red barrenwort). This hybrid of *E. alpinum* × *E. grandiflorum* has predominantly bright crimson flowers.

Epimedium ×*youngianum* 2 (Young's barrenwort). This hybrid of *E. grandiflorum* × *E. diphyllum* has relatively large, to 2.5 cm/1 in. across, white or pink flowers. The selection 'Niveum' (synonym: *E. grandiflorum* 'Niveum') has pure white flowers, and 'Roseum' has lilac-rose flowers.

Podophyllum peltatum 2 (mayapple). This distinctive groundcover plant in the Barberry Family (Berberidaceae) grows wild in the woods of most of eastern North America, from Quebec to Florida and Texas. Its uniquely lobed, umbrellalike leaves form a loose or dense canopy about 30–40 cm/12–16 in. above the ground, and the white flowers and yellowish fruits hang underneath, largely out of sight. Mayapple is more often conserved than planted, but in any case it makes a superb woodland groundcover in Zones 4a–9a.

Erica herbacea 2

Synonym: *E. carnea*
Spring heath
Evergreen groundcover
Ericaceae (Heath Family)

Native Range. Central and southern Europe.

Useful Range. USDA Zones 6b−7b, north to Zone 5a in areas having reliable snow cover for protection from winter wind, and south to Zone 8b in areas having mild summers.

Function. Rock garden, front of ericaceous border.

Size and Habit

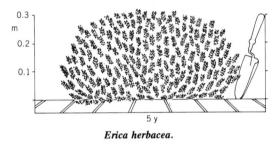

Erica herbacea.

Adaptability. This plant requires a combination of well-drained but not excessively dry, acid soil, high humidity, moderate temperatures, and full sun during the growing season for best growth and flowering. Relatively few places in eastern North America can supply all of these conditions. The southern and middle Atlantic coast, southern Appalachians, and northern areas with snow cover are the regions where this plant is most likely to be successful.

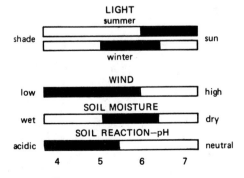

Seasonal Interest. *Flowers:* Red, pink, or white; small but numerous, in short (to 5 cm/2 in.), upright clusters in early spring, or winter in very mild climates. *Foliage:* Evergreen, needlelike, deep green, yellow in at least one cultivar.

Problems and Maintenance. Once the rather specific conditions for establishment have been met, this plant is relatively trouble-free. A light mulch should be maintained in all seasons to stabilize soil moisture.

Cultivars. 'Aurea' has golden-yellow foliage, especially toward the outside of the plant, and pink flowers. 'King George,' 'Ruby Glow,' and 'Vivellii' have bright rosy red flowers over a long blooming period. 'Praecox' (= 'Praecox Rubra') and 'Sherwoodii' are early flowering with deep rosy red flowers. 'Springwood Pink' and 'Winter Beauty' are popular cultivars with early pink flowers. 'Springwood White' shares the popularity of 'Springwood Pink' and has white flowers.

Related Species

Erica cinerea 2 (twisted or Scotch heath).   This heath is slightly less cold-hardy than *E. herbacea*, to Zones 7a−8a, some cultivars flowering very early in summer, some continuing through midsummer. The best cultivars include 'Atrorubens' and 'C.D. Eason,' which have unusually rich red flowers in midsummer, and 'Golden Drop,' with pink flowers in early summer and coppery gold foliage that turns reddish in winter.

Erica ×*darleyensis* 2 (Darley or winter heath). This hybrid between *E. herbacea* and *E. mediterranea* appears as an oversize version of *E. herbacea*, commonly reaching heights of 0.5 m/1.6 ft and taller, with similar but not outstanding flowering interest. It is useful in Zones 7a−8a.

Erica mediterranea 3 (synonyms: *E. erigena*, *E. hibernica*; Mediterranean heath).   This species bears pink flowers in spring, and is taller, more upright, and less hardy (Zones 7b−8b) than the other species included here. It probably is not useful in eastern North America.

Erica tetralix 2 (crossleaf heath, bog or bell heath).   This is one of the most cold-hardy of all *Erica* species, useful in Zones 4b–7a, with cultivars having soft pink, red, or white flowers in summer and woolly, gray-green foliage.

Erica vagans 2 (Cornish heath).   This plant is similar in size and hardiness to *E. herbacea*, but flowers from summer through early autumn. Some of the best cultivars include 'Alba Minor' and 'Nana,' low growing with white flowers; 'Lyonesse,' much taller (60 cm/2 ft) with pure white flowers; 'Mrs. D. F. Maxwell,' relatively tall (40 cm/1.3 ft) with long clusters of bright rose-pink flowers; and 'St. Keverne,' similar in height to 'Mrs. D. F. Maxwell' but with lighter, clear pink flowers.

The summer flowering heaths tend to be somewhat taller than is desirable for groundcover use, but they can be kept lower by annual pruning in spring. This treatment is not appropriate for spring flowering heaths, since it interferes with flowering.

In addition to the relatively small number of *Erica* species that are hardy in the cold temperate zone, there are hundreds of additional species, mostly from South Africa, that can be used in climates where minimum temperatures drop only a few degrees below freezing. Unfortunately, these large flowered *Erica* species are not adapted to our area.

Bruckenthalia spiculifolia 2 (spike heath).   This dwarf shrub from the eastern Mediterranean region is similar to *Erica* in landscape use and requirements and has pink flowers in midsummer. It is seldom used in our area, and its useful range is not clearly known, but it is at least suited to Zones 6b–7b, perhaps also Zone 8 where moisture is available.

Calluna vulgaris 2 (heather).   This close relative of *Erica* is native to much of Europe and naturalized in a few places in the northeastern United States. Its site requirements are very similar to those of *Erica herbacea*, and it is useful, given those requirements, in Zones 5b–7b, perhaps Zone 8a as well, and as far north as Zone 4b in areas with reliable snow cover. Flowers, opening in late summer or early autumn, are white, pink, reddish, or purple, and the scalelike leaves are golden-yellow, light or dark green, silvery or bronze-purple. Many cul-

Calluna vulgaris, Erica spp., as groundcovers.

tivars are available from specialty nurseries in the United States and Canada. The following are a few of the most common. 'Alba' has white flowers and gray-green foliage. 'Alportii' has rose-red flowers and is 50 cm/20 in. tall and vigorous. 'Aurea' and 'Cuprea' have purple flowers and yellow foliage, bronzing in winter. 'Coccinea' has deep red flowers and green foliage. 'County Wicklow' has double, shell pink flowers and is relatively tall growing, to 40 cm/16 in. 'H. E. Beale' has double, silvery pink flowers in long spikes and grows vigorously to 50 cm/20 in. tall. 'Hirsuta' (= 'Tomentosa') has purplish flowers and fuzzy grayish foliage but probably is not commercially available. 'J. H. Hamilton' has double, bright salmon pink flowers, and is vigorous but low growing, to 25 cm/10 in. 'Mrs. Ronald Gray' has rosy pink flowers and is very low growing, to only 10 cm/4 in. tall. 'Nana' (= 'Pygmaea') has purple flowers and grows to no more than 15 cm/6 in. tall but probably is not available. 'Searlei' has white flowers and green foliage and is rather tall (to 40 cm/16 in.) and

Calluna vulgaris 'Mrs. Ronald Gray.'

open in habit. 'Searlei Aurea' is similar to 'Searlei' except that it has yellow foliage and grows only 30 cm/12 in. tall.

Daboecia cantabrica 3 (Irish heath).   This low evergreen shrub from maritime western Europe, with dark green needlelike foliage and purple flowers over a long period from early summer to autumn, is similar in hardiness, site requirements, and landscape effect to *Erica herbacea* but has larger flowers and grows taller, to about 60 cm/24 in. Availability is limited, but the following cultivars have been available at one time or another. 'Alba' has white flowers. 'Atropurpurea' has deep purple flowers. 'Bicolor' (= 'Versicolor') has bicolored purple and white flowers. 'Multiflora,' 'Pallida,' and 'Rubra' have pink or rose-pink flowers.

Eriobotrya japonica 6

Loquat, Japanese plum
Evergreen shrub or small tree
Rosaceae (Rose Family)

Native Range. China.

Useful Range. USDA Zones 8a−9a+.

Function. Specimen, patio tree, border, screen.

Size and Habit

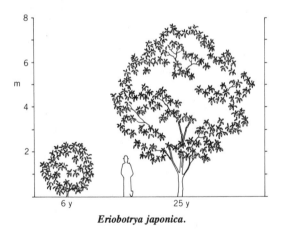

Eriobotrya japonica.

Adaptability

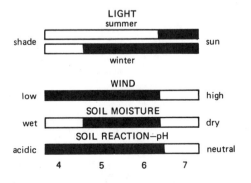

Seasonal Interest. *Flowers:* Small, fragrant, creamy white, partly hidden in large, brown, woolly clusters in late autumn and early winter. *Foliage:* Large (to 30 cm/12 in. long), evergreen, leathery, dark green leaves with woolly tan undersides and coarsely toothed margins; their coarse texture gives a tropical appearance. *Fruits:* Orange-yellow, slightly pear shaped, 3−4 cm/ 1.2−1.6 in. long, in late spring. Fruit is aromatic and edible, with a tart-sweet flavor. Fruits are seldom able to ripen north of Zone 8b or 9a.

Problems and Maintenance. This shrub is seriously affected by fire blight disease in some areas. Consult local professionals concerning its performance. Other than this it is trouble-free, given perfectly drained soil.

Related Species

Eriobotrya deflexa 6 (bronze loquat).   This species is somewhat less cold-hardy (Zone 9a+) than *E. japonica*, with smaller leaves and fruits, and its new leaves are bronze at emergence, turning green as they mature.

Escallonia virgata 3

Synonym: *E. philippiana*
Twiggy escallonia
Evergreen shrub
Saxifragaceae (Saxifrage Family)

Native Range. Chile.

Useful Range. USDA Zones 8b–9a+.

Function. Foundation, border, massing.

Size and Habit

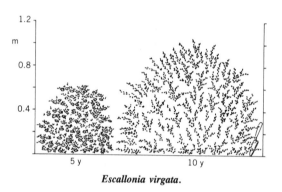

Escallonia virgata.

Adaptability. This is more tolerant of salt than most shrubs and is therefore useful in seashore situations.

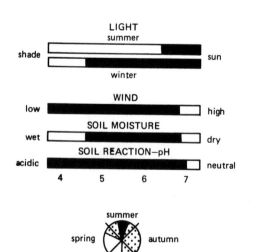

Seasonal Interest. *Flowers:* Small (1 cm/0.4 in.), white (or pink) in short clusters. *Foliage:* Fine-textured (leaves are about as large as flowers), leathery, semievergreen.

Problems and Maintenance. This shrub is relatively trouble-free where it is adapted.

Cultivars. 'Gwendolyn Anley' has pink flowers and low, compact growth habit.

Related Species. The following are less cold-hardy than *E. virgata*, marginally hardy at best in Zone 9a, but worthy of trial there. All are evergreen.

Escallonia bifida 6 (synonyms: *E. floribunda, E. montevidensis*; Montevideo or white escallonia). This tall-growing, evergreen, fall-flowering species can be pruned into tree form.

Escallonia ×exoniensis 5. This hybrid of *E. rosea × E. rubra* is a tall evergreen shrub, but it can be kept in size group 4 with pruning. The selection 'Frades' (= 'Pink Princess') has rich pink flowers in summer and compact form. It is useful for foundation or hedge planting.

Escallonia laevis 6 (synonym: *E. organensis*; Organ Mountain escallonia). Another tall shrub, this species has bronzed green leaves and pink flowers in early summer and can be trained into a small tree form. 'Jubilee' (*E. laevis × E. rubra*) is a compact selection with rosy pink flowers in summer.

Escallonia ×langleyensis 4–5 (synonym: *E. edinensis*; Langley escallonia). This hybrid of *E. rubra × E. virgata* is evergreen and variable with several popular cultivars, including 'Apple Blossom,' a slow growing, compact form with pale pink flowers, 'Slieve Donard,' a shrub to 2 m/6.6 ft with pale pink flowers, and several other "Donard" cultivars with pale to deep pink flowers and compact to arching growth habit.

Eucalyptus gunnii 6–7

Cider gum
Evergreen tree
Myrtaceae (Myrtle Family)

Native Range. Tasmania.

Useful Range. USDA Zone 9a+.

Function. Specimen, fast (temporary) shade tree, screen, or windbreak.

Size and Habit. Trees reach heights of 30 m/98 ft in good sites in their native habitat but seldom exceed 20 m/66 ft in North America and 10–15 m/33–49 ft in even the mildest parts of Zone 9a.

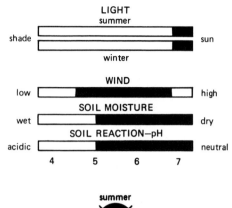

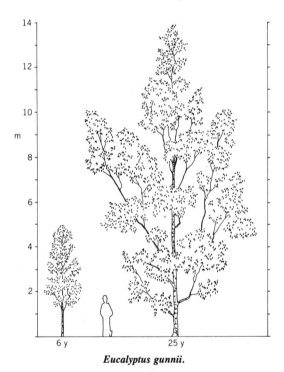

Eucalyptus gunnii.

Adaptability. *Eucalyptus* species grow best in full sun in relatively dry sites, where they tolerate conditions that would dehydrate many other trees. Too much moisture may encourage active growth in autumn, predisposing trees to freezing injury.

Seasonal Interest. *Flowers:* Yellow, about 1.5 cm/0.6 in. across, borne in large numbers in early autumn. *Foliage:* Evergreen, blue-green, nearly circular, to 6 cm/2.4 in. across, the loose canopy giving mottled shade. *Trunk and branches:* Smooth bark is peeling, bicolored green and white.

Problems and Maintenance. Mites and mealy bugs sometimes can be troublesome enough to require control measures. But the most serious problem of *Eucalyptus* species in our area, even Zone 9a, is freezing damage. Even though the hardier species such as *E. gunnii* perform well in comparable hardiness zones in California, they do not do as well in southeastern North America, probably because autumn weather is conducive to growth rather than acclimation for winter. Withholding fertilizer and water (when possible) in early autumn may be helpful in promoting slowed growth and acclimation, but results have been spotty at best. It is therefore not realistic to expect these trees to attain full size here or to develop without occasionally suffering freezing injury.

Related Species

Eucalyptus cinerea 6 (silverdollar eucalyptus). The silvery leaves, nearly circular, with the pairs often fused across the stem, give this tree from southeastern Australia its "silverdollar" name. A small tree at best and not very functional, this species usually is used as a specimen for accent or for cutting of foliage. Its trunk is covered with fibrous, reddish brown bark but often is too weak to support a canopy of any size unless it is staked. Useful in Zone 9a+, especially in the southwestern parts of our area.

Eucalyptus globulus 7 (blue gum).   This potentially huge tree from Tasmania is physically weak, surface-rooted, and excessively fast growing, and it is frequently damaged by freezes, leaving it ungainly in form. The selection 'Compacta' is very compact and more useful. Both forms have silvery white immature leaves, turning dark blue-green, giving the tree a blue cast. It

is barely useful in Zone 9a in our area, but well adapted to the warmer parts of California, where it has become naturalized.

Eucalyptus niphophila 6 (snow gum).   From high elevations in southeastern Australia, this is thought by some to be the hardiest species of *Eucalyptus* currently cultivated in North America. Even though it may be hardy in Zone 8a on the West Coast, like other *Eucalyptus* species it is subject to the problem of delayed acclimation in the moister climate of the Southeast.

Eucommia ulmoides 7

Hardy rubber tree
Deciduous tree
Eucommiaceae (Eucommia Family)

Native Range. Central China.

Useful Range. USDA Zones 6a−8b.

Function. Shade, street tree.

Size and Habit

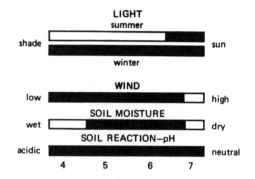

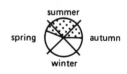

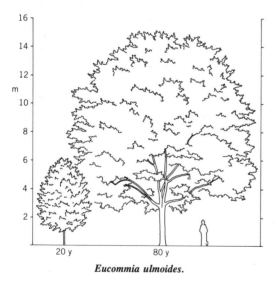

Eucommia ulmoides.

Adaptability. This tree is well adapted to hot, dry summers. This and its freedom from insect and disease problems are the principal reasons for its use.

Seasonal Interest. *Foliage:* Bright green, lustrous, lightly wrinkled when mature, falling in midautumn with little color change. Leaves and

Eucommia ulmoides.

other parts contain latex, which appears in long strands when a leaf is carefully broken apart. *Fruits:* Small but numerous, encircled by a leathery wing, adding marginal seasonal interest to female trees in late summer and autumn.

Problems and Maintenance. This tree's freedom from insect and disease problems is one of its best features. It has a strong tendency to produce vertical "water sprouts" from main branches and may require pruning to remove them where branching pattern is an important asthetic concern. But pruning only increases the vigor of such sprouting in the following year. A more satisfactory solution where this is a problem is to select a different tree.

Euonymus alata 5

Winged euonymus, winged spindletree, burning bush
Deciduous shrub
Celastraceae (Staff-tree Family)

Native Range. Northeastern Asia.

Useful Range. USDA Zones 4a−8a.

Function. Border, massing, screen, hedge, specimen.

Size and Habit

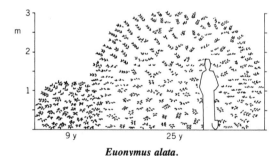

Euonymus alata.

Adaptability

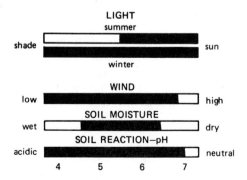

Seasonal Interest. *Foliage:* Medium green, crisp, turning scarlet to purplish red in autumn, fading to delicate shades of pink. *Fruits:* Lobed capsules opening to show scarlet arils covering seeds in autumn, toxic if eaten. *Twigs and branching:* Corky wings or ridges on twigs add interest in winter and early spring during leafing out. Branching is more-or-less horizontal, resulting in a mass as broad as it is tall.

Euonymus alata.

Problems and Maintenance. This is one of the least susceptible *Euonymus* species to scale, but occasionally it is found infested. Otherwise it is trouble-free, requiring little pruning except for restricting its size or in a formal hedge.

Cultivars. 'Compacta' is slower growing and more compact in form than the species type, with narrow wings that offer less winter interest. Its brilliant red fall foliage is too strong for some situations, and it is somewhat less cold-hardy than the species type, but useful in Zones 4b−8a.

Related Species

Euonymus phellomana 6.   Like *E. alata*, this species has large corky wings on the twigs, but the

similarity ends there, since this shrub is taller and more rangy, without very striking fall foliage color but with showy, pink fruits. It is rarely seen and probably not available commercially, but potentially useful in Zones 5b−8a.

Euonymus bungeana 6

Winterberry euonymus
Deciduous shrub or small tree
Celastraceae (Staff-tree Family)

Native Range. Northern China and Manchuria.

Useful Range. USDA Zones 4b−7b.

Function. Specimen shrub or small patio tree, border, screen (with pruning).

Size and Habit

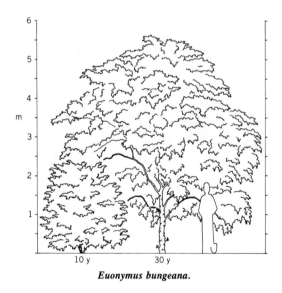

Euonymus bungeana.

Adaptability

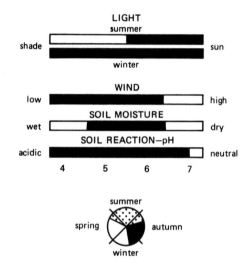

Seasonal Interest. *Foliage:* Light green, long-petioled and relatively long and drooping leaves, to 10 cm/4 in., turning dull yellow before falling. *Fruit:* Lobed capsules turn light pink in early autumn, open in midautumn to show orange-scarlet arils, and remain persistent and colorful after leaves fall. Toxic if eaten. *Trunk and branches:* Striped with light and dark gray, especially noticeable on old specimens.

Problems and Maintenance. This shrub is not as susceptible to euonymus scale as some species, but occasionally it is found infested. Otherwise it is relatively trouble-free but may require pruning to maintain fullness if used as a screen and to remove suckers.

Varieties and Cultivars. 'Pendula' has long, pendulous branches, making it useful only as a specimen. Var. *semi-persistens* has semievergreen foliage and fruits sparsely.

Euonymus europaea 6

European spindletree, European euonymus
Deciduous shrub
Celastraceae (Staff-tree Family)

Native Range. Europe to western Asia; naturalized in the northeastern United States.

Useful Range. USDA Zones 4a–7b.

Function. Screen, border.

Size and Habit

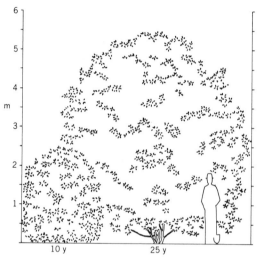

Euonymus europaea.

Adaptability

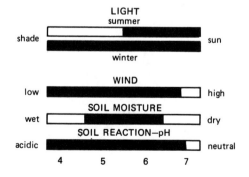

Seasonal Interest. *Foliage:* Medium to dark green leaves are relatively large (to 8 cm/3 in.) and turn dull reddish in autumn. *Fruits:* Showy, lobed capsules vary from pink to red, open to expose orange arils in midautumn. They are toxic if eaten.

Problems and Maintenance. This species is not as susceptible to scale as some *Euonymus* species but occasionally is infested. Aphids are a more common pest, causing leaf disfiguration. Occasional pruning is necessary to maintain form in all but the compact cultivars.

Varieties and Cultivars. Several cultivars have been selected for outstanding fruiting interest and compact growth. A few of the more common cultivars and varieties follow. 'Alba' has whitish fruits. 'Aldenhamensis' has unusually showy, bright rose-pink fruits in pendulous clusters. 'Atrorubens' has showy, bright crimson fruits. Var. *intermedia* has dark green, rounded leaves and bright red fruits. 'Nana' and 'Pumila' are dwarf forms, to about 1 m/3.3 ft in height, somewhat taller in time. They may be slightly less hardy than the species type. 'Red Cascade' has unusually large, bright red fruits in very heavy clusters.

Related Species

Euonymus americana 5 (strawberry bush). This upright shrub, smaller and less cold-hardy (Zones 6b–9a) than *E. europaea*, is known chiefly for its large, warty, crimson fruits, toxic if eaten. Not commonly planted, but sometimes preserved in development where native, from New York to Florida and Texas.

Euonymus atropurpurea 6 (wahoo, burning bush). This tall shrub or very small tree suckers heavily and is not commonly planted, but it can be preserved in native stands in most of our area. The small purple flowers are inconspicuous but are a distinctive means of identification in late spring. The principal seasonal interest is the bright crimson fruits, which are toxic if eaten. Useful in Zones 3b–7b.

Euonymus hamiltoniana var. *yedoensis.*

Euonymus hamiltoniana var. *yedoensis* 6 (synonym: *E. yedoensis*; Yeddo euonymus, burning bush).   This tall shrub has a flat-topped growth habit and unusually large leaves, to 12 cm/5 in. long. Its pinkish fruits are colorful but should not be eaten, and the bright red autumn foliage is outstanding. Useful in Zones 4a−7b.

Euonymus latifolia 6 (broadleaf euonymus). This tall shrub has large leaves, to 12 cm/5 in.

long, reddish underneath and turning completely red in autumn. Its pink fruits are comparable with those of *E. hamiltoniana* var. *yedoensis*, and it is useful at least in Zones 5b−7b.

Euonymus obovata 2 (running euonymus). This excellent, deciduous groundcover is native to the northeastern and central United States and adjacent Canada and useful in Zones 4a−7b. It forms a mass quickly in sun or partial shade and will tolerate full shade. Fruits and red foliage add autumn interest in sunny sites.

Euonymus sachalinensis 6 (synonym: *E. planipes*; Sakhalin euonymus).   This tall shrub is notable for its large, angular, lanternlike fruits, large, red-scaled winter buds, and rosy purple autumn foliage. One of the earliest of all *Euonymus* species to leaf out in spring, it is little-used but worthy of wider trial. Its useful range is not well established but includes at least Zones 6a−7b.

Euonymus fortunei 1 and 2−4

Synonym: *E. radicans* var. *acuta*
Wintercreeper
Evergreen vine, groundcover, or shrub
Celastraceae (Staff-tree Family)

Native Range. China, Japan, Korea.

Useful Range. USDA Zones 4b−9a, but not all cultivars are hardy in Zone 4b. Even though adaptable to the Deep South, susceptibility to scale insects and better alternative plants limit its use in Zones 8 and 9.

Function. Groundcover, vine, foundation shrub (some cultivars). The climbing types cover chimneys, masonry walls or tree trunks (without injury to the tree).

Size and Habit. 'Colorata' (left) and 'Sarcoxie' (right) are illustrated.

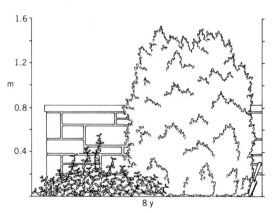

Euonymus fortunei.

Adaptability. Protection from full winter sun and wind is necessary in the northern extremes of its useful range to reduce desiccation of foliage.

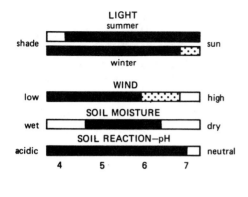

Euonymus fortunei 'Colorata.'

Euonymus fortunei 'Colorata.'

Seasonal Interest. *Flowers:* Small, pale green, inconspicuous. *Foliage:* Evergreen, leathery, variegated, with white or yellow in cultivars, turning purplish in winter in at least one cultivar, 'Colorata.' *Fruits:* Light orange, opening to show the red-orange aril and showy in autumn, but many cultivars have little or no fruiting interest.

Problems and Maintenance. This plant's only real problem, euonymus scale, is so serious in some areas that it limits its use. At best, the need for periodic spraying to control this pest should be expected. Once such maintenance is provided, this species is trouble-free and durable. Control of scale is especially important when this plant is used as a climber, since infestations above eye level may not be noticed until serious damage has been done.

Varieties and Cultivars. Var. *acuta* (= 'Acuta') is the species type, an excellent mat-forming groundcover or rock-climbing vine with relatively narrow leaves, to 5 cm/2 in. long.

'Carrierei' (Carriere wintercreeper) is a loosely shrubby form to 1.5 m/5 ft or higher with support. Fruits are colorful but not consistently displayed in all areas and probably toxic if eaten. It is cold-hardy to Zone 5b.

'Colorata' (purpleleaf wintercreeper) is a groundcover to 0.3 m/1 ft, with deep green foliage of medium texture, turning red-purple in winter, but without fruiting interest. It is cold-hardy to Zone 4b.

'Emerald Cushion' is dwarf and moundlike, eventually growing to 1 m/3.3 ft tall and twice as broad. It is cold-hardy to Zone 5a.

'Emerald Gaiety' is upright with spreading branches, to 1.5 m/5 ft tall, with white variegated foliage and no fruiting interest. It is cold-hardy to Zone 5b.

'Emerald 'n Gold' is similar to 'Emerald Gaiety' except for its yellow variegated foliage and slightly lower form. It is cold-hardy to Zone 5b.

'Emerald Pride' is erect in form, to 1.2 m/4 ft tall and nearly as broad. It is cold-hardy to Zone 5b.

'Golden Prince' (Plant Patent No. 3211, 1972) has golden-yellow variegated foliage in early summer, later turning mostly green. It is vigorous, yet remains low, perhaps not exceeding 0.8 m/2.6 ft in height. It is cold-hardy at least to Zone 5b.

'Gracilis' (= 'Argenteo-marginata,' = 'Pictus,' = 'Tricolor') is an outstanding groundcover form with white variegated foliage sometimes tinged with pink or yellow. It is cold-hardy to Zone 5b.

'Longwood' is an excellent groundcover, prostrate but tending to "pile up" in the center to a height of 15 cm/6 in., with small, dark green leaves (to 2 cm/0.8 in. long). It is cold-hardy in Zone 5a.

'Minimus' (= 'Kewensis') is a prostrate form with dark green leaves, only 0.5–0.8 cm/0.2–0.3 in. long, an excellent cultivar for small-scale display on rocks or masonry. It is cold-hardy in Zone 5a.

Var. *radicans* has smaller, thicker leaves that are leathery and distinctly toothed. This variety is confused in commerce, the name being applied to several other forms of *E. fortunei*.

'Sarcoxie' is a dense, vigorous, upright form with deep green foliage, growing to 1.5 m/5 ft or taller with ideal conditions or support. It is more tolerant of hot, dry summers than other upright forms, less troubled by scale, and cold-hardy in Zone 5b and sheltered sites in Zone 5a.

'Silver Queen' is a handsome, shrubby form with white variegated foliage, believed to be a mutant from 'Carrierei'' and similar in form except somewhat less vigorous and more compact. It is cold-hardy at least to Zone 6a.

Var. *vegeta* (= 'Vegeta'; bigleaf wintercreeper) functions as a climber or a loose shrub, useful as a wall cover or foundation specimen, with rounded, medium green leaves and outstanding fruiting interest. It is cold-hardy to Zone 4b.

Related Species

Euonymus nana 3 (synonym: *E. nana* var. *turkestanica*; dwarf euonymus).   This vigorous but open small shrub has very narrow leaves, to 6 cm/2.4 in. long, turning bright red in autumn and persisting late. Fruiting interest is also significant, making this an interesting small specimen shrub in Zones 3b–6b. However, it is highly susceptible to euonymus scale infestations.

Euonymus japonica 5

Evergreen euonymus
Evergreen shrub
Celastraceae (Staff-tree Family)

Native Range. Southern Japan.

Useful Range. USDA Zones 8b–9a+.

Function. Hedge, screen, specimen.

Size and Habit

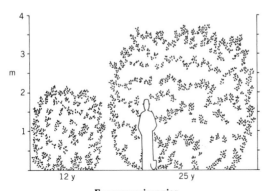

Euonymus japonica.

Adaptability. Protection from extreme summer sun eases stress and improves performance.

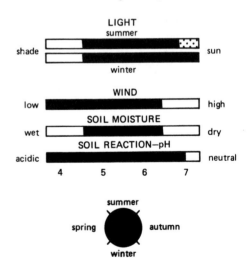

Seasonal Interest. *Flowers:* Pale green in early summer, inconspicuous. *Foliage:* Glossy and leathery, bright to deep green or strikingly variegated in cultivars. *Fruits:* Pink, opening to expose orange aril, showy in fall when present in great numbers, but this often does not occur because of pruning to maintain vigor.

Problems and Maintenance. Scale insects are a serious enough problem to rule this plant out in low-maintenance situations in the Deep South. These and other insects (white fly, aphids) require a careful pest-control program. Pruning will also be necessary to maintain size and form.

Euonymus japonica 'Aureo-picta.'

Euonymus japonica 'Argenteo-variegata.'

Cultivars. 'Albomarginata' and 'Silver King' have green leaves with white margins. 'Albovariegata' and 'Argenteo-variegata' have green leaves edged and irregularly marked with white. 'Aurea' has

yellow leaves but is seldom available. 'Aureo-marginata' has green leaves with yellow margins. 'Aureo-variegata,' 'Aureo-picta,' 'Gold Spot,' 'Mediopicta', and 'Yellow Queen' have green leaves blotched with yellow. 'Microphylla' (dwarf evergreen euonymus) has very small leaves (to 2.5 cm/1 in.), about one third the usual length and narrow. The plant is upright, rounded, and compact, to about 1 m/3.3 ft.

Euonymus kiautschovica 5

Synonym: *E. patens*
Spreading euonymus
Semievergreen shrub
Celastraceae (Staff-tree Family)

Native Range. Eastern and central China.

Useful Range. USDA Zones 6a−9a. Even though adaptable to the Deep South, other shrubs with better foliage in late winter are usually preferred in Zones 8 and 9.

Function. Border, hedge, specimen.

Size and Habit

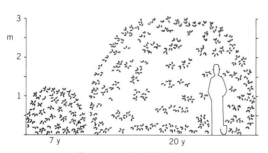

Euonymus kiautschovica.

Adaptability

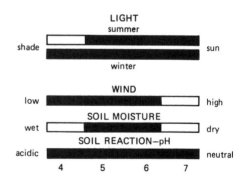

Seasonal Interest. *Flowers:* Small but numerous, pale green, in late summer, not showy. *Foliage:* Lustrous, deep green, somewhat leathery but less so than that of *E. fortunei* and *E. japonica*, semievergreen in the North to nearly evergreen in the South, persisting until the first severe cold of winter, then drying and looking ragged until new growth begins. *Fruits:* Pink, opening to show the orange arils, colorful in late autumn until the first severe cold, sometimes ineffective in the North because of early severe freezes.

Problems and Maintenance. Perhaps because it is not fully evergreen, this species is less susceptible to scale than *E. fortunei* and *E. japonica*, but it can be troubled occasionally and so cannot be considered trouble-free. Pruning usually is not necessary except for formal hedges and controlling growth in small-scale situations.

Cultivars. 'DuPont,' 'Manhattan,' and 'Newport' are compact forms of uncertain parentage, with lustrous leaves to 6 cm/2.4 in. All have superior foliage quality and are about as hardy as the species type.

Evodia daniellii 6

Korean evodia
Deciduous tree
Rutaceae (Rue Family)

Native Range. Korea and northern China.

Useful Range. USDA Zones 5b–8a.

Function. Specimen, patio tree.

Size and Habit

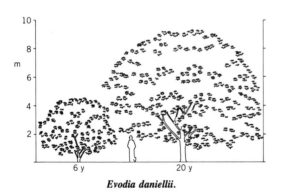

Evodia daniellii.

Adaptability

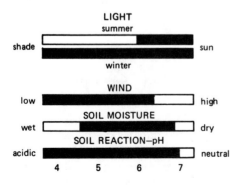

Seasonal Interest. *Flowers:* Small, whitish, in large, flat clusters in late summer. This tree is greatly favored by beekeepers for its nectar and late flowering. *Foliage:* Medium dark green, compound leaves, showing off flowers and fruits to advantage. *Fruits:* Pinkish to dull red, opening in autumn to disclose small, shiny black berries. *Trunk and branches:* Smooth, light gray bark adds mild winter interest.

Evodia daniellii.

Problems and Maintenance. *Evodia* species are relatively trouble-free as young trees but are relatively short-lived. Their weak wood is subject to damage from high winds and heavy ice and snow.

Related Species

Evodia hupehensis 7 (Chinese evodia). This tree from central China serves as a larger (to 15 m/49 ft) version of *E. daniellii*, with similar landscape interest. Since it is weak-wooded, it is better used as a lawn specimen or for naturalizing than as a street tree.

Zanthoxylum americanum 6 (northern prickly ash, toothache tree). This thicket-forming shrub or small tree will seldom be deliberately planted, but it is encountered as a wild species in site development through much of our area from Quebec to North Dakota and southward to Florida and Oklahoma. Its suckering habit and small but wicked thorns make it effective as a barrier, but other, equally effective shrubs can be controlled more easily and are more pleasing

visually. Its useful range includes Zones 4a−9a.

Zanthoxylum clava-herculis 6 (southern prickly ash, Hercules' club). This more southern counterpart of *Z. americanum* is native from coastal Virginia to Florida and Texas. It is no more useful as a landscape plant than the northern species but could be used, if there were reason, in Zones 8a−9a+.

Zanthoxylum schinifolium 6. This large shrub or small tree from northeastern Asia is limited in its usefulness by the same characteristics as *Z. americanum*, but it has much more handsome, glossy, dark green foliage. If any species of prickly ash is to be planted deliberately, this exotic species might well be first choice. It is potentially useful in Zones 6a−9a.

Exochorda ×macrantha 5

Hybrid pearlbush
Deciduous shrub
Rosaceae (Rose Family)

Hybrid origin. *E. racemosa* × *E. korolkowii.*

Useful Range. USDA Zones 5b−9a.

Function. Border, specimen.

Size and Habit

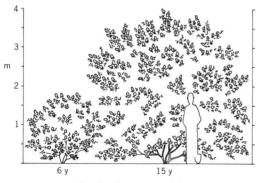

Exochorda ×macrantha.

Adaptability

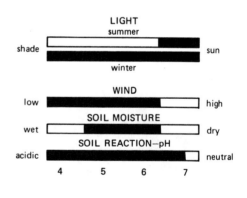

Seasonal Interest. *Flowers:* White, pearl-shaped in bud, opening to 5 cm/2 in. across. *Foliage:* Dull light green, of medium fine texture, not distinctive. *Fruits:* Interesting but inconspicuous, small, dull green, winged capsules.

Problems and Maintenance. This shrub is relatively trouble-free but not a very interesting plant during the 50 weeks of the year when it is not flowering.

Cultivars. 'The Bride' is low growing (to 1.5 m/5 ft), compact, and semiweeping with numerous flowers, somewhat larger than typical for *E. ×macrantha*.

Related Species

Exochorda giraldii var. *wilsonii* 6 (Wilson pearlbush).   This native of central China is at least as floriferous as *E. ×macrantha* 'The Bride,' but more upright and much taller, to 4−5 m/13−16 ft.

Exochorda racemosa 6 (common pearlbush). This native of eastern China is similar to *E. giraldii* in size and habit. It has smaller flowers (to 4 cm/1.6 in.) but is more widely available commercially, and it is the most cold-hardy species of *Exochorda*, to Zone 5a.

Fagus grandifolia 8

American beech
Deciduous tree
Fagaceae (Beech Family)

Native Range. Eastern North America.

Useful Range. USDA Zones 4a−9a. Adaptability in Zones 8 and 9 depends on having a site with adequate moisture, and local or regional seed sources should be used in all zones. Not useful as a street tree because of low-branching habit and site requirements.

Function. Shade tree, specimen, naturalizing.

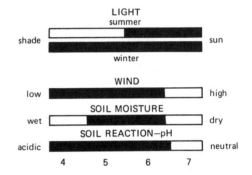

tree should be selected. Less drought-tolerant than its European counterpart, *F. sylvatica*.

Size and Habit

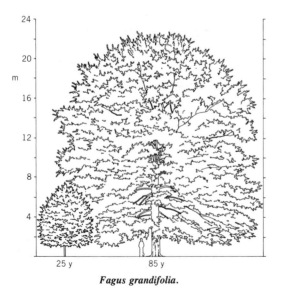

Fagus grandifolia.

Seasonal Interest. *Foliage:* Dense, medium green, crisp and clean, turning golden bronze in autumn, then drying to a warm tan color and persisting into early winter, especially on young trees. *Fruits:* Small triangular nuts, one or two in

Fagus grandifolia.

Adaptability. Best performance requires a well-aerated, at least slightly acidic soil with a good moisture supply. If this is not possible, another

a small burr. Although inconspicuous, they are interesting and edible. *Trunk and branches:* Smooth, light gray bark is an asset in all seasons, especially striking in winter.

Problems and Maintenance. Surface roots preclude establishment of vegetative groundcovers underneath. Mulch may be used as an alternative, but unpruned trees grown in the open will be clothed in foliage to the ground, eliminating the need for any other groundcover. This tree is reputedly difficult to transplant. This is true of wildling trees, but nursery-grown trees in the hands of competent landscapers are not difficult to transplant. Commercial availability is more of a problem, but even this is not insurmountable.

Fagus sylvatica 8

European beech
Deciduous tree
Fagaceae (Beech Family)

Native Range. Europe.

Useful Range. USDA Zones 5a−9a. Adaptability in Zones 8 and 9 depends on adequate moisture.

Function. Shade tree, specimen.

Size and Habit

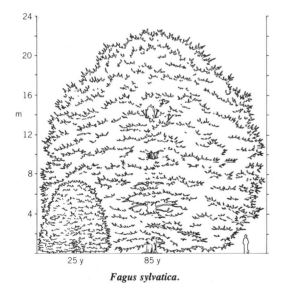

Fagus sylvatica.

Adaptability. Best performance requires a well-aerated, at least slightly acidic soil with a good moisture supply.

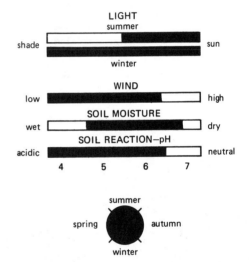

Seasonal Interest. *Foliage:* Dense, dark green—other colors in cultivars (below)—turning more-or-less bronze in autumn. *Fruits:* Small, triangular nuts in small burrs, inconspicuous but interesting. Reports that they are poisonous, although perhaps not true, should be checked out before eating. Good crops of seeds are not often produced in landscape sites outside the native range. *Trunk and branches:* Smooth gray bark is interesting in all seasons, especially winter, lending an elephantine appearance to the trunks of older trees.

Problems and Maintenance. Surface roots preclude the use of vegetative ground covers, and they are seldom needed, since the tree's leafy branches typically reach the ground. Mulches may be used where necessary. Usually free of pests, although woolly aphids can be troublesome in some areas.

Cultivars. Named variants of *F. sylvatica* include bronze, red-purple, yellow, variegated, and cut-leaved foliage, and fastigiate, pendulous, dwarf, and contorted form. A few of the more commonly available are listed here.

'Asplenifolia' (fernleaf beech) and 'Laciniata' (cutleaf beech) have very finely divided foliage and fine texture; 'Asplenifolia' is the finer of the two.

'Atropunicea' (= 'Cuprea,' = 'Purpurea,' = 'Riversii'; purple or copper beech) has red to purple foliage, variable in intensity since some trees are grown from seed and are only partially true to type. Thus this is more properly a group name than a cultivar.

'Fastigiata' (= 'Dawyckii') is fastigiate and narrowly columnar in form, useful for vertical accent.

'Pendula' (weeping beech) has a striking weeping growth habit.

Fagus sylvatica 'Fastigiata.'

Fagus sylvatica 'Pendula.'

'Rohanii' (Rohan purple beech) has foliage similar to that of 'Laciniata' but is purple rather than green.

'Spaethiana' (Spaeth purple beech) has the best purple foliage color of any beech, holding throughout the growing season.

'Tricolor' (tricolored beech) has leaves heavily variegated with white and with a pink margin. Because of the limited photosynthetic leaf area, it is very slow growing and best shaded from hot sun.

Fatsia japonica 4−5

Japanese fatsia, paper plant
Evergreen shrub
Araliaceae (Aralia Family)

Native Range. Southeastern Asia.

Useful Range. USDA Zones 7b−9a+, but only in protected sites in Zones 7b and 8a.

Function. Specimen, border, espalier.

Size and Habit. Except for espalier use, this shrub is best pruned to keep it below six feet in height and in good form. Without pruning it will eventually become a straggling small tree.

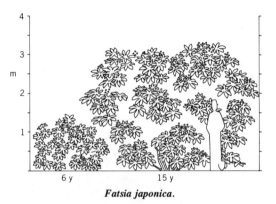

Fatsia japonica.

Adaptability. More winter shade is needed in Zones 7b and 8a than farther south. Tolerant of seashore conditions if protected from wind.

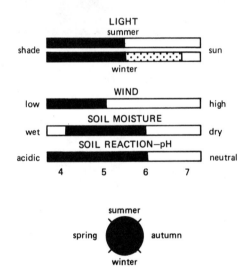

Seasonal Interest. *Flowers:* Greenish white, small but in large (to 5 cm/2 in.), globular clusters (umbels) in autumn. *Foliage:* Large, glossy, evergreen, palmately lobed leaves, to 35 cm/14 in. or more wide and long. *Fruits:* Small, blue-black, in globular clusters in winter, interesting but not colorful.

Problems and Maintenance. This plant is trouble-free except for occasional minor insect infestations but needs fertilization and pruning to maintain vigor, form, and leaf size. For best foliage display, fertilize lightly in spring and again in summer during periods of rapid growth. Prune in early spring to remove any winter-injured foliage and encourage vigorous new growth.

Cultivars. 'Moseri' is more compact in growth habit than the species type. 'Variegata' has creamy yellow variegation toward the ends of leaves.

Related Species

×*Fatshedera lizei* 4 *(fatshedera).* This intergeneric hybrid *(Hedera helix* × *Fatsia japonica)* is intermediate in most respects between its parents and more vinelike in its habit than *Fatsia.* It grows upward to about eye level; then the main stem usually falls over and starts growing upward again. Because of this, regular pruning is necessary to maintain a shrubby form. This plant is used in much the same way as *Fatsia* but is even more popular as a subject for espalier training. The handsome, lustrous, evergreen leaves are about two thirds the size of those of *Fatsia,* with only five lobes. The flowers are interesting but mostly sterile. The useful range corresponds with that of *Fatsia* but may be extended into Zone 7a with sufficient protection. The selection 'Variegata' has white variegated leaves.

Feijoa sellowiana 6

Pineapple guava
Evergreen shrub or small tree
Myrtaceae (Myrtle Family)

Native Range. Central South America.

Useful Range. USDA Zones 8a–9a+. Needs a protected site in Zone 8 and functions in size group 4 or 5 there.

Function. Screen, hedge, specimen.

Size and Habit

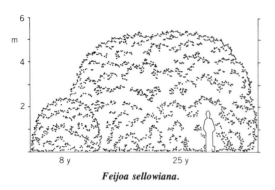

Feijoa sellowiana.

Adaptability

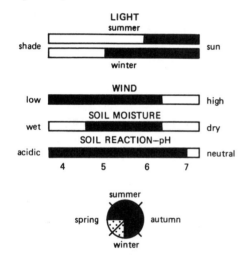

Seasonal Interest. *Flowers:* Whitish with deep red stamens, to 3.5 cm/1.4 in. across, numerous in small clusters in spring and continuing into early summer. *Foliage:* Small, evergreen leaves, to 7 cm/2.8 in. long, green above, white and downy underneath, giving a blue-green, fine-textured effect in the landscape. *Fruits:* Greenish, red tinged when ripe, about the same size as leaves, edible and popular for jellies. Produced in milder climates in its useful range and normally requires cross-pollination. A few commercial cultivars apparently do not require pollination by another clone.

Feijoa sellowiana.

Problems and Maintenance. This shrub is relatively trouble-free, requiring occasional pruning to maintain form and vigor.

Cultivars. Several selections for good fruiting have been made, but they are not readily available, and apparently selections have not been made primarily for landscape character.

Ficus pumila 1

Creeping or climbing fig
Evergreen vine
Moraceae (Mulberry Family)

Native Range. Southeastern Asia.

Useful Range. USDA Zones 8b–9a+.

Function. Wall cover, creeping vine covering the surface of any object it encounters, holding by aerial rootlets to form a solid, flat mat of leaves, and climbing to heights of 5–15 m/16–49 ft, depending on support and climate. Use only on southern exposures in Zone 8b.

Size and Habit

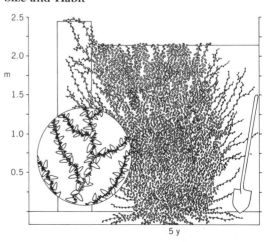

Ficus pumila.

Adaptability

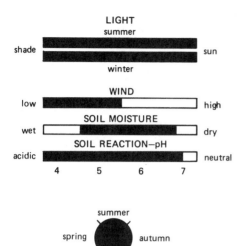

Seasonal Interest. *Foliage:* Evergreen leaves are a rich dark green, relatively small (to 2.5 cm/1 in. long) on juvenile (creeping) growth, larger on fruiting branches, which grow outward from the support, increasing the thickness of the vine cover from less than 2 cm/0.8 in. (juvenile) to 50 cm/16 in. (mature). *Fruits:* Light green, neither ornamental nor edible, in fact unattractive.

Problems and Maintenance. Fruiting branches with their coarse foliage detract from the appearance of the plant on masonry walls, so prune heavily every two or three years to delay maturity and cut out fruiting branches as they appear if a uniformly fine-textured cover is desired. This vine will damage wood or painted surfaces if allowed to cling to them.

Cultivars. 'Minima' has smaller leaves and slower growth. 'Variegata' has white variegated foliage.

Related Species. Many species of *Ficus* grow from Zone 9 into the tropics but fall outside the scope of this book.

Ficus carica 5—6 (common fig). This species is the hardiest of all figs, growing as a tree in Zones 8b—9a+ and as a shrub controlled by winter killback in Zones 6b—8a. Its distinctively coarse foliage and branching give it a unique appearance but leaf and fruit litter and winter killback (in colder zones) make it an untidy plant. The edible fruits often are the primary reason for

Ficus carica.

Ficus carica.

growing *F. carica*, with the landscape value considered in addition. This species performs best in full sun and tolerates dry soil.

Firmiana simplex 6—7

Synonyms: *F. platanifolia*, *Sterculia platanifolia*
Chinese parasol tree, phoenix tree, Japanese
varnish tree
Deciduous tree
Sterculiaceae (Sterculia Family)

Native Range. China and Japan.

Useful Range. USDA Zones 7b—9a+, but marginally functional in Zone 7b and 8a.

Function. Shade tree for quick effect. Reaches full size, to 15 m/49 ft, only in Zone 9a+, but will function as a small tree, irregular in size because of periodic winter killback, in Zones 7b—8b. Reaches functional size rapidly.

Seasonal Interest. *Flowers:* Small, white, in showy upright clusters, sometimes to 50 cm/20 in. long, in midsummer. *Foliage:* Very large leaves, to 30 cm/1 ft across, palmately lobed, reminiscent of those of *Platanus orientalis*, rusty pubescent as they emerge and begin to expand, turning bright yellow in autumn. Relatively few leaves are needed to provide dense shade. *Fruits:* Unusual greenish capsules turn brown and open when ripe. Small black seeds are borne on edges of capsule segments. Interesting but not showy. *Trunk and branches:* Smooth, lustrous, green bark adds interest at all seasons. Branches are arranged in accentuated whorls.

Size and Habit

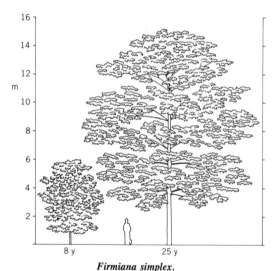

Firmiana simplex.

Adaptability. This tree is at its best in full sun and fairly moist soil, but out of strong wind, which can damage the foliage.

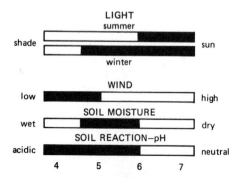

Firmiana simplex.

Firmiana simplex.

Problems and Maintenance. This tree is unusually free of pest problems. Pruning is necessary only to remove winterkilled parts and occasionally for rejuvenation. Otherwise it is trouble-free and easy to grow.

Fontanesia fortunei 5

Fortune fontanesia
Deciduous shrub
Oleaceae (Olive Family)

Native Range. China.

Useful Range. USDA Zones 5b−8b.

Function. Hedge, screen (with pruning to maintain fullness).

Size and Habit

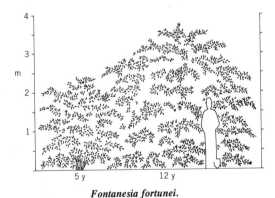

Fontanesia fortunei.

Adaptability

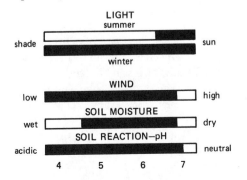

Seasonal Interest. *Flowers:* Small, greenish white, not showy. *Foliage:* Bright green, similar in general effect to that of deciduous *Ligustrum* species, falling early in autumn with little color change.

Problems and Maintenance. This shrub is relatively trouble-free and needs little maintenance other than annual pruning to maintain fullness for screening. Since there are many equally good and more colorful shrubs for this purpose, this cannot be considered a high priority landscape plant except in difficult situations where its broad adaptability serves it well.

Related Species

Fontanesia phillyreoides 5. This deciduous shrub from Asia Minor is more dense and compact than *F. fortunei* but much less cold-hardy, useful only in Zones 7b−9a+ and not valued highly in that region, since there are so many better alternatives.

Forestiera acuminata 5−6 (swamp privet). This deciduous shrub, also in the Olive Family, is native to the southeastern United States but is seldom available for planting except in sites where it can be transplanted from the wild. Its flowers have no petals, so are inconspicuous when they appear in early spring, and the plant has little seasonal interest other than the deep purple, olivelike fruits on female plants. Useful as a neutral border shrub or for naturalizing on moist to wet soils in Zones 6b−9a.

Forsythia ×intermedia 5

Showy border forsythia
Deciduous shrub
Oleaceae (Olive Family)

Hybrid origin. *F. suspensa* × *F. viridissima*.

Useful Range. USDA Zones 5b–8a, and will grow successfully in Zones 4b and 5a, but the flower buds are usually winterkilled there, so flowering occurs only after very mild winters or below the snow line.

Function. Specimen, border, screen.

Size and Habit

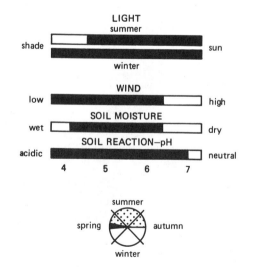

Forsythia ×intermedia.

Adaptability

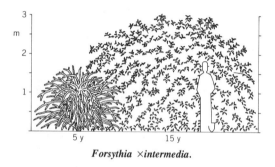

Seasonal Interest. *Flowers:* Brilliant yellow, before the foliage in early to middle spring, very showy. *Foliage:* Rich green, lustrous leaves per-

sist well into autumn with little color change, sometimes turning yellow or purplish before falling.

Problems and Maintenance. This shrub is relatively trouble-free except for the killing of flower buds in severe winters. Flowers are initiated during the summer before bloom and so must survive winter to open in spring. Flower buds unprotected by snow are usually killed at temperatures of about −25° to −27°C/−13° to −17°F. Pruning is needed for renewal every few years.

Cultivars. 'Arnold Dwarf,' actually a hybrid between *F. ×intermedia* and *F. japonica*, remains below 1 m/3.3 ft for several years and makes a good, large-scale groundcover in Zones 5a–8a. Unfortunately it is sparse-flowering.

'Beatrix Farrand' has large, deep yellow flowers that make a strong display, but less so than if they were more erect on the flowering stems. The plant is stiff and coarse.

'Karl Sax' is a polyploid with numerous large flowers, slightly more hardy in bud than those of 'Beatrix Farrand.'

'Lynwood' (= 'Lynwood Gold') is one of the most showy cultivars with bright yellow flowers somewhat smaller than the above two cultivars but held well erect and wide open.

'Spectabilis' was one of the earliest selections of *F. ×intermedia*, from which several other cultivars have been derived. It is still one of the most showy and satisfactory.

'Spring Glory' has lighter yellow flowers than the above cultivars but is equally showy.

Related Species

Forsythia suspensa 4–5 (weeping forsythia). This Chinese shrub, long cultivated in Japan, varies in height from about 1.5 m/5 ft in the strongly pendulous form, to more than 2 m/6.6 ft in the upright var. *fortunei*, which differs little from *F. ×intermedia*. The flowers are also very similar in general effect and in hardiness to those of *F. ×intermedia* cultivars. The typical weeping form, sometimes called var. *sieboldii*, gives a strikingly different landscape effect, especially when it is planted at the tops of banks and walls,

Forsythia suspensa.

Forsythia suspensa.

where its long branches can trail for some distance. The selection 'Aurea' has yellowish foliage in early summer but is not one of the best yellow-leaved shrubs. *F. suspensa* is generally useful in Zones 5b−8a, flowering in the majority of years.

Forsythia viridissima 5 (greenstem forsythia). This Chinese species differs from *F. ×intermedia* in that it is less showy in flower and has greenish stems of some interest in winter. It is about equal in hardiness to the hybrid. The variety *koreana*, from Korea, is more showy and may hold some promise for colder climates but has not been tested thoroughly and is not widely available. The dwarf selection 'Bronxensis' remains below 0.5 m/1.6 ft in height for several years, bears

Forsythia viridissima 'Bronxensis.'

fair quantities of pale yellow flowers, and has excellent summer foliage texture, making an effective groundcover.

Forsythia ovata 4

Early forsythia
Deciduous shrub
Oleaceae (Olive Family)

Native Range. Korea.

Useful Range. USDA Zones 5a–7a, and will grow in Zone 4, but the flower buds usually are winterkilled there, so flowering occurs only after very mild winters or below the snow line.

Function. Specimen, border.

Size and Habit

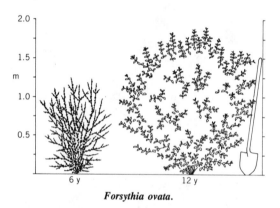

Forsythia ovata.

Adaptability

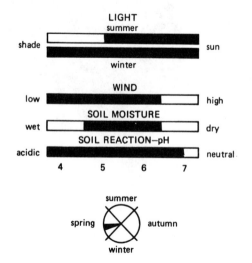

Seasonal Interest. *Flowers:* Light yellow, about half the size of those of *F.* ×*intermedia*, and somewhat earlier, displayed on stiffly upright

branches. *Foliage:* Dull green, less handsome than that of *F.* ×*intermedia*.

Problems and Maintenance. This shrub is relatively trouble-free except for the killing of flower buds in extreme winters. Flower buds are slightly more cold-hardy than those of *F.* ×*intermedia*, killing at about −28° to −30°C/−18° to −22°F. Occasional pruning is needed to maintain good form and should be done soon after flowering.

Cultivars. In Zones 4 and 5 there is considerable interest in developing *Forsythia* cultivars with hardier flower buds, and evaluation of selections of *F. ovata*, related species, and at least one hybrid, is underway.

F. ovata 'Ottawa' is rapidly becoming popular for its excellent, round, compact growth habit, far better than average for the species. Its flowers are similar to those of most other plants of *F. ovata*.

Hybrids of *F. ovata* × *F. europaea* have been obtained on at least two occasions. The selection 'Northern Gold,' originating as a hybrid between these two species in Ottawa, has shown considerable promise in Canada, and an as-yet-unnamed selection from a cross made at the Arnold Arboretum is showing great promise in early trials in the north-central states. These may prove usefully hardy in all or part of Zone 4.

Related Species

Forsythia europaea 5 (Albanian forsythia). This little-known shrub has relatively hardy flower buds and deep yellow flowers that do not open fully enough to give a display comparable with the showier species. It is seldom if ever used except as a parent in breeding for winter-hardy cultivars.

Forsythia giraldiana 5 (Giraldi forsythia). This native of northern China is seldom encountered but has been available commercially in the past. Like *F. europaea* and *F. ovata*, it has relatively cold-hardy flower buds, so it may be of interest in colder regions.

Forsythia mandshurica 4 (Manchurian forsythia). This species seems to have unusually cold-hardy flower buds, making it of interest in some of the coldest parts of our area. The selection 'Vermont Sun,' recently introduced by the University of Vermont, has flowers similar in color to those of *F. ovata* but larger and slightly earlier, and unusually large leaves. *F. mandshurica* has been under observation in Canada for several years and is useful in Zones 5a–7a and probably also in at least parts of Zone 4.

Abeliophyllum distichum 4 (Korean abelialeaf). This close relative of *Forsythia*, sometimes called white forsythia, has fragrant flowers, white or pink tinged in some years, smaller than those of *F. ovata*, about 1.5 cm/0.6 in. across, but otherwise similar, opening in early spring with or ahead of those of *F. ovata*. Its foliage is lustrous and dark green, turning purplish before falling in middle to late autumn. Under ideal conditions it remains full at the base, functioning as a low-

Abeliophyllum distichum.

maintenance facing shrub or foundation plant in Zones 4b–7b, but this does not always hold true, and flowering is uncertain in Zones 4b to 5b because of killing of flower buds in some winters.

Fothergilla major 5

Large fothergilla or witch-alder
Deciduous shrub
Hamamelidaceae (Witch Hazel Family)

Native Range. Northern Alabama and Georgia, southwestern North Carolina.

Useful Range. USDA Zones 5b–9a.

Function. Specimen, border, naturalizing.

Size and Habit

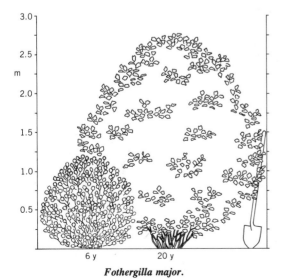

Fothergilla major.

Adaptability

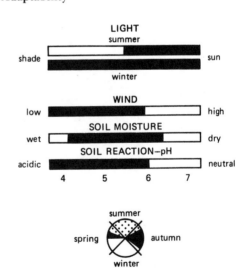

Seasonal Interest. *Flowers:* Fragrant, creamy white, in terminal, bottlebrushlike clusters to 6 cm/2.4 in. long, flowering with the new foliage in middle spring at the same time as *Cercis canadensis. Foliage:* Leaves resemble those of witch hazel, but are somewhat smaller, turning bright yellow in autumn, some overlaid with scarlet.

Problems and Maintenance. This is one of the most trouble-free of flowering shrubs, seldom needing pruning except perhaps to rejuvenate very old plants.

Related Species

Fothergilla gardenii 3 (dwarf fothergilla).   This shrub is native from Virginia to Georgia and smaller than *F. major* in all respects. It seldom exceeds a height of 1 m/3.3 ft and bears flower clusters no more than 3 cm/1.2 in. long, which appear before the foliage a little earlier than those of *F. major*. It is useful for small-scale plantings in the same zones and sites as *F. major*.

Fothergilla monticola 4 (Alabama fothergilla). This shrub, native from North Carolina to Alabama, differs from *F. major* only in being slightly lower and wider-spreading in habit and having less pubescent foliage. Some botanists currently include this in *F. major* rather than consider it a separate species. Since the two are somewhat confused in nursery practice, lumping them may solve the nomenclatural problem, but some distinction still needs to be made between upright and wide-spreading forms.

Fothergilla gardenii.

Fothergilla parviflora 3 (creeping fothergilla or witch-alder).   This low shrub (to 0.5 m/1.6 ft), native from North Carolina to Florida, forms large clumps by underground stems on sandy soil and probably is useful in Zones 7a−9a+. It is seldom available commercially but can be preserved in its native habitat.

Franklinia alatamaha 6

Synonym: *Gordonia alatamaha*
Franklinia, Franklin tree
Deciduous shrub or small tree
Theaceae (Tea Family)

Native Range. Originally found growing wild in southeastern Georgia by John Bartram, one of the earliest plant collectors and nurserymen in North America. He transplanted it to his Philadelphia nursery and sent plants to England. Named in honor of Benjamin Franklin, this plant was seen in the wild for the last time in 1790 and has been preserved through cultivation.

Useful Range. USDA Zones 6b−7b. It does not perform very well in Zones 8 and 9, even though those zones include its last known native habitat.

Function. Specimen, border.

Size and Habit

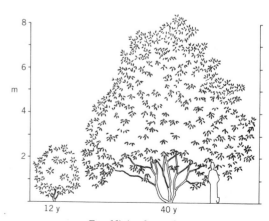

Franklinia alatamaha.

Adaptability

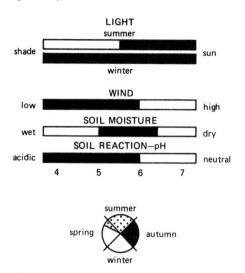

Seasonal Interest. *Flowers:* Large, showy, white with yellow centers, resembling single white *Camellia japonica* flowers, in late summer and autumn until frost. *Foliage:* Lustrous, dark green leaves turn wine-red in autumn, making a fine background in both green and red phases for the white flowers. *Trunk and branches:* Dark and light gray striped bark adds interest.

Franklinia alatamaha.

Franklinia alatamaha.

Problems and Maintenance. The most serious problem of *Franklinia* is a vascular wilt disease. The best means of protection is to plant in soil where the disease has not been active or in fumigated soil and to provide acidic, highly organic, perfectly drained soil. The plant has been difficult to establish in some areas, perhaps because of the disease problem. In any case, it probably is best reserved for situations where its distinctive landscape interest is particularly desired and where good maintenance can be carried out.

Related Species

Gordonia lasianthus 7 (Loblolly bay gordonia). The name *Gordonia*, sometimes erroneously used in referring to *Franklinia*, is correctly applied to this plant. A handsome evergreen tree, or shrub in very poor soil, it is native to the Coastal Plain of the southeastern United States but is seldom used in landscaping. With its large (to 6 cm/2.4 in. across), fragrant, white flowers in summer, its tolerance of moist to swampy soils, and its dense mass of leathery leaves (to 15 cm/6 in. long), it appears to be an overlooked plant useful for screening in Zones 8a−9a+ and for a patio tree in Zones 8b−9a+. Limited experience suggests that it is rather difficult to transplant and slow in establishment, but the evidence for this is not complete.

Fraxinus americana 8

White ash
Deciduous tree
Oleaceae (Olive Family)

Native Range. Eastern United States and adjacent Canada.

Useful Range. USDA Zones 4a–9a, with selection of appropriate genetic material.

Function. Shade, street tree.

Size and Habit

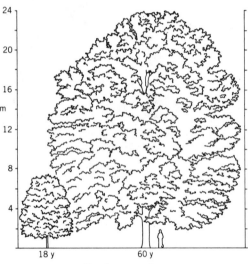

Fraxinus americana.

Adaptability. This tree is widely adapted to different soils and environments provided full sun is available.

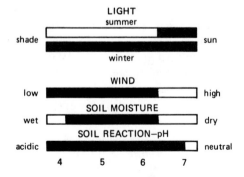

Seasonal Interest. *Foliage:* Dark green in summer, turning yellowish in autumn with a deep or rosy purple overlay, at an early stage appearing hazy gray-purple.

Problems and Maintenance. The litter and weed potential of fruiting trees is the greatest problem of most ashes. Fortunately, nonfruiting cultivars exist. *F. americana* is somewhat prone to storm damage, yet is a good combination of fast growth with reasonable durability.

Cultivars. 'Autumn Purple' is a nonfruiting selection with outstanding fall foliage color found in Wisconsin and cold-hardy as far north as Zone 5a. It is fast growing and seems to be an excellent selection for northern landscapes. 'Rosehill' (Plant Patent No. 2678, 1966) is another nonfruiting selection, a little slower growing in northern areas than 'Autumn Purple' and less cold-hardy in early tests. If that should prove to be the case, it may be better adapted in the southern parts of the useful range. For Zones 8 and 9, however, selections from the Deep South probably would hold more promise than either of the above cultivars.

Related Species

Fraxinus biltmoreana 7 (Biltmore ash). This species is sometimes included in *F. americana* and is similar except not as large, to 15 m/49 ft tall, and with pubescent foliage. It is native from New Jersey to Alabama and worth preserving in development there but seldom available for planting.

Fraxinus profunda 8 (synonym: *F. tomentosa*; pumpkin ash). This species is also similar to *F. americana* but with larger leaves (to 25 cm/10 in.). It is native in a spotty range from western New York to Illinois and south to Louisiana and northern Florida. It is seldom if ever available for planting but worth preserving when possible.

Fraxinus texensis 7 (Texas ash). This native of Texas is sometimes planted near its native range in the extreme southwestern part of our area. With good yellow autumn foliage color, it is useful at least in Zones 7b–9a.

Fraxinus excelsior 8

European ash
Deciduous tree
Oleaceae (Olive Family)

Native Range. Europe and Asia Minor.

Useful Range. USDA Zones 4b–8b. Insect problems preclude very wide use in Zones 6b–8b.

Function. Shade, street tree.

Size and Habit

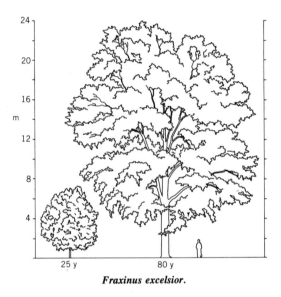

Fraxinus excelsior.

Seasonal Interest. The species type has little seasonal interest other than its dark green foliage that does not change color in autumn. Some selections have better foliage and twig color (see Cultivars).

Problems and Maintenance. The most serious problem of this tree is borers, which can kill a tree within a few years if they are not controlled. Scale insects also can be troublesome but can be controlled without difficulty in the North.

Cultivars. 'Aurea' has yellow twigs, showy in winter. 'Hessei' has simple, dark green, and lustrous leaves, and is more resistant to borers than the species type. 'Pendula' has strongly weeping branches but is not graceful compared with some other weeping trees. It is primarily a curiosity and seldom seen.

Related Species

Fraxinus holotricha 7. This tree from the Balkans is noteworthy only for the cultivar 'Moraine,' which bears very few fruits and is relatively low in stature. In many areas it is seriously affected by borers.

Adaptability

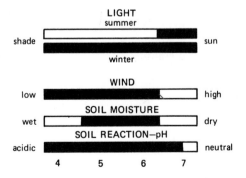

Fraxinus ornus 7

Flowering ash
Deciduous tree
Oleaceae (Olive Family)

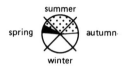

Native Range. Southern Europe and adjacent Asia.

Useful Range. USDA Zones 6a–8b. Some trees are hardy in Zone 5b. Usefulness in the Deep South is not well known.

Function. Shade, street tree.

Size and Habit

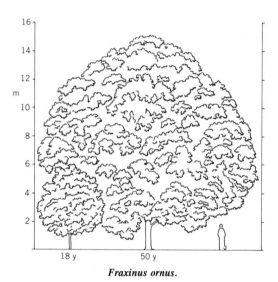

Fraxinus ornus.

Adaptability

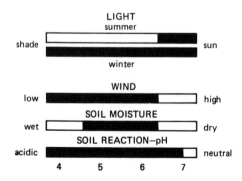

Seasonal Interest. *Flowers:* Fragrant, white, small, in dense clusters to 12 cm/5 in. long. Showy, unlike those of most ashes, in late spring. *Foliage:* Rich green leaves make a dense canopy and remain green or yellowish until they fall in autumn.

Problems and Maintenance. A popular street tree in Europe for years, *F. ornus* has not been used widely enough in eastern North America to be fully evaluated here. When it has been tried more widely, its susceptibility to scale and borers will be better known.

Related Species

Fraxinus bungeana 6 (Bunge ash). This very small, shrubby tree from northern China, to 4–5 m/13–16 ft tall, is rare and probably not in landscape use in our area. With flowering similar to that of *F. ornus* and small in stature, it might be a useful tree for small-scale situations in Zones 5a–8b, perhaps also Zone 4.

Fraxinus cuspidata 6 (Mexican ash). Another small, shrubby tree with showy, fragrant flowers, this species is native to Mexico, southern Arizona, New Mexico, and Texas and is useful in Zones 8b–9a+, perhaps also Zone 8a.

Fraxinus mariesii 6 (Maries ash). Yet another small, shrubby tree with flowering interest similar to *F. ornus* and its relatives, this Chinese species has an added summer attraction in its purplish fruits and is useful in Zones 8a–9a, perhaps also Zone 7.

Fraxinus pennsylvanica 8

Green or red ash
Deciduous tree
Oleaceae (Olive Family)

Native Range. Eastern United States and adjacent Canada and northern Great Plains.

Useful Range. USDA Zones 2a−9a with selection of appropriate genetic material.

Function. Shade, street tree.

Size and Habit

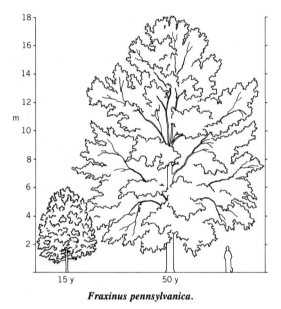

Fraxinus pennsylvanica.

Adaptability. This tree is one of the most widely occurring in the wild and most adaptable in landscape use in North America. It is especially useful in the Great Plains of the United States and Canada, where tolerance of climatic extremes determines success.

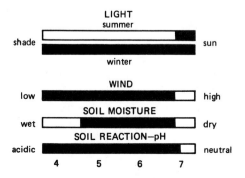

Seasonal Interest. *Foliage:* Medium to dark green in summer, turning clear yellow in autumn, falling rather early.

Problems and Maintenance. As with *F. americana*, fruit litter and weed seedlings are the principal problems of this tree. Fortunately, nonfruiting cultivars are available (see Cultivars). Both *F. americana* and *F. pennsylvanica* are far less troubled by borers than some of the European species.

Cultivars. There is considerable interest in nonfruiting selections of *F. pennsylvanica*.

'Marshall's Seedless,' the first selection made, has been tested widely and is common in landscape use. It has unusually dark green, glossy foliage and good form and growth rate, but its most important feature is its nonfruiting character. It is useful in Zones 3b−8b and perhaps in 9a as well.

'Summit' has finer textured foliage and is more upright in form than the species type.

Related Species

Fraxinus caroliniana 7 (water ash). This rather small tree, native from Virginia and Florida westward to Texas, is tolerant of wet soil and potentially useful in Zones 8a−9a+, but it probably is not commercially available.

Fraxinus velutina 7 (velvet ash). This small tree, native to the southwestern United States and Mexico, is best known for the var. *glabra* (Modesto ash), a useful, small, shade or street tree for the dry and alkaline soils of the south-central United States and other areas in Zones 6a−9a+, but it is troubled by borers and other insects and requires a spray program.

Fraxinus quadrangulata 8

Blue ash
Deciduous tree
Oleaceae (Olive Family)

Native Range. Central United States, Michigan to Arkansas and Tennessee.

Useful Range. USDA Zones 4a–8a, perhaps also Zones 8b and 9a.

Function. Shade, street tree.

Size and Habit. This tree is very high-branching, making it a good avenue tree.

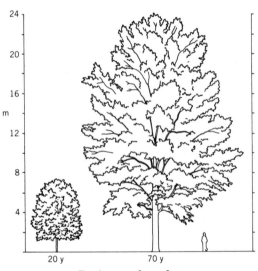

Fraxinus quadrangulata.

Adaptability. This tree is widely adapted in the central United States but not as tolerant of dry sites as *F. pennsylvanica*.

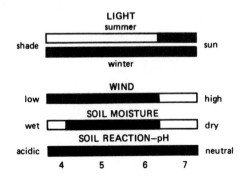

Seasonal Interest. *Foliage:* Dark green in summer, turning pale yellow or yellow-bronze in autumn. *Twigs:* four-angled in cross section, sometimes slightly winged, adding minor winter interest. *Trunks and branches:* Inner bark is light orange-brown, sometimes adding winter interest.

Fraxinus quadrangulata.

Problems and Maintenance. Nonfruiting cultivars are not yet available and probably will not be in the future since this tree is not dioecious, but the numbers of fruit set are not as great as those of *F. americana* or *F. pennsylvanica*. The extent of pest problems is not yet well known.

Cultivars. 'Urbana' is a large, high-branching selection with distinctly orange-brown inner bark, probably not yet available commercially.

Related Species

Fraxinus nigra 8 (black ash).   This large tree, native from Newfoundland to Manitoba and southward to West Virginia and Arkansas, grows wild in wet places. Its ability to grow in poorly drained soils and its hardiness make it potentially useful in Zones 3a–6b with selection of appropriate genetic material, but it is presently little used and perhaps not commercially available.

Fuchsia magellanica 3—4

Magellan fuchsia
Semievergreen subshrub
Onagraceae (Evening Primrose Family)

Native Range. Peru to southern Chile.

Useful Range. USDA Zones 7a—9a. A few cultivars may be hardy in Zone 6 in protected sites. Can be grown only in areas with relatively cool summers such as coastal and mountain areas.

Function. Specimen, border.

Size and Habit

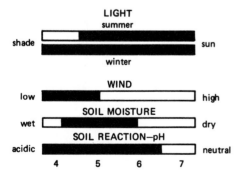

Fuchsia magellanica.

Adaptability

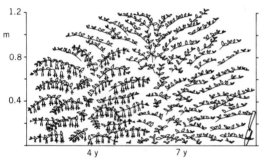

Seasonal Interest. *Flowers:* Red and purple-pink or violet, pendulous in clusters resembling small hanging lanterns, and very showy. *Foliage:* Handsome and lustrous, marked with red or purple in some cultivars.

Problems and Maintenance. The top of this plant kills back to the ground in winter and should be cut off in spring before new growth starts. Since a flowering plant must be formed in only a few weeks, attention to soil fertility and moisture is crucial. Mounding with mulch material around the crown is usually recommended for winter protection.

Cultivars. Several cultivars exist, varying in habit and flower color and size. Availability is haphazard at best in eastern North America, and it is best to seek local advice on cultivars for specific areas or to stay with the species type.

Related Species. Many other species of *Fuchsia* exist, but *F. magellanica* is the only one adapted to our area. A considerable number of cultivars of *F. ×hybrida*, hybrids probably involving *F. magellanica* as a parent, are useful in Zone 9a+ and subtropical areas on the West Coast, but they are seldom practical in our area except when used as annual plants.

Galax urceolata 2

Synonym: G. *aphylla*
Galax
Evergreen, herbaceous groundcover
Diapensiaceae (Diapensia Family)

Native Range. Southern Appalachian Mountains: Virginia to Georgia.

Useful Range. USDA Zones 5a−8b in cool, moist sites, and perhaps colder zones where snow cover is reliable.

Function. Naturalizing, small-scale groundcover (does not spread rapidly).

Size and Habit

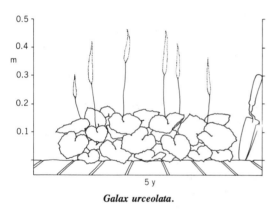

Galax urceolata.

Adaptability. Requires essentially full shade in summer, and at least light shade in winter helps to keep the foliage in good condition.

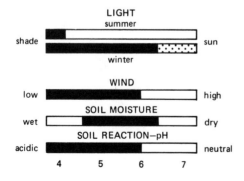

Seasonal Interest. *Flowers:* Small, white, in vertical, taperlike clusters, 50 cm/20 in. or more long, in early summer. *Foliage:* Evergreen, lustrous leaves to 12 cm/5 in. across, heart-shaped to rounded and slightly cupped, providing unusual texture, medium green in full shade, turning reddish bronze in direct sun and in autumn.

Problems and Maintenance. Once established, galax is trouble-free and requires no maintenance except for removal of competing weeds. But establishment can be difficult and should not be attempted if the site requirements cannot be satisfied.

Related Species

Shortia galacifolia 2 (Oconee bells).   This close relative of galax has a very limited natural habitat within the same range. Its foliage is similar to that of galax but its white flowers in spring are much larger, to 2.5 cm/1 in. across, borne singly on vertical stalks. This plant is even less vigorous than galax and useful only in very small-scale situations in cool, moist locations in Zones 5a−8b.

Galium odoratum 2

Synonym: *Asperula odorata*
Sweet woodruff
Herbaceous groundcover
Rubiaceae (Madder Family)

Native Range. Europe, Asia, and northern Africa.

Useful Range. USDA Zones 5a−9a+.

Function. Groundcover.

Size and Habit

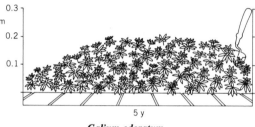

Galium odoratum.

Adaptability. This is one of the few groundcovers that will tolerate full shade and dry soil simultaneously.

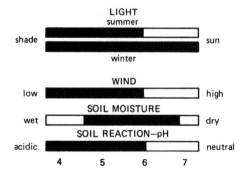

Seasonal Interest. *Flowers:* White, only 0.5 cm/0.2 in. across, but daintily attractive against the rich green foliage in late spring. *Foliage:* Narrow leaves, 2.5 cm/1 in. long, are borne in whorls of six to eight on sticky, angular stems, rich green and fragrant, providing a dense, fine-textured mass until the tops die down in autumn.

Galium odoratum.

Problems and Maintenance. This groundcover is trouble-free once established, needing only weeding or sometimes to be weeded out itself to control its spread.

Related Species. Several other species of *Galium* (bedstraw) have been introduced to our area from Europe and are potential groundcovers, but most are more coarse and weedy than *G. odoratum*. *G. verum* (yellow bedstraw) is especially well adapted to dry soils but is very weedy, escaping cultivation in many areas.

Gardenia jasminoides 4

Gardenia, Cape jasmine
Evergreen shrub
Rubiaceae (Madder Family)

Native Range. China.

Useful Range. USDA Zones 8b−9a+.

Function. Specimen, massing, border, cutting.

Size and Habit

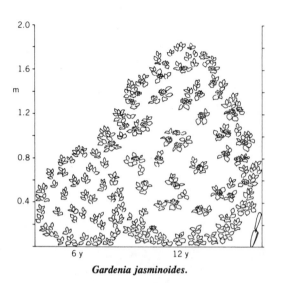

Gardenia jasminoides.

Adaptability. Grows and flowers better with light shade than in full sun in areas with hot summers.

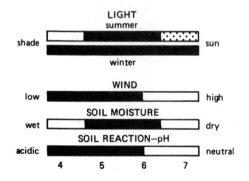

Seasonal Interest. *Flowers:* Highly fragrant, waxy appearing, white, often double, 5−8 cm/2−3 in. across, in early summer and intermittently later in the summer. *Foliage:* Evergreen, leathery, glossy, and distinctive, with wavy margins and impressed veins.

Problems and Maintenance. Use of this plant in southern landscapes has declined because of insect and nematode problems. Plants grafted on nematode-resistant rootstocks, or at least plants free of nematodes, should be used if available. In areas known or suspected to be nematode-infested it is essential to fumigate the soil in which gardenias are to be planted. A regular spray program will also be needed to control white fly and the resulting sooty mold as well as occasional scale and mealybug infestations.

Varieties and Cultivars. Var. *fortuniana* has unusually large, double flowers, well filled with petals in the center. 'Radicans,' called dwarf gardenia, grows no taller than 1 m/3.3 ft, usually remains at about 0.5 m/1.6 ft, and is considered a choice small shrub for Zone 9a+. Maintenance requirements are similar to those of the species type.

Gaultheria procumbens 2

Checkerberry, wintergreen
Evergreen groundcover
Ericaceae (Heath Family)

Native Range. Northern United States and adjacent Canada, northeasterly to Newfoundland, southerly to northern Georgia.

Useful Range. USDA Zones 3a−7a.

Function. Groundcover (small-scale), naturalizing.

Size and Habit

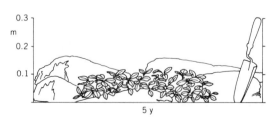

Gaultheria procumbens.

Adaptability

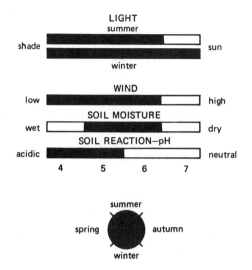

LIGHT
summer

shade ▮▮▮▮▮▮▮▮▮▮▮▮▮▮▮▮▮▮□ sun

winter

WIND

low ▮▮▮▮▮▮▮▮▮▮▮▮▮▮▮□ high

SOIL MOISTURE

wet □▮▮▮▮▮▮▮▮▮▮□ dry

SOIL REACTION–pH

acidic ▮▮▮▮▮▮▮□ neutral

    4   5   6   7

summer

spring ● autumn

winter

Seasonal Interest. *Flowers:* Small (to 0.7 cm/0.3 in.), white, bell-shaped, in late spring, partly hidden by foliage. *Foliage:* Evergreen, 2–4 cm/ 0.8–1.6 in. long, lustrous and bright green, aromatic (wintergreen flavor). *Fruits:* Small (to 1.0 cm/0.4 in.), bright red, aromatic when crushed, colorful from late summer throughout the winter.

Problems and Maintenance. Establishment is the only problem, and that is not difficult in woodland sites similar to its native habitat. Use pot-grown plants or sods and give especial attention to soil drainage.

Related Species

Gaultheria hispidula 2 (synonym: *Chiogenes hispidula*; creeping snowberry, maidenhair berry). This creeping plant, native to much of northern North America, has evergreen leaves less than half as large as those of *G. procumbens*, smaller flowers, and snow-white berries to 0.7 cm/0.3 in., adding interest in late summer and autumn. Useful only as a rock garden plant in partial shade in areas having cool summers in Zones 4a–6b.

Gaultheria shallon 3 (shallon or salal). This tall groundcover occasionally reaches heights of 1.5 m/5 ft or greater in native stands in the Pacific Northwest, has handsome evergreen foliage with leaves 5–12 cm/2–5 in. long, white or pink, bell-shaped flowers in late spring, and purple-black berries in autumn. In the past it has been

largely restricted to landscapes in its native region, but it is being tried increasingly in the milder climates of the East in Zones 7 and 8. It grows well in full sun or shade in its native habitat but needs some protection from full sun in the Southeast. It should be considered experimental in eastern North America.

Gaultheria shallon.

Mitchella repens 2 (partridgeberry, squawberry). This trailing, hardy, herbaceous plant grows wild over much of eastern North America from Nova Scotia and Minnesota to Florida and Texas, even into eastern Mexico. It is not an assertive groundcover and will not persist in full sun, but in a naturalized, partially shaded woodland setting it adds small-scale interest with its small (1–2 cm/0.4–0.8 in.), dark green, white-marked, evergreen leaves and bright red fruits (to 0.8 cm/0.3 in.), which persist all winter or until eaten by wildlife. Even though it belongs to the Rubiaceae (Madder Family), its requirements are similar to such members of the Ericaceae as *Gaultheria* and *Pernettya*.

Pernettya mucronata 3 (Chilean pernettya). This low shrub from the southern tip of South America has small (1–2 cm/0.4–0.8 in.), sharply pointed, lustrous evergreen leaves, very small white or pink flowers, and highly showy berries in white, pink, rosy red, or deep purple. For good fruiting, plant more than one cultivar, since cross-pollination seems to be necessary. Although not widely available commercially, this plant is potentially useful in Zones 7b–9a in areas having mild summers, but it should be considered experimental in eastern North America.

Gelsemium sempervirens 1 and 2

Carolina jessamine
Evergreen vine or groundcover
Loganiaceae (Logania Family)

Native Range. Southeastern United States to Central America.

Useful Range. USDA Zones 8a−9a+.

Function. Screen (with support), fence or bank cover, groundcover.

Size and Habit. Climbs by twining to heights of 5−10 m/16−33 ft.

Seasonal Interest. *Flowers:* Fragrant, bright golden-yellow, trumpetlike flowers in masses, early spring to early summer. *Foliage:* Evergreen and lustrous but usually arranged sparsely, turning purplish in winter.

Problems and Maintenance. This vine is free of insect and disease problems. The foliage is arranged rather sparsely on wiry stems, and the plant looks ragged as a groundcover or screen unless pruned back heavily occasionally to promote fullness. Unfortunately, plants and flowers of *Gelsemium* are toxic when ingested. There are reports of children being poisoned by pulling the tubular flowers from the plant and sucking nectar from them. There are some situations where this plant clearly should be avoided, and children should be taught to avoid potentially dangerous plants at an early age.

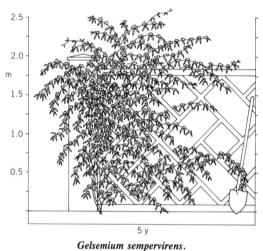

Gelsemium sempervirens.

Adaptability

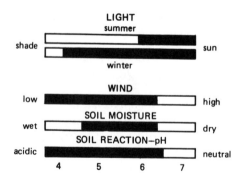

Genista tinctoria 3

Dyer's greenweed, woadwaxen
Deciduous shrub
Leguminosae (Legume Family)

Native Range. Europe, western Asia.

Useful Range. USDA Zones 3a–8a, perhaps somewhat warmer zones as well.

Function. Groundcover (on poor soils), specimen, rock garden.

Size and Habit

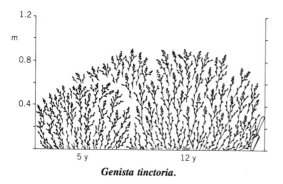

Genista tinctoria.

Adaptability. Especially valuable in poor, dry soils in full sun.

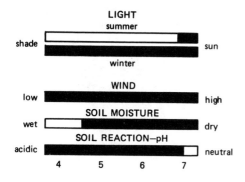

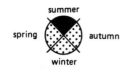

Seasonal Interest. *Flowers:* Bright yellow, pealike in early summer and continuing variably during the remainder of summer. *Foliage:* Narrow, bright green leaves, to 2.5 cm/1 in. long, falling

without color change in autumn. *Twigs and branches:* Green, adding mild winter interest.

Genista tinctoria.

Problems and Maintenance. Relatively trouble-free, this plant requires little maintenance other than cutting back winterkilled stems after severe winters. *Genista* species all have the reputation of being difficult to transplant, so pot-grown plants should be specified.

Cultivars. 'Plena' has showy, double flowers.

Related Species. The following species are not widely available but may be found offered for sale by specialists or rare plant nurseries.

Genista cinerea 3–4 (ashy woadwaxen). This Mediterranean species, with twigs and leaves grayed with silky hairs, is useful in Zones 7b–9a+. In the mildest climates it may approach 2 m/6.6 ft in height. Yellow flowers appear in early summer in upright clusters to 20 cm/8 in. long.

Genista germanica 3 (German woadwaxen). This more-or-less spiny, low species (to 0.5 m/1.6 ft) from central Europe is useful in Zones 5a–7b, but not as showy in flower as *G. tinctoria*, with gray, silky twigs and undersides of leaves.

Genista hispanica 2 (Spanish gorse or broom). This low-growing plant from southwestern Europe is one of the most showy of *Genista* species in bloom, with intensely yellow flowers in early summer. It also has many long, slender, green spines that add winter interest along with the green twigs. Useful in Zones 7a–9a+.

Genista pilosa 2 (silkleaf woadwaxen). This European species, like *G. cinerea* and *G. germanica,* has silky, hairy, and gray-green twigs and leaf undersides, but it is more cold-hardy, more shade-tolerant, and more prostrate in growth than either. Useful in Zones 5b–8b.

Genista sagittalis 3 (winged broom). This low-growing (to 0.5 m/1.6 ft) plant from European and western Asia has few leaves, but broadly winged bright green twigs that give it the appearance of being evergreen and bright yellow flowers like those of *G. tinctoria.* It is useful in Zones 3a–8a, perhaps colder zones as well.

Spartium junceum 5 (Spanish broom). This is a tall shrub from the Mediterranean region and Canary Islands, resembling *Cytisus* and *Genista,* with very small, blue-green leaves and fragrant yellow flowers, to 2.5 cm/1 in. long, from late spring through summer. This plant is very showy in flower, useful in Zones 7b–9a+, and similar in its requirements to *Cytisus* and *Genista* except that it must be pruned more frequently to maintain good form.

Ginkgo biloba 8

Ginkgo, maidenhair tree
Deciduous tree
Ginkgoaceae (Ginkgo Family)

Native Range. Eastern China.

Useful Range. USDA Zones 4b–8b and possibly also warmer zones.

Function. Shade or street tree, specimen.

Size and Habit

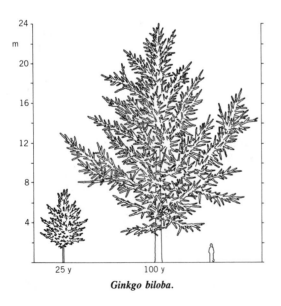

Ginkgo biloba.

Adaptability. Especially well adapted to most city conditions.

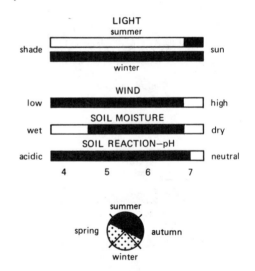

Seasonal Interest. *Foliage*: Distinctive, fan-shaped leaves turn bright yellow in autumn in some years. *Fruits*: Dioecious; the fruits (on female trees) are interesting but pose a serious problem (see Problems and Maintenance). *Twigs and branches*: Spurlike side shoots add textural interest in winter and result in a very sparse and open growth habit that gives the entire tree a distinctive winter aspect.

Problems and Maintenance. This tree is singularly free of insect and disease problems and physically durable. Because of its neat, open branching, it seldom if ever requires pruning

Ginkgo biloba.

Ginkgo biloba 'Fastigiata.'

Ginkgo biloba.

except where too little space is available for normal development. The fallen fruits constitute a serious litter problem and give off an unpleasant odor as they decay if they are not removed promptly.

Cultivars. Because of the fruiting problem, any male tree can be considered superior to any female tree for most sites. Trees propagated by cuttings or grafts from known male parents are sometimes available, and the following male cultivars have other useful characteristics.

'Autumn Gold' is more full in form than typical trees of G. *biloba* and has outstanding, yellow fall foliage. It eventually grows to be a large tree.

'Fastigiata' (sentry ginkgo) has excellent, narrowly pyramidal form. Some trees sold under this name are not the original cultivar, thus not true to name and somewhat variable.

'Lakeview' has a compact, conical form.

'Princeton Sentry' (Plant Patent No. 2726, 1967) is generally similar to true 'Fastigiata' but somewhat narrower, nearly columnar in form.

The interest in selection of cultivars of *Ginkgo* probably will continue, and this list is not intended to be comprehensive.

Gleditsia triacanthos 8

Honey locust
Deciduous tree
Leguminosae (Legume Family)

Native Range. Central United States.

Useful Range. USDA Zones 4b−9a. Certain selections will also succeed in Zone 4a if properly grown (see Problems and Maintenance).

Function. Shade or street tree.

Size and Habit. Var. *inermis* is illustrated.

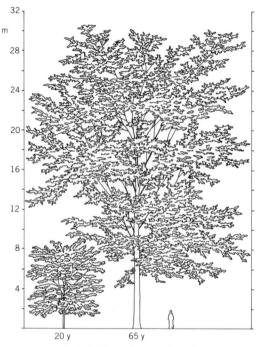

Gleditsia triacanthos var. *inermis*.

Adaptability. This tree is tolerant of most city conditions.

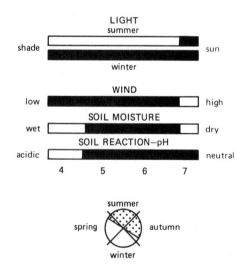

Seasonal Interest. *Foliage:* Bright to deep green, compound to doubly compound, typically with more than 100 small (less than 2.5 cm/1 in. long) leaflets on a single leaf. Leaves turn golden bronze in autumn in some but not all years.

Fruits: Long (to 45 cm/18 in.), leathery, twisted, flat pods, absent from the better selections (see Varieties and Cultivars).

Problems and Maintenance. Unless cultivars are used, the seed pods are a major litter problem, and unless cultivars—or at least var. *inermis*—are used, the huge, branched thorns are a hazard. Once these problems are eliminated by selection of cultivars, the greatest remaining problem is the mimosa webworm, which can damage the foliage severely in some years if not controlled. In spite of their good landscape qualities, *G. triacanthos* and its cultivars have been overused in many areas. At the northern edge of the useful range, winter hardiness can be improved by avoiding cultural practices such as heavy fertilization or late pruning and regular irrigation that promote overly vigorous growth and by maintaining sod over the feeding root system to compete for water and nutrients.

Varieties and Cultivars. Var. *inermis* (thornless honey locust) is thornless but not necessarily nonfruiting. Seeds from this variant generally produce thornless seedlings. The following cultivars are selections from var. *inermis* and are nonfruiting as well as thornless.

'Bujotii' is a gracefully weeping form selected more than a century ago. An interesting specimen, it is limited in functional value and probably is no longer commercially available.

'Imperial' is round-headed with evenly spaced, wide-spreading branches. It is somewhat resistant to webworm infestation, at least in the Midwest.

'Majestic' has a straight trunk and compact, upright growth. Its foliage remains green later in autumn than that of most other cultivars.

'Moraine,' one of the earliest thornless, nonfruiting selections, has a less pronounced central trunk, often growing vertically in a vaguely zigzag pattern. It is graceful and wide-spreading at maturity with some of the character of the American elm yet much different because of the finely textured foliage. It is the most resistant to mimosa webworm of at least the older cultivars.

'Rubylace' has purple foliage in early summer, turning to bronze later. As the foliage emerges it is a delightful lacy mass of red-purple, but it is much less handsome in late summer and autumn. Unfortunately, it does not grow reliably well and has poor form.

'Shademaster' has a strong, straight central trunk and is upright in form and intermediate in resistance to webworm.

'Skyline' develops a strong central leader with well-spaced branches. It is outstanding for its bright gold autumn foliage.

'Sunburst' is a delightful, lacy mass of golden foliage when leaves emerge in early summer. Young foliage at twig tips remains more-or-less yellow during summer, but the mass of foliage usually turns green. Slow growing and rather compact, this cultivar has performed inconsistently in different localities, but it is generally useful in Zones 4b–9a. Unfortunately, it is the most highly susceptible to webworm infestations of all the established cultivars.

Newer cultivars have been introduced and additional ones probably will follow. Such ones as 'Continental,' 'Cottage Green,' 'Emerald Lace' (Plant Patent No. 3260, 1972), 'Green Glory' (Plant Patent No. 2786, 1968), and 'Halka' (Plant Patent No. 3096, 1972) may turn out to be superior forms after enough time has elapsed for thorough trial.

Gymnocladus dioica 8

Kentucky coffee tree
Deciduous tree
Leguminosae (Legume Family)

Native Range. Central United States.

Useful Range. USDA Zones 4a–7b, assuming selection of appropriate genetic material.

Function. Shade tree, specimen.

Size and Habit

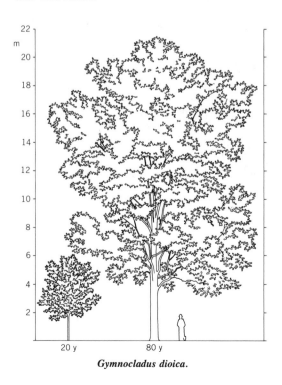

Gymnocladus dioica.

Adaptability

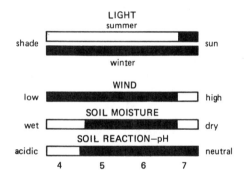

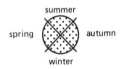

Seasonal Interest. *Foliage:* Dark green, doubly compound, individual leaves to 35 cm/14 in. long and of up to 100 leaflets, much larger (5–8 cm/2–3 in. long) than those of *Gleditsia triacanthos.* Foliage is not attractive in autumn and constitutes a litter problem when it falls. *Fruits:* short (seldom over 15 cm/6 in. long), but thick and broad pods (on female trees only) offer seasonal interest after leaves fall in autumn, posing a litter problem later. The pulp that surrounds the seeds has been reported to be poisonous. *Trunk and branches:* covered with handsomely textured gray bark, the coarse, stubby branches offer an interesting texture in winter.

Problems and Maintenance. This tree is trouble-free, requiring little maintenance other than cleaning up litter in late autumn. Grows slowly the first few years after planting.

Varieties and Cultivars. No named cultivars or varieties are known, but considerable variation exists in this wide-ranging species, and it is probably a good idea to select landscape trees from seedlings grown from local or nearby seed trees.

Halesia carolina 7

Synonym: *H. tetraptera*
Deciduous tree
Carolina silverbell
Styracaceae (Styrax Family)

Native Range. Southeastern United States.

Useful Range. USDA Zones 5a−9a.

Function. Small shade or patio tree, naturalizing.

Size and Habit

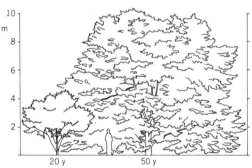

Halesia carolina.

Adaptability

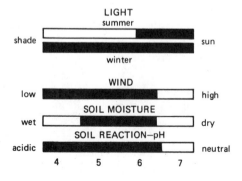

Seasonal Interest. *Flowers:* White, bell-shaped, pendulous, 1−1.5 cm/0.4−0.6 in. long, in clusters of up to five in late spring. *Foliage:* Clean, dark green leaves, turning yellowish in autumn. *Fruits:* Pendulous, four-winged, green, ripening brown, 2−3.5 cm/0.8−1.4 in. long, adding quiet interest in late summer and early autumn. *Trunk and branches:* Smooth with a molded appearance, covered with subtly striped bark, whitish on dark gray.

Halesia carolina.

Problems and Maintenance. Relatively trouble-free, requiring little or no maintenance.

Related Species

Halesia diptera 7 (two-winged silverbell).   The fruits of this species have two instead of four wings, and the tree has the reputation of being somewhat less free-flowering. It is seldom available commercially but worth preserving in its native habitat (southeastern United States) and similar enough to *H. carolina* to be considered interchangeable for landscape use except in Zone 5, where it may not be fully hardy.

Halesia monticola 8 (mountain silverbell).   This is a large tree (to 20 m/66 ft and occasionally taller) with larger flowers and fruits than *H. carolina*. It probably is less tolerant of the climate of the Deep South (useful in Zones 5a—8a), but otherwise similar in requirements to *H. carolina*. The selection 'Rosea' has pale pink flowers.

Halesia monticola.

Hamamelis mollis 6

Chinese witch hazel
Deciduous shrub
Hamamelidaceae (Witch Hazel Family)

Native Range. Central China.

Useful Range. USDA Zones 5b—9a. Best in areas having mild summers in the South.

Function. Specimen, border.

Size and Habit

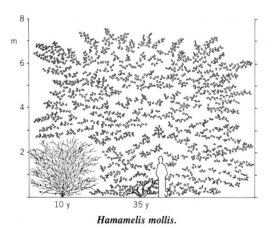

Hamamelis mollis.

Adaptability

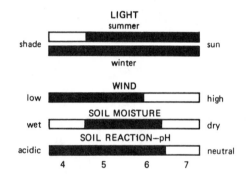

Seasonal Interest. *Flowers:* Fragrant, yellow, with narrow, ribbonlike petals in late winter or very early spring. *Foliage:* Downy, gray-green, turning rich yellow in midautumn. *Fruits:*

Hamamelis mollis.

Interesting but inconspicuous dry capsules opening explosively and discharging seeds for some distance in autumn.

Hamamelis mollis.

Problems and Maintenance. This shrub is relatively trouble-free and requires little or no maintenance other than light selective pruning where space is limited.

Cultivars. 'Brevipetala' is notable for its orange-gold flowers.

Related Species

Hamamelis ×*intermedia* 6 (hybrid witch hazel). This includes all hybrids between *H.*

mollis and *H. japonica.* One of the most showy, 'Arnold Promise,' has bright golden yellow flowers, at least as large as those of *H. mollis*, to 4 cm/1.5 in. across, and reddish yellow fall foliage. It is useful in Zones 5b−9a. Several selections for red or orange flowers, including 'Jelena' and 'Ruby Glow,' have appeared in Europe, but these are seldom available in the United States at present, and their hardiness has not been well established.

Hamamelis japonica 6 (Japanese witch hazel). This species is similar to *H. mollis* except for its smooth foliage, turning reddish in autumn. The selection 'Flavo-purpurascens' bears flowers with petals reddened toward the base and deeply purple tinted inner calyx.

Hamamelis vernalis 5 (vernal witch hazel). This native of the south-central United States flowers at about the same time as the Asian species but has smaller flowers and less reliable autumn foliage color. Its dense growth makes it more useful for screening than most *Hamamelis* species. Few cultivars exist, but 'Rubra' has red-bronze flowers and 'Orange Glow' has orange-bronze flowers.

Hamamelis virginiana 6

Common witch hazel
Deciduous shrub
Hamamelidaceae (Witch Hazel Family)

Native Range. Eastern and central United States.

Useful Range. USDA Zones 4a−9a.

Function. Border, screen, naturalizing.

Size and Habit

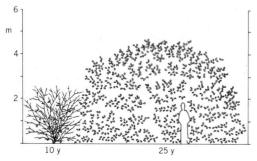

Hamamelis virginiana.

Adaptability. Grows best with at least light shade in the South and Midwest.

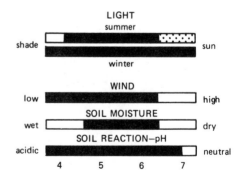

Seasonal Interest. *Flowers:* Yellow, with narrow, ribbonlike petals and light, spicy fragrance, showy in middle to late autumn, especially after leaves have fallen. *Foliage:* Clean, bright green, turning clear yellow in early to midautumn. *Fruits:* Explosive capsules discharge seeds for

some distance in autumn a year after flowering and add mild seasonal interest.

Problems and Maintenance. This plant is relatively trouble-free and requires little or no maintenance.

Forms and Cultivars. F. *rubescens* has reddish petals but is little known. Cultivars have not been developed, but sufficient variation exists to justify selection for form and foliage quality and late flowering, since flowers are largely masked by the leaves until they fall. Hybridization with spring flowering *Hamamelis* species might accomplish this.

Hedera helix 1 and 2

English ivy
Evergreen vine or groundcover
Araliaceae (Aralia Family)

Native Range. Europe, western Asia, North Africa.

Useful Range. USDA Zones 6a−9a+. A few cultivars are hardy northward to Zone 5a, a few tender in Zone 6.

Function. Groundcover, wall cover, vine climbing by aerial rootlets.

Size and Habit

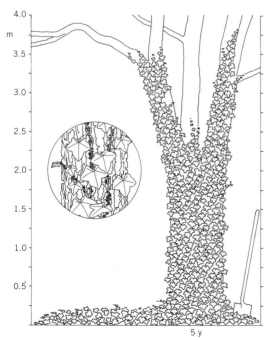

Hedera helix.

Adaptability. Some protection from full winter sun and wind is necessary at the northern edges of the useful range (Zone 5b) to avoid winter drying of foliage.

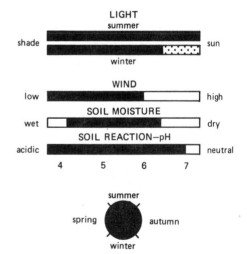

Seasonal Interest. *Flowers:* Present only on the mature (arborescent) form, in interesting but not conspicuous round clusters (umbels). *Foliage:* Handsome, evergreen, lobed leaves, unlobed in

Hedera helix, mature foliage.

the mature form, 4−10 cm/1.6−4 in. long, with lighter vein markings in some cultivars. *Fruits:* Also only on the mature form, the small black berries, in round clusters about golf-ball size, are poisonous if eaten. The fact that cases of actual poisoning are not known probably attests to their lack of appeal.

Problems and Maintenance. Relatively trouble-free, but susceptible to infestation by mites in areas with hot, dry summers and by scale insects and slugs in warm, moist climates.

Cultivars. In the South, some 50 cultivars, varying from cutleaf to curled and crinkled leaves, to white and yellow variegated forms, are available at one time or another, and it is best to rely on local information on performance and availability. In Zone 9a, *Hedera canariensis* may be preferable to any cultivar of *H. helix.* In the North, the number of adapted cultivars is much more limited. The following are among the hardiest available, useful as groundcovers northward to Zone 5b, but not fully hardy there as wall covers.

'Baltica,' from Latvia, is notably hardy.

'Bulgaria' and 'Rumania,' from the named countries, are notably hardy and drought resistant.

'Ogalalla' has proved hardiest of several hardy strains under trial at the University of Minnesota Landscape Arboretum, succeeding there (Zone 4b) with careful attention to site.

'Thorndale' is an unusually handsome form with veins clearly marked with white. It is valued highly in the Central Plains area (Zone 5b−6b).

Related Species

Hedera canariensis 1 and 2 (Algerian or Canary ivy). This species is useful and usually preferred over *H. helix* from Zone 9a southward. It is marginally hardy in Zone 8. It is more vigorous than *H. helix,* with larger leaves (to 15 cm/6 in.), and makes a thick mat of vegetation to 0.5 m/1.6 ft deep. Several cultivars exist but the most commonly used is 'Variegata,' with white variegated leaves.

Hedera colchica 1 and 2 (Colchis or Persian ivy). This species from western Asia is notable for its large, leathery leaves, 10−25 cm/4−10 in. long. It is not as widely available as the other *Hedera* species listed, but is useful in Zones 8a−9a+ and in protected sites in Zone 7b.

Hemerocallis fulva 3

Orange or tawny daylily
Herbaceous groundcover
Liliaceae (Lily Family)

Native Range. Eurasia, naturalized in North America.

Useful Range. USDA Zones 3b−9a+.

Function. Groundcover, massing, specimen.

Size and Habit

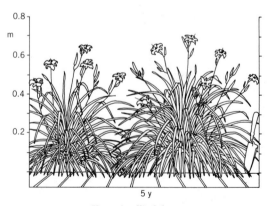

Hemerocallis fulva.

Adaptability. Full sun is best for heaviest flowering, but as much as half shade can be tolerated if the sunny part of the day is in morning or midday.

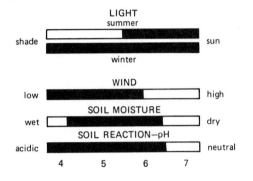

Seasonal Interest. *Flowers:* Orange (and many other colors in hybrids), lilylike, each flower normally remaining open only for a day, very

Hemerocallis fulva, as groundcover.

colorful for most of midsummer. *Foliage:* Medium to bright green, narrowly straplike, making a dense mass 0.5−0.7 m/1.6−2.8 ft high, dying down over winter (some hybrids, useful in mild climates, have persistent foliage).

Problems and Maintenance. Daylilies are essentially trouble-free but may occasionally be infected with a leaf-spot disease. They require little or no maintenance once established, even when tightly matted. Dividing and fertilizing old plantings undoubtedly will improve flowering, but temporarily reduces the effectiveness of groundcover plantings in resisting weed encroachment.

Species and Hybrids

Hemerocallis lilioasphodelus 3 (synonym: *H. flava*; yellow daylily, lemon lily). This species, widely distributed across Asia, has become naturalized in our area. It differs from *H. fulva* in being somewhat less vigorous, not quite so tall, and in having clear yellow flowers somewhat earlier in summer.

Several other *Hemerocallis* species have been involved in a very active breeding effort in the United States, much of the effort the work of amateur specialists, and a very large number of cultivars now exists. Many have been developed for flowering characteristics, some also for good foliage, and the effectiveness of most for massing in landscape use is not well known. In selecting cultivars, it is best to rely on local experience and availability.

Hibiscus syriacus 5

Shrub althea, Rose of Sharon
Deciduous shrub
Malvaceae (Mallow Family)

Native Range. China, India.

Useful Range. USDA Zones 5b–9a.

Function. Border, specimen.

Size and Habit

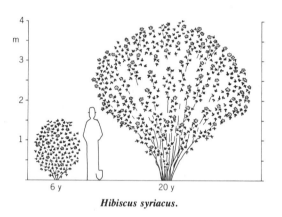

Hibiscus syriacus.

Adaptability. This shrub is tolerant of seashore conditions.

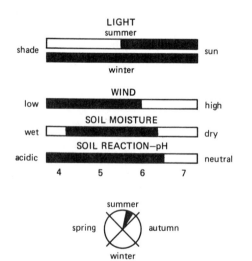

Seasonal Interest. *Flowers:* Large (6–10 cm/ 2.4–4 in. across) and showy, single or double, white, pink, red, violet, or blue in late summer. *Foliage:* Smooth, lobed, bright green leaves are sparsely arranged on stems.

Problems and Maintenance. Stems are occasionally killed back in spring in Zones 5b–6b. Although it is necessary to remove the deadwood, this does not interfere with flowering, which occurs on new growth. In fact, heavy pruning in spring may improve flowering by increasing the general vigor and length of new growth. Regular annual pruning to enhance flowering results in a shrub functioning in size group 4 (1–1.5 m/3.3–4.9 ft) rather than the size group 5 that would otherwise be attained.

Cultivars. A few of the most popular color variants are listed below. Many others are available at different times in different localities.

'Ardens' has semidouble, light orchid-purple flowers. 'Bluebird' has single flowers with pale blue petals, crimson at the base. 'Coelestis' has single, pale violet flowers. 'Lady Stanley' has semidouble, white flowers, with petals red-marked at the base and occasionally streaked up the petal. 'Totus Albus' and 'W. R. Smith' have single, pure white flowers. 'Woodbridge' has single, rose-pink petals, marked deep red at the base.

Related Species

Hibiscus rosa-sinensis 6 (Chinese hibiscus). This species is, practically speaking, out of our range, but it is sometimes grown with protection in Zone 9a. It is a large shrub, to 5 m/16 ft or more under good growing conditions, with large flowers, 10–20 cm/4–8 in. across, white, pink, or red, depending on the cultivar.

Hippophaë rhamnoides 6

Sea buckthorn
Deciduous shrub or small tree
Elaeagnaceae (Oleaster Family)

Native Range. Europe and Asia.

Useful Range. USDA Zones 3a−7a.

Function. Specimen, border, barrier, massing.

Size and Habit

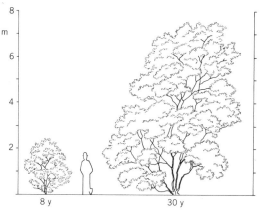

Hippophaë rhamnoides.

Adaptability. Like some other members of the Oleaster Family, this is a nitrogen-fixing species, adaptable to very poor, dry soil. It is one of the best shrubs for cold climates on dry, even somewhat alkaline soils. It grows well in seaside sites and is relatively tolerant of road salt as well.

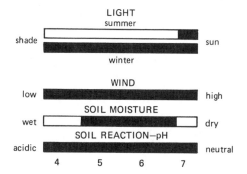

Seasonal Interest. *Flowers:* Dioecious, pale yellow, small and inconspicuous in early spring. *Foliage:* Narrow, silvery green leaves on spiny branches give distinctive color and fine texture in summer. *Fruits:* Bright yellow-orange, only 0.8 cm/0.3 in. across but borne in great numbers on female plants, very showy well into winter.

Hippophaë rhamnoides.

Hippophaë rhamnoides, as accent.

Problems and Maintenance. Establishment has sometimes been difficult, but this probably is not a serious problem if pot-grown plants are specified. Requires occasional pruning to maintain fullness, if this is desired, and to remove root suckers as they develop if a thicket-type growth is to be avoided.

Hosta plantaginea 2

Synonym: *H. subcordata*
Fragrant plantain lily
Herbaceous groundcover
Liliaceae (Lily Family)

Native Range. China and Japan.

Useful Range. USDA Zones 3b−9a+.

Function. Groundcover, massing, specimen.

Size and Habit

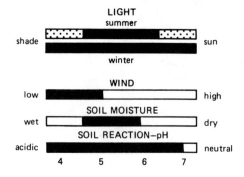

Hosta plantaginea.

Adaptability. Partial shade is best for growth, but this plant tolerates complete shade, with lessened flowering, and full sun, although growth is stronger and leaf color better in light shade, especially in the Midwest and South.

Seasonal Interest. *Flowers:* Fragrant, pure white, funnel-shaped, to 12 cm/5 in. long, in clusters on stalks to at least 60 cm/2 ft tall in late summer and early autumn, persisting longer than those of other species. *Foliage:* Bright green, the leaf blades 15−25 cm/6−10 in. long and 10−15 cm/4−6 in. broad, conspicuously parallel veined, making a solid, pleasingly coarse mass from late spring until late autumn, dying down over winter.

Problems and Maintenance. Garden slugs and leaf-spot diseases may be troublesome in very wet years. Otherwise, plantain lilies are trouble-free and require practically no maintenance.

Related Species. The species listed below are only a few of the more common plantain lilies. All are similar to *Hosta plantaginea* in their general requirements and useful range, but they offer considerable variety in landscape effect.

Hosta fortunei 3 (Fortune plantain lily). This Japanese species has leaf blades to 12 cm/5 in. long and 7 cm/3 in. wide, and pale lavender flowers to 4 cm/1.6 in. long in upright spikes occasionally to nearly 1 m/3.3 ft tall in late spring and early summer. The selection 'Marginato-alba' has white-edged leaves.

Hosta sieboldiana 3 (synonym: *H. glauca,* Siebold plantain lily). This striking plant from Japan has dull blue-gray, conspicuously parallel-veined leaf blades, 25−35 cm/10−14 in. long and 15−25 cm/6−10 in. wide, and small clusters of pale violet flowers in early summer.

Hosta undulata 2 (wavy leaved plantain lily). This low-growing plant from Japan is known only in cultivation. With its wavy, bright green leaves irregularly variegated with white, it is best used for accent and in shade where the variegation develops best. The pale lavender flowers are of minor interest.

Hydrangea anomala ssp. *petiolaris* 1 and 2

Synonym: *H. petiolaris*
Climbing hydrangea
Deciduous vine
Saxifragaceae (Saxifrage Family)

Native Range. Japan, Taiwan.

Useful Range. USDA Zones 5a−7b. May be used in Zone 8 in relatively cool, moist sites.

Function. Wall cover, specimen, groundcover. Vine climbing by aerial rootlets, sometimes to heights of 20−25 m/66−82 ft.

Size and Habit

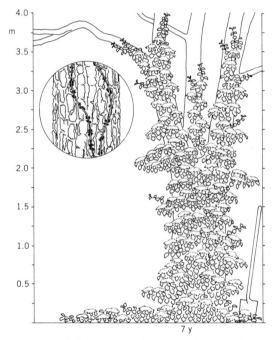

Hydrangea anomala ssp. *petiolaris*.

Seasonal Interest. *Flowers:* White, in large flat clusters, inconspicuous fertile flowers in the center and more showy sterile flowers around the margin of the cluster, conspicuous against the handsome foliage in late spring and early summer. *Foliage:* Dark green, lustrous, neat in appearance, the leaves, 5−10 cm/2−4 in. long, fall in autumn with little color change. *Twigs and branches:* Covered with flaky tan bark, interesting with the aerial rootlets only at very close range.

Problems and Maintenance. Relatively trouble-free and requiring almost no maintenance, although it is very slow-growing for the first few years. It can be troubled by mites occasionally, especially in dry sites or dry years, but this is not a serious problem with attention to soil and site conditions. Plant parts are poisonous but of little appeal and apparently not troublesome.

Subspecies. Ssp. *anomala*, the species type from China, differs little from ssp. *petiolaris* except in being less showy in flower and slightly less cold-hardy (Zones 6b−7b). It is seldom commercially available.

Related Species

Decumaria barbara 1 and 2 (decumaria, wood vamp). This vine, climbing by aerial rootlets, is a close relative of *Hydrangea*, native to the southeastern United States. It has much the same growth habit as *H. anomala* but less vigor,

Adaptability

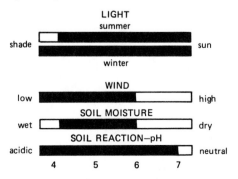

Decumaria barbara.

Decumaria barbara.

evergreen leaves, to 15 cm/6 in. long, and climbs by aerial rootlets much like the related *H. anomala*, to heights of 10–15 m/33–49 ft. It grows best in at least some shade and tolerates deep shade, even flowering well there. The small, white flowers appear in large clusters from midsummer through early autumn. It is useful in Zones 8a–9a+, but probably not commercially available in eastern North America.

Schizophragma hydrangeoides 1 and 2. This Japanese species is a close relative of *H. anomala* and often is confused with it, but it can be distinguished easily by two features: its marginal, sterile, white flowers each have only a single large sepal, rather than four or five as in *Hydrangea*; and its leaves are more coarsely toothed, less lustrous, and usually lighter green. Its requirements are similar to those of *H. anomala*, and it is useful in Zones 6a–7b.

Schizophragma hydrangeoides.

seldom climbing higher than 5–10 m/16–33 ft. The leaves are smaller than those of *H. anomala* but equally lustrous and handsome. It has white flowers in late spring, less showy than those of *H. anomala*, and grows best in fairly moist sites in partial shade in Zones 6b–9a.

Pileostegia viburnoides 1 and 2. This vigorous vine from Southern China and Taiwan has

Hydrangea arborescens 3

Smooth hydrangea
Deciduous shrub or subshrub
Saxifragaceae (Saxifrage Family)

Native Range. Eastern and central United States.

Useful Range. USDA Zones 4a–9a.

Function. Border, specimen, informal low hedge.

Size and Habit. 'Grandiflora' is illustrated.

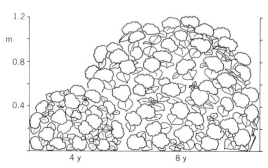

Hydrangea arborescens 'Grandiflora.'

Adaptability

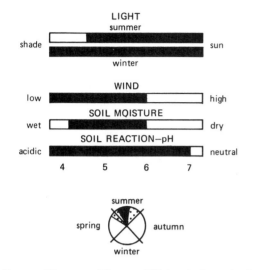

Seasonal Interest. *Flowers:* White, in large (to 15 cm/6 in.), flat clusters, inconspicuous fertile flowers in the center and more showy sterile flowers around the margin of the clusters, or in globose clusters of sterile flowers in cultivars.

Showy from early to midsummer. *Foliage:* Coarse, dark green, forming a good background for flowering but usually not attractive thereafter.

Problems and Maintenance. Relatively trouble-free, but kills to the ground in most winters in the North. Even when it does not, it is best pruned close to the ground in spring, since it returns vigorously to flower in the same year and retains a more-or-less regular, moundlike form. Plant parts are poisonous (see *Hydrangea anomala*).

Subspecies and Cultivars. Ssp. *radiata* (synonym: *H. radiata*; silverleaf hydrangea) is similar to ssp. *arborescens*, the species type, except that its leaves are white and fuzzy underneath, giving the lower surface a silvery appearance.

'Annabelle' has unusually large, globose flower clusters, to 20 cm/8 in. or more across, composed almost entirely of sterile flowers.

'Grandiflora' (hills-of-snow hydrangea) is a long-cultivated selection with sterile flowers in globose clusters, 5–15 cm/2–6 in. across.

Hydrangea macrophylla 3

Bigleaf or florist hydrangea
Deciduous shrub
Saxifragaceae (Saxifrage Family)

Native Range. Japan.

Useful Range. USDA Zones 6b–9a.

Function. Specimen, border.

Size and Habit

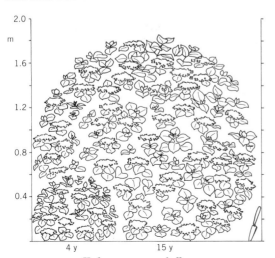

Hydrangea macrophylla.

Adaptability. In the South, this shrub does best in relatively cool, moist sites, for instance, on the north sides of buildings. Flower color in blue and pink cultivars is controlled by the amount of soluble aluminum in the plant—in turn controlled by soil acidity. For clear blue color, soil pH should be no higher than 5.5, for clear pink color, no lower than 6.0. In the intermediate range, some cultivars produce mauve or magenta flowers, not usually very attractive. Plant growth is usually best below about pH 6.5, leaving a rather narrow range of optimal acidity for both good growth and pink flowers.

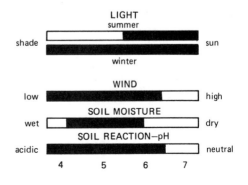

Seasonal Interest. *Flowers:* White, pink, or blue, in large clusters, those composed of fertile flowers are flattened and those of sterile flowers are globose, both very showy in summer. *Foliage:* Lustrous, bright green, somewhat leathery, falling without color change in autumn.

Problems and Maintenance. Relatively trouble-free, but may require regular adjustments of soil acidity in some areas. Pruning should be done as soon as possible after flowering to allow time for new stem growth and initiation of flower buds for the next year. In no case should live stems be pruned back in spring because *H. macrophylla*, unlike *H. arborescens*, usually does not produce flowers in a single growing season. Typically, flower buds are initiated in summer, then must survive winter and receive their chilling requirement before opening the following summer. Plant parts are poisonous (see *Hydrangea anomala*).

Subspecies, Varieties, and Cultivars. Ssp. *macrophylla*, the typical subspecies, has smooth stems and leathery leaves tending to be evergreen in very mild climates. It includes the following varieties.

Var. *macrophylla*, the so-called hortensia types, with entirely sterile flowers in large, globose heads. Many cultivars have been selected from var. *macrophylla*, some not fully cold-hardy in Zone 6b. A few of the most common follow. 'All Summer Beauty' is a relatively recent selection for heavy flowering and compact growth. It usually is grown in acid soil for blue flowers, but is interesting with multicolored blooms in the transitional zone around pH 6.0. 'Blue Prince' is effective in either the blue or pink pH range. 'Domotoi' is unique in having large clusters of double flowers and useful in either the blue or pink pH ranges but usually most effective with light blue flowers in acid soil since it grows

weakly in soil of higher pH. Hardy northward to Zone 6b. 'Mandshurica' is effective in either the blue or pink pH range and is unusually cold-hardy, to Zone 6a in protected sites. 'Nikko Blue' is most effective in acid soil, with deep blue flowers. 'Otaksa' is effective in either the blue or pink pH range but most color-stable in acid soil with large clusters of blue flowers and compact growth habit.

Var. *normalis*, the wild type of *H. macrophylla*, includes many of the so-called lacecap cultivars, having small, fertile flowers in the center of the flattened flower cluster and large, sterile flowers around the outer edge. A few of the most common selections follow. 'Blue Wave' has showy, flat clusters of flowers, most effective in the blue phase in acid soil. 'Coerulea' also is best in acid soil, with central, fertile flowers of deep blue, the outer, sterile flowers lighter. 'Mariesii' has large, rosy pink flowers in moderately acid to neutral soil, blue flowers in very acid soil. 'Variegated Mariesii' is similar to 'Mariesii' except that its leaves have white margins. The blue color phase is perhaps more attractive in combination with this foliage than the pink phase.

Hydrangea macrophylla var. *normalis*.

Ssp. *serrata* (synonyms: *H. acuminata*, *H. serrata*; tea-of-heaven) differs from ssp. *macrophylla* in having smaller, less leathery leaves, and more hairy foliage and stems. Its flowers are typically borne in flattened, "lacecap" clusters.

Hydrangea paniculata 6

Panicle hydrangea
Deciduous shrub
Saxifragaceae (Saxifrage Family)

Native Range. Japan.

Useful Range. USDA Zones 4a–8a.

Function. Specimen, border.

Size and Habit. 'Grandiflora' is illustrated.

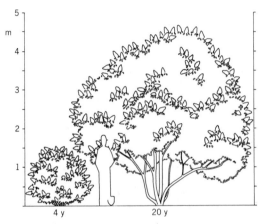

Hydrangea paniculata 'Grandiflora.'

Adaptability

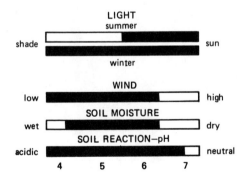

Seasonal Interest. *Flowers:* White, in large (to 25 cm/10 in. long), upright pyramidal clusters, mostly of small fertile flowers but with showy sterile flowers at the base or mostly sterile flowers in a cultivar. Clusters turn pinkish in late summer, light brown in autumn. *Foliage:* Coarse, medium green, adding little landscape interest.

Problems and Maintenance. This shrub is relatively trouble-free. Plant parts are poisonous but probably not troublesome (see *Hydrangea anomala*).

Cultivars. 'Grandiflora' (peegee hydrangea) has clusters of mostly sterile flowers resembling huge, pyramidal snowballs. This is by far the most common form of *H. paniculata* in landscape use. Sometimes pruned into treelike forms and called tree hydrangea, it has been widely promoted by mail-order houses and disseminated more widely than is justified by its landscape value. Individual plants occasionally assume dwarf or compact growth habit for no clear reason, then may revert to the typical vigorous growth just as mysteriously.

'Praecox' (early panicle hydrangea) flowers about 20 days earlier than the species type and has a few more sterile flowers in each cluster.

'Tardiva' (late panicle hydrangea) flowers later than the species type.

Hydrangea quercifolia 4−5

Oakleaf hydrangea
Deciduous shrub
Saxifragaceae (Saxifrage Family)

Native Range. Southeastern United States.

Useful Range. USDA Zones 5b−9a. Tops are winterkilled frequently in Zones 5b and 6a, occasionally in Zone 6b.

Function. Border, specimen, massing, naturalizing.

Size and Habit

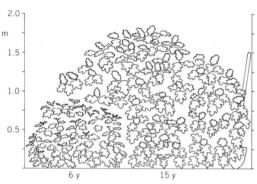

Hydrangea quercifolia.

Adaptability

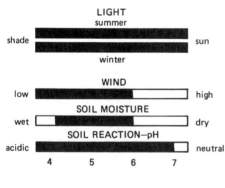

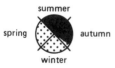

Seasonal Interest. *Flowers:* White, in upright, pyramidal clusters, to 25 cm/10 in. long, composed mostly of small, fertile flowers but with showy, sterile flowers at the base or mostly of sterile flowers in some cultivars. Clusters turn pinkish in late summer, brown in autumn. Flower buds are initiated the previous summer as in *H. macrophylla* and are often winterkilled with stems in colder zones, eliminating flowering interest for the year. *Foliage:* Coarse but handsome, oaklike leaves, to 20 cm/8 in. long, provide strong landscape interest in summer even in nonflowering years in the North and turn a rich russet-red in autumn. *Twigs and branches:* New twig growth is covered with a dense mat of short, reddish brown hairs.

Hydrangea quercifolia.

Problems and Maintenance. This shrub is relatively trouble-free. In the North in some years, annual pruning will be necessary to remove winterkilled branches. This should be done at about the same time that new growth starts to see the extent of injury. Winter injury has the effect of maintaining the functional height of the shrub below eye level in northern zones and contributes to fuller, more shapely form there. Plant parts are poisonous (see *Hydrangea anomala*).

Cultivars. 'Harmony' and 'Roanoke' differ from the species type in having large influorescences, mostly composed of showy, sterile flowers, resembling huge, elongated snowballs, usually heavy enough to weigh branches down, giving the plant an irregularly pendulous form. 'Snowflake' (Plant Patent No. 3047, 1972) has been selected for large inflorescences with extremely large double flowers.

Hypericum calycinum 2

Aaronsbeard St. John's-wort
Evergreen or semievergreen groundcover
Hypericaceae (Hypericum Family)

Native Range. Southeastern Europe and adjacent Asia.

Useful Range. USDA Zones 6b−9a.

Function. Groundcover, useful for large areas, making a dense mat of foliage.

Size and Habit

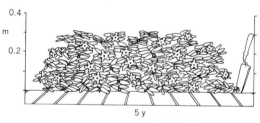

Hypericum calycinum.

Adaptability

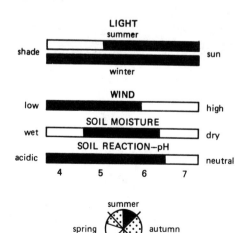

Seasonal Interest. *Flowers:* Large (to 8 cm/3 in. across), bright golden yellow with prominent reddish stamens in center, middle to late summer. *Foliage:* Handsome, rich green, rounded leaves, 5−10 cm/2−4 in. long, semievergreen in Zones 6 and 7, evergreen in the Deep South.

Hypericum calycinum.

Problems and Maintenance. Relatively trouble-free and requiring no maintenance other than occasional to annual pruning (in spring) in small-scale sites. St. John's-worts are toxic to some animals if eaten (by photosensitization), so keep plantings away from farm animals.

Related Species

Hypericum buckleyi 2 (Buckley or Blueridge St. John's-wort). This American species is similar to *H. calycinum* in form and function, but deciduous, having smaller flowers (to 2.5 cm/1 in.) appearing a little earlier in summer, and slightly more cold-hardy. It is useful in Zones 6a−8a.

Hypericum ×*moseranum* 3 (gold flower). This hybrid *(H. calycinum* × *H. patulum)* is intermediate in height (to 0.6 m/2 ft) and flower size (to 6 cm/2.4 in.) between its parents and functions as a rather tall groundcover for mild climates (Zones 7a−9a+). It flowers over most of the summer.

Hypericum patulum 3

Goldencup St. John's-wort
Semievergreen shrub
Hypericaceae (Hypericum Family)

Native Range. Japan, China.

Useful Range. USDA Zones 7a—9a.

Function. Border, specimen, massing.

Size and Habit

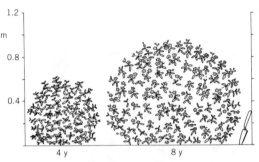

Hypericum patulum.

Adaptability

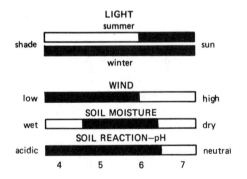

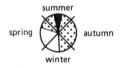

Seasonal Interest. *Flowers:* Bright golden-yellow, to 5 cm/2 in. across, with prominent stamens in small clusters in midsummer. *Foliage:* Semievergreen, rich green, rounded leaves 3—6 cm/1.2—2.4 in. long.

Problems and Maintenance. Relatively trouble-free and requiring no maintenance other than pruning to remove deadwood after severe winters in Zone 7. Plant parts are toxic to some animals if eaten (see *Hypericum calycinum*).

Related Species

Hypericum beanii 3 (synonym: *H. patulum* var. *henryi;* Henry or Bean St. John's-wort).   This Chinese species is similar to *H. patulum* except more vigorous, with larger flowers, to 6 cm/2.4 in. across, and slightly more cold-hardy, to Zone 6a.

Hypericum forrestii 3 (synonym: *H. patulum* var. *forrestii;* Forrest St. John's-wort).   This species, native from western China to Burma, is similar to *H. patulum* except more vigorous, with larger flowers, to 6 cm/2.4 in. across, and slightly more cold-hardy, to Zone 6a. The selection 'Hidcote,' of uncertain parentage but perhaps a hybrid of *H. forrestii* × *H. calycinum*, has fragrant, golden-yellow flowers to 5 cm/2 in. across and semievergreen to evergreen foliage and is useful northward to Zone 6b.

Hypericum 'Hidcote'.

Hypericum hookeranum 4 (Hooker St. John's-wort).   This species, native to western China and the Himalayas, is similar to *H. patulum* but taller, more showy, and somewhat less cold-hardy. It is useful in Zones 7b—9a+.

Hypericum kouytchense 3 (synonym: *H. patulum* 'Sungold;' Sungold St. John's-wort). Another native of western China, very similar to *H. forrestii* in form and flower and interchangeable in landscape use.

Hypericum prolificum 3

Shrubby St. John's-wort
Deciduous shrub
Hypericaceae (Hypericum Family)

Native Range. Eastern United states and adjacent Canada.

Useful Range. USDA Zones 4b−8b.

Function. Border, specimen, massing.

Size and Habit

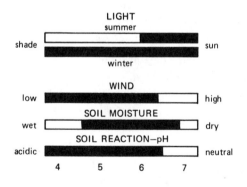

Hypericum prolificum.

Adaptability. This is one of the most widely adaptable of all *Hypericum* species.

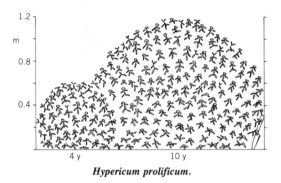

Seasonal Interest. *Flowers:* Bright yellow, to 2 cm/0.8 in. across, in clusters, very colorful in misdummer. *Foliage:* The handsome, bright green leaves (3−8 cm/1.2−3 in. long and much

narrower) give relatively fine texture and fall in autumn with little color change. *Twigs and branches:* Light brown peeling bark adds minor winter interest.

Hypericum prolificum.

Problems and Maintenance. This shrub is relatively trouble-free and requires no maintenance other than removal of deadwood after severe winters in Zones 4 and 5a. Plant parts are toxic to some animals if eaten (see *Hypericum calycinum*).

Related Species

Hypericum frondosum 3 (golden St. John's-wort). This native of the southeastern United States has larger flowers (to 5 cm/2 in. across) and slightly smaller leaves than *H. prolificum*, and is somewhat less cold-hardy. It is useful in Zones 5b−9a.

Hypericum kalmianum 3 (Kalm St. John's-wort). This shrub is more northern in origin than *H. prolificum*, growing wild well into Canada from the Great Lakes area. It is lower growing and has smaller flowers, to 2.5 cm/1 in. across. Useful in Zones 4b−8b.

Iberis sempervirens 2

Evergreen candytuft
Evergreen groundcover
Cruciferae (Mustard Family)

Native Range. Mediterranean region: southern Europe, western Asia, North Africa.

Useful Range. USDA Zones 5a–7b.

Function. Groundcover (small-scale), rock garden.

Size and Habit

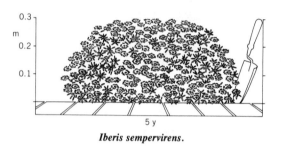

Iberis sempervirens.

Adaptability

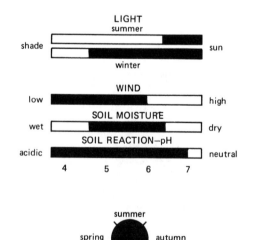

Seasonal Interest. *Flowers:* Pure white, in small rounded clusters about 2.5 cm/1 in. across, showy for two to four weeks in late spring. *Foliage:* Fine textured, very dark green, evergreen, and leathery.

Problems and Maintenance. Relatively trouble-free, requiring little maintenance. Foliage may become less attractive by midsummer, but clipping after flowering to promote new growth will help to avoid this.

Varieties and Cultivars. Var. *correifolia* has flat flower clusters and seldom grows taller than 15 cm/6 in. The species type grows to twice that height in good sites.

The following cultivars have been selected. 'Christmas Snow' flowers at the usual time in late spring and again in early autumn. 'Little Gem' is among the lowest growing forms, 10–15 cm/4–6 in. tall. 'Purity' is also low growing with large flower clusters. 'Snowflake' is perhaps the most showy in flower, with large numbers of large, compact flower clusters, and reaches heights of 20–25 cm/8–10 in.

Related Species

Iberis gibraltarica 2 (Gibraltar candytuft). This evergreen groundcover grows somewhat taller and looser than *I. sempervirens*, with pink to light rosy purple flowers in middle spring. Less cold-hardy than *I. sempervirens*. Useful in Zones 6b–9a and perhaps colder zones as well.

Iberis pruitii 2 (synonym: *I. tenoreana*). Another Mediterranean species, this plant from Italy has pink-tinged flowers. It is useful in Zones 7a–9a and perhaps in colder zones but it is seldom if ever available.

Iberis saxatilis 2. Another native of southern Europe, this is similar to and often confused with *I. sempervirens* but has narrower leaves and more consistently low habit. It is useful in Zones 6b–9a and perhaps also colder zones.

Idesia polycarpa 7

Idesia, Iigiri tree
Deciduous tree
Flacourtiaceae (Flacourtia Family)

Native Range. China, southern Japan.

Useful Range. USDA Zones 7b−9a and perhaps colder zones as well, but may not fruit well in Zone 7.

Function. Shade or patio tree.

Size and Habit

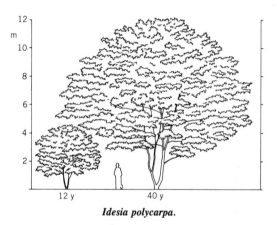

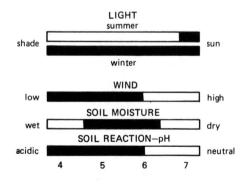

Idesia polycarpa.

Adaptability

Seasonal Interest. *Flowers:* Inconspicuous but fragrant, in pendulous clusters to 25 cm/10 in.

long in late spring. *Foliage:* Large, bright green leaves, 15−25 cm/6−10 in. long, vaguely resembling those of *Catalpa* but not as coarse in texture, falling in autumn with little color change. *Fruits:* Red-orange berries, small but borne in large, pendent clusters and showy in early autumn. Some plants are dioecious, some monoecious (both male and female flowers on the same plant). Plants with at least some female flowers should be used for colorful fruiting.

Idesia polycarpa.

Problems and Maintenance. This tree has so seldom been used in the past that any problems are not yet well known, but it appears relatively trouble-free in trial plantings. Its useful range is also not accurately known, and after further trial it may be found to include more than the Zones 7b−9a indicated. It is seldom commercially available as yet.

Related Species

Stachyurus praecox 5 (early spiketail). This rare native of Japan, in its own family but closely related to the Flacourtiaceae (Flacourtia Family), is popular in Europe but little known in North America. Its usefulness depends on questionable availability, but it has good potential for specimen use because of its pale yellow flowers in very early spring in pendulous clusters 5−8 cm/2−3 in. long, semievergreen foliage, and reddish winter twigs. It is useful in Zones 7a−9a+, but effective in flower only in areas where hard freezes are not common.

Ilex aquifolium 6

English holly
Evergreen shrub or small tree
Aquifoliaceae (Holly Family)

Native Range. Asia, southern Europe, North Africa.

Useful Range. USDA Zones 7a−9a+.

Function. Specimen, screen, hedge.

Size and Habit. This plant seldom attains the size in our area that it reaches in its native habitat and rarely exceeds heights of 4−6 m/13−20 ft except in mild coastal climates.

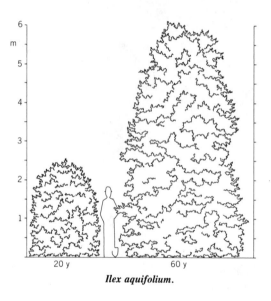

Ilex aquifolium.

Adaptability. Shade in summer improves performance in the South and in winter reduces foliage burn in Zone 7.

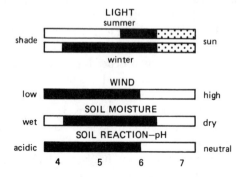

Seasonal Interest. *Flowers:* Small, white, dioecious, insignificant in the landscape. *Foliage:* Handsome, spiny and glossy, evergreen leaves. *Fruits:* Bright red berries (on females) remain colorful during fall and winter, occasionally until spring in the South. Male plants must be located nearby for pollination, except for a few parthenocarpic cultivars that set fruits (not seeds) without pollination.

Ilex aquifolium.

Problems and Maintenance. The most troublesome holly insects are holly leaf miners, mites, and scale insects. These are not often major problems for *I. aquifolium.*

Cultivars. Many cultivars have been selected in Europe, but only a small number are available in the United States. A sampling of the variation in this species is seen in the following list.

'Albomarginata,' 'Argenteo-marginata,' 'Argentea Regina' (= 'Silver King,' = 'Silver Queen'), and 'Silver Beauty,' have white or silvery variegated leaves. Some are properly collective names rather than cultivars.

'Angustifolia' (narrowleaved English holly) has narrow leaves. Properly a collective name rather than a cultivar name, applied to both male and female clones.

'Aureo-marginata,' 'Aurea Medio-picta,' 'Aurea Regina' (= 'Golden King,' = 'Golden Queen'), and 'Muricata,' have yellow or golden-yellow variegated leaves.

'Bacciflava' (= 'Fructu Luteo') has yellow berries.

'Camelliaefolia' has leaves with few spines and large red fruits.

'Crispa' (= 'Contorta,' = 'Revoluta,' = 'Tortuosa') has spirally twisted leaves with thickened, nonspiny margins.

'Ferox' (hedgehog or porcupine holly) has small spines on the upper leaf surface. Actually a collective name, including silver and gold variegated cultivars 'Ferox Argentea' and 'Ferox Aurea.'

Related Hybrids

Ilex aquifolium × *I. cornuta* 'Nellie R. Stevens' 6. This vigorous and handsome hybrid is upright and pyramidal in form. Its ultimate height is not known, but it has been known to reach 6 m/20 ft in less than 20 years. It bears heavy crops of orange-red fruits and is useful in Zones 7a−9a+.

Ilex ×*aquipernyi* 'Brilliant' 6 (brilliant holly). This hybrid of *I. aquifolium* × *I. pernyi* becomes a pyramidal tree to 5−8 m/16−26 ft tall, with small, glossy, spiny leaves and large, bright red berries (without the need for a male pollinator). Useful in Zones 7a−9a, perhaps in 6b with further trial.

Ilex ×*altaclarensis* 7. This hybrid of *I. aquifolium* × *I. perada* includes many cultivars often lumped with *I. aquifolium* cultivars in use but tending to be less cold-hardy. Useful in Zones 7b−9a+.

Ilex ×*koehneana* 7. This supposed hybrid between *I. aquifolium* and *I. latifolia* becomes a large tree, eventually at least 15 m/49 ft tall, but functions in smaller size for a considerable time. Its leaves are large, leathery, and densely spiny toothed like those of *I. latifolia*.

Ilex cassine 6

Dahoon
Evergreen shrub or small tree
Aquifoliaceae (Holly Family)

Native Range. Southeastern United States.

Useful Range. USDA Zones 7b−9a+.

Function. Specimen, massing, naturalizing.

Size and Habit

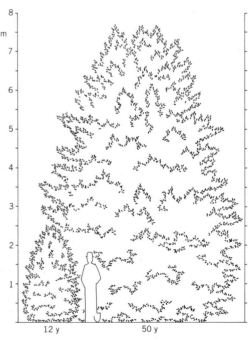

Ilex cassine.

Adaptability. This shrub is well adapted to seashore planting.

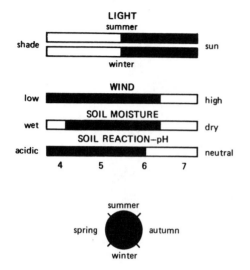

Seasonal Interest. *Flowers:* Small, white, dioecious, insignificant in the landscape. *Foliage:* Evergreen leaves, variable in length, 4–10 cm/ 1.6–4 in., and narrow, not toothed or slightly toothed at leaf apex, light to dark green, turning purplish in winter. *Fruits:* Red berries (on females) in clusters, colorful in autumn and winter.

Problems and Maintenance. Relatively trouble-free and requiring no maintenance except for pruning if greater fullness is desirable.

Varieties. Var. *cassine*, the typical form, has light green leaves to 10 cm/4 in. long and small berries, to 0.6 cm/0.25 in., colorful in autumn and early winter. Several cultivars for superior foliage have been selected. Var. *myrtifolia* (myrtle-leaved holly) has small, dark green leaves, to 4 cm/1.6 in. and larger berries, to 0.8 cm/0.3 in., lasting through the winter. The selection 'Lowei' has yellow berries and dark green foliage.

Related Hybrids

Ilex ×attenuata 6. This hybrid group (*I. cassine* × *I. opaca*), useful in Zones 7a–9a+, includes several excellent narrowly conical hollies with foliage intermediate between the parents and red fruits (females). A few of the most popular selections are listed here:

'East Palatka' has light green foliage and is not very spiny. It is loose in habit unless sheared.

'Foster No. 2' (= 'Fosteri') is the most popular of all *I. ×attenuata* selections, with spiny, dark green foliage, growing vigorously more than 0.3 m/1 ft annually.

'Hume No. 2' (= 'Hume' and sometimes listed as a cultivar of *I. opaca*), is broadly pyramidal in form, with glossy, spine-tipped leaves and heavy crops of red berries.

'Savannah' has spiny, light green foliage and heavy crops of red berries. Foliage color can be improved with careful fertilization.

Ilex cornuta 5—6

Chinese holly
Evergreen shrub
Aquifoliaceae (Holly Family)

Native Range. Eastern China.

Useful Range. USDA Zones 7a–9a+, with selection of appropriate cultivars.

Function. Specimen, screen, massing.

Size and Habit. 'Burfordii' is illustrated.

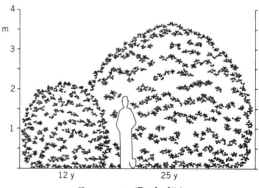

Ilex cornuta 'Burfordii.'

Adaptability. This shrub grows well in full sun to half shade, but for best fruiting (female plants) full sun is best.

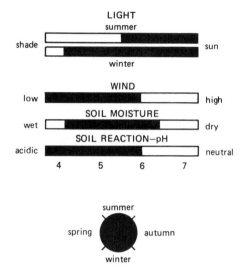

Ilex cornuta 'Dwarf Burford.'

Seasonal Interest. *Flowers:* Small, white, dioecious, insignificant in the landscape. *Foliage:* Handsome, evergreen leaves, with few large, spined lobes (or none in cultivars), easily recognized by the downturned spines at the ends of the leaves. *Fruits:* Bright red berries (on females) are colorful well into winter, occasionally until spring in the South. Through parthenocarpy, fruits appear without benefit of pollination, and it is not necessary to include males in the same planting.

Problems and Maintenance. The most serious problem is scale insects, which can be controlled with carefully timed sprays. Because of the vigor of this species, occasional pruning may be necessary to keep it within bounds. When this is the case, avoid shearing, since this removes newly formed fruits and reduces future color as well as losing the form of the plant. Prune by cutting out individual branches selectively as necessary. Soil fertility must be maintained for heavy annual fruiting.

Cultivars. 'Burfordii' (Burford holly) is probably the best known of all *I. cornuta* cultivars, first described in 1934. It is vigorous, upright, and full, reaching heights of 3–5 m/10–16 ft in less than 20 years. Unlike the species type, each leaf has only a single terminal spine and has a distinctly convex upper surface. It bears very heavy crops of bright red berries. Useful in Zones 7a–9a.

'Dwarf Burford' (= 'Burfordii Compacta,' = 'Burfordii Nana') is, as the name suggests, very full and compact, reaching heights of 2 m/6.6 ft and more if not pruned. It can be kept below eye level for several years with annual pruning, but this reduces fruiting. Useful in Zones 7a–9a, marginal in 6b.

'D'Or' is similar to the species type of *I. cornuta* except that it has bright yellow berries, displayed handsomely against dark green, single-spined leaves.

'Rotunda' differs greatly from other cultivars of *I. cornuta* in form and growth rate, but has typical spiny foliage. It makes a tightly globose plant, functioning below eye level for several years but eventually reaching a height of 2 m/6.6 ft or perhaps more. Pruning may be necessary to control size, but not to maintain the dense form. It is a male, nonfruiting clone.

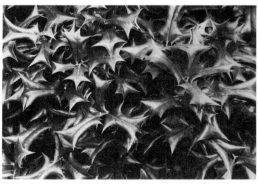

Ilex cornuta 'Rotunda'.

Ilex cornuta 'Rotunda', with *Pachysandra terminalis*.

Related Hybrids

Ilex cornuta × *I. ciliospinosa.*   A series of cultivars has resulted from this fairly recent cross made at the U.S. National Arboretum. 'Albert Close,' 'William Cowgill,' and 'Edward Goucher' are female clones, and 'Howard Dorsett' and 'Harry Gunning' are male clones. These cultivars are still in the evaluation stage.

Ilex cornuta × *I. pernyi.*   At least one female clone, 'Doctor Kassab,' has resulted from this cross.

Ilex cornuta 'Burfordii' × *I. pernyi.*   This cross has produced several cultivars, notable among them 'John T. Morris' and 'Lydia Morris,' male and female clones, respectively, introduced by the U.S. National Arboretum in 1961. Both are dense, conical plants reaching heights of 5 m/16 ft and 4 m/13 ft, respectively, in less than 25 years. Both have excellent foliage and are useful in Zones 6b–9a. 'Lydia Morris' has bright red fruits from autumn until midwinter.

Ilex crenata 3–5

Japanese or box-leaved holly
Evergreen shrub
Aquifoliaceae (Holly Family)

Native Range. Japan.

Useful Range. USDA Zones 6a–9a, with appropriate site, culture, and selection of cultivars (see Adaptability and Problems and Maintenance).

Function. Specimen, hedge, border, rock garden.

Size and Habit

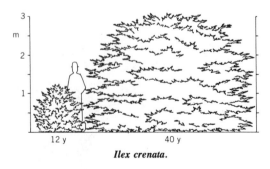

Ilex crenata.

Adaptability. This shrub is best in full sun in the North and tolerant of partial shade as well, but it performs best in partial shade in summer in Zones 8 and 9. Protection from winter wind is important in Zone 6.

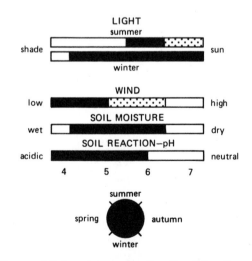

Seasonal Interest. *Flowers:* Small, white, dioecious, insignificant in the landscape. *Foliage:* Glossy, bright to deep green, leathery, evergreen leaves, to 3 cm/1.2 in. long with indefinitely toothed margins, some cultivars with convex-rounded upper surfaces. *Fruits:* Small black berries (on females), with little landscape interest.

Problems and Maintenance. Mite infestations can be troublesome, especially in areas having hot, dry summers. Because of this and a limited tolerance of summer heat and dryness, *I. crenata* is best reserved for areas where summers are less extreme or else grown with some shade and irrigation as necessary. In poor soil, annual fertilization is helpful. The roots of *Ilex* species are very susceptible to freezing injury. Those such as *I. crenata* that are grown in Zones 6 and 7a should be protected from root killing in severe winters by mulching, because soil temperatures as high as −5°C to −7°C (20° to 23°F) are low enough to cause damage.

Cultivars. A large number of variants exist, but most of the basic forms available can be summarized by the following cultivars.

'Buxifolia' has strongly convex leaves, much like the foliage of 'Convexa,' but a distinctly upright growth habit.

'Compacta' has dark green, only slightly convex leaves and compact growth habit. It usually functions below 1 m/3.3 ft but will grow much taller in time.

'Convexa' (= 'Bullata,' convexleaf Japanese holly) has strongly convex upper leaf surfaces giving distinctive texture as each leaf is highlighted from any perspective. Usually functions below or slightly above 1 m/3.3 ft but will grow to at least twice that height and at least half again as wide in time. Cold-hardy to Zone 6b, 6a with protection.

Ilex crenata 'Convexa.'

'Green Cushion' (= 'Kingsville Green Cushion') is very dwarf and fine-textured, useful as an edging or rock garden plant.

'Helleri' is moundlike and compact with very small leaves, taking many years to exceed 1 m/3.3 ft in height. Its form is twiggy and interesting,

making it a choice landscape plant. It is cold-hardy to Zone 6a.

'Hetzi' is very similar to 'Convexa' except with larger leaves and faster growth, reaching a height of 1 m/3.3 ft almost as rapidly as 'Rotundifolia.' Cold-hardy to Zone 6b.

'Kingsville' is loose-growing, functioning below 1 m/3.3 ft and seldom exceeding 1.5 m/5 ft in height but at least half again as broad.

'Latifolia' (= 'Fortunei') is a vigorous, fast-growing selection with relatively large leaves, reaching heights of 3–5 m/10–16 ft in 10 to 15 years. It is an excellent plant for hedges and massing, cold-hardy to Zone 6b.

'Microphylla' has leaves almost as small as those of 'Helleri,' but is vigorous, growing almost as fast as 'Latifolia.' It is stiffly upright and picturesque when left unpruned.

'Rotundifolia' is little if any different from 'Latifolia' and can be considered interchangeable in landscape use.

'Stokesii' is comparable to 'Helleri' in form and growth rate and is among the hardiest cultivars of *I. crenata*.

Ilex crenata 'Stokesii.'

Related Species

Ilex sugerokii 5 (Sugeroki holly).   This native of China and Japan has handsome leaves to 4 cm/1.6 in. long, red berries (on female plants), and is useful in Zones 7b–9a but not generally available.

Ilex yunnanensis 5 (Yunnan holly).   This native of western China resembles *I. crenata* except in its pyramidal habit and red berries (on female plants) and is useful in Zones 6b–9a.

Ilex decidua 6

Possum haw
Deciduous shrub
Aquifoliaceae (Holly Family)

Native Range. Southeastern and south-central United States.

Useful Range. USDA Zones 5b−9a+.

Function. Border, screen, massing, hedge, naturalizing.

Size and Habit

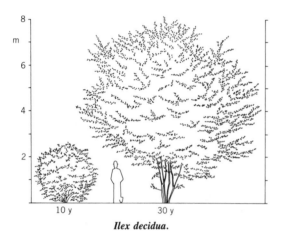

Ilex decidua.

Adaptability

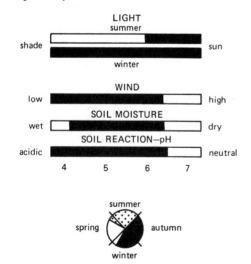

Seasonal Interest. *Flowers:* Small, white, dioecious, insignificant in the landscape. *Foliage:* Lus-

trous, medium green, deciduous in late autumn with little color change. *Fruits:* Red to orange-red berries (on female plants), to 0.8 cm/0.3 in. across, borne in great numbers on some plants and remaining colorful late, often all winter. Occasional male plants are needed for pollination and fruiting effectiveness of females. *Twigs and branches:* Light gray, contrasting well with berries.

Problems and Maintenance. This shrub is relatively trouble-free and requires little or no maintenance other than pruning for fullness when used as a hedge or for screening.

Varieties and Cultivars. Var. *longipes* (synonym: *I. longipes;* Georgia haw) differs little from *I. decidua* except that its berries are borne on long stalks, to 2 cm/0.8 in. long, and it is less tolerant of wet soils. It is seldom available commercially but may be encountered and preserved in the development of wild areas.

Var. *decidua* is the typical form of the species. Several cultivars have been selected for superior fruiting including 'Byer's Golden,' with golden yellow berries, and 'Fraser's Improved,' 'Oklahoma,' and 'Warren's Red,' with superior red or orange-red fruiting interest. 'Warren's Red' is one of the finest of all deciduous hollies.

Related Species

Ilex ambigua 6 (synonym: *I. montana;* mountain holly or mountain winterberry).   This is a tall, sparse shrub or small tree native to the Appalachian Mountains from Massachusetts to Alabama. Not often available, but of some landscape interest in its native habitat.

Nemopanthus mucronatus 5 (mountain holly, catberry).   This thicket-forming shrub, growing above eye level, is a close relative of the true hollies, native to the northeastern United States and adjacent Canada to Newfoundland. With dull red berries in summer, it is not of great landscape value, but it is useful in natural and naturalistic landscapes within the native range in Zones 4b−6a.

Ilex glabra 6

Inkberry, gallberry
Evergreen shrub
Aquifoliaceae (Holly Family)

Native Range. Eastern coastal United States and northward to Nova Scotia.

Useful Range. USDA Zones 5a−9a with selection of appropriate genetic material.

Function. Border, hedge, massing.

Size and Habit

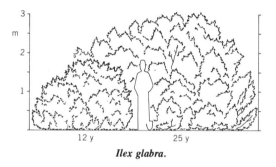

Ilex glabra.

Adaptability. This shrub is well adapted to seashore planting and relatively tolerant of de-icing salt.

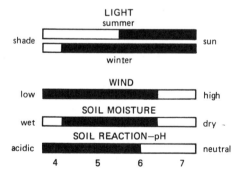

Seasonal Interest. *Flowers:* Small, white, dioecious, insignificant in the landscape. *Foliage:* Evergreen, lustrous, flat leaves are small (2.5−5 cm/1−2 in.), not spiny, and have only a few teeth toward the apex. *Fruits:* Small black berries (on females), interesting but not a significant landscape feature except in the white variants (see Cultivars).

Ilex glabra.

Problems and Maintenance. This shrub usually is trouble-free, but mites can be a problem in dry sites. It needs pruning for fullness in hedging or screening and responds well to shearing into hedge form.

Cultivars. 'Compacta' is an excellent female selection for compact growth, easily maintained below eye level with occasional pruning. 'Ivory Queen' and 'Leucocarpa' are white-fruited selections, interesting in autumn.

Ilex latifolia 6

Lusterleaf holly
Evergreen shrub
Aquifoliaceae (Holly Family)

Native Range. Japan.

Useful Range. USDA Zones 8a−9a+.

Function. Screen, specimen.

Size and Habit

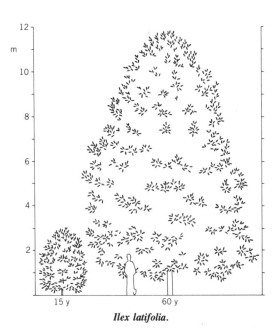

Ilex latifolia.

Handsome, leathery leaves, 18 cm/7 in. long, finely toothed but not lobed or sharp-spined. *Fruits:* Red berries in clusters, showy in autumn, but not as striking as the fruits of some other hollies.

Ilex latifolia.

Adaptability. Unlike most hollies, this species requires light shade for best growth. It is less tolerant of poor, dry soil than most hollies.

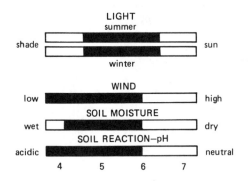

Seasonal Interest. *Flowers:* Small, white, dioecious, insignificant in the landscape. *Foliage:*

Problems and Maintenance. Scale insect infestations can be troublesome but are controlled with carefully timed sprays.

Related Species

Ilex fargesii 6.   This species from western China has long (6−12 cm/2.4−4.8 in.), narrow leaves with fine teeth toward the apex and fruiting interest (on females) similar to that of *I. latifolia*. It is useful in the same range as *I. latifolia*.

Ilex integra 6 (mochi tree).   This shrub or small tree from Japan, to 6 m/20 ft, has moderately large leaves (5−10 cm/2−4 in.), seldom with teeth or spines, and large red fruits (on females). It is useful in the same range as *I. latifolia*.

Ilex ×meserveae 4−5

Meserve or blue holly
Evergreen shrub
Aquifoliaceae (Holly Family)

Hybrid origin. *Ilex rugosa* × *I. aquifolium*.

Useful Range. USDA Zones 5a−8a and perhaps colder and milder zones as well with further trial.

Function. Specimen, foundation, massing.

Size and Habit

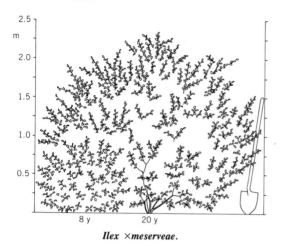

Ilex ×meserveae.

Adaptability. Grows well in full sun to half shade in summer, but for best fruiting (female cultivars) and most compact growth, full sun is best. At the northern extremes of the useful range (not well known, but probably in Zone 5) light shade will reduce winterburn of foliage.

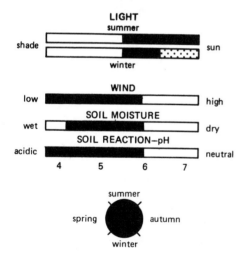

Seasonal Interest. *Flowers:* Small, white, dioecious, insignificant in the landscape. *Foliage:* Spiny evergreen leaves are deep, glossy blue-green, purpling slightly in winter, borne on bluish purple stems. *Fruits:* Small, to 0.8 cm/0.3 in., bright red and shiny (on females). Because of the dioecious condition, an occasional male must be present within about 100 meters (about 300 ft) for reliable pollination.

Problems and Maintenance. Limited experience to date shows this species to be among the most trouble-free of evergreen hollies and little or no maintenance other than mulching should be needed. Pruning normally is not necessary.

Cultivars. The following cultivars have been introduced, and additional selections have followed.

'Blue Boy' (Plant Patent No. 2435, 1964) and 'Blue Girl' (Plant Patent No. 2434, 1964), male and female, respectively, were the first two selections to be named. They have largely been replaced by more recent introductions, below.

'Blue Prince' (Plant Patent No. 3517, 1972), as the name suggests, is male. Since its introduction, it has quickly developed a reputation as a highly effective pollinator, not just for other *I. ×meserveae* selections but for a wide range of hollies. It has excellent, deep green foliage, deep bluish stems, and low, compact growth.

'Blue Angel' (Plant Patent No. 3662, 1973) and 'Blue Princess' (Plant Patent No. 3675, 1973) are female selections, considered superior to 'Blue Girl.' 'Blue Angel' was developed by back crossing *I. ×meserveae* with *I. aquifolium* and shows the dominant influence of that species in its larger leaves and reduced cold hardiness. It is probably useful in Zones 7a–8a and perhaps in somewhat colder zones as well.

Related Species

Ilex rugosa 3 (prostrate or Tsuru holly). This species from northern Japan and Sakhalin is one of the hardiest of evergreen holly species. Plants are low and spreading with wrinkled, leathery, evergreen leaves to 5 cm/2 in. long, spineless and barely toothed. Although it is best known as the parent of *I. ×meserveae*, it is a useful landscape plant in its own right in Zones 4a–7a, but it is little known and seldom available at present.

Ilex rugosa.

Ilex opaca 7

American holly
Evergreen shrub or tree
Aquifoliaceae (Holly Family)

Native Range. Eastern United States.

Useful Range. USDA Zones 6a–9a, but the same cultivars do not grow well at both range extremes.

Function. Specimen, screen, hedge.

Size and Habit

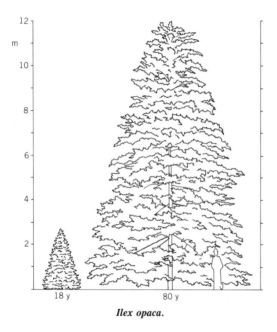

18 y   80 y
Ilex opaca.

Adaptability. Grows well in full sun to half shade in summer, but for best fruiting (female plants) and most compact growth, full sun is best. At the northern extremes of the useful range light shade may reduce winterburn of foliage.

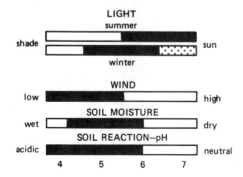

Seasonal Interest. *Flowers:* Small, white dioecious, insignificant in the landscape. *Foliage:* Evergreen, spiny leaves are dull or lustrous, depending on cultivar. *Fruits:* Bright red berries (on females) are colorful in fall and early winter, throughout winter in certain cultivars. For best fruiting, occasional male plants should be nearby (within a few hundred feet) to serve as pollinators.

Ilex opaca.

Problems and Maintenance. The most serious insect pest of *I. opaca*, leaf miner, can be controlled with carefully timed sprays; so can occasional scale infestations. Leaf-spot diseases are also troublesome. Some, primarily tar-spot disease in the South, are caused by fungi. Spine-spot is simply damage from spines of one leaf blowing against the surface of another leaf. Purple blotch seriously disfigures foliage of some plants and is considered a physiological disorder, the cause of which is as yet unknown. It can be avoided by careful selection of cultivars.

Cultivars and Forms. There are at least 300 named cultivars of *I. opaca*. Some are very similar to others. Generally it is a good practice to rely on local experience, since the same cultivars do not perform well in all areas. A few of the most popular are listed here.

'Amy' is one of the best in foliage and form for northern areas, with large fruits borne singly.

'Arden' is broad and open in habit with strongly horizontal branching, leaves light to medium green, bronzing in winter, and heavy crops of fruit, ripening early.

'Bountiful' has dark green foliage and heavy crops of berries annually.

'Cardinal' is unusually hardy and bears extremely heavy crops of berries.

'Croonenberg' is distinctive because it is self-fruitful, bearing a few male flowers. It may be a hybrid with *I. aquifolium*.

'Dauber' has very dark green, lustrous leaves, bears heavy crops of berries, and is very hardy.

'Fruitland Nursery' has saffron-yellow fruits.

'Hedgeholly' has smaller than normal leaves, dense growth that responds well to pruning in hedge form, and dark red berries.

'Howard' is columnar and dense, with leaves having one to five spines (or none), and heavy crops of bright red berries. This is an excellent selection for the southern Coastal plain.

'Isaiah' is a broadly conical male form, an effective pollinator.

'Jersey Knight' is a hardy male selection with lustrous leaves, an effective pollinator.

'Judge Brown' is a conical form with glossy foliage, bearing heavy crops of scarlet berries.

'MacDonald' is a vigorous selection with good crops of red berries, easy to transplant and well adapted to the central Midwest.

'Merry Christmas' is a very hardy selection with good crops of glossy, bright red berries.

'Old Heavy Berry' is a vigorous, hardy selection with dark green, lustrous, textured foliage and good crops of red berries.

'Taber No. 3' is a narrow, fastigiate selection with heavy crops of glossy red berries.

'Taber No. 4' is a slightly pendulous, large growing selection with dark green foliage and very large, bright red berries.

F. *xanthocarpa* includes all yellow-fruited cultivars of *I. opaca*. The first record is of a plant in Massachusetts, but yellow-fruited forms have been found in several other areas as well. Base selection on local experience and availability.

Related Species

Ilex pedunculosa 6 (longstalk holly). This large Japanese species is densely to loosely pyramidal in habit, reaching heights of 4−6 m/13−20 ft or more, with pointed leaves, 3−7 cm/1.2−2.8 in. long, without teeth or spines. Bright red berries are borne on stalks, 2−4 cm/0.8−1.6 in. long, giving a different fruiting effect than that of other hollies. This is one of the hardiest of evergreen hollies, useful in Zones 6a−9a and perhaps protected sites in Zone 5b.

Ilex pedunculosa.

Ilex pedunculosa.

Ilex pernyi 6

Perny holly
Evergreen shrub
Aquifoliaceae (Holly Family)

Native Range. China.

Useful Range. USDA Zones 7a–9a.

Function. Specimen, border. Upright, often sparse growth gives the plant distinctive character but eliminates it for screening use.

Size and Habit

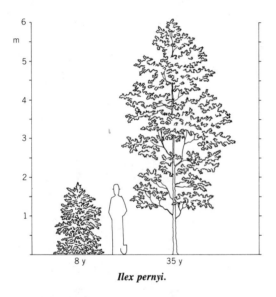

Ilex pernyi.

Adaptability. This shrub grows well in full sun to half shade, but for best fruiting (female plants), full sun is best.

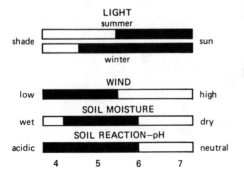

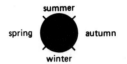

Seasonal Interest. *Flowers:* Small, white, dioecious, insignificant in the landscape. *Foliage:* Relatively spiny, evergreen leaves borne close to the sparsely branching stems. *Fruits:* Small, bright red berries (on females) in clusters, showy in autumn and early winter. Occasional male plants must be located nearby for pollination to have a significant show of fruits.

Problems and Maintenance. This plant is relatively trouble-free and requires little maintenance, although light pruning for shaping may be desirable in some situations.

Related Species

Ilex bioritensis 6 (synonym: *I. pernyi* var. *veitchii;* Veitch holly).   This species differs from *I. pernyi* in having larger leaves with 9–11 spines rather than the 3–7 typical of *I. pernyi*. Although it is available, some plants sold under the name *I. pernyi* var. *veitchii* probably are not truly of this species. The form most commonly available is male.

Ilex ciliospinosa 6.   Closely related to *I. pernyi*, this species is more shrubby and compact but eventually reaches heights of 4 m/13 ft and taller.

Both *I. ciliospinosa* and *I. pernyi* are better known for their hybrids with *I. aquifolium* and *I. cornuta* than in themselves.

Ilex verticillata 5

Winterberry, black alder
Deciduous shrub
Aquifoliaceae (Holly Family)

Native Range. Eastern North America.

Useful Range. USDA Zones 4a−9a with selection of appropriate genetic material.

Function. Border, screen, massing, stream banks (forms thickets).

Size and Habit

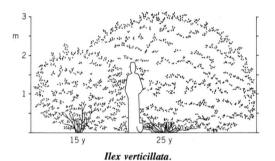

Ilex verticillata.

Adaptability

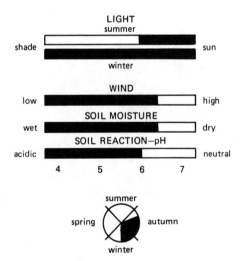

Seasonal Interest. *Flowers:* Small, white, dioecious, insignificant in the landscape. *Foliage:* Pale to rich green, turning yellowish and blackening in early autumn, then falling early. *Fruits:* Bright red and glossy, borne close to the twigs, adding striking interest (to female plants) in late autumn and early winter. Occasional males are needed for pollination and fruiting effectiveness of females. *Twigs and branches:* Dark gray or brown in winter.

Problems and Maintenance. Foliage is frequently affected by leaf spots and mildew, but it is seldom completely disfigured. Susceptibility varies considerably from plant to plant. Otherwise, this shrub is relatively trouble-free.

Cultivars. There has been considerable interest in selecting variants of *I. verticillata* for superior fruit color, heavy fruiting, and late retention in winter, as well as superior foliage. A few of the best known are listed here. 'Aurantiaca' has orange berries. 'Cacopon,' 'Fairfax' and 'Shaver' all were selected in West Virginia for outstanding fruiting. 'Chrysocarpa' has yellow berries. 'Afterglow' and 'Nana' are excellent, heavy fruiting selections that remain relatively low (to 1 m/3.3 ft) for many years. 'Winter Red' (Plant Patent No. 29912, 1979) is a relatively recent selection for superior fruiting and fruit retention in winter.

Related Species

Ilex laevigata 5 (smooth winterberry). This species differs from *I. verticillata* in having slightly larger, orange-red berries, forming in considerable numbers through parthenocarpy (without fertilization or development of seeds). It is useful in Zones 4b−7b and perhaps farther southward but seldom available commercially. The selection 'Hervey Robinson' has yellow berries.

Ilex serrata 5 (Japanese winterberry or finetooth holly). This is the Asian counterpart of *I. verticillata* and differs from that species in having slightly smaller berries that ripen earlier in autumn and sometimes are taken quickly by birds and in being less cold-hardy. It is useful in Zones 6a−9a and perhaps in somewhat colder zones. White- and yellow-fruited forms, f. *leucocarpa* and f. *xanthocarpa*, are, to a limited extent, available.

Several hybrids involving various combinations of *I. laevigata*, *I. serrata* and *I. verticillata* have been produced and may prove useful as they are tried more widely.

Ilex vomitoria 6

Yaupon
Evergreen shrub
Aquifoliaceae (Holly Family)

Native Range. Southern United States.

Useful Range. USDA Zones 8b−9a+ in tree form; 7b−9a+ as a shrub.

Function. Specimen, massing, hedge.

Size and Habit

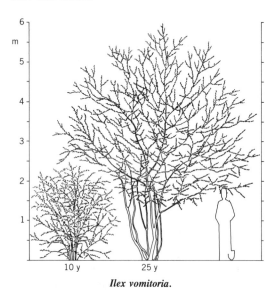

Ilex vomitoria.

Adaptability. This species is especially well adapted to seashore planting and is better adapted to wind and hot climates than most evergreen hollies.

LIGHT
summer
shade ▭▬ sun
winter
shade ▭▬ sun

WIND
low ▬▭ high
SOIL MOISTURE
wet ▭▬▭ dry
SOIL REACTION−pH
acidic ▬▭ neutral
4   5   6   7

Seasonal Interest. *Flowers:* Small, white, dioecious, insignificant in the landscape. *Foliage:* Evergreen and lustrous, medium to gray-green leaves averaging about 2.5 cm/1 in. long, arranged sparsely on the stems. *Fruits:* small (to 0.6 cm/0.25 in.) berries in clusters, borne in very large numbers (on female plants). An occasional nearby male pollinator is necessary for heavy fruiting.

Problems and Maintenance. Leaf miner infestations occasionally can be a problem, especially to the selection 'Nana,' and mites can be troublesome in dry sites. Regular pruning is necessary when this plant is to be used as a hedge or in other situations where fullness of form is desired.

Cultivars and Forms. 'Nana' (= 'Compacta;' dwarf yaupon) is a female clone with dark green foliage and compact, moundlike form, usually remaining below 1 m/3.3 ft for many years, but sometimes becoming twice that height and very broad. Popular in the South as a low hedge or edging plant, it is useful in Zones 7b−9a+, but it is thoroughly confused in commerce with 'Schilling's Dwarf' (= 'Stokes Dwarf,') and other dwarf selections.

Ilex vomitoria 'Nana.'

F. *pendula* (weeping yaupon) is a strongly pendulous tree form of striking habit. Several cultivars have been selected, including 'Folsom Weeping' and 'Grey's Littleleaf' (= 'Grey's Weeping'). These are useful in Zones 8b−9a+ but are questionable in colder zones except in sheltered sites.

Illicium anisatum 6

Japanese anise tree
Evergreen shrub
Illiciaceae (Illicium Family)

Native Range. Japan and southern Korea.

Useful Range. USDA Zones 8a−9a+.

Function. Screen, massing, specimen.

Size and Habit

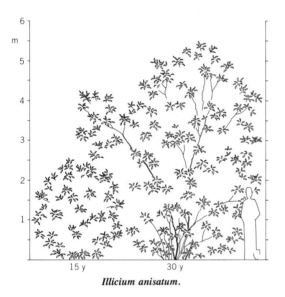

Illicium anisatum.

Adaptability

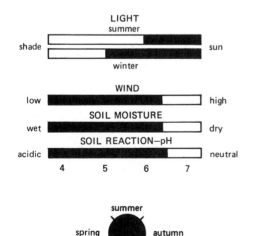

Seasonal Interest. *Flowers:* Fragrant, white to yellow, to 4 cm/1.6 in. across in late spring.

Fruits: Flattened terminal capsules, rarely produced in cultivation in North America. *Foliage:* Evergreen, smooth, leathery, olive green, dense, making the plant effective as a screen. Leaves are pleasantly aromatic when crushed and as much as 10 cm/4 in. long.

Illicium anisatum.

Problems and Maintenance. This species seems to be free of trouble and requires no maintenance other than occasional pruning for shaping when desirable, but even this is seldom necessary.

Related Species

Illicium floridanum 5 (Florida anise tree). This shrub seldom exceeds 3 m/10 ft in height and functions at a smaller size than this in our range. It is useful from Zone 9a southward or in Zone 8 in protected sites. Deep reddish flowers, reminiscent of those of *Calycanthus*, about 5 cm/2 in. across, appear in midspring. Leaves are aromatic, up to 15 cm/6 in. long.

Illicium parviflorum 5. This native of northern Florida is intermediate in size between *I. anisatum* and *I. floridanum* with white, starlike flowers and flattened leaves borne semierect at narrow angles with the stems. The interesting texture and fullness of the foliage makes this species a valuable addition to the list of evergreen shrubs for the Deep South, that is, Zones 8b−9a+ and perhaps also Zone 8a, but it is seldom commercially available as yet.

Illicium parviflorum.

Illicium parviflorum.

Kadsura japonica 1 (scarlet kadsura).   This twining vine from Japan and Korea, a member of the Schisandraceae (Schisandra Family), has leathery, dark green leaves, 5–10 cm/2–4 in.

long, semievergreen in Zone 8 and northward, evergreen in Zone 9a+, turning reddish in winter. Its flowers are not conspicuous, but the bright scarlet fruits, in clusters about 2.5 cm/1 in. across on pistillate (female) plants, are very showy in autumn and early winter. An occasional staminate (male) plant should be planted for pollination. This vigorous vine is useful for screening on fence support in Zones 7b–9a+ but is seldom commercially available.

Schisandra chinensis 1 (Chinese magnolia vine).   This deciduous relative of S. *propinqua* from northeastern Asia is notable for its greater cold hardiness, at least to Zone 6a, and autumn show of red fruits in rather long, drooping clusters on female plants (with occasional males for pollination).

Schisandra propinqua 1 (magnolia vine).   This deciduous to semievergreen vine from central China was once classified in the Magnoliaceae (Magnolia Family) but now has been split off, with Kadsura, into the closely related Schisandraceae (Schisandra Family). Orange flowers, to 1.5 cm/0.6 in. across, add color in summer, but the main seasonal interest is the bright red berries, in elongated, drooping clusters to 15 cm/6 in. long on pistillate (female) plants in autumn. Occasional staminate (male) plants must be planted for pollination to produce fruits. Useful in Zones 8a–9a+ and perhaps Zone 7b.

Indigofera kirilowii 3

Kirilow indigo
Deciduous shrub or subshrub
Leguminosae (Legume Family)

Native Range. Northern China and Korea.

Useful Range. USDA Zones 5a–7b.

Function. Groundcover, massing.

Size and Habit

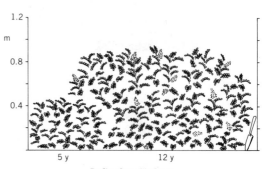

Indigofera kirilowii.

Adaptability

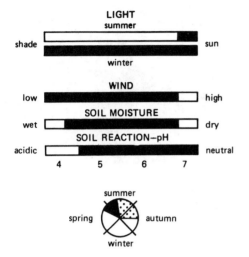

Seasonal Interest. Flowers: Small, purplish rose, in elongated clusters, 10—12 cm/4—5 in. long, in early summer. *Foliage:* Compound, of interesting texture.

Problems and Maintenance. Stems are winter-killed regularly in Zone 5, frequently in Zone 6, and occasionally farther south, and occasional pruning is necessary to remove dead twigs and avoid a ragged appearance. Since new growth and flowers return quickly in spring, plants can be pruned to a few inches from the ground in early spring, annually if desired. If allowed to grow unpruned in mild climates, this species may reach heights of 1 m/3.3 ft or more.

Related Species

Indigofera divaricata 3 (spreading indigo). This little-known plant from China and Japan is used in southern Louisiana as a tall, rather loose groundcover in partially shaded sites. Its regularly compound foliage provides a lacy appearance, and its flowers, in clusters similar to those of *I. kirilowii*, open intermittently during most of the growing season. Useful in Zone 9a+, this plant may be hardy in slightly colder zones as well.

Indigofera incarnata 3 (Chinese indigo). This plant is slightly lower than *I. kirilowii* and more tender, regularly topkilling in winter, but useful in Zones 6a—8a. It is commercially available only as the white flowered form 'Alba,' flowering in midsummer.

Indigofera incarnata 'Alba.'

Itea virginica 4—5

Virginia sweetspire
Deciduous shrub
Saxifragaceae (Saxifrage Family)

Native Range. Southeastern United States and north to New Jersey.

Useful Range. USDA Zones 6b—9a+.

Function. Naturalizing, border, specimen.

Size and Habit. The irregular habit of this shrub is best in naturalized situations. It remains mostly below 1 m/3.3 ft in height in northern zones and poor sites, but it can reach 3 m/10 ft in moist sites in the South.

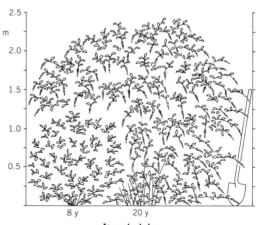

Itea virginica.

Adaptability. Performs best with at least light shade in areas having hot summers.

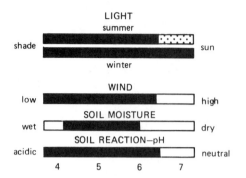

Itea virginica.

other than occasional pruning to maintain form when used as a specimen.

Related Species

Itea ilicifolia 4 (holly leaf sweetspire).   This Chinese species, unlike *I. virginica*, is evergreen and useful only in the southern extremities of our area, perhaps no farther north than Zone 9a. As the name suggests, it has spiny toothed leaves to 8−10 cm/3−4 in. long and greenish white flowers in hanging clusters, 15−30 cm/6−12 in. long. This is a handsome landscape plant but little known and probably not commercially available in our area.

Seasonal Interest. *Flowers:* Fragrant, white, small, in upright to drooping spikes to 10−15 cm/4−6 in. long, attractive in late spring and early summer. *Foliage:* Dull green but turning bright red in autumn before falling.

Problems and Maintenance. This shrub is relatively trouble-free and requires little maintenance

Jasminum mesneyi 4

Synonym: *J. primulinum*
Primrose jasmine
Evergreen, scrambling shrub
Oleaceae (Olive Family)

Native Range. Western China.

Useful Range. USDA Zone 9a+, and Zone 8 with protection.

Function. Massing, bank cover, trailing over walls or fences, specimen.

Size and Habit. Branches trail to lengths of 2−3 m/6.6−10 ft if not pruned.

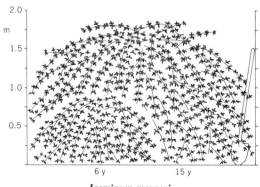

Jasminum mesneyi.

Adaptability

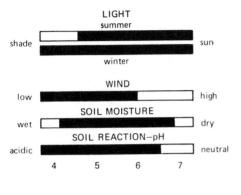

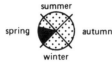

Seasonal Interest. *Flowers:* Soft yellow, large (to 4 cm/1.6 in. across), single to semidouble, mostly in spring but appearing occasionally at most other seasons. *Foliage:* Evergreen, trifoliolate leaflets to 8 cm/3 in. long.

Problems and Maintenance. This plant is relatively trouble-free but requires pruning to maintain its graceful form—frequent pruning if it is to be kept in a restricted space. Shearing completely destroys its graceful landscape effect; prune by thinning out a few of the older branches to the ground every year or by cutting the entire plant back in spring every four or five years.

Related Species

Jasminum floridum 4 (flowering jasmine).   This species differs from *J. mesneyi* in its somewhat lower stature, greater cold hardiness (Zones 7b-9a+), and smaller (to 1.3 cm/0.5 in.), fragrant, bright yellow flowers, borne in clusters of five and more in late spring and intermittently in summer. Like *J. mesneyi* it is evergreen, but with finer textured foliage, moundlike and graceful in habit, and it may be trained as a scrambling climber over fences and walls.

Jasminum floridum.

Jasminum nudiflorum 4—5

Winter jasmine
Deciduous, scrambling shrub
Oleaceae (Olive Family)

Native Range. China.

Useful Range. USDA Zones 6b−9a+.

Function. Massing, bank cover, trailing over walls or fences, specimen.

Size and Habit. Branches trail to lengths of 3−5 m/10−16 ft if not pruned.

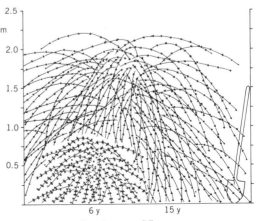

Jasminum nudiflorum.

Adaptability

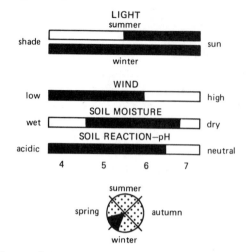

Seasonal Interest. *Flowers:* Fragrant, bright yellow, to 2.5 cm/1 in. across, in late winter on leafless stems resembling a rather sparse, early-flowering forsythia. Favored for forcing indoors. *Foliage:* Deciduous but remaining green well into autumn, trifoliolate with leaflets to 2.5 cm/1 in. long. *Twigs and branches:* Green, adding quiet winter interest even before flowering begins.

Problems and Maintenance. This plant is relatively trouble-free but requires occasional pruning to maintain its graceful form. This should be done carefully by removing a few older branches each year rather than by shearing, which destroys its graceful landscape effect. An alternative pruning method is to cut the entire top back close to the ground every few years, if the appearance of the plant deteriorates enough to make renewal necessary. This should be done in spring at or before the time new growth is beginning, to allow maximum time for regrowth before winter.

Jasminum officinale 1 and 3

Common jasmine, poet's jasmine
Semievergreen, scrambling, vinelike shrub
Oleaceae (Olive Family)

Native Range. Iran to western China.

Useful Range. USDA Zones 7b−9a+.

Function. This procumbent, scrambling shrub has weak stems that need support at first, but it can be trained as a rambling climber to cover banks, walls, fences, and trellises.

Size and Habit. Branches trail to lengths of 5−10 m/16−33 ft if not pruned.

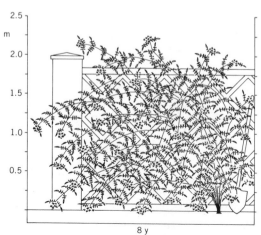

Jasminum officinale.

Adaptability

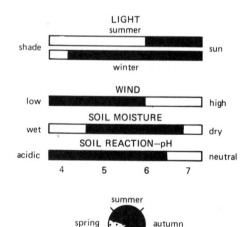

Seasonal Interest. *Flowers:* Fragrant, white, to 2.5 cm/1 in. across, in clusters of up to 10, most showy in late spring and summer but continuing with occasional bloom well into autumn. *Foliage:* Glossy and dark green, compound with five to nine leaflets, tending to be semievergreen. *Twigs and branches:* Green, adding quiet winter interest after leaves fall.

Problems and Maintenance. This plant is relatively trouble-free but requires occasional pruning for control of size and for thinning and

Jasminum officinale.

shaping. Since it is a weak climber, its branches must be tied to their support if trained on trellis or wire.

Forms and Cultivars. 'Aureo-variegatum' has yellow variegated foliage. 'Grandiflorum' (= f. *affine*) has larger flowers, to 4 cm/1.6 in. across, and relatively stout stems, not as easily trained as the species type.

Related Species and Hybrids

Jasminum beesianum 3. This low, moundlike shrub or weakly scrambling climber, to 2 m/6.6

ft, has fragrant, pink to rosy red flowers, unusual in this genus, in middle to late spring. It is seldom available commercially but is potentially useful in Zones 7b−9a+.

Jasminum humile 1 and 4 (Italian jasmine). In spite of its common name, this is another Chinese species of *Jasminum*, usually grown as a scrambling climber. It has nearly evergreen, fine textured foliage and fragrant yellow flowers in late spring and is useful in Zones 7b−9a+.

Jasminum multiflorum 1 (synonym: *J. pubescens*; furry jasmine). This scrambling climber from India is one of the most satisfactory species for use on fences and trellises. It has evergreen foliage and fragrant white flowers during the summer but is useful only in Zone 9a+.

Jasminum ×stephanense 1 and 3 (Stephan jasmine). This hybrid between *J. beesianum* and *J. officinale* 'Grandiflorum' combines the pink flower color (although paler) of the female parent with the scrambling habit of the male parent, but is rank-growing and not easily trained, and so of limited interest in its useful range of Zones 8b−9a+.

Juglans nigra 8

Eastern black walnut
Deciduous tree
Juglandaceae (Walnut Family)

Native Range. Eastern United States and southern Ontario.

Useful Range. USDA Zones 4b−9a, with selection of appropriate genetic material.

Function. Shade tree, naturalizing.

Size and Habit

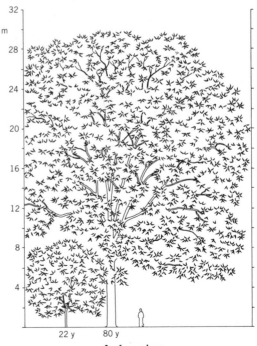

Juglans nigra.

Adaptability

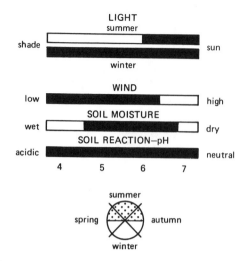

Seasonal Interest. *Flowers:* Hanging catkins (male) to 8 cm/3 in. long, add mild spring interest. *Foliage:* Coarse, compound, bright green leaves give the tree unique character in summer, and fall with little color change in autumn. *Fruits:* Large edible nuts in husks add interest in early autumn. *Trunks and branches:* Thickly ridged, dark gray-brown bark is distinctive but not a major source of landscape interest.

Juglans nigra.

Problems and Maintenance. The nuts are a serious litter problem when they fall to the ground in autumn along with occasional twigs, ruling this tree out for use in street plantings or in other intensive sites. Its overall size rules it out for small properties. In short, *J. nigra* is best planted only in parklike or naturalized situations, but existing trees are worth preserving in development elsewhere.

For many years, *J. nigra* and other walnuts have been known to exert toxic effects on certain other plants under some conditions. There is still some uncertainty about the required conditions, but the toxic material, *juglone,* is thought to be formed by the oxidation of *hydrojuglone,* a material present in large amounts in walnut roots, when roots of sensitive plants come in contact with those of walnut. Sensitive plants include tomato, potato, alfalfa, blackberry, red pine, and several members of the Ericaceae (Heath Family). Lack of information on compatibility of walnut with the great bulk of other landscape plants suggests a cautious approach to the use of walnuts in mixed plantings and provides an additional reason for using them in parklike situations in preference to intensive landscapes.

Cultivars. 'Laciniata' has finely dissected foliage but is similar to the species type otherwise. It is seldom if ever commercially available at present. Several cultivars selected for superior nut quality are available from specialized nut tree nurseries.

Related Species

Juglans ailanthifolia 7 (synonym: *J. sieboldiana;* Japanese walnut). This is a relatively small tree, usually growing to only about 15 m/50 ft. Useful in Zones 5a–8b, it is otherwise subject to the same limitations as *J. nigra. J. ailanthifolia* var. *cordiformis* 7 (synonyms: *J. cordiformis, J. sieboldiana* var. *cordiformis;* heartnut) differs little from the species type as a landscape tree.

Juglans cinerea 8 (butternut). This native of the northeastern and north-central United States and adjacent Canada is generally similar to *J. nigra* but slightly more cold-hardy (Zones 3b–7a), somewhat less impressive as a shade tree, and relatively short-lived because of its susceptibility to blight and canker diseases. Seldom if ever is this tree planted, but it is worthy of preservation in development in some situations.

Juglans regia 8 (English or Persian walnut). This tree from southeastern Europe and Asia, used primarily for nut production, is potentially useful as a lawn or park shade tree, with its rugged trunk and branches covered with light tan-gray bark, bright green, compound leaves, and open branching habit. This tree poses the same litter problem as *J. nigra* and is generally useful in Zones 7a–7b, but the so-called Carpathian walnut, a seed source found in the Carpathian Mountains, is more cold-hardy, useful northward to Zone 6a and good sites in Zone 5b.

Juniperus chinensis 2–7

Chinese juniper
Evergreen shrub or tree
Cupressaceae (Cypress Family)

Native Range. China, Japan.

Useful Range. USDA Zones 4a–9a with selection of appropriate cultivars.

Function. Screen, specimen, massing, groundcover.

Size and Habit. 'Keteleeri' (left rear), 'Armstrongii' (right rear), 'Pfitzerana' (left front) and var. *sargentii* (right front) are illustrated in the lower set of drawings.

Adaptability

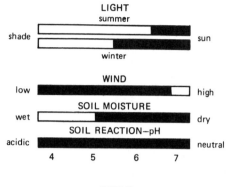

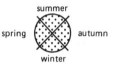

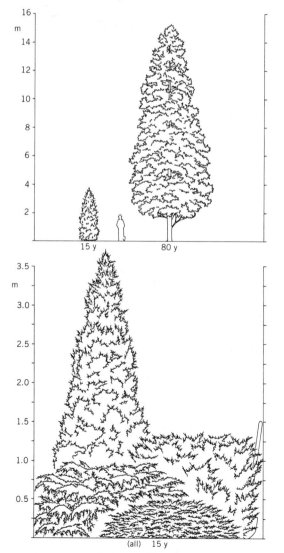

Juniperus chinensis.

Seasonal Interest. *Foliage:* Evergreen, dull olive green to bluish green, occasionally bright green. Commonly both juvenile (needlelike) and mature (scalelike) forms are present on the same plant, but occasionally the foliage is entirely juvenile or predominantly mature. The foliage usually undergoes little or no color change in winter. *Fruits:* Relatively large (to 0.8 cm/0.3 in. across), whitish blue at first, ripening brownish in the second year, on female plants (dioecious).

Problems and Maintenance. This evergreen is relatively trouble-free in most areas at most times, but bagworms are a serious problem in some areas, and mites and *Phomopsis* twig blight (juniper blight) can be troublesome occasionally. Pruning is seldom needed except to control the size of spreading forms. It should be done by cutting back individual branches rather than by shearing so as not to destroy the form of the plant.

Varieties and Cultivars. More than 60 varieties and cultivars have been selected. Many are no longer available, but some of the more common and useful are listed here:

'Ames,' 'Iowa,' and 'Maney' are semierect, vigorous forms, to 2–3 m/6.6–10 ft, selected at Iowa State University, Ames, Iowa. They have dull blue-green needles, mostly juvenile (needlelike) and are unusually well adapted to the region in which they were selected. 'Maney' is well adapted to planting in containers—this is fortunate, since its vase shape is difficult to use in many other settings. All three are considered very cold-hardy—'Maney' at least to Zone 3b—and they are subject to juniper blight in damp years. 'Iowa' fruits very heavily in most years.

'Armstrongii' is compact and blocky in form, about equal in height and breadth, to 1 m/3.3 ft or somewhat greater with time, and is nonfruiting (staminate). Foliage is fairly bright olive green, mostly mature (scalelike). This is fully cold-hardy only to Zone 5b.

Juniperus chinensis 'Armstrongii.'

'Blaauw' is upright, to about 1.5 m/5 ft tall and no more than 1 m/3.3 ft in width, with dull, dark green foliage. It is an interesting specimen for accent, but its somewhat urnlike form is difficult to assimilate into some plantings. Hardy northward to Zone 4a.

'Columnaris' is a handsome, dark green, narrowly conical form, excellent for screening. It reaches heights of at least 10 m/33 ft in time, with a height/width ratio of about 4:1.

'Hetzii' is an extremely vigorous, wide-spreading form, eventually reaching 4—5 m/13—16 ft in height and width. With handsome, silvery blue-green, mostly scalelike foliage and blue berries, it is an excellent shrub for large-scale situations. Unfortunately, it is most commonly used in foundation plantings, where it rapidly overgrows the site and requires drastic pruning or replacement. Useful northward to Zone 4a.

'Iowa,' see 'Ames.'

'Kaizuka' (= 'Torulosa;' Hollywood juniper) is a compact, upright, roughly conical, spiraled form with irregular branching, bright green foliage (mostly juvenile), and bluish berries. It is useful only as a specimen for accent in formal

landscapes in Zones 6a—9a. It can reach heights of 3—4 m/10—13 ft but usually is seen in the 1—2 m/3.3—6.6 ft range.

'Keteleeri' is similar to the treelike species type's pistillate (fruiting) form except that it has denser, brighter green foliage. This is one of the best junipers for screening, growing to heights of 3—4 m/10—33 ft, useful in Zones 4a—8a and perhaps more widely.

'Maney,' see 'Ames.'

'Mint Julep' is similar in form to 'Pfitzerana' but with brighter green foliage and more compact growth.

'Mountbatten' is dense and narrowly pyramidal in form, nonfruiting, with grayish or bluish green foliage, mostly juvenile. Useful for vertical accent or a narrow screen in Zones 4b—8a, perhaps more widely.

'Old Gold' is similar to 'Pfitzerana Aurea,' except that it is more compact, with golden bronze outer foliage that holds its color in winter.

'Parsonii' (= 'Expansa;' synonym: *J. davurica* 'Expansa') is a rather tall (to 0.5 m/1.6 ft) groundcover type, dense and with interestingly textured gray-green foliage.

Juniperus chinensis 'Pfitzerana' (front) and 'Hetzii.'

'Pfitzerana' is an extremely popular, staminate, spreading form with gracefully arching branches and dark to bright green foliage, predominantly mature (scalelike). It functions below eye level in most landscape situations but eventually reaches heights of at least 2–3 m/6.6–10 ft and spreads to more than twice that distance. Useful in Zones 4a–9+, its size can be held to less than 1.5 m/5 ft for years with careful pruning (not shearing). More compact forms are appropriate for low maintenance.

'Pfitzerana Aurea' is very similar to 'Pfitzerana,' with bright, golden-yellow outer foliage in early summer turning to yellowish green by autumn and winter.

Juniperus chinensis var. *procumbens.*

Juniperus chinensis 'Pfitzerana Aurea.'

'Pfitzerana Compacta' (Nick's compact juniper) is similar in habit to 'Pfitzerana' except in being more compact, remaining well under 1 m/3.3 ft in height for many years while spreading to 2–3 m/6.6–10 ft or more.

'Pfitzerana Glauca' (blue Pfitzer juniper) is similar to 'Pfitzerana' except that it has blue-green foliage, silvery to purplish blue in winter. It is intermediate between 'Pfitzerana' and 'Pfitzerana Compacta' in growth rate.

Var. *procumbens* (synonym: *J. procumbens*; Japanese garden juniper) has been treated as a distinct species by many writers and will be found in nurseries almost universally as *J. procumbens* at present. It is a low, moundlike, broad-spreading plant, to 0.5 m/1.6 ft or occasionally 0.7 m/2.3 ft and eventually very broad, with entirely needlelike, pale to bright green foliage and ascending branch tips. The form 'Nana' is very compact and lower, an excellent small-scale groundcover. Both forms are useful in Zones 5a–9a and perhaps colder zones as well.

'Pyramidalis,' often incorrectly labeled *J. excelsa* 'Stricta' (spiny Greek juniper), is mentioned here as a warning rather than a recommendation. It is stiffly upright, nonfruiting, with juvenile, very prickly, steely blue foliage, much too positive for any but very formal landscapes, and after a few years its lower foliage begins to brown and drop. Even though it is commonly grown and sold, usually it is best avoided. True *J. excelsa* 'Stricta' is much less cold-hardy (Zones 7b–9a) and probably not available in our area.

'Robusta Green' is a dull, deep green, compactly upright selection, similar in texture to 'Kaizuka.'

'San Jose' is a low, spreading form with predominantly juvenile foliage but often with considerable scalelike foliage as well. It usually remains below 0.5 m/1.6 ft for many years, but spreads widely.

Var. *sargentii*, a distinctive, natural variety from the Kurile Islands, north of Japan, grows to 0.5 m/1.6 ft or a little taller with age, spreading to 3 m/10 ft or more in diameter where space is available. Its foliage is bright to deep green or

Juniperus chinensis var. *sargentii.*

blue-green, usually with only needlelike leaves, much shorter than those of most junipers. This is an excellent, neat groundcover for Zones 4a–9a. Several selections have been made, including 'Compacta' with compact growth, 'Glauca' with blue-green foliage, and 'Viridis' with bright green foliage.

'Shoosmith' is a dwarf selection with a "patchy" mixture of scalelike and needlelike, blue-green foliage, upright in form but remaining under 1.5 m/5 ft in height and spread for many years.

Related Species

Juniperus squamata 2–5 (singleseed juniper). This species includes several shrubby forms,

ranging from 'Prostrata' a creeping, mat-forming groundcover, to 'Wilsonii,' a bright green, conical shrub eventually reaching 3 m/10 ft in height. But the cultivar most commonly in landscape use is 'Meyeri,' an irregularly upright shrub with steely blue, all needlelike foliage. 'Meyeri' is strikingly colorful but difficult to use because of its positive accent and irregular form. It is adapted to Zones 5a–8a and possibly warmer zones as well. The newer cultivar, 'Blue Star,' with foliage similar to that of 'Meyeri' but lower and moundlike in form, promises to be more useful as a landscape plant than 'Meyeri.'

Juniperus communis 2–6

Common juniper
Evergreen shrub
Cupressaceae (Cypress Family)

Native Range. Northern parts of Asia, Europe, North America.

Useful Range. USDA Zones 3a–8a with selection of appropriate cultivars.

Function. Groundcover, specimen, rock garden.

Size and Habit. 'Hibernica' (left), var. *depressa* (right), and var. *saxatilis* (front) are illustrated.

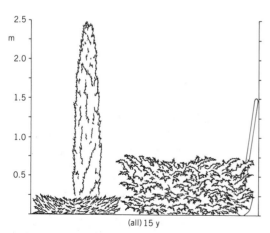

Juniperus communis: 'Hibernica' (left), var. *depressa* (right), and var. *saxatilis* (front).

Adaptability. This species is relatively tolerant of salt in seashore sites and where de-icing salt is used.

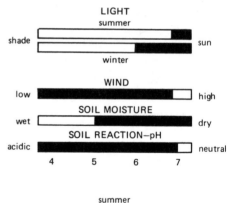

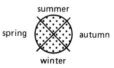

Seasonal Interest. *Foliage:* Evergreen, sharply needlelike, dull yellowish green to deep blue-green, mostly turning brownish in winter. *Fruits:* Blue-black with a waxy bloom, to 0.6 cm/0.24 in. across, usually dioecious.

Problems and Maintenance. Relatively trouble-free in most cases, but mites and bagworms can be troublesome. Pruning should be carried out, if at all, in the manner described for *J. chinensis*. Most individuals of this species have poor color and form and are of little landscape value, but selected cultivars and varieties are useful.

Varieties and Cultivars. 'Compressa' is a very slow-growing, tightly columnar selection with deep green foliage, useful for accent in small-scale situations. It remains below 1 m/3.3 ft for many years.

Var. *depressa* is the spreading shrub distributed widely in old fields and pastures across North America, usually lower than 1 m/3.3 ft but several times as broad after many years. Individual plants with better form and color than average have been selected for landscape use in cold climates (Zones 3a–5a).

'Depressa Aurea,' selected from var. *depressa*, has typical form, the new foliage bright golden yellow as it emerges, then dull yellow, changing to deep green by the second year.

Juniperus communis 'Depressa Aurea.'

'Gold Beach' is an excellent creeping form selected from the mountains of the Pacific Northwest, not exceeding 10–15 cm/4–6 in. in height. It makes a dense, matlike groundcover with bright yellow-green foliage.

'Hibernica' (= 'Stricta'; Irish juniper) and 'Suecica' (Swedish juniper) are both vigorous, tightly columnar forms, reaching heights of 3–5 m/10–16 ft, in width seldom exceeding 1 m/3.3 ft even at mature size. 'Hibernica' has more upright branch tips than 'Suecica,' but both are prone to breakage and pulling apart by snow and wind in winter unless carefully tied together, and to winterburning of foliage as well. They are useful in Zones 5b–8a and frequently marred by winter damage farther north except in protected sites.

'Hornibrookii' is a selection from var. *saxatilis* for compact but spreading growth habit. It is one of the most successful groundcover types, growing to 0.5 m/1.6 ft tall and very broad in time, with deep green foliage that takes on a brownish cast in winter.

'Jackii' (= var. *jackii*, = 'Montana') is a creeping form selected from the mountains of the Pacific Northwest. It has shorter needles than the species type and more pleasing texture as a small-scale groundcover. It is useful in Zones 5b–8a and very likely in colder zones as well.

'Repanda' is a low-growing selection from var. *saxatilis*, growing to 1.5 m/5 ft or more in width although only 0.3 m/1 ft tall.

Var. *saxatilis* includes the prostrate or low-growing forms native to the sub-Arctic or mountainous parts of Europe and North America and perhaps interior Asia as well. Most forms have unusually good blue-green foliage color and make effective groundcovers in Zones 3a–7a.

Related Species

Juniperus rigida 6 (needle juniper).   This tall shrub or small tree from northeastern Asia has foliage very similar to that of *J. communis* but arranged loosely on drooping branches. It is seldom available for landscape use but potentially useful in Zones 5a–8a and perhaps also colder zones.

Juniperus conferta 2

Shore juniper
Evergreen groundcover
Cupressaceae (Cypress Family)

Native Range. Japan, Sakhalin.

Useful Range. USDA Zones 6a–9a+. Selec-

tions from northern extremes of the natural range may prove useful in Zone 5.

Function. Groundcover, specimen, rock garden. In appropriate sites, this is one of the fastest evergreen groundcovers to become established.

Size and Habit

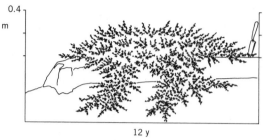

Juniperus conferta.

Adaptability. This plant is unusually tolerant of seashore conditions and de-icing salts and is usually at its best in infertile soil.

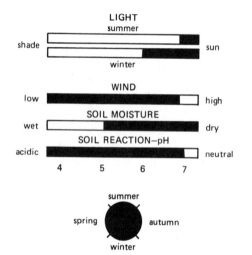

Seasonal Interest. *Foliage:* Evergreen, sharply needlelike, bright green to slightly bluish, not

changing appreciably in winter. *Fruits:* Black with a waxy bloom, to 1.2 cm/0.5 in. across. Dioecious.

Juniperus conferta.

Problems and Maintenance. This groundcover is relatively trouble-free in most situations, but mites occasionally can be troublesome.

Cultivars. The following two cultivars are relatively new, and their limits of cold hardiness have not been fully determined. 'Blue Pacific' is blue-green and fully prostrate, remaining below 15 cm/6 in. 'Emerald Sea' is equally prostrate but a soft green.

Juniperus horizontalis 2

Creeping juniper
Evergreen groundcover
Cupressaceae (Cypress Family)

Native Range. Northern North America: Nova Scotia to Alaska, southward to New Jersey, Minnesota, and Montana.

Useful Range. USDA Zones 2a–9a with selection of appropriate genetic material.

Function. Groundcover, specimen, rock garden.

Size and Habit. 'Douglasii' is illustrated.

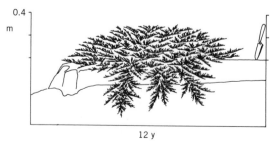

Juniperus horizontalis 'Douglasii.'

Adaptability. This species is unusually tolerant of seashore conditions and de-icing salts.

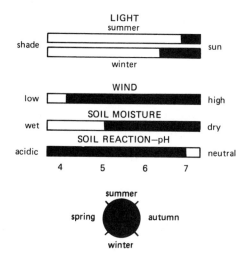

Seasonal Interest. *Foliage:* Evergreen, bluish green to soft, gray-green or rich, deep green, usually mostly scalelike at maturity with some juvenile (needlelike) foliage, but some variants are entirely or predominantly juvenile. *Fruits:* Light blue berries (on female plants), to 0.8 cm/0.3 in. across, add landscape interest. Dioecious.

Problems and Maintenance. Many cultivars are susceptible to *Phomopsis* twig blight (juniper blight) under environmental conditions favorable for the disease (moist weather in spring). This disease can be a serious problem, especially since it is difficult to control. The problem is somewhat localized, so selection of cultivars should be guided by local experience. Mites can be troublesome in hot, dry weather.

Cultivars. Only a few of the many useful cultivars are listed here.

'Alpina' is similar to 'Plumosa,' nonfruiting with needlelike foliage and purple winter color, but its branches grow and stand vertically to a height of up to 0.5 m/1.6 ft before falling into a prostrate position, giving a vertically planar texture. It is highly susceptible to twig blight but useful in Zones 4a–9a.

'Bar Harbor' is a creeping, nonfruiting selection from Maine with bluish leaves, both needlelike and scalelike. It is rather thoroughly confused with other variants in the nursery trade. When specifying this cultivar, one can be reasonably sure only that some creeping form of *J.*

horizontalis will be supplied. Useful in Zones 3a–8b, perhaps more widely.

'Douglasii' (Waukegan juniper) is an excellent, nonfruiting creeping form of midwestern origin with steely blue-green foliage that turns silvery purple in winter, on twig tips ascending to no more than 0.5 m/1.6 ft high, usually about half that height. This is less confused in the nursery trade than most older cultivars and seems to be less susceptible to twig blight. Useful in Zones 3a–8b and perhaps more widely.

Juniperus horizontalis 'Douglasii.'

'Emerald Spreader' (Plant Patent No. 2752, 1967) is a matlike, spreading selection with rich green foliage, useful in Zones 4a–9a and perhaps colder zones as well.

'Glauca' is a creeping selection similar to 'Bar Harbor' and 'Wiltonii' but not as widely used. Useful in Zones 3b–8a and perhaps more widely.

'Glenmore' is a slow-growing groundcover that originated in Wyoming. It makes a dense mat 10 cm/4 in. high, with bluish green foliage, browning slightly in winter. Useful in Zones 4a–8b, perhaps more widely.

'Hughes' is a recent selection for its extremely vigorous dense, low, moundlike growth (15–30 cm/6–12 in. high) and exceptionally blue foliage. Its distinctive texture results from straight branchlets radiating from main branches, seen also in other cultivars such as 'Douglasii,' but accentuated in 'Hughes.' Useful in Zones 4a–8b and perhaps more widely.

'Plumosa' (Andorra juniper) is a nonfruiting, spreading form with branches ascending to 25–40 cm/10–16 in. Foliage is entirely needlelike, soft green in summer and deep silvery purple (fertile soil) to rosy plum-purple (infertile soil) in winter. It is notably susceptible to twig blight. Useful in Zones 4a–8b.

'Plumosa Compacta' (compact Andorra juniper) is similar to 'Plumosa' except lower branching and remaining below 25 cm/10 in. tall.

'Prince of Wales' is an excellent, low, mat-forming, nonfruiting selection introduced in 1967 by the Agriculture Canada Research Station at Morden, Manitoba, and originating in Alberta. Its foliage is bright medium green with a silvery purple cast on exposed parts in winter. Useful in Zones 2a–8a, perhaps in warmer zones as well.

'Turquoise Spreader' (Plant Patent No. 2773, 1967) is a vigorous, mat-forming groundcover, to 20–25 cm/8–10 in., with blue-green foliage. Useful in Zones 4a–9a and perhaps colder zones as well.

'Wiltonii' (blue rug juniper) is an excellent, dense, nonfruiting, creeping form with silvery blue foliage, so low that it assumes the form of the surface that it covers except for slight mounding toward plant centers, giving it a subtly irregular surface. Originating in Maine, it is useful in Zones 3a–9a.

'Youngstown' is very similar to 'Plumosa Compacta.'

Juniperus sabina 2–5

Savin juniper
Evergreen shrub
Cupressaceae (Cypress Family)

Native Range. Southwestern Europe to Siberia.

Useful Range. USDA Zones 3b–8b with selection of appropriate cultivars. May be useful farther south as well.

Function. Groundcover, specimen, massing. The taller cultivars are not easy to use because of their vase-shaped form.

Size and Habit. 'Von Ehren' (rear), 'Tamariscifolia' (right), and 'Broadmoor' (left) are illustrated.

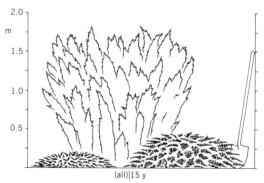

Juniperus sabina: 'Von Ehren' (rear), 'Tamariscifolia' (right), and 'Broadmoor' (left, front).

Adaptability

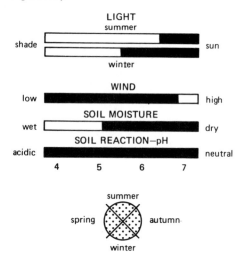

Seasonal Interest. *Foliage:* Evergreen, bright yellowish green to deep green, blue-green occasionally, usually predominantly scalelike but in some cultivars mostly needlelike with scale leaves toward the branch tips. Foliage gives off a pungent (unpleasant?) odor when crushed. *Fruits:* Blue-black with whitish, waxy bloom, inconspicuous. Dioecious.

Problems and Maintenance. *Phomopsis* twig blight can be a problem for some cultivars. Consult people with local experience when making selections. Mites can be troublesome, especially in dry climates and years.

Cultivars. A few of the most common and useful cultivars are listed here.

'Arcadia' is a low, spreading form with ascending branch tips, to about 0.5 m/1.6 ft tall, originating in the Ural Mountains of Russia. Foliage is predominantly scalelike, a bright, pale green. Nonfruiting, it is useful in Zones 3b−7b and probably more widely.

'Broadmoor,' from the Ural Mountains, is one of the lowest growing *J. sabina* cultivars, reaching a height of only about 40 cm/16 in. after many years and spreading to at least two to three times its height. The foliage is bright green, feathery in texture, with mostly needlelike leaves. This nonfruiting selection is useful in Zones 4a−8b, perhaps more widely.

'Skandia,' another selection from the Ural Mountains, is similar to 'Arcadia' but with mostly needlelike foliage, blue-green in color. It is useful in Zones 3b−7b and probably more widely.

'Tamariscifolia' (tamarix juniper) is a handsome, broad-spreading selection, to about 0.5

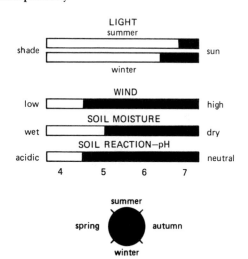

Juniperus sabina 'Broadmoor.'

m/1.6 ft tall, with bright green, feathery foliage consisting mostly of short, needlelike leaves, giving a distinctive texture. This common nonfruiting selection is useful in Zones 4a−8b, perhaps more widely.

'Von Ehren' is an excessively vigorous, vase-shaped selection, difficult to use in the landscape.

Juniperus scopulorum 7

Rocky Mountain juniper, western red cedar
Evergreen tree
Cupressaceae (Cypress Family)

Native Range. Western United States and southwestern Canada.

Useful Range. USDA Zones 3b−6b with selection of appropriate cultivars or other genetic material. May be useful in warmer zones as well.

Function. Specimen, screen, massing.

Size and Habit

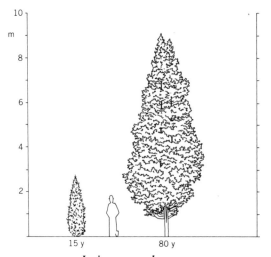

15 y   80 y

Juniperus scopulorum.

Adaptability

Seasonal Interest. *Foliage:* Evergreen, medium green to striking silvery blue, predominantly scalelike except in young seedlings. Little color change in winter. *Fruits:* Bright blue with whitish, waxy bloom similar in color to the foliage in silvery blue selections, to 0.6 cm/0.24 in. across or slightly larger. Dioecious.

Problems and Maintenance. In some areas, this species and its cultivars are made almost useless by a twig blight (probably *Phomopsis* blight). Its best performance seems to be in the western part of our range (western Central Plains and Great Plains), especially in the northern portions, but good specimens can be found in certain sites all the way to the Atlantic Coast. Bagworms can be a serious problem in some areas. Before selecting this species, it is advisable to inquire about local experience or to proceed on a small scale.

Cultivars. There has been considerable interest in variants of this species in the Northern Plains and Rocky Mountain areas of the United States and Canada, and at least 25 cultivars have been selected and named. A few of the most common or most widely adaptable are listed here.

'Blue Heaven' (sometimes incorrectly listed as 'Blue Haven') is a vigorous, silvery blue, pyramidal form selected in Nebraska. It seems to be more widely adapted in our range than some other cultivars.

'Cologreen' is a vigorous columnar form with green foliage selected in Colorado and at its best west of our range.

'Gray Gleam' is a relatively slow-growing, pyramidal form with blue-gray foliage, becoming grayer in winter.

'Hill's Silver' is a compact, narrowly pyramidal form originating in South Dakota. This is one of the earliest cultivars selected (1922 or earlier) and may no longer be commercially available.

'Medora' is a vigorous pyramidal form with blue-green foliage that has been tested thoroughly in Zone 3b and found fully winter-hardy (not to exclude the possibility that any others listed here will prove equally hardy).

'Moffetii' is dense and pyramidal in form, with

Juniperus scopulorum 'Medora.'

silvery blue-green foliage. Selected in Nebraska (1937), it may no longer be available.

'Pathfinder' is a very narrowly pyramidal form with blue-gray foliage, selected in Nebraska. It is typically at least five times as tall as it is wide.

'Silver King' is one of relatively few compact and spreading forms of *J. scopulorum*, making a dense mass at least 2 m/6.6 ft across and 0.5 m/1.6 ft high in time, with silvery-blue foliage.

Juniperus virginiana 3–8

Eastern red cedar
Evergreen shrub or tree
Cupressaceae (Cypress Family)

Native Range. Eastern United States and adjacent southern Ontario.

Useful Range. USDA Zones 3b–9a with selection of appropriate cultivars or other genetic material.

Function. Specimen, screen, massing.

Size and Habit

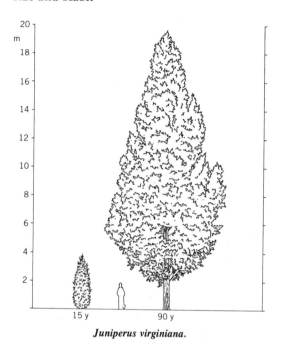

Juniperus virginiana.

Adaptability

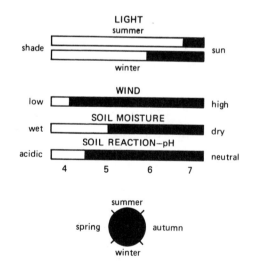

Seasonal Interest. *Foliage:* Evergreen, deep green to silvery blue-green in a few cultivars, usually predominantly scalelike except in young seedlings, turning purplish or brownish in winter. *Fruits:* Bright blue to grayish, to 0.6 cm/0.24 in. across, colorful in some cultivars, especially in combination with bright green foliage. Dioecious.

Juniperus virginiana.

Problems and Maintenance. Mites can be troublesome occasionally, and bagworms are a potential problem in certain areas and must be controlled to avoid serious damage. *J. virginiana* is susceptible to *Phomopsis* blight and is also a principal alternate host to the fungus that causes cedar apple rust. The fruiting bodies of this fungus can be considered either interesting or unsightly but do little harm to the tree except in the cases of very heavy infections. But the disease is a serious problem of the other alternate hosts: the pome fruits such as apples and hawthorns, and selection of *J. virginiana* should be done with other susceptible species in mind. This species should at least be avoided in the vicinity of commercial apple orchards.

Cultivars. More selections have been made from this species than from *J. scopulorum.* A few of the most useful and commonly available are listed here.

‘Burkii’ is one of the finest blue selections with both scalelike and needlelike foliage types of fine texture, turning deep purple in winter. It is a staminate (nonfruiting) clone, pyramidal in form. Useful in Zones 5a−8a and perhaps more widely as well.

'Canaertii' is one of the most popular and distinctive cultivars with irregular branching, tufted deep green foliage year-round, and bright blue fruits. Useful in Zones 3b−8a, perhaps in warmer zones as well. Notoriously sensitive to certain spray chemicals; check tolerance before planning spray programs.

'Glauca' has irregular branching and fine-textured, tufted, strikingly blue-green foliage.

'Grey Owl' bears a striking resemblance to *J. chinensis* cultivars 'Hetzii' and 'Pfitzerana Glauca.' P. den Ouden and B. K. Boom, in *Manual of Cultivated Conifers*, point out that it originated as a seedling from a plant of *J. virginiana* 'Glauca,' which was standing near a plant of *J. chinensis* 'Pfitzerana' in a nursery in the Netherlands, suggesting the possibility that it is an interspecies hybrid. Whatever its parentage, it is a fine, wide-spreading shrub with silvery blue foliage, eventually reaching heights of at least 1.5 m/5 ft and much greater spread. Useful at least in Zones 4a−8a, there seem to be at least two clones in commerce, one fruiting and one non-fruiting, but the latter may be mislabeled *J. chinensis* 'Pfitzerana Glauca.'

'Hillii' is a slow-growing, pyramidal selection with blue-green foliage turning purple in winter. It is useful in Zones 4a−8a and perhaps warmer zones as well.

'Hillspire' (= 'Cupressifolia,' = 'Cupressifolia Green') is an exceptionally tightly columnar form with rich green foliage, growing three to five times as tall as it is wide.

'Kosteri' is one of the lowest growing forms of *J. virginiana*, spreading broadly but remaining

Juniperus virginiana 'Hillspire.'

below 1 m/3.3 ft in height for many years, with soft green or blue-green foliage. It is useful for massing, much like *J. chinensis* 'Pfitzerana Compacta.'

'Skyrocket' is perhaps the narrowest of all cultivars of *Juniperus* in commerce, with a height:spread ratio of 8:1 or greater, and silvery blue-green foliage. It is useful for vertical accent in formal landscapes but susceptible to breakage by heavy snow.

Kalmia latifolia 5

Mountain laurel
Evergreen shrub
Ericaceae (Heath Family)

Native Range. Eastern North America.

Useful Range. USDA Zones 5a−9a with selection of appropriate genetic material.

Function. Border, specimen, screen, naturalizing, roadside.

Size and Habit

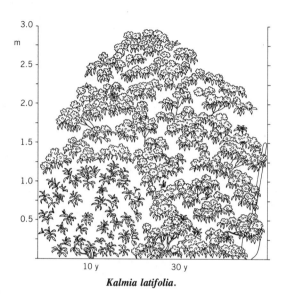

Kalmia latifolia.

Adaptability. This shrub is tolerant of full sun or shade in summer in the North, but flowering is reduced by shade. In the South it is useful only in relatively cool sites: northern exposures with at least some shade. Light shade in winter reduces winterburn of foliage in Zone 5.

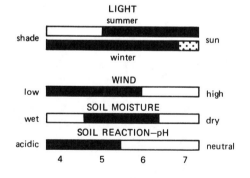

Seasonal Interest. *Flowers:* White to rosy pink, to 2.5 cm/1 in. across, in showy terminal clusters in late spring to early summer. *Foliage:* Evergreen, leathery, and dark green, slightly lustrous, individual leaves to 10 cm/4 in. long.

Problems and Maintenance. Relatively trouble-free, given a cool site and acidic soil, but subject to a controllable leaf-spot disease. Removal of flowers after they fade prevents fruiting and enhances flowering in the following year. Foliage of this and most other members of the Ericaceae is toxic to cattle, sheep, and humans.

Forms and Cultivars. F. *rubra* includes plants with deep pink flowers. Several clones have been selected and are under test, and several cultivars with distinctive flower color patterns also have been selected but are not yet widely available.

Kalmia poliifolia 3

Bog laurel
Evergreen shrub
Ericaceae (Heath Family)

Native Range. Northeastern North America to Pennsylvania and Minnesota in bog habitats.

Useful Range. USDA Zones 2a–6a, perhaps in warmer zones in cool microclimates.

Function. Specimen, bog, or rock garden with ample moisture.

Size and Habit

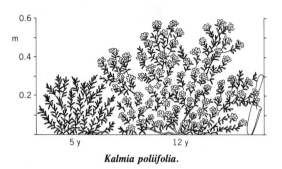

Kalmia poliifolia.

Adaptability. This plant is tolerant of full sun or partial shade, but flowering is reduced by shade. Acidic and well-drained but moist soil is essential for success. Limited to relatively cool sites, even in Zone 5.

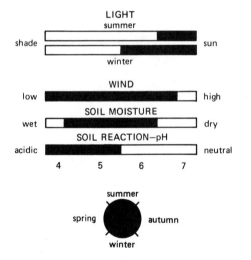

Seasonal Interest. *Flowers:* Rosy purple, to 1.5 cm/0.6 in. across, in terminal clusters in late spring or early summer. *Foliage:* Small, narrow, evergreen leaves to 3.5 cm/1.4 in. long, with edges rolled underneath, the upper side deep green to whitish, the lower side waxy and whitened. Toxic to animals.

Problems and Maintenance. This species is relatively trouble-free given a good site (cool, moist, but well-drained acidic soil). It is not commonly available but can be found in some northern nurseries.

Related Species

Andromeda polifolia 2 (bog rosemary). This evergreen, moundlike shrub, usually remaining below 0.5 m/1.6 ft, is native to northern Eurasia as well as northern North America. It is similar to *Kalmia poliifolia* in landscape use, useful range and requirements, and its limited availability. Its flowers appear at the same time as those of *Kalmia poliifolia* or slightly later, but are only half as large.

Cassiope tetragona 2. This evergreen, moundlike shrub is similar to *Kalmia poliifolia* in native and useful ranges, adaptability, and landscape use. It differs in having finer textured foliage with leaves only 0.4 cm/0.15 in. long, arranged on the stem to give a four-angled form.

Kalmia angustifolia 3 (lamb kill, sheep laurel). This small, straggling shrub, native to northeastern North America, has pale green, evergreen foliage and small purplish flowers in lateral clusters. Not a greatly valued landscape plant, it is worthy of preservation in some natural landscapes. Its foliage is highly toxic to sheep and cattle, as the name suggests. Useful in Zones 2b–7b. The var. *caroliniana* (southern sheep laurel) is useful southward to Zone 8b.

Loiseleuria procumbens 2 (alpine azalea). This low alpine shrub from northern Eurasia and North America varies from a tight mat of foliage only a few centimeters thick on mountain summits to somewhat taller in more protected sites. Its small, clear, rosy pink flowers are exquisite in early to midsummer, and its very fine textured foliage is evergreen. Its landscape usefulness is limited to rock gardens, probably only in Zones 2b–5b or in unusually cool microclimates in Zone 6.

Kalopanax pictus 8

Castor aralia
Deciduous tree
Araliaceae (Aralia Family)

Native Range. China, Japan, Korea.

Useful Range. USDA Zones 5a—8a.

Function. Shade tree, specimen.

Size and Habit

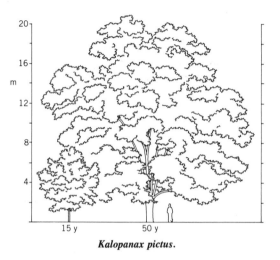

Kalopanax pictus.

Seasonal Interest. *Flowers:* White, small, in large clusters (compound umbels), very striking in middle to late summer. *Foliage:* Individual leaves similar in shape to those of sweetgum but larger, the blades 25 cm/10 in. or more across, and petioles sometimes an additional 25 cm/10 in. or more. Deep green, forming a dense, irregular canopy in summer, turning reddish in autumn. *Fruits:* Small, shiny, black, in clusters, interesting in early autumn but usually taken quickly by birds. *Twigs and branches:* Heavy and coarse, with large terminal buds and many large and sharp prickles, even on trunks of young trees

Problems and Maintenance. This tree is unusually trouble-free but appears stark and sparse when young, becoming round-headed in a few years. Prickles on lower trunk and branches must be removed where small children are present, but once this is done no further attention is necessary.

Varieties. Var. *maximowiczii* has more deeply lobed leaves than the species type.

Adaptability

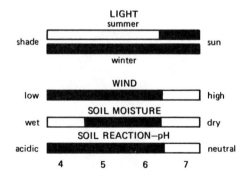

Kerria japonica 4

Kerria
Deciduous shrub
Rosaceae (Rose Family)

Native Range. China.

Useful Range. USDA Zones 5b—9a.

Function. Border, specimen.

Size and Habit

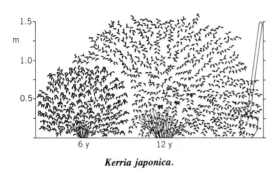

Kerria japonica.

Adaptability

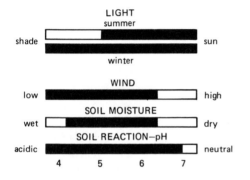

Seasonal Interest. *Flowers:* Bright yellow and showy, to 4.5 cm/1.8 in. across, in midspring.

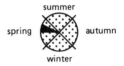

Often a few flowers will open intermittently during late summer and autumn. *Foliage:* Bright green with crisp texture; leaves long tapered and sharply toothed, to 5 cm/2 in. long, sometimes turning yellow before falling in autumn. *Twigs and branches:* Pale green, adding considerable winter interest.

Problems and Maintenance. This shrub is relatively trouble-free but needs to be thinned every few years to maintain form. This is especially true of the double-flowered cultivar.

Cultivars. 'Picta' has white-edged foliage and is much daintier and slower growing than the species type. But it is genetically unstable, fairly often undergoing bud mutations back to the species type, which, because of its greater vigor, soon takes over. 'Picta' is best reserved for small-scale gardens where the plant is frequently inspected so that reversions to the species type can be cut out promptly.

'Pleniflora' has double flowers, almost globose in form, remaining colorful for considerably longer than the single flowers of the species type and gradually turning to a deep orange-yellow.

Koelreuteria paniculata 7

Golden rain tree
Deciduous tree
Sapindaceae (Soapberry Family)

Native Range. China and Korea.

Useful Range. USDA Zones 5b–9a.

Function. Specimen, patio tree, small shade tree.

Size and Habit

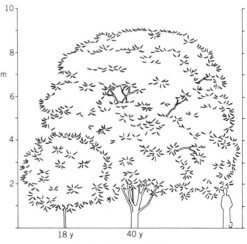

Koelreuteria paniculata.

Adaptability

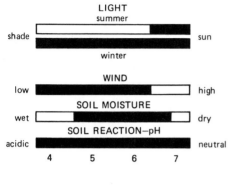

Seasonal Interest. *Flowers:* Yellow with red centers, small but borne in large, loose, upright clusters; showy in midsummer on most trees, but in late summer on some. *Foliage:* Deep green, deeply cut, compound with a few leaflets doubly compound, falling in autumn without color change. *Fruits:* Large (to 5 cm/2 in. long), papery, inflated capsules, pale yellow-green in late summer, later turning brown and persisting well into autumn.

Problems and Maintenance. This tree is trouble-free except for being weak wooded and subject to damage during ice and wind storms.

Cultivars. 'September' is a recent introduction selected for its late flowering, a full five weeks or more later than typical trees of *K. paniculata*. Not yet widely available but useful in Zones 6b−9a and perhaps Zones 5b−6a as well. Other late-flowering individual trees are known in certain localities.

Related Species

Koelreuteria bipinnata 7 (golden rain tree). This tree gives much the same landscape effect as its more cold-hardy relative, *K. paniculata*. Its papery, bladderlike pods, similar to those of *K. paniculata*, are pink at first, drying a warm tan color, and its foliage turns yellowish before falling. Useful in Zone 9a+ and perhaps Zone 8 as well in protected sites.

Koelreuteria elegans 7 (synonym: *K. formosana*; Chinese flame tree, flamegold). Generally similar to *K. bipinnata* and often confused with it, but less cold-hardy. It is useful in Zone 9a+ and most common south of our range in Florida.

Sapindus drummondii 7 (western soapberry, wild China tree). This native of the south-central and southwestern United States from southern Missouri to Arizona and adjacent Mexico is drought-resistant and trouble-free, potentially useful as a street tree in Zones 6b−9a+, but little used and seldom available. It reaches heights of up to 15 m/49 ft, the trunk and branches covered with scaly bark showing reddish orange inner bark. The lustrous, medium green, compound leaves turn golden yellow before falling in midautumn. Very small, yellowish white flowers are borne in loose clusters to 25 cm/10 in. long in late spring, and the yellow, translucent fruits, to 1.5 cm/0.6 in. across, ripen in early autumn, then turn black and hang on for some time. The seeds occasionally send up weed seedlings much like those of the related *Koelreuteria*.

Xanthoceras sorbifolium 6 (xanthoceras). This small, shrubby tree, to 8 m/25 ft tall, native to China, is little used and not generally available. But it has good landscape qualities, including white flowers, yellow to red in the center, in clusters 15−25 cm/6−10 in. long in midspring, and lustrous foliage that remains dark green late into autumn. It has broad soil and environmental tolerance and is useful in Zones 6b−9a.

Kolkwitzia amabilis 5

Beautybush
Deciduous shrub
Caprifoliaceae (Honeysuckle Family)

Native Range. Central China.

Useful Range. USDA Zones 5a–8a.

Function. Border, specimen.

Size and Habit

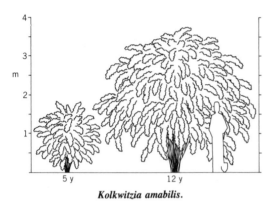

Kolkwitzia amabilis.

Adaptability

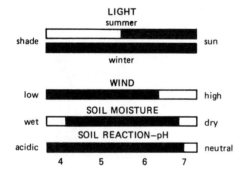

Seasonal Interest. *Flowers:* Pale pink with yellow-orange throat, only 1.5 cm/0.6 in. long but borne in great numbers all along the arching branches, making this one of the most spectacular of flowering shrubs in late spring. *Foliage:* Medium green, pointed leaves resemble those of the small-leaved mock oranges and turn reddish in autumn in some years. *Fruits:* Brown or pinkish and bristly, adding little to the plant's interest in summer and early autumn. *Twigs and branches:* Light tan bark peels off in large strips and patches, giving a ragged winter appearance.

Problems and Maintenance. This shrub is relatively trouble-free but requires regular pruning (thinning by removal of large branches) to maintain the potentially graceful form. Pruning for control of size is not practical. Rather the plant should be used only where there is enough space to accommodate its height and spread. At the northern edge of its useful range (Zone 5) it suffers occasional twig kill, requiring some additional pruning to remove winterkilled branch tips.

Laburnum ×watereri 6

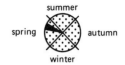

Synonym: *L. vossii*
Deciduous tree
Waterer laburnum, golden chain tree
Leguminosae (Pea Family)

Hybrid origin. *L. anagyroides* × *L. alpinum.*

Useful Range. USDA Zones 6a−7b and relatively cool sites in Zone 8.

Function. Specimen, patio tree, border accent.

Size and Habit. 'Vossii' is illustrated.

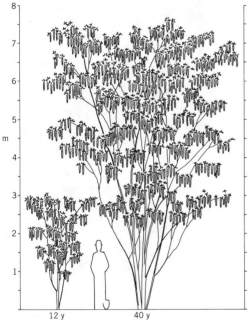

Laburnum ×watereri 'Vossii.'

Seasonal Interest. *Flowers*: Bright yellow, individually to 2.5 cm/1 in., in pendulous clusters, 25−50 cm/10−20 in. long, in late spring, lasting for only a week or two. *Foliage*: Bright green leaves of three leaflets, each 3−8 cm/1−3 in. long, falling without color change in autumn. *Twigs and branches*: Smooth, olive green bark is distinctive in the landscape in winter.

Problems and Maintenance. This tree is relatively trouble-free where it is fully hardy. At the edges of its useful range it is prone to sun-scald of the bark where exposed to afternoon sun in winter. Foliage "burning" may occur in summer if used in dry or windy sites. The seeds are poisonous to both livestock and humans.

Cultivars. 'Vossii,' sometimes incorrectly listed as *L. vossii* in nursery catalogs, is a selection (or perhaps more than one) for fullness, good form, and large flower clusters.

Related Species

Laburnum alpinum 6 (Scotch laburnum). This tree, from the mountains of southern Europe in spite of its common name, is similar to *L. ×watereri* except somewhat less showy in flower and at least slightly more cold-hardy, to Zone 5b.

Laburnum anagyroides 6 (golden chain, bean tree). This tree is less showy in flower and probably less cold-hardy than either *L. alpinum* or *L. ×watereri*. There is little reason for using it when the other species are available.

Adaptability

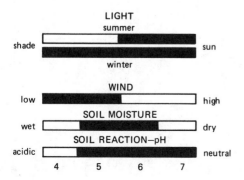

Lagerstroemia indica 6

Crape myrtle
Deciduous shrub or small tree
Lythraceae (Loosestrife Family)

Native Range. China.

Useful Range. USDA Zones 7b−9a+.

Function. Specimen, border.

Size and Habit

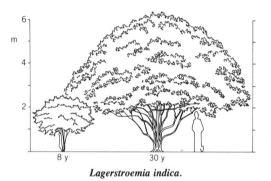

Lagerstroemia indica.

Adaptability. Performs best in well-drained soil of good water-holding capacity rather than sandy soils that tend to dry out rapidly.

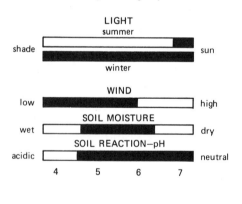

Seasonal Interest. *Flowers:* Brilliant red, pink, lavender, or white, crinkly textured, in showy clusters of 15 cm/6 in. and larger in middle to late summer. *Foliage:* Neatly textured oval leaves are deep reddish bronze as they unfold, quickly turn rich medium green, and then turn reddish

or yellowish before falling in autumn. *Trunk and branches:* Smooth, silvery gray to pinkish tan bark and sinewy main branches add strong winter interest.

Problems and Maintenance. North of Zone 7b this plant will persist, but tops will frequently winterkill and must be removed each spring. Since this plant flowers on new growth, it will return and give a flowering display in late sum-

Lagerstroemia indica.

Lagerstroemia indica.

mer but will not attain full size or develop trunk and bark interest. Powdery mildew can be troublesome, especially for plants in shaded sites, but resistant cultivars are being developed (see Cultivars). In areas where Japanese beetle has spread, this insect can cause severe damage to the flowers.

Cultivars. At least 50 cultivars are in the U.S. market, but their availability varies locally. Some of the best and most commonly used are listed here.

'Alba' is a full-size selection with white flowers.

'Carolina Beauty' is full-size with dark red flowers.

'Catawba,' a U.S. National Arboretum (USNA) introduction, is mildew-resistant, compact, and globose, to 3 m/10 ft tall with dark purple flowers and orange-red autumn foliage.

'Centennial' is compact and globose, 2–3 m/6.6–10 ft tall with deep red-purple flowers and yellow to red autumn foliage, useful northward to Zone 7a and highly resistant to powdery mildew.

'Cherokee,' another USNA introduction, is open in growth habit, to 2.5 m/8 ft tall, and has brilliant red flowers.

'Conestoga,' also a USNA introduction, is open in growth habit, to 3 m/10 ft tall (and broader than tall), with medium to pale lavender flowers.

'Dixie Brilliant' is full size, with deep, watermelon pink flowers.

'Hope' is mildew-resistant, a semidwarf with open branching, and has white flowers.

'Low Flame' is a semidwarf, 1.5–2 m/5–6.6 ft tall, with early red flowers.

'Majestic Orchid' is full-size with orchid-purple flowers.

'Muskogee,' a USNA introduction, is a large selection, to 7 m/23 ft tall, mildew-resistant, with lavender flowers and brown, exfoliating bark. This is a hybrid of *L. indica* and *L. fauriei.*

'Natchez,' a USNA introduction, is a large plant, to 7 m/23 ft, mildew-resistant, with white flowers and rich red-brown, exfoliating bark. This is a hybrid between an *L. indica* selection and *L. fauriei.*

'Near East' has great quantities of delicately pale pink flowers.

'New Snow' is semidwarf with white flowers.

'Petite Embers' and 'Petite Red Imp' are semidwarf, 1.5–2 m/5–6.6 ft tall, with rose-red and dark red flowers, respectively.

'Petite Orchid' is similar to 'Petite Embers' but has deep orchid-purple flowers.

'Petite Pinkie' and 'Pink Ruffles' are similar to 'Petite Embers' but with pink flowers.

'Petite Snow' is similar to 'Petite Embers' but has snow white flowers.

'Potomac,' another USNA selection, is treelike, to 5 m/16 ft tall, mildew-resistant, and has pink flowers.

'Powhatan,' a USNA introduction, is compact and globose, to 3 m/10 ft tall, with lavender flowers and mildew resistance.

'Purpurea' is full-size and vigorous with bright purple flowers.

'Royalty' is a semidwarf with royal purple flowers.

'Rubra' and 'Rubra Grayi' (= 'Gray's Red') are full-size selections with red flowers.

'Seminole,' a USNA introduction, is compact and globose, to 2.5 m/8 ft tall, with medium pink flowers.

'Tiny Fire' is very dwarf with rich red flowers.

'Twilight' is full-size, vigorous, with dark purple flowers.

'Victor' is compact and globose, 2–3 m/6.6–10 ft tall, with deep red flowers. It is useful northward to Zone 7a.

'Watermelon Red' (= 'Watermelon Pink') and 'Wm. Toovey' are full-size plants with deep watermelon-pink flowers.

Introduction of new selections is continuing and the list of available cultivars is constantly changing. Check local availability and performance in making selections.

Lamium maculatum 2

Spotted dead nettle
Herbaceous groundcover
Labiatae (Mint Family)

Native Range. Europe.

Useful Range. USDA Zones 5a−9a.

Function. Groundcover.

Size and Habit

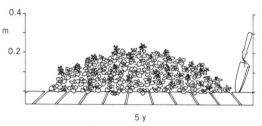

Lamium maculatum.

Adaptability. Widely adapted to full sun or shade except that light shade or snow cover reduces winter injury in Zone 5.

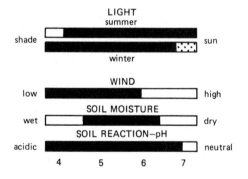

Seasonal Interest. *Flowers:* Small, purplish rose or white, in short, erect clusters from late spring to midsummer. *Foliage:* Deep sage green leaves, to 4 cm/1.6 in. long, each with a whitish stripe

down the center, making a solid mat of attractive color and texture.

Problems and Maintenance. This groundcover is trouble-free and needs no maintenance other than to restrict its growth occasionally, since it can be weedy.

Cultivars. 'Album' has creamy white flowers. 'Aureum' has a yellow, rather than white, stripe down the center of the leaf. Neither of these cultivars is widely available.

Related Species

Lamiastrum galeobdolon 2 (synonym: *Lamium galeobdolon*; golden dead nettle, yellow archangel). This close relative of *Lamium* from southern Europe and adjacent Asia, has bright green leaves and brown-marked yellow flowers to 2 cm/0.8 in. long in summer. The selection 'Variegatum' with silvery white blotched leaves is most commonly seen. This species has trailing stems, making it an effective groundcover but also enabling it to grow out of control if neglected. Its useful range is not accurately known, but probably includes Zones 5b−9a.

Nepeta mussinii 2 (catmint). This native of the Caucasus region of western Asia has gray-green foliage and masses of small lavender flowers in early summer, and again in late summer or autumn if the plant is cut back after the first flowering. This effective groundcover needs a little more maintenance than *Lamium* species to keep it neat and within bounds, but it is useful in the same range as *Lamium maculatum*.

Larix decidua 8

European larch
Deciduous tree
Pinaceae (Pine Family)

Native Range. Northern and central Europe.

Useful Range. USDA Zones 4a−6b and possibly colder and warmer zones as well.

Function. Specimen, massing, naturalizing.

Size and Habit

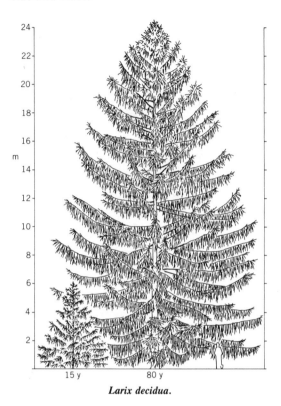

Larix decidua.

Adaptability

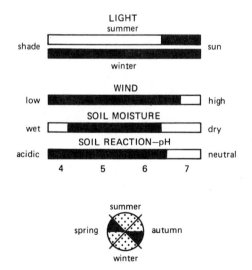

Seasonal Interest. *Foliage:* Deciduous, pale green needles, giving a lacy effect in spring, dark green later in summer, turning dull to bright yellow in late autumn before falling. *Fruits:* Cones to 3.5 cm/1.4 in. long in autumn and into winter; not adding greatly to the landscape interest of the tree. *Trunk and branches:* Branches are thickly spaced and the branchlets hang gracefully, especially noticeable in spring when accentuated by the new foliage.

Problems and Maintenance. The larch casebearer insect occasionally can seriously disfigure trees and must be controlled except in naturalized situations. Larches drop twig and cone litter but fallen needles are scarcely noticeable.

Cultivars. 'Pendula' has gracefully weeping branches but is seldom available. 'Pyramidalis' is narrowly pyramidal in form, also seldom available.

Related Species

Larix laricina 8 (eastern larch or tamarack). This species is native to North America from eastern Canada and adjacent United States to Alaska and useful in Zones 2−6b. It differs from *L. decidua* in having much smaller cones, clearer yellow autumn foliage, and somewhat narrower growth habit, and is especially well adapted to wet soils.

Larix kaempferi 8 (synonym: *L. leptolepis*; Japanese larch). This tree differs from *L. decidua* in having heavier lateral branches more widely spaced on a massive central trunk, giving a more open growth habit. It is somewhat faster growing and is useful in Zones 4a−6b.

Larix kaempferi.

Lavandula angustifolia 3

Synonyms: *L. officinalis, L. spica, L. vera*
English lavender
Herbaceous groundcover or subshrub
Labiatae (Mint Family)

Native Range. Mediterranean region.

Useful Range. USDA Zones 6a–8b. Some cultivars useful in Zone 5.

Function. Groundcover, specimen, front of border, rock garden.

Size and Habit

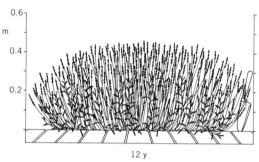

Lavandula angustifolia.

Adaptability

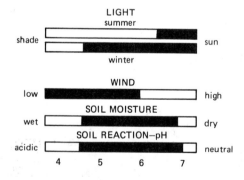

Seasonal Interest. *Flowers:* Lavender to purple, fragrant, very small, in erect spikes to 8 cm/3 in. long from early to late summer. *Foliage:* Very fine textured, the narrow, semievergreen leaves are grayish green and fragrant when crushed.

Problems and Maintenance. Trouble-free, requiring no maintenance other than pruning back after severe winters in the North.

Subspecies and Cultivars. *L. angustifolia* includes two subspecies, each until recently considered a species in its own right. Ssp. *pyrenaica* (synonym: *L. pyrenaica*) is little used, but ssp. *angustifolia*, the species type, is commonly used and available. Several cultivars have been selected, including those listed here.

'Alba' has white flowers.

'Hidcote' is compact in growth habit, to 30 cm/12 in. tall, with deep purple flowers and silvery gray foliage. It is somewhat more cold-hardy than average for the species, probably to Zone 5b.

'Munstead' is compact in growth habit, with lavender flowers.

'Nana' is the lowest of all cultivars with foliage mass seldom exceeding 20 cm/8 in. high and flower stalks less than twice that height. It is one of the most cold-hardy of all lavenders, to Zone 5a in protected sites, and even colder zones where snow cover is reliable.

Ledum groenlandicum 2–3

Labrador tea
Evergreen groundcover
Ericaceae (Heath Family)

Native Range. Northern North America.

Useful Range. USDA Zones 2b–6b.

Function. Specimen, rock garden.

Size and Habit

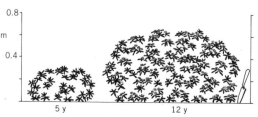

Ledum groenlandicum.

Adaptability

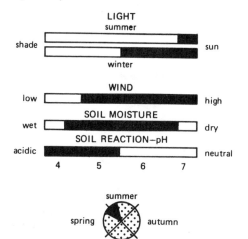

Seasonal Interest. *Flowers:* Small, white, in flat clusters, making an interesting contrast with the foliage in late spring and early summer. *Foliage:* Evergreen, medium green and wrinkled on upper

Ledum groenlandicum.

surface with dense, rusty pubescence underneath and on stems. Leaves are about 2.5–5 cm/1–2 in. long, and narrow, almost linear.

Problems and Maintenance. Once established in a proper site, it is trouble-free and requires no maintenance other than weed control, preferably by mulching.

Cultivars. 'Compactum' is more compact than the species type, remaining well below 0.5 m/1.6 ft for many years, with wider leaves and smaller flower clusters.

Related Species

Ledum palustre 2–3 (wild rosemary). This Eurasian species differs little from *L. groenlandicum*, its North American counterpart, and can be considered interchangeable in landscape use when available.

Ledum palustre.

Leiophyllum buxifolium 2 (box sandmyrtle). This low, moundlike native of the Atlantic Coast from New Jersey to South Carolina eventually grows to about 0.5 m/1.6 ft tall and several feet wide, but for the first few years it remains small. It is useful in rock gardens, in acidic, well-drained to dry soil. Probably its greatest value is that it gives the same general effect as several ericaceous bog species but tolerates drier soil. However, it requires ample moisture following transplanting. Since it is considered somewhat difficult to establish, start with pot-grown plants. The small pinkish or white flowers appear at the same time as those of *Ledum groenlandicum* with about the same effect. This plant is useful at least in Zones 6a–8b.

Leitneria floridana 5−6

Corkwood
Deciduous shrub
Leitneriaceae (Corkwood Family)

Native Range. Southeastern United States from Florida to Texas and northward to Missouri.

Useful Range. USDA Zones 6a−9a+.

Function. Naturalizing in wet areas.

Size and Habit. In Zones 8 and 9 this plant eventually forms a loosely open, suckering tree to 5 m/16 ft; in colder zones it usually remains below 3 m/10 ft because of winter injury.

Seasonal Interest. *Foliage:* Long, rather narrow, bright green leaves, smooth with a faint silky pubescence, giving a clean, somewhat coarse texture, falling in autumn without color change.

Leitneria floridana.

Problems and Maintenance. This shrub's greatest limitation is that it is seldom commercially available. When preserved in the wild or naturalized, it is trouble-free and requires no maintenance beyond establishment.

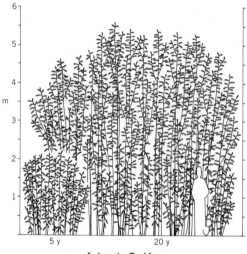

Leitneria floridana.

Adaptability

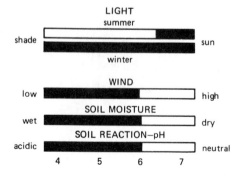

Lespedeza bicolor 5

Shrub bush clover
Deciduous shrub or subshrub
Leguminosae (Pea Family)

Native Range. China, Japan.

Useful Range. USDA Zones 5a−7b.

Function. Border, specimen, massing.

Size and Habit

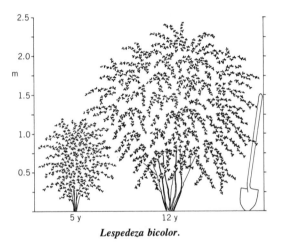

Lespedeza bicolor.

Adaptability

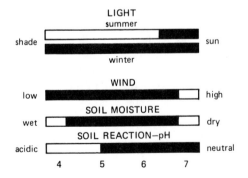

Seasonal Interest. *Flowers:* Small, rosy purple, in small to large, loose clusters in late summer and early autumn. *Foliage:* Medium to fine textured

and airy, of three leaflets, each to 4 cm/1.6 in. long, upper surface dark green, lower paler gray-green.

Problems and Maintenance. This shrub is subject to winter dieback of branches, especially in Zone 5, so it requires some pruning in most years, in spring after new growth begins so that the extent of winter injury can be seen. In warmer zones, occasional pruning (thinning out of large stems and selective tip pruning) is necessary to maintain form. When necessary, it can be cut back to the ground and will return and flower in the same year.

Related Species

Lespedeza cuneata 3 (synonym: *L. sericea;* Chinese bush clover, sericea). This low subshrub, to 1 m/3.3 ft, with wandlike, ascending branches and whitened, fine textured foliage, is useful for roadside planting in Zones 6a−9a+ and is recommended by the U.S. Soil Conservation Service for use as a roadside cover and for stabilizing stripmine spoils as well as for forage.

Lespedeza cyrtobotrya 5. This shrub has dense clusters of red-purple flowers very late in summer and into autumn. It is slightly less hardy than *L. bicolor,* Zones 6a−8a, and not as commonly available.

Lespedeza japonica 5 (Japanese bush clover). This shrub differs from *L. bicolor* in having white flowers that open later. It is slightly less cold-hardy, useful in Zones 6a−8a.

Lespedeza thunbergii 5 (Thunberg bush clover). This subshrub is similar to *L. japonica* except that it has rosy purple flowers.

Leucophyllum frutescens 5

Synonym: *L. texanum*
Ceniza, Texas sage
Semievergreen shrub
Scrophulariaceae (Figwort Family)

Native Range. Texas to Mexico.

Useful Range. USDA Zones 8a–9a+, perhaps slightly colder areas as well, useful primarily in the southwestern parts of our area.

Function. Hedge, specimen.

Size and Habit

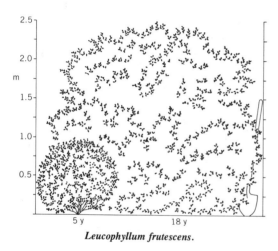

Leucophyllum frutescens.

Adaptability. Outstanding for tolerance of high-limestone soils, drought, and heat.

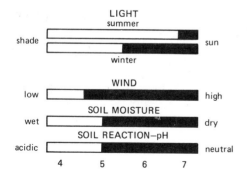

Seasonal Interest. *Flowers:* Rosy purple, funnel shaped, to 2 cm/0.8 in. across, in great numbers in summer. *Foliage:* Silvery felted, to 2.5 cm/1 in. long, giving color and textural interest, nearly evergreen but becoming dingy by late winter.

Problems and Maintenance. This shrub is trouble-free but little known and seldom available outside its native habitat, which includes the southwestern corner of our area. It may not perform well in the more humid climate of the southeastern states but is worth trying experimentally there.

Cultivars. 'Compactum' is lower-growing and more compact than the species type, remaining below 1.5 m/5 ft for some time.

Related Species

Lycium halimifolium 4 (common matrimony vine). This large, rambling, vinelike shrub from southeastern Europe and adjacent Asia has become naturalized in some parts of our area. It is one of the few woody members of the Solanaceae (Nightshade Family), loosely allied to the Scrophulariaceae (Figwort Family). Its spiny, arching branches make it an effective barrier, but it is potentially troublesome in the same way as *Rosa multiflora*, suckering and spreading quickly to become a weed. Its small purple flowers, beginning in early summer and continuing sporadically, give it minor added interest, and its orange-red fruits, each only up to 2 cm/0.8 in. long but borne in large numbers, add color in late summer and autumn. Its usefulness, in Zones 5a–9a, comes from its effectiveness as a barrier and its tolerance of very dry soil and salt.

Leucothoë fontanesiana 4

Synonyms: *L. catesbaei, L. editorum*
Fountain or drooping leucothoe
Evergreen shrub
Ericaceae (Heath Family)

Native Range. Virginia to Georgia and Tennessee.

Useful Range. USDA Zones 5b–9a.

Function. Border, naturalizing. Especially useful as a facing shrub in combination with rhododendrons in a border or screen.

Size and Habit

Leucothoë fontanesiana.

Adaptability. Protection from full winter sun is necessary, at least in the North, to prevent winterburn.

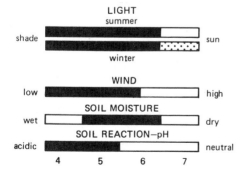

Seasonal Interest. *Flowers:* Waxy, white, in drooping spikes, 4–8 cm/1.6–3 in. long, in late spring. *Foliage:* Evergreen, leathery, dark green and sharp-pointed, arranged in double rows on

the arching branches, turning deep bronze-purple when exposed to direct sun in winter.

Problems and Maintenance. This shrub is relatively trouble-free and requires little maintenance other than occasional pruning, which must be done carefully by removing older stems close to the base of the plant and letting them be replaced by suckers from the roots, since there are few lateral buds on the lower stems. The plant is toxic to animals (see *Kalmia latifolia*).

Cultivars. 'Rainbow' is a slow-growing selection with leaves variegated with creamy yellowish white and pink tinged new growth. Because of its slower growth it needs little pruning.

Leucothoë fontanesiana 'Rainbow.'

Related Species

Leucothoë axillaris 4 (synonym: *L. catesbaei;* coast leucothoe).   This evergreen shrub is very similar to *L. fontanesiana*, easily confused with it, and interchangeable in landscape use except in Zone 5, where it is not fully hardy.

Leucothoë populifolia 5 (synonym: *L. acuminata*).   This rangy shrub from the far southeastern United States is less valued for landscape planting than *L. axillaris* and *L. fontanesiana* but can be preserved or naturalized to good effect in Zones 7b–9a.

Leucothoë racemosa 5 (sweetbells). Unlike the other species of *Leucothoë* mentioned, this is a deciduous shrub, tall and rangy, with white to pinkish flowers in early summer and bright green foliage that turns red before falling in late autumn or early winter. It is useful in Zones 6a–9a for massing and screening.

Leucothoë racemosa.

Ligustrum japonicum 5–6

Synonyms: *L. texanum*, and often confused with *L. lucidum* (see Cultivars and Related Species)
Japanese privet, wax leaf ligustrum
Evergreen shrub or small tree
Oleaceae (Olive Family)

Native Range. Japan and Korea.

Useful Range. USDA Zones 7b–9a+.

Function. Hedge, screen, small specimen tree, containers.

Size and Habit

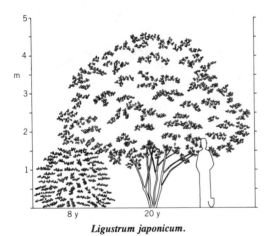

Ligustrum japonicum.

Adaptability. This is one of the most widely adaptable broadleaved evergreens for the South.

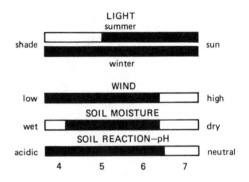

Seasonal Interest. *Flowers:* Small, in upright clusters, fragrant as is characteristic of *Ligustrum* species, not universally considered pleasantly so; interesting but not truly showy, in late summer. *Foliage:* Deep green with a waxy luster, evergreen and leathery, elegant in color and texture, and striking in the landscape, especially in winter. *Fruits:* Small, green and ripening black, of little landscape significance.

Problems and Maintenance. Sooty mold and accompanying aphids, white flies, and scale insects can disfigure this plant if not controlled. Nematodes can also be troublesome in certain areas in Zone 9a and southward. In such areas, only plants grafted on nematode-resistant rootstocks such as *L. quihoui* (see *L. vulgare*) should be used. This plant, for all its good landscape qualities, tends to be overused in the Deep South to the point of monotony.

Varieties and Cultivars. Var. *rotundifolium* (synonym: *L. coriaceum*; curlyleaf ligustrum) has rounded leaves, slightly notched at the apex. 'Suwannee River' (Plant Patent No. 1402, 1955) is a selection for outstanding foliage character, compact growth, and greater cold hardiness than the species, to Zone 7a, not reliably tall enough for screening. So-called *L. texanum* is not a species but a selection for highly waxy foliage and a tolerance of dry soil. It probably should be considered a cultivar.

Other cultivars are on the market in Florida, southern Texas, and on the West Coast. This species is variable, with large-leaved and small-leaved selections, treelike and shrubby forms. In some cases, large-leaved and treelike or small-leaved and shrubby forms have been variously, and incorrectly, called *L. lucidum*. For true *L. lucidum*, see Related Species.

Related Species

Ligustrum lucidum 6 (glossy privet). This tall shrub or small tree, to 8–10 m/25–33 ft but most often seen in the 5–8 m/16–25 ft range, has large, evergreen leaves, not as glossy as those of *L. japonicum* in spite of its name. It is rank growing with less landscape character than *L. japonicum*, but does produce a display of huge clusters of purple-black fruits on orange stems in autumn and throughout winter.

Phillyrea decora 5 (synonym: *P. vilmoriniana*; lanceleaf phillyrea). This large, evergreen shrub with glossy, leathery, lance-shaped leaves to 12 cm/5 in. long is useful for background and screening in Zones 8b–9a+, but it has been used very little in the southeastern United States and probably is commercially available only from West Coast sources. Even though it bears clusters of small white flowers in late spring and red fruits that ripen black in late summer and early autumn, the handsome foliage is its most important landscape feature.

Ligustrum obtusifolium 4–5

Border privet
Deciduous shrub
Oleaceae (Olive Family)

Native Range. Japan.

Useful Range. USDA Zones 4b–8a.

Function. Informal hedge, border, specimen.

Size and Habit. Var. *regelianum* is illustrated.

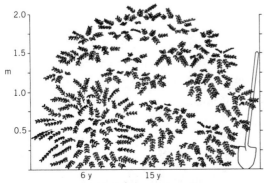

Ligustrum obtusifolium var. *regelianum.*

Adaptability

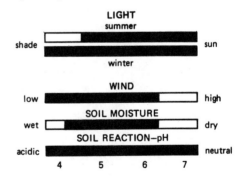

Seasonal Interest. *Flowers:* Small, white, in small clusters, fragrant but not pleasantly so to some people, in late spring. *Foliage:* Deciduous, medium green to lustrous deep green, the individual leaves about 5 cm/2 in. long, turning yellow to purplish in autumn in some locations and years. *Fruits:* Small, blue-black, adding quiet autumn interest.

Problems and Maintenance. This shrub is about as trouble-free as any privet and requires less maintenance than most deciduous privets, since pruning is seldom necessary except for renewal.

Varieties. Var. *regelianum* (Regel privet) is the preferred variety, with gracefully arching branches when young, compact, blocky form at maturity, and handsome, lustrous foliage. This plant should not be pruned into a formal hedge,

since such treatment destroys its landscape character, and there are much better plants for use as formal hedges.

Related Species

Ligustrum amurense 5 (Amur River privet). This privet is usefully hardy northward to Zone 4b. It is trouble-free in northern areas except for occasional killing back in winter, has bright green to light green foliage, and is easily pruned into a formal hedge. Fertilization improves foliage color but predisposes the plant to winter injury, as does shearing later than midsummer.

Ligustrum ovalifolium 5

California privet
Deciduous or semievergreen shrub
Oleaceae (Olive Family)

Native Range. Japan.

Useful Range. USDA Zones 6a–9a.

Function. Hedge, screen, border.

Size and Habit

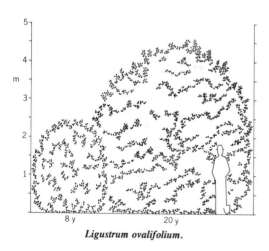

Ligustrum ovalifolium.

Adaptability

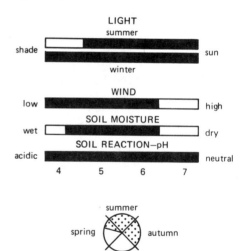

Seasonal Interest. *Flowers:* Small, white, in small upright clusters, fragrant but not pleasantly so to some people, in late spring or early summer. *Foliage:* Lustrous, bright to deep green, deciduous (North) to semievergreen (South), somewhat leathery. *Fruits:* Small, blue-black, adding quiet autumn interest.

Problems and Maintenance. This shrub is occasionally troubled with aphids and scale insects but is not nearly as susceptible to insect problems as the fully evergreen privets. In Zone 6 it can be damaged severely in occasional very cold winters, and this susceptibility to cold injury is heightened by late season pruning or overfertilization.

Cultivars. 'Aureo-marginata' (= 'Aureum') has yellow-margined leaves. Contrast between the green and yellow is enhanced by high soil fertility levels, but this predisposes the plant to winter injury in the north, so this cultivar probably should be used only from Zone 7a southward.

Ligustrum ovalifolium 'Aureo-marginata.'

Related Species

Ligustrum ×ibolium 5 (Ibolium privet). This hybrid (*L. ovalifolium* × *L. obtusifolium*) is very similar to *L. ovalifolium* except it is deciduous earlier and noticeably more cold-hardy. It is useful in Zones 5b−8b and is a good substitute for *L. ovalifolium* in Zones 5b and 6.

Ligustrum ×vicaryi 5 (Vicary or golden Vicary privet). This hybrid (*L. ovalifolium* 'Aureo-marginata' × *L. vulgare*) is slower growing and somewhat broader spreading than either of its parents. Its principal feature is its foliage, which is golden yellow where exposed to full sun. It remains yellow throughout the growing season but is especially bright in early summer. This is an effective accent plant, useful in Zones 5b−8b, overused in some parts of our area, especially the Midwest. The so-called Hillside Strain, selected for use in Minnesota, is cold-hardy to Zone 4b.

Ligustrum sinense 5

Chinese privet
Deciduous or semievergreen shrub
Oleaceae (Olive Family)

Native Range. China.

Useful Range. USDA Zones 7a−9a+.

Function. Screen, hedge, massing, border.

Size and Habit

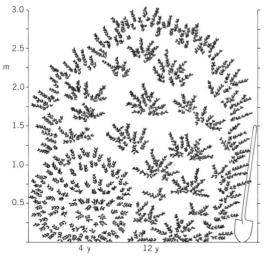

Ligustrum sinense.

Adaptability

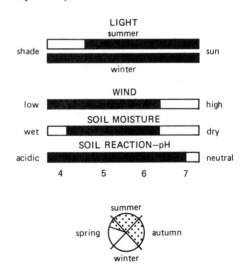

Seasonal Interest. *Flowers:* Small, white, in many large clusters, fragrant but not pleasantly so to some people. Unusually showy in flower for a privet, in early to midsummer. *Foliage:* Medium green, not distinguished except in the variegated cultivar. Tends to be semievergreen in the South. *Fruits:* Small, blue-black, adding quiet autumn interest.

Problems and Maintenance. This shrub is fairly trouble-free but occasionally becomes infested by aphids or white flies. It can be a problem in itself, as a weed, in the Deep South, but this is less true of 'Variegatum.'

Cultivars. 'Pendulum' has somewhat pendulous branches, giving it a gracefully moundlike form. 'Variegatum' has white variegated foliage and is a most striking plant in the landscape in late spring and early summer with a shining, yellow-white appearance. In late summer and autumn it fades

to a pale gray-green color. As with most variegated plants it is less vigorous than the green species type.

Related Species

Ligustrum indicum 6 (synonym: *L. nepalense*; India or Nepal privet).   This shrub or small tree is semievergreen, with leaves slightly recurved or puckered, to 8 cm/3in. long. Useful in Zones 7b−9a+, in the same conditions as *L. sinense* but in larger scale situations.

Ligustrum vulgare 4−6

Common privet
Deciduous shrub
Oleaceae (Olive Family)

Native Range. Europe and North Africa. Naturalized in eastern North America.

Useful Range. USDA Zones 4b−8a with selection of appropriate cultivars.

Function. Hedge, screen, border.

Size and Habit

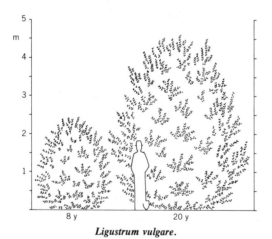

Ligustrum vulgare.

Adaptability

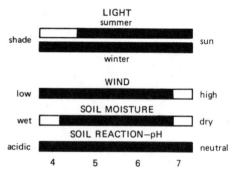

Seasonal Interest. *Flowers:* Small, white, in upright clusters, fragrant but not pleasantly so to some people, in early summer. *Foliage:* Dark green and lustrous, holding the color well until it falls in late autumn. *Fruits:* Small, black, and shiny, holding well into winter and adding quiet interest.

Problems and Maintenance. Relatively trouble-free in most areas but subject to a serious blight disease in some localities and to be avoided where experience dictates. As with other *Ligustrum* species, *L. vulgare* is prone to occasional severe winter dieback in the northern part of its useful range (Zones 4b and 5).

Cultivars. 'Cheyenne,' selected in the Great Plains, is notably more resistant to cold and drought than most other privets and is possibly useful as far north as Zone 4a.

'Densiflorum' is a narrowly upright, compact growing selection with very dark green foliage.

'Lodense' (= 'Nanum') is a dwarf form with smaller leaves, making a dense, moundlike plant only 0.5–1 m/1.6–3.3 ft tall and one and a half to two times as broad after many year's growth. Unfortunately, it often has been grafted on understock of the species type, which frequently suckers and overgrows the dwarf plant unless the suckers are pruned out promptly. It is useful northward to Zone 5b.

'Pyramidale' is narrowly upright and dense. Apparently at least two different selections are being sold under this name. One of them is more formal in outline and branching, but both have the same general form.

Related Species

Ligustrum quihoui 5. This vigorous species from China differs from *L. vulgare* in its more stiffly upright form, lower ultimate height of 2–3 m/6.6–10 ft, late summer flowers, and large fruits in heavy clusters. Best known as a nematode-resistant understock for the southern evergreen privets, it is considerably better adapted to the North than is often supposed. Useful in Zones 5b–9a+ and perhaps slightly colder zones as well.

Lindera benzoin 5

Synonym: *Benzoin aestivale*
Spicebush
Deciduous shrub
Lauraceae (Laurel Family)

Native Range. Northeastern North America to Florida and Texas.

Useful Range. USDA Zones 5b–9a and Zone 5a using native plants in northeastern North America.

Function. Naturalizing, specimen.

Size and Habit

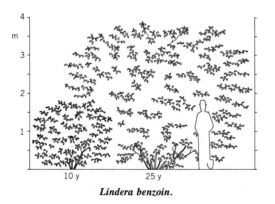

Lindera benzoin.

Adaptability

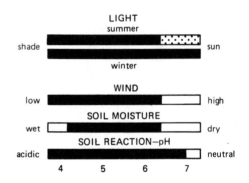

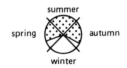

Seasonal Interest. *Flowers:* Small, fragrant, yellow, interesting but not showy, in early spring. Dioecious. *Foliage:* Clean, medium green, aromatic when crushed, turning clear yellow in autumn. *Fruits:* Shiny, bright red berries are fairly showy in autumn, especially after the leaves fall, when they persist until taken by birds.

Problems and Maintenance. This shrub is essentially trouble-free, given a favorable site with some shade and at least moderately moist soil. It requires little or no maintenance, especially since its primary use is in naturalized landscapes.

Lindera benzoin.

Related Species

Lindera melissifolia 4 (synonym: *Benzoin melissifolium*; southern spicebush). Similar to *L.benzoin* but more restricted to the South in natural distribution and lower growing, making a low thicket in wet sites. Not available for planting but useful in natural sites in Zones 7a−9a.

Lindera obtusiloba 6 (synonym: *Benzoin obtusilobum*). This native of China, Japan, and Korea is a large shrub or small tree with handsome, lobed leaves, gray-green in summer and golden-yellow in autumn. Flowers are yellow and appear almost as early as those of *L. benzoin*, in somewhat larger clusters but still not showy.

Probably not available commercially, although it can be found in arboreta in the United States and is potentially useful in Zones 6a−9a.

Lindera obtusiloba.

Liquidambar styraciflua 8

Sweet gum
Deciduous tree
Hamamelidaceae (Witch Hazel Family)

Native Range. Southeastern, east-central and south-central United States, southern Mexico, and Central America.

Useful Range. USDA Zones 5b−9a+, with selection of appropriate genetic material.

Function. Shade, street tree, specimen.

Size and Habit

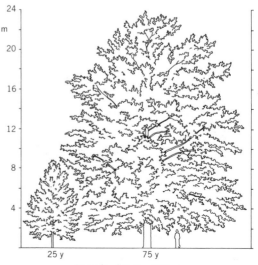

Liquidambar styraciflua.

Adaptability. Tolerates seaside sites if protected from high winds.

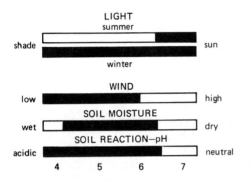

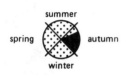

Liquidambar styraciflua.

Seasonal Interest. *Flowers:* Small, greenish yellow, in tightly globose clusters, not striking in the landscape. *Foliage:* Star-shaped leaves emerge pale green, turn deep green, lustrous, and rather leathery in summer. Foliage turns yellow to red or bronze in autumn, sometimes displaying all of these colors with green as well, at a single time in autumn. Individuals vary greatly in time of leaf coloring. Trees of northern origin usually color early, those from the south later. *Fruits:* Globose clusters with horny projections, green at first, ripening brown, interesting as they ripen in autumn and persist into winter, releasing the seeds through openings in the fruit. *Trunk and branches:* Massive, the smaller branches covered with smooth, silvery gray bark and sometimes corky winged.

Problems and Maintenance. This tree is relatively trouble-free and requires little maintenance. It is reputedly difficult to transplant, but

this is not a major problem for experienced landscapers except with large trees. Fruits constitute a litter problem in some sites. The most important limitation relates to adaptability. It is important to select trees of northern origin (Kentucky and Virginia northward) for use in Zones 5 and 6 and probably equally important to select trees of southern origin for Zones 8b and 9.

Cultivars. Several cultivars have been selected for outstanding form and fall foliage color, and additional selections probably will be made. Since these selections are not adaptable rangewide and have been incompletely observed, selection of cultivars is probably best done on the basis of local experience or experimentally.

Related Species

Liquidambar formosana 8 (Formosa sweet gum). This tree has been little used to date in eastern North America but offers possibilities for street and shade use in the South. It probably is useful from Zone 7b or 8a southward. Breeding efforts at the U.S. National Arboretum may produce useful cultivars of this species as well as *L. styraciflua*.

Liriodendron tulipifera 8

Tulip tree, yellow poplar
Deciduous tree
Magnoliaceae (Magnolia Family)

Native Range. Eastern United States and adjacent Ontario.

Useful Range. USDA Zones 5a–9a and 4b with selection of appropriate genetic material.

Function. Shade or specimen tree, street tree where enough space is available to accommodate its size and to provide the soil mass to hold enough moisture for good growth.

Size and Habit

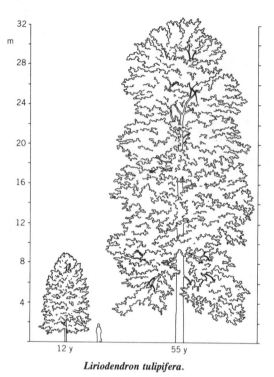

Liriodendron tulipifera.

Adaptability

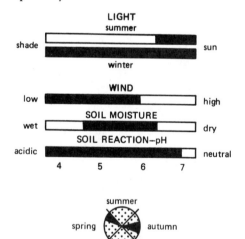

Seasonal Interest. *Flowers:* Tulip-shaped, to 5 cm/2 in. long, borne upright, singly at the ends of twigs. Petals are pale green, deep orange at the base, showy when they open before the unfolding foliage is fully expanded in late spring. *Foliage:* Clean, medium green, turning clear yellow in late summer and autumn, moderately coarse textured. Distinctive lobed leaves are squared off at the end as though the tip had been cut off with

scissors. *Fruits:* Conelike, made up of overlapping scales, the tan bottom scales persisting well into winter, adding quiet seasonal interest after the foliage has fallen. *Trunk and branches:* Gray bark, finely striped with light gray or off-white on branches and trunks of young trees, adds quiet winter interest.

Liriodendron tulipifera.

Problems and Maintenance. This tree is relatively free of serious problems, but the foliage is sometimes affected by aphids and a leaf spot disease that causes early fall of older leaves. Its principal limitations relate to its size, site requirements, and geographical variation. Trees grown from seed sources in the same region usually should be specified. This is especially important at the northern and southern range extremes. Unless ample space and reasonably good soil are available, other trees should be used. Branches are somewhat prone to wind breakage; not a serious problem but reason to use other species in very windy sites.

Cultivars. 'Fastigiatum' (= 'Pyramidale') is narrowly upright in form. Not widely available, it is usually grafted on seedlings of the species, and suckering from the rootstock then can be a nuisance in some cases.

Related Species

Liriodendron chinense 8 (Chinese tulip tree). This rare tree may have future value in the Deep South, but it is not commercially available at present. It is smaller than *L. tulipifera*, growing only to about 15 m/60 ft tall, with smaller, more deeply lobed leaves and smaller flowers, and is useful only from about Zone 7b and 8a southward.

Liriope spicata 2

Creeping lilyturf or liriope
Evergreen, herbaceous groundcover
Liliaceae (Lily Family)

Native Range. China and Vietnam.

Useful Range. USDA Zones 6a−9a+, but not fully evergreen and therefore loses much of its effectiveness in Zones 6 and 7.

Function. Groundcover on a large or small scale, edging, accent plant.

Size and Habit

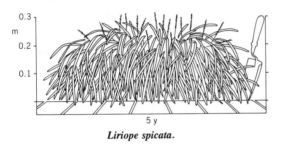

Liriope spicata.

Adaptability. Broadly adapted to light and soil conditions and relatively salt-tolerant.

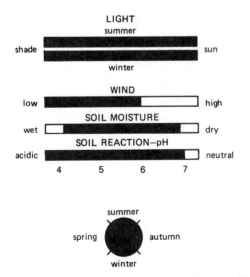

Seasonal Interest. *Flowers:* Lavender or nearly white, very small, borne tightly clustered in upright spikes to 10 cm/4 in. long in middle or late summer. *Foliage:* Evergreen leaves are medium green, narrowly straplike, 25−40 cm/ 10−16 in. long and 0.6 cm/0.25 in. wide. *Fruits:* Blue-black berries are round, less than 1 cm/0.4 in. across, ripening in autumn.

Problems and Maintenance. This plant is trouble-free and requires little or no maintenance once established. Thinning is seldom necessary but can be done for propagation of new plants.

Related Species

Liriope muscari 2 (big blue lilyturf or liriope). This native of China and Japan is larger, with straplike leaves to 50 cm/20 in. long and 2 cm/0.8 in. wide, allowing for variety in texture with other lilyturfs and deep violet flowers. Several cultivars have been selected, including 'Majestic,' with narrow leaves and large spikes of violet flowers, 'Munroe White,' with pure white flowers, and 'Variegata,' with yellow striped leaves. The last two cultivars are best restricted to at least partly shaded spots in Zones 8a−9a+, but the species type can be used northward to Zone 7b.

Ophiopogon japonicus 2 (dwarf liriope or Mondo grass). This fine-textured, almost grasslike plant from Japan and Korea has lustrous, very dark green leaves 25−35 cm/10−14 in. long but only 0.3 cm/0.12 in. wide. Its requirements and uses are basically the same as those of *Liriope* species and it is useful in the same range as *Liriope muscari*, Zones 7b−9a+, but less cold-hardy than *Liriope spicata*.

Ophiopogon japonicus.

Lonicera alpigena 5

Alps honeysuckle
Deciduous shrub
Caprifoliaceae (Honeysuckle Family)

Native Range. Mountains of south-central Europe.

Useful Range. USDA Zones 4b–8b.

Function. Screen, border.

Size and Habit

Lonicera alpigena.

Seasonal Interest. *Flowers:* Yellowish, tinged dull red, not showy, in late spring. *Foliage:* Deep green, relatively large leaves, to 10 cm/4 in. long. *Fruits:* Bright red, hanging on slender stalks, colorful in late summer and early autumn.

Problems and Maintenance. This shrub is relatively trouble-free, requiring little maintenance other than pruning, either by annual thinning or radical renewal every five to eight years. Not as weedy as some other shrub honeysuckles.

Cultivars. 'Nana' is an excellent dwarf, mound-like selection, seldom exceeding 1.5 m/5 ft in height but becoming considerably wider than that.

Adaptability

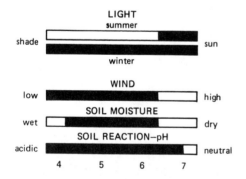

Lonicera fragrantissima 5

Fragrant honeysuckle
Semievergreen shrub
Caprifoliaceae (Honeysuckle Family)

Native Range. China.

Useful Range. USDA Zones 5b–9a.

Function. Screen, hedge, specimen, border.

Size and Habit

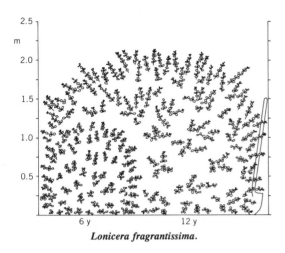

Lonicera fragrantissima.

Lonicera fragrantissima.

Adaptability. Retains foliage quality in dry soil better than most *Lonicera* species.

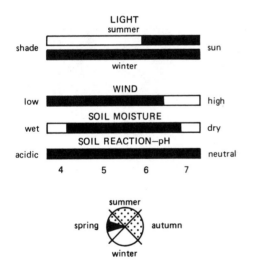

Seasonal Interest. *Flowers:* Fragrant, white, before the new foliage in early spring. *Foliage:* Blue-green, leathery, semievergreen. *Fruits:* Red berries in early summer.

Problems and Maintenance. Relatively trouble-free and requiring little maintenance other than annual thinning or radical renewal every 5 to 8 years. It is not as weedy as some other shrub honeysuckles but occasionally escapes cultivation in the South.

Related Species and Hybrids

Lonicera caerulea 4 (blue honeysuckle). This Eurasian species, naturalized in North America,

is useful in Zones 3a–8a for massing or as a specimen. Its landscape interest is not striking, but its compact growth habit requires little pruning and its elongated, dark blue berries are edible.

Lonicera ×purpusii 5 This hybrid of *L. standishii × L. fragrantissima* is similar to *L. fragrantissima* with its fragrant flowers and semievergreen foliage. Its leaves are larger than those of *L. fragrantissima*, and it is useful in Zones 6a–9a and perhaps also parts of Zone 5.

Lonicera standishii 4 (Standish honeysuckle). This Chinese semievergreen shrub functions as a lower-growing version of the related *L. fragrantissima*, with larger leaves, to 10 cm/4 in. long, and fragrant flowers in early spring. Useful in Zones 6a–9a.

Leycesteria formosa 4 (Himalayan honeysuckle, flowering nutmeg). This relative of *Lonicera* from southwestern China and the Himalayas is useful for massing or as a specimen for its whitish flowers, borne in the axils of colorful red-purple bracts, in hanging clusters to 10 cm/4 in. long in

Leycesteria formosa.

late summer. Its bright green leaves give the plant an interestingly coarse texture. This shrub is seldom available but potentially useful in Zones 7b–9a+. The tops are frequently killed back in

winter in Zones 7 and 8, causing new, arching branches to develop low on the plant. The best way to prune is drastic renewal: cutting the entire top down to stubs each spring.

Lonicera japonica 1 and 2

Japanese honeysuckle
Evergreen or semievergreen vine
Caprifoliaceae (Honeysuckle Family)

Native Range. Eastern Asia, naturalized in eastern United States.

Useful Range. USDA Zones 5b–9a+, but too aggressive a weed in the South to recommend for most uses in Zones 7 through 9.

Function. Groundcover, especially on banks and rough terrain, screen (with support), cover for stone walls and fences, climbing by scrambling and twining, to 5–10 m/16–33 ft.

Size and Habit

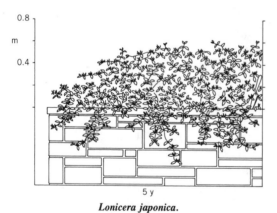

Lonicera japonica.

Adaptability. Partial shade helps to prolong retention of foliage in winter in northern areas (Zones 5 and 6).

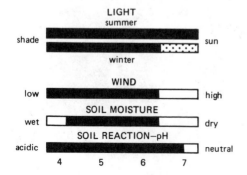

Seasonal Interest. *Flowers:* Fragrant, white, tinged with purple in some plants, turning yellowish with age, beginning in late spring and continuing intermittently through the summer. *Foliage:* Semievergreen in the North, evergreen in the South, handsome, leathery, and deep green in summer, bronzing in winter.

Lonicera japonica.

Problems and Maintenance. This vine is relatively trouble-free but requires pruning to restrict its growth because of its extreme vigor. In the South this is so serious a problem that it cannot be recommended for planting (see *L. henryi* under Related Species).

Cultivars. 'Aureo-reticulata' has smaller leaves, net-veined in golden-yellow, and is much less vigorous than the species type, a striking variegated climber. 'Halliana' (Hall's honeysuckle) differs little from the species, but its fragrant white flowers turn clear, pale yellow only a few days after opening. This probably is the most common form found in the United States.

Related Species

Lonicera henryi 1 and 2 (Henry honeysuckle). This handsome, semievergreen to evergreen, weakly twining vine has most of the good qualities of *L. japonica* and is not as weedy, but it is more effective as a groundcover than as a climber. Its leaves are more elongated and sharp-pointed than those of *L. japonica* and do not bronze so much in winter, and its yellowish or reddish flowers are fairly interesting in early summer. It is useful in Zones 6a–9a and perhaps also part of Zone 5.

Lonicera maackii 6

Amur honeysuckle
Deciduous shrub
Caprifoliaceae (Honeysuckle Family)

Native Range. Northeastern Asia.

Useful Range. USDA Zones 3a–8a.

Function. Border, specimen, screen (with pruning).

Size and Habit

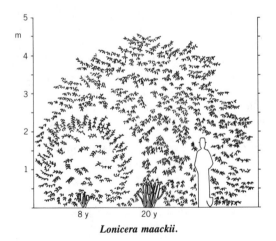

Lonicera maackii.

Seasonal Interest. *Flowers:* Fragrant, white, turning yellow, in late spring to early summer. *Foliage:* Lustrous, deep green, long-pointed, remaining green well into autumn, serving as a background for the late red berries as well as the flowers. *Fruits:* Bright red berries, ripening in autumn and providing strong, late autumn landscape interest.

Problems and Maintenance. Relatively trouble-free, but requires occasional pruning to thin out the main stems and maintain vigor. Although tall enough to function as a small tree, this plant's suckering tendency is so strong that it requires almost constant pruning to hold it to tree form. Its size, far too great for many landscape situations, limits its usefulness, and it seeds profusely, giving rise to many weed seedlings.

Forms. F. *podocarpa* differs little from the species. It is claimed that this variant holds its foliage and fruits later in autumn than the species type, but individually both types are highly variable, and it is unlikely that specifying either will give any specific result.

Adaptability

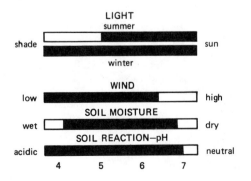

Lonicera morrowii 4

Morrow honeysuckle
Deciduous shrub
Caprifoliaceae (Honeysuckle Family)

Native Range. Japan; naturalized in eastern United States.

Useful Range. USDA Zones 5a−8b.

Function. Border, specimen, informal hedge.

Size and Habit

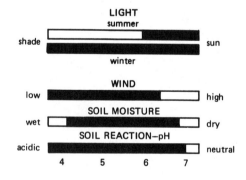

Lonicera morrowii.

Adaptability

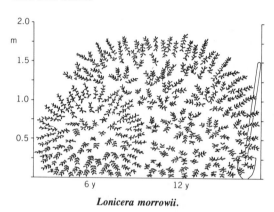

Seasonal Interest. *Flowers:* White, turning yellow, late spring. *Foliage:* Soft gray-green, downy, effectively fine textured on horizontally spreading branches. *Fruits:* Red (or golden yellow) berries in middle to late summer.

Problems and Maintenance. This shrub is relatively trouble-free and requires little pruning because of its dense, moundlike growth habit, but it can be weedy in some areas.

Cultivars. 'Xanthocarpa' has golden yellow to orange-yellow berries, otherwise does not differ from the species type.

Related Species

Lonicera spinosa var. *alberti* 3 (Albert honeysuckle). This nonspiny variety of the spiny honeysuckle from west-central Asia has narrow, blue-green leaves, rosy purple flowers in early summer, and deep red-purple berries in late summer. Like *L. morrowii*, it is gracefully widespreading, effective in the front of a shrub border or for foundation planting. It is useful in Zones 3b−8a, but most highly valued in Zones 3 and 4.

Lonicera syringantha 5 (lilac honeysuckle). This wide-spreading, moundlike shrub from northern China has fragrant, pink to rosy purple flowers in late spring and red berries in late summer, and is useful in Zones 5a−8a.

Lonicera pileata 3

Privet honeysuckle
Evergreen shrub
Caprifoliaceae (Honeysuckle Family)

Native Range. China.

Useful Range. USDA Zones 7b−9a+.

Function. Massing, specimen, rock garden.

Size and Habit

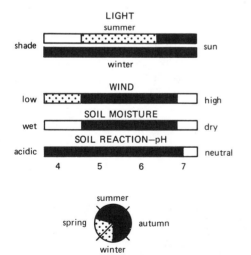

Lonicera pileata.

the leaves 1−4 cm/0.4−1.6 in. long and two-ranked on the stem, giving an interesting texture. *Fruits:* Small, violet-purple, translucent, not showy but interesting at close range.

Lonicera pileata.

Adaptability. This shrub grows vigorously in moist, partly shaded sites but functions better in the landscape and requires less pruning when grown more slowly in rather dry, windy sites in full sun.

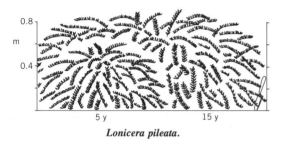

Seasonal Interest. *Flowers:* Fragrant, white, small, not showy, in middle spring. *Foliage:* Evergreen or nearly so, lustrous and dark green,

Problems and Maintenance. This shrub is largely trouble-free, but aphids occasionally can become a problem. It tends to accumulate dead twigs low on the plant, especially when growing vigorously, requiring occasional renewal pruning in intensive situations.

Related Species

Lonicera nitida 4 (synonym: *L. pileata* f. *yunnanensis*). This shrub is a slightly taller-growing version of *L. pileata* with more uniformly small evergreen leaves. It functions better than *L. pileata* as a small clipped hedge, and equally well as an informal garden specimen, except that it becomes taller and is more cold-hardy, useful in Zones 6a−9a. These two similar species are often confused.

Lonicera sempervirens 1 and 2

Trumpet honeysuckle
Evergreen or semievergreen vine
Caprifoliaceae (Honeysuckle Family)

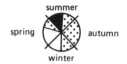

Native Range. Eastern United States, west to Nebraska and Texas.

Useful Range. USDA Zones 4a−9a, with selection of appropriate genetic material.

Function. Fence cover, screen (with support and pruning), groundcover, twining specimen, to 4−6 m/13−20 ft.

Seasonal Interest. *Flowers:* Scarlet and yellow-orange in showy clusters in summer. *Foliage:* Semievergreen or evergreen in the Deep South, bluish-green, the terminal pairs of leaves perfoliate (two opposite leaves fused into a single blade, surrounding the stem). *Fruits:* Red berries in autumn, not particularly showy.

Problems and Maintenance. This plant can be disfigured by serious aphid infestations in certain years and localities, but they can be controlled by spraying if necessary. Density for screening usually depends on pruning to encourage filling-in of open areas.

Cultivars. 'Magnifica' is a selection for late and free flowering. 'Sulphurea' has clear sulfur-yellow flowers. 'Superba' has bright red flowers and is free-flowering. Other cultivars are listed in catalogs. Some probably are duplicate names for some of the above.

Related Species

Lonicera ×*brownii* 1 and 2 (Brown's honeysuckle). This hybrid of *L. sempervirens* × *L. hirsuta* differs little from *L. sempervirens* and can be used interchangeably when available. It is useful in Zones 3b−9a. 'Dropmore Scarlet' *(L, hirsuta* × *L.sempervirens)*, with large numbers of red flowers, is one of the finest of the vine honeysuckles, especially for cold climates. It is useful in Zones 3a−8a.

Size and Habit

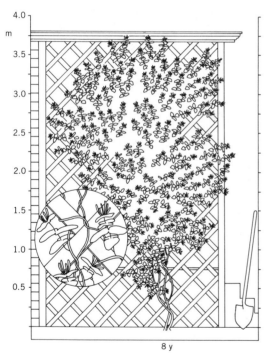

Lonicera sempervirens.

Adaptability

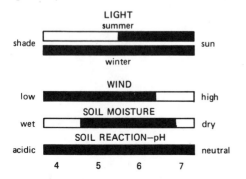

Lonicera 'Dropmore Scarlet.'

Lonicera etrusca 1 and 2 (Etruscan honeysuckle). This climbing species from the Mediterranean area is somewhat more showy than most cultivars of *L. sempervirens*, but much less cold-hardy and useful in Zones 7b−9a+. The selection 'Superba' has very showy, yellowwhite, purple-tinged flowers and tends to be less evergreen.

Lonicera flava 1 and 2 (yellow honeysuckle). Native in the southeastern United States and to Oklahoma, this weakly twining vine has showy and fragrant orange-yellow flowers and is useful in Zones 6a−9a.

Lonicera ×*heckrottii* 1 and 2 (everblooming or goldflame honeysuckle). This weakly climbing, deciduous vine of uncertain hybrid origin is one of the heaviest and longest-flowering of twining honeysuckles, and next to *L. sempervirens* the most widely available. Its flowers are pinkish purple and yellow, borne in large clusters from early summer until early autumn, and it is nearly as cold-hardy as *L. sempervirens*, useful in Zones 4b−9a. Like *L. sempervirens*, it can be seriously troubled by aphids.

Lonicera ×*heckrottii.*

Lonicera hildebrandiana 1 and 2 (Hildebrand, giant or Burmese honeysuckle). This extremely vigorous evergreen twining and high-climbing vine probably is not cold-hardy in our area, but it might be tried in sheltered sites in Zone 9a, since it returns rapidly after being killed back to the ground. Mounding around the base may be helpful in winters when temperatures remain below −2° to −3°C/26 to 28°F for several hours. With large clusters of fragrant, creamy yellowwhite flowers, turning to red-orange as they mature in late summer, it is by far the showiest and most vigorous of the twining honeysuckles.

Lonicera hirsuta 1 and 2 (hairy honeysuckle). This high-climbing twiner native to the northern United States and Canada is as hardy as *L. sempervirens*, but less effective as a landscape plant and seldom used or available.

Lonicera periclymenum 1 and 2 (woodbine). This long-cultivated, weakly climbing twiner from Europe and the Mediterranean area is similar to several other vining honeysuckle species. It has yellowish flowers, purplish outside in varieties: var. *belgica* (Dutch woodbine) has leathery foliage, and is sometimes used as a substitute for *L. japonica*, as it is easier to control; var. *serotina* (autumn woodbine) has fragrant flowers, dark purple outside and yellow inside, eventually fading entirely to yellow. Both varieties are useful in Zones 5b−9a.

Lonicera tragophylla 1 and 2 (Chinese woodbine). This Chinese native has very large yellow, unscented flowers, to 8 cm/3 in. long in large clusters, and is useful in Zones 6b−9a+. The related *L.* ×*tellmanniana* (Tellmann redgold honeysuckle), a hybrid of *L. tragophylla* × *L. sempervirens*, tends to be more deciduous, with unscented but very showy deep pink-flushed yellow flowers, and is useful in Zones 6a−9a+.

Lonicera tatarica 5

Tatarian honeysuckle
Deciduous shrub
Caprifoliaceae (Honeysuckle Family)

Native Range. Southwestern Soviet Union to the Altai Mountains.

Useful Range. USDA Zones 3b—8a.

Function. Border, screen, specimen, hedge.

Size and Habit

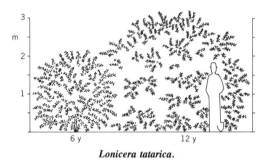

Lonicera tatarica.

Adaptability

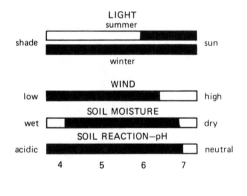

Seasonal Interest. *Flowers:* White to pink or rose-red, in late spring. *Foliage:* Dull to lustrous, dark green, falling in autumn without color change. *Fruits:* Red (or yellow) berries in middle to late summer.

Problems and Maintenance. This shrub is essentially trouble-free and requires little or no maintenance other than pruning for renewal every five to eight years. Seedlings can be a weed problem, since this species often escapes cultivation.

Cultivars. 'Alba' has pure white flowers. 'Arnold Red' has dark purplish red flowers, the deepest in color of any cultivar, but not as colorful from a distance as those of 'Rosea' or 'Zabelii.' 'Lutea' has bright yellow berries and pink flowers. 'Morden Orange' has a moderate growth rate, compact form, bright orange berries, and pale pink flowers. 'Rosea' has rosy pink flowers. 'Zabelii' (synonym: *L. korolkowii* 'Zabelii') is an excellent plant with rather bluish green foliage, and fuller growth, especially at the base.

At least 30 other cultivars have been named and are available, either commercially or in arboretum collections in the United States and Canada. Many are equivalent in landscape use to those listed, and selection can be made on the basis of local experience and availability.

Related Species and Hybrids

Lonicera ×*amoena* 5. This hybrid of *L. tatarica* × *L. korolkowii* is best known for the cultivar 'Arnoldiana,' which has pink-flushed, white flowers and is very similar to *L. tatarica* except for more gracefully arching branches. Useful in Zones 4b—8a.

Lonicera ×*bella* 5 (belle honeysuckle). This group of hybrids of *L. morrowii* × *L. tatarica* has the upright growth of *L. tatarica* and grows very rapidly but not at the expense of fullness. Flower color varies from white in 'Candida' to rosy pink in 'Rosea.' Useful in about the same area as *L. tatarica* (Zones 4a—8a), and its seedlings constitute at least as much of a weed problem as those of *L. maackii* and *L. tatarica*.

Lonicera korolkowii 5 (blueleaf honeysuckle). This distinctive shrub has blue-green foliage, sometimes almost bluish white, and rose-pink to white flowers. It is seldom available commercially, but potentially useful in Zones 5a—8a. The selection sold as *L. korolkowii* 'Zabelii' more closely resembles *L. tatarica* and is considered a cultivar of that species here.

Lonicera ×*xylosteoides* 5.   This hybrid of *L. tatarica* × *L. xylosteum* is represented in commerce by the compact growing selection 'Clavey's Dwarf.' This excellent, dense, rounded shrub eventually will function as a screen above eye level, but since plants may require 10 years to attain that height, faster growing cultivars may be preferred for that function. In the short term, 'Clavey's Dwarf' is most commonly used for massing or foundation planting and can be kept below eye level for many years with a little pruning. It has creamy white flowers, blue-green foliage, and bright red fruits and is useful in Zones 3b−8a.

Lonicera xylosteum 5 (European fly honeysuckle).   This shrub, common in the wild from Europe through Asia to the Altai, has relatively inconspicuous yellowish white flowers, but shiny, beadlike, dark red berries that are displayed effectively against the deep green foliage in late summer. The dwarf selection 'Nana' (emerald mound honeysuckle) is truly dwarf, remaining below 1 m/3.3 ft in height without pruning for many years while spreading to nearly twice that distance. It is useful in Zones 3b−8a.

Lonicera ×*xylosteoides* 'Clavey's Dwarf.'

Lonicera ×*xylosteoides* 'Clavey's Dwarf.'

Lonicera xylosteum 'Nana.'

Loropetalum chinense 5

Loropetalum
Evergreen shrub
Hamamelidaceae (Witch Hazel Family)

Native Range. China.

Useful Range. USDA Zones 8a−9a+ and protected sites in Zone 7b.

Function. Border, specimen, espalier, screen (with pruning).

Size and Habit

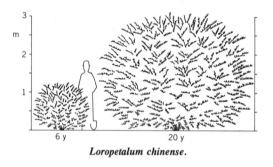

Loropetalum chinense.

Seasonal Interest. *Flowers:* Creamy white, with narrow petals like those of *Hamamelis* species, effective against the dark green foliage on arching branches in early to middle spring. *Foliage:* Deep green leaves, reminiscent of those of *Hamamelis* but evergreen and only about 5 cm/2 in. long.

Loropetalum chinense.

Adaptability. Performs best when protected from full sun in summer and from sun and wind in winter in Zone 8a and colder.

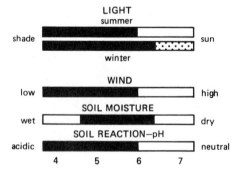

Problems and Maintenance. This shrub is trouble-free, given a relatively cool, moist soil and at least partial shade. Foliage may suffer winter burn in the northern parts of the useful range, but the plant usually recovers quickly in the spring.

Lyonia lucida 4

Fetterbush
Evergreen shrub
Ericaceae (Heath Family)

Native Range. Southeastern United States.

Useful Range. USDA Zones 7b−9a+.

Function. Border, specimen, naturalizing.

Size and Habit

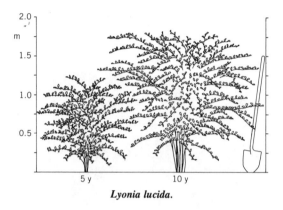

Lyonia lucida.

Adaptability

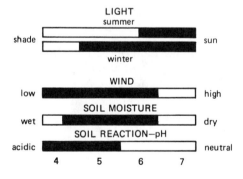

Seasonal Interest. *Flowers:* Small, white to pink, in axillary clusters in late spring. *Foliage:* Evergreen, bright green and lustrous, 2.5−8 cm/1−3 in. long on wandlike stems, the leaves typically smaller toward the ends of stems. *Fruits:* Inconspicuous dry capsules.

Problems and Maintenance. Relatively trouble-free and requires little or no maintenance.

Forms. F. *rubra* has deep pink flowers.

Related Species

Lyonia mariana 4 (staggerbush). This deciduous counterpart of *L. lucida*, native from southern New England to Florida and west to Arkansas, has large numbers of small, white to pink flowers in late spring or early summer. It is useful primarily for naturalizing in boglike sites or to be preserved in natural areas.

Chamaedaphne calyculata 3−4 (leatherleaf, cassandra). This low evergreen shrub functions as a lower, more northern counterpart of *L. lucida*. Native to northern Eurasia, the Pacific Northwest, and eastern North America as far south as northern Georgia, it probably is variable in adaptability to heat and cold. In our area, assuming selection of appropriate genetic material, it is useful in Zones 3a−7b and perhaps farther south. Its small white flowers appear in late spring.

Maclura pomifera 7

Osage orange, hedgeapple
Deciduous tree
Moraceae (Mulberry Family)

Native Range. South-central United States.

Useful Range. USDA Zones 5b−9a+.

Function. Windbreak, barrier, hedge, shade tree.

Size and Habit

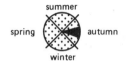

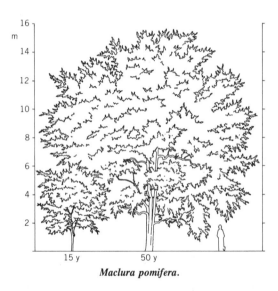

Maclura pomifera.

Seasonal Interest. *Foliage:* Lustrous, bright green leaves on spiny branches, turning clear yellow in autumn. *Fruits:* Massive, compound fruits, to 13 cm/5 in. across, on female trees, at first are green then ripen yellow-orange. *Trunk and branches:* One-year-old branches are yellow-brown; sinewy trunk has orange-brown inner bark, seen through the shredding, gray outer bark.

Maclura pomifera.

Adaptability. Unusual in its broad adaptability to difficult soils and environments. Because of this, it is valued in the Central and Great Plains as a windbreak and livestock barrier hedge.

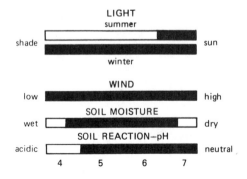

Problems and Maintenance. This tree is free of serious diseases and insect problems, but fallen branches and fruits (from female trees) constitute a serious litter problem. This, the spiny branches, and a tendency for roots to grow into and clog drainage lines, prohibit the use of this tree in intensive situations.

Forms. F. *inermis* is free of spines but is seldom if ever commercially available.

Magnolia acuminata 8

Cucumbertree magnolia
Deciduous tree
Magnoliaceae (Magnolia Family)

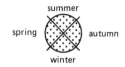

Native Range. East-central United States and adjacent Ontario.

Useful Range. USDA Zones 4b–8b.

Function. Shade tree.

Size and Habit

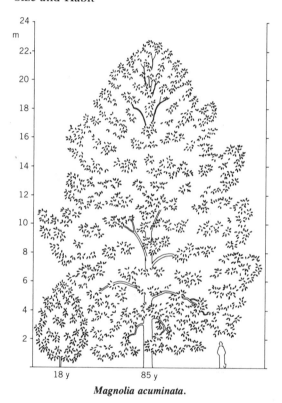

Magnolia acuminata.

Adaptability

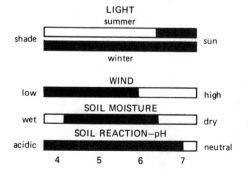

Seasonal Interest. *Flowers:* Silvery blue-green in bud, opening greenish yellow, to 8 cm/3 in. long, six petals, loosely cup-shaped, interesting but inconspicuous, with or after the leaves in late spring. *Foliage:* Large, deep green leaves, 10–25 cm/4–10 in. long, form a dense canopy with pleasingly coarse texture, falling with little color change in early autumn. *Fruits:* Reddish, knobby, to 8 cm/3 in. long, opening by slits to expose the red-orange seeds in late summer. *Twigs and branches:* Smooth, silvery gray bark on stout branches and twigs adds landscape interest in winter.

Problems and Maintenance. This tree is somewhat soft-wooded and prone to breakage by severe icing conditions and wind, but less so than most other magnolias, and it usually recovers quickly because of its rapid growth. Some old trees show evidence of considerable breakage in earlier years; others show none. It is not clear whether this is a genetic trait or merely results from differences in microclimate and soil fertility. Otherwise, this tree is remarkably trouble-free. Some maintenance is required in raking up the large leaves in autumn along with any fruit and branch litter. Because of brittleness and litter, *M. acuminata* is not a good choice for street planting. Because of its ultimate size, it is not an appropriate tree for small urban or suburban sites.

Varieties and Cultivars *Var. acuminata* (cucumbertree). This is the species type.

Var. subcordata (synonym: *M. cordata*; yellow cucumbertree). This tree typically is smaller than the species type, reaching heights of up to 10–12 m/33–39 ft, but occasional trees become nearly as large as the species type. The clear yellow flowers are more showy than those of the species type and appear slightly earlier, so are hidden less by the partially expanded foliage. Useful in Zones 5a–9a.

'Golden Glow' is a selection from var. *acuminata* for more brightly colored, yellowish flowers than typical.

'Miss Honeybee' is a selection from var. *sub-cordata* for larger, paler yellow flowers than typical.

Related Species

Magnolia ×brooklynensis 7.   This hybrid group (*M. acuminata* × *M. quinquepeta* 'Nigra') is represented by the cultivars 'Evamaria' and 'Woodsman,' both too recent for their ultimate size and hardiness to be known. These hybrids combine the hardiness and late flowering tendency of *M. acuminata* with the showy flowers of *M. quinquepeta*. They should prove useful as late flowering, and so less frost prone, equivalents of the popular saucer magnolia, *M. × soulangiana*. 'Woodsman' is especially interesting with an unusually wide mixture of flower colors including yellow-green, pink, and purple.

Magnolia grandiflora 8

Southern magnolia, bull bay
Evergreen tree
Magnoliaceae (Magnolia Family)

Native Range. Southeastern United States.

Useful Range. USDA Zones 7a−9a+ with selection of appropriate genetic material. Foliage burn occurs in some winters in Zone 7.

Function. Shade tree, specimen.

Size and Habit

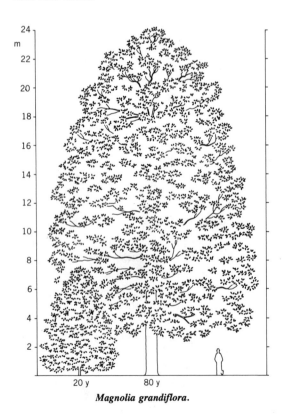

Magnolia grandiflora.

Adaptability

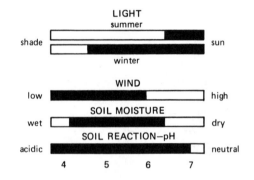

Seasonal Interest. *Flowers:* Fragrant, white, to 15−20 cm/6−8 in. across, in late spring and intermittently through summer. *Foliage:* Evergreen, lustrous, and leathery, dark green, to 20

Magnolia grandiflora.

cm/8 in. long, varying in shape from tree to tree, the undersides varying from gray-green to rusty red. *Fruits:* Rusty red-brown, 8 cm/3 in. long, opening by slits to expose the red-orange seeds in early autumn.

Problems and Maintenance. This tree is free of problems but requires maintenance in the form of cleaning up leaf and twig litter, and for this reason not the best choice as a street tree, although it is often used for this purpose in the South.

Cultivars. Many cultivars have been selected and named, so local experience and availability should be considered. A few of the most widely available are listed here.

'Majestic Beauty' has been selected for outstanding form and foliage.

'Russet' (Plant Patent No. 2617, 1966) is a selection for compact growth and leaves with a russet colored tomentum underneath.

'Samuel Sommer' has outstanding foliage, russet underneath, large flowers over a long season, and better than average cold-hardiness.

'St. Mary' is a selection for outstanding flower and foliage character, noted for flowering very young.

'Victoria' has little tomentum underneath its leaves and is considered one of the most cold-hardy cultivars.

Magnolia ×loebneri 6−7

Synonym: see nomenclatural note under Related Species, *M. kobus*
Loebner magnolia
Deciduous tree
Magnoliaceae (Magnolia Family)

Hybrid origin. *M. stellata* × *M. kobus.*

Useful Range. USDA Zones 5a−9a.

Function. Specimen, patio tree, border accent.

Adaptability

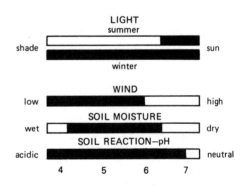

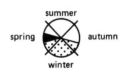

Size and Habit

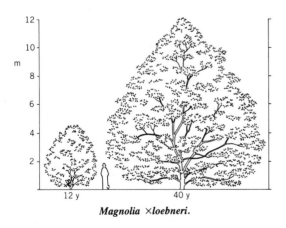

Magnolia ×loebneri.

Seasonal Interest. *Flowers:* Fragrant, white, 8−10 cm/3−4 in. across, of approximately 12 tepals (petals and petallike sepals) in early to middle spring. *Foliage:* Medium green, not a major landscape feature but forming a rather dense canopy, falling in early autumn with little color change. *Fruits:* Reddish, knobby, to 8 cm/3 in., seldom developing fully but opening by slits to expose a few red-orange seeds in early autumn. *Trunk and branches:* Smooth, silvery gray bark adds winter interest.

Problems and Maintenance. This tree has few problems other than the general tendency of magnolias to be soft-wooded and somewhat prone to breakage in ice storms.

Cultivars. 'Ballerina' is a hybrid originating from seeds of M. ×loebneri, possibly back-crossed by M. stellata. Its flowers are unusual in having 30 or more petals and petalloid sepals and they are longer lasting than average for this group. Although too recently selected for a good estimate of ultimate size, it appears that it will function at a height of at least 6–8 m/20–25 ft.

'Leonard Messel' has lilac-pink flowers.

'Merrill' (= 'Dr. Merrill') reaches a functional height of about 10–15 m/33–49 ft, with much of the precocious and heavy flowering of the M. stellata parent, and has become popular and widely available.

'Spring Snow' is a more recent selection with fragrant, unusually long-lasting flowers, appearing slightly later than those of 'Merrill' and marginally less susceptible to frost damage.

Other selections of M. ×loebneri exist, some not yet named. It seems likely future selections will be made from this hybrid group.

Related Species

Magnolia kobus 6–7 (Kobus magnolia).   This species varies from a shrubby small tree, about 8 m/25 ft, to a medium size tree, to about 20 m/65 ft. Because it often does not flower appreciably until it is relatively old, this species is being replaced by the similar but more floriferous M. ×loebneri in many landscape situations. Nevertheless, it is a handsome tree, useful in Zones 5a–8b.

Nomenclatural note.   In recent taxonomic treatments, *Magnolia kobus* has been broadened to include M. stellata and M. ×loebneri. Since it remains to be seen how widely this treatment will be accepted, this book treats these species in the more traditional way, following *Hortus Third*. If the recent changes are accepted in the future, present M. kobus will become M. kobus var. kobus, M. stellata will become M. kobus var. stellata, and M. ×loebneri will become M. kobus var. loebneri, unless a more satisfactory solution for the latter hybrid group can be found.

Magnolia macrophylla 7

Bigleaf magnolia
Deciduous tree
Magnoliaceae (Magnolia Family)

Native Range. Southeastern United States.

Useful Range. USDA Zones 5b–9a.

Function. Specimen, shade, or patio tree.

Size and Habit

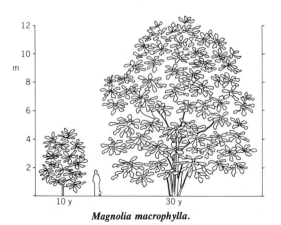

Magnolia macrophylla.

Adaptability

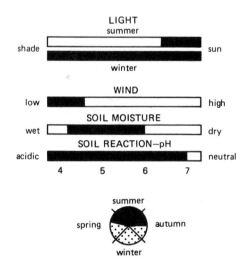

Seasonal Interest. *Flowers:* Fragrant, creamy white, to 20–25 cm/8–10 in. or more across, in middle to late spring. *Foliage:* Very large, papery leaves, to 80 cm/30 in. long and 30 cm/12 in. across, forming an umbrellalike canopy and falling without much color change in autumn.

Fruits: Reddish, knobby, to 8 cm/3 in. long, opening by slits to expose the red-orange seeds in early autumn. *Trunk and branches:* Smooth, silvery gray bark adds winter interest to the coarse, upright branches.

Magnolia macrophylla.

Problems and Maintenance. The fragility of the leaves and stems is the only serious problem of this species but this is sufficient to limit its use to sites sheltered from winds that would dry and tear the leaves, and having ample soil moisture.

Related Species

Magnolia fraseri 7 (Fraser magnolia).   This native of the southeastern United States functions as a smaller edition of *M. macrophylla*, with leaves about half the size. It is useful in Zones 5b−9a but not often available.

Magnolia hypoleuca 7−8 (synonym: *M. obovata*; white-leaf Japanese magnolia).   This is the Asian counterpart of the American large-leaved magnolias such as *M. fraseri*, *M. macrophylla*, *M. tripetala*. It is potentially a larger tree than any of the others, to 20 m/66 ft or even taller in good sites, and its leaves, to 40 cm/16 in. long, are distinctly whitened underneath. It is useful in Zones 6a−9a, perhaps also Zone 5, but not widely available.

Magnolia sieboldii 6 (Oyama magnolia).   This Japanese species has large, fragrant, white flowers with red stamens, opening over a relatively long period in early summer. It is less tolerant of limestone soil and full sun than most magnolias. Unfortunately, its growth habit is awkward and open and it is seldom available commercially.

When available it is useful in Zones 6a−9a. The selection 'Charles Coates,' a hybrid of **M.** *sieboldii* × **M.** *tripetala*, is at least as hardy as **M.** *sieboldii* and, like the parent, requires partial shade.

Magnolia ×*thompsoniana* 7 (Thompson magnolia).   This handsome hybrid *(M. tripetala* × *M. virginiana)* has smaller leaves than *M. tripetala*, to about 20 cm/8 in. long, of better substance, and bears pleasantly fragrant, creamy white flowers over a relatively long period in early summer in Zones 7a−9a+. The selection 'Urbana' is outstanding in cold hardiness, useful in Zones 5b−9a.

Magnolia tripetala 7 (umbrella magnolia). This native of the southeastern and south-central United States as far north as Pennsylvania is the most cold-hardy of the large-leaved magnolias, useful in Zones 5a−9a, and protected sites in Zone 4. It is open and umbrellalike in growth habit, functioning well as a patio tree

Magnolia tripetala.

Magnolia tripetala.

away from strong winds. Its large flowers are similar to those of *M. macrophylla*, except with a disagreeable odor.

Magnolia ×*wieseneri* 6 (synonym: *M.* ×*watsonii*; Watson magnolia). This hybrid (*M. hypoleuca* × *M. sieboldii*) is outstanding for its large, fragrant, pink flowers with crimson stamens in late spring to early summer and for its modest size. But it is not very widely available, and it has inherited a poor growth habit from *M. sieboldii*. Nevertheless, its low stature and late, showy flowers make it potentially useful in Zones 5b−9a.

Magnolia salicifolia 7

Anise magnolia
Deciduous tree
Magnoliaceae (Magnolia Family)

Native Range. Japan.

Useful Range. USDA Zones 5a−9a.

Function. Specimen, border accent.

Size and Habit

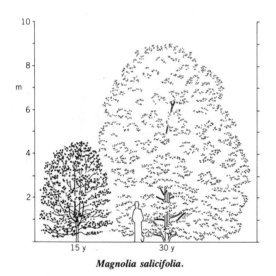

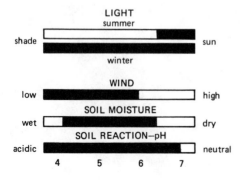

Magnolia salicifolia.

Adaptability

Seasonal Interest. *Flowers*: Fragrant, white or purplish at base, to 12 cm/5 in. across, with six petals, in early to middle spring. Flowers appear on relatively young trees. *Foliage*: Light green leaves about 8−10 cm/3−4 in. long and narrow, giving neater, finer foliage texture than most other magnolias and yet a fairly dense, upright foliage mass. *Fruits*: Reddish, knobby, to 7 cm/3 in. long, opening by slits to expose red-orange seeds in early autumn. *Trunk and branches*: Smooth, silvery gray bark adds winter interest.

Problems and Maintenance. This tree is relatively trouble-free and requires little maintenance. It is less prone to storm breakage than most deciduous magnolias.

Cultivars. 'Wada's Memory' has unusually large flowers, 12−15 cm/5−6 in. across. There is some evidence that it may be a hybrid with *M. kobus*. It is not yet widely available.

Related Species. The following two hybrid groups are, in recent taxonomic treatment, considered part of the species *M. liliflora*. They are listed here simply to note their identity, without judgment as to taxonomic treatment:

Magnolia ×*kewensis* 7 (Kew magnolia). Plants in this group traditionally have been considered hybrids of *M. kobus* × *M. salicifolia*. 'Wada's Memory' has been associated with this cross. Its adaptability has not yet been widely tested.

Magnolia ×*proctoriana* 6 (Proctor magnolia). Plants in this group traditionally have been considered hybrids of *M. salicifolia* × *M. stellata*.

Like *M. salicifolia*, they are upright and pyramidal in growth habit, but they are showier in flower than *M. salicifolia*, with as many as twice the number of petals in each flower. They are similar in adaptability to the parent species, but less commonly available.

Magnolia ×soulangiana 7

Saucer magnolia
Deciduous tree
Magnoliaceae (Magnolia Family)

Hybrid Origin. *M. heptapeta* (synonym: *M. denudata*) × *M. quinquepeta* (synonym: *M. liliflora*).

Useful Range. USDA Zones 5a–9a.

Function. Specimen, patio tree, border accent.

Size and Habit

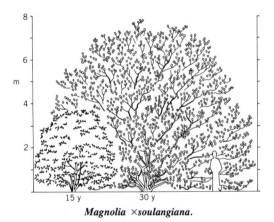

Magnolia ×soulangiana.

Adaptability

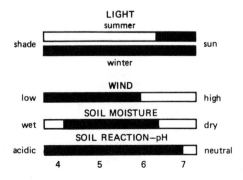

Seasonal Interest. *Flowers:* White, pink to purple, cuplike, 8–12 cm/3–5 in. long, fragrant in a few cultivars, in middle to late spring. *Foliage:* Light green, rather coarse, falling in autumn with little color change. *Fruits:* Reddish, knobby, to 8 cm/3 in., seldom developing fully but opening by slits to expose a few red-orange seeds in early autumn. *Trunk and branches:* Smooth, silvery gray bark adds winter interest.

Problems and Maintenance. This tree is relatively trouble-free and requires little maintenance. It is moderately prone to storm breakage.

Cultivars

At least 20 cultivars are currently available in the United States and Canada, and considerably more than that number have been named. Seldom are more than five or six available in a locality except through a few specialists, and local availability and experience should be followed. A few of the most popular cultivars are listed here.

'Alba Superba' (= 'Alba') has large, white flowers, early. 'Alexandrina' has large, early flowers, rose purple outside and white inside; an outstanding cultivar. 'Brozzonii' has huge white flowers flushed with pink at the base. 'Grace McDade' has huge lavender-pink flowers with white inside and a rather loose growth habit. 'Lennei' has huge, deep purple flowers with white inside. 'Lilliputian' has small, light pink-purple flowers and is a slow growing, shrubby form. 'Rustica Rubra' (= 'Rustica,' = 'Rubra') has moderately large, deep red-purple flowers, whitish inside. 'Speciosa' has large, ivory to white flowers very late. 'Verbanica' has moderately large flowers, clear rosy pink, whitish inside, very late. Slow growing and compact.

Related Species

Magnolia heptapeta 7 (synonyms: *M. denudata*, *M. conspicua*; Yulan magnolia). This long-cultivated Chinese species has fragrant, ivory-white flowers in middle spring along with the earliest *M. ×soulangiana* cultivars. It is an excellent specimen for show but requires considerable space since it grows to at least 10 m/33 ft in height and width under good conditions in Zones 6a−9a.

Magnolia quinquepeta 5 (synonym: *M. liliflora*; lily magnolia). This shrubby species from China has showy purple flowers in late spring, with or following the latest *M. ×soulangiana* cultivars such as 'Speciosa' and 'Verbanica.' The selection 'Nigra,' with deep purple flowers opening two weeks later than *M. ×soulangiana*, is useful in Zones 5b−9a, primarily for its late flowering effect.

Magnolia sprengeri 7 (Sprenger magnolia). This Chinese native is one of the most showy and

***Magnolia quinquepeta* 'Nigra.'**

impressive of flowering trees, with rich pink flowers, tapered at the base and streaked inside. Although the species type is rather tender (Zones 6b−9a+), the selection 'Diva,' with deeper pink flowers, has been cold-hardy as far north as Zone 5b or 6a in limited trials.

Magnolia stellata 5

Synonym: (see nomenclatural note under *M. ×loebneri*, Related Species)
Star magnolia
Deciduous tree
Magnoliaceae (Magnolia Family)

Native Range. Japan.

Useful Range. USDA Zones 5a−9a.

Function. Specimen, patio, border accent.

Size and Habit

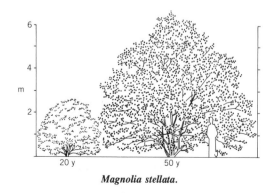

Magnolia stellata.

Adaptability

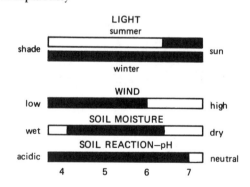

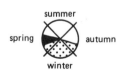

Seasonal Interest. *Flowers:* Fragrant, white (or pink), 8−10 cm/3−4 in. across of 12−18 tepals (petals and petal-like sepals) in early spring. *Foliage:* Medium green, finer textured than that of most other magnolias, forming a dense mass, falling in early autumn with little color change.

Fruits: Reddish, knobby, to 5 cm/2 in., seldom developing fully but opening by slits to expose a few red-orange seeds in early autumn. *Twigs and branches:* Smooth, silvery gray bark adds winter interest.

Magnolia stellata.

Problems and Maintenance. This plant is relatively trouble-free and requires little maintenance but is soft-wooded and prone to breakage in ice storms.

Cultivars. 'Rosea' has clear, light pink flowers, otherwise is similar to the species type. 'Royal Star' has larger flowers than is typical for the species and is among the hardiest clones. 'Rubra' has purple-pink flowers, a color more difficult to use in the landscape than that of other cultivars. 'Waterlily' has large flowers, pink in bud and opening white.

Related Species and Hybrids. The following hybrids between *M. quinquepeta* (synonym: *M. liliflora*) and *M. stellata* were introduced by the U.S. National Arboretum in 1968. They are mostly shrubby forms, flowering later than *M. stellata*. Although they have yet to be fully evaluated, they should prove useful at least in Zones 6a–9a and perhaps in Zone 5 as well.

'Ann' and 'Susan' are shrubby, compact plants with red-purple flowers in early to middle spring. 'Judy' is shrubby, compact, and broad, with small flowers, red-purple outside and white inside. 'Pinkie' is compact and broad-spreading, with large, cuplike flowers, to 15 cm/6 in. across, pale red-purple outside and white inside, in late spring.

'Betty,' 'Jane,' 'Randy', and 'Ricki' are shrubby plants but larger than the other cultivars listed. Their flowers are red-purple outside and white inside. 'Betty' has unusually large flowers, to 20 cm/8 in. across, in early to middle spring.

Magnolia virginiana 6–7

Synonym: *M. glauca*
Sweet bay
Evergreen to semievergreen tree
Magnoliaceae (Magnolia Family)

Native Range. Southeastern and eastern United States coastal areas, Massachusetts to Florida and Texas.

Useful Range. USDA Zones 5b–9a+ with selection of appropriate genetic material.

Function. Specimen tree or shrub, border.

Size and Habit

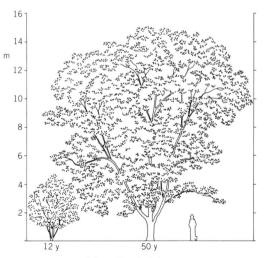

Magnolia virginiana.

Adaptability

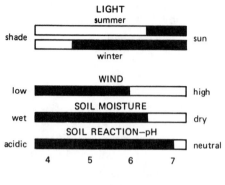

Magnolia virginiana.

Seasonal Interest. *Flowers:* Fragrant, creamy white, 5–8 cm/2–3 in. across with 9–12 petals in late spring and early summer. *Foliage:* Evergreen or semievergreen, to 12 cm/5 in. long, smooth and lustrous, bright green on the upper surface and strongly whitened underneath. *Twigs and branches:* Bright green, adding quiet winter interest when foliage does not persist. *Fruit:* Dark red, to 5 cm/2 in. long, opening by slits to expose the red-orange seeds in early autumn.

Problems and Maintenance. This is a trouble-free plant, susceptible only to mechanical damage from severe ice storms, and less so than most other magnolias.

Varieties and Cultivars. Var. *australis,* occurring in the southern coastal plain, tends to be more nearly evergreen than the species type and may be less cold-hardy on the average. 'Henry Hicks' is a selection from var. *australis* with fully evergreen foliage and unusual cold hardiness, making it useful in Zones 5b–9a+.

Mahonia aquifolium 3–4

Oregon holly-grape
Evergreen shrub
Berberidaceae (Barberry Family)

Native Range. Pacific Northwest from British Columbia to Oregon.

Useful Range. USDA Zones 5b–9a with selection of appropriate genetic material.

Function. Border, specimen, massing.

Size and Habit

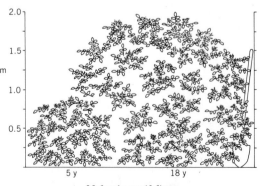

Mahonia aquifolium.

Adaptability. Grows best in at least light shade in the South.

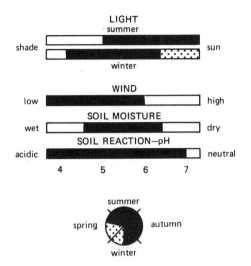

LIGHT
summer
shade · · · · · · · · · · · sun
winter

WIND
low · · · · · · · · high

SOIL MOISTURE
wet · · · · · · · · dry

SOIL REACTION—pH
acidic · · · · · · · · neutral
4   5   6   7

summer
spring · · · autumn
winter

Seasonal Interest. *Flowers:* Bright yellow, in clusters to 8 cm/3 in. across in midspring. *Foliage:* Evergreen, leathery, compound with spiny margined leaflets, lustrous and dark green or dull in some plants, turning purplish green in winter, often suffering winterburn in the North. *Fruits:* Blue-black with a whitish waxy bloom, resembling purple grapes, effective in summer.

Mahonia aquifolium.

Problems and Maintenance. Relatively trouble-free in good sites but highly susceptible to foliage dehydration in some winters in Zones 5b and 6, occasionally killing back in Zone 5b. Shade from winter sun and snow cover reduce winterburn of foliage in Zone 5.

Cultivars. 'Compacta' has glossy, dark green foliage, remains under 0.5 m/1.6 ft for several years, and is more cold-hardy than average for the species.

Much variation exists in this species, and new selections are appearing that may be found superior when more fully tested in eastern North America.

Related Species and Hybrids

Mahonia nervosa 3. This handsome, low-growing species, also from the Pacific Northwest, has larger leaves than *M. aquifolium*, with as many as nine pairs of leaflets as compared with the four pairs usually found in *M. aquifolium*. It is seldom available, and its limits of adaptability in eastern North America are not well known, but its useful range includes Zones 6b—9a.

Mahonia pinnata 4—5 (California or cluster holly-grape). This densely upright evergreen serves as a larger version of *M. aquifolium*, especially useful for its vertical growth habit. Foliage is not as lustrous as that of *M. aquifolium*, but otherwise it is rather similar, turning purplish in winter. Useful in Zones 7a—9a+ and generally available.

Mahonia repens 2 (creeping mahonia). This creeping groundcover with dull bluish green foliage is less handsome than *M. aquifolium* but well adapted as a groundcover on rather dry soils and similar in general adaptability to the most cold-hardy plants of *M. aquifolium* (Zones 5b—9a).

×*Mahoberberis aquisargentii* 4. This intergeneric hybrid between *Mahonia aquifolium* and *Berberis sargentiana* has glossy, deep green leaves, varying widely in shape, either simple or compound (three leaflets). It is the most interesting and useful ×*Mahoberberis* hybrid to date, but has not been fully evaluated. It reaches heights of at least 1.5 m/5 ft in Zones 6b—9a and may eventually reach screening height in mild climates. Its cold hardiness in Zone 6a is uncertain.

A few other ×*Mahoberberis* hybrids exist. The oldest, ×*M. neubertii* (*Berberis vulgaris* × *Mahonia aquifolium*) has been known for well over 100 years in Europe, but has little or no landscape value. ×*M. aquicandidula* (*Mahonia aquifolium* × *Berberis candidula*) is somewhat slower growing than ×*M. aquisargentii*, is less full and attractive in form, and probably is not commercially available.

Mahonia bealei 5

Leatherleaf mahonia
Evergreen shrub
Berberidaceae (Barberry Family)

Native Range. China.

Useful Range. USDA Zones 6b−9a+.

Function. Specimen, border accent, massing; especially useful in formal, architectonic settings.

Size and Habit

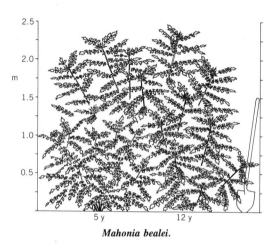

Mahonia bealei.

Adaptability. Grows best in at least light shade in the South.

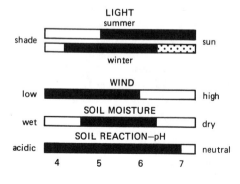

Seasonal Interest. *Flowers:* Fragrant, pale to lemon yellow, in large (to 15 cm/6 in.) upright clusters, several radiating from one branch, early to middle spring. *Foliage:* Evergreen, leathery, to 40 cm/15 in. long, compound with up to 15 spiny margined leaflets, deep blue-green, giving striking textural effect, and remaining green in winter. *Fruits:* Blue-black with a whitish waxy bloom, elongated, in large, semipendulous clusters, striking in early summer.

Problems and Maintenance. This shrub is trouble-free but eventually needs pruning to maintain fullness toward the base. It is susceptible to winterburn, especially in Zones 6 and 7, and should be planted in sites protected from sweeping winds.

Related Species

Mahonia fortunei 4 (Fortune or Chinese mahonia). This evergreen shrub has finer textured foliage than other *Mahonia* species, because its leaflets are only about 1 cm/0.4 in. wide and up to 12 cm/5 in. long. Foliage emerges bright green and remains deep green in winter. Flowers and fruits are less showy than those of *M. bealei*, and the entire plant is less cold-hardy, useful in Zones 8b−9a+.

Mahonia lomariifolia 5 (Chinese or Burmese mahonia). This striking shrub is not greatly different from *M. bealei* in general appearance but has larger leaves than any other *Mahonia* species discussed here, sometimes 50 cm/20 in. long, with more than 25 leaflets, giving a strong textural accent valued in highly architectonic landscapes. Flowering and fruiting interest is comparable with that of *M. bealei*, but *M. lomariifolia* is no more cold-hardy than *M. fortunei*.

Malus baccata 7

Siberian crabapple
Deciduous tree
Rosaceae (Rose Family)

Native Range. Northeastern Asia.

Useful Range. USDA Zones 3a−7a.

Function. Specimen, shade tree, screen.

Size and Habit

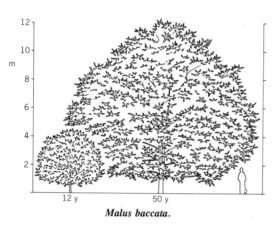

Malus baccata.

Adaptability

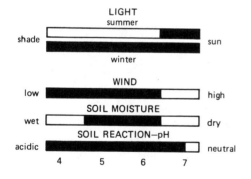

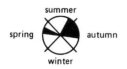

Seasonal Interest. *Flowers:* Fragrant, white, showy, to 4 cm/1.6 in. across in middle spring, borne annually. *Foliage:* Bright green and quietly attractive, except when infected by apple scab. Falls in early to midautumn without color change. *Fruit:* Red or yellow, very small, to 1 cm/0.4 in. across, borne annually and remaining on the tree after leaves have dropped until early winter. *Trunk and branches:* Bark is yellow-brown, a small but sometimes appreciable contribution to winter color.

Problems and Maintenance. Many trees of the species type are moderately susceptible to apple scab disease. Resistant cultivars have been selected (see Varieties and Cultivars). The better *M. baccata* selections generally are resistant to the other important diseases of crabapples. Scale insects and borers can be troublesome, especially in warmer parts of the useful range, and may need to be controlled there.

Varieties and Cultivars. 'Columnaris' (columnar Siberian crabapple) is actually narrowly oval in form, but as close to columnar as any crabapple. It has showy white flowers annually, and red-blushed yellow fruits. It is highly resistant to scab but, unfortunately, susceptible to fire blight and probably should be avoided in areas where that disease is known to be serious.

Var. *jackii* (Jack flowering crabapple), native to Korea, is outstanding for its deep red fruits and disease resistance, and equal to the species type in coldhardiness. It should be used in preference to the species type in most cases.

A recently introduced cultivar of unknown parentage that gives the effect of *M. baccata* is 'White Angel' (= 'Inglis'). This tree is upright with an open branching habit and masses of white flowers annually in middle spring and small scarlet fruits, showy in autumn and lasting well into winter. Although not disease-free, 'White Angel' is only occasionally troubled by fire blight and is useful in Zones 4a−7a.

Hybrids of *Malus baccata*

Malus ×adstringens 7. This hybrid group has resulted from crosses of *M. baccata* × *M. pumila* 'Niedzwetzkyana,' the converse cross, and open-pollinated seedlings from these hybrids. Included are the Morden Rosybloom cultivars originated by the Canada Department of Agriculture at Morden, Manitoba, and probably at least some of the original Rosybloom group that originated at the C.D.A. Central Experimental Farm at Ottawa, although the full parentage of most members of that group is not known. The Rosybloom crabapples in general are very cold-hardy (Zones 3a−7a) and large and spreading in habit. They tend to flower well only in alternate years and to be highly susceptible to apple scab, but there are important exceptions to these generalizations noted below. Their flowers are red-purple and their foliage more or less purple, at least in spring. A few of the better known Rosybloom cultivars are listed here.

'Almey,' a second generation hybrid of M. baccata × M. pumila 'Niedzwetzkyana,' was once very popular but is very susceptible to apple scab and has largely been replaced by newer selections with greater resistance and better flower color such as 'Selkirk.'

'Hopa,' an open-pollinated hybrid of M. pumila 'Niedzwetzkyana,' probably by M. baccata, has become more popular than justified by its landscape value. Its magenta flowers fade quickly and it is very susceptible to apple scab, so it now should be replaced by better selections.

'Kelsey,' a complex hybrid with 'Almey' in its background, was introduced by the C.D.A. Morden station in honor of the Manitoba centennial observation in 1969. It has semidouble, purplish red flowers and deep red fruits persisting well into winter. Its disease resistance throughout our area has yet to be fully determined, but it is at least moderately susceptible to apple scab.

'Makamik' is perhaps the best of the original Rosybloom group, and one of the showiest of all flowering crabapples in bloom. It is highly resistant to apple scab and has no other serious disease problems. Its relatively large (to 2 cm/0.8 in.), purplish red fruits remain effective throughout autumn and into early winter.

'Radiant,' an open-pollinated seedling of 'Hopa,' has foliage that is red-purple only as it unfolds in spring, deep pink flowers that make a reliable show annually, and bright red fruits that last through early winter. Originally it was thought to be completely disease resistant; there is now some doubt about the extent of its scab resistance. Useful in Zones 4a−7b.

'Red Silver' has very deep purple flowers, foliage, and fruits. Its unfolding leaves are silvery, giving rise to the name. Unfortunately it is susceptible to apple scab.

'Red Splendor' originated as an open-pollinated seedling from 'Red Silver' and has red-purple foliage, bright rose-red flowers, and dark red fruits lasting well into winter. It is more disease-resistant than 'Red Silver.'

'Royalty' was selected from open-pollinated Rosybloom seedlings in Saskatchewan. It is notable for its outstanding red-purple foliage, the most intensely colored of any crabapple cultivar. Its flowers and fruits, also deep red-purple, are almost inconspicuous because of the intensely colored foliage. Useful in Zones 3b−7a. It is susceptible to apple scab.

'Selkirk' resulted from a controlled cross of M. baccata × M. pumila var. 'Niedzwetzkyana' at Morden, Manitoba. Even though not formally introduced until 1962, it had been tested under number at other places for several years at that time, so that it is better known and more adequately observed than many selections of comparable age. It is one of the most handsome of all Rosybloom crabapples, with upright, rounded growth habit, ultimately reaching heights of 7−9 m/23−29 ft. Its large flowers are bright rose, contrasting with the bronze-purple new foliage, which soon turns to bronze-green. Fruits are 2 cm/0.8 in. across, remaining showy through early autumn, and persisting in winter until eaten by birds. It is somewhat susceptible to apple scab and mildew but useful in Zones 3a−7a.

'Strathmore,' another Morden Rosybloom selection, is narrowly vase-shaped, one of very few crabapples with this form. Its flowers are similar to those of 'Hopa' but fade less with age, and its foliage emerges deep red-purple, fades to dull reddish in summer, and turns to a brighter red in autumn. Unfortunately, it is highly susceptible to apple scab and is mentioned here only because of its unique combination of form and color.

Another excellent cultivar, similar in some ways to the Rosybloom crabapples is 'Adams,' a selection of unknown parentage found in Massachusetts, not to be confused with 'Adam,' a very different selection. 'Adams' has single, purplish red flowers fading to rose-pink, and medium-size (to 1.5 cm/0.6 in.), bright red fruits that are colorful in early autumn. It flowers and fruits well annually and is essentially disease-free and useful in Zones 4a−7a.

Malus ×*micromalus* 6 (midget crabapple). This hybrid, probably *M. spectabilis* × *M. baccata*, is notable for its deep rosy pink flowers that fade very little with age and its very small red fruits that remain showy only into midautumn but persist until early winter. The name refers to the small fruits, not the size of the tree, although it seldom exceeds 4–5 m/13–16 ft in height. Useful in Zones 4a–7b but susceptible to fire blight.

Malus ×*robusta* 6 (cherry crabapple). This group of vigorous and hardy hybrids of *M. baccata* × *M. prunifolia* includes several excellent selections valued in cold climates. A few of the best known are listed here.

'Beauty,' originated as an open-pollinated seedling of *M.* ×*robusta*, and is upright, to 6–8 m/19–26 ft tall. This is an excellent dual-purpose tree, with showy white flowers and rather large (2.5 cm/1 in.) bright red fruits that make excellent jelly. It is very resistant to scab and fire blight and useful in Zones 3b–7a.

'Dolgo' is similar to 'Beauty' in parentage, landscape interest, and jelly-making potential, but it is considerably larger, sometimes to 10–12 m/33–39 ft tall and 8–9 m/26–29 ft broad. Like 'Beauty,' it is resistant to scab and fire blight and useful in Zones 3b–7a.

'Persicifolia' (peachleaf crabapple) is a rather shrubby tree, to 6 m/19 ft tall, flowering and fruiting very heavily. It holds its bright red fruits, 2 cm/0.8 in. across, well into winter and is fairly disease resistant and useful in Zones 3b–8a.

Related Species and Their Hybrids

Malus ×*magdeburgensis* 6 (Magdeburg crabapple). This hybrid of *M. spectabilis* × *M. pumila* resembles *M. spectabilis*, with large, semidouble pink flowers but without significant fruiting interest. Useful in Zones 4a–7b.

Malus prunifolia 6 (plumleaf or pearleaf crabapple). This native of eastern Asia is closely related to *M. baccata*, but is slightly less cold-hardy. It is best known for its hybrids, notably *M.* ×*robusta* and *M.* ×*scheideckeri*. *M. prunifolia* 'Pendula' differs from the species type only in its pendulous growth habit. It is probably not available itself but is prominent through its parentage of other pendulous cultivars (see Weeping

crabapples, under *M. floribunda*). *M. prunifolia* var. *rinkii* (Ringo or Chinese pearleaf crabapple) has been planted frequently in the past but it is highly susceptible to apple scab and of limited interest for that reason if no other.

Malus prunifolia.

Malus pumila 7 (common apple). Although best known for commercial fruiting apples, *M. pumila* has been involved in the parentage of many flowering crabapples as well, especially as represented by the interesting but disease susceptible *M. pumila* 'Niedzwetzkyana,' a shrubby, small tree with reddish flowers, fruits, flesh of fruits, and wood of twigs. Commercial fruiting cultivars of *Malus pumila* and *Malus sylvestris* also can be functional landscape plants, used as shade trees or in allée or bosque plantings in situations where the fruits are considered an asset rather than a liability. For successful fruit production, at least a minimal spray maintenance program probably will be necessary. Consult state, provincial, or county extension service offices about local requirements and procedures.

Malus ×*purpurea* 6 (purple crabapple). This variable group of hybrids of *M. pumila* 'Niedzwetskyana' × *M.* ×*atrosanguinea* (*M. halliana* × *M. sieboldii*), is noted for early red-purple flowers and fruits, and, to varying degrees, purple foliage, fading to greenish in late summer. Most members are susceptible to apple scab. Several cultivars useful in Zones 3b–7a have been selected and named, and a few of the most common are listed below.

'Aldenhamensis' is a popular selection for purple foliage, now largely replaced because of its susceptibility to apple scab.

'Eleyi,' a selection for outstanding rosy purple flowers like 'Aldenhamensis' is falling out of favor because of its susceptibility to apple scab.

'Lemoinei' has the deepest red-purple flowers of all M. ×purpurea selections and is still valued for this quality, even though the resistance to apple scab that it was once thought to possess is being questioned. Useful in Zones 4a−7b.

'Liset,' a hybrid of M. ×purpurea 'Lemoinei' × M. sieboldii, is similar to 'Lemoinei' except that it flowers as a younger tree, has more deeply purple foliage, and is more disease resistant.

Malus spectabilis 6 (Chinese flowering crabapple). This species, not known in the wild, has very showy single, semidouble, or double, pale pink flowers, rosy pink in bud. But the yellowish fruits have little ornamental value. As a result, other double-flowered crabapples with yellow fruiting interest (e.g., 'Blanche Ames' and 'Dorothea') may be used preferentially. The fol-lowing selections are most commonly used in landscape plantings.

'Albi-plena' has double white flowers, to 4 cm/1.6 in. across. This cultivar is fairly resistant to disease and is useful in Zones 5b−8b.

'Blanche Ames' is presumably a hybrid, originating as an open-pollinated seedling of M. spectabilis 'Riversii.' Its semidouble, pink to white flowers are borne annually and its small fruits are more colorful than the larger ones of M. spectabilis. It is highly disease resistant and useful in Zones 4a−8a.

'Riversii,' selected in England more than a century ago, is one of the most spectacular of all crabapples in bloom, with double pink flowers to 5 cm/2 in. across, appearing rather early in the crabapple flowering sequence. It is fairly resistant to disease but has fallen from favor to some extent for the lack of colorful fruiting interest.

Malus floribunda 6

Japanese flowering crabapple
Deciduous tree
Rosaceae (Rose Family)

Native Range. Japan.

Useful Range. USDA Zones 4b−8b, possibly colder zones as well.

Function. Specimen, massing, patio tree.

Size and Habit

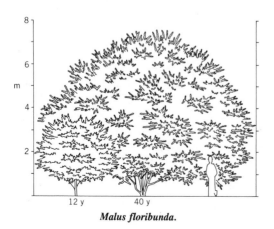

Malus floribunda.

Adaptability

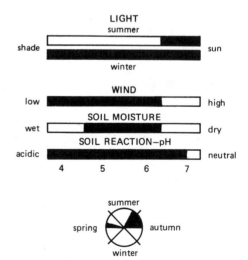

Seasonal Interest. *Flowers:* Fragrant, red in bud, opening rosy pink and fading to white, to 3−4 cm/1.2−1.6 in. across, borne in great numbers in middle spring annually. *Foliage:* Bright green, neat and attractive, falling without color change. *Fruit:* Yellow with slight red blush, only to 0.8 cm/0.3 in. across, borne annually but remaining on the tree for only a short time after leaves drop, in part because they are favored by birds.

Problems and Maintenance. This tree is fairly resistant to apple scab, rust, and mildew, and usually is not troubled with fire blight, although damage has occurred in some years. It needs little or no pruning, and the fruits are less of a litter problem than those of many crabapples. While crabapples in general cannot be considered low maintenance plants, *M. floribunda* usually requires very little attention.

Hybrids of *Malus floribunda*

Malus ×*arnoldiana* 6 (Arnold crabapple). This hybrid of *M. floribunda* × *M. baccata* is a smaller tree than either parent, seldom exceeding 5 m/16 ft in height, with strongly horizontal to moundlike growth habit. Its flowers are similar to those of *M. floribunda* except slightly larger and deeper red in bud, and it is similar to *M. floribunda* in useful range and site requirements. Unfortunately, it is very susceptible to apple scab. *Malus* ×*arnoldiana* has been further hybridized with other species, yielding very showy cultivars, most as susceptible to apple scab as the common parent. Two of the most common are listed here.

'Dorothea' (*M.* ×*arnoldiana* × *M. halliana* 'Parkmanii') has large, semidouble flowers, deep red in bud, opening rose-pink, and fading very little. It is very susceptible to both apple scab and fire blight. Useful in Zones 4a−7a.

'Van Eseltine' (probably *M.* ×*arnoldiana* × *M. spectabilis*) is distinctively vase-shaped in growth habit, very narrow when young, with very showy, double flowers, deep red in bud and opening pink, fading to pale pink, to 5 cm/2 in. across. It is somewhat more resistant to apple scab than *M.* ×*arnoldiana*, but it can be devastated by fire blight in some years and some localities. Useful in Zones 4a−7a.

Malus ×*scheideckeri* 6 (Scheidecker crabapple). This hybrid of *M. floribunda* × *M. prunifolia* is a small tree, 4−6 m/13−19 ft tall, with slender branches, graceful when allowed to assume its natural form. Its semidouble, rosy pink flowers appear at about the same time as those of the parents, relatively early among crabapples, and its small yellow fruits are effective in early autumn. It is useful in Zones

5a−8b, but moderately susceptible to apple scab and highly susceptible to fire blight.

Weeping crabapples. The following three hybrids involving *M. floribunda* are the best known of the pendulous flowering crabapples. They are best used as specimens for accent, singly or in small groups.

'Exzellenz Thiel' (probably *M. floribunda* × *M. prunifolia* 'Pendula') is a gracefully pendulous small tree with flowering interest similar to *M. floribunda* and yellow, angular fruits slightly larger than those of *M. floribunda*. Because of the slender trunk and branches, young trees must be grafted on an upright standard or else staked for the first few years after planting to ensure an upright trunk.

'Oekonomierat Echtermeyer' ('Exzellenz Thiel' × *M. pumila* 'Niedzwetzkyana') is sometimes called by the invalid but simpler and commercially more acceptable name "Pink Weeper." It has large, pink-purple flowers and

Malus 'Red Jade.'

Malus 'Red Jade.'

deep purple fruits, foliage that emerges purple but soon changes to bronze-green. It is usually grafted on a standard. Unfortunately, it is susceptible to apple scab, but only the fruits seem to be affected.

'Red Jade,' an open-pollinated hybrid of 'Exzellenz Thiel,' has much of the latter's delicate growth habit and sparkling red fruits in autumn. It is reasonably resistant to the common crabapple diseases except fire blight and useful in Zones 3b–7a. It is usually grafted on a standard.

Other Hybrids. 'Beverly,' a compact tree with the approximate form of *M. floribunda* and pink flowers, has excellent, small, bright red fruits and is resistant to most diseases but susceptible to fire blight.

'Ormiston Roy' is a handsome selection of unknown parentage, selected in Iowa, bearing at least some resemblance to *M. floribunda* but possibly not closely related. Its flower buds are at first rosy red, turning to rose-pink as they expand, finally opening white, to 4 cm/1.6 in. across. Red-blushed, yellow-orange fruits, about 1.2 cm/0.5 in. across, remain colorful into midwinter. Flowers and fruits are borne annually, and this tree is essentially disease free and useful in Zones 4a–7a.

'Seafoam' is a semipendulous tree that arose as an open-pollinated seedling of 'Oekonomierat Echtermeyer.' Its flowers are much lighter in color than those of the weeping parent, rosy-pink in bud and opening white, flushed pink, to 3.5 cm/1.4 in. across. Its small yellow fruits add autumn interest. 'Seafoam' is not widely available, but is essentially disease-free and probably will become more popular in time.

Malus hupehensis 6

Synonym: *M. theifera*
Tea crabapple
Deciduous tree
Rosaceae (Rose Family)

Native Range. China.

Useful Range. USDA Zones 4b–8b.

Function. Specimen, patio tree.

Size and Habit

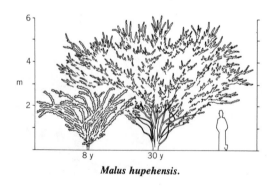

Malus hupehensis.

Adaptability

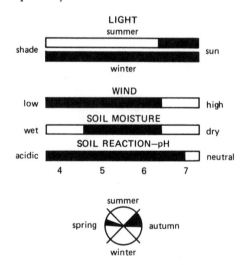

Seasonal Interest. *Flowers:* Fragrant, deep pink in bud, opening blush pink and fading to white, to 4 cm/1.6 in. across, borne in alternate years. *Foliage:* Deep green, displayed to good advantage by the picturesque, open branching habit. *Fruits:* Greenish yellow with red blush, giving significant but not outstanding interest in early autumn in alternate years. *Habit:* Open branching habit is among the most picturesque of all crabapples, with long, irregularly spreading, sparsely branching limbs.

Malus hupehensis.

Malus hupehensis.

Problems and Maintenance. This species is resistant to most crabapple diseases but is occasionally troubled by fire blight.

Related Species and Hybrids. The following are related to *M. hupehensis* more in landscape effect than genetically.

Malus ×atrosanguinea 6 (carmine crabapple). This hybrid of *M. halliana* × *M. sieboldii* is a small, shrubby tree with deep red flower buds, opening bright rose, to 3 cm/1.2 in. across, midway in the flowering season. It has little fruiting interest. It is resistant to apple scab but can be seriously affected by fire blight in some areas and is useful in Zones 5a–8b.

Malus halliana 5 (Hall flowering crabapple). This small tree, cultivated in the Far East but not known in the wild there, is gracefully spreading to vase-shaped and has relatively early, bright rose flowers, to 3.5 cm/1.4 in. The most commonly used cultivar, 'Parkmanii' (Parkman flowering crabapple), has semidouble flowers and is highly resistant to apple scab and other diseases. *M. halliana* has very small, dull, deep red fruits in early autumn, of much less interest than the flowers, and is among the least cold-hardy of crabapples, useful only in Zones 5b–8b.

'Katherine' is an open-branching, extremely showy tree with very large (to 5 cm/2 in. or slightly larger), double flowers, light pink and fading to white, and large numbers of dull red fruits, to 0.8 cm/0.3 in. across. Its parentage is thought to be *M. halliana* × *M. baccata*. It is moderately susceptible to apple scab, otherwise trouble-free, and useful in Zones 5a–8b.

Malus ioensis 6

Iowa or prairie crabapple
Deciduous tree
Rosaceae (Rose Family)

Native Range. North-central United States.

Useful Range. USDA Zones 4a–6b.

Function. Specimen, massing, patio tree.

Size and Habit

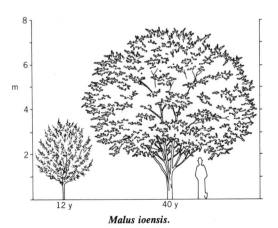

Malus ioensis.

Adaptability

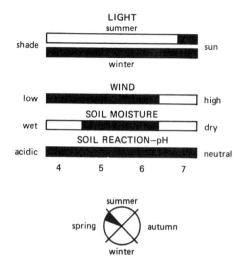

Seasonal Interest. *Flowers:* Fragrant, clear, light pink, single or double, to 4–5 cm/1.6–2 in. across in late spring after most flowering crabapples have finished flowering, borne annually. *Foliage:* Medium to light green, rather coarse. *Fruits:* Greenish and inconspicuous. *Twigs and*

Malus ioensis.

branches: Bark is more or less light silvery gray, adding winter interest.

Problems and Maintenance. *Malus ioensis* and the other native American crabapples, including *M. angustifolia* and *M. coronaria*, are alternate hosts for the cedar apple rust fungus and should be grown only in areas free of native American junipers, especially eastern red cedar (*Juniperus virginiana*), or where intensive spraying maintenance is available. In areas free of cedar apple rust, members of this group still have other disease problems. They are generally susceptible to apple scab and fire blight. Because of their susceptibility to disease, native American crabapples should only be used when there are compelling reasons or when preserved in natural or naturalized settings.

Cultivars and Hybrids. 'Evelyn' originated as an open-pollinated seedling of *M. ioensis* and is thought to be a hybrid of *M.* ×*purpurea*. It has single flowers, rose red in bud and opening rosy pink, to 3.5 cm/1.4 in. across, and is resistant to apple scab but somewhat susceptible to fire blight.

'Fiore's Improved' has extremely large, semidouble flowers and unusually smooth, silvery gray bark.

'Nova' is similar to 'Plena' except that its flowers are deeper pink and it may differ in resistance to apple scab and fire blight.

'Plena' (Bechtel crabapple) is the original double-flowered selection of *M. ioensis*, with fragrant flowers to 5 cm/2 in. and having as many as 30 petals. It is mostly being replaced by improved selections such as 'Fiore's Improved' and 'Nova,' or even more frequently by oriental crabapple selections for similar but earlier flowering interest coupled with greater fruiting interest and disease resistance.

'Prairie Rose' originated as an open-pollinated seedling of *M. ioensis*, and so may be a hybrid. It resembles 'Plena' except for having deeper pink flowers.

'Prince Georges' is thought to be a hybrid of *M. ioensis* 'Plena' × *M. angustifolia*. It is notable for extremely double flowers with close to 60 petals—approximately twice as many as 'Plena'—and appears to be sterile.

Related Species

Malus angustifolia 6 (southern or wild sweet crabapple).   This wild tree native to the southeastern United States as far south as northern Florida is the only flowering crabapple that performs well as far south as the Gulf Coast, and it is useful in Zones 6b–9a. It is not a highly functional landscape tree there, but with its gracefully irregular form and fragrant, pale pink single flowers (to 2.5 cm/1 in.) it has distinctive charm in natural and naturalized settings. Like the more northern native American crabapples, it is susceptible to cedar apple rust, and it is often defoliated before autumn when growing in the same area as *Juniperus virginiana* or its cultivars.

Malus coronaria 6 (wild sweet crabapple).   This native of the eastern United States, from New York and Ontario to Alabama and Indiana can be considered the northeastern counterpart of *M. angustifolia* and *M. ioensis*, from which it differs very little. It is useful in Zones 5a–7a. Several selections have been made but only the following cultivars have become at all well known. 'Charlottae' has fragrant, clear pink, semidouble flowers, to 2.0–2.5 cm/0.8–1 in. across, appearing at about the same time in late spring as those of *M. ioensis*. It is susceptible to cedar apple rust, apple scab, and fire blight. 'Nieuwlandiana' is similar to 'Charlottae' but has deeper pink, larger, more fully double flowers. 'Klehm's Improved Bechtel,' with large, double pink flowers, is often listed as a variant of *M. ioensis* 'Plena' (Bechtel crabapple), but crabapple experts classify it as *M. coronaria*.

Other less commonly used species in the native American group include *M. glaucescens* and *M. platycarpa*. These and the hybrid groups *M.* ×*heterophylla* (*M. coronaria* × *M. pumila*) and *M.* ×*soulardii* (*M. ioensis* × *M. pumila*) all share the disease problems common to the group.

Malus sargentii 5

Sargent crabapple
Deciduous tree
Rosaceae (Rose Family)

Native Range. Japan.

Useful Range. USDA Zones 4b–8b.

Function. Specimen, massing.

Size and Habit

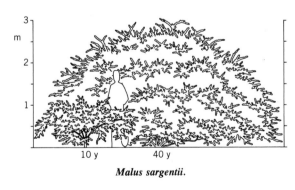

Malus sargentii.

Adaptability

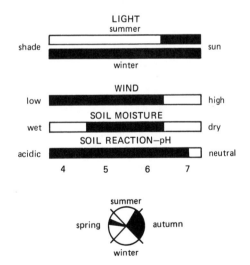

Seasonal Interest. *Flowers:* Fragrant, light pink in bud, opening pure white, no more than 2.5 cm/1 in. across, flowering heavily only in alternate years. *Foliage:* Deep green, partly lobed, neat in texture. *Fruits:* Shiny, deep red, small, about 1 cm/0.4 in. across, adding interest throughout autumn in alternate years.

Problems and Maintenance. Biennial flowering and fruiting is a limitation in any flowering crabapple and is often sufficient reason for discarding one cultivar in favor of another. *M. sargentii* has remained in favor in spite of this drawback because of its uniqueness in size, form, and function. The species and the selection 'Rosea' (see Cultivars) are highly resistant, but not immune, to apple scab and fire blight. Pruning is seldom necessary, except to remove dead, damaged, or rubbing branches.

Cultivars. 'Mary Potter' is actually a hybrid of *M. sargentii* 'Rosea' × *M. ×atrosanguinea*. It tends to breed true from open-pollinated seed, presumably by apomixis (development of an embryo without fertilization), which is known to occur in the parent, *M. sargentii*. This selection has flowers and fruits generally similar to those of *M.*

sargentii 'Rosea,' and the form of a larger version of *M. sargentii*, reaching a mature height of 3–4 m/10–13 ft, with spread of 5–6 m/16–19 ft, compared with heights of 2–2.5 m/6–8 ft for *M. sargentii*. In a few locations it has been reported as flowering and fruiting biennially, but most frequently it flowers and fruits well annually.

'Rosea' (pinkbud Sargent crabapple) is similar to *M. sargentii* except that it grows larger and its flower buds are rosy red before opening white. A few observers have listed this selection as being more susceptible to apple scab than the species type, but this does not seem to be consistently true.

'Tina' is a selection for dwarf, spreading growth habit, and is even smaller than the species type, not exceeding 2 m/6.6 ft in height for many years.

Malus sieboldii 6

Toringo crabapple
Deciduous tree
Rosaceae (Rose Family)

Native Range. Japan and Korea.

Useful Range. USDA Zones 4a–8b (see Varieties).

Function. Specimen, massing, patio tree.

Size and Habit. M. ×*zumi* (synonym: *M. sieboldii* var. *zumi*) is illustrated.

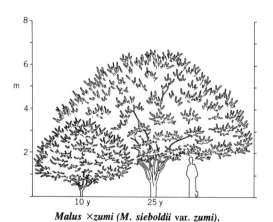

Malus ×*zumi* (*M. sieboldii* var. *zumi*).

Adaptability

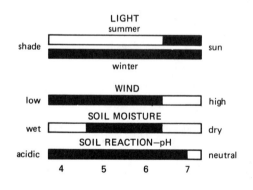

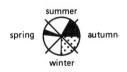

Seasonal Interest. *Flowers:* Fragrant, single, pink in bud, opening pale pink or white, 2 cm/0.8 in. across, borne annually in middle to late spring (see Varieties). *Foliage:* Medium green, variously lobed. *Fruits:* Small (0.8 cm/0.3 in. across), brownish yellow or red, borne annually.

Problems and Maintenance. This species is resistant to most diseases. Some pruning for establishment of structure may be desirable in var. *arborescens*.

Varieties. Var. *arborescens* (tree Toringo crabapple) is distinctly a tree form, to 8−10 m/25−23 ft tall and equally wide at maturity. It is valued primarily for its annual display of fragrant, small, pink to white flowers opening in late spring and for its disease resistance. Useful in Zones 5a−8a and perhaps in colder zones as well.

Related Hybrids

Malus ×*zumi* 6 (synonym: *M. sieboldii* var. *zumi*; Zumi crabapple). This hybrid of *M. baccata* var. *mandshurica* × *M. sieboldii* has large numbers of white flowers, pink in bud, borne biennially in middle spring, and small, bright red fruits. The selection 'Calocarpa' holds its fruits well into winter and is valued especially for winter color, but unfortunately this is only a biennial display. In some locations in some years, foliage will turn orange before falling. 'Calocarpa' is more resistant to fire blight than average for *M.* ×*zumi* and is useful in Zones 4a−8a.

Hybrids of *M.* ×*zumi* are noted for their colorful fruits, retained into late autumn or winter. A few of the best known follow.

'Indian Magic' and 'Indian Summer,' two of several flowering crabapples developed by Mr. Robert C. Simpson of Vincennes, Indiana, have rose-red flowers and bright red fruits that remain colorful through autumn and persist all winter.

'Indian Summer' has greater scab resistance and later fruiting interest than 'Indian Magic.'

'Snowdrift' has outstanding, upright growth habit when young, grows to 6 m/20 ft tall, has white flowers, pink in bud, and very small (1 cm/0.4 in.) and persistent orange-red fruits. This selection is one of the best crabapples for street planting, but is susceptible to fire blight.

Two other fine cultivars are thought to have originated from *M.* ×*zumi*, even though their parentage is not documented.

'Bob White' was selected in Massachusetts more than a century ago and is still valued for its fragrant white flowers, opening from red buds in middle spring, and small yellow fruits that persist all winter. Unfortunately, it usually flowers and fruits well only in alternate years, but it is very nearly disease-free, suffering only occasional outbreaks of fire blight.

'Golden Hornet' was selected more recently in England and is thought to be an open-pollinated seedling of *M.* ×*zumi* 'Calocarpa.' It is similar in flowering and fruiting interest except that its bright yellow fruits are somewhat larger, to 2 cm/0.8 in., and last only through about half the winter. In 1974, 'Golden Hornet' was listed among the 20 best flowering crabapple cultivars at the University of Minnesota Landscape Arboretum, in part because of its freedom from disease, but it has since proved susceptible to fire blight and it does not have good form.

Malus toringoides 6

Cutleaf crabapple
Deciduous tree
Rosaceae (Rose Family)

Native Range. Western China.

Useful Range. USDA Zones 4b−8a.

Function. Specimen, massing, patio tree.

Size and Habit

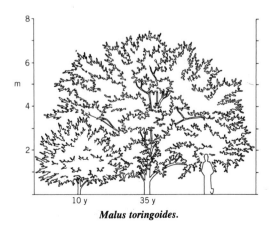

Malus toringoides.

Adaptability

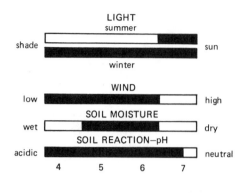

Seasonal Interest. *Flowers:* Fragrant, white, to 2.5 cm/1 in. across, borne in quantity only in alternate years in late spring. *Foliage:* Medium green, usually lobed, making a fairly dense canopy. *Fruits:* Distinctively pear shaped, yellow with a red blush on the sunny side, to 1.2 cm/0.5 in. long, very striking, late summer to late autumn in alternate years.

Problems and Maintenance. This tree is reasonably resistant to apple scab and rust but highly susceptible to fire blight in some areas. Fire blight has been reported less frequently in the selection 'Macrocarpa' (see Cultivars), but the cultivar may be less important as a variable than the geographical location. The dense, twiggy growth habit of M. *toringoides* tends to discourage pruning, which is hardly necessary anyway.

Cultivars. 'Macrocarpa, a selection for larger fruits, to 2.5 cm/1 in. long, is one of the most ornamental of all crabapples in fruit.

Related Species. Some of the following are no more closely related to M. *toringoides* than to any other crabapples but fall into the generalized category of species with lobed or coarsely toothed foliage. All can be considered minor species in use at present.

Malus ×*dawsoniana* 6 (Dawson crabapple). This tall-growing hybrid of M. *fusca* × M. *pumila* is noteworthy only for its greatly elongated fruits, to 3.5 cm/1.4 in. long and only 2.2 cm/0.9 in. across, bright yellow and more or less pink-blushed, adding significant landscape interest from late summer until late autumn. This tree is susceptible to apple scab but not troubled appreciably by other disease. It is useful in Zones 5a–8b.

Malus florentina 5 (Italian crabapple).   This native Italian species, long cultivated in Europe, is very different from any other flowering crabapple. It is a small tree, to about 3 m/10 ft tall, upright and round-headed or pyramidal in habit. Its deeply lobed leaves resemble those of some hawthorns more than those of other crabapples, and its small, single, white flowers open in late spring at about the same time as those of M. *ioensis*. Its small (1 cm/0.4 in.) red fruits are colorful in early autumn, and in some years its foliage turns red-orange before falling. This species has been so little used in the United States that its disease susceptibility is not well documented, and it probably is not commercially available. It is mentioned here because of its distinctness and the possibility that it might be useful in the South if it passes the test of disease resistance. Useful in Zones 6a–8b, perhaps also 9a.

Malus tschonoskii 7 (Tschonoski crabapple). This Japanese tree is unlike any other crabapple, primarily because of its foliage interest. Young leaves are covered with a thick felt of silvery white hairs, which gradually disappears from the upper leaf surface, remaining on the lower surface. In some locations and in some years, the leaves turn bright shades of yellow, red, and purple in autumn. The foliage interest, unhampered by apple scab, and its regularly pyramidal form give this species value as a landscape tree, but it has only minor flowering and fruiting interest and unfortunately is susceptible to fire blight. It is gradually becoming more widely available and is useful in Zones 4b–8b.

Menispermum canadense 1 and 2

Common moonseed
Deciduous vine
Menispermaceae (Moonseed Family)

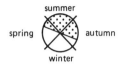

Native Range. Eastern North America: Quebec to Manitoba and south to Georgia and Arkansas.

Useful Range. USDA Zones 5a−9a+.

Function. Groundcover, screen (with support). Climbs by twining to heights of 3−4 m/10−13 ft, in Zones 5−8, kills back almost to the ground each winter, returning rapidly the following spring and summer.

mass, remaining green until the tops are killed back by hard freezes. *Fruits:* Blue-black, 0.8 cm/0.3 in. across, in clusters resembling grapes on pistillate (female) plants, adding both landscape interest and potential hazard, since they are toxic and may be taken for grapes by children.

Menispermum canadense.

Size and Habit

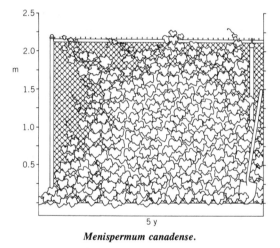

Menispermum canadense.

Adaptability

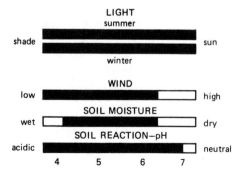

Problems and Maintenance. This trouble-free vine requires no maintenance except to remove winterkilled tops and to prune back the vine when it threatens to become overly aggressive, which it commonly does. This is not a plant to be used in intensive situations.

Related Species

Cocculus carolinus 1 (Carolina moonseed). This native of the southeastern United States, also in the Menispermaceae (Moonseed Family), resembles *Menispermum canadense* generally but has smaller, rounded leaves, 5−8 cm/2−3 in. long, and red fruits (on pistillate plants), 0.8 cm/0.3 in. across, in showy clusters in late summer and autumn. Carolina moonseed climbs by twining to about the same height as common moonseed and is useful as a partial screen, with support, in Zones 7a−9a+. Like *Menispermum canadense*, it can become a weed in some areas.

Seasonal Interest. *Foliage:* Lustrous, dark green, distinctively round-lobed, 10−20 cm/4−8 in. long, making a handsomely textured, dense

Metasequoia glyptostroboides 8

Dawn redwood
Deciduous tree
Taxodiaceae (Taxodium Family)

Native Range. Western China.

Useful Range. USDA Zones 5b−9a.

Function. Specimen, screen (summer).

Size and Habit

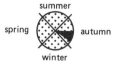

Seasonal Interest. *Foliage:* Deciduous, needlelike, giving fine, feathery texture; lacy and light green in spring, medium green in summer, and turning delicate shades of pinkish tan to brown before falling in late autumn. *Metasequoia* can easily be distinguished from

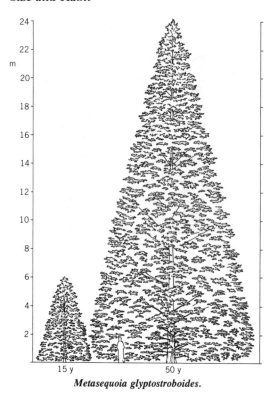

Metasequoia glyptostroboides.

Metasequoia glyptostroboides.

Adaptability. *Metasequoia* is notable for its ability to grow close to the edges of ponds or streams, but it will also grow well in soil of average moisture content.

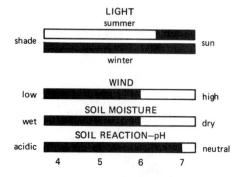

Metasequoia glyptostroboides.

Taxodium distichum (common bald cypress) by the opposite arrangement of lateral branchlets and large winter buds; in *Taxodium* the arrangement is mostly alternate and the winter buds are small and inconspicuous. *Trunk and branches:* Lower branches are borne horizontally on the strong, straight, tapered, and eventually buttressed central trunk with interestingly fissured and shredded bark.

Special note. One of the most interesting features of *Metasequoia glyptostroboides* is its story. Known only in the fossil record as a presumably extinct tree of North America and Asia before 1941, it was found in the wild in that year in Szechwan province, China. Seeds were received by the Arnold Arboretum of Harvard University in 1948 and quickly disseminated to other arboreta around the world. As a result, it quickly became cultivated as a landscape tree and is now fairly readily available in most areas. In landscape function it differs little from *Taxodium distichum* (common bald cypress) except that it is slightly

less cold-hardy than genetic material of *Taxodium* of northern origin.

Problems and Maintenance. Although this tree grows well in soils that are wet to moderately moist, it should not be used in distinctly dry sites, sinces the foliage will be damaged by drought stress and mite infestations. Avoid planting in frost pockets, since this tree often makes late growth and is prone to early autumn freezes. In recent years a trunk-canker disease has appeared in a few locations, and this could become a more general problem in time.

Cultivars. 'National,' a selection made at the U.S. National Arboretum, is narrow in form, growing rapidly in height. 'Sheridan Spire,' introduced by Sheridan Nurseries near Toronto, Canada, is at least as narrow as 'National' and more compactly columnar. Other form variants presumably will be selected and named in the future, and will need to be observed for several years for adequate evaluation.

Michelia figo 5

Synonyms: *Magnolia fuscata, Michelia fuscata*
Banana shrub
Evergreen shrub
Magnoliaceae (Magnolia Family)

Native Range. China.

Useful Range. USDA Zones 8b−9a+ and protected sites in Zone 8a.

Function. Specimen, massing, screen, border.

Size and Habit

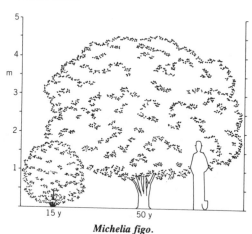

15 y   50 y

Michelia figo.

Adaptability. Although this plant will tolerate a considerable amount of wind, for full benefit of the fragrance it is better used in sites where the air is fairly still.

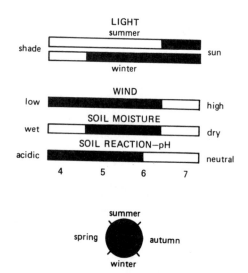

Seasonal Interest. *Flowers:* Pale yellow with crimson margins and brown outside, from brown velvety winter buds, opening to 3.5 cm/1.4 in. across, with a bananalike fragrance. *Foliage:*

Evergreen, neatly textured, medium green, with leaves about 4−6 cm/1.6−2.5 in. long on stems covered with a scurf of rusty colored hairs. *Fruits:*

Michelia figo.

Small, brown, magnolialike pods with fleshy orange seeds are seldom seen in cultivation.

Problems and Maintenance. This plant seems to be completely trouble-free. Its slow growth probably has discouraged its use to some extent, but for many landscape situations this is outweighed by its permanence and freedom from maintenance.

Related Species. Several other species of *Michelia* are known in cultivation, some for ornament, some for lumber, in the subtropics and tropics.

Morus alba 7−8

White mulberry
Deciduous tree
Moraceae (Mulberry Family)

Native Range. China; widely naturalized in Eurasia and North America.

Useful Range. USDA Zones 5a−9a; some selections in Zone 4 as well.

Function. Small shade tree.

Size and Habit

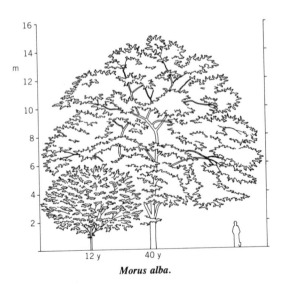

Morus alba.

Adaptability. Unusually well adapted to the difficult climates of the Great Plains within its useful range.

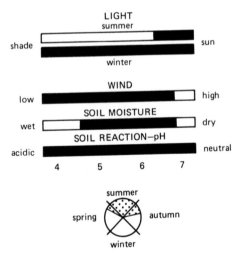

Seasonal Interest. *Foliage:* Variously lobed, usually more or less lustrous and bright green, falling in early autumn with little color change. *Fruits:* Small, blackberrylike, edible, crimson, pink or white, borne on most trees and constituting a major litter problem, but some trees are dioecious (all flowers on a tree of only one sex), giving rise to nonfruiting selections. *Trunk and branches:* Bark is orange-brown, a slight but sometimes appreciable contribution to winter color.

Morus alba.

Problems and Maintenance. This tree requires little or no maintenance except for light pruning to maintain form and remove low-hanging branches. Its most serious problem is the fruit litter, which discolors pavement, and the seedlings, generated by bird-carried seeds, which appear in flower beds, alleys, and anywhere else they happen to land. Nonfruiting cultivars (below) are, of course, free of both these problems.

Cultivars. 'Kingan' and 'Striblingii' (= 'Mapleleaf') are nonfruiting forms, useful in more intensive landscape sites than the fruiting species type. 'Pendula' (weeping mulberry) is one of the most strongly pendulous trees known, useful only

where such strong accent is desired. 'Tatarica' (Russian mulberry) is a selection for unusual cold hardiness. It is valued for planting in the northern Great Plains, where it is cold-hardy to Zone 4a. It has small fruits, an added advantage in most landscape situations.

Related Species

Morus rubra 7—8 (red mulberry).   This native North American mulberry is generally similar to *M. alba* except that it has fairly good yellow autumn foliage color. No nonfruiting cultivars have been selected to date. Useful in Zones 4b—9a with selection of appropriate genetic material, but nursery-grown plants are seldom available.

Broussonetia papyrifera 7 (paper mulberry). This native of China and Japan is occasionally naturalized in the central and southeastern United States. Like *Morus* species, it is well adapted to difficult site conditions within its useful range of Zones 6b—9a. Its gray-green, irregularly lobed leaves make a dense canopy, and trunks of old trees are irregular and picturesque with smooth, gray bark. On the negative side, it suckers freely and is soft-wooded and drops considerable twig and fruit (female trees) litter, so it is neither durable nor a low-maintenance tree.

Myrica pensylvanica 4— 5

Bayberry
Deciduous or semievergreen shrub
Myricaceae (Bayberry Family)

Native Range. Eastern North America, mostly the Atlantic Coast.

Useful Range. USDA Zones 4b—9a, with occasional winter damage in Zone 4.

Function. Border, massing, foundation, screen (in good soil).

Size and Habit

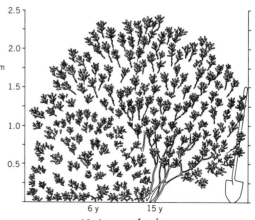

Myrica pensylvanica.

Adaptability. This shrub is unusually tolerant of seaside and roadside salt and infertile soil. All *Myrica* species are capable of fixing and using atmospheric nitrogen, and they do this most effectively in soils low in fertility.

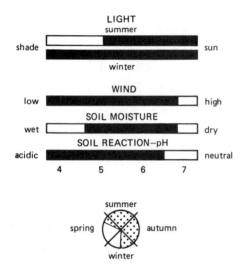

Seasonal Interest. *Foliage:* Clean, bright to dull green as summer progresses, persisting well into early winter. Strongly and pleasantly aromatic when crushed. *Fruits:* Borne only on female plants (dioecious), but male plants are needed nearby for pollination to have significant fruiting interest, a reason for using this plant in mass plantings. The gray, waxy berries, only 0.5 cm/0.2 in. across but borne in great numbers close to the twigs, add significant fall and winter interest before and after leaves drop. Fruits, like the foliage, are aromatic, and the wax covering them can be removed and added to candle wax to make bayberry candles.

Problems and Maintenance. This shrub is unusually trouble-free and requires little or no maintenance. It does not require pruning unless used as a formal hedge, and this is not an appropriate use for this plant, since shearing destroys its character. It is reputedly difficult to transplant, but this is no problem with pot-grown or even field-grown plants if properly handled.

Related Species

Myrica cerifera 6–7 (synonym: *M. caroliniensis*; wax myrtle). This tall shrub or small tree is native to eastern North America, northward only to New Jersey, but far southward well into Florida and Texas. It resembles *M. pensylvanica* closely except that it is more fully evergreen and usually considerably taller. Useful in Zones 6b–9a+, it is a serviceable, low-maintenance plant for the South, especially in coastal areas, where its salt-resistance is a great asset. It is somewhat more tolerant of wet soils than *M. pensylvanica*.

Myrica gale 4 (sweet gale). This fine-textured, thicket-forming shrub is less handsome than *M. cerifera* or *M. pensylvanica*, with small, dull, dark green leaves on upright branches. Native to edges of lakes and streams in the northern parts of both Eurasia and North America, its cold-hardiness and tolerance of wet soils are its most important qualities. It is useful in Zones 1–8a with selection of appropriate genetic material, but is seldom available in nurseries.

Comptonia peregrina 2 (synonyms: *C. asplenifolia*, *Myrica asplenifolia*; sweet fern). This low, thicket-forming shrub is native from the northeastern United States and Canada to the Great Lakes area and south on the Atlantic Coast to North Carolina. Its graceful, dissected foliage is pleasantly scented, like that of the closely related *Myrica* species. It is useful primarily on sandy, infertile soils, where, like *Myrica* species, it uses atmospheric nitrogen through bacteria associated with its roots. This plant has grown rapidly in popularity for highway landscaping in the Northeast, but its commercial availability is still limited. Useful in Zones 4a–8a, it is difficult to establish unless pot-grown.

Comptonia peregrina.

Nandina domestica 4—5

Nandina, heavenly bamboo
Evergreen shrub
Berberidaceae (Barberry Family)

Native Range. China and Japan.

Useful Range. USDA Zones 7a—9a+ and sheltered sites in Zone 6b.

Function. Specimen, border. If allowed to reach full height for screening, it becomes leggy and open.

Size and Habit

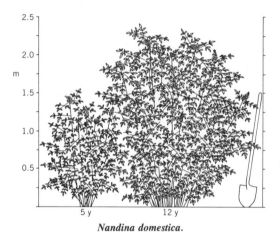

Nandina domestica.

Adaptability

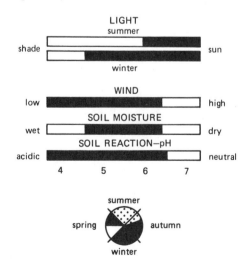

Seasonal Interest. *Flowers:* Small, white, in loose clusters, 20—30 cm/8—12 in. long, in late spring. *Foliage:* Evergreen, doubly or triply com-

pound with small, sharp-pointed, leathery leaflets, forming an attractive open pattern. New leaves emerge bronze to red in spring, and foliage turns dull red-purple to bright red in autumn in full sun. *Fruits:* Bright red berries, to 0.8 cm/0.3 in., in large clusters add striking landscape color in autumn and throughout winter. *Branches:* Little-branched canes give the superficial appearance of a bamboo (hence the common name), and contribute to the leggy growth habit (see Problems and Maintenance).

Nandina domestica.

Problems and Maintenance. This shrub has a rank, open growth habit and requires regular pruning (annual removal of older canes) to maintain good form. With pruning, it functions in size group 4 instead of the 5 indicated. Mildew can be a problem with some plants, especially in humid coastal areas.

Cultivars. 'Alba' has white berries, strikingly different in effect from other selections. 'Com-

Nandina domestica 'Compacta.'

pacta' is more compact and lower than the species type, with many more stems growing from the rootstock and finer textured foliage.

Several other dwarf or semidwarf cultivars with fine textured foliage are on the market and more may emerge. They should be used on a trial basis, since the nomenclature is somewhat confused.

Nerium oleander 6

Oleander
Evergreen shrub
Apocynaceae (Dogbane Family)

Native Range. Mediterranean region to Japan.

Useful Range. USDA Zone 9a+. A few cultivars can be used in Zone 8 in protected sites, functioning in size group 4 or 5.

Function. Screen, hedge, border, massing, specimen: permanent or in containers.

Size and Habit

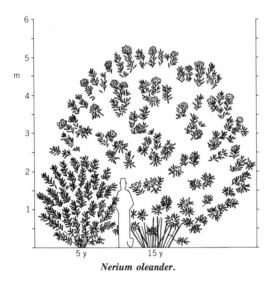

Nerium oleander.

Seasonal Interest. *Flowers:* Fragrant, single or double, 3−5 cm/1−2 in. across, white, pink, red, or yellow, in early summer and continuing to a lesser extent into late summer and autumn. *Foliage:* Evergreen, dark green, long (10−15 cm/4−6 in.) and narrow (2−4 cm/0.8−1.6 in.), smooth. *Fruits:* Elongated green pods to about 15 cm/6 in., not adding significant landscape interest.

Problems and Maintenance. All parts of this plant are poisonous to humans, and even smoke from burning wood can cause serious irritation, so prunings should be disposed of in other ways than burning. Otherwise, this plant is trouble-free. Winter hardiness can be maximized by withholding fertilizer and water in late summer so that growth slows and hardening takes place in autumn. This is especially important in Zone 8.

Cultivars. Variants in flower color are frequently sold by color and whether double or single (e.g., 'Double Red,' 'Single White,' 'Hardy Pink' or 'Hardy Red').

Adaptability. Widely adaptable to strong sun and wind, dry soil, and salt spray in seashore sites.

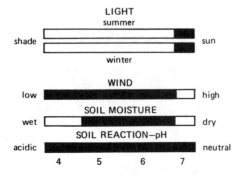

Nyssa sylvatica 8

Tupelo, sour gum, black gum, pepperidge
Deciduous tree
Nyssaceae (Tupelo Family)

Native Range. Eastern North America.

Useful Range. USDA Zones 5a−9a+ with selection of appropriate genetic material.

Function. Shade tree, specimen, massing.

Size and Habit

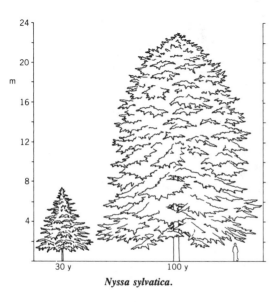

Nyssa sylvatica.

Adaptability. One of the best shade trees for swampy sites, but grows well with average soil moisture as well. Relatively resistant to seashore conditions except where exposed to strong winds.

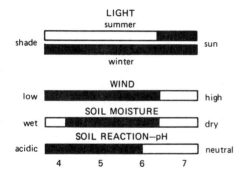

Seasonal Interest. *Foliage:* Glossy, bright to deep green, medium-fine texture, with leaves to 10 cm/4 in. long and half as wide, turning yellow-orange to blazing scarlet in autumn. *Fruits:* Small, blue-black, in clusters or pairs, ripening in autumn but inconspicuous in the landscape. Trees are mostly dioecious. *Twigs and branches:* Silvery gray bark adds winter interest along with the distinctly horizontal branching.

Problems and Maintenance. This tree is generally trouble-free and requires little maintenance but is relatively difficult to transplant, so it should be specified in relatively small sizes, preferably in containers.

Varieties. Var. *biflora* grows wild in the southern part of the range and otherwise differs only in botanical details. The more important distinction that should be made in landscape use is that trees for extreme northern areas should be of northern origin and those for the Deep South should be of southern origin.

Related Species

Nyssa aquatica 8 (water tupelo, cotton gum). This tree is native to the southeastern United States and northward in the Mississippi Basin to southern Illinois and on the Atlantic Coast to Virginia. It can be considered equivalent to *N. sylvatica* for wet soil sites in full sun in the South, but is seldom available except by accident when the two species are confused.

Orixa japonica 5

Japanese orixa
Deciduous shrub
Rutaceae (Rue Family)

Native Range. Japan.

Useful Range. USDA Zones 5b–8b, perhaps 5a and 9a as well.

Function. Screen, specimen, border. Occasional winter dieback limits its use as a screen in Zones 5 and 6.

Seasonal Interest. *Foliage:* Glossy, bright green, oval leaves, to 10 cm/4 in. long, are slightly puckered, giving a distinctive texture. They are strongly aromatic when crushed, and they fall with little or no color change in midautumn.

Size and Habit

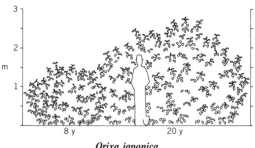

Orixa japonica.

Adaptability

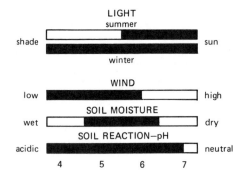

Problems and Maintenance. This shrub is relatively trouble-free and requires no maintenance except occasional pruning to remove dead twigs and maintain form. Availability is limited.

Orixa japonica.

Osmanthus fragrans 5–6

Sweet olive, tea olive
Evergreen shrub or tree
Oleaceae (Olive Family)

Native Range. Eastern Asia.

Useful Range. USDA Zones 8b–9a+.

Function. Border, specimen tree. Functional height varies from about 3 m/10 ft in Zone 8b to 8–10 m/26–33 ft in warmer zones, after some time.

Size and Habit

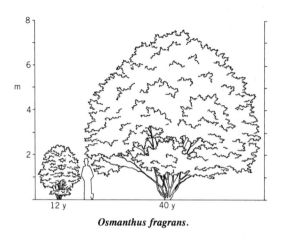

Osmanthus fragrans.

Adaptability

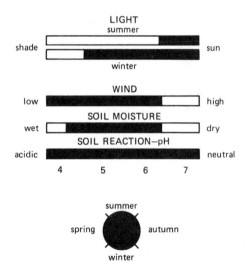

Seasonal Interest. *Flowers:* Very small, white, highly fragrant, year-round but most heavily in spring and autumn. *Foliage:* Evergreen, leathery,

to 10 cm/4 in. long. *Fruit:* Small, blue-black, seldom seen and not adding significant landscape interest when they do develop.

Osmanthus fragrans.

Problems and Maintenance. This plant is trouble-free, requiring little maintenance when properly used in a formal shrub border or as a specimen. It does not respond well to pruning, so it should not be used as a hedge or screen.

Related Species

Osmanthus americanus 5−6 (devilwood osmanthus). This native of the southeastern United States becomes a small tree, to 8−10 m/26−33 ft, from Zone 8b southward, but functions as a large shrub to one third that height as far north as Zone 6b. Its very small flowers are fragrant in early spring, but less so than *O. fragrans*. Its blue-black fruits, to 1.3 cm/0.5 in. long, are more conspicuous than those of *O. fragrans*. Otherwise, except for the difference in cold-hardiness, the two species are functionally similar.

Osmanthus heterophyllus 5

Synonym: *O. ilicifolius*
Holly osmanthus
Evergreen shrub
Oleaceae (Olive Family)

Native Range. Japan.

Useful Range. USDA Zones 7b−9a+.

Function. Hedge, screen, specimen.

Size and Habit

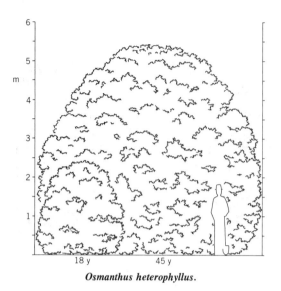

Osmanthus heterophyllus.

Adaptability

Osmanthus heterophyllus.

Problems and Maintenance. This shrub is trouble-free and requires little or no maintenance except when pruned as a formal hedge.

Cultivars. Several foliage variants have been selected, including the following. 'Aureus' has yellow leaf margins. Some plants sold by this name are really 'Variegatus,' and true 'Aureus' may not be commercially available. 'Gulftide' has relatively small leaves and a dense, erect growth habit. 'Rotundifolius' has nearly round, slightly crinkled leaves with few teeth. 'Variegatus' has white variegated leaf margins and is widely available.

Related Species

Osmanthus delavayi 4 (synonym: *Siphonosmanthus delavayi*; Delavay osmanthus). This compact, fine-textured shrub has leaves less than 2.5 cm/1 in. long, more-or-less holly-toothed, and fragrant white flowers, larger than those of other *Osmanthus* species listed here, in small clusters in early spring (and sometimes with scattered flowering in late autumn). This plant is not

Seasonal Interest. *Flowers:* Very small, white or yellowish, fragrant, in middle to late summer. *Foliage:* Evergreen, dark green, leathery, mostly toothed and spiny tipped, resembling holly leaves but easily distinguished by the opposite arrangement (hollies have alternate leaves). Degree of toothing varies greatly from leaf to leaf on the same plant. *Fruits:* Blue-black, to 1.5 cm/0.6 in. long, adding significant landscape interest only at close range in autumn.

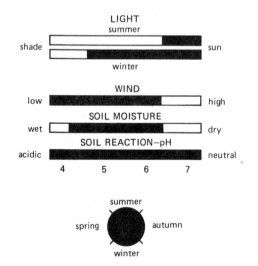

Osmanthus ✕fortunei.

widely available but deserves greater use in Zones 8b−9a+ and possibly in sheltered sites in colder zones.

Osmanthus ×*fortunei* 6 (Fortune osmanthus). This hybrid of *O. heterophyllus* × *O. fragrans* has generally shallowly toothed, spiny tipped leaves, and very fragrant flowers in midsummer to autumn. It is nearly as cold-hardy as *O. heterophyllus*, useful in Zones 7b−9a+. In form, it is dense and compact, almost as broad as tall, and functions in size group 5 for several years before growing into size group 6, where it can be trained into a small tree form if desired.

Ostrya virginiana 7−8

Hop hornbeam, ironwood
Deciduous tree
Betulaceae (Birch Family)

Native Range. Eastern North America.

Useful Range. USDA Zones 3b−9a with selection of appropriate genetic material.

Function. Shade tree, specimen, naturalizing.

Size and Habit

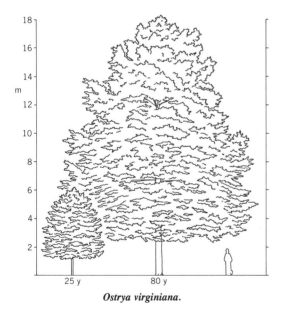

Ostrya virginiana.

Adaptability. This tree is unusually intolerant of salt so should not be used in roadside plantings in the North.

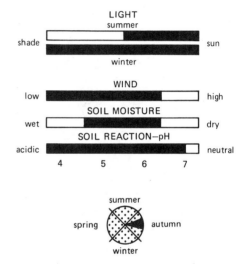

Seasonal Interest. *Foliage:* Medium to dark green, finely toothed, similar to those of birch and elm, making a rather dense canopy, turning yellow before falling in midautumn. *Fruits:* Small, inflated pods in tight, hanging clusters, to 6 cm/2.4 in. long, resembling fruits of the hop vine, hence the name hop hornbeam, quietly interesting in midsummer to early autumn in South and North, respectively. *Trunk:* Finely shredded bark and "muscled" conformation of the trunk add quiet interest in all seasons.

Problems and Maintenance. This is one of the most trouble-free of all deciduous trees, requiring little or no maintenance. As the name ironwood suggests, this is one of the most hard-wooded of temperate zone trees, seldom injured by wind or ice storms. But this strength is the result of a slow growth rate, which has kept the tree from being widely and easily available. It also has the reputation of being difficult to transplant, so it should be nursery-grown and moved in small sizes. Container-grown trees should be specified if they are available. In spite of these problems, this is a high quality tree that deserves greater landscape use for its permanence and low maintenance.

Related Species. Counterpart species from Asia and Europe exist but are rare in North America and certainly not available commercially.

Oxydendrum arboreum 7−8

Sourwood, sorrel tree
Deciduous tree
Ericaceae (Heath Family)

Native Range. Eastern United States.

Useful Range. USDA Zones 5b−9a.

Function. Specimen, patio tree, naturalizing.

Size and Habit

Seasonal Interest. *Flowers:* Small, white, resembling lilies of the valley, in gracefully nodding clusters 10−25 cm/4−10 in. long, in middle to late summer. *Foliage:* Lustrous and leathery, pale to deep green, turning rich maroon to scarlet in autumn and persisting late. *Fruits:* Small capsules carry the flower cluster interest into autumn.

Problems and Maintenance. This tree is trouble-free and requires little or no maintenance if planted in well drained, acidic soil. It is sometimes considered difficult to transplant, but this is only true in large sizes. Specify relatively small sizes, preferably container-grown, and transplant in the spring. Like other members of the heath family, *Oxydendrum* has a fibrous root system that is easily dug and handled when the tree is young. Very light pruning occasionally may be needed to maintain good form, but generally the less pruning the better. Even though this tree is ordinarily hardy northward to Zone 5b, trees recently planted can be damaged in exposed sites even in Zone 6.

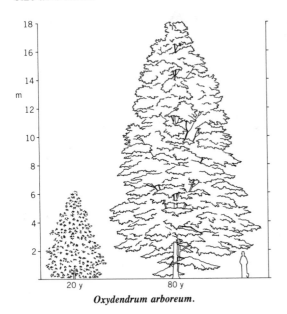

Oxydendrum arboreum.

Adaptability

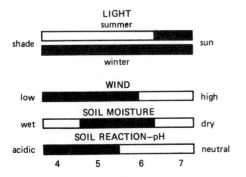

Pachysandra terminalis 2

Japanese spurge
Evergreen groundcover
Buxaceae (Box Family)

Native Range. Japan.

Useful Range. USDA Zones 5a–7b.

Function. Groundcover.

Size and Habit

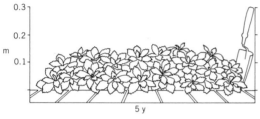

Pachysandra terminalis.

Adaptability. Not only tolerates but requires shade from full sun for satisfactory performance. Will tolerate half sun in the North, but not in the South.

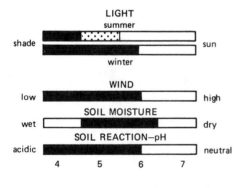

Seasonal Interest. *Flowers:* Small, white, in short spikes, not showy, in spring. *Foliage:* Lustrous and dark green, forming a dense, evergreen groundcover.

Pachysandra terminalis.

Problems and Maintenance. This groundcover is relatively trouble-free once established in a proper site. Because of its dense foliage canopy, this is one of the most effective groundcovers in resisting encroachment of weeds, so little maintenance is required once the canopy is established. A light mulch will reduce the need for weed control during establishment.

Cultivars. 'Green Carpet' has unusually dark green, glossy foliage and is lower-growing than the species type. 'Variegata' has white variegated leaves and is somewhat lower, finer-textured, and slower-growing than the species type.

Related Species

Pachysandra procumbens 2 (Alleghany pachysandra). This native of the southern Appalachian Mountains is deciduous to semievergreen, with dull green but interesting leaves. It is less vigorous than *P. terminalis* and less versatile as a groundcover but excellent in a naturalized woodland setting, with spikes of white or pinkish purple flowers, more showy than those of *P. terminalis*, appearing before the new leaves in middle to late spring. Useful in Zones 5a–7b.

Paeonia suffruticosa 4

Tree peony
Deciduous subshrub
Ranunculaceae (Buttercup Family)

Native Range. China to Bhutan and long cultivated in much of eastern Asia.

Useful Range. USDA Zones 6a−7b, protected
sites in the milder parts of Zone 5, and cool sites
in Zone 8.

Function. Specimen, border.

Size and Habit

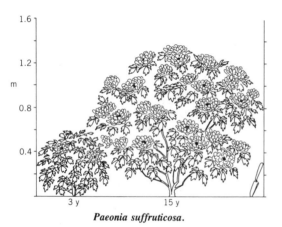

Paeonia suffruticosa.

Adaptability. Exposure to full sun for a major
part of the day, preferably morning, is necessary
for good flowering, but partial shade during the
hottest part of the day is desirable except in
coastal areas that have hazy, mild summers. In
winter, protection from full sun will reduce
dehydration of the stems in areas where that is a
problem. Soil drainage must be perfect for best
results.

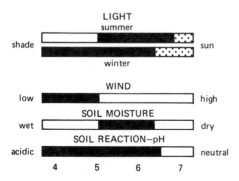

Seasonal Interest. *Flowers:* White, pink, rose, or
rich red, double or single, with bright yellow
centers, 10−30 cm/4−12 in. across, spectacular
in bloom. *Foliage:* Dull blue-green and distinctive in texture, but deciduous early and not a
major landscape feature.

Problems and Maintenance. Like many other
plants that have been bred for extreme showiness
(e.g., hybrid tea roses), tree peonies have several
insect problems and should be watched carefully
during the growing season. When pest control is
necessary, instructions can be obtained through
county, state, or provincial extension service
offices.

Cultivars. Several hundred cultivars have been
developed in China and Japan, and a substantial
number are now available in the United States.
Since few are available in a specific time and
place, they must be selected for availability above
all else. Most cultivars are hybrids of *P. suffruticosa* with other tree peony species, *P. delavayi*
and/or *P. lutea* (see Related Species).

Related Species

Paeonia delavayi 4 (Delavay tree peony).   This
subshrub has relatively small (8 cm/3 in.), dark
red flowers and is best known as a parent of
hybrids. Like *P. suffruticosa*, it is from China and
it is comparable in hardiness.

Paeonia lutea 4 (yellow tree peony).   This plant
is not greatly different from other tree peony
species except in having yellow flowers, about 5
cm/2 in. across. Like *P. delavayi*, it is best known
through its parentage of hybrids with *P. suffruticosa*, and it, too, is from China and comparable
in hardiness to other tree peonies.

Parkinsonia aculeata 6

Jerusalem thorn, Mexican palo verde
Deciduous tree
Leguminosae (Pea Family)

Native Range. Tropical America.

Useful Range. USDA Zone 9a+.

Function. Shade, patio, or specimen tree, barrier hedge.

Size and Habit

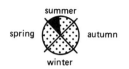

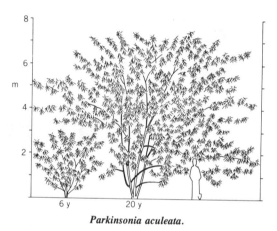

Parkinsonia aculeata.

Adaptability. Resistant to salt spray in seashore sites.

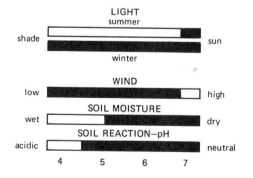

Seasonal Interest. *Flowers:* Fragrant, bright yellow, about 2.5 cm/1 in. across, borne in great numbers in loose clusters in early summer in Zone 9a, and later as well in warmer climates. *Foliage:* Long, whiplike, compound leaves, to 30 cm/12 in. or longer with up to 50 tiny leaflets, giving very light, filtered shade until they fall in autumn. *Twigs and branches:* Loose and open branching with many thorns, to 2.5 cm/1 in. long, borne on twigs and branches that remain smooth and green year-round.

Problems and Maintenance. This tree is at its best south of our area, and smaller branches occasionally will be winterkilled in Zone 9a. Nevertheless, it is usefully hardy there. The sharp thorns can be troublesome when people come in contact with branches, so lower limbs will need to be pruned away or cleaned of thorns in patio situations. *Parkinsonia* is a short-lived tree at best, in our area sometimes dying suddenly following temporary flooding or excessive wetting of the soil. Plant in sites with maximum soil drainage. Because of the rapid growth rate of this species, dead trees can be replaced fairly quickly.

Parrotia persica 6–7

Persian parrotia
Deciduous tree or large shrub
Hamamelidaceae (Witch Hazel Family)

Native Range. Iran.

Useful Range. USDA Zones 6a–9a, and Zone 5b in protected sites.

Function. Specimen, shade tree.

Size and Habit

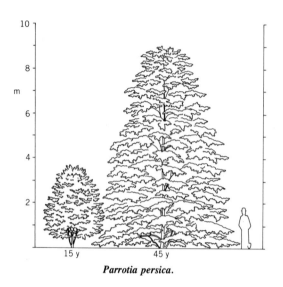

Parrotia persica.

Adaptability

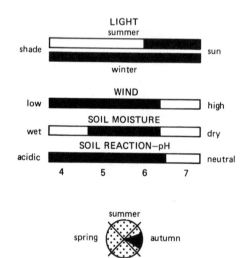

Parrotia persica.

Seasonal Interest. *Flowers:* Small, inconspicuous except when the stamens first emerge ruby-red, adding color at close range very early in spring. *Foliage:* Medium bright green, lustrous, providing interesting medium texture, similar to foliage of the witch hazels but more handsome, turning to bright yellow, orange, and scarlet in autumn, when in full sun. *Trunk and branches:* Bark on trunks and main branches of older trees flakes off, leaving a handsomely mottled pattern of gray and off-white.

Problems and Maintenance. This plant is relatively free of problems and requires little maintenance beyond initial pruning to establish form. This involves a decision, however: whether to gradually remove lower branches to expose the interesting bark year-round and allow the tree to serve in a patio situation, or to allow the lower branches to remain and the tree to attain its greatest gracefulness. In this case, the ground surface beneath should be mulched and turfgrass limited to the outer periphery, where it can be cut without trimming under the tree. This tree deserves much wider use, but is not as available as desirable.

Related Species

Disanthus cercidifolius 5. This member of the witch hazel family is a graceful, tall shrub with heart-shaped leaves strongly resembling those of *Cercis* species. Deep blue-green and leathery, they turn deep red in autumn with orange overtones. Seldom if ever available commercially, it may become better known in the future. It is potentially useful in Zones 7a—9a in semishaded sites with at least moderately acid, well-drained soil with a good supply of moisture.

Disanthus cercidifolius.

Parrotiopsis jacquemontiana 6.   This small tree is closely related to and resembles *Parrotia* except that it flowers in late spring and its inconspicuous flowers are surrounded by showy whitish bracts to 5 cm/2 in. across, giving a little of the effect of *Davidia* (dove tree). Foliage is similar to that of the witch hazels and turns yellow in autumn. This tree, like *Disanthus*, deserves much wider trial, but it is seldom commercially available at present. It is potentially useful in Zones 8a—9a+.

Parthenocissus quinquefolia 1 and 2

Synonym: *Ampelopsis quinquefolia*
Virginia creeper, woodbine
Deciduous vine
Vitaceae (Grape Family)

Native Range. Eastern United States and adjacent Canada.

Useful Range. USDA Zones 3b—9a+.

Function. Cover for walls and fences, rambling large-scale groundcover.

Size and Habit. Climbing vine, holding by branched tendrils, some with adhesive discs, climbing to heights of 15 m/50 ft and more on tree trunks; selections with adhesive discs will also climb on masonry to great heights.

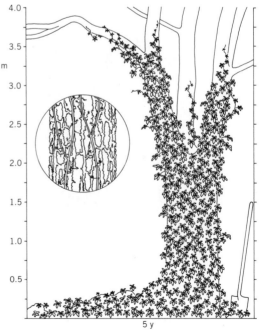

Parthenocissus quinquefolia.

Adaptability

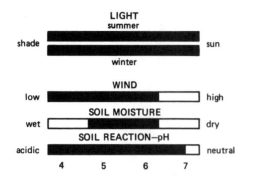

Seasonal Interest. *Flowers:* Inconspicuous, in early summer. *Foliage:* Deep green, dull to lustrous, palmately compound, with five leaflets to 10 cm/4 in. long, giving an interesting, coarse texture, turning brilliant red in sun in early autumn. *Fruits:* Small, blue-black with a whitish, waxy bloom, resembling wild grapes, in loose clusters on mature, high-climbing plants, fairly conspicuous after the leaves have fallen in autumn.

Parthenocissus quinquefolia.

Problems and Maintenance. This vine is relatively trouble-free and usually requires no maintenance other than pruning to control growth in small-scale situations.

Cultivars. 'Engelmannii' has smaller leaves, giving more refined texture appropriate to smaller-scale use. 'Saint-Paulii' has smaller leaves than average and more highly-branched tendrils with greater numbers of adhesive discs and so is more effective for use on masonry walls.

Related Species

Parthenocissus henryana 1 and 2 (silvervein creeper). This weakly climbing vine is used for its striking foliage. Leaves are about 10 cm/4 in. or less across, bright red as they open, dark green and leathery in summer with white-marked veins, and finally bright red again before falling. The white vein markings, which only develop well in the shade, make it a striking specimen, but too open in growth habit to function as a solid groundcover or wall cover. It is much less cold-hardy than *P. quinquefolia*, useful only in Zones 8b−9a+.

Parthenocissus inserta 1 and 2. This vine is very similar to *P. quinquefolia* in general appearance and range, differing in that its tendrils do not bear adhesive discs and so it is not effective in holding to masonry. When a vine is needed for this purpose, care should be taken to obtain *P. quinquefolia*, not *P. inserta*. Otherwise the two are equivalent as landscape plants.

Parthenocissus tricuspidata 1 (synonym: *Ampelopsis tricuspidata*; Boston ivy). This neatly textured, deciduous vine, with three-lobed leaves similar to those of some grapes, is not useful as a groundcover but is one of the most satisfactory vines for covering masonry walls, holding by branched tendrils with adhesive discs and climbing to heights of 15 m/50 ft and more. The foliage turns orange-red in autumn and the fruits, similar to those of *P. quinquefolia*, add interest

Parthenocissus tricuspidata.

after the leaves fall. This plant is trouble-free, well adapted to most city conditions, and useful in Zones 4b−8b. When used as a wall cover, some maintenance is required to keep it from covering windows. Selections with smaller leaves and finer texture (e.g., 'Lowii' and 'Veitchii') are occasionally available.

Passiflora caerulea 1 and 2

Bluecrown passionflower
Semievergreen to evergreen vine
Passifloraceae (Passionflower Family)

Native Range. Southern Brazil and Argentina.

Useful Range. USDA Zones 8a−9a+, perhaps also Zone 7b.

Function. Specimen, groundcover, screen (with support). Climbs by tendrils to heights of 5−10 m/16−33 ft, but kills back to the ground in severe winters in Zone 8.

Size and Habit

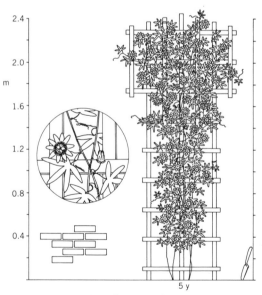

Passiflora caerulea.

Adaptability

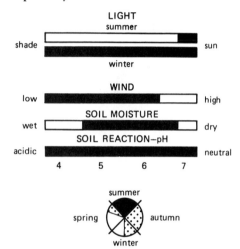

Seasonal Interest. *Flowers:* Lightly fragrant, blue, pale pink, and white, complex in structure and remarkably radially symmetrical, to 10 cm/4 in. across, opening during most of the summer. *Foliage:* Distinctive, five-lobed leaves are medium green, semievergreen in Zone 8, fully evergreen farther south.

Problems and Maintenance. This is one of the most trouble-free *Passiflora* species, seldom requiring any maintenance other than pruning for restraint when it begins to grow out of bounds and to remove the dead tops after severe winters. Nematodes can be troublesome in the Deep South.

Cultivars. 'Constance Elliott' has pure white flowers. 'Grandiflora' has unusually large flowers, to 15 cm/6 in. across.

Related Species

Passiflora incarnata 1 (maypop, wild passionflower). Native to the southeastern United States and northward to Missouri and Virginia, this vine has purple-marked, pinkish white flowers to 5 cm/2 in. across, opening from midsummer to early autumn, and edible yellow fruits, about the size of apricots. It is useful as a screen (with support) in Zones 7b−9a+ and sheltered sites in Zone 7a, but does not make a dense groundcover.

Passiflora lutea 1 (yellow passionflower).   Native to the southeastern United States, northward to Pennsylvania and westward to Texas, this is the most cold-hardy of the *Passiflora* species, useful in Zones 7a−9a+ and sheltered sites in Zone 6b, but its greenish yellow flowers, only 2 cm/0.8 in. across, are not nearly as showy as those of other passionflowers, and it finds little landscape use.

Paulownia tomentosa 7

Empress tree
Deciduous tree
Bignoniaceae (Bignonia Family); some authors place it in the Scrophulariaceae (Figwort Family)

Native Range. China; escaped to the wild in east-central United States.

Useful Range. USDA Zones 6b−9a+.

Function. Specimen, shade tree.

Size and Habit

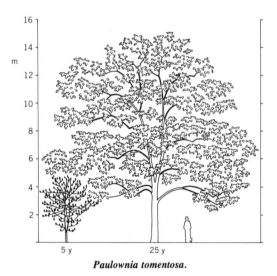

Paulownia tomentosa.

Adaptability

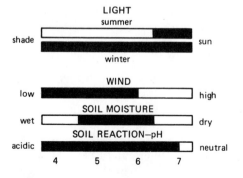

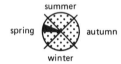

Seasonal Interest. *Flowers:* Fragrant, pale violet-purple, tubular, individually 5 cm/2 in. long, borne in loosely pyramidal clusters of 10 or more, making this one of the showiest flowering trees of the temperate zone. *Foliage:* Deep green, downy, heart shaped, to 25 cm/10 in. long (and even larger on vigorous young trees), giving an unusually coarse textural effect, falling without color change. *Fruits:* Rounded capsules to 4 cm/1.6 in. across, pale green, ripening brown in early autumn and breaking open to release large numbers of small seeds, the opened capsules then persisting well into winter. *Winter buds:* Flower buds form in summer and are conspicuous on the tree all winter, rounded and covered with rusty pubescence, 0.5 cm/0.2 in. across and expanding to twice that size before opening in spring.

Problems and Maintenance. Unfortunately, this spectacular, fast-growing tree is soft-wooded, short-lived, and weedy, in mild climates rivaling *Ailanthus* as a source of weed seedlings. In the North (Zones 5 and 6) the tree will persist but be killed back severely in winter, sometimes to the ground. Following this drastic pruning by winter cold, plants recover rapidly, often producing stems 2−4 m/7−13 ft tall during the following growing season. Such growth is exceptionally soft, even for this tree, and even more prone to damage the next winter. Since flower buds form one year and open the next, winterkilling of the stems eliminates flowering interest. Considering all of this, *Paulownia* should be considered a high maintenance tree and questionable as a functional tree.

Paxistima canbyi 2

Synonym: *Pachistima canbyi*
Canby paxistima
Evergreen groundcover
Celastraceae (Staff-tree Family)

Native Range. Eastern United States: central Appalachian Mountains.

Useful Range. USDA Zones 4a−7b, only in cool microclimates in Zone 7, and with snow cover or other protection in Zone 4.

Function. Groundcover, specimen, rock garden.

Seasonal Interest. *Foliage:* Very small leaves, to 2.5 cm/1 in., are evergreen, leathery, toothed, and dark green, making a very effective, fine-textured, year-round groundcover that bronzes when it is exposed to winter sun. *Flowers and fruits:* Inconspicuous.

Size and Habit

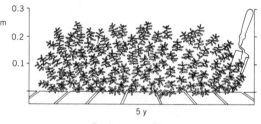

Paxistima canbyi.

Paxistima canbyi.

Adaptability. Grows well in full sun to half shade in the North, but needs at least light shade for good performance in Zone 7. Foliage may winterburn in full sun in the North. Often referred to as an acid-soil plant, actually it also grows well in nearly neutral soils, provided they are well drained.

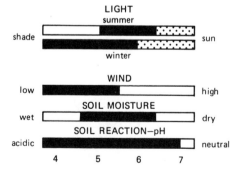

Problems and Maintenance. This groundcover usually is relatively trouble-free but is occasionally subject to infestations of euonymus scale insects. Once established in a good site, it requires little maintenance, but old plantings may become ragged with a mass of leafless stems underneath. If they are otherwise in good condition, they can be rejuvenated by pruning back heavily and fertilizing the soil lightly in spring.

Related Species

Paxistima myrsinites 3 (Oregon paxistima). This low shrub, native from British Columbia to New Mexico, is very similar to its eastern relative in general appearance but so little cultivated that its performance in eastern North America is not well known. It may be useful in Zones 6b−8b, but probably is never available in our area.

Phellodendron amurense 7−8

Amur corktree
Deciduous tree
Rutaceae (Rue Family)

Native Range. Northern China and Manchuria.

Useful Range. USDA Zones 4b−7b, also Zone 3 if appropriate genetic material is available, and possibly Zone 8a as well.

Function. Shade tree, specimen.

Size and Habit

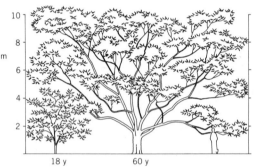

Phellodendron amurense.

Adaptability

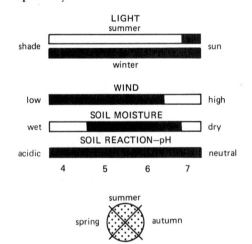

Seasonal Interest. *Flowers:* Inconspicuous, dioecious. *Foliage:* Dark green, compound, with a turpentine odor when crushed, forming an effective canopy of mottled shade, in some locations and years turning yellow before falling early and suddenly in autumn. *Fruits:* Small, black, and aromatic when crushed. *Trunk and branches:* Bark on trunks and main limbs of older

trees is corky and heavily furrowed. Branching is picturesque and open, with few massive side branches, adding landscape interest at all seasons.

Phellodendron amurense.

Problems and Maintenance. This tree is trouble-free, requiring almost no maintenance. Dropping fruits and foliage constitute a minor litter problem in some situations.

Related Species

Phellodendron sachalinense 8 (Sakhalin corktree). This close relative of *P. amurense* differs very little but tends to have less corky bark, and so less winter interest. The two species may be confused in commerce, and both are variable in height and bark character. Except for degree of bark interest, they can be considered to be equivalent for most landscape use.

Other species of *Phellodendron* exist, all from eastern Asia, but they are seldom if ever available and are usually considered to be inferior in landscape use to the two listed above.

Philadelphus coronarius 5

Sweet mockorange
Deciduous shrub
Saxifragaceae (Saxifrage Family)

Native Range. Southwestern Europe.

Useful Range. USDA Zones 4a−7b.

Function. Border, screen, specimen. Functional as a visual screen only in full sun and with some pruning.

Size and Habit

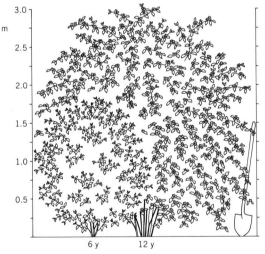

Philadelphus coronarius.

Adaptability

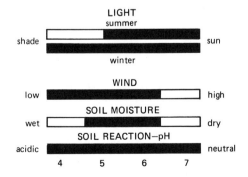

Seasonal Interest. *Flowers:* Fragrant, white, single, about 3 cm/1.2 in. across, in late spring. *Foliage:* Deep green leaves, 6−8 cm/2.3−3.2 in.

long, widely spaced on wiry stems, giving rather coarse texture, usually making a rather loose mass.

Problems and Maintenance. This shrub is essentially trouble-free but requires occasional careful pruning to maintain fullness.

Cultivars. 'Aureus' has bright yellow new foliage, which fades during the growing season to green. Plants are less vigorous than the species but eventually reach heights of close to 2 m/6.6 ft. Flowering is not profuse, the primary landscape color coming from the yellow foliage in late spring and early summer.

Related Species

Philadelphus inodorus 5 (scentless mockorange). This native of the southern Appalachian Mountains is unusual for its unscented flowers, but also for having better than average form in the landscape. The species type and its varieties all are more-or-less moundlike in form with foliage and flowers right down to the base of the plant. The species type and var. *grandiflorus* (synonym: *P. grandiflorus*; bigleaf scentless mockorange) are tall, broadly moundlike shrubs to 3m/10 ft, and somewhat broader than tall at maturity. Var. *laxus* (synonym: *P. laxus*; drooping mockorange) has drooping branches, as the name suggests, and seldom exceeds 2 m/6.6 ft in height, but may be 3 m/10 ft wide. *P. inodorus* and its varieties are useful in Zones 5b−9a and perhaps in Zone 5a as well.

Philadelphus lewisii 4−5 (Lewis mockorange). This variable species is native to western North America from Alberta and British Columbia to northern California, and includes several populations that have sometimes been considered to be separate species: *P. columbianus*, *P. gordonianus*, and *P. californicus*, now *P. lewisii* ssp. *californicus*. The northern forms are of special interest since they include individuals with unusual cold-hardiness, useful in the northwestern parts of our area. The best known example is *P. lewisii* 'Waterton,' selected in Alberta and useful northward at least to Zone 3b and probably to Zone 2. This cultivar is compact in growth yet reaches heights of about 2 m/6.6 ft under good conditions. Its flowers are displayed well but are unscented like those of the species.

Philadelphus purpurascens 5–6 (purplecup mockorange). This native of China is one of the largest of mockoranges, to 4 m/13 ft tall under good conditions, spreading widely with arching branches. The fragrant flowers are borne in purple, cuplike calyces and are displayed very effectively since they are not covered by the relatively small (to about 2–3 cm/1 in. long) leaves. Useful in Zones 5b–8a, but seldom available. Except for the purple calyces, *P. purpurascens* has little advantage over *P. coronarius* or any of the other scented, large-growing mockoranges.

Philadelphus schrenkii 5 (Schrenk mockorange). This hardy shrub from Korea and Manchuria is well adapted to the northern plains

of our area: useful in Zones 3a–7a, perhaps even in Zone 2. The var. *jackii* may be somewhat less cold-hardy but is useful in Zone 3b, and it is one of the earliest of all mockoranges to flower, as much as two weeks earlier than *P.* ×*lemoinei* and *P.* ×*virginalis.*

Philadelphus ×*splendens* 5. This hybrid of *P. inodorus* var. *grandiflorus*, probably by *P. lewisii*, has large flowers, to 5 cm/2 in. across but only slightly fragrant, and excellent moundlike form, to 2.5 m/8 ft tall and greater in width, branching well to the ground. Useful in Zones 5b–8a and perhaps colder zones as well.

Several other species of *Philadelphus* exist in collections but add little to the range of characteristics offered by those mentioned and are seldom if ever commercially available. In fact several of those listed will be found difficult to obtain, since large mockoranges are, at best, limited in function and seasonal interest.

Philadelphus ×*lemoinei* 4

Lemoine mockorange
Deciduous shrub
Saxifragaceae (Saxifrage Family)

Hybrid origin. *P. microphyllus* × *P. coronarius.*

Useful Range. USDA Zones 4b–8a, but some cultivars are cold-hardy only to Zone 5.

Function. Border, specimen (those selections having good form).

Size and Habit

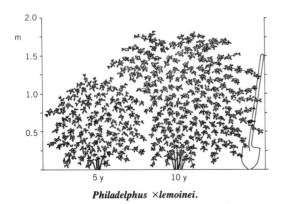

Philadelphus ×*lemoinei.*

Adaptability

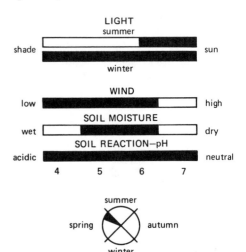

Seasonal Interest. *Flowers:* Fragrant, white, single to double, 2.5–5.5 cm/1.0–2.2 in. across, from late spring to very early summer. *Foliage:* Deep green, leaves are variable, 1.5–4 cm/0.6–1.6 in. long, but usually small, the most consistent difference between *P.* ×*lemoinei* and *P.* ×*virginalis* cultivars.

Problems and Maintenance. This shrub is relatively trouble-free but mostly requires pruning to maintain form, and some cultivars have poor form in spite of pruning. Prune in spring or after flowering has ended in early summer by removing a few older branches at or near ground level and cutting tips of other branches back to encourage branching. Do not prune later than early summer, since this encourages rank growth and reduces winter hardiness.

Cultivars. 'Avalanche' is a low-growing selection, to a little over 1 m/3.3 ft, with gracefully arching branches and single, highly fragrant flowers, about 2.5 cm/1 in. across. Useful in Zones 4b−8a. 'Belle Etoile' and 'Boule d'Argent' have extremely large (to 5.5 cm/2.2 in.), fragrant flowers, single and double, respectively. Both are useful in Zones 5a−8a. 'Erectus' is upright, to a little over 1 m/3.3 ft tall, and compact in form with single flowers. 'Innocence' is tall growing, to 2 m/6.6 ft, with large, single, exceptionally fragrant flowers. 'Mont Blanc' has unusually good, moundlike form, growing to a little over 1 m/3.3 ft, and fragrant, single flowers. Useful in Zones 4b−8a.

Other cultivars exist, but those listed are most likely to be available.

Related Species

Philadelphus microphyllus 4 (little-leaved mockorange). This small, sparse shrub, native to the southern United States and Mexico, is notable only as an important parent of many smaller-growing hybrid mockoranges. In itself it has little landscape usefulness and probably is not available commercially.

Philadelphus ×*virginalis* 4−5 (virginal mockorange). This group of hybrids of *P. ×lemoinei* by an unknown parent, possibly *P. nivalis*, includes some of the showiest mockorange cultivars, but mostly with poor form, along with an occasional one with good form as well as showy flowers. A few of the better cultivars are listed here:

'Albatre,' 'Argentine,' and 'Glacier' are relatively low-growing, to about 1.5 m/5 ft tall, with large, double flowers and undistinguished landscape form. These old cultivars, originating in the Lemoine Nursery in France, are seldom available in North America but are potentially useful in Zones 5a−8a.

'Bouquet Blanc,' usually associated with *P. ×virginalis* but so different as to cause speculation about its true origin, has outstanding landscape form and is one of the few mockoranges that are very useful as functional landscape plants. This one is moundlike and useful for massing, but at best it is barely tall enough to function as a visual screen. Useful in Zones 4b−8a.

'Frosty Morn' is a more-or-less dwarf selection, 1−1.5 m/3.3−5 ft tall, with large, double, fragrant flowers. Selected in Minnesota, it is useful in Zones 4a−8a. Since its origin has not been disclosed, it is not certain that it is a *P. ×virginalis* selection.

'Miniature Snowflake' is a compact selection with upright form, to 1 m/3.3 ft or somewhat taller, and large, double flowers, useful in Zones 4b−8a.

'Minnesota Snowflake' is a vigorous selection with upright, leggy form and very large, fragrant, double flowers, to 5 cm/2 in. across, useful in Zones 4b−8a and possibly 4a as well.

'Silver Showers' is an unusually fragrant and freeflowering selection that remains below 1 m/3.3 ft in height with excellent bright green foliage. It is useful at least in Zones 5a−8a and perhaps colder zones as well.

'Virginal' is the original *P. ×virginalis* hybrid and one of the most commonly available commercially. It has very large, fragrant, double flowers, to 5 cm/2 in. across, but very poor, leggy form and is too sparse for visual screening even though it is tall enough. It is best relegated to a background role in the shrub border. Useful in Zones 4b−8a.

Phlox subulata 2

Moss pink, mountain pink
Semievergreen herbaceous groundcover
Polemoniaceae (Phlox Family)

Native Range. Eastern United States from New York to Michigan and southward to North Carolina.

Useful Range. USDA Zones 3b–8a, and to a limited extent in Zone 8b.

Function. Groundcover, rock garden.

Size and Habit

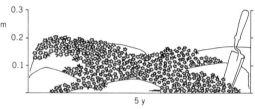

Phlox subulata.

Adaptability

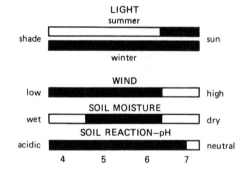

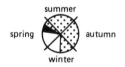

Seasonal Interest. *Flowers:* Bright magenta, pale violet, pink, or white, to 2 cm/0.8 in. across, borne in such great numbers that they form a solid carpet of bloom on the ground in mid-spring. The magenta colors are so strong that they can be overpowering and fail to harmonize with other colors. Use strong colors on a small scale or at a distance, with careful attention to companion flower colors. *Foliage:* Bright green, sharp, needlelike leaves are less than 2.5 cm/1 in. long, remaining green well into the winter but suffering winterburn and deteriorating in late winter, especially in the North.

Problems and Maintenance. This plant occasionally is subject to several diseases, but these are seldom serious enough to require control. Some maintenance is required, however, primarily to renovate old plantings that eventually develop dead spots at the centers of old plants. Need for replanting can be forestalled for years by cutting back the tops after flowering to force vigorous new growth.

Cultivars. Many selections have been made for superior foliage, vigor, and flower color in white and shades of pink and lavender. Few are available at any one time and place. Select for local availability.

Related Species

Phlox nivalis 2 (trailing phlox).   This plant has a more southerly native range than *P. subulata*, from Virginia to Alabama and Florida, and may be better adapted to landscape use in the Deep South. It is so similar in appearance to *P. subulata* that the two are often confused. The selections 'Azurea' and 'Camla' are outstanding, with pale blue and salmon pink flowers, respectively. Both are useful in Zones 5b–8b, perhaps colder zones, and probably Zone 9a.

Photinia ×fraseri 6

Fraser photinia
Evergreen shrub
Rosaceae (Rose Family)

Hybrid origin. *P.serrulata × P.glabra.*

Useful Range. USDA Zones 8a−9a+ and protected sites in Zone 7b.

Function. Screen, specimen, border, hedge, massing.

Size and Habit

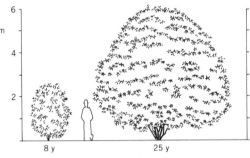

Photinia ×fraseri.

Adaptability. Full sun and good air circulation help to control severity of leaf diseases, and root rot diseases are less troublesome in exceptionally well-drained soil.

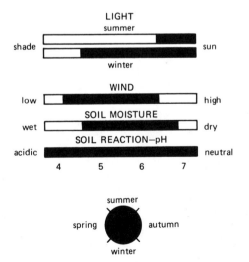

Seasonal Interest. *Flowers:* Small, white, in flat clusters about 10−15 cm/4−6 in. across in late spring. *Foliage:* New foliage and stems emerge

glossy and flame-red in spring, turn green as they mature, and remain deep green and lustrous until leaves fall in spring or summer of the following year. Leaves are large, to 10−12 cm/4−5 in., giving a coarse texture year-round.

Problems and Maintenance. *P. ×fraseri* is intermediate between its parents in susceptibility to disease (see *P. serrulata*, Problems and Maintenance). It is more seriously troubled by root rot and leaf spot diseases than *P. serrulata*, less so than *P. glabra*. And it is less troubled by mildew than *P. serrulata*. All photinias should be planted in perfectly drained sites with good air circulation. Annual pruning stimulates vigor and maximum development of the flame-red color of the new shoots. This is routinely done in hedges, but must be done more selectively where some of the form of the plant is to be retained. Irrigation may be needed in some sites during drought periods, but water should be withheld in autumn to promote hardening.

Related Species

Photinia glabra 5 (Japanese or red leaf photinia). This large shrub is frequently used in the South for color accent, alone or in borders or hedges. Like *P. ×fraseri*, its chief seasonal interest is the bright red, newly emerging foliage in middle to late spring. Flowering interest is less significant than in *P. ×fraseri* or *P. serrulata*, since the clusters are only about half as large, and fruiting is seldom as prominent as in *P. serrulata*. It is slightly less cold-hardy than *P. ×fraseri* and *P. serrulata*, but useful in Zones 8a−9a+. As with the other two species, close attention to soil

Photinia villosa var. *maximowicziana.*

drainage is crucial to the success of this species. In fact, root rot disease is so serious a problem that *P. ×fraseri* is increasingly being substituted for *P. glabra*.

Photinia villosa 6 (oriental photinia).   This tall deciduous shrub or small tree from China, Japan, and Korea is too open to function as a screen, but its bright red berries and foliage add substantial autumn interest. Fire blight can be a serious problem in some areas. Otherwise this plant is useful in Zones 6a−8a. The var. *maximowicziana* from Korea is somewhat more cold-hardy, to Zone 5b, but probably is not available.

Photinia serrulata 6

Chinese photinia
Evergreen shrub or small tree
Rosaceae (Rose Family)

Native Range. China.

Useful Range. USDA Zones 7b−9a+.

Function. Screen, specimen, border, patio tree (with pruning).

Size and Habit

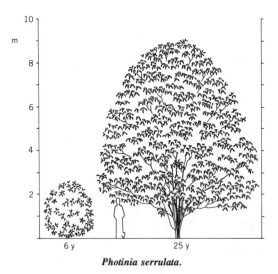

Photinia serrulata.

Adaptability. Full sun and good air circulation help to control the severity of leaf diseases. Root rot diseases are less troublesome in well-drained soil.

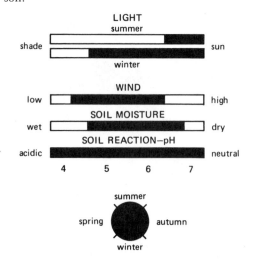

Seasonal Interest. *Flowers:* Small, white, in flat clusters to 10−15 cm/4−6 in. across in middle to late spring. *Foliage:* New foliage emerges glossy

Photinia serrulata.

reddish or bronze in spring, turns green as it matures, and remains deep green and lustrous until spring or summer of the following year, when it falls, often reddening first. Leaves are leathery, to 15–18 cm/6–7 in. long, sharply and finely toothed, giving a relatively coarse texture year-round.

Problems and Maintenance. *P. serrulata* has the usual problems of evergreen photinias in general. Fire blight and a leaf-spot disease are highly destructive in some areas, and mildew can be serious in shaded sites with little air movement or in humid coastal areas. Observe local experience

when selecting this plant. In good sites, plants are often trouble-free for many years. Pruning will eventually be needed to promote vigor and is sometimes done routinely to maintain high vigor and maximum bronzing of the new foliage. Water should be withheld in autumn to promote hardening.

Cultivars. 'Aculeata' (red-twig Chinese photinia) has more sharply and deeply toothed leaves, new twigs that are very red, and a more compact growth habit, reaching an ultimate height of little over 3 m/10 ft, less than half that of the species type.

Physocarpus opulifolius 4–5

Eastern ninebark
Deciduous shrub
Rosaceae (Rose Family)

Native Range. Northeastern and north-central United States and adjacent Canada.

Useful Range. USDA Zones 3a–6b with selection of appropriate genetic material.

Function. Border, massing, hedge, bank cover (dwarf variety).

Size and Habit

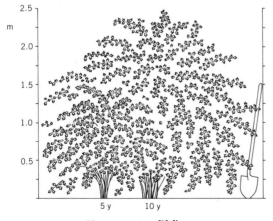

Physocarpus opulifolius.

Adaptability. This is one of the most broadly adaptable shrubs to different soil conditions.

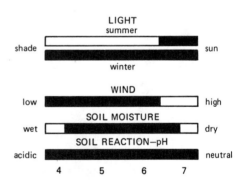

Seasonal Interest. *Flowers:* White or off-white, small, in clusters to 5 cm/2 in. across, adding significant color very early in summer. *Foliage:* Deep to olive green (or yellowish in a cultivar) on wiry branches. Texture is somewhat coarse, even though leaves are seldom much over 5 cm/2 in. long, falling without much color change, occasionally turning reddish first. *Fruits:* Small dried pods, fused, two to five together, almost insignificant in autumn, but briefly reddish in late summer. *Twigs and branches:* Shredding bark adds slight winter interest.

Problems and Maintenance. This shrub is more trouble-free than most members of the rose family but requires regular pruning to maintain any gracefulness of form. More often than not, it is encountered as a rather ragged specimen for lack of pruning.

Varieties and Cultivars. Var. *intermedius* (synonym: *P. intermedius*) is a low-growing, more compact form, seldom exceeding 1.5 m/5 ft and easily kept below 1 m/3.3 ft with radical renewal pruning (cutting back to short stubs in spring or early summer) every three to five years. Primary function is as a large-scale groundcover, especially for banks, where it tolerates a wide range of soil moisture. The foliage is finer textured than in the species type, giving a much neater effect.

'Luteus' differs from the species type only in that its leaves emerge golden-yellow in spring, fading during summer, until almost green in late

Physocarpus opulifolius var. *intermedius*.

summer. It is just as coarse as the species type; yet well-pruned plants with their arching branches make striking specimens in late spring and early summer.

'Nanus' is even more dwarf than var. *intermedius* but less effective as a groundcover and seldom if ever commercially available.

Picea abies 3–8

Synonym: *P. excelsa*
Norway spruce
Evergreen tree or shrub
Pinaceae (Pine Family)

Native Range. Northern and central Europe.

Useful Range. USDA Zones 3a–8a.

Function. Screen, specimen, hedge, corner and foundation planting (dwarf cultivars).

Size and Habit

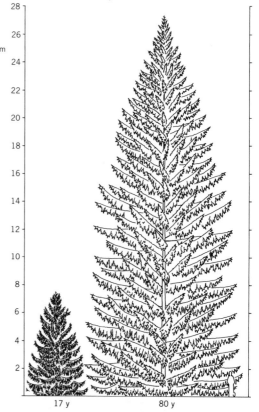

Picea abies.

Adaptability

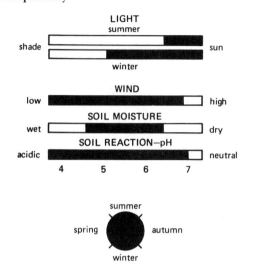

Seasonal Interest. *Foliage:* Evergreen, needlelike, lustrous, and deep green, no more than 2.5 cm/1 in. long, usually shorter, not harsh to the touch, on pendulous branchlets hanging from the ascending main branches. *Cones:* Large, to 15 cm/6 in. long, cylindrical, light brown, with many thin scales, pendulous from upper branches of mature trees.

Problems and Maintenance. This tree is relatively trouble-free, but mites can be troublesome in hot, dry sites, and insect infestation occasionally can require spraying. Pruning is seldom if ever necessary except for hedges. The greatest single limitation of the species type is its ultimate size; frequently it is planted where too little space is available. It is ironic that the greatest limitation to commercial acceptance of the dwarf cultivars is their slow growth.

Cultivars. Several full-sized cultivars, varying in foliage color, columnar form, and pendulous or sparsely branched habit are known, but most are considered curiosities or collectors' items and few are generally available.

The following may be found in at least a few nurseries. 'Columnaris' and 'Cupressina' are rather narrowly pyramidal to columnar forms. 'Pendula' has more pendulous branches as well as branchlets. 'Viminalis' and 'Virgata' are sparsely branched with a ropy appearance, striking in the landscape but not effective for screening.

Conifer manuals list at least 40 different dwarf or slow-growing forms, most of which are not available commercially. A few of those that usually are available are listed here. 'Clanbrassiliana' is a true dwarf, irregularly rounded in form, remaining below 1 m/3.3 ft for many years. 'Gregoryana' is cushionlike and very dwarf, remaining below 0.5 m/1.6 ft for many years and useful only in very small-scale situations such as rock gardens. 'Maxwellii' tends to be dwarf and cushionlike, remaining below 1 m/3.3 ft for many years, but eventually may reach 2 m/6.6 ft in height and at least twice that in width. Its needles are radially arranged and sharp-pointed, giving it a prickly texture. This is one of the most useful and widely available cultivars. 'Nidiformis' (nest spruce) probably is the most commonly available dwarf of *P. abies*. As the name suggests, it superficially resembles a bird's nest, ultimately to 2 m/6.6 ft high and twice as wide, but it remains below 1 m/3.3 ft for many years. 'Procumbens' is more procumbent than dwarf in habit, not exceeding 1.5 m/5 ft in height but spreading to several times that distance. It is very useful for massing but probably will not be found widely available, especially in quantity. 'Pumila' is pillowlike in form and lower than most of the other cultivars listed, comparable with 'Maxwellii' but without the prickly texture, reaching a height of only 0.6 m/2 ft while spreading to three times that distance. 'Pygmaea' has bright green foliage with ascending branches and unevenly globose to broad pyramidal form. It is one of the most dwarfed of all *P. abies* cultivars, seldom attaining 0.5 m/1.6 ft in height even after many years. 'Repens' is one of the most distinctive and useful cultivars, with light blue-green foliage and twigs arching outward and downward to face the ground and create a symmetrical, pillowlike form. It remains under 0.5 m/1.6 ft for at least 10 to 15 years while spreading to 1.5 m/5 ft, but it eventually becomes larger, so it probably should be considered slow-growing or procumbent rather than dwarf.

At a glance there appears to be little variation among *P. abies* cultivars, but this assortment shows that there is some variety, especially in growth rate and form. Omission from this list does not mean that a particular cultivar is unsuitable, and other good ones can be found in specialty nurseries.

Related Species

Picea asperata 8 (dragon spruce). This Chinese spruce is similar in general appearances to

P. abies except that it has foliage prickly to the touch and grows more slowly in our area. It is seldom available but useful in Zones 6a−8a when it can be found.

Picea glauca 8 (white spruce).   This native North American spruce is similar in general appearance to *P. abies,* but it has much smaller cones, to no more than 5 cm/2 in. long, and usually lighter blue-green foliage. Although it can be substituted for *P. abies* in Zones 2a−7a, and sometimes is, it is perhaps slightly less handsome in most sites. The juvenile dwarf, *P.*

Picea glauca 'Conica.'

glauca var. *albertiana* 'Conica' (dwarf Alberta spruce), is useful for formal effect with tightly conical form and tightly packed, slender needles. Since it grows at a rate of only 3−5 cm/1.2−2 in. per year, it is likely to be expensive, but even small specimens have the desired formal character. Because of the fine-textured juvenile needles, it is more susceptible to winter dehydration than most spruces and is most useful in Zones 5b−7a. Another tightly conical form, *P. glauca* var. *densata* (Black Hills spruce) grows faster than Alberta spruce, but only about half as fast as the species. It has heavy needles, is better adapted to the Northern Plains area than most evergreens, and is widely used in shelter-belt plantings.

Picea mariana 7−8 (black spruce).   This North American tree is native from Labrador to Alaska, southward to the northern states, and in the Appalachian Mountains to Virginia. It is often found in bog habitats and, predictably, grows well in wet landscape sites in the North, but is at best a thin, small tree with little landscape function. A few dwarf cultivars (e.g., 'Beissneri' and 'Doumetii') exist and are useful in small-scale situations. Useful, with these limitations, in Zones 1b−6b.

Picea rubens 8 (red spruce).   This species is native to the northeastern United States and adjacent Canada, from Newfoundland to the North Carolina mountains. It is not a very useful or handsome landscape plant outside the immediate environs of its native habitat and seldom if ever is available commercially. Care should be taken to preserve native stands, however, especially the fragile 'Krummholz' or low, shrubby, or cushion forms assumed in mountaintop treeline climates in the Appalachians.

Picea omorika 8

Serbian spruce
Evergreen tree
Pinaceae (Pine Family)

Native Range. Southeastern Europe.

Useful Range. USDA Zones 4b−8a.

Function. Screen, specimen. Requires less space than most spruces because of its narrow habit.

Size and Habit. Most branches are so strongly pendulous that the form of the tree is held to narrowly pyramidal or almost columnar in older trees.

Seasonal Interest. *Foliage:* Evergreen, needlelike, flattened, and sharp pointed, lustrous, deep green underneath, the upper surface whitened, giving a bicolored appearance. *Cones:* Lustrous, purple, about 5 cm/2 in. long, not an important landscape feature.

Problems and Maintenance. This tree is relatively trouble-free and requires essentially no maintenance other than occasional spraying for mites in warm climates. Foliage winterburns in exposed sites in Zones 4b and 5a in some years.

Cultivars. 'Nana' is a handsome, bright, green-white bicolored true dwarf, densely pyramidal to globose, remaining below 0.5 m/1.6 ft for 15−20 years but probably reaching 1.5 m/5 ft or taller in time. 'Pendula' is a striking, slow-growing variant that grows about half as fast as the species type with a pendulous branching habit.

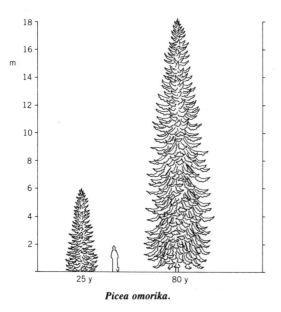

Picea omorika.

Adaptability

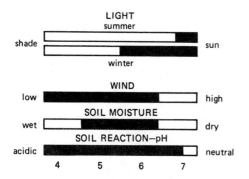

Picea orientalis 8

Oriental spruce
Evergreen tree
Pinaceae (Pine Family)

Native Range. Southeastern Europe and Asia Minor.

Useful Range. USDA Zones 5b–8a.

Function. Screen, specimen, hedge.

Size and Habit

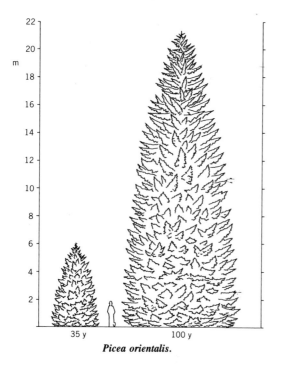

Picea orientalis.

Adaptability

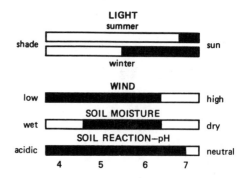

Seasonal Interest. *Foliage:* Evergreen, needlelike, lustrous, and dark green, short and blunt, less than 1 cm/0.4 in. long, on gracefully pendulous branches. *Cones:* Colorful, red-purple as they begin to develop in spring, later turning brown and growing to 6–9 cm/2.4–3.6 in. long.

Problems and Maintenance. This tree is relatively trouble-free and probably superior to *P. abies* in the South (Zones 6b–8a) even with its slower growth. It is not yet widely used or available in most nurseries.

Cultivars. Selections have been made for yellow foliage, but they are seldom if ever available and are of limited landscape interest.

Picea pungens 8

Colorado spruce
Evergreen tree
Pinaceae (Pine Family)

Native Range. Rocky Mountains of the western

United States and northern Mexico.

Useful Range. USDA Zones 3a–7b

Function. Screen, specimen.

Size and Habit

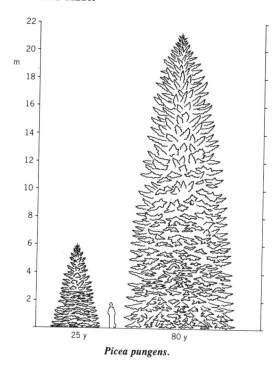

Picea pungens.

Adaptability

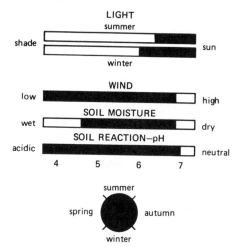

Seasonal Interest. *Foliage:* Evergreen, needlelike, with thick, sharp pointed needles to 3 cm/1.2 in. long, spreading radially around the twigs, dull green to striking silvery blue, with all intermediates. *Cones:* Cylindrical, light brown, 6−10 cm/2.4−4 in. long, with many thin scales, not a striking landscape feature.

Problems and Maintenance. Insect and mite infestations occasionally can be serious problems if not controlled, since the formal symmetry of the tree can be destroyed.

Forms and Cultivars. F. *glauca* includes all individual trees having a heavy, white and waxy (glaucous) coating over the needles, giving them a more-or-less bluish appearance. Such individuals vary widely in color and are not easily or clearly separated from the species type.

'Globosa' is a more-or-less dwarf selection with an informally globose outline and distinctly glaucous foliage, reaching heights of about 1 m/3.3 ft and greater spread after 20−30 years.

'Hoopsii' is one of the most intensely silvery blue forms, growing relatively rapidly for this species.

'Hunnewelliana' is densely pyramidal and slow-growing, with foliage blue-green as it first expands, turning silvery blue later. Plants usually remain below 3 m/10 ft for 20−30 years, but they probably attain tree stature eventually. This cultivar is not very commonly available.

'Koster,' with silvery white foliage and striking, stiffly formal outline, is one of the most commonly available cultivars.

'Moerheimii' is dense and relatively narrow and spirelike with strikingly blue foliage and is commonly available.

Seed propagation of f. *glauca* or any of the above cultivars yields seedlings ranging from the green of the species type to a wide range of blue shades, but few individuals rival the intensity of blue of the parent. When strikingly blue forms are required for accent, it is best to specify vegetatively propagated plants of one of the blue cultivars, even at the considerably greater cost entailed by grafting or rooting of cuttings and subsequent nursery care.

Blue Colorado spruce cultivars frequently are misused by planting in quantity rather than for specific landscape accent. For screens and other mass plantings there are better choices.

Related Species

Picea engelmannii 8 (Engelmann spruce). This tree from the Rocky Mountain region is similar to the closely related *P. pungens*, but its bluer forms are slightly softer and less positive in appearance. Useful in Zones 3a−7b and possibly in Zone 2, but seldom available commercially in eastern North America.

Pieris floribunda 4

Synonym: *Andromeda floribunda*
Mountain andromeda
Evergreen shrub
Ericaceae (Heath Family)

Native Range. Virginia to Georgia.

Useful Range. USDA Zones 5a−7b, sites with reliable snow cover in Zone 4, and sites with mild, moist summers in Zone 8.

Function. Border, specimen, massing.

Size and Habit

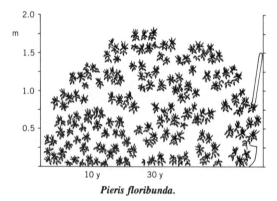

Pieris floribunda.

Adaptability. Needs protection from full winter sun in the North (Zones 4−5). For best growth, the soil must be acidic and extremely well drained yet not excessively dry.

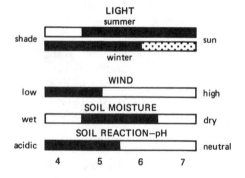

Seasonal Interest. *Flowers:* Waxy white, resembling those of lily of the valley, in semierect clusters 5−10 cm/2−4 in. long in early to middle spring. *Foliage:* Evergreen, lustrous, leathery, and deep green, making a loose mass of interesting texture. *Fruits:* Small, round capsules, green in summer, ripening dull brown, not a significant landscape feature. Moreover, if allowed to develop, they repress formation of flower buds for the following year.

Problems and Maintenance. This plant is relatively trouble-free in good sites, but a stem-rot disease has become a serious problem in some areas, especially where soil drainage and air circulation are not perfect. In northern areas, foliage can be damaged if plants are exposed to sweeping winds and full sun in winter. Pruning is necessary to remove deadwood and occasionally for light shaping of the plant. Removal of old flower heads immediately after flowering, called dead-heading, promotes formation of new flower buds for the following year.

Cultivars. 'Millstream' is low-growing and compact, with good annual flowering, even when fruits and seeds are allowed to develop. In 15 years plants can be expected to attain a height of approximately 0.5 m/1.6 ft and spread of about 1.5 m/5 ft under favorable growing conditions. Full extent of its useful range has not yet been determined.

Related Species

Pieris phillyreifolia 1 and 3.   This native vine or shrub of swamps and other wetlands of Alabama, Florida, and Georgia has been reintroduced into cultivation and is commercially available. It can be a climber in native habitat, moving up tree trunks with its stems virtually imbedded in the bark, but functions as a small shrub in landscape use. In spite of its wet native habitats, it will also grow well in acid soils of normal moisture given proper care. It is useful in Zone 9a+, and perhaps in Zone 8 as well.

Pieris japonica 4–5

Japanese andromeda
Evergreen shrub
Ericaceae (Heath Family)

Native Range. Japan.

Useful Range. USDA Zones 6a–8a, protected sites in Zone 5, and moist, cool sites in Zones 8b–9a+.

Function. Border, specimen, screen (under ideal growing conditions).

Size and Habit

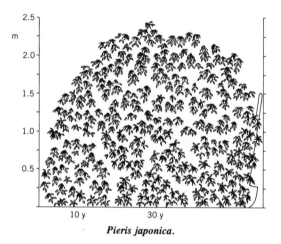

Pieris japonica.

up to 12 cm/5 in. long, displayed effectively against the dark green foliage in early spring. *Foliage:* Evergreen foliage first emerges glossy red, bronze, or yellow-green, then turns deep green and lustrous for the remainder of the year. *Fruits:* Small, round capsules, green in summer, ripening dull brown, not a significant feature in the landscape. If allowed to develop, they may interfere with formation of flower buds for the following year.

Pieris japonica.

Adaptability. Needs protection from full winter sun in the North (Zones 5–6).

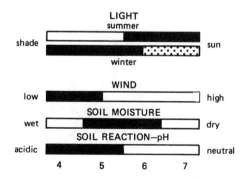

Seasonal Interest. *Flowers:* Dormant flower buds are more or less reddish, adding additional winter color. The flowers open waxy white, resembling those of lily of the valley, in pendulous clusters

Problems and Maintenance. The most serious problem of this shrub in northern areas is dehydration by winter sun and wind. Sites should be selected carefully to avoid exposure to sweeping winds and strongest sun. Damaged plants may be invaded by secondary disease organisms. The greatest limitation is moisture in the South, where irrigation is needed regularly. Insects such as lace bugs and mites can be troublesome at times, but are less so in sites with adequate moisture. Pruning is necessary to remove deadwood and occasionally for light shaping of the plant. Removal of old flower heads immediately after color fades (dead-heading) allows formation of new flower buds for the following year.

Cultivars. More than 20 cultivars have been selected and named, and selection of new forms continues. A few of those most likely to be available are listed here.

'Dorothy Wyckoff' has dark red winter flower buds that turn lighter red as they swell in early spring and then clear pink to white as they open. The foliage is dark green, taking on a reddish bronze color in winter.

'Forest Flame,' not a selection of P. *japonica* but rather a hybrid of P. *forrestii* 'Wakehurst' (see Related Species) by P. *japonica*, is notable because its new foliage emerges bright red, then reverts to green through pink and whitish stages. It also has large flower clusters and excellent form. Full extent of its useful range is not known, since it is a fairly recent introduction, but it is not as cold-hardy as P. *japonica*, probably only to Zone 7a.

'Pygmaea' has small, very narrow leaves, giving very fine texture and much slower growth rate than the species type, not exceeding 0.5 m/1.6 ft for years. It seldom flowers but is useful for its foliage and dwarfness in Zones 6b–9a.

'Variegata' has leaves with narrow white margins and is slightly less vigorous in growth yet far from dwarf. Its ultimate height is similar to that of the species type.

'White Cascade' flowers very heavily, and its

Pieris japonica 'Variegata.'

flowers have unusual keeping quality, sometimes remaining colorful four to five weeks.

Related Species

Pieris forrestii 5 (synonym: P. *formosa* var. *forrestii*; Chinese or Forrest pieris). This handsome plant from China and the Himalayas has large, showy, pendulous flower clusters, to 15 cm/6 in. long, and bright red new foliage. The selection 'Wakehurst' has broader leaves, even brighter red in the immature stage than the species type, and is useful in Zone 8 and moist, cool sites in Zone 9a+.

Pinus aristata 4–6

Bristlecone pine
Evergreen shrub or small tree
Pinaceae (Pine Family)

Native Range. High mountains of the southwestern United States.

Useful Range. USDA Zones 4a–7a, probably Zone 3 as well.

Function. Specimen for accent.

Size and Habit

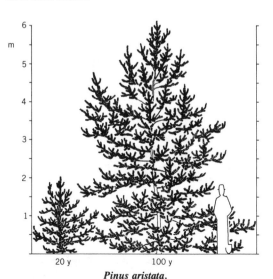

Pinus aristata.

Adaptability

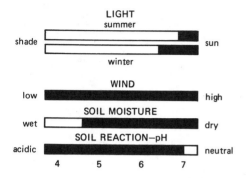

Seasonal Interest. *Foliage:* Evergreen and persisting for several years, dark green, the needles in fascicles of five, packed tightly on sparsely branching stems, giving an irregular, picturesque form. White resin dots on needles are normal but may be confused with scale insects.

Problems and Maintenance. Slow growth is this plant's most serious limitation in landscape use, yet it is also the greatest source of landscape value: trees are very long-lived and remain in scale in landscape situations for a great many years. Wild trees on west-facing slopes of the White Mountains of California are known to be at least 4000 years old and are thought by some to be the oldest living trees on earth, surpassing even the sequoias.

Pinus banksiana 8

Jack pine
Evergreen tree
Pinaceae (Pine Family)

Native Range. Far northern and northeastern North America.

Useful Range. USDA Zones 2a−6a.

Function. Massing or large-scale screening on dry sites.

Size and Habit

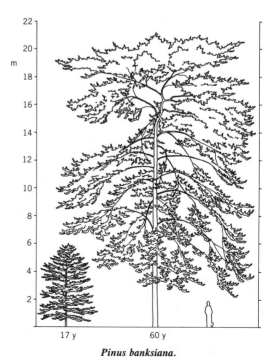

Pinus banksiana.

Adaptability

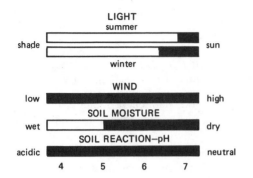

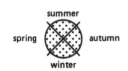

Seasonal Interest. *Foliage:* Evergreen, medium green to yellow-green needles are short (averaging 2.5−3.5 cm/1−1.4 in. long), in fascicles of two, arranged sparsely and persisting for only 2−4 years. Foliage usually is fuller and more handsome in the northern parts of the useful range than in the southern parts, but even there turns yellowish in winter. *Cones:* Lustrous, yellow-brown, 2.5−5 cm/1−2 in. long, persisting on the tree for several years but adding little to its landscape interest.

Problems and Maintenance. This tree is relatively trouble-free and requires little maintenance. Needle-fall is so light that it provides little mulch, so weed encroachment may be a problem. But in the large-scale dry sites where this tree is most useful, weed growth is not strong enough to be very competitive or objectionable visually.

Cultivars. Probably no cultivars are commercially available, but dwarf, pillowlike forms exist and may become available in the future. A dwarf, pendulous form, 'Uncle Fogey,' has been selected but probably is not available.

Related Species

Pinus contorta 6−8 (shore pine). This native of the Pacific Northwest from Alaska to California and eastward to Colorado exists in two principal types:

Var. *contorta*, the species type from Pacific coastal areas, is an interesting, contorted, low-growing tree that reaches heights of 4−8 m/13−26 ft. It is valued on the West Coast, especially in Japanese gardens, where it seems appropriate in spite of its North American origin. It has been used very little in the eastern United States and may not be adapted to the climate of any of our area.

Var. *latifolia* (lodgepole pine), the mountain counterpart, grows wild farther inland, is a much larger tree, to 20 m/65 ft or sometimes more than 30 m/98 ft, and is relatively narrow in outline. Even though it is not commonly used in eastern North America and may be less useful than native species, it is at least reasonably well adapted here in Zones 5b−8a.

Pinus bungeana 6−7

Lacebark pine
Evergreen tree
Pinaceae (Pine Family)

Native Range. Northern China.

Useful Range. USDA Zones 5a−9a. Limited to areas with moderate summer temperatures in Zones 8 and 9.

Function. Specimen.

Size and Habit. Grows slowly and remains shrubby for many years.

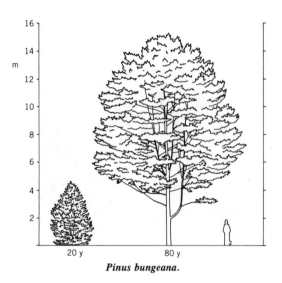

Pinus bungeana.

Adaptability

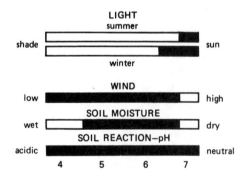

Seasonal Interest. *Foliage:* Evergreen, medium green needles, 5–10 cm/2–4 in. long, in fascicles of three, persistent for only 3–4 years and seldom dense enough to make an effective visual screen. *Trunk and branches:* Bark is smooth, and on branches more than about 5–10 cm/2–4 in. across it flakes off in large, irregular, rounded patches, giving a gray, green, and off-white tricolored effect.

Pinus bungeana.

Problems and Maintenance. Bark interest, the primary reason for using this tree, seldom becomes significant until the tree is at least 10–15 years old, and the tree has little interest as a specimen until that time. Careful pruning to expose the bark more fully may be desirable. Otherwise, the tree is relatively free of maintenance and troubles.

Related Species

Pinus edulis 7(pinyon or nut pine). This native of the southwestern United States, from Wyoming and Texas to California has been considered in the past to be var. *edulis* of *Pinus cembroides.* It has strikingly glaucous, blue foliage as a young seedling, but soon outgrows this character and becomes an undistinguished tree of little value in our area except for the edible seeds. Useful, when of interest, in Zones 5a–8a.

Pinus cembra 6−8

Swiss stone pine
Evergreen tree
Pinaceae (Pine Family)

Native Range. Central Europe to northern Asia.

Useful Range. USDA Zones 3b−6b and high elevations (with moderate summers) in Zone 7 with selection of appropriate genetic material.

Function. Specimen, screen (in time).

Size and Habit

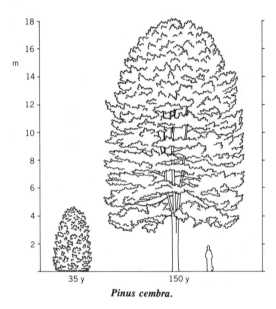

Pinus cembra.

Adaptability

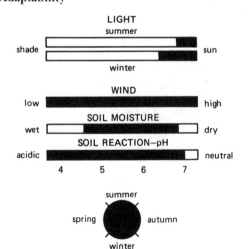

Seasonal Interest. *Foliage:* Evergreen, dense, with needles in fascicles of five, usually 5−10

cm/2−4 in. long, occasionally longer, retained for four to five years, dark green with whitened stomatal lines evident.

Pinus cembra.

Problems and Maintenance. This tree is relatively trouble-free and requires little or no maintenance. Its principal limitation is its slow growth, and it is most useful in small-scale landscapes.

Related Species

Pinus koraiensis 8 (Korean pine). This five-needled pine from Korea is highly reminiscent of *Pinus strobus*, to which it is also closely related, but with more pronounced lateral branching when young. Not widely available at present, but increasingly recognized as one of the most useful and handsome pines for northern climates with a relatively fast growth rate. Useful in Zones 4a−7b and perhaps Zones 3 and/or 8 as well.

Pinus pumila 4−5 (dwarf stone pine). This spreading shrub usually is seen below 1 m/3.3 ft, but in time can reach 2−2.5 m/6.6−8.4 ft with

Pinus pumila.

Pinus pumila.

greater spread under good conditions. Native to northeastern Siberia and Japan, it has been in cultivation for many years but still is rarely commercially available in our area. It is useful in Zones 4a–7a and perhaps also in Zone 3.

Pinus sibirica 8 (synonym: *P. cembra* var. *sibirica*; Siberian stone pine). This tree from Siberia and adjacent Russia is faster growing than *P. cembra*, becoming 30–40 m/98–131 ft tall under ideal conditions. It is useful in the North, in Zones 2b–5b, but it seldom is commercially available.

Pinus densiflora 7–8

Japanese red pine
Evergreen tree
Pinaceae (Pine Family)

Native Range. Japan.

Useful Range. USDA Zones 5b–7b, and northward to Zone 4b with careful selection of genetic material.

Function. Specimen, massing.

Size and Habit

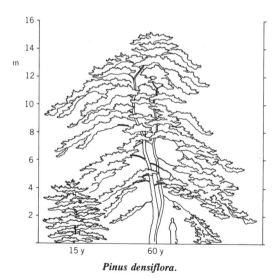

Pinus densiflora.

Adaptability

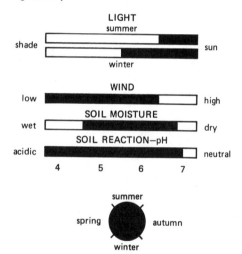

Seasonal Interest. *Foliage:* Evergreen, usually rather sparse, bright bluish to olive green with slender needles, mostly 8–10 cm/3–4 in. long, occasionally longer, in fascicles of two, persisting for three years. *Cones:* Yellow-brown, to 5 cm/2 in. long, persisting on the tree for two or three years. *Trunk and branches:* Bark on large branches and trunks is distinctly orange-red, adding interest at all seasons. This and the picturesque growth habit are the distinctive reasons for using this species.

Problems and Maintenance. This tree usually is trouble-free and requires little maintenance. Growth is relatively slow for a pine, but not slow enough to discourage its use.

Cultivars. 'Oculus-draconis' (dragon's eye pine) is unusual for its variegated needles, each with two yellow bands. It is useful primarily as a striking specimen while young and is slower growing than the species type. Useful in Zones 6a–7b.

'Umbraculifera' (Tanyosho pine) has many branches in a vase shaped arrangement and a

Pinus densiflora 'Umbraculifera.'

foliage canopy more flattened even than the species type and umbrella like. The striking branching is accentuated by the orange-red bark. Slower growing than the species type, but ultimately reaches heights of 3–4 m/10–13 ft in Zones 5b–7b.

Related Species

Pinus thunbergiana 6–7 (synonym: *P. thunbergii*, Japanese black pine). This picturesque tree, occasionally growing to 20 m/66 ft or taller in native habitat in Japan and Korea, seldom is seen exceeding 10 m/33 ft in landscape use in our area. Its irregular, open form gives it special character for appropriate situations, and its tolerance of salt spray and wind makes it especially useful in coastal sites in Zones 6a–9a, but it does not perform well in poorly drained soil or in sites that are periodically flooded.

Pinus flexilis 8

Limber pine
Evergreen tree
Pinaceae (Pine Family)

Native Range. Mountains of western United States and adjacent Canada.

Useful Range. USDA Zones 4b–7b with selection of appropriate genetic material.

Function. Specimen, screen.

Size and Habit

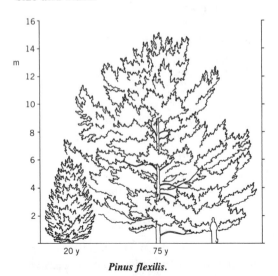

Pinus flexilis.

Adaptability. Better adapted to dry soil and windy sites than the related *P. strobus*.

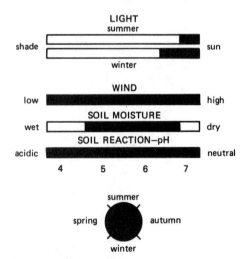

Seasonal Interest. *Foliage*: Evergreen, blue-green, fine-textured but making a dense mass, with slender needles, 3.5–8 cm/1.4–3 in. long, in fascicles of five, persisting for five years. Foliage of some trees is twisted, giving texture similar to that of *Pinus parviflora* 'Glauca.' *Cones*: Light brown and lustrous, to 15 cm/6 in. long. *Trunk and branches*: Branches are very flexible, covered with dark greenish gray bark; trunk bark is roughened, dark gray.

Problems and Maintenance. This tree is trouble-free and requires little or no maintenance but is rather slow-growing. It is noticeably less susceptible to winterburn and salt injury than most other five-needled pines.

Cultivars. 'Glenmore' is highly glaucous, with silvery blue-green color, selected and used in Colorado but not widely available in our area. Other variants have been selected locally, but few have entered commerce to date.

Related Species

Pinus albicaulis 6 (white bark pine).   This native of the mountains of the Pacific Northwest, where it is shrubby to prostrate at high elevations, occasionally has found its way into landscape use in Zones 4a–7a, but it is much less likely to be

Pinus flexilis.

available in our area than the related *P. flexilis* is. It receives its name from its distinctly whitened bark.

Pinus mugo 4–6

Synonym: *P. montana*
Mugho or mountain pine
Evergreen shrub
Pinaceae (Pine Family)

Native Range. Mountains of southern Europe.

Useful Range. USDA Zones 3a–7b.

Function. Foundation, massing, specimen, border.

Size and Habit. Growth rate and height are highly variable, even when plants of the dwarf variety are specified (see Varieties and Cultivars).

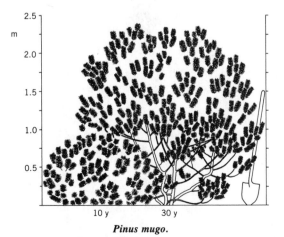

Pinus mugo.

Adaptability

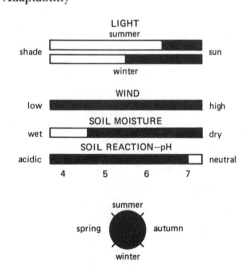

Seasonal Interest. *Foliage:* Evergreen, dense, with thick, dark green needles, 3–8 cm/1.2–3.2 in. long, in fascicles of two, persisting for four years or longer in some plants. *Cones:* Dull brown, to 6 cm/2.4 in. long.

Problems and Maintenance. This shrub is often trouble-free, requiring little maintenance, but insects (pine shoot moth, mugho pine scale) occasionally are troublesome in some areas. Follow local experience. Growth is usually rather slow, but this is seldom as much a problem as the overly fast, rank growth of seedlings that were expected to remain low and compact.

Varieties and Cultivars. Var. *mugo* (synonym: *mughus*), the species type, is more-or-less shrubby with ascending branches that usually do not exceed 1−4 m/3.3−13 ft in height. Seedlings vary widely in growth rate and compactness within this range. When definitely low and compact plants to 1 m/3.3 ft are needed, it is best to try to obtain vegetatively propagated cultivars such as 'Compacta,' 'Slavinii', or unnamed dwarf clones or selections when available. If specification by individual plant is possible, select unsheared plants that have maintained compact form for several years.

There is considerable confusion about var. *pumilio*. Even though it has been described as a population of shrubby to prostrate plants, the name is also being used to describe a very dwarf, pillowlike form in the nursery trade.

Related Species

Pinus uncinata 7−8 (synonym: *P. mugo* var. *rostrata*). Until recently, this tree, to 20 m/66 ft or taller, was considered to be a tall-growing variety of *P. mugo*, along with *P. uncinata* var. *rotundata* (synonym: *P. mugo* var. *rotundata*), a shrubby tree to 10 m/33 ft. Both are similar to *P. mugo* in foliage characteristics and in adaptation, but obviously not in function. They probably are not commercially available except perhaps by accident resulting from nomenclatural confusion.

Pinus nigra 8

Black pine
Evergreen tree
Pinaceae (Pine Family)

Native Range. Central and southern Europe and adjacent Asia.

Useful Range. USDA Zones 4a−8a with selection of appropriate genetic material.

Function. Specimen, screen, windbreak.

Size and Habit

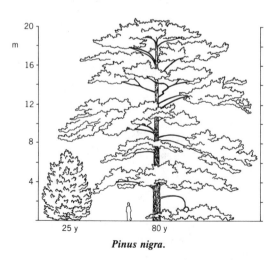

Pinus nigra.

Adaptability. Tolerates city situations better than most other pines.

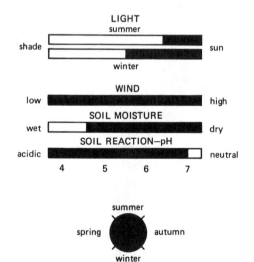

Seasonal Interest. *Foliage:* Evergreen, dense, with thick, dark green needles, 8−15 cm/3−5 in. long, in fascicles of two, persistent for three years. *Cones:* Shiny, yellow-brown, to 8 cm/3 in. long, persisting for two years. *Trunk:* Bark of large trees is coarsely marked with irregular plates, deep gray-brown and almost white.

Problems and Maintenance. Until recently this tree has been relatively trouble-free, but it now has serious disease problems, especially a twig blight *(Diplodia)*, and in some areas it can be severely damaged by sapsuckers. It may require spraying as well as removal of cone and twig litter. Its use as a screen is limited to the first decade or two of its life, since its lower branches usually remain no longer than this. Top pruning may lengthen this period somewhat.

Subspecies and Varieties. Several subspecies and varieties have been described over this species' wide range in southern Europe. Ssp. *nigra* (synonym: *P. nigra* var. *austriaca*; Austrian pine) is the typical form of the species, and the one ordinarily encountered in landscape use in North America.

Pinus palustris 8

Longleaf pine
Evergreen tree
Pinaceae (Pine Family)

Native Range. Southeastern United States.

Useful Range. USDA Zones 7b−9a+.

Function. Specimen, massing, shade tree.

Size and Habit

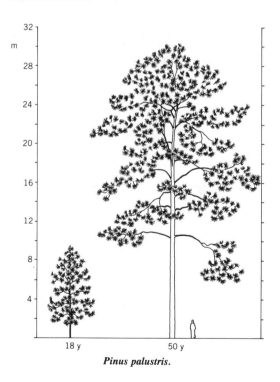

Pinus palustris.

Adaptability

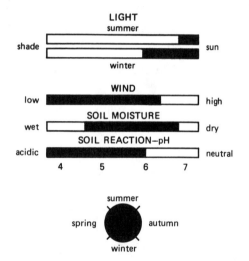

Seasonal Interest. *Foliage:* Evergreen with bright green needles, 20−40 cm/8−16 in. long, usually in fascicles of three, in "tufts" of many fascicles giving an open, picturesque appearance. *Cones:* Large, 15−30 cm/6−12 in. long, add interest but considerable litter. *Trunk:* Orange-brown, scaled bark adds interest to large trees.

Problems and Maintenance. This tree is generally trouble-free, but in the colder parts of its useful range occasional snow and ice can break branches and destroy the form of the tree. Slow growth during the first three years can be discouraging, but an extensive root system is formed during this period, and later growth is rapid. Cones cause a modest litter problem.

Related Species

Pinus elliottii 8 (slash pine).   This native of the southeastern Coastal Plain differs from *P. palus-*

tris in having somewhat shorter needles (15—25 cm/6—10 in.) in fascicles of two and three, with less "tufting." Like *P. palustris*, it is a tall, upright tree, to 30 m/98 ft. It is useful in Zones 8b—9a+ and performs best in those areas where it is native: coastal Mississippi to southern South Carolina.

Pinus glabra 8 (spruce pine).   This tree is native to much of the same area as *P. elliottii* and *P.*

palustris. It, too, is a tall tree, but differs in being a little slower-growing and more tolerant of wet soils, but does not grow well in coastal sites. Its foliage is finer textured than that of the other species, with slender, twisted needles to 8 cm/3 in. long, mostly in fascicles of two. In spite of its slender needles, it produces a dense mass of foliage, effective for screening.

Pinus ponderosa 8

Ponderosa or western yellow pine
Evergreen tree
Pinaceae (Pine Family)

Native Range. Western United States and adjacent Canada and Mexico.

Useful Range. USDA Zones 3b—8a with selection of appropriate genetic material.

Function. Specimen, screen, windbreak.

Size and Habit

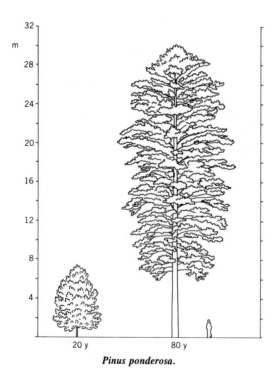

Pinus ponderosa.

Adaptability. Frequently does not perform as well in eastern North America as pines that are native here, but worth trying in problem areas, especially in the Central Plains.

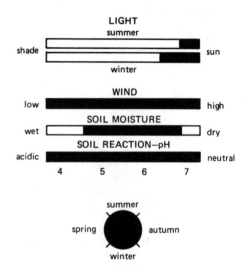

Seasonal Interest. *Foliage:* Evergreen with deep green needles, 10—25 cm/4—10 in., in fascicles of two and three, persisting for three years. *Cones:* Reddish or yellowish brown and lustrous with curved spines (umbos) on the outside of the scales, 8—15 cm/3—6 in. long. *Trunk:* Yellow-brown to cinnamon-brown bark is irregularly and lightly fissured on older trees.

Problems and Maintenance. This tree is relatively trouble-free and requires little or no maintenance, but a disease of the needle fascicles occasionally can be troublesome, especially in humid areas. Cones constitute a minor litter problem, and this is one of the most difficult pines to transplant.

Related Species

Pinus jeffreyi 8 (Jeffrey pine).   This species from high elevations in California and adjacent Nevada and Oregon is very similar to *P. pon-* *derosa* and functionally equivalent, but it is much less likely to be commercially available than *P. ponderosa*.

Pinus resinosa 8

Red pine, Norway pine (so-called in spite of its native origin)
Evergreen tree
Pinaceae (Pine Family)

Native Range. North-central and northeastern United States and adjacent Canada.

Useful Range. USDA Zones 3a−6b.

Function. Screen, specimen, windbreak.

Size and Habit

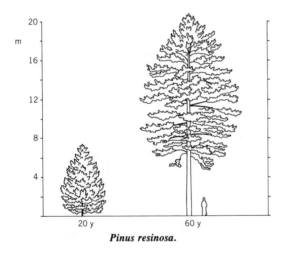

Pinus resinosa.

Seasonal Interest. *Foliage:* Medium to yellow-green with soft texture and slender needles, 12−18 cm/5−7 in. long, in fascicles of two, persisting for four years. *Cones:* Brown, about 5 cm/2 in. long, ripening the first year, persisting for two to three years, but not adding significant interest. *Trunk and branches:* Inner bark is reddish brown.

Problems and Maintenance. This tree is relatively trouble-free and requires little or no maintenance other than removal of cone litter.

Varieties. No varieties and hardly any cultivars are known, although occasionally columnar or globose forms can be found. This species is notable among the pines for its low variability.

Adaptability

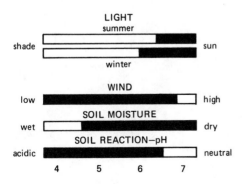

Pinus strobus 8

Eastern white pine
Evergreen tree
Pinaceae (Pine Family)

Native Range. North-central and northeastern United States, and adjacent Canada, and southward in the Appalachian Mountains to Georgia.

Useful Range. USDA Zones 3a−9a with selection of appropriate genetic material.

Function. Specimen, shade tree, screen, hedge.

Size and Habit

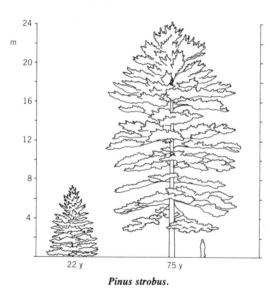

Pinus strobus.

Seasonal Interest. *Foliage:* Evergreen, soft, blue-green, fine textured with very slender needles, 5−12 cm/2−5 in. long, persisting for three years. *Cones:* Dull brown, cylindrical, 8−20 cm/3−8 in. long, persisting for two years or longer. *Trunk and branches:* Bark on branches is smooth, olive green to gray; trunk bark is smoother than that of most pines, dark gray.

Problems and Maintenance. This is one of the most satisfactory and trouble-free evergreen trees in most of our area, except for urban centers. White pine blister rust is a serious disease that has been eliminated largely from the native range by the elimination of its alternate host, certain species of *Ribes* (currants). Foliage is subject to winter desiccation. Recently transplanted trees are especially sensitive but usually recover after establishment. This tree is very sensitive to road salt and ocean salt spray.

Adaptability. Grows best in good soil of moderate moisture content. Not a good choice for roadsides, urban plantings, very dry or windswept areas (see Problems and Maintenance), or for planting in heavy soils.

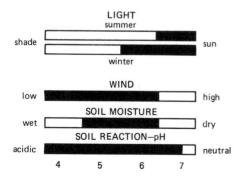

Pinus strobus 'Fastigiata.'

Cultivars. 'Fastigiata' is almost columnar as a young tree, its width about one third of its height, but broadening with age to become narrowly pyramidal to ovate. Useful when young for vertical accent.

'Nana' is a densely compact dwarf, remaining below 0.5 m/1.6 ft in height and spread for 10 years or more and not exceeding 1 m/3.3 ft for many years. Many such dwarfs have been found as witch's brooms or their progeny, and they appear under other cultivar names as well (e.g., 'Brevifolia' and 'Globosa'). They are useful for rock gardens or foundation planting.

'Pendula' is a strongly pendulous, graceful plant, reaching heights of at least 3 m/10 ft, usually with greater spread. Available commercially only from a few specialists, but useful for accent where there is enough space.

Related Species

Pinus lambertiana 8 (sugar pine).   This handsome tree reaches heights of more than 60 m/200 ft in its native habitat in California and is notable for its huge cones, to 50 cm/20 in. long. Seldom used or available in eastern North America, it probably could be used in areas protected from strong wind in Zones 6b–8a.

Pinus monticola 8 (western white pine).   This close relative of *P. strobus* from the Pacific Northwest is somewhat denser in growth habit but not distinctive enough to justify selecting it over the native *P. strobus* in eastern North America. It is potentially useful in Zones 5a–6b and perhaps farther south as well, but it is seldom available at present.

Pinus sylvestris 7–8

Scots pine
Evergreen tree
Pinaceae (Pine Family)

Native Range. Europe through Siberia.

Useful Range. USDA Zones 3a–8b with selection of appropriate genetic material.

Function. Specimen, massing, screen (when young).

Size and Habit

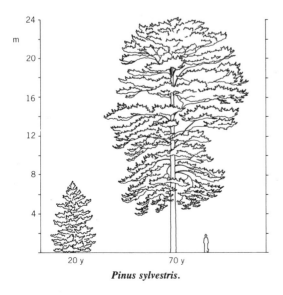

Pinus sylvestris.

Adaptability. Grows best in reasonably fertile soil but tolerates relatively infertile soil as well as wet or dry sites.

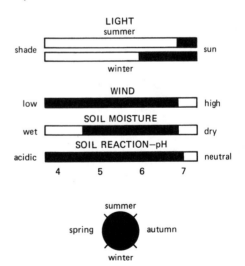

Seasonal Interest. *Foliage:* Evergreen, blue-green to yellow-green, with flattened and twisted needles, 2.5–8 cm/1–3 in. long, in fascicles of two, persisting for three years. *Cones:* Yellowish brown, 2.5–8 cm/1–3 in. long, falling at maturity. *Trunk and branches:* Inner bark is bright orange-tan, adding year-round interest to mature trees.

Problems and Maintenance. This tree is subject to a twig blight disease *(Diplodia)* that can be a serious problem if not controlled, especially in humid climates. Pruning is needed to control size and maintain fullness in screen plantings. Otherwise, screens become open and nonfunctional with age.

Cultivars. 'Beuvronensis' is very dwarf and pillowlike, remaining below 0.5 m/1.6 ft in height for many years. 'Fastigiata' is a tall-growing, narrowly pyramidal plant, its height commonly four to five times its width, holding this form better than *P. strobus* 'Fastigiata' with age. 'Watereri' is a slow-growing, globose to broadly ovate plant, ultimately exceeding 3 m/10 ft in height and spread, with silvery blue-green foliage.

Many other variants in color and growth rate exist, but few are available commercially in our area. In addition, seed strains available to Christmas tree growers sometimes yield superior landscape forms.

Related Species

Pinus halepensis 7 (Aleppo pine). This open-branched Mediterranean species has been widely planted in southern Europe and may have promise for seashore sites in our Gulf Coast area.

Pinus pinaster 7–8 (cluster pine). This tree from southwestern Europe and Morocco is well adapted to the sandy soils and salt spray of seashore sites but needs further trial in Zones 7b–9a before its adaptability to our area is known. It is reputedly difficult to transplant, but this presumably can be overcome by the use of container-grown plants of small size.

Pinus taeda 8

Loblolly pine
Evergreen tree
Pinaceae (Pine Family)

Native Range. Southeastern to south-central United States.

Useful Range. USDA Zones 7b–9a.

Function. Specimen, massing, shade tree, fast but temporary screen.

Size and Habit

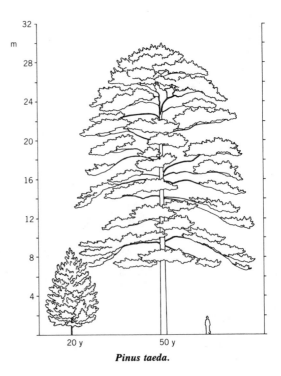

Pinus taeda.

Adaptability. Tolerates very poor soil and exposed sites.

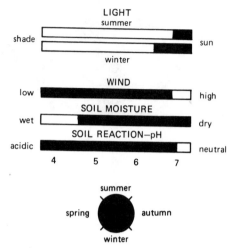

Seasonal Interest. *Foliage:* Evergreen with bright green needles, 15−25 cm/6−10 in. long, in fascicles of three. *Cones:* Light brown, shiny, 6−10 cm/2.4−4 in. long, adding minor landscape interest. *Trunk:* Handsome, reddish brown bark is fissured into heavy scaly plates, interesting in all seasons.

Problems and Maintenance. This is among the most durable and trouble-free of the southern pines in landscape use. Borers occasionally are troublesome, usually when trees have been damaged by pruning or other breakage in spring and summer. *P. taeda* is difficult to transplant in larger sizes, so specify young seedlings or container-grown trees. Growth is so rapid that trees quickly attain functional size even when starting as young seedlings.

Varieties. Apparently there has been little interest in selecting particular forms of this useful tree. Considerable variation has been found in forestry trials, but for landscape purposes it seems sufficient at present to try to obtain trees from nearby seed sources.

Related Species

Pinus echinata 8 (shortleaf pine).   This is one of the most northerly ranging of the southern pines, growing wild from New Jersey, Ohio, and Illinois to Texas, and recognizable from a distance by the presence of young branches growing from the trunk inside the main canopy. As this tendency suggests, it recovers better from pruning than most other pines. Useful for shade, massing, or naturalizing in Zones 6a−9a.

Pinus virginiana 7

Virginia pine, scrub pine
Evergreen tree
Pinaceae (Pine Family)

Native Range. East-central United States from New Jersey to Alabama.

Useful Range. USDA Zones 5b−9a.

Function. Massing, naturalizing, large-scale screening, roadside bank planting.

Size and Habit

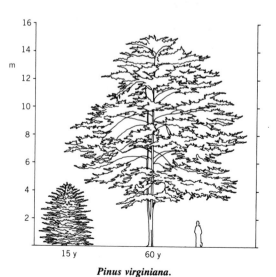

Pinus virginiana.

Adaptability. Especially useful on poor, dry soils.

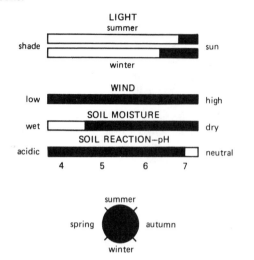

Seasonal Interest. *Foliage:* Evergreen, twisted needles, 5–8 cm/2–3 in. long, in fascicles of two, persisting for three to four years, deep green in summer but yellowing in winter. *Cones:* Lustrous, reddish brown, to 5 cm/2 in. long, maturing in the second year but persisting longer.

Pinus virginiana.

Problems and Maintenance. This tree is relatively trouble-free and requires little maintenance other than spraying if insect infestations become heavy.

Related Species

Pinus rigida 7–8 (pitch pine). This native of the east-central United States from Maine to the southern Appalachian Mountains is useful on very poor, dry soils in Zones 4b–7a. Usually it is less attractive for this purpose than *P. virginiana* or *P. banksiana*, but it can become picturesque with age.

Pinus virginiana.

Pinus wallichiana 8

Synonyms: *P. excelsa, P. griffithii*
Himalayan or Bhutan pine
Evergreen tree
Pinaceae (Pine Family)

Native Range. Himalayas westward to Afghanistan.

Useful Range. USDA Zones 5b–9a with selection of appropriate genetic material.

Function. Specimen, shade tree, screen.

Size and Habit. Resembles a more massive edition of *Pinus strobus* and so needs plenty of space.

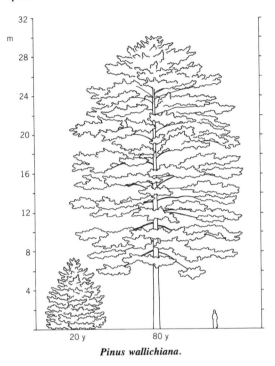

Pinus wallichiana.

Adaptability. Foliage is very sensitive to winter windburn in Zones 5 and 6.

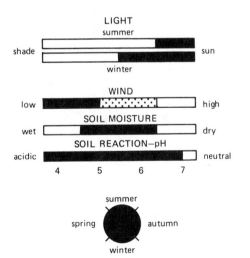

Seasonal Interest. *Foliage:* Evergreen, soft blue-green, fine-textured, with very slender needles, 10–20 cm/4–8 in. long, drooping and giving distinctive texture. *Cones:* Cylindrical, 15–25 cm/6–10 in. long, ripening yellow-brown and pendulous, adding interest because of their size. *Trunk and branches:* Bark on branches is smooth,

olive green to gray; trunk bark is roughened, dark gray.

Pinus wallichiana

Problems and Maintenance. Young trees may need protection from winter wind until they have been established for several years. Even older trees will not tolerate extreme exposures in colder zones.

Related Species

Pinus armandii 8 (Chinese white pine). This variable tree usually is picturesque and irregular in form, smaller than *P. wallichiana*, yet wide-spreading in relation to its height (15–20 m/60–80 ft). It is seldom available commercially at present but is potentially useful in Zones 5a–9a.

Pinus parviflora 7–8 (Japanese white pine). This picturesque, rather slow-growing tree has much shorter needles than either *P. armandii* or *P. wallichiana*, usually 2.5–8 cm/1–3 in. long. Its branching habit is often markedly tiered, giving strong horizontal accents. The selection 'Glauca' has more distinctly whitened, blue-green foliage, peculiarly clumped and twisted, with interesting textural effect. 'Glauca' is slower growing than the species type, but eventually may reach heights of 10 m/33 ft or greater. Useful as a striking specimen while young, or ultimately for screening, in Zones 5b–9a.

Pinus peuce 7 (Macedonian pine). This native of the Balkans is little used and seldom available but potentially useful in Zones 5a–9a. Compact and slower growing than most of the white pines, yet not as slow as *P. cembra*. It can be maintained as an effective screen for many years, since it retains its lower branches longer than most pines. It is apparently resistant to white pine blister rust.

Pistacia chinensis 8

Chinese pistachio
Deciduous tree
Anacardiaceae (Cashew Family)

Native Range. China.

Useful Range. USDA Zones 7b−9a+; individual trees reportedly are hardy northward to Zone 6b.

Function. Shade tree, rootstock for edible pistachio nut tree, *P. vera*.

Seasonal Interest. *Flowers:* Small and inconspicuous, dioecious. *Foliage:* Rich green, compound leaves with narrow leaflets 5−8 cm/2−3 in. long turn red to golden-orange in autumn virtually every year. *Fruits:* Red, later purple, round, 0.5 cm/0.2 in. across in showy clusters 15−20 cm/6−8 in. long in autumn on female trees.

Size and Habit

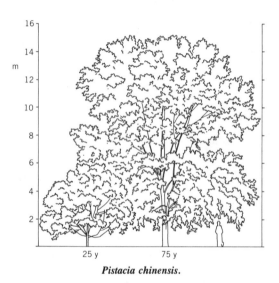

Pistacia chinensis.

Adaptability. One of the most widely adaptable of all shade trees within its useful range. Much more resistant to wind than its relatives the *Rhus* species, and relatively salt tolerant and resistant to extreme heat and drought.

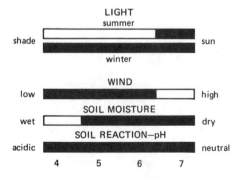

Pistacia chinensis.

Problems and Maintenance. This tree is essentially trouble-free, requires little or no maintenance, and is unusually free of insects and diseases.

Cultivars. Few cultivars are yet available, but the increasing popularity of this tree in the South and lower Mississippi Basin along with variation in form, hardiness, and the desirability of heavily fruiting forms suggests that more cultivars may be developed in the future.

Pittosporum tobira 5

Japanese pittosporum
Evergreen shrub
Pittosporaceae (Pittosporum Family)

Native Range. China and Japan.

Useful Range. USDA Zones 8b−9a+ and in sheltered sites in Zone 7b and 8a.

Function. Screen, massing, specimen, foundation.

Size and Habit

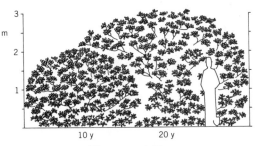

Pittosporum tobira.

Adaptability. Tolerates seaside wind and salt spray.

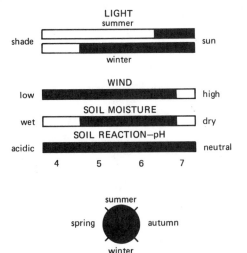

Seasonal Interest. *Flowers:* White to pale yellow, very fragrant, individually 1.3 cm/0.5 in. across, in clusters to 8 cm/3 in. across, in midspring. *Foliage:* Evergreen, bright to deep green, rounded leaves to 10 cm/4 in. long in full shade, but more commonly half that length, giving

rather fine texture. *Fruits:* Capsules, developing in summer, are not conspicuous but in some years add autumn interest as red seeds are exposed. *Branching:* Sympodial branching, as in most azaleas and flowering dogwood, accentuates the broad-spreading growth habit.

Problems and Maintenance. This shrub is usually trouble-free, but occasionally is subject to disease and insect problems, the most serious of which are aphids and scale insects, which must be controlled early to prevent serious damage.

Cultivars. 'Variegata' has gray-green foliage, variegated creamy white. It is a striking specimen plant, considerably slower growing than the species type, and seldom exceeding heights of about 1.5 m/5 ft, so it is not suitable for screening.

Pittosporum tobira 'Variegata.'

Pittosporum tobira 'Variegata.'

'Wheeler's Dwarf' is compact in growth, remaining below 0.5 m/1.6 ft for several years, and can be kept below 0.8 m/2.6 ft indefinitely with occasional pruning. The deep green leaves are about as large as those of the species type, packed into a dense mass of distinctive texture. This handsome and useful dwarf plant is popular for foundation planting and massing in Zones 8a−9a+ and may prove adapted to sheltered sites in Zone 7b.

Related Species. Many other species of *Pittosporum* are known, primarily from Australia, New Zealand, and southeastern Asia, and a few are used as landscape plants in California. *P. tobira* is the only one in general use in the eastern United States.

Pittosporum tobira 'Wheeler's Dwarf.'

Platanus occidentalis 8

Sycamore, American planetree
Deciduous tree
Platanaceae (Planetree Family)

Native Range. Eastern North America.

Useful Range. USDA Zones 5a−9a and to Zone 4b with selection of northern seed sources.

Function. Shade tree, street tree, specimen.

Size and Habit

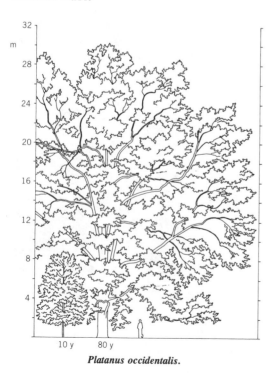

Platanus occidentalis.

Adaptability. This tree is one of the most tolerant to city conditions.

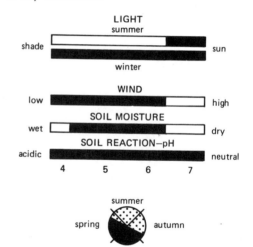

Seasonal Interest. *Foliage:* Medium green, lobed, adding coarse texture in summer, turning brown before falling in autumn. *Fruits:* Globose heads, green, ripening tan, about 2.5 cm/1 in. across, pendulous on long stalks, adding quiet interest in autumn and early winter. *Trunk and branches:* Smooth bark exfoliates in large flakes, exposing patterns of creamy white inner bark with contrasting areas of gray and brown, providing striking interest during the leafless season and mild interest the rest of the year.

Problems and Maintenance. Anthracnose is a serious disease of this tree, causing twig blight and occasionally cankers, sometimes weakening trees but seldom killing them. The seriousness of the disease in any year depends to a great extent on weather conditions. Cool, moist weather following leaf emergence favors the disease. Minimum control consists of cleaning up and burning of leaf and twig litter in autumn. When necessary, appropriate spraying will further reduce the incidence and extent of the disease. The tendency of this species to litter the ground with leaves, twigs, bark, and fruits makes it far from an ideal street tree. But its tolerance of difficult city conditions has resulted in its widespread use for this purpose, and it is admittedly functional where there is enough space for it, in spite of its disadvantages, especially in the Midwest.

Varieties. There are no commercially available selections of this species, but the general rule for selection of seed source applies: when possible, use trees grown from seed parents native to the region in question.

Related Species

Platanus ×acerifolia 8 (synonyms: *P. ×hybrida, P. ×cantabrigiensis*; London planetree). This hybrid *(P. occidentalis × P. orientalis)* has been planted widely as a street and shade tree in its useful range (Zones 6a–9a) in the eastern and central United States. Its popularity has been derived largely from its anthracnose resistance, although it is noticeably less cold-hardy than *P. occidentalis*. It has been observed by professional plantsmen that the London planetree appears in some areas to be more prone to anthracnose than previously believed, and somewhat more cold-hardy, evidence that accidental backcrossing with *P. occidentalis* may have occurred in areas where *P. occidentalis* grows wild. Genetic studies at the U.S. National Arboretum may yield superior selections or hybrids of *Platanus* for use as city trees in our area.

Unfortunately, *P. ×acerifolia* is subject to a still more serious, in fact lethal, disease called cankerstain, which seems to be less of a problem with *P. occidentalis*. At this writing, the native *P. occidentalis* seems to be the better prospect of the two for use as a shade tree.

Platanus orientalis 8 (oriental planetree). This native of southeastern Europe and adjacent Asia is a common street tree in European cities, often kept in scale by pollarding. It does not grow as tall

Platanus orientalis.

Platanus orientalis.

Platanus orientalis.

as the other *Platanus* species mentioned, reaching heights of about 25 m/82 ft, but it is fully as wide-spreading when left unpruned. In the past, *P. orientalis* has been relatively resistant to disease but is considerably less cold-hardy than its American relative, with a useful range of Zones 7a–9a, perhaps including protected sites in Zone 6b.

Podocarpus macrophyllus 5–7

Yew podocarpus
Evergreen tree or shrub
Podocarpaceae (Podocarpus Family)

Native Range. Japan.

Useful Range. USDA Zones 8b–9a+ and sheltered sites in Zones 7b and 8a.

Function. Specimen, hedge, screen.

Size and Habit. Size is limited by climate; this plant remains in size group 5 in Zones 7b and 8a, but reaches size group 7 in Zone 9a.

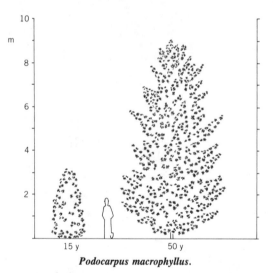

Podocarpus macrophyllus.

Seasonal Interest. *Foliage:* Evergreen, broad-needlelike, to 10 cm/4 in. long and 0.8 cm/0.3 in. broad, glossy dark green on upper surface, light green underneath, handsome in all seasons. *Fruits:* Greenish to purple, on female plants, inconspicuous.

Problems and Maintenance. This plant is relatively trouble-free and requires little or no maintenance. Light pruning may be necessary in the Deep South to restrict size in some sites. This should be done by removing individual branch tips, not by shearing, except when used as a formal hedge. Scale insects may occasionally be troublesome in warm areas.

Varieties. Var. *angustifolius* has narrow leaves and narrow growth habit but is seldom commercially available. Var. *macrophyllus* is the species type described above. Var. *maki* (synonym: *P. chinensis*) is a shrubby plant, seldom exceeding 2–3 m/7–10 ft tall, dense and erect. It is commonly used in foundation plantings.

Related Species. Several other species of *Podocarpus* are used on the West Coast, but most material in use in the southeastern states belongs to *P. macrophyllus*.

Adaptability. Partial shade from full summer sun is beneficial, especially in the Deep South. In Zones 7b and 8a, protection from full sun and wind in winter reduces leaf scorch.

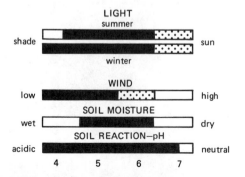

Polygonum aubertii 1

China or silver fleecevine, silverlace vine
Deciduous vine
Polygonaceae (Buckwheat Family)

Native Range. Western China.

Useful Range. USDA Zones 4b–8b and to Zone 3b where snow cover is reliable.

Function. Screen (with support), specimen; vine growing rapidly and climbing by twining to heights of 5–10 m/16–33 ft, but not effective as a screen near the ground without training.

Size and Habit

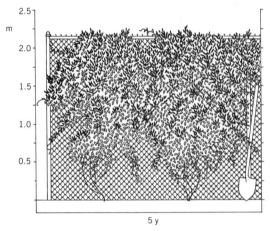

Polygonum aubertii.

Adaptability

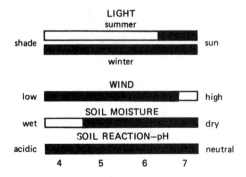

Seasonal Interest. *Flowers:* Greenish white at first, then white or sometimes pinkish at maturity; small but numerous, making a solid mass of bloom over the upper parts of the plant. *Foliage:*

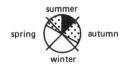

Reddish as it unfolds, quickly turning bright green, falling without color change in autumn.

Polygonum aubertii.

Problems and Maintenance. Japanese beetles can be troublesome in areas within the range of this insect. In northern areas, vines may kill to the ground during winter but return vigorously during the following summer. When used as a visual screen (e.g., on a chainlink fence) coverage near ground level depends on the vine reaching the top of its support and falling back to the ground as it continues to grow. For this reason, low coverage may never be complete in Zones 4 and 5, and other species may be preferred for screening.

Related Species

Polygonum cuspidatum 3–5 (Japanese knotweed, Mexican bamboo). This clump-forming plant to 2 m/6.6 ft or more tall, spreads vigorously by underground stems and is extremely difficult to eradicate, so it should be used and contained very carefully. In most instances, better plants can be found, but few plants are as effective in stabilizing soil on steep banks. This plant kills to the ground at the first hard freeze in autumn, looks unsightly until the dead stalks are removed, then returns with seemingly redoubled vigor during the next growing season. It is useful in Zones 4b–9a.

The var. *compactum* (synonym: *P. reynoutria*)

grows in much the same manner as the species type, but usually to heights of 0.2−1 m/0.7−3.3 ft. It has reddish flowers, is slightly less difficult to control, and is just as effective in slope stabilization. There is considerable variation in the height and vigor of this variety, leading to confusion. The lowest forms are considered by some to be a

Polygonum cuspidatum var. *compactum*.

separate species, *P. reynoutria*, but probably are not commercially available.

Antigonon leptopus 1 (coralvine, mountain rose, rosa de montana, confederate vine).   This Mexican member of the Polygonaceae makes a vigorous screen with support and pruning, climbing loosely by tendrils to heights of 5−10 m/16−33 ft, and higher well south of our area. It is unusual in its tolerance of hot, dry climates and poor, dry soils, and produces masses of bright coral-pink flowers in midsummer. This otherwise trouble-free vine usually freezes back in winter in Zone 8b, where it reaches its northern limit, and requires annual pruning for renewal, usually done by cutting back close to the ground after the first frost, then adding a winter mulch. From the southern extremes of our area (Zone 9a) to the tropics, severe pruning is necessary to control size and promote vigor, but this practice delays flowering if overdone. The selection 'Album' has white flowers.

Poncirus trifoliata 6

Trifoliate orange, hardy orange
Deciduous shrub
Rutaceae (Rue Family)

Native Range. Northern China and Korea.

Useful Range. USDA Zones 6b−9a+, and Zone 6a in sheltered sites.

Function. Specimen, barrier, hedge, rootstock for citrus fruits.

Size and Habit

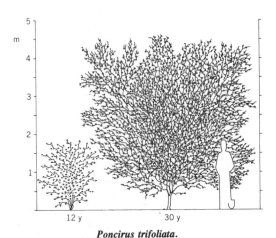

Poncirus trifoliata.

Adaptability. Best in full sun, and grows well in hot, dry sites.

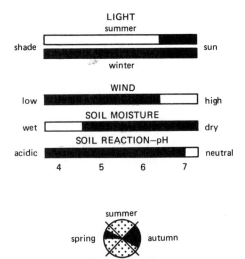

Seasonal Interest. *Flowers:* Fragrant, white, similar to those of *Citrus* species, 3−5 cm/1.2−2 in. across. *Foliage:* Compound leaves with three leaflets and winged petiole. Not dense enough in mass to function as a visual screen, falling in midautumn with little or no color change. *Fruits:* Yellow-orange, globose, to about 5 cm/2 in. across, resembling small oranges, fragrant but not edible. *Twigs and branches:* Heavy, angled, deep green twigs and smaller branches bear sharp, rugged thorns.

Poncirus trifoliata.

Problems and Maintenance. This plant is relatively trouble-free and requires little maintenance other than pruning for use as a hedge or to keep the thorny branches out of contact with people. The heavy, thorny branches make this plant a highly effective barrier, but it can be troublesome in intensive situations, especially where children are present.

Related Species

-*Choisya ternata* 5 (Mexican orange). This evergreen shrub from Mexico with foliage mass denser than that of *Poncirus* reaches heights of 2–3 m/6.6–10 ft, occasionally taller. It is useful for barrier plantings in hot, dry sites in Zones 8b–9a+ and in protected sites in Zones 7b and 8a, with fragrant white flowers, to 3 cm/1.2 in. across, borne in showy clusters in late spring. The dark blue fruits, to 1.5 cm/0.6 in. across, are not showy.

Populus alba 8

White poplar
Deciduous tree
Salicaceae (Willow Family)

Native Range. Central Europe to central Asia.

Useful Range. USDA Zones 4a–9a.

Function. Specimen, shade tree, screen.

Size and Habit

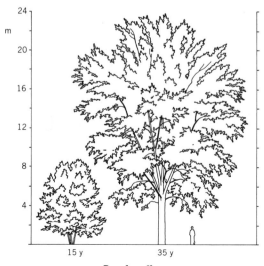

Populus alba.

Adaptability

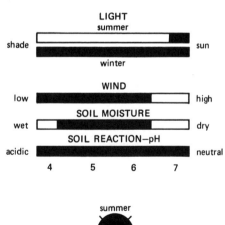

Seasonal Interest. *Foliage:* Three-lobed, maplelike leaves are lustrous and deep green above and white and felty underneath, giving a striking glitter effect as they are tumbled over by even light breezes. In autumn, the green is dulled, sometimes giving way to a reddish or russet color before they fall in midautumn. *Trunk and branches:* Whitish gray-green bark is interesting at all seasons.

Problems and Maintenance. Poplars as a group are soft-wooded, short-lived, and prone to storm breakage, usually aggravated by their susceptibility to serious stem and trunk canker diseases. They quickly send roots into moist areas, frequently clogging drainage lines and disrupting pavement. In fact, they are prohibited in many places by city ordinances. *Populus alba* is not as prone to serious diseases as many other poplars, and for this reason usually is longer-lived, yet it has enough problems to justify caution in planting it. On the other side of the ledger, this and other poplars are extremely fast growing and handsome as young trees. *P. alba* is certainly one of the most satisfactory of this group.

Cultivars. 'Nivea' has unusually thick, white pubescence underneath the leaves and is especially striking in summer but becomes unsightly where large amounts of dust or soot are present. 'Pyramidalis' (synonym: 'Bolleana'; Bolleana poplar) is fastigiate and columnar in outline when young, later narrowly pyramidal. It is a more durable alternative to the lombardy poplar, *P. nigra* 'Italica.'

Populus alba 'Pyramidalis.'

Populus balsamifera 8

Synonyms: *P. candicans, P. tacamahaca*
Balsam poplar, tacamahac
Deciduous tree
Salicaceae (Willow Family)

Native Range. Northern North America.

Useful Range. USDA Zones 2–5; will grow in southern zones also, but not as a useful landscape tree.

Function. Shade tree.

Size and Habit

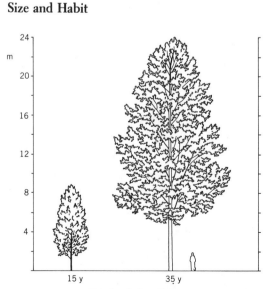

Populus balsamifera.

Adaptability

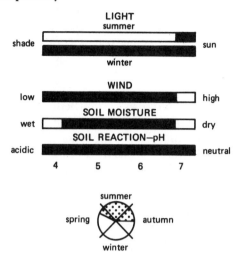

Seasonal Interest. *Foliage:* Bright green with brownish pubescence giving a "brassy" appearance and medium-coarse texture, falling in midautumn with little color change.

Problems and Maintenance. This tree is subject to the problems of poplars in general (see *P. alba*) and not very long-lived, but a fairly satisfactory shade tree in the far North (Zones 2–4).

Related Species

Populus angustifolia 7 (narrow-leaved cottonwood). This rather narrow tree from the Great Plains and eastern Rocky Mountain region has potential value as a landscape tree for the Northern Plains to Zone 3a, even though it is little used at present. It has narrow leaves, to 10 cm/4 in. long, smooth bark, and orange branches.

Populus maximowiczii 8 (Japanese poplar). This tree is one of the least disease-prone of all poplars, growing to about the same size as *P. balsamifera*, with handsome, dark green foliage and light green bark, useful in Zones 4a–5b, perhaps also in colder areas.

Populus simonii 7 (Simon poplar). This native of northern China is a medium-size tree, similar to *P. angustifolia* in general form. It is represented in landscape use by the cultivar 'Fastigiata,' which is narrowly pyramidal in form and sometimes substituted for *P. alba* 'Pyramidalis' or *P. nigra* 'Italica,' even though it is not as strikingly columnar as those cultivars. Useful in Zones 3a–5b and perhaps farther south as well.

Populus trichocarpa 8 (western balsam poplar, black cottonwood). This large, western North American tree is potentially useful in the Northern Plains in Zones 2–4 and perhaps elsewhere, but it probably is not in use or available in our area at present.

Populus deltoides 8

Cottonwood
Deciduous tree
Salicaceae (Willow Family)

Native Range. Eastern United States and adjacent Canada.

Useful Range. USDA Zones 3a–9a.

Function. Shade tree.

Size and Habit

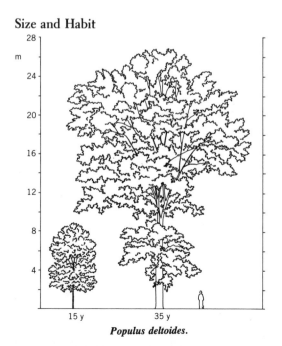

Populus deltoides.

Adaptability

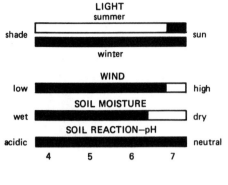

Seasonal Interest. *Foliage:* Lustrous, bright to deep green leaves, to 12 cm/5 in. long and broad, giving a rather coarse texture. *Fruits:* Catkins on female trees bear many seeds surrounded by silky or cottony hairs. Their release in late spring gives rise to the common name, cottonwood. Fruits and seeds of other *Populus* species are much the same but not so noticeably "cottony."

Problems and Maintenance. Cottonwood is subject to the problems of poplars in general (see *P. alba*) but longer-lived than most. It is primarily of value as a massive shade tree in the far North (Zones 3−4), and fairly effective in this role, but it drops a considerable amount of branch and leaf litter, and female trees also release seeds that germinate as fast-growing weed seedlings.

Cultivars. At least one nonfruiting (male) selection, 'Siouxland,' has been made. This cultivar apparently is somewhat rust-resistant but perhaps not far superior to other male cultivars and not widely available.

Related Species

Populus ×*berolinensis* 7−8 (Berlin poplar). This hybrid *(P. laurifolia* × *P. nigra* 'Italica') is narrowly pyramidal or oval, but not as narrow as *P. nigra* 'Italica.' Seldom available commercially, it probably is no better than several other similar forms but useful in Zones 3a−9a.

Populus ×*canadensis* 8 (Carolina poplar). This group of extremely vigorous hybrids *(P. deltoides* × *P. nigra)* includes several forms, the most common of which is 'Eugenei,' a narrowly pyramidal tree with glossy, deep green leaves and smooth, gray-green bark. Its unusually rapid growth is offset by the fact that it clogs drains and disrupts pavement even more rapidly than most other poplars, and it is not dependably long-lived. Useful in Zones 3a−9a.

Populus nigra 8 (black poplar). This large Eurasian tree is best known in our area as the narrowly columnar form 'Italica' (Lombardy poplar), commonly planted for its striking vertical effect. Its most appropriate use is as a temporary screen or windbreak. Unfortunately, in this role it is seldom removed soon enough but usually left until rather large, disease-ridden, and costly to remove. It is useful in Zones 3a−9a.

Quaking or trembling aspen
Deciduous tree
Salicaceae (Willow Family)

Native Range. Northern North America.

Useful Range. USDA Zones 2b−6b, but so short-lived that it is barely useful in zones warmer than 5b.

Function. Naturalizing, massing.

Size and Habit

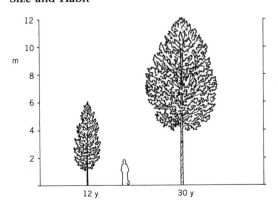

Populus tremuloides.

Adaptability

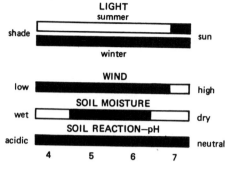

Seasonal Interest. *Foliage:* Casts light, mottled shade. Leaves are small, 3–8 cm/1.2–3 in. long, the upper surface dull or deep green, whitened underneath, giving a glittering, bicolored effect as they are turned over by even slight wind, because of the flattened petioles typical of all *Populus* species. Foliage turns clear, bright yellow in autumn. *Trunk and branches:* Smooth, pale gray-green bark becomes almost white with age, adding significant year round interest.

Problems and Maintenance. Like other *Populus* species, *P. tremuloides* is weak-wooded, disease susceptible, and short-lived, and so is best used in naturalized plantings. Unlike many poplars, *P.*

tremuloides and its close relatives (see Related Species) are not easily propagated by cuttings.

Cultivars. 'Pendula,' with weeping branches, probably is not commercially available. *P. tremuloides* is one of the widest ranging of all trees, suggesting that much genetic variation exists, but few selections have been made, probably because of the difficulty of propagating them as well as the minor importance of this species as a landscape tree in most heavily populated areas. Most plants used are seedlings, and selection of nearby seed sources probably is a useful precaution, as with other wide ranging species.

Related Species

Populus grandidentata 6–7 (bigtooth aspen). This tree has larger leaves than *P. tremuloides,* to 8–10 cm/3–4 in. long, coarsely toothed, and giving less of the mobile effect of those of *P. tremuloides.* This species is more tolerant of warm sites and moist and heavy soils than *P. tremuloides,* has similar bark interest, and is equally short-lived. It is useful in Zones 4a–7a.

Populus tremula 6–8 (European aspen). This tree is the European counterpart of *P. tremuloides.* It is almost never used in our area and is noteworthy only for the narrowly columnar cultivar 'Erecta,' which is being tested in Canada and the United States and thus far seems to be more trouble-free and durable than other narrow poplars.

Potentilla fruticosa 3–4

Shrubby cinquefoil
Deciduous shrub
Rosaceae (Rose Family)

Native Range. Northern North America and Eurasia.

Useful Range. USDA Zones 2b–7b and good sites in Zone 8.

Function. Border, massing.

Size and Habit

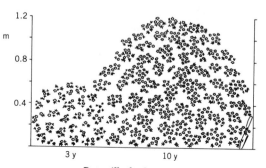

Potentilla fruticosa.

Adaptability. One of the most widely tolerant of all shrubs to soil extremes and to seashore or de-icing salts. Planting in sites with good air circulation helps control mildew disease.

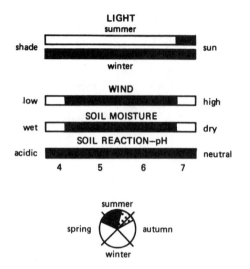

Seasonal Interest. *Flowers:* Yellow, red-orange, or white, to 2–3 cm/0.8–1.2 in. across, showy in early summer and continuing intermittently until fall. *Foliage:* Bright to gray-green, fine textured, hairy, compound leaves, falling in autumn with little or no color change. *Fruits:* Inconspicuous dry capsules.

Potentilla fruticosa.

Problems and Maintenance. Leaf-spot diseases, mildew, and chewing insects occasionally are troublesome. Pruning is seldom if ever necessary, but older plants that have become ragged can be renewed by pruning close to the ground in spring.

Cultivars. More than 40 cultivars of *Potentilla* are currently in use in North America. A few of the more common are listed here.

'Abbotswood' has large white flowers and deep blue-green foliage and is probably the best white-flowered cultivar available.

'Goldfinger' has bright yellow flowers, to 3 cm/1.2 in. across, in large numbers, and is perhaps the showiest of all *P. fruticosa* selections in flower.

'Jackmanii' has relatively few but large flowers and unusually deep green foliage.

'Katherine Dykes' has lemon-yellow flowers and may belong to *P. ×friedrichsenii* (see Related Species and Hybrids).

'Longacre' has lemon-yellow flowers and low growth habit.

'Moonlight' (= 'Maanelys') has pale yellow flowers.

'Mount Everest' has relatively large white flowers and erect, open growth habit, and may belong to *P. davurica* or *P. ×friedrichsenii* (see Related Species and Hybrids).

'Primrose Beauty' has pale yellow flowers and excellent foliage.

'Red Ace' has vermillion (reddish orange) flowers and bright green foliage. It is a recent selection, not fully evaluated at this writing, but apparently very low-growing.

'Tangerine' has orange tinted yellow flowers, but not as orange as the name suggests, and a low, spreading form.

Related Species and Hybrids

Potentilla davurica 3 (synonyms: *P. fruticosa* 'Arbuscula' and 'Davurica,' var. *arbuscula*, var. *davurica*; Dahurian cinquefoil). This low-growing species (to 0.5 m/1.6 ft) from central Siberia has white or yellow flowers. 'Sutter's Gold' has brighter yellow flowers than most selections from this species.

Potentilla ×friedrichsenii 3 (Friedrichsen cinquefoil). This tall hybrid (*P. davurica* × *P. fruticosa*) has pale yellow flowers.

Potentilla parvifolia 3 (often listed as *P. fruticosa* 'Parvifolia' or var. *parvifolia*). This Chinese species closely resembles *P. fruticosa* except in having finer textured, silkier foliage. 'Gold Drop' (= 'Farreri') has golden yellow flowers, low stature, and excellent foliage; 'Klondyke' has large, deep golden yellow flowers.

Potentilla tridentata 2 (wineleaf cinquefoil). This woody native of eastern North America from Labrador and Manitoba to eastern Tennes-

Potentilla tridentata.

see has lustrous, leathery, evergreen, compound leaves, each with three notched leaflets, turning wine-red in winter. In well-drained, acidic soil and in full sun it forms a solid mass of foliage and serves as a handsome, small-scale groundcover. Useful in Zones 3a–7b and perhaps also in coastal sites in Zone 8.

Several low-growing herbaceous *Potentilla* species are useful as groundcovers during the growing season, with strong displays of yellow flowers in spring or early summer. A few of the most common species are: *P. cinerea* 2 (synonym: *P. tommasiniana*; rusty cinquefoil) and *P. crantzii* 2 (synonym: *P. verna*). These two species are useful in Zones 4b–6b, *P. cinerea* to colder zones as well, and *P. crantzii* southward to Zone 7b.

Prinsepia sinensis 4–5

Cherry prinsepia
Deciduous shrub
Rosaceae (Rose Family)

Native Range. Manchuria.

Useful Range. USDA Zones 2b–6b, perhaps farther south as well.

Function. Barrier hedge, screen, massing, specimen.

Size and Habit

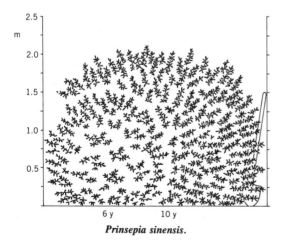

Prinsepia sinensis.

Adaptability. Well-adapted to wind, cold, and heavy, neutral soils of the Northern Plains.

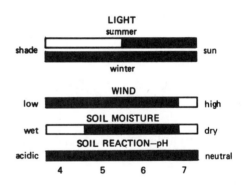

Seasonal Interest. *Flowers:* Yellow, small, and inconspicuous, in small clusters in midspring. *Foliage:* Bright green leaves, to 8 cm/3 in. long, unfolding very early and remaining green until heavy frosts in autumn. *Fruits:* Red to red-purple, resembling small cherries, to 1.5 cm/0.6 in. across, showy against the green foliage in midsummer. *Branches:* Gracefully arching with many small, sharp spines; bark on older branches peels, adding slight winter interest.

Prinsepia sinensis.

Problems and Maintenance. This shrub is occasionally troubled by insects and diseases but seldom seriously so in the North. It is easily pruned as an informal hedge and may require severe renewal pruning after several years of growth. This is best done when growth begins in spring, especially in the far North.

Related Species

Prinsepia uniflora 4 (hedge prinsepia). This native of northern China resembles *P. sinensis* in growth habit but has narrower leaves and finer foliage texture. It is not tall enough or dense enough to function as a visual screen but is about as effective a barrier as *P. sinensis.* Useful in Zones 4a–6b and perhaps farther south as well.

Prunus americana 5

American plum
Deciduous shrubby tree
Rosaceae (Rose Family)

Native Range. Eastern North America to Utah and New Mexico.

Useful Range. USDA Zones 3b–9a, perhaps Zone 3a as well with selection of northern genetic material.

Function. Naturalizing, border, edible fruits.

Size and Habit

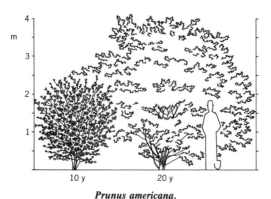
Prunus americana.

Adaptability

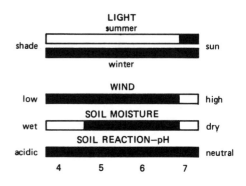

Seasonal Interest. *Flowers:* White, fairly showy for a short period in midspring. *Foliage:* Medium green, not distinctive or particularly ornamental, changing to yellow or orange before falling in early autumn. *Fruits:* Red or yellowish with a minimal blush, about 2.5 cm/1 in. across, in late summer; sometimes used to make excellent preserves and jellies.

Problems and Maintenance. This tree is subject to several disease problems, usually is not long-lived, and tends to form thickets. It is best restricted to naturalized areas to reduce the need for intensive maintenance.

Cultivars. Several cultivars selected for good fruiting are in commerce but are not widely available.

Related Species

Prunus alleghaniensis 5 (Alleghany plum). This small, thicket-forming tree from the northeastern United States resembles *P. americana* but has smaller, dark purple fruits. It is seldom planted but worth preserving in natural and naturalized landscapes. Useful in native habitat in Zones 5b—6b.

Prunus angustifolia 5 (Chickasaw plum). This small tree from the southeastern United States also forms thickets and is useful in much the same way as *P. alleghaniensis.* It is useful in Zones 6a—9a.

Prunus maritima 4 (beach plum). This straggling shrub or very small tree, usually remaining below 2 m/6.6 ft in height, is valued near its native habitat on the Atlantic Coast from Maine to Delaware for its salt tolerance, flowering interest, and edible fruits, much like those of *P. americana* but slightly smaller. Useful in Zones 4b—7a and perhaps farther south in coastal areas.

Prunus mexicana 6 (Mexican or big-tree plum). This tree does not form thickets like the other plums listed and is native from the Mississippi Basin of Kentucky to Oklahoma and into Mexico. Relatively drought-resistant, it is seldom used in landscape planting but may be preserved in natural and naturalized areas. The fruits are valued locally for preserves. Useful (and native) in Zones 7a—9a.

Prunus nigra 5—6 (Canada plum). This native of eastern Canada and adjacent United States is very similar in general effect and usefulness to *P. americana* but is probably significantly more cold-hardy and useful in Zones 3a—6b and perhaps Zone 7 as well.

Prunus avium 6—8

Mazzard cherry, sweet cherry
Deciduous tree
Rosaceae (Rose Family)

Native Range. Eurasia.

Useful Range. USDA Zones 6a—8b in sites near bodies of water or otherwise protected from temperature extremes for effective flowering and fruiting; tree will grow well without fruiting in Zone 5 as well.

Function. Shade tree, specimen, edible fruits.

Size and Habit

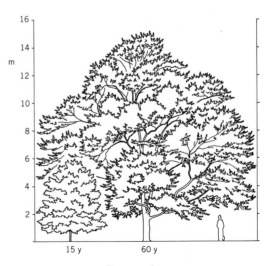

Prunus avium.

Adaptability

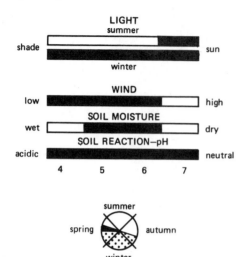

Seasonal Interest. *Flowers:* White, single or double, 2.5–3.5 cm/1–1.4 in. across, in clusters in midspring. *Foliage:* Medium green, not distinctive or particularly ornamental and not changing color before falling in autumn. *Fruits:* Very deep red and sweet at maturity. Commercial sweet cherries belong to this species. For fruit production, more than one cultivar or clone usually is needed for cross-pollination. *Trunk and branches:* Typical "cherry" bark, deep red-brown with horizontal lenticels, but not nearly as striking as that of some other cherry species.

Problems and Maintenance. Stone fruits are subject to a variety of insect and disease problems and require at least a minimal spray program for best results, even when used as landscape trees. Consistent production of good quality fruits re-

quires a more detailed spray schedule and a moderate climate free of severe temperature fluctuations, since flower buds are susceptible to freezes in winter and early spring. For most landscape purposes there are better and more trouble-free *Prunus* species, and this species probably should only be used where the edible fruits are also desired, except for the cultivars below.

Cultivars. 'Plena' has double flowers. Since extra petals are derived by modification of functional organs, this cultivar is sterile. As a result, the flowers are considerably longer lasting, barring freezes, than single flowers of the species type and there are, of course, no fruits.

'Scanlon' is a smaller, double-flowered selection, remaining below 6 m/20 ft in height.

Many cultivars have been selected for outstanding commercial fruit production. For more information on cultivars and other aspects of fruit production, consult the nearest county, state, or provincial extension service office.

Related Species

Prunus cerasus 6–7 (sour cherry). This small Eurasian tree is the parent species of commercial sour cherry cultivars. Although it is reasonably effective as a small shade tree, there are better choices for most situations where edible fruit production is not a concern, and in many situations the presence of fruit can cause problems with litter and birds. It is more shade tolerant than most cherry species yet requires at least partial sun for effective flowering and fruiting, and it is useful in Zones 5a–8b.

Prunus besseyi 3

Western sand cherry
Deciduous shrub
Rosaceae (Rose Family)

Native Range. Northern Great Plains of the United States and Canada.

Useful Range. USDA Zones 3a–6a; can be grown somewhat farther south but is not particularly useful there.

Function. Massing, edible fruits.

Size and Habit

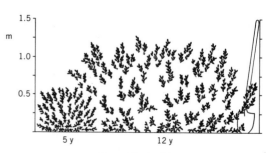

Prunus besseyi.

Adaptability

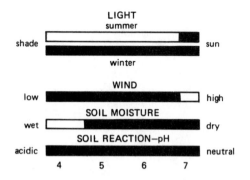

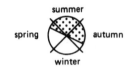

Seasonal Interest. *Flowers:* Small, white, adding minor landscape interest in middle to late spring. *Foliage:* Gray-green leaves are whitish underneath, 2.5−5 cm/1−2 in. long. *Fruits:* Deep purple, nearly black, 1.5 cm/0.6 in. across, borne in great numbers in native habitat, valued locally as edible fruits.

Problems and Maintenance. Brown rot disease may be troublesome in moist years and must be controlled to avoid serious damage. In relatively dry areas where this plant finds its greatest value, the disease may not often be severe.

Selections. "Hansen bush cherries" are selected seed strains from superior parent plants but are much more variable than vegetatively propagated cultivars would be. Occasional plants of *P. besseyi* have whitish or yellowish fruits and such selections have been made but not distributed widely.

Related Species

Prunus pumila 4 (sand cherry). This native of the Great Lakes region is similar to *P. besseyi* in appearance and function, but less prostrate and a little more shrubby. It is seldom available commercially.

Prunus caroliniana 6−7

Carolina laurelcherry, cherry laurel
Evergreen tree
Rosaceae (Rose Family)

Native Range. Southeastern United States.

Useful Range. USDA Zones 7b−9a+ and limited use as a shrub in Zone 7a.

Function. Garden or patio tree, screen, hedge.

Size and Habit

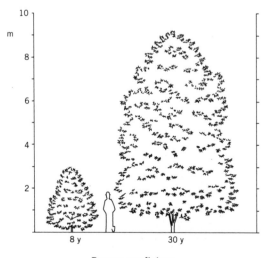

Prunus caroliniana.

Adaptability. Unusually sensitive to poorly drained soil but tolerant of salt in seashore situations.

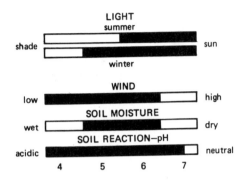

Seasonal Interest. *Flowers:* Very small, white, in racemes to 2.5 cm/1 in. long in midspring. *Foliage:* Evergreen, lustrous, leathery leaves, 5–10 cm/2–4 in. long, pointed. *Fruits:* Blue-black, shiny, cherrylike, 0.8 cm/0.3 in. across in

autumn, adding minor landscape interest until eaten by birds.

Prunus caroliniana.

Problems and Maintenance. This plant has fewer problems than most *Prunus* species but is susceptible to white fly infestations in the Deep South and occasionally is attacked by borers. It requires pruning for maximum fullness as a visual screen but only for removing damaged wood when it is left to assume a small tree form. It is rather susceptible to physical breakage, especially from occasional ice and heavy snow in the northern parts of its useful range.

Prunus cerasifera 6

Cherry plum, Myrobalan plum
Deciduous tree
Rosaceae (Rose Family)

Native Range. Southeastern Europe to central Asia.

Useful Range. USDA Zones 4b–9a with selection of appropriate cultivars.

Function. Specimen, patio tree, border accent.

Size and Habit

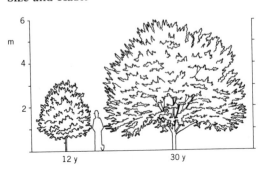

Prunus cerasifera.

Adaptability. Tolerates light shade, but the purple-leaved cultivars need full sun for best development of foliage color.

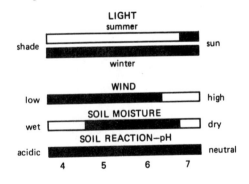

Seasonal Interest. *Flowers:* Pale to deep pink, small (1.8 cm/0.7 in. across) but numerous, showy in spring except for cultivars with deep pink flowers masked by emerging foliage. *Foliage:* Medium green in the seldom-used species type, cultivars vivid maroon-purple, fading to bronze-purple by late summer, variable depending on cultivar. *Fruits:* Maroon-purple plums are hardly noticeable among the leaves but are useful for jellies.

Problems and Maintenance. The better purple-leaved cultivars, at least, seem to be less troubled by insects and diseases in the Midwest, where they are most popular, than most plums and most other *Prunus* species. They require little maintenance other than occasional pest control.

Cultivars. 'Atropurpurea' (= 'Pissardii') was the first selection made and is still satisfactory in comparison with newer cultivars. It may not hold its purple color as well as some of the newer selections, especially in the Midwest, but it is useful in Zones 5a−9a.

Prunus cerasifera 'Atropurpurea.'

'Hollywood' is distinctive because its foliage first emerges green, then quickly turns purple, much like *P. virginiana* 'Schubert,' but it is not as commonly used as 'Atropurpurea,' 'Newport,' and 'Thundercloud.' Useful in Zones 5a−9a.

'Newport' is considered one of the hardiest selections in the Northern Plains to Zone 4a. Its origin is controversial. Some consider it a hybrid, either a *P.* ×*blireiana* selection, which seems unlikely considering its hardiness, or *P. americana* × *P. cerasifera* 'Atropurpurea.'

'Nigra' is not widely used but is similar to 'Newport' in general appearance.

'Thundercloud' reputedly holds its color longer than average and is useful in Zones 5b−9a.

Related Species

Prunus ×*blireiana* 6 (blireiana plum). This hybrid of *P. cerasifera* 'Atropurpurea' × *P. mume* is similar in general effect to the other purple-leaved plums, but has wider leaves and semidouble, pink flowers. It is not as well adapted to the extreme North but is useful in Zones 6a−9a.

Prunus ×*cistena* 5 (purple-leaved sand cherry). This strongly purple-leaved hybrid of *P. pumila* × *P. cerasifera* 'Atropurpurea' is distinctly shrubby rather than a tree, reaching heights of 2 m/6.6 ft and somewhat taller in fertile soil. Its flowers are white, contrasting with the newly emerging purple foliage, which is intensely red-purple at this stage and holds a fairly good red-purple color throughout the growing season. It is somewhat more cold-hardy than the purple plums, presumably owing to the *P. pumila* parentage, useful in Zones 3b−8a, but with occasional winter dieback in Zones 3b and 4a. This is less a problem than it would be for the purple-leaved plums, since *P.* ×*cistena* requires occasional pruning to maintain form and vigor, and removal of small amounts of deadwood constitutes little additional maintenance.

Prunus domestica 6−7 (garden plum). This Eurasian species includes the blue or purple fruited commercial plum cultivars. Except for the fruit, it probably will not find much value in landscape planting. It is useful in Zones 5a−8b as a landscape tree, but for information on region and site for commercial fruit production as well as cultivars, consult county, state, or provincial extension service offices.

Prunus salicina 6−7 (Japanese plum). This native of China includes the so-called Japanese or Oriental red plum cultivars grown commercially primarily on the West Coast, the south Atlantic coast, and the lower Mississippi Basin. As with *P. domestica*, there is little reason for including it in landscaping plantings other than for fruit production.

Prunus glandulosa 4

Dwarf flowering almond, almond cherry
Deciduous shrub
Rosaceae (Rose Family)

Native Range. China and Japan.

Useful Range. USDA Zones 4b−9a+.

Function. Specimen, border, massing.

Size and Habit

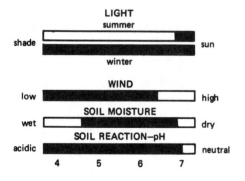

Prunus glandulosa.

Adaptability

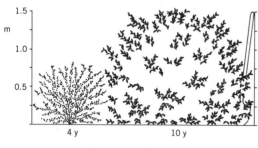

Seasonal Interest. *Flowers:* Very showy, white or pink, single or double, to 1.5 cm/0.6 in. across, borne in large numbers in midspring just as leaves are beginning to unfold. *Foliage:* Medium green, lustrous but not especially interesting, falling without color change. *Fruits:* Small (to 1.2 cm/0.5 in. across) red cherries in summer. Not developed in double-flowered cultivars.

Problems and Maintenance. This shrub is occasionally subject to several insect and disease problems, but its principal problems are borers in the South and mice in the North. When damaged, it can be pruned to the ground in spring or early summer and will return but will not flower for a year.

Cultivars. 'Alboplena' has double, white flowers. 'Rosea' has single, pink flowers. 'Sinensis' has double, pink flowers and is the most common form in landscape use.

Related Species

Prunus tenella 4 (dwarf Russian almond). This low shrub is of value for its extreme cold-hardiness, to Zone 3a. Its flowering interest is similar to that of the single-flowered forms of *P. glandulosa*, but it produces many root suckers, making it difficult to contain. The selection 'Fire Hill' is similar except that it has brighter pink flowers, a more upright habit, a lesser tendency to sucker, and excellent orange autumn foliage color.

Prunus triloba 5−6 (flowering almond). This tall shrub from China is striking in bloom in early spring, with large, double, pink or white flowers up to 2.5 cm/1 in. across. But, like the other members of this group, it is not very interesting in other seasons. It is susceptible to several insect and disease problems common to the stone fruits, and to rabbit damage as well, making it a questionable selection where little maintenance will be provided. The selection 'Multiplex,' with bright pink, double flowers, is most commonly seen; f. *simplex* is the single-flowered wild form, found after the species type had been described as the double flowered form. Useful in Zones 4a−9a and sheltered sites in Zone 3b.

Prunus laurocerasus 4–6

Cherry laurel, English laurel
Evergreen shrub
Rosaceae (Rose Family)

Native Range. Southeastern Europe and adjacent Asia.

Useful Range. USDA Zones 7a–9a+ and protected sites in Zone 6 with selection of appropriate cultivars (see Cultivars).

Function. Massing, border, hedge, screen.

Size and Habit

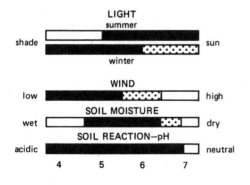

Prunus laurocerasus.

Adaptability. In northern areas, protection from full winter sun and wind is necessary to reduce leaf scorch. Even though this plant grows best with average soil moisture, allowing soil to become drier in late summer and autumn reduces the tendency to grow late and enables the plant to harden properly for winter.

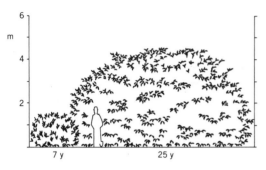

Seasonal Interest. *Flowers:* Small, white, in racemes 5–12 cm/2–5 in. long, in midspring. *Foliage:* Evergreen, lustrous and leathery, bright to deep green, to 15 cm/6 in. long and 4–8 cm/1.6–3.2 in. wide, variable with cultivar. *Fruits:* Green, 0.8 cm/0.3 in. across, ripening purple-black in autumn.

Prunus laurocerasus.

Problems and Maintenance. This species is relatively trouble-free as *Prunus* species go, but is subject to a blight caused by the brown rot fungus that infects many stone fruits and may be infested by white flies and occasionally borers. Pruning may be necessary to control size unless ample space is provided for this wide-ranging plant, but it responds well to pruning, even shearing.

Cultivars. 'Angustifolia' has glossy, deep green leaves to 12 cm/5 in. long but only about 4 cm/1.6 in. wide, and a wide, spreading habit. It remains below eye level for many years.

'Nana' is slower growing than the other cultivars listed and has much smaller leaves, making it preferable for small-scale situations. It is not widely available.

'Otto Luyken' is slow-growing, remaining below 1 m/3.3 ft in height for many years, but spreading laterally to at least 2–3 m/6.6–10 ft.

'Schipkaensis' has been selected for its hardiness. It has deep green, lustrous leaves, slightly smaller than average for the species. It is useful in sheltered sites in Zone 6 as well as in the South, and intermediate in growth rate, reaching a height of 1–1.5 m/3.3–5 ft and width of 2 m/6.6 ft or greater in 5–10 years.

'Salicifolia' and 'Zabeliana,' like 'Angustifolia,' have long, narrow leaves and a low, wide-spreading habit. 'Zabeliana' may be the most widely available of the three.

Related Species

Prunus lusitanica 5−6 (Portuguese laurel). This native of Spain and Portugal is generally similar in appearance and landscape function to *P. laurocerasus* but is more easily trained into tree form and has larger flower clusters, to 25 cm/10 in. long. Useful in Zones 7b−9a+.

Prunus maackii 7

Amur chokecherry
Deciduous tree
Rosaceae (Rose Family)

Native Range. Korea and Manchuria.

Useful Range. USDA Zones 3b−7a and possibly farther south.

Function. Specimen, border, small shade tree.

Size and Habit

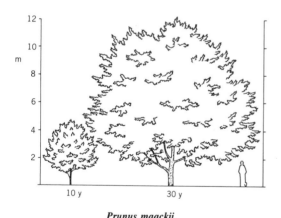

Prunus maackii.

Adaptability

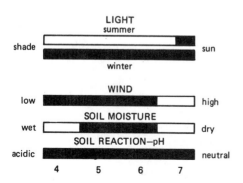

Seasonal Interest. *Flowers:* Small, white, in racemes to 8 cm/3 in. long in middle to late spring. *Foliage:* Medium to bright green, dense but not distinctive, appearing early and falling early with little color change. *Fruits:* Black, inconspicuous. *Trunk and branches:* The bright amber to coppery orange bark curls as it peels off, lending striking winter interest.

Prunus maackii.

Problems and Maintenance. This tree is relatively trouble-free for a cherry in the far North, but more subject to disease and insect problems when used in Zones 6 and 7. It may assume either a single or multiple trunked form and may need initial pruning to ensure that the desired form is taken, but it is relatively free of maintenance thereafter.

Related Species

Prunus padus 7 (European bird cherry).   This Eurasian tree (Europe through northern Asia to Japan) has fragrant white flowers in upright to drooping racemes 10−15 cm/4−6 in. long in middle spring after the leaves have expanded, giving mature trees a distinctive, billowy appearance at this season. The small black cherries are inconspicuous in midsummer, the foliage is not distinctive either in summer or autumn, and the tree has little or no winter interest. Useful in Zones 3b−7b and perhaps farther south as well, but highly susceptible to black knot disease. The variety *commutata* differs little except in leafing out earlier in spring than the species type.

Prunus pensylvanica 7 (pin cherry, wild red cherry).   This native of much of North America from Newfoundland to British Columbia and southward to Colorado and high elevations in North Carolina usually is rather short-lived, and so it is best used in naturalizing or temporary plantings. It is one of the first woody species to return to disturbed sites on poor soil, so there should be increasing use for this purpose (e.g., revegetating road cuts). It is a handsome tree with shiny, mahogany-red bark, small, shiny red cherries in late summer, and bright, yellow-orange to red fall foliage. Useful in Zones 3a−7a and perhaps farther south as well.

Prunus virginiana 6 (chokecherry).   This shrub or small tree native to much of North America from Newfoundland to Saskatchewan and southward to Kansas and North Carolina has little landscape character and is so susceptible to the eastern tent caterpillar that it has been partially eradicated in parts of the northeastern United States to reduce caterpillar infestations. Its tendency to sucker heavily completes the case for eliminating the species type from planting lists. Its fruits are astringent but not bitter and have been used to make preserves and wine. The selection 'Schubert' and, more recently, 'Canada Red,' are of interest as small landscape trees, at least in the Northern Plains. Their leaves emerge pale green but turn red-purple as soon as they are fully expanded, making striking specimens. The objection of suckering habit remains but is overcome by grafting on a nonsuckering rootstock, *P. padus*. These selections are useful in Zones 3a−5a but seldom perform well much farther south and are susceptible to black knot disease.

Prunus persica 6

Peach
Deciduous tree
Rosaceae (Rose Family)

Native Range. China.

Useful Range. USDA Zones 6a−9a.

Function. Patio tree, edible fruits.

Size and Habit

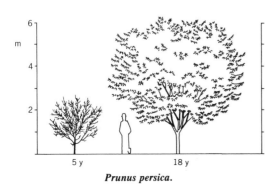

Prunus persica.

Adaptability

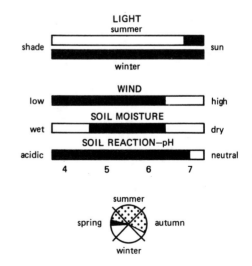

Seasonal Interest. *Flowers:* Pink to red or white, single or double, 2.5−3.5 cm/1−1.4 in. or more across in midspring. *Foliage:* Lustrous, somewhat leathery leaves are long (to 15 cm/6 in.), down-curving, and pointed, giving striking textural effect until they fall with little color change in late autumn. *Fruits:* Aside from their obvious edible value, the yellow-red fruits have some small landscape value. But when edible fruits are not wanted, they may be more a liability than an asset in the landscape, since they litter the ground. Double-flowered cultivars do not bear fruit.

Problems and Maintenance. Peaches are subject to a wide array of insect and disease problems, the most serious of which is borers, which can kill trees in a short time. Peaches, whether for fruit or as an ornamental flowering tree, should be avoided unless a maintenance program is provided, at least for protection against borers. In addition, peach trees and flower buds frequently suffer freezing damage in winter or early spring in much of the useful range and probably are best planted only in the South and in northern areas that are considered suitable for commercial peach production.

Cultivars. A few single-flowering, but mostly double-flowering, ornamental selections have been made, along with a few selections for red or purple foliage and dwarf habit. A list of all selections without regard for possible duplication would be very long, and only a few cultivars are available at any one time or place. Some of the more common cultivars are listed here to illustrate the variety that exists, not to recommend these over others. Select cultivars according to general type, availability, and known performance in the locality in question.

'Alba' has single, white flowers.

'Alboplena' and 'Iceberg' have double, white flowers.

'Atropurpurea' has deep red-purple leaves, changing to bronze, then green during the growing season.

'Bonanza' 'Flory Dwarf' are dwarf fruiting cultivars used primarily as curiosities or specimens for accent rather than as functional landscape plants.

'Cardinal,' 'Early Double Red,' 'Late Double Red' and 'Rubroplena' have double red flowers.

'Peppermint Stick' and 'Versicolor' have double flowers variegated respectively in red-white and pink-white.

'Pink Charming' and 'Roseoplena' have double, pink flowers.

'Rubra' has single, red flowers.

Related Species

Prunus armeniaca 7 (apricot). Although primarily used for fruit production, this tree from western Asia is also occasionally used as a landscape tree. In fact, it is more reliable in northern areas as a landscape tree than for fruiting, since flower buds open so early in spring that they frequently are frozen, preventing fruit set. In southern areas, brown rot disease may be very difficult to control. It is useful in Zones 5b−9a with reservations, but the Japanese apricot (*P. mume*) usually is preferred in the South. Var. *mandshurica* is a smaller tree, to 4−5 m/13−16 ft, cold-hardy, with its fruiting cultivars, to Zone 3b.

Prunus dulcis 6 (synonym: *P. amygdalus*; almond). Several double flowered cultivars of this species have been selected for landscape use, but they are not as commonly used as the flowering peach cultivars and are less cold-hardy, useful in Zones 7a−9a.

Prunus mume 6−7 (Japanese apricot). Single and double flowered selections are occasionally used in Zones 7a−9a but are not nearly as common as the flowering peach cultivars. These trees usually assume greater stature than *P. persica*, sometimes to 8−10 m/26−33 ft.

Prunus sargentii 7−8

Sargent cherry
Deciduous tree
Rosaceae (Rose Family)

Native Range. Japan, Korea, Sakhalin.

Useful Range. USDA Zones 5a−9a, and will grow without reliable flowering in Zone 4b.

Function. Shade tree, specimen.

Size and Habit

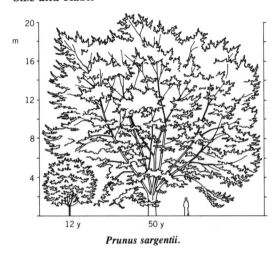

Prunus sargentii.

Adaptability

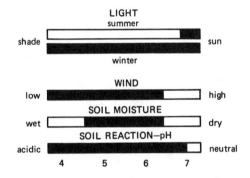

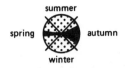

Seasonal Interest. *Flowers:* Single, rose-pink, to 4 cm/1.6 in. across, borne in large numbers before the foliage in midspring. *Foliage:* Reddish as it unfolds, turning deep green in summer and orange-red in autumn. One of the few *Prunus* species with reliable autumn color. *Fruits:* Small, purple-black cherries, inconspicuous. *Trunk and branches:* Bark is deep red-brown and lustrous with prominent horizontal lenticels, handsome in winter.

Problems and Maintenance. This is one of the most trouble-free of the flowering cherries, yet it is occasionally subject to some insect and disease problems, and it sometimes is short-lived. Pruning is seldom if ever necessary, provided enough space is given to this fairly large tree.

Cultivars. 'Columnaris' is distinctly narrower than the species type, with more upright branching. It is not truly columnar but narrowly oval in outline.

Prunus serotina 8

Black, rum, or wild cherry
Deciduous tree
Rosaceae (Rose Family)

Native Range. Eastern United States and adjacent Canada.

Useful Range. USDA Zones 3b–9a.

Function. Shade tree, naturalizing.

Size and Habit

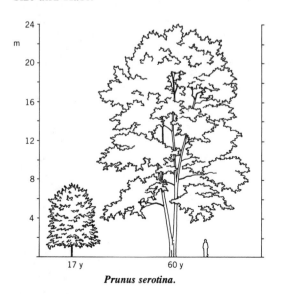

Prunus serotina.

Adaptability

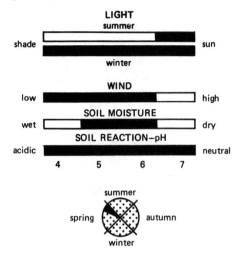

Seasonal Interest. *Flowers:* Small, white, lightly fragrant, in drooping clusters about 12 cm/5 in. long in late spring. *Foliage:* Deep green, slightly leathery leaves, 5−12 cm/2−5 in. long, turning yellowish or orange in autumn in northern areas. *Fruits:* Small cherries, to 1 cm/0.4 in. across, red in midsummer, then ripening black in late summer, slightly bitter but used for wines and preserves. *Trunk and branches:* Lenticular bark, cracking and curling back, adds quiet winter interest.

Problems and Maintenance. This is one of the more trouble-free of the cherries, usually not seriously enough affected by insects and diseases to require corrective spraying, especially in naturalized or parklike situations where this tree is at its best, but it may be seriously damaged by the eastern tent caterpillar and black knot in some areas. The wood is somewhat brittle and susceptible to breakage in ice storms.

Prunus serrulata 6

Oriental cherry, Japanese flowering cherry
Deciduous tree
Rosaceae (Rose Family)

Native Range. China, Japan, Korea.

Useful Range. USDA Zones 6b−8b, some cultivars hardy northward to Zone 6a.

Function. Specimen, patio tree, massing.

Size and Habit. Becomes a large tree, occasionally to 20m/66 ft in its native range but seldom exceeds 6−8 m/20−26 ft in landscape use in our area, since it tends to be short-lived. 'Kwanzan' is illustrated.

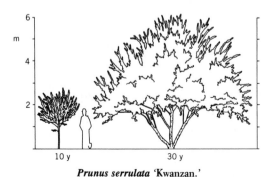

Prunus serrulata 'Kwanzan.'

Adaptability

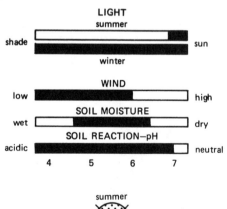

Seasonal Interest. *Flowers:* White or pink, single or double, in certain cultivars fragrant, 4−6 cm/1.6−2.4 in. across in clusters of three to five, extremely showy in midspring. *Foliage:* Leaves are briefly bronze as they unfold, then deep green until they fall in midautumn, rather coarse in texture. *Fruits:* Small, black, inconspicuous. *Trunks and branches:* Bark is deep red-brown, lustrous, with prominent horizontal lenticels, handsome in winter, but not as striking as that of some of the other cherries (e.g., *P. serrula*).

Problems and Maintenance. Like other cherries, this species is affected by many diseases and insects, but most occur only occasionally. For good performance of flowering cherries, it is best to follow a careful maintenance program consisting of necessary spraying and removal and destruction of affected parts. Otherwise pruning is seldom necessary and should be avoided, since it is easy to disfigure these trees by excessive pruning. Several cultivars of this species can be carriers of serious cherry virus diseases without showing symptoms themselves. Trees of this species are seldom long-lived.

Varieties and Cultivars. Var. *hupehensis* is the wild Chinese variety of this species, with small, single, white flowers, seldom if ever available for landscape use.

Var. *lannesiana*, a Japanese wild variety with fragrant flowers, has given rise to cultivars with more showy, fragrant flowers (e.g., 'Amanogawa,' 'Sirotae' and 'Ukon').

Var. *pubescens*, from northern Japan and Korea, is not presently available for landscape use but probably includes forms that could be used to extend the cold hardiness of this species at least into Zone 5.

Var. *serrulata*, considered the "typical" form of the species simply because it was this form to which the species name was first applied, is not a wild variety but rather a collection of cultivars with large, double flowers, mostly not fragrant.

Var. *spontanea* is a wild Japanese variety, probably that from which var. *serrulata* was derived, seldom if ever used in the landscape in our area.

'Amanogawa' is a very narrow-growing form, to about 6 m/20 ft tall and not over 2 m/6.6 ft wide, with light pink, semidouble, fragrant flowers, to 4.5 cm/1.8 in. across.

'Fugenzo' (= 'Kofugen,' = 'James H. Veitch') is a broad-spreading form with very double, unscented pink flowers to 6 cm/2.4 in. across.

'Kwanzan' (='Sekiyama') is by far the most common *P. serrulata* cultivar in landscape use. With unscented, double, pink flowers to 6 cm/2.4 in. across and borne in large numbers, and a stiffly upright, vase-shaped growth habit, it lacks the delicacy usually associated with

Japanese cherries. But for outright showiness it is impressive, and it is more cold-hardy than most other *P. serrulata* cultivars that are presently in use, to Zone 6a and protected sites in Zone 5b.

'Shirofugen' is fast-growing and wide-spreading, with unscented, double flowers, to 6 cm/2.4 in., pink in bud and opening white.

'Shirotae' (= 'Mt. Fuji') has fragrant, pure white, semidouble to double flowers, to 6 cm/2.4 in. across, and a wide-spreading growth habit. Generally acknowledged to be one of the most handsome of the oriental cherries, the Mt. Fuji cherry performs better in the southern parts of our area than in the North, perhaps because of a shorter bud-chilling requirement.

'Shogetsu' is unusually broad and flat-topped, with very double, pale pink flowers to 5 cm/2 in. across.

'Takasago' (synonyms: *P. sieboldii*, 'Sieboldii'; Naden cherry) has bright pink, semidouble flowers to 5 cm/2 in. across and probably is equal to 'Kwanzan' in cold hardiness (to Zone 6a) but is much less common and seldom available for landscape use.

'Ukon' is unusual among flowering cherries for its fragrant, semidouble, pale yellow flowers, to 5 cm/2 in. across, accompanied by bronze unfolding leaves.

Related Species

Prunus yedoensis 6 (Yoshino cherry, Potomac cherry). This and *P. serrulata* are the predominant species in the famous planting of Japanese cherries in the Tidal Basin area of Washington, D.C. *P. yedoensis* is one of the most showy of all cherries in flower, with many fragrant single flowers, about 3 cm/1.2 in. across, opening pale pink, then fading to white. Because it tends to be short-lived, it seldom exceeds heights of about 8 m/26 ft in our area, with somewhat greater spread, but it becomes larger in Japan. Useful in Zones 6a–8b and perhaps also 9a. The botanical status of this tree is not clear, since it is not known in the wild state but only in cultivation. It has been speculated that it may be a hybrid of *P. serrulata* × *P. subhirtella*, but its tendency to breed relatively true from seeds makes this questionable. The selection 'Akebono' (= 'Daybreak') is magnificent in bloom, with soft pink flowers, translucent in overall effect.

Prunus subhirtella 6

Higan cherry
Deciduous tree
Rosaceae (Rose Family)

Native Range. Japan

Useful Range. USDA Zones 6a–8b and some cultivars in Zones 5b, or 9a.

Function. Specimen, patio tree.

Size and Habit

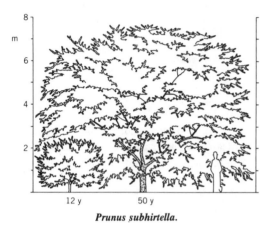

Prunus subhirtella.

Adaptability

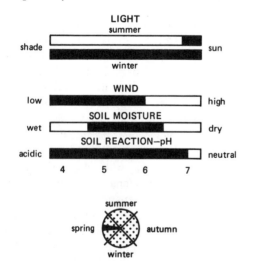

Seasonal Interest. *Flowers:* Pale to deep pink, single or double, about 2.5 cm/1 in. across, giving a loose, airy effect in early to middle spring. *Foliage:* Deep green, falling in autumn

with little color change. *Fruits:* Small, black, inconspicuous. *Trunks and branches:* Bark is deep red-brown with prominent horizontal lenticels, distinctive but not offering the strong winter interest of some other flowering cherries.

Problems and Maintenance. This species is not as seriously affected by diseases and insects as some other Asian cherries, but for good performance, it is best to follow a careful maintenance program (see *P. serrulata*).

Varieties and Cultivars. Var. *ascendens* is a much larger, upright tree with white flowers, seldom if ever available for landscape use.

'Autumnalis' differs little from the species type except that part of its flowers often open during warm periods in autumn, the remainder in spring. The autumn interest derived from this tendency is indisputable, but it may make the remaining flower buds more cold-sensitive, reducing the chances of good spring flowering in northern zones. There is some variation in trees exhibiting this behavior, suggesting that perhaps they should be considered f. *autumnalis* with selection of superior cultivars under new names.

'Pendula' is the commonly grown weeping cherry, widely used in many areas in Zones 6a–8b. It is one of the most graceful of all flowering trees. Since it is rather variable, including even double-flowered forms, perhaps, like 'Autumnalis,' it ought to be given forma status (f. *pendula*), with selection of individual types under new cultivar names, a practice that, in fact, has been started.

Prunus subhirtella 'Pendula.'

'Yae-shidare-higan' (= 'Pendula Plena;' double weeping cherry) has double flowers and a weeping growth habit.

The related cultivar 'Hally Jolivette,' actually a hybrid [*P. subhirtella* × (*P. subhirtella* × *P. yedoensis*)], is a small, shrubby tree, to 3–5 m/10–16 ft tall, upright but loosely graceful in flower, outstanding because its semidouble, pink and white flowers open gradually over about a three week period, giving it a longer flowering period than most flowering cherries. It is also more cold-hardy than its close relatives, useful in Zones 5b–8b, and protected sites in Zone 5a.

Related Species

Prunus campanulata 6 (Taiwan cherry).   This small tree from Japan and Taiwan is outstanding in bloom very early in spring, with white to pink flowers, 2.5 cm/1 in. across, borne in large numbers. It is not an especially functional landscape tree but justifiable for its early flowering interest alone in Zones 8b–9a+.

Prunus nipponica 6 (Nippon cherry).   This rather uncommon tree makes a showy display of single, white or pink flowers in early to middle spring, but its yellow to orange autumn foliage is the feature that distinguishes it from most other cherries. Useful in Zones 6a–8b but seldom if ever available.

Prunus serrula 6 (paperbark cherry).   The principal justification for including this uncommon tree from western China is its lustrous, deep red bark, handsomely marked with large horizontal lenticels. It is so outstanding in this respect that its small white flowers become almost incidental in their landscape interest. Unfortunately, it is not commonly available and is susceptible to some of the most destructive virus diseases. But it is unique for its bark interest and useful in Zones 6a–8a, perhaps in Zone 5 as well.

Prunus serrula.

Prunus tomentosa 5

Nanking or Manchu cherry
Deciduous shrub
Rosaceae (Rose Family)

Native Range. Northeastern Asia to the Himalayas.

Useful Range. USDA Zones 3a–6b, but may suffer serious injury in some years in Zones 5 and 6 from spring freezes following premature activity during warm periods in late winter.

Function. Screen, hedge, border, specimen.

Size and Habit

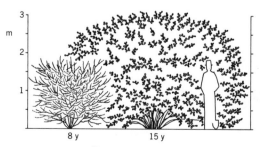

Prunus tomentosa.

Adaptability. One of the best adapted shrubs to the Northern Plains, tolerating extreme cold and considerable wind and dryness.

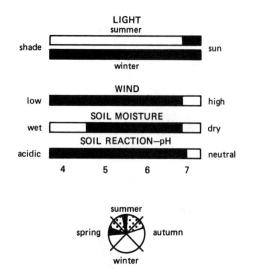

Prunus tomentosa.

Seasonal Interest. *Flowers:* Small but numerous, white or pinkish, in early to middle spring. *Foliage:* Dull, deep green leaves are hairy and wrinkled, giving distinctive texture but no great seasonal interest. *Fruits:* Red cherries are tart but edible in much the same way as those of sour cherry *(P. cerasus)*, in pies and preserves. They tend to be borne in large numbers in alternative years when more than one plant (seedling) is present for cross-pollination. Isolated plants do not always fruit well.

Problems and Maintenance. This shrub is subject to damage by rodents and to many of the diseases and insects of cherries in general, but this does not rule it out in low-maintenance situations, at least in the far North (Zones 3 and 4).

Cultivars. Selections for outstanding flowering and fruiting have been made but are not widely available. One such selection is 'Geneva.'

Related Species

Prunus japonica 4 (Chinese or Japanese bush cherry, Korean cherry).   This hardy shrub from northeastern Asia serves as a smaller edition of *P. tomentosa* in the landscape, with comparable fruiting value, without which it would have little landscape value. It is useful in about the same range as *P. tomentosa* but is seldom available.

Pseudolarix kaempferi 8

Synonyms: *P. amabilis, Chrysolarix amabilis*
Golden larch
Deciduous tree
Pinaceae (Pine Family)

Native Range. Eastern China.

Useful Range. USDA Zones 6a−7b, perhaps sheltered sites in Zone 5, also Zone 8 in moist sites with moderate summer temperatures.

Function. Specimen, screen.

Size and Habit

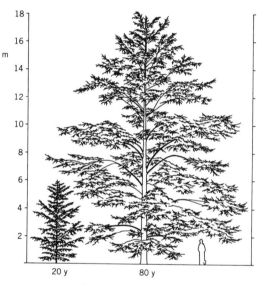

Pseudolarix kaempferi.

Seasonal Interest. *Foliage:* New leaves, flattened needles, to 6 cm/2.4 in. long and 0.3 cm/0.12 in. broad, emerge a delicate light green in middle to late spring, turn a soft medium green in summer, and then, briefly, yellow to russet-gold before falling in middle to late autumn. *Cones:* Yellow-green, ripening red-brown, 5−8 cm/2−3 in. long, borne erect on the upper surfaces of main branches of older trees, composed of fleshy scales that disintegrate on the tree in midautumn. *Branching:* Horizontally spreading to gracefully descending main branches and somewhat pendulous side branches add interest at all seasons.

Pseudolarix kaempferi.

Adaptability

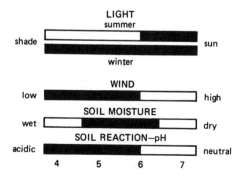

Problems and Maintenance. This is one of the most trouble-free of all trees given proper site and soil conditions. It seldom requires even pruning provided it has ample space in which to grow and assume its graceful form.

Pseudotsuga menziesii 8

Synonyms: *P. douglasii, P. taxifolia*
Douglas fir
Evergreen tree
Pinaceae (Pine Family)

Native Range. Western United States and adjacent Canada and Mexico.

Useful Range. USDA Zones 3b–6b with selection of appropriate genetic material, and Zone 7, perhaps even Zone 8, in areas with moderate summer temperatures.

Function. Screen, specimen.

Size and Habit

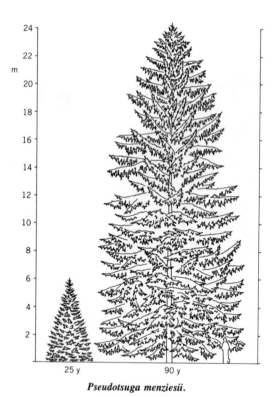

Pseudotsuga menziesii.

Adaptability. Trees from Rocky Mountain seed sources probably tolerate wind and high soil pH better than Pacific Coast types.

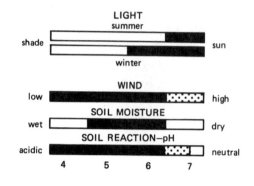

Seasonal Interest. *Foliage:* Deep green or slightly blue-green needles, 2–3 cm/0.8–1.2 in. long and slightly flattened, form a dense mass, handsome in all seasons. *Cones:* Medium brown, 5–10 cm/2–4 in. long, with distinctive forked bracts protruding from between scales.

Problems and Maintenance. Several diseases and insects can be troublesome, but not enough to require control measures except in occasional cases of severe outbreaks. Maintenance requirements are much the same as for spruces (*Picea* species).

Varieties and Cultivars. Var. *glauca* is generally considered to include the Rocky Mountain forms, which are generally slower-growing, with a heavier waxy layer on the needles, hence more bluish green, and more tolerant of cold and probably wind than the typical coastal form. This variety and its selections are most common in landscape use in our area. Several dwarf and slow-growing cultivars have been selected, mostly in Europe, but few are available for landscape use in our area.

Ptelea trifoliata 6

Wafer ash, hop tree
Deciduous shrub or small tree
Rutaceae (Rue Family)

Native Range. New York to Minnesota, south to Florida and Texas.

Useful Range. USDA Zones 4a–9a, with selection of appropriate genetic material.

Function. Border, patio tree, naturalizing.

Size and Habit

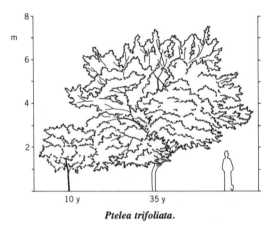

Ptelea trifoliata.

Adaptability

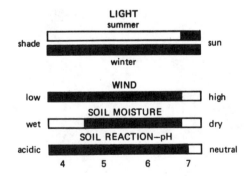

Seasonal Interest. *Flowers:* Male and female flowers occur on the same tree, small, greenish white, inconspicuous. *Foliage:* Bright to deep green, trifoliate leaves are aromatic when crushed, fall without color change in midautumn. *Fruits:* Thin, waferlike, winged fruits, to 2.5 cm/1 in. across, are pale yellowish green, adding quiet interest from late summer through autumn and into winter in some areas.

Ptelea trifoliata.

Problems and Maintenance. This is one of the most trouble-free small trees, some compensation for its lack of striking seasonal interest, but occasionally it is infected with a leaf-spot disease, especially in warm, moist climates. It may require initial training when used in tree form, but needs little maintenance thereafter except to control occasional insect infestations.

Pterocarya fraxinifolia 8

Caucasian wing nut
Deciduous tree
Juglandaceae (Walnut Family)

Native Range. Caucasus to Iran.

Useful Range. USDA Zones 6a−9a, and possibly some sites in Zone 5, but little-tried.

Function. Shade tree and street tree, but only where sufficient space is available.

Size and Habit

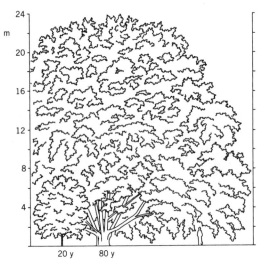

Pterocarya fraxinifolia.

Adaptability

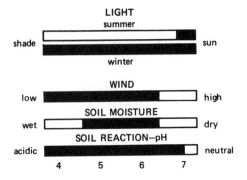

Seasonal Interest. *Flowers:* Male and female catkins occur on the same tree and are inconspicuous. *Foliage:* Rich, deep green, compound leaves, 20−40 cm/8−16 in. long, of 11−19 leaflets with moderately coarse texture, remaining deep green until they fall in late autumn. *Fruits:* Winged nutlets, borne in pendulous chains to 40 cm/16 in. long, add light green contrast to deep green foliage in summer.

Problems and Maintenance. This tree seems to be generally trouble-free, but it is so infrequently used that there has been little opportunity to observe potential disease problems. Pruning is necessary only to remove any damaged wood and for size control in situations where space limitations should have deterred planting.

Related Species

Pterocarya ×rehderana 8 (Rehder wingnut). This hybrid (*P. fraxinifolia* × *P. stenoptera*) differs little from *P. fraxinifolia* except in having a winged leaf axis (rachis). It is generally believed to be slightly more cold-hardy and vigorous than *P. fraxinifolia*, but the difference, if any, is small. It can be considered equivalent to *P. fraxinifolia* as a landscape tree in Zones 6a−9a, but neither is widely available.

Pterocarya ×rehderana.

Pterocarya stenoptera 8 (Chinese wingnut). This Chinese counterpart differs very little functionally from the above species, except that it is somewhat less cold-hardy. It is useful in Zones 7a−9a, perhaps also in Zone 6b, but is almost never available.

Pterostyrax hispidus 7

Epaulette tree
Deciduous tree
Styracaceae (Styrax Family)

Native Range. Japan.

Useful Range. USDA Zones 6a—9a+.

Function. Specimen, patio tree.

Size and Habit

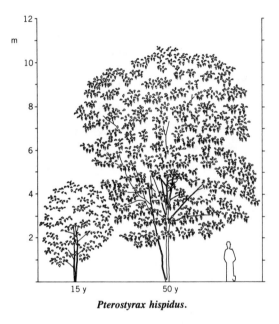

Pterostyrax hispidus.

Seasonal Interest. *Flowers:* Fragrant, creamy white, in pendulous, fringelike panicles, to 20 cm/8 in. long, in late spring or early summer. *Foliage:* Light green leaves give a rather coarse effect and fall with little color change in midautumn. *Fruits:* Small dry fruits are bristly and hang on after leaves fall but add little additional landscape interest.

Problems and Maintenance. This tree seems to be relatively trouble-free but is so little used that there has not been much opportunity to observe potential disease and insect problems. Pruning is not necessary other than to remove dead and damaged wood. It is seldom available commercially, but it is a distinctive tree that might be used more widely, especially in the South.

Related Species

Pterostyrax corymbosus 6 (shrubby epaulette tree). This shrubby species is smaller than *P. hispidus* but can be trained into a very small tree, to 3—5 m/10—16 ft. Its flower clusters are somewhat smaller (to about 10—12 cm/4—5 in. long), and it may be slightly less cold-hardy. It is useful at least in Zones 7b—9a+ but is less likely to be available than *P. hispidus.*

Adaptability

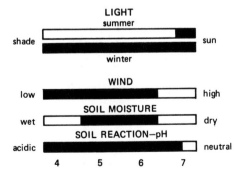

Pueraria lobata 1 and 3

Synonym: *P. thunbergiana*
Kudzu vine
Deciduous vine
Leguminosae (Pea Family)

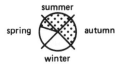

Native Range. China and Japan.

Useful Range. USDA Zones 6b−9a+, killing back to the ground and returning from the roots in most winters in Zones 6b−7b and frequently in Zone 8.

Function. Screen (with support), twining loosely, climbing to heights of 15 m/50 ft in mild climates; large-scale groundcover for erosion control. Since it grows extremely rapidly, it has attracted some interest in revegetation of strip-mined areas.

Seasonal Interest. *Flowers:* Violet-purple, pealike, in upright clusters to 25 cm/10 in. long in late summer in zones where winter dieback is not complete. *Foliage:* Compound, with three leaflets, the largest (central) to 18 cm/7 in. long, medium to light green and hairy, borne on coarse, heavy, loosely twining stems.

Pueraria lobata.

Size and Habit

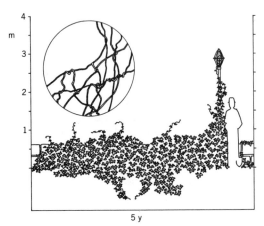

Pueraria lobata.

Adaptability

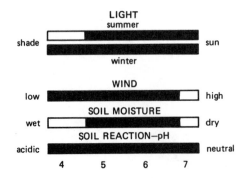

Problems and Maintenance. Trouble-free but itself a problem because of its rampant growth, Kudzu vine should only be planted in large-scale situations where other plants will not function as well. In some areas of the South, this plant has covered acres of land, climbing over utility poles and lines, trees, and anything else standing in its way.

Punica granatum 6

Pomegranate
Deciduous shrub
Punicaceae (Pomegranate Family)

Native Range. Southeastern Europe to the Himalayas.

Useful Range. USDA Zones 7b–9a+.

Function. Hedge, specimen, border.

Size and Habit

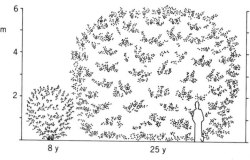

Punica granatum.

Adaptability. This is one of the most successful shrubs in hot, dry sites and calcareous soils, but not in poorly drained soils.

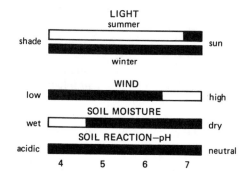

Seasonal Interest. *Flowers:* Scarlet, yellow, or white, single or double, to 3 cm/1.2 in. across from late spring to early summer. *Foliage:* Deciduous but glossy and somewhat leathery leaves, reddish as they unfold, then bright green, 2.5–8 cm/1–3 in. long, borne on stiff, somewhat spiny branches, falling in autumn with little color change. *Fruits:* Domelike, deep yellow, burnished red-orange, scarlet, or purplish red, 5–8 cm/2–3 in. across, rather dry, with tart, edible, red seeds, the whole fruit colorful in autumn.

Problems and Maintenance. One of the most trouble-free shrubs, pomegranate requires practically no care other than occasional pruning for shaping if it is to be used as an informal hedge.

Cultivars. 'Alba Plena' (= 'Multiplex') has creamy white, double flowers but no fruits. 'Chico' is low-growing, usually only to 2 m/6.6 ft, with bright orange-red, double flowers over the entire summer but no fruiting interest. 'Flavescens' has single, yellow flowers, but seldom is available commercially. 'Nana' is a dwarf, seldom exceeding 1 m/3.3 ft in ultimate height, with considerably smaller leaves, flowers, and fruits than the species type. This is a very popular and useful landscape plant, especially for small-scale situations. 'Wonderful' is a full-size plant selected for outstanding fruit production.

Pyracantha coccinea 4–5

Scarlet firethorn
Semievergreen or evergreen shrub
Rosaceae (Rose Family)

Native Range. Southern Europe and western Asia.

Useful Range. USDA Zones 6a–9a and a few cultivars in Zone 5 as well.

Function. Border, wall shrub (espalier), foundation, hedge.

Size and Habit. Most cultivars remain below eye level in the North but grow taller in the South, some to 4 m/13 ft or taller if given espalier training.

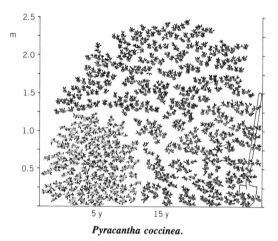

Pyracantha coccinea.

Adaptability. Planting in sites with good air circulation helps to control diseases in the South, but strong winds, especially in winter, should be avoided in the northern extremes of its useful range.

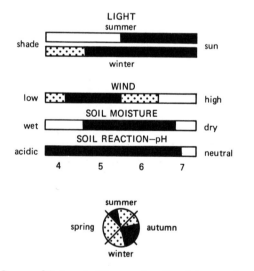

Seasonal Interest. *Flowers:* Small, white, in clusters, effective against the new foliage in early summer. *Foliage:* Rich green leaves are variable in size and shape, up to 4 cm/1.6 in. long and rather narrow, semievergreen in the North (Zones 6 and 7), evergreen in the South (Zones 8 and 9). *Fruits:* Bright orange, red-orange, or yellow, about 0.6 cm/0.25 in. across, borne in large numbers in good sites and showy from early autumn into early winter, depending on cultivar. *Branching:* Stiffly irregular branching pattern is

interesting and lends well to training in a vertical plane (espalier), especially against a south-facing wall.

Problems and Maintenance. Several insects and diseases occasionally are troublesome but can be controlled. The most consistent problems are fire blight, difficult to control when weather conditions are favorable, and scab, which can disfigure fruits during prolonged moist periods, especially in sites with poor air circulation. Cultivars vary in their resistance to these diseases. Aphids, lace bugs, mites, and scale insects are occasionally troublesome.

Cultivars and Hybrids. 'Government Red' is a popular, red-fruited selection with handsome large leaves and red berries. There is some question about the species parentage of this cultivar, which is useful in Zones 7a–9a+.

'Kasan' has rather compact growth habit (but not dwarf) and orange fruits and has proved to be among the most cold-hardy *Pyracantha* cultivars, useful in Zones 5b–9a and sheltered sites in Zone 5a.

'Lalandei' is the most common cultivar in northern landscapes, having been in use for many years. Its fruits are deep orange, and it has considerable vigor. It is useful in Zones 5b–9a. 'Lalandei Thornless' differs little from 'Lalandei' except that it is less thorny and easier to use in public areas where people may brush against it.

'Lowboy,' as the name suggests, is low-growing but wide-spreading, with bright orange fruits. Useful in Zones 7a–9a+.

'Monrovia' is a vigorous, upright form with bright orange fruits and excellent foliage. Useful in Zones 6a–9a+.

'Teton' is a recent introduction by the U.S. National Arboretum, with strikingly upright growth habit, bright orange fruits, and high resistance to fire blight. It reaches heights of up to 4 m/13 ft, presumably deriving its vigor from its hybrid parentage with larger growing species: *P. fortuneana* and *P. rogersiana*. Useful in Zones 6b–9a+ but not fully evergreen in Zone 6b.

'Watereri' is a hybrid (*P. coccinea* 'Lalandei' × *P. crenulata*) with full growth habit, excellent foliage, and bright red fruits. Generally believed to be the most cold-hardy red-fruited *Pyracantha* cultivar, it is useful in Zones 7a–9a+.

'Wyattii' is another selection for hardiness, wide-spreading growth habit, and orange fruiting interest, useful in Zones 6a–9a.

Pyracantha koidzumii 5

Synonym: *P. formosana*
Formosa firethorn
Evergreen shrub
Rosaceae (Rose Family)

Native Range. Taiwan.

Useful Range. USDA Zones 7b−9a+.

Function. Screen, wall shrub (espalier), hedge, specimen.

Size and Habit

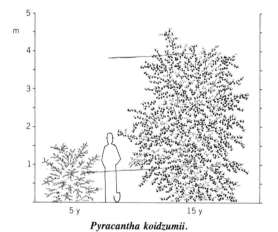

Pyracantha koidzumii.

Adaptability. Planting in breezy sites helps control diseases by reducing air stagnation.

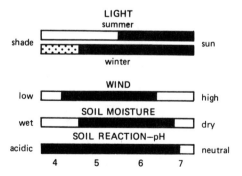

Seasonal Interest. *Flowers:* Small, white, in clusters, effective against the deep green foliage in late spring. *Foliage:* Rich, deep green leaves are similar to those of *P. coccinea* except more distinctly rounded on the end, evergreen except when occasionally winterburned in the northern extremes of its useful range. *Fruits:* Orange-red to deep red, about 0.6 cm/0.25 in. across, borne

in very large numbers in good sites, and showy from early autumn well into winter.

Problems and Maintenance. Troubles are generally similar to those of *P. coccinea* and other *Pyracantha* species. Fire blight is the most serious problem, although less so than on *P. coccinea*. It can be partly controlled by removing and burning new infections as soon as they appear, but it is difficult to control fully during severe outbreaks. Selection of resistant cultivars is a more satisfactory solution. Scab frequently disfigures the fruits, especially in sites with poor air circulation and in wet seasons.

Cultivars and Hybrids. 'Mohave' is a hybrid of *P. koidzumii* × *P. coccinea* selected at the U.S. National Arboretum for vigor and resistance to both scab disease and fire blight. It has deep orange-red fruits, lasting well into midwinter, and heavy evergreen or nearly evergreen foliage. It is useful in Zones 6b−9a+.

'Red Elf' is a recent selection for dwarf growth habit, reaching about 0.5−1 m/1.6−3.3 ft in height. It has intensely red fruits and small leaves and is useful in Zones 7b−9a+.

'San Jose' is a wide-spreading hybrid selection, probably *P. koidzumii* × *P. fortuneana*, with bright red fruits. Useful in Zones 7b−9a+.

'Santa Cruz' (= 'Santa Cruz Prostrate') is a very low, spreading, almost prostrate selection, seldom exceeding 1 m/3.3 ft in height, with strong red fruiting interest. Useful in Zones 7b−9a+.

'Shawnee,' introduced by the U.S. National Arboretum, was selected as a seedling from 'San Jose.' It has a spectacular show of yellow fruits from late summer until late winter, semievergreen foliage, large and dense growth habit, and is resistant to both scab and fire blight and useful in Zones 7b−9a+.

'Tiny Tim' (Plant Patent No. 2684, 1966) was selected for dwarf growth habit, remaining below 1 m/3.3 ft in height with light annual pruning. It has rich green foliage and bright red fruits and is useful in Zones 7b−9a+.

'Victory' is a fast-growing selection for large

masses of deep red fruits and good foliage and is useful in Zones 7b−9a+.

'Walderi' (= 'Walderi Prostrata') is a low-growing, wide-spreading form with red fruits, useful in Zones 7b−9a+.

Related Species

Pyracantha angustifolia 5 (narrow-leaved firethorn). This native of southwestern China differs from *P. koidzumii* primarily in having narrow leaves, usually bristle-tipped or notched, and rather large (0.8 cm/0.3 in.), red-orange fruits, persistent through most of the winter. It is useful in Zones 7b−9a. The selection 'Gnome' is dwarf and dense in growth habit, remaining below 1 m/3.3 ft for several years and probably not exceeding 2 m/6.6 ft in ultimate height. More cold-hardy than the species type, it is useful in Zones 6a−9a. The selection 'Variegata,' with variegated foliage, is perhaps not available under this name, but may be similar or identical to 'Harlequin,' which is available. This cultivar has creamy white variegated leaves, taking on a pink winter color in some areas, and is useful in Zones 8a−9a+ and perhaps also in Zone 7.

Pyracantha atalantioides 6 (Gibbs firethorn). The red fruits of this large-growing (to 5−6

m/16−20 ft) native of China persist longer than those of *P. koidzumii*, often through the entire winter. Useful in Zones 7b−9a+. The selection 'Aurea' has golden-yellow fruits.

Pyracantha crenulata 6 (Nepal firethorn). This large-growing species, to 5−6 m/16−20 ft tall, is of interest primarily as a parent of hybrids, although a few cultivars have been selected. *P. rogersiana*, once classified as *P. crenulata* var. *rogersiana*, is of greater interest.

Pyracantha fortuneana 5 (synonyms: *P. crenatoserrata*, *P. yunnanensis*; Chinese firethorn). This native of western China has remotely sawtoothed leaves and is very vigorous and heay-fruiting, with red berries. The selections 'Graberi' and 'Rosedale' are outstanding for vigor and heavy fruiting. Fruits of 'Rosedale' turn red earlier than those of most *Pyracantha* cultivars, in late summer. Both cultivars are useful in Zones 7b−9a+, perhaps also in Zone 7a.

Pyracantha rogersiana 5 (synonym: *P. crenulata* var. *rogersiana*; Rogers firethorn). The leaves of this native of southwestern China are among the smallest of any firethorn, exposing the relatively large (0.8 cm/0.3 in.), red-orange fruits fully. Useful in Zones 7b−9a+, perhaps also Zone 7a. The selection 'Flava' has yellow fruit.

Pyrus calleryana 7

Callery pear
Deciduous tree
Rosaceae (Rose Family)

Native Range. China.

Useful Range. USDA Zones 5a−9a.

Function. Small shade, street, or patio tree.

Size and Habit. 'Bradford' is illustrated.

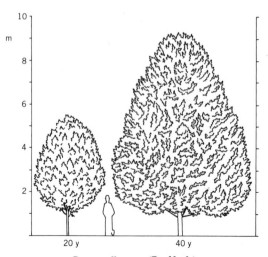

Pyrus calleryana 'Bradford.'

Adaptability

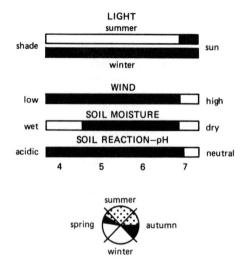

Seasonal Interest. *Flowers:* White, in clusters, beginning in midspring before the foliage. *Foliage:* Lustrous and leathery, unfolding pale green, turning deep green when fully expanded, then mahogany-red and sometimes finally bright orange-red in late autumn after foliage of many other trees has fallen. *Fruits:* Round, brown, only about 1 cm/0.4 in. across, insignificant either as litter or landscape interest.

Problems and Maintenance. Unusually trouble-free for a pear, *P. calleryana* is highly resistant (although not immune) to fire blight. Other disease and insect problems are minor. In some areas in some years, flower buds become activated during warm periods in early spring and are then damaged by freezes.

Cultivars. 'Aristocrat' (Plant Patent No. 3193, 1972) is vigorous, faster-growing in height, and somewhat less dense than 'Bradford.' After a limited time in use, its disease resistance seems to be high, but its most distinctive feature is its handsome, leathery leaves with crinkled edges, turning deep red in late autumn.

'Bradford,' the first selection of *P. calleryana*, was introduced by the U.S. Plant Introduction Station, Glenn Dale, Maryland. It is unusually symmetrical and compact, with handsome, dense foliage, coloring well in late autumn. When used by itself, this largely self-sterile clone bears very few fruits and is valued as a city street tree.

'Chanticleer' (= 'Select;' Plant Patent No. 2489, 1965) is similar to 'Bradford' in its symmetry and denseness, but more narrow in outline and apparently more cold-hardy in early tests.

Newer selections of *P. calleryana* are available but have yet to be fully evaluated.

Related Species

Pyrus fauriei 6 (synonym: *P. calleryana* var. *fauriei;* Korean Callery pear) is a round-headed tree to only about 5m/16 ft tall but to 6m/20 ft broad. Useful in Zones 5a−8b, perhaps also 9a.

Pyrus ussuriensis 7 (Ussuri pear). This tree from northeastern Asia (Manchuria and eastern Siberia) is the only *Pyrus* species found fully cold-hardy at the Agriculture Canada research station at Morden, Manitoba. Like *P. calleryana*, it has considerable resistance to fire blight. Its fruits are larger than those of *P. calleryana*, but only 4 cm/1.6 in. across, not posing as much of a litter problem as those of most pears. Because of its extreme hardiness, it may have a place as a small shade tree in northern parts of our area. Useful in Zones 3b−6b, perhaps farther south.

Quercus acuta 7

Japanese evergreen oak
Evergreen tree
Fagaceae (Beech Family)

Native Range. China, Japan, Korea.

Useful Range. USDA Zones 8b−9a+, and at least certain sites in Zone 8a.

Function. Small shade tree, specimen, screen.

Size and Habit

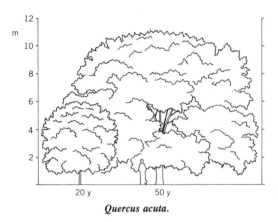

Quercus acuta.

Adaptability

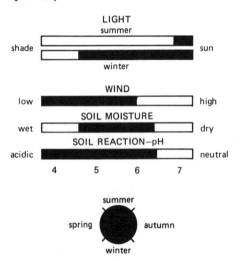

Seasonal Interest. *Flowers:* Small and inconspicuous. *Foliage:* Evergreen, leathery, olive green, gray-green underneath, 10−12 cm/4−5 in. long, not lobed or toothed, but with wavy margins, making a dense canopy year-round. *Fruits:* Small acorns add little landscape interest or litter.

Quercus acuta.

Problems and Maintenance. There is reason to suspect that several diseases and insects of oaks in general affect this species under some conditions, but experience is so limited that such problems have not been evaluated adequately. Experience to date has been favorable. *Q. acuta* is not yet generally available.

Related Species

Quercus glauca 7 (blue Japanese oak). This tree from China, Japan and Taiwan is generally similar to *Q. acuta* and sometimes confused with it. The leaves of *Q. glauca* are more bluish green and lightly toothed above the middle. The useful range of *Q. glauca* is similar to that of *Q. acuta*, and the two might be considered interchangeable for most landscape situations given the present state of knowledge.

Quercus glauca.

Quercus glauca.

Quercus acutissima 7

Sawtooth oak
Deciduous tree
Fagaceae (Beech Family)

Native Range. China, Japan, and Korea.

Useful Range. USDA Zones 6a−9a, possibly also Zone 5 with selection of hardy genetic material. Trees of undetermined geographic origin have survived in Zone 5b for up to 15 years, only to be devastated by occasional severe winters.

Function. Shade tree, specimen.

Size and Habit

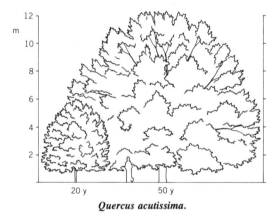

Quercus acutissima.

Adaptability

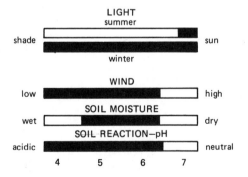

Seasonal Interest. *Flowers:* Small and inconspicuous. *Foliage:* Toothed leaves, resembling those of chestnut, pale green as they unfold, expanding and remaining deep green and lustrous well into autumn, then drying light brown and persisting, sometimes until midwinter. *Fruits:* Small acorns add little landscape interest or litter.

Problems and Maintenance. Disease and pest problems are relatively minor, requiring attention only in intensive situations or where outbreaks are severe. Pruning is needed only for removal of any deadwood.

Related Species

Quercus cerris 8 (Turkey oak). This large, Eurasian tree has relatively small leaves, 5−12 cm/2−5 in. long, with small, bristle-tipped lobes, themselves toothed. Useful in Zones 7a−9a, perhaps also Zone 6a with selection of hardy genetic material, but seldom available for use in our area.

Quercus cerris.

Quercus variabilis 8 (oriental oak). This tree, native to the same region as *Q. acutissima* and closely related to it, has chestnutlike foliage and corky bark, of minor landscape interest. It is useful in about the same range as *Q. acutissima* and functions as a larger version of that species but is less likely to be commercially available.

Quercus alba 8

White oak
Deciduous tree
Fagaceae (Beech Family)

Native Range. Eastern United States from Maine and Minnesota southward to Florida and Texas.

Useful Range. USDA Zones 4b–9a.

Function. Shade tree, specimen, naturalizing.

Size and Habit

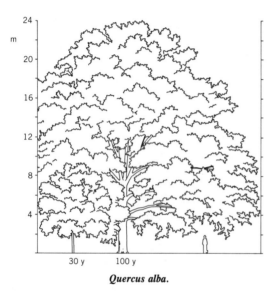

Quercus alba.

Adaptability

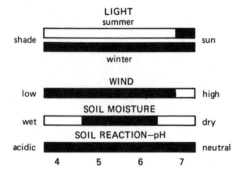

Seasonal Interest. *Flowers:* Small, pale greenish yellow catkins are interesting along with newly expanding leaves in spring. *Foliage:* Dull, deep green leaves with rounded lobes turn purplish in middle to late autumn before falling. *Fruits:* Relatively small acorns are borne in great num-

bers in some years but add little landscape interest and pose a litter problem. *Trunks and branches:* Rugged framework of massive branches and light colored, slightly shaggy bark make this a majestic and interesting tree in all seasons.

Problems and Maintenance. Disease and pest problems are minor, requiring attention only when severe outbreaks occur. *Q. alba* is resistant to oak wilt, a serious disease in the Midwest. Pruning is needed only for removal of any deadwood. The most serious limitation to acceptance is its slow growth, but this can be hastened somewhat by early attention to fertilization and irrigation during prolonged drought, and it is compensated for by the tree's longevity. Even when not planted, *Q. alba* should receive high priority for protection during site development, since it is highly sensitive to disturbance.

Related Species

Quercus bicolor 8 (swamp white oak). This tree has much of the character of *Q. alba* but is more tolerant of wet soil and slightly more cold-hardy, useful in Zones 4a–8b.

Quercus bicolor.

Quercus falcata 8

Southern red oak, Spanish oak
Deciduous tree
Fagaceae (Beech Family)

Native Range. Southern and south-central United States.

Useful Range. USDA Zones 6b–9a.

Function. Shade tree, specimen, naturalizing.

Size and Habit

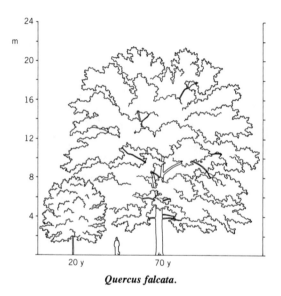

Quercus falcata.

Adaptability

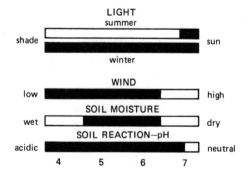

Seasonal Interest. *Flowers:* Yellow-green catkins add interest to newly expanding foliage in middle spring. *Foliage:* Deeply cut leaves with narrow, bristle-tipped lobes, often curved (falcate), lustrous, deep green, not forming a dense mass of foliage but allowing light penetration, turning orange-russet to red-orange in autumn. *Fruits:* Small acorns add little landscape interest or litter.

Problems and Maintenance. Problems such as oak galls are minor, requiring attention only when severe outbreaks occur. Pruning is seldom needed, only for removing any deadwood. Transplanting is easier than for *Q. alba* or *Q. coccinea*, for example, and this species should receive high priority for preservation during site development.

Varieties. Var. *pagodifolia* (cherrybark or swamp Spanish oak) differs from the species type in having more evenly lobed leaves and bark vaguely resembling that of *Prunus serotina* (black cherry). It is much more tolerant of wet soil than the species type and most other oaks.

Related Species

Quercus marilandica 7 (blackjack oak). This relatively small tree, usually not over 8–10 m/26–33 ft tall, is irregularly and narrowly upright. Its leaves are irregularly club-shaped in outline, leading to its common name. Native to the southeastern United States, it is worth preserving in development and of value for planting in very poor, dry soils where few other trees will perform well. It is useful in Zones 5b–9a with selection of appropriate genetic material.

Quercus imbricaria 8

Shingle oak
Deciduous tree
Fagaceae (Beech Family)

Native Range. East-central United States from Pennsylvania to Nebraska and south to Georgia and Arkansas.

Useful Range. USDA Zones 5a–9a and perhaps certain sites in Zone 4b with selection of hardiest genetic material.

Function. Shade tree, specimen, naturalizing, screen (as a hedge).

Seasonal Interest. *Flowers:* Pale yellow-green catkins add interest to newly-expanding foliage in middle spring. *Foliage:* Leaves are neither lobed nor toothed, but dark green and leathery, 8–16 cm/3–6 in. long and 2.5–4 cm/1–1.6 in. wide, drying a warm tan color in late autumn and usually persisting past midwinter. *Fruits:* Small acorns add little landscape interest or litter.

Size and Habit

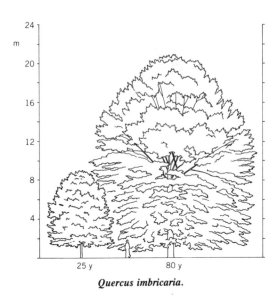

Quercus imbricaria.

Adaptability. This tree is more tolerant of calcareous, neutral, or slightly alkaline soil than *Q. palustris*, which it resembles in form and function (although not in foliage character).

Quercus imbricaria.

Problems and Maintenance. Problems such as oak galls are minor, requiring attention only when severe outbreaks occur. Pruning is needed only for removing any deadwood and gradually removing lower branches when necessary to allow access underneath. Since foliage falls gradually in late winter, there is a slight, continuing litter problem.

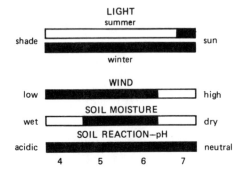

Quercus macrocarpa 8

Bur oak, mossycup oak
Deciduous tree
Fagaceae (Beech Family)

Native Range. Northeastern North America from Nova Scotia to Manitoba and southward to Texas.

Useful Range. USDA Zones 3a−9a with selection of appropriate genetic material.

Function. Shade tree, specimen.

Size and Habit

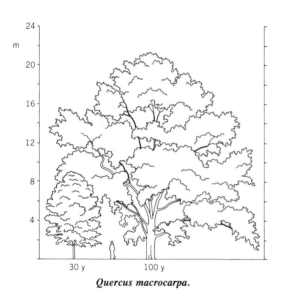

Quercus macrocarpa.

Adaptability. This is one of few trees that are well adapted to the Northern Plains. It is and was native to the prairies and is presumably able to tolerate periodic fires because of its heavy bark.

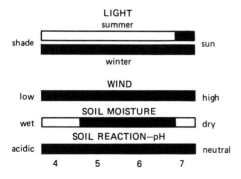

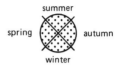

Seasonal Interest. *Flowers:* Small, pale yellowish catkins add minor interest along with newly expanding leaves of the same color. *Foliage:* Deeply round-lobed leaves turn deep green and leathery when fully expanded, grayish underneath with a felt of fine hairs, falling in autumn without color change. *Fruits:* The large acorns, to 3.5 cm/1.4 in., are about half covered by the heavy cup. *Trunks and branches:* The bark is unusually thick, heavily furrowed on the trunk, and irregularly ridged on the branches, giving the framework a massive appearance in winter.

Quercus macrocarpa.

Problems and Maintenance. Problems, most commonly oak galls, are minor, requiring attention only when severe outbreaks occur. Pruning is seldom necessary. Principal limitation to use is slow growth and difficulty in transplanting.

Related Species

Quercus lyrata 8 (overcup oak, swamp post oak). This close relative of *Q. macrocarpa*, native to the southeastern states and northward to New Jersey and Missouri, functions as a large shade tree with large acorns, to 2.5 cm/1 in. long, usually almost completely covered by the cup, hence the common name. It seldom is planted but is worthy of greater use and certainly is worth preserving in site development. It has the reputation of being more tolerant of wet soil than either *Q. macrocarpa* or *Q. stellata*, yet usually grows wild in well-drained sites. Useful in Zones 6a−9a with selection of appropriate genetic material.

Quercus stellata 7−8 (post oak). This wide-ranging tree from Massachusetts and Florida west to Nebraska and Texas is seldom planted but worthy of preservation in site development. Foliage is dark green, forming a densely rounded canopy. Useful in Zones 6a−9a.

Quercus nigra 8

Synonym: *Q. aquatica*
Water oak
Semievergreen tree
Fagaceae (Beech Family)

Native Range. Southeastern United States.

Useful Range. USDA Zones 6b−9a+.

Function. Shade and street tree, specimen.

Size and Habit

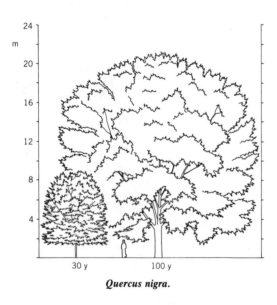

Quercus nigra.

Adaptability. Even though tolerant of wet or poorly drained soils, *Q. nigra* does best on well-drained soils in landscape situations.

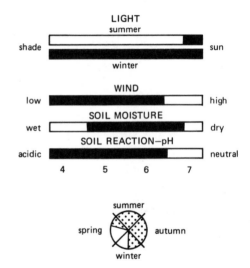

Seasonal Interest. *Flowers:* Small, pale yellowish green catkins add minor landscape interest along with newly expanding foliage. *Foliage:* Pale green at first, then deep to olive green, leaves varying in shape from unlobed to remotely three-lobed to occasionally strongly lobed, persisting well into winter in the Deep South before falling with little color change. *Fruits:* Small acorns add little seasonal interest and minimal litter.

Problems and Maintenance. This tree is subject to several disease and insect problems including galls, leaf spots, scale insects, and borers. Mistletoe infestations sometimes are severe enough to damage host trees of *Q. nigra*. This species is softer-wooded and more prone to storm damage than most oaks, perhaps a by-product of its rapid growth. All things considered, it is not as maintenance-free as its wide use suggests. Therefore, other species such as *Q. ilex*, *Q. imbricaria*, *Q. phellos* and *Q. virginiana* should be considered as possible alternative street trees in the Deep South.

Related Species

Quercus laurifolia 8 (laurel oak). This native of the southeastern states is widely used in the southeastern Coastal Plain as a fast growing shade or street tree. But it is relatively weak-wooded and short-lived as compared with most other oaks. Its lustrous, narrow leaves are not quite evergreen, persisting through much of the winter. Useful in Zones 8a−9a+ and in some sites in Zone 7b.

Quercus palustris 8

Pin oak
Deciduous tree
Fagaceae (Beech Family)

Native Range. Northeastern to central United States.

Useful Range. USDA Zones 5a−8b and some sites in Zones 4b−9a.

Function. Shade tree, specimen.

Size and Habit

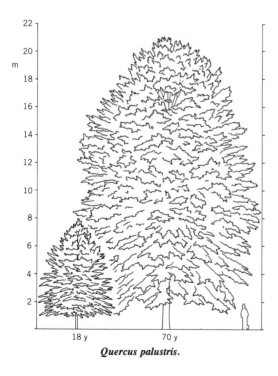

Quercus palustris.

Adaptability. *Q. palustris* is strikingly intolerant of neutral or calcareous soils, developing chlorosis (foliar yellowing) because of insufficient iron uptake.

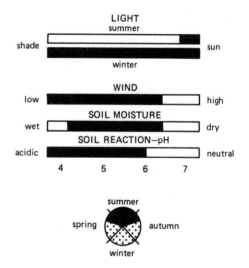

Seasonal Interest. *Flowers:* Pale yellow-green catkins add interest to newly expanding foliage in midspring. *Foliage:* Leaves are about 10 cm/4 in. long, deeply incised, with narrow, bristled lobes, giving a rather fine texture. They are yellow-green as they expand, then deep green and lustrous in proper soil, yellowing or bronzing slightly before drying a warm tan color in late autumn, some of the leaves usually persisting into winter. *Fruits:* Small acorns add little seasonal interest but may produce considerable litter in heavy fruiting years. *Trunk and branches:* Striking form with drooping to ascending branches and often mastlike trunk add interest even in winter.

Problems and Maintenance. Most insect and disease problems are not serious, and this is one of the easiest oaks to transplant. The greatest maintenance problem is that of correcting iron chlorosis in trees planted on calcareous soil. This usually can be done with some success through foliar sprays of soluble iron, but it requires repeated applications over the years. A better solution is to substitute other trees when soil conditions are not favorable for pin oak. Other oaks with more or less similar branching and general functional effect include *Q. imbricaria* and *Q. phellos*. These differ in foliage character but, like the pin oak, do not form a dense canopy that interferes with turfgrass growth underneath.

Cultivars. 'Sovereign' (Plant Patent No. 2662, 1966) is a selection for outstanding vigor, form, and foliage. Some initial difficulties, perhaps related to unsuccessful matching of grafting un-

derstock material, have been experienced. When these have been fully overcome, this cultivar will probably serve as a uniform superior form of pin oak. Since there is considerable interest in pin oaks in the landscape industry, other selections are appearing.

Related Species

Quercus ellipsoidalis 8 (northern pin oak). This northern counterpart of *Q. palustris*, native from the northern lake states to Manitoba, resembles *Q. palustris* and extends the useful range of this form northward to Zone 3b. Presumably the two species can be used interchangeably in Zones 5–6. *Q. palustris* is the preferred species in Zones 7 and 8 and probably will be used in preference to *Q. ellipsoidalis* in most areas because it is more widely available and easier to transplant.

Quercus phellos 7–8

Willow oak
Deciduous tree
Fagaceae (Beech Family)

Native Range. Eastern and central United States.

Useful Range. USDA Zones 6a–9a.

Function. Shade and street tree, naturalizing.

Size and Habit

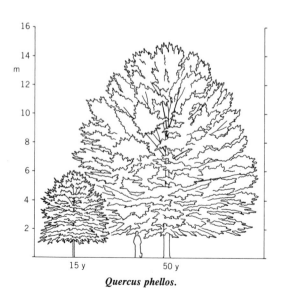

Quercus phellos.

Adaptability

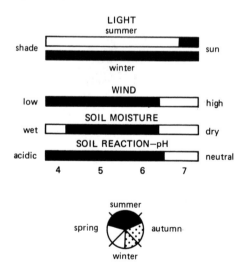

Seasonal Interest. *Flowers:* Pale yellow-green catkins add interest in midspring along with the newly expanding leaves. *Foliage:* Leaves are very narrow, almost willowlike, 5–10 cm/2–4 in. long and seldom over 1 cm/0.4 in. wide, yellow-green as they emerge in spring, then remaining bright green through summer, turning dull yellow to reddish in midautumn and persisting well into winter in the Deep South. *Fruits:* Small acorns add little landscape interest or litter.

Trunk and branches: Form is reminiscent of the pin oak, making the tree mildly interesting even while not in leaf.

Problems and Maintenance. Most insect and disease problems are not serious, and this is one of the easiest oaks to transplant. Maintenance is minimal, but the pendulous lower branches, like those of the pin oak, may have to be removed in small-scale situations to accommodate pedestrian traffic. This changes the landscape character of the tree and should be done carefully to avoid disfiguring it.

Quercus prinus 8

Synonym: *Q. montana*
Chestnut oak
Deciduous tree
Fagaceae (Beech Family)

Native Range. Eastern United States from Maine to Alabama.

Useful Range. USDA Zones 5a–9a.

Function. Shade tree, specimen, naturalizing.

Size and Habit

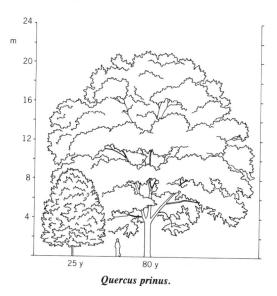

Quercus prinus.

Adaptability. This is one of the best oaks for use on dry soils.

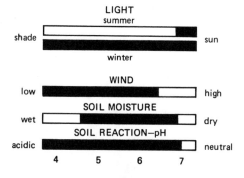

Seasonal Interest. *Flowers:* Pale green catkins add interest in midspring along with newly expanding foliage. *Foliage:* Leaves, 12–17 cm/5–7 in. long, shallowly round-lobed or round-toothed, vaguely resembling those of chestnuts, pale green as they unfold, turning and remaining dark green through summer and early autumn, then turning red-orange to golden brown before falling. *Fruits:* Relatively large acorns add only slight seasonal interest in early autumn and can pose a mild litter problem in some years. *Trunk and branches:* Bark is dark gray-brown and heavily ridged, adding slight additional interest.

Quercus prinus.

Problems and Maintenance. Most disease and insect problems are not usually serious and seldom require attention except in small-scale situations. This tree is more likely to be encountered as a subject for potential preservation in site development than it is to be planted. It is somewhat difficult to transplant and not widely available commercially.

Related Species

Quercus michauxii 8 (synonym: *Q. prinus*, but not to be confused with true *Q. prinus*, chestnut oak; basket oak, swamp chestnut oak). This native of central and southern parts of the eastern United States from Delaware to Missouri and Texas with foliage similar to that of chestnut oak is little used as a landscape tree and seldom available. Nevertheless, it is a beautiful, round-headed shade tree when grown in the open and should receive high priority for preservation in site development. When planted, it performs best in fairly moist soil and will tolerate occasionally wet soil. Useful in Zones 6b−9a.

Quercus mongolica 7−8 (Mongolian oak). This rare tree has been used experimentally in Minnesota and Manitoba and promises to be a very cold-hardy, small shade tree for the Northern Plains, somewhat resembling a smaller edition of *Q. macrocarpa* but with foliage more similar to that of *Q. prinus* or *Q. muehlenbergii*. It may take a number of years for this tree to become available commercially in any quantity, but it is presumably potentially useful in Zones 3a−5b and perhaps in warmer areas as well.

Quercus muehlenbergii 8 (Chinquapin oak, yellow chestnut oak). This native of much of the United States from the Northeast to the Midwest and as far southwest as Texas and New Mexico is seldom available for planting but definitely worth preserving in site development. It has foliage

Quercus muehlenbergii.

much like that of *Q. prinus* and is as adaptable to dry soil as that species but with a more narrow, vase-shaped growth habit. This species is more tolerant of neutral, calcareous soils than most oaks but is less desirable than several others where soils are acidic. Useful in Zones 5a−8b and perhaps 9a with selection of appropriate genetic material.

Quercus robur 7−8

English oak
Deciduous tree
Fagaceae (Beech Family)

Native Range. Europe, northern Africa, and western Asia.

Useful Range. USDA Zones 5b−9a with selection of appropriate genetic material (see Problems and Maintenance).

Function. Shade tree, specimen.

Size and Habit

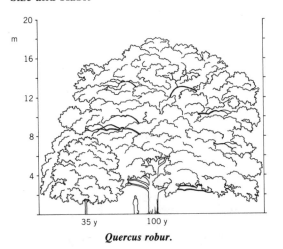

Quercus robur.

Adaptability

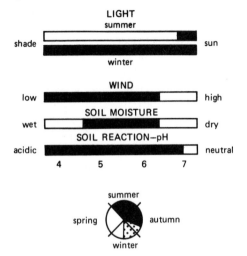

Seasonal Interest. *Flowers:* Small, pale yellowish green catkins add minor landscape interest along with newly expanding leaves. *Foliage:* Leaves are small, 5–12 cm/2–5 in. long, evenly round-lobed, giving uniform texture. They unfold pale green, turning to olive green or deep green in summer, and remain deep green long into autumn, finally drying a light brown color and persisting well into winter. *Fruits:* Elongated acorns, about 1–1.5 cm/0.4–0.6 in. across and 1.5–2.5 cm/0.6–1 in. long, hanging singly or in groups of as many as five on one long pendulous stalk, adding slight landscape interest in late summer and early autumn.

Problems and Maintenance. Disease and insect problems are not usually serious, but powdery mildew disfigures the foliage in warm, humid climates. Cold hardiness is precarious and probably depends on selection of genetically hardy stock, which is not available except through local experience. *Q. robur* seems to be a good example of imperfect adaptation, since mature trees in Zones 5 and 6 have been known to be killed outright by an occasional severe winter. And it appears that this species is not particularly well adapted to the hot, dry summers of our Zones 7, 8 and 9, even though it thrives in such zones in Europe. Best adaptation is to coastal areas and sites located on the east sides of the Great Lakes in Zones 6a–8b.

Cultivars. 'Fastigiata' is the only selection of much interest in our area. With columnar to narrowly pyramidal growth habit, it is an excellent choice where vertical accent is needed, with a greater degree of permanence than can be expected from the columnar poplars. Since this form comes largely true-to-type when propagated by seed, it perhaps should be considered to be var. *fastigiata* rather than a cultivar. Useful in Zones 5b–9a, but severe injury has been sustained in occasional winters in some sites in Zones 5b and 6a, and it is susceptible to powdery mildew where summers are humid, in all zones.

Quercus rubra 8

Synonyms: *Q. borealis*, *Q. borealis* var. *maxima*
Northern red oak
Deciduous tree
Fagaceae (Beech Family)

Native Range. Eastern North America from Nova Scotia to Minnesota, Kansas, and Georgia.

Useful Range. USDA Zones 3b–9a, with selection of appropriate genetic material.

Function. Shade and street tree, naturalizing.

Size and Habit

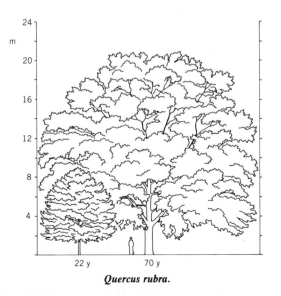

Quercus rubra.

Adaptability. *Q. rubra* is one of the best oaks for city street planting, out-performing many other tree species in relatively small soil volumes.

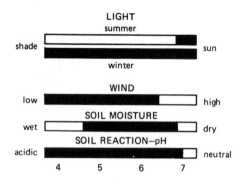

LIGHT
summer
shade ▭ sun
winter

WIND
low ▭ high

SOIL MOISTURE
wet ▭ dry

SOIL REACTION—pH
acidic ▭ neutral
4   5   6   7

summer
spring — autumn
winter

Seasonal Interest. *Flowers:* Pale yellow-green catkins add interest along with newly expanding foliage in midspring. *Foliage:* Relatively large leaves, 12−20 cm/5−8 in. long with broad, bristle-tipped lobes, pale green as they unfold, then a rich, deep lustrous green in summer, turning deep to bright red in midautumn. *Fruits:* Rather large acorns are borne in great quantities in some years. They add little landscape interest and pose a litter problem.

Problems and Maintenance. Most disease and insect problems are minor, but one, oak-wilt disease, has proved lethal to trees of *Q. rubra* and other species in the red oak group in certain parts of the Midwest. It was thought at one time that this disease might become more widespread, and this may yet happen, but its spread has so far been moderate where measures have been taken to reduce it, including prompt removal and destruction of infested trees, control of insects that can serve as vectors, and delaying pruning until summer to reduce spreading on pruning tools during the most active season for the disease, when the tree growth is also most active. In areas where oak-wilt has not developed, *Q. rubra* remains a popular and serviceable shade and street tree. Transplanting *Q. rubra* is not difficult when compared with many other oaks.

Related Species

Quercus velutina 8 (black oak).   This native of much of our area is seldom available commercially, probably because it is considered difficult to transplant. It is among the most susceptible species to oak-wilt disease but is worth preserving in site development. It is often untidy in appearance because it holds dead branches for a long time, but it performs somewhat better than *Q. rubra* in dry, sandy soils. Its glossy, dark green foliage is handsome in summer and turns red in autumn. Useful in Zones 4b−9a, with selection of appropriate genetic material.

Quercus shumardii 8

Shumard oak
Deciduous tree
Fagaceae (Beech Family)

Native Range. Southeastern and south-central United States: North Carolina and Florida west-

ward to Texas and Kansas, northward to Michigan.

Useful Range. USDA Zones 6a−9a.

Function. Shade tree, specimen, naturalizing.

Size and Habit

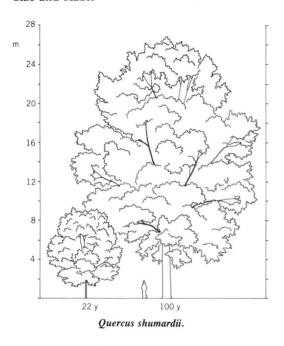

Quercus shumardii.

Adaptability

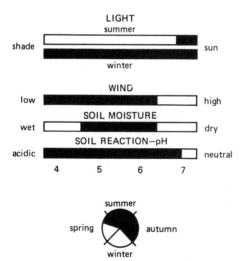

Seasonal Interest. *Flowers:* Pale yellow-green catkins add substantial interest along with newly expanding foliage in midspring. *Foliage:* Relatively large leaves, 8–18 cm/3–7 in. long with wide-spreading, bristle-tipped lobes, pale green as they unfold, then deep, glossy green in summer, turning bright red in midautumn. *Fruits:* Medium-size acorns provide little landscape interest and only a minor litter problem.

Problems and Maintenance. Disease and insect problems are minor, making this one of the more trouble-free oaks, although it remains to be seen whether oak-wilt disease will become serious in this species. *Q. shumardii* is about as easy to transplant as *Q. palustris* and *Q. rubra*, considerably easier than *Q. coccinea* and *Q. velutina.*

Related Species

Quercus coccinea 8 (scarlet oak). This fine tree, native to much of our area, would be far more commonly used if it were not considered very difficult to transplant. Nevertheless, some landscape nurserymen and contractors are moving scarlet oaks successfully. *Q. coccinea* resembles *Q. rubra* in general growth habit and *Q. palustris* in foliage texture and is more reliably colorful in autumn, with maroon to brilliant scarlet foliage. It grows best in somewhat acidic soil but is not as sensitive to limestone as *Q. palustris* is. Useful in Zones 5a–9a with selection of appropriate genetic material.

Quercus coccinea.

Quercus virginiana 8

Live oak
Evergreen tree
Fagaceae (Beech Family)

Native Range. Southeastern United States and Mexico.

Useful Range. USDA Zones 8b−9a+, and without full development in Zones 7b and 8a (see Problems and Maintenance).

Function. Shade tree, specimen (where plenty of space is available).

Size and Habit

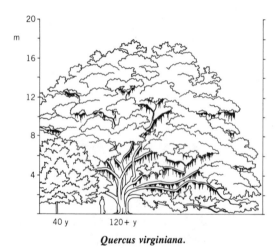

Quercus virginiana.

Adaptability

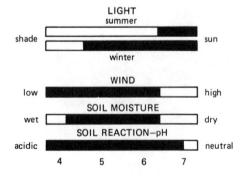

Seasonal Interest. *Flowers:* Yellow-green catkins add substantial interest in early to middle spring, just as new leaves begin to emerge. *Foliage:* Evergreen in Zones 8 and 9, but not always fully evergreen in Zone 7; unlobed new leaves emerge pale yellow-green in midspring and change to lustrous dark green when they fully expand to 5−10 cm/2−4 in. long. Old leaves begin to yellow and fall as new leaves expand and mature. *Fruits:* Acorns, about 2.5 cm/1 in. long, borne in clusters of one to five on long stalks, add minor landscape interest in late summer and autumn. *Trunk and branches:* Massive horizontal limbs give old trees a uniquely majestic character. In most sites in Zones 8b−9a+, limbs are draped with large quantities of the epiphytic Spanish moss. Full development is reliable only from Zone 8b southward, where ice storm damage is negligible (see Problems and Maintenance).

Problems and Maintenance. Live oak, like longleaf pine, generally tolerates cold extremes northward to Zone 7b but occasionally is severely damaged by ice storms in Zones 7b and 8a. The northern limits of its useful range depend on whether full development is necessary to fulfill the intended function. Most insect and disease problems usually are not serious enough to require attention, but stem cankers can occasionally be really troublesome, and stress-related dieback can occur on old specimens in dry years, with dry soil or with limited soil volume. Pruning is seldom needed other than to remove deadwood or as an adjunct to transplanting, which is not especially difficult if care is used, even for fairly large specimens.

Varieties. Even though varieties and cultivars are not recognized, much variation in size, growth rate, and form exists in different habitat sites. This dictates caution in selection but also offers opportunity for selection of distinct types.

Related Species

Quercus ilex 7 (Holm oak, holly oak). This native of southern Europe has long been a favorite shade tree in much of Europe but has not been much used in the southeastern United States, presumably because of the hot, dry summers. In areas with sufficiently mild, moist summers, it probably would be useful in Zone 9a, perhaps also in Zone 8. Further trial is justifiable on the chance that this excellent evergreen tree might be adaptable to our area. Its leaves, with lustrous, dark green upper surfaces and white-felted undersides, are only 2.5−8 cm/1−3 in. long and remotely toothed, and its growth habit is rounded, not exceeding 15−18 m/50−60 ft in height and less than that in spread for many years.

Quercus suber 7 (cork oak).   The bark of this tree is the source of commercial cork, and plantings have been made in the southeastern United States for this purpose. *Q. suber*, a Mediterranean native, has grown at least reasonably well in the southeastern United States as far north as Maryland. This tree is comparable in size to *Q. ilex*, the evergreen leaves are similar in size to those of *Q. virginiana*, and the heavy corky bark is a landscape asset as well. Useful in Zones 7b−9a+.

Quercus ilex.

Raphiolepis indica 3

Indian raphiolepis, Indian hawthorn
Evergeen shrub
Rosaceae (Rose Family)

Native Range. Southern China.

Useful Range. USDA Zones 8a−9a+, and sheltered sites in Zone 7b.

Function. Specimen, border, massing. Effective for accent against architectural materials.

Size and Habit

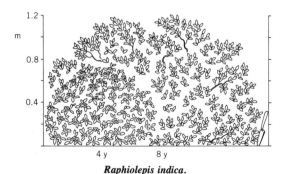

Raphiolepis indica.

Adaptability. Tolerates coastal salt spray and wind.

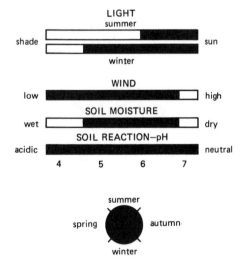

Seasonal Interest. *Flowers:* Fragrant, white or pink, to 2 cm/0.8 in. across, in loose clusters to 8 cm/3 in. across in middle spring, with or just before the new foliage. *Foliage:* Evergreen, deep green, and stiff, leathery leaves, about 5 cm/2 in. long, loosely arranged and turning purplish in full sun in winter. *Fruits:* Blue-black, about 1 cm/0.4 in. across, interesting but not showy in autumn. *Branching:* Twisting irregularly and picturesquely, giving a mildly striking accent.

Problems and Maintenance. Nematodes can be a problem in some areas. When this happens, it is necessary to fumigate and replant with nematode-free stock or other nematode-resistant species. Scale insects and a twig blight occasionally are troublesome but not major problems. Pruning is not necessary and should be avoided, except for removal of deadwood, so as not to interfere with the natural character of the plant.

Cultivars. Several outstanding cultivars have been selected over the past few decades, expanding the list considerably. Some of the most common are listed here.

'Bill Evans' has bright pink flowers and medium plant size.

'Enchantress' has bright rose-pink flowers in large numbers over a relatively long flowering season, glossy green foliage, and compact growth habit.

'Fascination' (Plant Patent No. 2644, 1966) has leathery foliage and bicolored flowers, pink with white centers, and relatively dense foliage.

'Flamingo' has light salmon-pink flowers and medium plant size.

'Jack Evans' has double pink flowers and compact growth habit.

'Pink Cloud' has deep rose-pink flowers in large numbers over a long flowering season and glossy foliage.

'Rosea' is the first cultivar selected for pink flowers, still widely used.

'Snow White' has pure white flowers in large quantities, bright, light green foliage, not pur-

pling in winter, and a relatively low, spreading growth habit.

'Springtime' has clear, light pink flowers in large numbers and graceful growth habit.

Related Species

Raphiolepis ×*delacourii* 4.   This hybrid group (*R. indica* × *R. umbellata*) is occasionally used in place of either parent, and some of the available cultivars may actually belong to this group, members of which are intermediate between the parents in size and landscape character, usually with more or less pink flowers.

Raphiolepis umbellata 4 (synonyms: *R. japonica*, *R. ovata*; Yedda hawthorn).   This native of Japan and Korea differs little from the Chinese *R. indica* except in size. It is more vigorously upright and can become sparse at the base in time, requiring smaller facing shrubs for basal cover in border situations. For this reason, it has gradually become less popular than *R. indica*. Its leaves are somewhat broader and its flowers are most commonly white and as fragrant as those of *R. indica*. It is useful in Zones 8a−9a+.

Raphiolepis umbellata.

Rhamnus frangula 6

Alder buckthorn
Deciduous shrub
Rhamnaceae (Buckthorn Family)

Native Range. Europe, western Asia, North Africa, naturalized in the eastern United States.

Useful Range. USDA Zones 4b−8a.

Function. Hedge, screen, border.

Size and Habit. 'Columnaris' is illustrated.

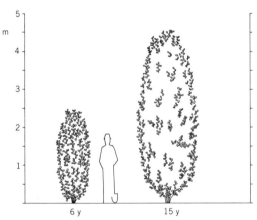

Rhamnus frangula 'Columnaris.'

Adaptability

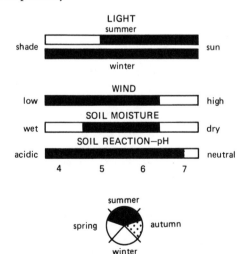

Seasonal Interest. *Flowers:* Very small, whitish yellow, inconspicuous. *Foliage:* Lustrous, rich deep green, pale green underneath, 3−8 cm/1−3 in. long, neatly textured, turning yellowish before falling in late autumn. *Fruits:* Red in midsummer, soon turning purplish black, about 0.6 cm/0.24 in. across, persisting into autumn. *Branches:* Dark gray bark marked with small white lenticels, inconspicuous but interesting at close range.

Problems and Maintenance. *R. frangula* is usually considered relatively trouble-free, but at least in some parts of the Midwest leaf-spot disease, possibly complicated by a twig blight, reduces the effectiveness of the narrow cultivar 'Columnaris' as a visual screen. Pruning may be necessary under some conditions to promote sufficient fullness for screening. The tendency of this species to spread spontaneously by seed propagation makes it a potential weed in some areas. *Rhamnus* species are prohibited in many areas where oats are grown, especially in Canada (see Related Species, *R. cathartica*).

Cultivars. 'Asplenifolia' is a relatively slow-growing form with very fine-textured, almost fernlike foliage. Leaves are about as long as those of the species type, but usually less than 0.5 cm/0.2 in. wide with wavy margins. This makes a fine specimen for accent against architectural material: stone, stucco, gravel mulch, and so forth, in formal and small-scale landscape situations, although plants probably will reach a height and spread of at least 2 m/6.6 ft in time. This specimen plant presently is seldom available but is worth introducing more generally into landscape use in the northern parts of our area.

'Columnaris' (tallhedge buckthorn) is by far

Rhamnus frangula 'Asplenifolia.'

the most common buckthorn in landscape use, valued for its narrowly upright growth habit and used primarily as a visual screen where lateral space is limited. Because of an apparent disease problem (see Problems and Maintenance), it is difficult in some areas to maintain foliage density toward the bottom of the plant, and lower facing plants or opaque fences must be used in combination for full visual screening. It is useful in Zones 4b–8a.

Related Species

Rhamnus caroliniana 6 (Carolina buckthorn, Indian cherry).   This large shrub or small tree is native over much of the eastern United States, north to New York and Nebraska and south to Florida and Texas. It is seldom if ever available commercially but worth preserving as a native plant in some situations. Its rather narrow leaves, to 15 cm/6 in. long and usually less than 2.5 cm/1 in. wide, are lustrous and bright green and its fruits are slightly larger and more colorful in the red stage than those of *R. frangula*. It is useful primarily for naturalizing in Zones 6b–9a, and in some sites in Zones 5b and 6a where native plants exist and can be used or preserved.

Rhamnus cathartica 6 (common buckthorn). This rather trouble-free, large, Eurasian shrub or small tree, like *R. frangula*, has become naturalized in the northeastern United States. It has very dark green leaves with prominent curved veins, dark gray bark, and black fruit borne in great numbers, but it has little other seasonal interest and is used primarily for hedges and informal screens (with some pruning to promote fullness). Since it is the alternate host to the crown rust disease of oats, it should be avoided or eradicated in areas where oats are grown. This and other *Rhamnus* species are prohibited by quarantine laws from many areas where oats are grown, especially in Canada. Moreover, *R. cathartica* is fully as likely to escape cultivation and become a weed as *R. frangula*. Useful, when these limitations do not prohibit it, in Zones 3b–6b.

Rhamnus davurica 6 (Dahurian buckthorn). This large shrub or small tree from north-central and northeastern Asia has light olive green leaves, to 10 cm/4 in. long, and form and fruiting similar to that of *R. cathartica*. It is unusually cold-hardy, useful in Zones 3a–6b, but seldom commercially available.

Rhamnus pallasii 4.   This native of western Asia has dark green leaves only about 2.5 cm/1 in. long and less than half as wide and is extremely cold-hardy, useful in Zones 3a–6b, but planted only experimentally in the Northern Plains, where it could become a popular, medium-size shrub if it were more widely available.

Rhododendron bakeri 3–5

Synonyms: *Azalea bakeri, R. cumberlandense*
Cumberland azalea
Deciduous shrub
Ericaceae (Heath Family)

Native Range. Appalachian Plateau, West Virginia to Alabama.

Useful Range. USDA Zones 5b–8b, probably also some sites in Zone 5a with selection of appropriate genetic material.

Function. Specimen, border, naturalizing.

Size and Habit. Height varies widely among seedlings, from about 1 m/3.3 ft or less to nearly 3 m/10 ft.

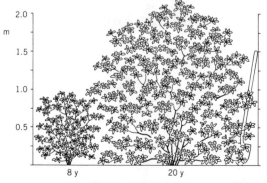

Rhododendron bakeri.

Adaptability. Light shade in summer is beneficial in the South and Midwest, especially to reduce fading in red-flowered cultivars. Shade provided by tall pine trees in the South is near-optimal.

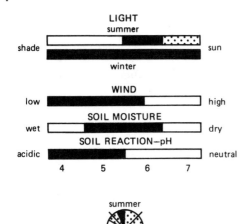

Seasonal Interest. *Flowers:* Red, orange-red, and through intermediate shades to yellow, in early summer, usually at least two weeks later than *R. calendulaceum.* Flowers are about 4 cm/1.6 in. across but are borne in large clusters, striking against the fully developed background foliage. *Foliage:* Medium green, falling in autumn with little color change.

Problems and Maintenance. This azalea apparently is as trouble-free as *R. calendulaceum* and requires little intensive care, but it has not yet been widely used, and more will be known about maintenance requirements in the future.

Cultivars. 'Camp's Red' is a selection for deep, rich red flower color and intermediate growth habit, probably size group 4.

Related Species

Rhododendron prunifolium 5 (synonym: *Azalea prunifolia;* plumleaf azalea). This native of southwestern Georgia and adjacent Alabama resembles *R. bakeri* except in its greater stature, and has forms with bright red flowers as well as intermediates to yellow that flower in midsummer and are useful in Zones 6b−9a.

Rhododendron calendulaceum 5

Synonym: *Azalea calendulacea*
Flame azalea
Deciduous shrub
Ericaceae (Heath Family)

Native Range. Mountains of eastern United States from Pennsylvania to Georgia.

Useful Range. USDA Zones 5a−8b.

Function. Specimen, border, naturalizing.

Size and Habit

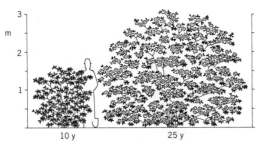

Rhododendron calendulaceum.

Adaptability. Light shade in summer is beneficial in the South and Midwest, especially to reduce fading in red-flowered cultivars. Shade provided by tall pine trees in the South is near-optimal.

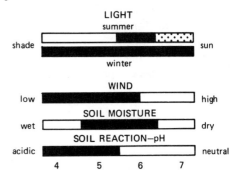

Seasonal Interest. *Flowers:* Yellow through orange to scarlet, not fragrant, to 5 cm/2 in. across, in very showy clusters with the immature foliage very late in spring. *Foliage:* Deep green, slightly lustrous, displayed to good effect by the

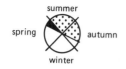

tiered branching pattern, falling in autumn with little color change. *Fruits:* Dried capsules, inconspicuous.

Rhododendron calendulaceum.

Problems and Maintenance. Several diseases and insects occasionally damage the foliage of *R. calendulaceum,* but these are minor and occasional problems. Pruning is not necessary and should be avoided, since the form of most azaleas is more likely to be destroyed than improved by pruning. Where space is limited, there are many other smaller-growing azaleas that can be used in preference to large types such as *R. calendulaceum.*

Cultivars. Even though many cultivars are hybrids of *R. calendulaceum,* few selections have been made directly from the wild species. Those that have been (e.g., f. *aurantium* and 'Croceum') have been more or less replaced by hardy hybrid cultivars and probably are no longer available.

Hybrids

Ghent Hybrids (R. ×gandavense). This large hybrid group has resulted from crosses among members of older hybrid groups: the Mortier Hybrids, involving *R. calendulaceum, R. luteum* (synonym: *R. flavum*), and *R. periclymenoides* (synonym: *R. nudiflorum);* the Ornatum Hybrids, involving *R. flammeum* (synonym: *R. speciosum), R. luteum, R. periclymenoides* and *R. viscosum;* and the Viscosepalum Hybrids,

which involved *R. flammeum, R. molle* and *R. viscosum.*

Most cultivars included in the Ghent Hybrids are useful in Zones 6b−7b. Many are cold-hardy northward to Zone 5b as well. Only a few seem to be heat-tolerant enough for Zone 8. At least 300 cultivars are included in this group, and selection should be based on local experience and availability. A few of the most common cultivars are listed here. All are among the best-adapted to cold climates (Zone 6); some are exceptionally cold-hardy.

'Altaclarensis' has single white flowers with an orange blotch. This is not to be confused with another clone sometimes sold under this name but having yellow flowers, probably a Molle Hybrid.

'Beaute Celeste' (= 'Cardinal') has fragrant, small, single, orange-red flowers.

'Charlemagne' has large, single, dull-orange flowers.

'Daviesii' has very large (to 5.5 cm/2.2 in. across), single, pale yellow flowers, opening late and finally fading to white. It is one of the most cold-hardy cultivars in this group, and at the same time is heat tolerant well into Zone 8.

'Fanny' (= 'Pucella' or 'Pucelle') is also unusually cold-hardy, with very large single purplish pink flowers, opening late.

'Flamboyant' has large flowers, red-orange and yellow, very showy and late-flowering in this group.

'Gloria Mundi' is unusually cold-hardy with very large, single, bright orange flowers, slightly frilled.

'Ignaeum Novum' has very large, single, orange and red-orange flowers and unusual cold hardiness in this group.

'Minerva' has very large, red flowers, opening late.

'Narcissiflorum' has fragrant, double, yellow flowers, opening late and remaining colorful for a relatively long period of time. It is unusually cold-hardy and heat-tolerant to Zone 8 as well.

'Pallas' has very large, single, orange-red flowers with a yellow-orange blotch and is unusually cold-hardy.

'Unique' has large, single, yellow-orange flowers that open late. It is unusually cold-hardy.

Knap Hill Hybrids. This is another large, complex hybrid group, made up of four subgroups: the original Knap Hill Hybrids, the Slocock (or Goldsworth) Hybrids, the Exbury Hybrids, and the Ilam Hybrids. The Ilam Hybrids have been developed in New Zealand, the others in England. They have been produced by crossing members of the Ghent and Molle Hybrid groups and their parents, and in some cases *R. occidentale*, the western azalea. Because of their large flowers (5−8 cm/2−3 in. across) in large clusters (up to 20 to 30 flowers in a cluster) and hardiness generally comparable with that of the Ghent Hybrids, cultivars in this group have been accepted increasingly since their introduction following World War II and now probably constitute the most important group of deciduous azaleas for the northern parts of our area, excepting the very coldest regions (Zones 3 and 4). Frequently, seedlings from Knap Hill Hybrids are offered for sale with the expected variation in color and other characteristics. Even though the quality of such progeny is variable, many of them are very acceptable as landscape plants. A few of the more popular cultivars in this large hybrid group are listed below. Selection should not be limited to those included here and should be based on local experience and availability.

'Balzac' (Exbury) has fragrant, orange-red flowers.

'Berry Rose' (Exbury) has fragrant, orange-blotched, rose-red flowers.

'Brazil' (Exbury) has brilliant, deep orange flowers.

'Brightstraw' (Exbury) has deep yellow flowers.

'Cecile' (Exbury) has salmon-pink flowers with a yellow blotch.

'Fawley' (Exbury) has white, pink-flushed flowers.

'Fireglow' (Slocock) has deep orange flowers.

'Gibraltar' (Exbury) has bright orange flowers.

'Golden Dream' (Exbury) has golden yellow flowers.

'Golden Eagle' (Knap Hill) has bright orange flowers.

'Golden Oriole' (Knap Hill) has light yellow flowers with a deep orange blotch.

'Klondyke' (Exbury) has golden yellow flowers with an orange blotch.

'Satan' (Slocock) has brilliant scarlet flowers.

'Scarlet Pimpernel' (Exbury) has bright red flowers.

'Seville' (Slocock) has bright orange flowers.

'Sun Chariot' (Exbury) has exceptionally large (9 cm/3.5 in. across), bright, golden yellow flowers.

'Whitethroat' (Knap Hill) has pure white flowers.

Related Species

Rhododendron austrinum 5 (synonym: *Azalea austrina*; Florida flame azalea). This southern counterpart of *R. calendulaceum*, native to northern Florida and adjacent Alabama and Georgia, has clusters of fragrant, golden yellow flowers in midspring (late March and early April in Zone 9a), and is useful in Zones 7a−9a+ and sheltered sites in Zone 6b.

Rhododendron flammeum 5 (synonyms: *Azalea flammea, A. speciosa, R. speciosum*; Oconee or sweet azalea). This native of Georgia and South Carolina has clusters of unscented flowers, red-orange to yellow and pink, in middle to late spring. Useful in Zones 7b−8b, and sheltered sites in Zone 7a.

Rhododendron luteum 5 (synonym: *Azalea lutea, A. pontica, R. flavum*; sweet or Pontic azalea). This Eurasian species with fragrant yellow flowers is seldom grown in our area but is important because of its inclusion in the Ghent and Knap Hill hybrids.

Rhododendron carolinianum 4

Carolina rhododendron
Evergreen shrub
Ericaceae (Heath Family)

Native Range. Southern Appalachians: North Carolina.

Useful Range. USDA Zones 5b−7b, areas with moderate summer temperatures in Zone 8, and protected sites in Zone 5a.

Function. Border, specimen, foundation.

Size and Habit

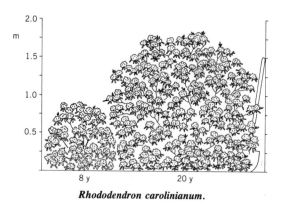

Rhododendron carolinianum.

Adaptability. Shade from full summer sun is necessary in Zones 7 and 8 except in areas where summer heat is tempered by high elevation or proximity to large bodies of water. This plant will tolerate full shade but will neither grow nor flower well. Protection from winter sun and wind is advisable, especially in Zones 5 and 6.

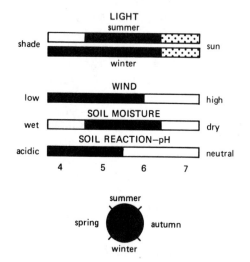

Seasonal Interest. *Flowers:* Pale pink to rosy purple (or white in a variety), to 4 cm/1.6 in. across, in terminal, rounded clusters of up to 10 flowers in the better horticultural forms, in middle to late spring. *Foliage:* Evergreen, leathery leaves are deep green with brownish scales underneath, 5–8 cm/2–3 in. long and about 2.5 cm/1 in. wide, curling tightly under drought or cold stress.

Problems and Maintenance. Relatively free of maintenance, but several pests and diseases occasionally become troublesome, so a minimal pest control program is necessary. Most common problems in northern areas are physiological and relate to improper soil preparation and/or site (see *Rhododendron catawbiense*), but *R. carolinianum* seems to be more tolerant of environmental stresses than most rhododendrons. For maximum flowering year after year, it is necessary to remove faded flower clusters to prevent fruit and seed development and the drain that this imposes on flowering in the following year.

Varieties and Cultivars. Var. *album* has pure white flowers, slightly larger than those of the species type, and can be reproduced true to type by seed propagation. It is considered a highly choice rhododendron. Selections for clear pink color have been made but not named or maintained in the nursery trade. There is room for selection of superior variants, not only for color, but also flower size, foliage, and form.

Hybrids

Rhododendron ×*laetevirens* 4 (synonym: *R.* ×*wilsonii*; Wilson rhododendron). This compact, moundlike hybrid (probably *R. carolinianum* × *R. ferrugineum*) is used primarily in borders and foundation plantings for the textural effect of the rich, bright green, evergreen foliage. The rosy-pink flowers are not borne in large numbers and appear so late in spring that they are partially obscured by the emerging new foliage. Useful in Zones 5a–7b and moderate climates in Zone 8.

Rhododendron P.J.M. Hybrids 4 (P.J.M. hybrid rhododendrons). This is a class of hybrids (*R. dauricum* var. *sempervirens* × *R. carolinianum*) with some variation in foliage, growth habit, and flower color (from pale to deep rose-pink), but it has been handled as a cultivar in the trade. Plants are consistently compact, usually more or less moundlike, with neatly textured foliage that turns deep mahogany-purple in winter. The name comes from the late Peter J. Mezitt, founder of Weston Nurseries in Massachusetts. His son, Edmund V. Mezitt, has selected and named several cultivars from this population: 'Elite' has bright pink-lavender flowers in midspring, later than average for this group; 'Regal' has strong, lavender-pink flowers at about the peak of the flowering season for this group, usually with the later *Forsythia* cultivars; 'Victor' is the earliest cultivar to flower, but all begin to flower within a week or so of each other. Unusually winter-hardy, these hybrids are useful in Zones 5a−7b and protected sites in Zone 4.

Related Species

Rhododendron chapmanii 4 (Chapman rhododendron). This native of northwestern Florida is notably more heat-resistant than R. *carolinianum* or, for that matter, most other rhododendrons. It is similar to R. *carolinianum*, so it can be considered a counterpart for the Deep South. Useful in Zones 8a−9a+, perhaps also in Zone 7 in protected areas. An endangered species, R. *chapmanii* should not be collected from the wild but grown from seeds or cultivated material.

Rhododendron minus 5−6 (Piedmont rhododendron). This close relative of R. *carolinianum* becomes a larger plant, frequently to 2−3 m/6.6−10 ft in height and spread, sometimes twice that in native habitat. Its flowers range from clear pink to rose-purple and occasionally white, in clusters of 10 to 30. As in R. *carolinianum*, and perhaps even more so, there is great potential for selection of superior clones, but such selections are not yet available and the species itself is not widely available. Useful in Zones 6a−8b.

Rhododendron catawbiense 5

Catawba rhododendron
Evergreen shrub
Ericaceae (Heath Family)

Native Range. Southern Appalachians: Virginia to Georgia.

Useful Range. USDA Zones 4a−7b, areas having moderate summer temperature in Zone 8, and protected sites in Zone 3b. Note that the Catawbiense Hybrids are considerably less cold-hardy than the species type.

Function. Border, screen, specimen, naturalizing.

Size and Habit

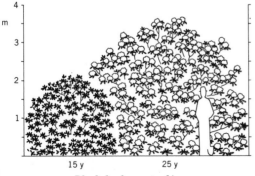

Rhododendron catawbiense.

Adaptability. Shade from full summer sun is necessary in Zones 7 and 8, the Midwest, and other areas having hot summers. Plants tolerate full shade but do not flower well. Protection from winter sun and wind is advisable in Zones 3b, 4, and 5.

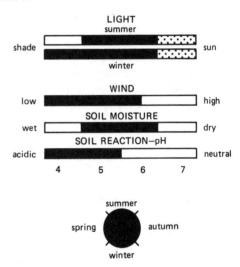

Seasonal Interest. *Flowers:* Lilac-purple (white in a variety), 6 cm/2.4 in. across, as many as 20 packed in tight, rounded, terminal clusters up to 15 cm/6 in. across, opening in late spring but before new leaves emerge. *Foliage:* Evergreen, leathery, dark green, 8−15 cm/3−6 in. long, forming a dense mass in plants that are growing well.

Rhododendron catawbiense.

Problems and Maintenance. Several insects and mites can be troublesome, but most are only occasionally serious and easily controlled. However, black vine and strawberry weevils and borers can be lethal if not controlled promptly, and nematodes can be a serious problem in the Deep South. Several diseases also can affect rhododendrons, and some of these can pose serious problems. The most destructive include twig blight, dieback, and wilt diseases. When rhododendrons are to be used in quantity, a thorough plant protection program should be available.

In many areas, plants more frequently show symptoms of physiological disorders than of pathogenic diseases. These include leaf scorch from winter sun and sweeping winds and chlorosis (leaf yellowing) or dieback from improper soil conditions. To prevent or reduce incidence of these problems, it is necessary to give careful attention to selection of soil and site. Protection from full sun on south and west sides of plantings and from winter wind from the north and west will go a long way to avoid leaf scorch, but remember that some sun or open sky above the plantings is necessary for full flowering.

If soils are not sufficiently acidic—below pH 5.5 or 6.0—acidification with sulfur, acid peat moss, and acid-residue fertilizer may help, as will foliar applications of ferrous sulfate or chelated iron. But in soils containing free limestone, such adjustments will be so transient as to be virtually useless. In such cases, the use of rhododendrons and their relatives may require building raised planting beds with acid-residue organic soil materials such as wood or bark chips or peat moss, alone or in combination. In areas having "problem" soils for such plants, more information can

be obtained from state universities or county, state, or provincial extension service offices.

For best flowering year after year, flower clusters should be removed as soon as they fade to prevent fruit and seed development and interference of these processes with formation of flower buds for the next year. This may not be practical on large plants.

Varieties. Var. *album* is a naturally occurring population within the species of plants with white flowers, delicately tinted with a trace of pink when they first open. This variety is among the finest of rhododendrons for landscape use, with excellent form and foliage as well as flowers and cold hardiness equal to the species type. It comes true from seed and should not be confused with the commonly available white-flowering hybrid of R. *catawbiense* called 'Catawbiense Album,' which is inferior in both cold hardiness and landscape character.

Var. *compactum* also occurs naturally at very high elevations in the Southern Appalachians, and is of interest for its low, dense growth habit, but this is seldom available commercially.

Hybrids. The cultivars listed below constitute a very limited sampling of those that are commercially available. Emphasis is on the most cold-hardy types, the so-called ironclad hybrids, but a few others, as noted, are included. Not all are Catawbiense Hybrids; some involve only the related species described below. Those that show greatest cold hardiness frequently have shown good heat resistance as well. Yet successful use of these plants south of Zone 7b is limited to areas with relatively moderate summers and requires careful maintenance, including irrigation when necessary.

'Album Elegans' has white flowers very late in spring. Useful in Zones 6a–7b.

'America' has fine, deep red color but poor form. Useful in Zones 6a–7b.

'Boule de Neige' has white flowers in middle to late spring, and compact growth, to only about 2 m/6.6 ft maximum. Useful in Zones 5b–7b.

'Catawbiense Album' has white flowers in late spring, midseason among Catawbiense Hybrids. Useful in Zones 6a–7b but not to be confused with the less commonly available R. *catawbiense* var. *album*, which is superior in both cold hardiness and landscape character.

'Charles Dickens' has deep red-purple flowers and is useful in Zones 6a−7b.

'Everestianum' has rosy lilac flowers with frilled petals and is useful in Zones 6a−7b.

'Lady Armstrong' has large, purplish pink flowers and is useful in Zones 6a−7b.

'Mrs. Charles S. Sargent' has very large, deep rose flowers with yellow-green markings and excellent plant form. Useful in Zones 5b−7b at least.

'Nova Zembla' is the best red-flowering rhododendron for northern areas, with good flower color and plant form. Useful in Zones 5b−7b.

'Purpureum Grandiflorum' does not have as strong a purple color as 'Purple Splendour' but is more cold-hardy, useful in Zones 5b−7b.

'Roseum Elegans' has large, lavender-pink flowers, good plant habit and is useful in Zones 6a−7b. Some plants sold under this name are not true and are inferior.

'Sappho,' perhaps not a R. catawbiense hybrid, has white flowers with a crimson blotch and is useful and popular in Zones 6b−7b and southward.

'Wellesleyanum' is a hybrid of R. maximum × R. catawbiense with pink-tinged white flowers. It is useful in Zones 5b−7b, probably Zone 5a as well, and possibly Zone 4.

Related Species

Rhododendron arboreum 7 (tree rhododendron).   This truly treelike native of the Himalayas is not considered to be useful in our area at present, since it is too cold-tender for any but our warmest zones. But hybrids have been successfully obtained with R. *catawbiense* and a few other related species, and in time such offspring may prove useful in our area. 'Goldsworth Yellow,' an outstanding example, has apricot-yellow flowers, a most unusual color in hardy rhododendrons. A complex hybrid involving R. *arboreum*, R. *caucasicum*, and R. *campylocarpum*, it is useful in Zones 6b−7b and in areas with moderate summers in Zone 8.

Rhododendron decorum 6 (sweetshell rhododendron).   This native of western China is not useful in much of our area and is seldom available. In coastal areas and high elevations in Zones 6b−7b its large, fragrant, pink or white flowers give it landscape value, but it is more likely to be encountered in the form of hybrids than as the species type. Some specialists believe R. *decorum* was a principal parent of the Dexter Hybrids (see below).

Rhododendron fortunei 5 (Fortune rhododendron).   This native of eastern China is a magnificent landscape plant in itself in Zones 6b−7b and southward, with fragrant pink to white flowers, up to 10 cm/4 in. across, and leaves 10−20 cm/4−8 in. long. There has been considerable interest in obtaining hybrids with R. *catawbiense* and other hardy rhododendrons, and the efforts of the late C. O. Dexter of Sandwich, Massachusetts in this direction are only beginning to be fully recognized. A few of the Dexter Hybrids have been introduced. 'Amethyst' has lavender flowers; 'Ben Moseley,' 'Mrs. W. R. Coe,' 'Scintillation,' and 'Westbury' have varying pink flowers. All are large-growing plants with large, fragrant flowers, useful in Zones 6b−7b and southward, some to Zone 6a and perhaps even 5b. Some of the earliest introductions, notably 'Mrs. W. R. Coe,' have received wide recognition, but others still under evaluation may eventually prove superior to some of those released earliest.

Earlier Fortune Hybrids were mostly developed in England under less stressful climatic conditions and may be more appropriate for the Pacific Northwest than our area.

Rhododendron griffithianum 6 (Griffith rhododendron).   This Himalayan species is best known for its huge flowers, 12−15 cm/5−6 in. across, white or pale pink with yellow throats. It is not sufficiently cold-hardy to be used in colder zones than 8b−9a, and there only with protection and on a trial basis. Its hybrids may be somewhat more useful in our area, but most should be used on a trial basis until hardiness limits are better defined. A few cultivars are already well established:

'Mars' is an excellent, deep red-flowering selection, useful in Zones 6b−7b and southward. It is especially important to provide shade from full summer sun for rhododendrons with dark colored flowers to reduce early fading.

'Vulcan' is similar to 'Mars' but with medium red flowers and is useful from Zone 7b (and perhaps 7a) southward.

Rhododendron ponticum 5 (Pontic rhododendron).   This relative of *R. catawbiense* from southern Europe and adjacent Asia is extremely vigorous and is commonly used for screening in Europe. Its flower color, similar to that of *R. catawbiense*, has the same limitation for use in combination with other colors, especially reds and pinks, but the plant could be used more than it is at present in the southeastern United States as a functional screening plant. Useful in Zones 7 and 8. Several hybrids exist; perhaps the most common is 'Cunningham's White,' believed to be *R. ponticum* var. *album* × *R. caucasicum*, not to be confused with 'Cunninghamii,' another hybrid (*R. maximum* × *R. arboreum* var. *cinnamomeum*) that probably is no longer in cultivation. 'Cunningham's White' is less cold-hardy than 'Boule de Neige,' but is valued in Zones 6a–7b for its outstanding, compact growth habit and early display of white flowers with yellow-green throats.

'Purple Splendour,' another fine *R. ponticum* hybrid, is considered the best deep purple rhododendron for moderate climates in our area by some specialists. Not to be confused with the azalea 'Purple Splendor,' it is useful in Zones 6b–7b and areas with moderate summer temperatures in Zone 8.

Rhododendron ferrugineum 3

Rock rhododendron, alpine rose
Evergreen shrub
Ericaceae (Heath Family)

Native Range. Central Europe, in the Alps.

Useful Range. USDA Zones 5b–6b and protected sites in Zone 5a and perhaps Zone 4, but only in areas having moderate summer temperatures: high elevations and coastal environments.

Function. Rock garden, foundation, massing.

Size and Habit

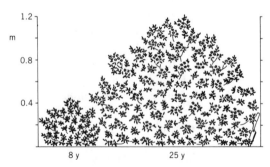

Rhododendron ferrugineum.

Adaptability. At least partial sun is necessary for best growth and flowering, but in winter, light shade and protection from extreme winds may be beneficial. This species and its close relatives (see Related Species) are more tolerant of calcareous soils than most rhododendrons.

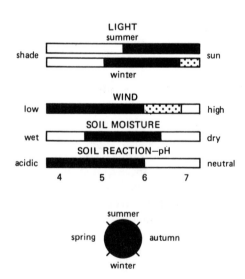

Seasonal Interest. *Flowers:* Pale to rosy pink or white, 1.5 cm/0.6 in. across, in clusters of 6 to 12, in midsummer. *Foliage:* Evergreen, lustrous, deep green, smooth but with rusty scales, the leaves to 4 cm/1.6 in. long and about 1 cm/0.4 in. wide.

Problems and Maintenance. This species is relatively trouble-free in sites meeting its environmental requirements, especially relatively even temperatures, but these conditions prevail in few parts of our area, mainly high elevations and maritime climates in the northeastern United States and the Canadian maritime provinces.

Forms. F. *album* has white flowers, outstanding against the lustrous, dark green foliage.

F. *atrococcineum* has deep rose flowers, nearly red, but is not likely to be found commercially.

Related Species

Rhododendron fastigiatum 2.   This close relative of the more commonly known R. *impeditum* and other species listed below is the most dwarf of the blue-flowering, scaly leaved rhododendrons from western China, with leaves only about 1 cm/0.4 in. long and a matlike growth habit that seldom exceeds 25–50 cm/10–20 in. tall. Its pale lavender to mauve to rose flowers, 2.5 cm/1 in. across, open in midspring. It is useful in protected sites in Zones 6 and 7 and may be slightly less demanding than R. *russatum* and R. *scintillans* in its requirement for cool summers. Two highly functional hybrids (R. *fastigiatum* × R. *carolinianum*) are 'Purple Gem' and 'Ramapo,' both low-growing cultivars, to 0.5–0.8 m/1.6–2.6 ft in ultimate height, with, respectively, deep and medium lavender-purple flowers, very showy in middle to late spring.

Rhododendron hirsutum 3 (garland rhododendron, hairy Alpine rose).   This species is similar to R. *ferrugineum* and virtually interchangeable in landscape use, differing in having fringes of hairs on the edges of the leaves and in other minor respects. The f. *albiflorum* has white flowers.

Rhododendron impeditum 3.   This dwarf rhododendron from very high elevations in western China forms a tight, cushionlike mass of fine-textured, blue-green foliage with individual leaves only about 1 cm/0.4 in. long. The light lavender-blue flowers, about 1.5 cm/0.6 in. across, appear in midspring. Useful primarily as a rock garden plant in Zones 5b–7b where summer temperatures are moderate.

Rhododendron lapponicum 2 (Lapland rhododendron).   This very dwarf plant ranges from 20–40 cm/8–16 in. tall in cultivation to less than 10 cm/4 in. tall in its native habitat in the Arctic of Eurasia and North America and a few mountaintops—in our area the summit of Mt. Washington, New Hampshire. The evergreen, deep green leaves are 1–2 cm/0.4–0.8 in. long, forming a background for the purplish flowers, about 1.5 cm/0.6 in. across, appearing in early summer. Useful in alpine gardens in Zones 1–6 where summers are moderate.

Rhododendron micranthum 5 (Manchurian rhododendron).   This native of northeastern Asia is distinctive because of its small, whitish flowers, appearing very late in spring, in clusters up to 5 cm/2 in. across, and sparsely arranged evergreen leaves to 3.5 cm/1.4 in. long. Its flowers certainly do not give it wide appeal, and its loosely straggling form is attractive only in rather specific settings. But its hardiness and durability make a place for it in northern landscapes. Useful in Zones 4a–6b, in areas having moderate summer temperatures.

Rhododendron micranthum.

Rhododendron russatum 3.   This close relative of R. *impeditum* and R. *lapponicum* forms a dense mass of rusty green leaves, each 2–4 cm/0.8–1.6 in. long, and bright blue-purple flowers, about 2.5 cm/1 in. across, in small clusters at about the same time as those of R. *impeditum*, in midspring. This plant has performed well in the Canadian Maritimes but probably is a poor risk in most of our area because of its need for cool summers and an abundant supply of moisture. Useful, given these conditions, in Zones 6a–7a.

Rhododendron scintillans 3. This handsome dwarf, with tiny, scaly leaves, and sparkling, lavender-blue to blue-purple flowers in midspring like its relatives *R. impeditum* and *R.*

russatum, comes from high elevations in western China. It is useful at least in Zone 7 and protected sites in Zone 6.

Rhododendron indicum 4

Synonyms: *Azalea indica*, A. *macrantha*, R. *macranthum*
Indian or macrantha azalea
Evergreen shrub
Ericaceae (Heath Family)

Native Range. Southern Japan.

Useful Range. USDA Zones 6b−9a.

Function. Specimen, border, naturalizing.

Size and Habit

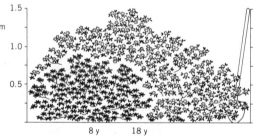

Rhododendron indicum.

Adaptability. Light shade in summer is beneficial, especially to reduce fading of red-flowered cultivars. Light shade in winter reduces leaf scorch in northern parts of the useful range (Zones 6 and 7).

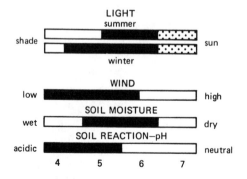

Seasonal Interest. *Flowers:* Rose-red to scarlet, 5−6.5 cm/2−2.6 in. across, very showy in very late spring or early summer against the deep green foliage. *Foliage:* Evergreen or nearly evergreen leaves, 2.5−3.5 cm/1−1.4 in. long, deep green and slightly lustrous. Those that are first to emerge fall in autumn, and those opening in summer usually remain until new growth begins in spring.

Problems and Maintenance. Several diseases and insects may damage foliage and flowers of azaleas, but these are seldom serious problems. Control may be needed for infestations of mites and scale insects, and soil treatments may be needed occasionally for soil-borne diseases such as rhododendron wilt and nematodes. Pruning is seldom necessary or desirable.

Cultivars. Most cultivars involving this species are hybrids with other species (see Hybrids), but a few selections have been made directly from the species, including the following.

'Balsaminaeflorum' has very double, orange-red flowers, to 4 cm/1.6 in. across.

'Flame Creeper' is a low growing form with orange-red flowers.

'J. T. Lovett' has orange-red, single flowers, to 6.5 cm/2.6 in. across, and a low, dense growth habit.

'Macranthum' (= 'Macrantha') is simply a synonym for *R. indicum*, probably a clone that has been carried along as representing the species.

Hybrids

Belgian Indian Hybrids. With large flowers (to 8 cm/3 in. across) in midspring, these cultivars are mostly hybrids involving *R. indicum*, *R.*

simsii, *R. mucronatum*, and *R. pulchrum* var. *phoeniceum* to a lesser degree. *R. simsii* is the major contributing species. They were selected in Belgium for greenhouse forcing and are relatively tender, but some cultivars have been found useful in Zones 8b and 9a. Few are commercially available in our area.

Rutherford Hybrids. These hybrids were developed in Rutherford, New Jersey, as greenhouse forcing cultivars from parentage not greatly different from that of the Belgian Indian Hybrids—primarily *R. indicum*, *R. mucronatum*, *R. pulchrum* var. *phoeniceum*, and *R. simsii*, but other minor influences as well, including the Kurume Hybrids (see *R. obtusum*). They were never intended as landscape plants and usually are sold as house plants. But several have been as useful in the landscape as the Belgian and Southern Indian Hybrids in Zones 8b and 9a.

Southern Indian Hybrids. This group originated from the importation of Belgian Hybrid cultivars to the southeastern United States with subsequent spontaneous and deliberate selection and hybridization. The word Indian as the name of both hybrid groups is a misnomer, since none of the species involved are from India, and the so-called Indian azalea (*R. indicum*) is not the major contributor to the hybrid cultivars. Over the years, a considerable number of new cultivars have been selected in the South. They range in height from 2−3 m/6.6−10 ft, depending on parentage, and mostly flower in midspring. A few are listed here.

'Album Maculatum' has single, white flowers to 8 cm/3 in. across with a faint, greenish-yellow blotch and a spreading growth habit, showing a strong influence of *R. mucronatum*.

'Criterion' has single, white and deep purple-red variegated flowers, to 6 cm/2.4 in. across, and a low, spreading growth habit.

'Duc de Rohan' has single, orange-red flowers, to 6 cm/2.4 in. across, with a spreading growth habit, showing a strong influence of *R. indicum*.

'Elegans Superbum' (= 'Pride of Mobile,' = 'Watermelon Pink') has single, light rosy pink flowers, to 6 cm/2.4 in. across, and an upright growth habit, showing an influence of *R. pulchrum* var. *phoeniceum*.

'Fielder's White' has single, frilled, white flowers, to 7 cm/2.8 in. across, with a faint, greenish yellow blotch and a spreading growth habit, showing a strong influence of *R. mucronatum*.

'Formosa' has violet-red flowers, to 9 cm/3.5 in. across, and an upright growth habit, showing the influence of *R. pulchrum* var. *phoeniceum* and *R. simsii*.

'George Lindley Taber' has white flowers, flushed violet-red with a deeper blotch, to 9 cm/3.5 in. across, with an upright growth habit, showing influence of *R. pulchrum* var. *phoeniceum*.

'Giant Ruffles' has large, rose-red flowers and an upright growth habit, an unusually large plant.

'Indica Alba' is only a synonym for *R. mucronatum*, sometimes mistakenly called an Indian Hybrid azalea.

'Iveryanum' has single flowers varying from white with rose-red flecking to solid rose, to 8 cm/3 in. across, and a low, spreading growth habit indicative of the strong influence of *R. indicum*.

'Judge Solomon,' a sport (bud mutation) of 'Formosa,' has pink flowers and an upright growth habit.

'Mrs. G. G. Gerbing,' a sport of 'George Lindley Taber,' has white flowers and upright growth habit.

'Pride of Dorking' has rose-red flowers, rather late, and a spreading growth habit.

'Watermelon Red' is very similar to 'Elegans Superbum' but with deeper red flowers.

Cultivars in this group are generally useful in Zone 9a, many are also cold-hardy in Zone 8b, and a few can be used in protected sites in Zone 8a. Base selection on local experience and availability of cultivars.

Glenn Dale Hybrids. This large group of evergreen azaleas, more than 400 in all, was developed at the U.S. National Arboretum in a very large breeding program carried out in the 1930s and 1940s. The objective of this program was to develop cultivars suitable for the Middle Atlantic region. Parent material included *R. indicum*, *R. kaempferi*, *R. mucronatum*, *R. obtusum*, *R. pulchrum* var. *phoeniceum*, *R. simsii*, *R. yedoense* var. *poukhanense*, the Indian and Kaempferi Hybrids, and several superior individual cultivars. Many of the resulting clones have become standard cultivars in the Middle Atlantic area and elsewhere in Zones 7a–8b. Because of the great variety of parent material, individual cultivars vary considerably in cold hardiness as well as adaptability to the southern extremes of our area. In selecting cultivars, consider local experience and availability. Only a small sampling of the more popular cultivars is presented here:

'Aphrodite' has large numbers of pale rose-pink flowers in midspring, dark green foliage, and broad-spreading habit. It reaches more than 1 m/3.3 ft in height.

'Beacon' is an erect to arching plant, eventually reaching 1.5 m/5 ft tall, with narrow, dark green leaves and rose-scarlet flowers, to 4.5 cm/1.8 in. across, that hold their color well in full sun, opening in middle to late spring.

'Buccaneer' has brilliant red flowers, 5 cm/2 in. across, in midspring, but they fade in full sun, so partial shade is important for this and many other red cultivars to perform well. Growth habit is spreading but developing in height to 1.5 m/5 ft.

'Copperman' has brilliant orange-red flowers, to 8 cm/3 in. across, in late spring, and a dense, spreading growth habit, reaching a height of more than 1 m/3.3 ft.

'Coquette' has rose-pink flowers, 5 cm/2 in. across, in middle to late spring and an erect to arching growth habit, to a height of 1.5 m/5 ft.

'Crusader' has orange-rose flowers, to 7 cm/2.8 in. across, in very late spring, in keeping with a large contribution of R. indicum parentage. Growth habit is spreading and ascending eventually to 0.9 m/3 ft.

'Fashion' has orange-red flowers, 5 cm/2 in. across, in middle to late spring and an erect to arching growth habit, eventually to nearly 2 m/6.6 ft.

'Festive' has white flowers striped dull rose, to 6 cm/2.4 in. across, in early spring and an erect to arching growth habit, eventually to nearly 2 m/6.6 ft tall.

'Gaiety' has rose-pink flowers, to 8 cm/3 in. across, in late spring and an erect to broad-spreading growth habit and narrow, dark green leaves, to 1.5 m/5 ft tall.

'Glacier' has shining white flowers, to 8 cm/3 in. across, in midspring, unusually lustrous, dark green foliage, and an erect to spreading growth habit, to 1.5 m/5 ft tall.

'Glamour' has bright rose-red flowers, to 8 cm/3 in. across, in middle to late spring, narrow, dark green leaves, and an erect to broad-spreading growth habit, to 1.5 m/5 ft tall.

'Greeting' has coral-rose flowers, to 5 cm/2 in. across, in midspring, dark green leaves, and an erect to broad-spreading growth habit, to more than 1 m/3.3 ft tall.

'Martha Hitchcock,' a Satsuki azalea, has white, red-purple margined flowers, to 8 cm/3 in. across, medium green leaves, and a broad-spreading growth habit, to about 1 m/3.3 ft tall.

'Treasure' has flowers pale pink in bud, opening nearly white, 9–11 cm/3.6–4.4 in. across, in midspring. It functions as an "improved" version of R. mucronatum, wide-spreading and vigorous, eventually reaching a height of 1.5 m/5 ft.

'Trophy' has light lavender-pink flowers to 8 cm/3 in. across with medium green leaves and a broad-spreading growth habit, to about 1 m/3.3 ft tall.

'Vestal' has white flowers with yellow-green blotches, 6 cm/2.4 in. across, and dark green leaves. The growth habit is broad-spreading, to 1 m/3.3 ft or taller.

Satsuki Azaleas. This group takes its name from the Japanese word for fifth month. As the name implies, these cultivars are late-flowering—about as late as R. indicum, the common parent, in late spring or early summer. Some cultivars usually included here may be simply forms of R. indicum, and those mentioned earlier (see R. indicum, Cultivars) are sometimes included in this group.

The terms Satsuki Hybrids or Chugai Hybrids usually are meant to apply to a specific group of hybrids involving R. indicum, R. simsii, and the Belgian Hybrids, developed in Japan and carrying Japanese cultivar names. More than 50 cultivars of this group were imported by the U.S. Plant Introduction Station in the late 1930s and distributed for evaluation during the following 25 years. These are low-growing, large-flowering forms, rather unstable with respect to flower color, often with striped or flecked petals (chimeras), and with flowers of different colors on the same plant, opening in late spring. These have proved useful in Zones 7b−9a and some in sheltered sites in Zone 7a, but most have not yet become available commercially. A few that have are listed below:

'Gunbi' has frilled, red-flecked white flowers, to 6 cm/2.4 in. across, and a low, spreading growth habit.

'Gyokushin' has pink-flushed white flowers, to 7.5 cm/3 in. across, and a low, spreading growth habit.

'Pink Gumpo' is similar to 'White Gumpo' except in having light pink flowers.

'Red Gumpo' is similar to 'White Gumpo' except in having rose-pink flowers.

'White Gumpo' (originally 'Gunpo') has frilled, red-flecked white flowers, to 7.5 cm/3 in. across, and low, compact growth.

Related Species

Rhododendron mucronatum 4 (synonyms: *Azalea indica alba*, A. *ledifolia*, R. *ledifolium*; snow azalea). This handsome, white-flowered azalea from Japan offers maximum nomenclatural confusion, since it is still frequently offered for sale under synonyms or even under cultivar names such as 'Indica Alba' and 'Ledifolia Alba.' Moreover, its common name causes it to be confused with the Kurume azalea 'Snow' (see under R. *obtusum*). A further source of confusion is the similarity in name to R. *mucronulatum*, the Korean rhododendron.

In spite of these potential difficulties, R.

mucronatum is an excellent plant, cultivated in Japan for centuries and no longer known in the wild. It remains below eye level for several years, eventually edging up to about 2 m/6.6 ft under ideal conditions, and usually is broader than tall. Its single, pure white flowers are about 7.5 cm/3 in. across and open in middle to late spring before those of R. *indicum*, and its dark green foliage is outstanding. It is useful in Zones 7a−9a+ and readily available from nurseries specializing in azaleas. Cultivars include 'Delaware Valley White,' which differs little from the species type, and several selections for pink-flushed or variegated petals, mostly uncommon in our area.

Rhododendron pulchrum 4. This species, like R. *mucronatum*, is not known in the wild but only in cultivation, and may even be a hybrid involving that species. It is best known for the var. *phoeniceum* (synonym: R. *phoeniceum*), which has magenta flowers and is itself best known for its contribution to the Indian Hybrids.

Rhododendron simsii 5 (Sims azalea). This common, wild species of China and Taiwan has more or less red flowers and at least superficially resembles a taller, looser-growing edition of R. *indicum*. In spite of the fact that it is a colorful and potentially useful landscape plant itself in Zones 7b−9a, it is hardly known in our area other than as the probable major parent of the Indian Hybrid azaleas.

Rhododendron japonicum 4

Synonym: *Azalea japonica*
Japanese azalea
Deciduous shrub
Ericaceae (Heath Family)

Native Range. Japan.

Useful Range. USDA Zones 4b−8b.

Function. Specimen, border.

Size and Habit

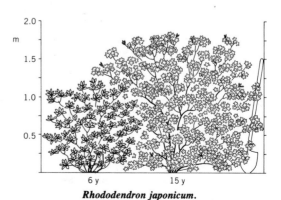

Rhododendron japonicum.

Adaptability. At least certain cultivars of *R. japonicum* and *R. ×kosteranum* (see Hybrids) do not require as strongly acid soil as many other azaleas.

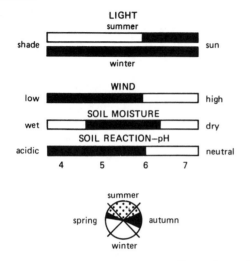

Seasonal Interest. *Flowers:* Yellow through orange to red, 5–8 cm/2–3 in. across, in late spring with the first expansion of foliage, with an odor that is not particularly pleasant. *Foliage:* Pale to medium green, hairy and rather coarse, turning reddish in autumn in sunny sites, in some areas and years.

Problems and Maintenance. Several diseases and insects occasionally cause minor damage, but *R. japonicum* and its hybrids usually are about as trouble-free as any azaleas. Pruning is seldom needed but can be used for renewal of old plants by pruning back a few main branches annually.

Cultivars. Cultivars involving *R. japonicum* mostly belong to the Molle Hybrids (see Hybrids), but this species is variable in both flower color and hardiness. The red-flowered forms from the northern parts of its natural range in Japan tend to be more cold-hardy than the more southern yellow-flowered forms, but this correlation is not perfect, and individual, yellow-flowered plants may be as hardy as most red-flowered plants.

Hybrids

Molle Hybrids (R. ×kosteranum). These are hybrids of *R. japonicum* and *R. molle* (Chinese azalea). The most common cultivars tend toward the greater cold hardiness of *R. japonicum* and are generally useful in Zones 5a–8b, but some other cultivars in this group are more tender because of the *R. molle* parentage. Even the best cultivars are used less than formerly, since they have not been very competitive with the handsome Exbury and Ghent Hybrids as functional landscape plants. Currently it is more common to find Molle Hybrid seedlings offered for sale than any great number of cultivars, with the expected variation in color and hardiness.

Rhododendron ×kosteranum.

Northern Lights Hybrids. This new group of hybrids (*R. ×kosteranum × R. prinophyllum*), developed at the University of Minnesota, promises to extend the useful range of showy azaleas substantially northward. First generation seedlings are produced by controlled pollination and so are relatively uniform. Flowers carry the delightful fragrance of *R. prinophyllum*, the roseshell azalea, and are similar in color: light to deep pink, and in time of bloom: late spring, but are much more showy. Individual flowers, 4 cm/1.6 in. across, are borne in clusters 8–10 cm/3.2–4 in. across. Plants are compact in growth habit but can be expected to reach heights of 2 m/6.6 ft within 20 years. They promise to be useful in Zones 3b–6b and perhaps somewhat colder and milder zones as well.

Related Species

Rhododendron molle 4 (synonyms: *Azalea mollis, R. sinense;* Chinese azalea). This native of China with yellow flowers to 5–6 cm/2–2.4 in. across is distinctly less cold-hardy than *R. japonicum* and probably exists in landscape use in our area only in the form of remaining plants of a few Molle Hybrids. Useful, if it were available, in Zones 7a–9a.

Rhododendron maximum 6

Rosebay rhododendron
Evergreen shrub
Ericaceae (Heath Family)

Native Range. Northeastern United States and adjacent Canada, southward in the Appalachian Mountains to Alabama.

Useful Range. USDA Zones 5a—6b, protected sites in Zone 4, and areas having moderate summer temperatures in Zone 7 with selection of appropriate genetic material.

Function. Naturalizing, border (background), screen, specimen.

Size and Habit

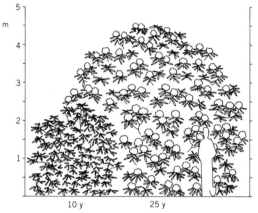

Rhododendron maximum.

Adaptability. Shade from full summer sun is necessary in Zones 6 and 7, but flowering may be reduced in full shade. Protection from winter sun and wind is advisable in all zones.

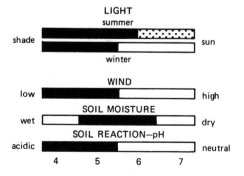

Seasonal Interest. *Flowers:* Rose-pink, pink-margined, or white, to 4 cm/1.6 in. across, in large trusses of up to 25 or more flowers under ideal conditions, in early summer to midsummer, partly obscured by the new foliage in southern areas. *Foliage:* Leaves are evergreen, leathery, smooth or with a light rusty undersurface, 10—20 cm/4—8 in. long and 5 cm/2 in. wide, providing a coarse texture.

Problems and Maintenance. This species is subject to the usual number of insects and diseases that trouble rhododendrons in general, but few are serious enough to require regular maintenance, especially in properly situated naturalized plantings. Leaf-scorch can be a serious problem in all zones if a protected site is not provided at the beginning. Availability is limited outside the natural range.

Varieties and Forms. F. *album* has green-spotted, white flowers. F. *purpureum* has green-spotted, deep rose-pink flowers.

Var. *leachii* from West Virginia is more compact in growth with smaller leaves having wavy margins.

Little has been done in selecting cultivars, perhaps because of difficulty in vegetative propagation or because flowering interest is usually considered secondary to the foliage effect.

Rhododendron mucronulatum 4

Korean rhododendron
Deciduous shrub
Ericaceae (Heath Family)

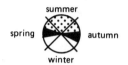

Native Range. Northeastern Asia, including northern Japan.

Useful Range. USDA Zones 5a−7b, sheltered sites in Zone 4b, and areas in Zone 8 having moderate summer temperatures.

Function. Border, specimen.

Size and Habit

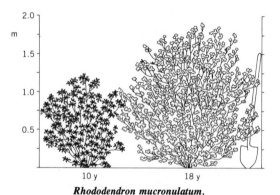

Rhododendron mucronulatum.

Adaptability. Shade from full summer sun is beneficial in areas having very hot summers. The plant will tolerate full shade but will not flower well or remain full.

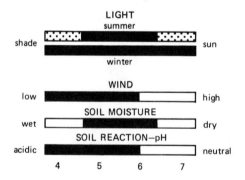

Seasonal Interest. *Flowers:* Light rosy purple (or pink), to 4 cm/1.6 in. across, in clusters of three to six at tips of branches, very showy, before the leaves emerge in early to middle spring. *Foliage:* Deciduous but leathery, about 6 cm/2.4 in. long, turning yellow to pink-bronze, or sometimes red, in autumn before falling.

Problems and Maintenance. This plant is subject to several disease and pest problems, but these are not as likely to be serious as on the evergreen rhododendrons. The deciduous character of this plant allows infected or infested foliage to be removed easily from the area annually if necessary. The tendency of flower buds to expand and open during favorable weather in early spring makes them susceptible to late spring freezes.

Cultivars. 'Cornell Pink' differs from the species type only in that the flowers are clear rosy pink, with little or none of the magenta color that makes the species type difficult to use in combination with some other colors, especially pinks and reds.

Related Species

Rhododendron dauricum 4 (Dahurian rhododendron). This deciduous to semievergreen rhododendron usually is considered inferior as a landscape plant to the closely related *R. mucronulatum*, which it resembles. Because of this it is seldom available. The var. *sempervirens*, almost fully evergreen, is important because of its involvement in the parentage of the P.J.M. Hybrid rhododendrons (see under *R. carolinianum*). Useful, when available, in Zones 5b−7b, perhaps also in Zone 5a with selection of appropriate genetic material, and areas in Zone 8 having moderate summers.

Rhododendron obtusum 3

Synonym: *Azalea obtusa*
Hiryu or Kirishima azalea
Evergreen, semievergreen, or deciduous shrub
Ericaceae (Heath Family)

Native Range. Japan.

Useful Range. USDA Zones 7a−9a, a few cultivars also in Zone 6.

Function. Specimen, border, foundation, naturalizing.

Size and Habit. 'Hinodegiri' (Kurume) is illustrated.

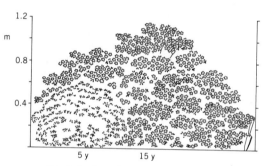

Rhododendron 'Hinodegiri' (Kurume).

Adaptability. Light shade in summer is beneficial in the South and in other areas having very hot summers for good growth and to reduce fading in red-flowered cultivars. Light shade in winter reduces leaf scorch in northern parts of the useful range (Zones 6 and 7).

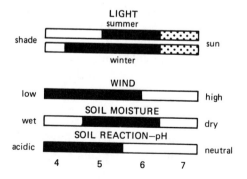

Seasonal Interest. *Flowers:* Orange-red to bright red to deep magenta, 2−3.5 cm/0.8−1.4 in. across, very showy in middle spring with the

partly expanded foliage. *Foliage:* Lustrous, evergreen or nearly evergreen leaves, 1−2.5 cm/0.4−1 in. long. The "summer leaves" that develop after flowering usually are retained through most or all of winter, the last of them falling as new leaves and flowers emerge in spring.

Problems and Maintenance. Problems include mites, scale insects, and several other diseases and insects. Most do not cause severe or permanent damage, but control measures are occasionally needed, especially in warmer zones. Pruning seldom is necessary or desirable. Bark splitting at the soil line can occur in late autumn when plants have not hardened properly. To minimize this, avoid overwatering or fertilizing in late summer and early autumn.

Cultivars. 'Album' has single, white flowers and upright growth and is seldom commercially available.

'Amoenum' (synonyms: *Azalea amoena*, *R. amoenum*, *R. obtusum* var. *amoenum*; originally known as "Hatsu-giri" in Japan) has small, double, magenta (red-purple) flowers, small, deep green leaves, and a dense, upright branching habit. This cultivar, generally considered to be the most cold-hardy form of *R. obtusum*, is useful in Zones 6b−9a and sheltered sites in Zone 6a.

'Amoenum Coccineum' is similar to 'Amoenum' except that it has bright rose-red flowers, a color that harmonizes more easily than the magenta of 'Amoenum.'

Additional cultivars have been selected from *R. obtusum*, but the greatest importance of this species is as a parent of the Kurume Hybrids (see Hybrids). A few cultivars sometimes listed under *R. obtusum* probably are more correctly assigned to the Kurume Hybrid group or to *R. kiusianum* (see Related Species).

Hybrids

Kurume Hybrids. The parentage of this group of excellent hybrids is not very clear but apparently consists of *R. kaempferi*, *R. kiusianum*, and

R. obtusum. Since the first of this group was developed in Japan almost 200 years ago, there has been great interest in producing new cultivars. The number currently in collections in the United States is in the hundreds, but relatively few are available commercially. These are mostly rather low-growing plants, but some will eventually attain heights of close to 2 m/6.6 ft after many years. They have fine-textured, lustrous, evergreen foliage, in some cultivars turning a rich mahogany-red in winter sun. These are among the best of all azaleas for year-round landscape effectiveness and are useful in the same range as *R. obtusum.* A few of the most commonly available cultivars are listed here:

'Blaauw's Pink' has salmon rose-pink flowers, and is reputed to be more cold-hardy than average for Kurume azaleas, to Zone 6b.

'Christmas Cheer' (= 'Ima-shojo,' = 'Fascination') has bright red flowers, to 3 cm/1.2 in. across, and a spreading but compact growth habit. It is cold-hardy to sheltered sites in Zone 6b.

'Coral Bells' has single, bright, shell-pink flowers, usually less than 3 cm/1.2 in. across, and low, spreading growth habit.

Rhododendron 'Coral Bells.'

'Hino-crimson' is similar to 'Hinodegiri' except in having slightly deeper red flowers and slightly smaller leaves.

'Hinodegiri' has ruby-red flowers, to 4 cm/1.5 in. across, compact growth, and excellent foliage. Although this is a very good selection, cold-hardy to Zone 6b, it has been overused at the expense of the variety of colors that can be obtained from other good Kurume cultivars.

'Hinomayo' has single, deep rose-pink flow-

ers, 3 cm/1.2 in. across, and an upright growth habit.

'Pink Pearl' has double, deep salmon-pink flowers. Technically it probably is not a Kurume azalea, but it is similar in form and function.

'Sherwood Red' has single, orange-red flowers, more than 4 cm/1.6 in. across, and a low, compact growth habit. It is cold-hardy to Zone 6b.

'Snow' has single, white flowers, more than 4 cm/1.6 in. across, and vigorous upright growth, eventually to 2 m/6.6 ft tall in good sites. The impressive flowers unfortunately remain on the plant after they have turned brown.

Kaempferi Hybrids (Malvaticum Hybrids). These are mostly hybrids of 'Malvaticum,' a seedling of unknown origin but perhaps involving *R. mucronatum* and *R. kaempferi* (see Related Species). These are of special interest in Zone 6a and sheltered sites in Zone 5b, just outside the useful range of the Kurume azaleas. They are vigorous, upright plants, sometimes to 2 m/6.6 ft tall.

A few of the most common cultivars are listed here. 'Alice' has salmon-red flowers with a deeper red center. 'Carmen' has deep rose-pink flowers to 6 cm/2.4 in. across with a brown blotch. 'Cleopatra' has lilac-rose flowers. 'Fedora' has deep violet-rose flowers, to 5 cm/2 in. across. 'Oberon' has soft, light pink flowers. 'Othello' has vivid red flowers, as bright as those of 'Hinodegiri' but larger, to 5 cm/2 in. across, and an upright growth habit.

Related Species

Rhododendron kaempferi 5 (synonyms: *Azalea kaempferi,* *R. obtusum* var. *kaempferi*; torch azalea). This native of northern Japan is deciduous. It is taller and rangier than *R. obtusum* and distinctly more cold-hardy, useful in Zones 6a—9a, protected sites in Zone 5b, and possibly even colder zones if hardiest genetic material can be obtained. Flowers are red to salmon-red to deep salmon-rose, 3—5 cm/1.2—2 in. across. It is a valuable landscape plant in its own right as well as a parent of the Kaempferi and Kurume Hybrids discussed here and the Gable Hybrids (see *R. yedoense*).

Rhododendron kiusianum 3 (synonym: *R. obtusum* f. *japonicum*; Kyushu azalea). This small, dense plant from high elevations in Japan has small deciduous leaves and small, pink to purple flowers. Useful in Zones 7a−9a, it is valued as a bonsai subject and is an important parent of the Kurume azaleas.

Rhododendron prinophyllum 5

Synonyms: *Azalea prinophylla*, *A. rosea*, *R. roseum*
Roseshell azalea
Deciduous shrub
Ericaceae (Heath Family)

Native Range. Northeastern United States and adjacent Canada, southwesterly to Arkansas.

Useful Range. USDA Zones 3b−6b.

Function. Border, specimen, naturalizing.

Size and Habit

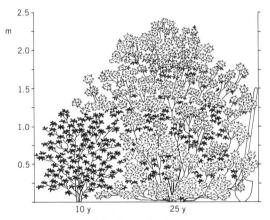

Rhododendron prinophyllum.

Adaptability

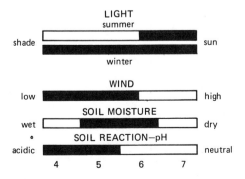

Seasonal Interest. *Flowers:* Highly fragrant, bright, clear pink, 4 cm/1.6 in. across, in clusters to 7.5 cm/3 in. across very late in spring. *Foliage:* Hairy, dull blue-green leaves are sparsely arranged, offering minor summer interest, and fall without color change in autumn.

Problems and Maintenance. This azalea is relatively trouble-free and requires little or no maintenance, although insects and mites that damage azaleas occasionally may be troublesome. Pruning is not necessary except for renewal of old plants and should not be done without good reason.

Hybrids

Northern Lights Hybrids. This new hybrid group (R. ×*kosteranum* × R. *prinophyllum*) is similar in most ways to R. *prinophyllum* but much more showy in flower. For a more complete description, see R. *japonicum*, Hybrids.

Related Species

Rhododendron alabamense 3−4 (*Azalea alabamensis*; Alabama azalea). This rare, deciduous species is a low, thicket-forming shrub, found on rather dry soils in northern Alabama and adjacent Georgia. It has deliciously fragrant white flowers, sometimes with yellow centers. It is not likely to be available in nurseries and should not be collected from the wild but should be preserved if encountered in development, primarily in Zones 7 and 8.

Rhododendron canescens 5 (synonym: *Azalea canescens*; Florida pinxter or Piedmont azalea). This tall, loose, deciduous shrub ranges commonly and widely in the southeastern United States from North Carolina to Florida and Texas. Its fragrant flowers are white with a pink tube, appearing in early spring before the new foliage or just as it begins to unfold, and it is more shade-tolerant than R. *prinophyllum*. It is not widely available for planting but worth preserving

Rhododendron canescens.

in development. Useful in Zones 7a−9a+ and perhaps also parts of Zone 6.

Rhododendron periclymenoides 4 (synonyms: *Azalea nudiflora*, *R. nudiflorum*; pinxter-bloom). This commonly occurring native of the Appalachians from Massachusetts to North Carolina and Tennessee is similar to R. *canescens* and R. *prinophyllum*, with pale pink to nearly white flowers. It is a thicket-forming shrub of varying height, more shade-tolerant than R. *prinophyllum*, and useful in Zones 5b−8b, but probably should be considered of secondary value to R. *canescens* in the South and to R. *prinophyllum* in the North because its flowers have little or no fragrance and its growth habit lends well only to naturalizing.

Rhododendron schlippenbachii 5

Synonym: *Azalea schlippenbachii*
Royal azalea
Deciduous shrub
Ericaceae (Heath Family)

Native Range. Japan, Korea, Manchuria.

Useful Range. USDA Zones 5b−8b and protected sites in Zone 5a.

Function. Specimen, massing, border.

Size and Habit

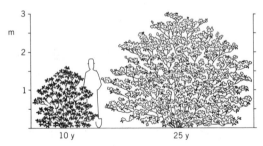

Rhododendron schlippenbachii.

Adaptability

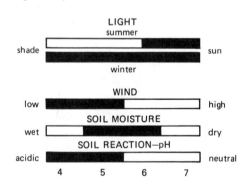

Seasonal Interest. *Flowers:* Fragrant, delicately tinted, pale to rosy pink, 6−8 cm/2.4−3 in. across, before the foliage, making an extraordinary show in midspring. *Foliage:* Broad, rounded leaves give distinctive texture and turn yellow to orange-red before falling in autumn.

Rhododendron schlippenbachii.

Problems and Maintenance. Foliage is sometimes affected by a leaf-spot disease and mites, but these usually are not serious. Flower buds are tender in Zone 5; for best flowering there, protect plants from strong winter winds as well as frost pockets. Northern exposures may be helpful in delaying flower bud activity in spring until threat of severe cold is past.

Rhododendron smirnowii 5

Smirnow rhododendron
Evergreen shrub
Ericaceae (Heath Family)

Native Range. Western Asia: Caucasus Mountains.

Useful Range. USDA Zones 5b—7b, areas with moderate summer temperatures in Zone 8, and protected sites in Zone 5a, perhaps also Zone 4.

Function. Border, specimen, foundation.

Size and Habit

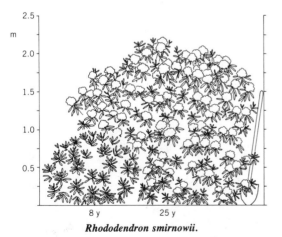

Rhododendron smirnowii.

Adaptability. Shade from full summer sun is necessary for good performance in Zones 7 and 8, the Midwest, and other areas having hot summers. Plants tolerate full shade but do not flower well. Protection from full winter sun is necessary in Zones 4 and 5.

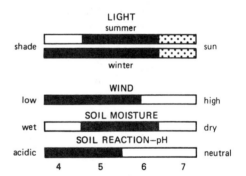

Seasonal Interest. *Flowers:* Pale to rosy pink, 6 cm/2.4 in. across, as many as a dozen packed together in clusters to 15 cm/6 in. across, opening in middle to late spring, before those of *R. catawbiense. Foliage:* Evergreen, leathery, 8—15 cm/3—6 in. long and rather narrow, dark green and lustrous on upper surfaces, heavily felted underneath, pure white at first, later rusty brown. Even the upper surfaces of newly emerging leaves are felted, and traces of white sometimes remain as leaves mature.

Rhododendron smirnowii.

Problems and Maintenance. Many of the insects and diseases that trouble R. *catawbiense* also affect R. *smirnowii*, but insects that feed on the undersides of leaves (e.g., lace bug) are inhibited by the heavy mat of hairs, which also help to make leaves less susceptible to damage from desiccation and rapid temperature changes. Nevertheless, attention to both site and soil is essential for good performance (see R. *catawbiense*).

Varieties and Cultivars. Varieties of R. *smirnowii* are not known, perhaps because of the limited native habitat of this species. Nevertheless, plants in commerce under this name are highly variable, probably because of inadvertent hybridization. While hybridization has diluted some of the desirable features of R. *smirnowii* (e.g., compact growth, heavy felting of foliage, and relatively clear pink flowers), it may also produce superior individuals differing from the species type in advantageous ways. Examination of known and speculative hybrids has produced a few useful hybrid cultivars and may produce more.

Related Species

Rhododendron brachycarpum 5. This relative of R. *smirnowii* from Japan and Korea is variable, with yellow-white to pink flowers and broad, elliptical leaves that are thinly felted underneath. Like R. *smirnowii*, this is one of the most cold-hardy *Rhododendron* species, useful in Zones 5b–7b but seldom commercially available.

Rhododendron caucasicum 3 (Caucasian rhododendron). This low, compact plant with yellowish white or pink-tinged flowers and leaves

5–10 cm/2–4 in. long and rusty felted underneath, probably is not in landscape use, but it is a parent of several fine hybrids such as the R. *catawbiense* hybrid 'Boule de Neige' and the R. *caucasicum* hybrid 'Goldsworth Yellow.' If available, it probably would be useful at least in Zones 6a–7b.

Rhododendron degronianum 4. This Japanese relative of the above species is notable for its variable habit with some broadly compact, moundlike forms and red-brown felted foliage. It is little known in commerce but has been used in producing relatively cold-hardy hybrids. If available, it probably would be useful at least in Zones 6a–7b.

Rhododendron keiskei 3–5 (Keisk rhododendron). This Japanese species is distinctive as the hardiest of all yellow-flowering species, useful in Zones 6b–7b and southward where summer heat is not extreme. If not for the yellow flowers, it probably would receive little attention, since its growth habit is gracefully open to straggling, ranging greatly in height. Even with the distinctiveness of its flower color, it is little used and seldom available. This species is of interest as a hybrid parent because of its flower color, and it may be used increasingly in producing distinctive and useful cultivars for landscape use.

Rhododendron yakusimanum 3 (Yakusima rhododendron). This close relative of R. *degronianum* and R. *smirnowii* functions as a smaller, more compact, and more elegant counterpart of those species. It remains below 1 m/3.3 ft in height for at least 10 to 15 years, usually longer, and is typically broader than tall, with lustrous, dark green leaves, to 8 cm/3 in. long,

Rhododendron yakusimanum.

with very heavy buff felting underneath. This fine plant, with light pink or white flowers in clusters about 10 cm/4 in. across, has been rediscovered recently by gardeners. Even though it is being propagated in much greater numbers, it may be some time before supply catches up with demand. Meanwhile, selection of indi-

vidual clones and hybridizing are going on, promising considerable variety in highly functional, low-growing rhododendrons in the future. Useful at least in Zones 6a–7b, Zone 5b in protected sites, and areas in Zone 8 having moderate summer temperatures.

Rhododendron vaseyi 5

Synonym: *Azalea vaseyi*
Pinkshell azalea
Deciduous shrub
Ericaceae (Heath Family)

Native Range. Mountains of North Carolina.

Useful Range. USDA Zones 5a–8b.

Function. Border, naturalizing, massing, specimen, screen (in good sites).

Size and Habit

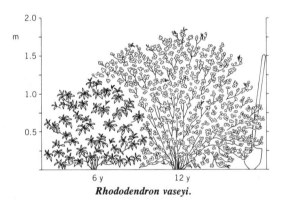

Rhododendron vaseyi.

Adaptability. Tolerance of wet soils does not extend to heavy clay soils, but this species is a good choice for pond and stream bank sites in lighter soils.

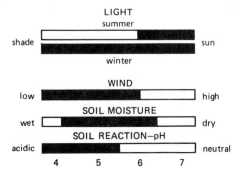

Seasonal Interest. *Flowers:* Fragrant, light pink, two-lipped, to at least 2.5 cm/1 in. long, in clusters before the new foliage in middle to late spring. *Foliage:* Smooth leaves, to at least 10 cm/4 in. long, bright green but turning light red before falling in autumn, differing from most azalea leaves in smoothness and texture.

Rhododendron vaseyi.

Problems and Maintenance. This shrub is relatively trouble-free and requires little maintenance, although minor insect and mite problems may arise occasionally. Usually does not need to be pruned except for rejuvenation of very old plantings, and even this is not necessary in naturalized plantings in good, moist sites. An endangered species, *R. vaseyi* should not be collected from the wild.

Forms. F. *album* has white flowers.

Related Species

Rhododendron canadense 3 (synonyms: *Azalea canadensis*, *Rhodora canadensis*; rhodora).

This native of moist to wet sites in northeastern North America from Newfoundland and Labrador to northern Pennsylvania has two-lipped, rosy-purple flowers, to 2 cm/0.8 in. long, and dull blue-green foliage. Not as showy in flower as most azaleas, *R. canadense* is useful primarily in naturalized plantings, especially in the Far North. Useful in Zones 3a–5b, probably also Zone 2, and cool, moist sites in Zone 6.

Rhododendron viscosum 5

Synonym: *Azalea viscosa*
Swamp azalea
Deciduous shrub
Ericaceae (Heath Family)

Native Range. Eastern United States, Maine to Georgia and Alabama.

Useful Range. USDA Zones 4b–9a, with selection of appropriate genetic material.

Function. Border, naturalizing.

Size and Habit

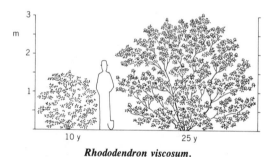

Rhododendron viscosum.

Adaptability. Tolerance of wet soil gives this plant added usefulness but does not make it suitable for wet clay soils. In the wild, it occurs in swamps on hummocks. In wet soils in landscape sites, it should be planted in shallow planting holes or in artificial hummocks or mounds of organic material such as wood chips or peat moss, or a combination of these.

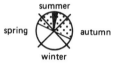

Seasonal Interest. *Flowers:* Highly fragrant, white or pink-flushed, to 2.5 cm/1 in. long, opening from early summer to midsummer. *Foliage:* Bright green, sparse, turning dull orange before falling in autumn.

Rhododendron viscosum.

Problems and Maintenance. This shrub is relatively trouble-free and requires little maintenance, comparable with R. *prinophyllum* in this respect. Pruning is neither necessary nor desirable in naturalized situations, but in more formal landscapes the strong tendency to form thickets may make occasional pruning necessary.

Cultivars. No cultivars of this species are available, but considerable variation in flower numbers and color exists, and selection of superior individuals, when feasible, gives much more colorful plants than average. Hybrids with R.

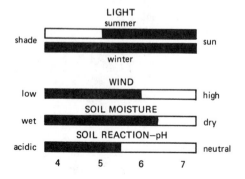

arborescens, some with rosy pink flowers, exist in the wild and could be propagated for landscape use.

Related Species

Rhododendron arborescens 5 (synonym: *Azalea arborescens*; sweet azalea). This mountain counterpart of *R. viscosum* grows wild in the Appalachians from Pennsylvania to northern Alabama and is useful in Zones 5a–9a. Its flowers are fragrant, like those of *R. viscosum*, but slightly earlier, and its glossy, bright green leaves turn red in autumn. It is less tolerant of wet soils than *R. viscosum*. The selection 'Rubescens' has rosy tinted flowers but is not yet widely available.

Rhododendron atlanticum 3 (synonym: *Azalea atlantica*; coast azalea). This native of the Atlantic Coast from Delaware to South Carolina tolerates dry sites better than either *R. arborescens* or *R. viscosum* but is less shade-tolerant than those species. As a low, thicket-forming shrub, it is not as useful as the other two species except for naturalizing in its native area, but it can be grown in Zones 5a–9a. Its flowers, highly fragrant and similar to those of *R. arborescens* and *R. viscosum*, appear in middle to late spring.

Rhododendron serrulatum 6 (synonym: *Azalea serrulata*; hammocksweet azalea). This southern counterpart of *R. viscosum* is native from southeastern Georgia to central Florida and Louisiana, and more fully extends the useful range of this complex of species into Zone 9a+. It probably is useful northward to Zone 7a, but is no better there than *R. viscosum*.

Rhododendron yedoense 4

Yodogawa azalea
Deciduous shrub
Ericaceae (Heath Family)

Native Range. This species is a cultivated form that, according to the International Code of Botanical Nomenclature, must be assigned the species name. The wild type, var. *poukhanense*, is native to Korea.

Useful Range. USDA Zones 5b–8b and sheltered sites in Zone 5a.

Function. Specimen, border, massing, foundation.

Size and Habit. Var. *poukhanense* is illustrated.

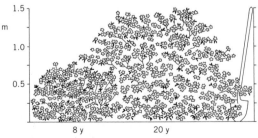

Rhododendron yedoense var. *poukhanense*.

Adaptability. Light shade in summer is beneficial in the South and other areas having very hot summers for best performance.

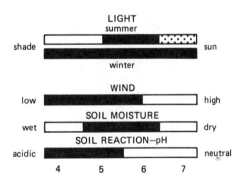

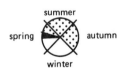

Seasonal Interest. *Flowers*: Rosy lavender, double (single in var. *poukhanense*), to 5 cm/2 in. across, in middle to late spring. *Foliage*: Medium green, slightly silky, remaining green late, then turning purplish before falling in late autumn.

Problems and Maintenance. Disease and insect problems, mostly not serious, are much the same as for *R. obtusum*. Pruning is neither necessary nor desirable. Bark splitting and resulting death of the plant can occur in late autumn if plants have not hardened adequately. To reduce the chances of this happening, avoid overwatering and fertilization in late summer and early autumn.

Varieties. Var. *poukhanense* (synonyms: *Azalea poukhanensis, R. poukhanense;* Korean azalea) is the wild type of this species. Ordinarily the wild type would be considered the species type, but in this case the garden form with double flowers was described before Western botanists were aware of the single-flowered wild type. According to the International Code of Botanical Nomenclature, the first-named type becomes the species type. The var. *poukhanense* is an excellent landscape plant in itself, freely bearing purplish lavender flowers and making a low, mounded mass of foliage and bloom. It is at least as cold-hardy as the Yodogawa azalea and at least reasonably successful in good sites in Zone 5a. Moreover, it has been used as a parent in breeding many hardy hybrids, including most of the Gable Hybrids and a few of the hardier Glenn Dale Hybrids (see *R. indicum*).

Hybrids

Gable Hybrids. These hardy and varied hybrids mostly originated from the breeding program of Joseph B. Gable in Pennsylvania, beginning in the 1920s and continuing into the 1950s, but some are products of continuation of this program by others. Parentage includes *R. yedoense* var. *poukhanense, R. kaempferi, R. mucronatum,* and others. Most of the resulting cultivars have flowers similar in size to those of *R. yedoense* and flower at approximately the same time. Most cultivars are cold-hardy to Zone 6a and a few to Zone 5b. When selecting cultivars, rely on local experience and availability. A few of the more common cultivars are listed here. 'Boudoir' has single, violet-rose flowers, 4 cm/1.6 in. across. 'Cameo' has single, shell-pink flowers, 4 cm/1.6 in. across. 'Campfire' has single, red flowers, to 4.5 cm/1.8 in. across. 'Elizabeth Gable' has single, frilled, rose-red flowers, to 6 cm/2.4 in. across, and a spreading growth habit. It is one of the most cold-hardy of the Gable Hybrids. 'Herbert' has single, reddish purple flowers, to 4.5 cm/1.8 in. across, and a low, spreading growth habit. 'Louise Gable' has semidouble, purplish red flowers, to 5.5 cm/2.2 in. across, and a low, dense growth habit. 'Polaris' has single, white flowers, to 6 cm/2.4 in. across, with yellow-green centers. 'Purple Splendor' has single, red-purple flowers, to 4.5 cm/1.8 in. across, and a low, spreading growth habit. 'Robert Lee' has ruffled, white flowers, to more than 6 cm/2.4 in. across, and a low, spreading growth habit. 'Rosebud' has double, rose-red flowers, to 4.5 cm/1.8 in. across, and a low, dense growth habit. 'Rose Greeley' has fragrant, single, white flowers with a yellow-green blotch, to 5.5 cm/2.2 in. across, and a low, dense growth habit. 'Springtime' has single, rose-red flowers, 5 cm/2 in. across, and a tall, upright growth habit. 'Stewartstonian' has single, bright red flowers and wine-red winter foliage.

Rhodotypos scandens 4

Synonyms: *R. kerrioides, R. tetrapetala*
Jetbead
Deciduous shrub
Rosaceae (Rose Family)

Native Range. China and Japan.

Useful Range. USDA Zones 5a–8a and areas in Zone 8b having moderate summers.

Function. Border, massing, foundation.

Size and Habit

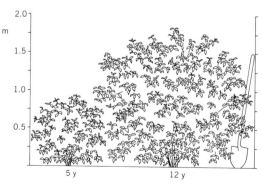

Rhodotypos scandens.

Adaptability

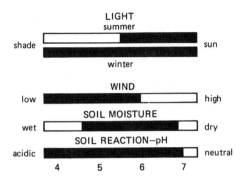

Seasonal Interest. *Flowers:* Single, white, 3 cm/1.2 in. across, moderately showy in combination with the handsome foliage. *Foliage:* Dark green, prominently veined and sharply toothed leaves, 5–8 cm/2–3 in. long, provide distinctively crisp texture and fall in autumn with little color change. *Fruits:* Shiny, black, beadlike fruits, 0.5 cm/0.2 in. across, produced in clusters usually of four at the twig ends, persist after the leaves fall and through much of the winter, adding quiet interest during part of the leafless season.

Problems and Maintenance. A twig-blight disease occasionally becomes troublesome but can be controlled by pruning off and burning infected stems. Otherwise pruning is necessary only to promote vigor and fullness in older plants, and overall need for maintenance is minimal.

Related Species

Neviusia alabamensis 4 (snow-wreath). This close relative of *Rhodotypos*, native to Alabama, is planted occasionally in the mid-South for its display of masses of white flowers with many stamens, giving a feathery appearance about the same time as the flowering of *Rhodotypos*. It has little other seasonal interest but is a good neutral plant for the shrub border or naturalizing in Zones 6b–8b.

Neviusia alabamensis.

Rhus aromatica 4–5

Synonym: *R. canadensis*
Fragrant sumac
Deciduous shrub
Anacardiaceae (Cashew Family)

Native Range. Eastern United States and adjacent Canada.

Useful Range. USDA Zones 3b–9a.

Function. Border, massing, foundation, large-scale groundcover (low forms).

Size and Habit

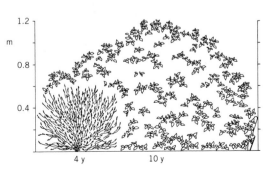

Rhus aromatica.

Adaptability

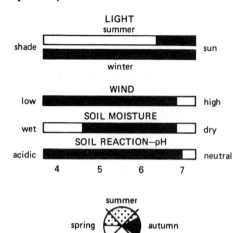

Rhus aromatica.

Seasonal Interest. *Flowers:* Small, pale yellow, in terminal clusters 0.5−2 cm/0.2−0.8 in. long, not showy but fairly conspicuous because they appear before the leaves unfold in early to middle spring. *Foliage:* Softly hairy, trifoliate leaves, aromatic when crushed, with leaflets 2.5−8 cm/1−3 in. long, soft green as they unfold, then lustrous deep green in summer, turning orange to scarlet in autumn, at least in some forms in light soils. *Fruits:* Red, rounded, and hairy, about 0.6 cm/0.25 in. across, adding quiet interest in late summer.

Rhus aromatica.

Problems and Maintenance. Leaf spot and mildew can be minor problems, but generally this plant is trouble-free. Pruning is necessary every few years for renewal and maintenance of vigor.

Varieties and Cultivars. Var. *serotina,* ranging naturally from Indiana to Texas, differs from the species type in flowering later and in its height, frequently to almost 2 m/6.6 ft. It does not seem to color as reliably in autumn as the lower species type, but holds its deep green foliage rather late. The species type is usually preferred in landscape use, since its lower stature, to about 1 m/3.3 ft, is frequently more useful.

'Green Globe' is an upright selection with rounded form.

'Gro-Low' is a low, spreading form that remains below 0.6 m/2 ft in height for years and is an excellent large-scale groundcover.

Related Species

Rhus trilobata 4−5 (ill-scented sumac, skunkbush). This shrub, native from Illinois westward to California, is seldom intentionally planted but sometimes inadvertently offered as *R. aromatica.* Although it is essentially interchangeable with *R. aromatica,* it is usually more stiffly upright and not as functional as a groundcover. This plant is useful in the same zones as *R. aromatica* but is seldom available in our area.

Two additional species with three-leaflet leaves, *R. radicans* (poison ivy) and *R. toxicodendron* (poison oak), are poisonous to touch, strongly so to many persons. In spite of their fine autumn foliage, they obviously must be avoided.

Rhus copallina 6

Shining sumac
Deciduous shrub
Anacardiaceae (Cashew Family)

Native Range. Eastern United States and parts of adjacent Canada: Maine to Florida and westward to Ontario, Minnesota, and Texas.

Useful Range. USDA Zones 4b–9a.

Function. Border, specimen, large-scale massing.

Size and Habit

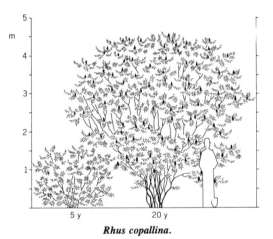

Rhus copallina.

Adaptability

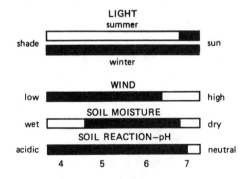

Seasonal Interest. *Flowers:* Pale yellowish green in dense, erect, terminal clusters to 15 cm/6 in. long, fairly conspicuous against the dark green foliage in late summer. Dioecious. *Foliage:* Glossy, dark green, pinnately compound with

9–12 leaflets, each up to 10 cm/4 in. long, more striking in summer than that of most *Rhus* species, with a distinctive winged rachis (leaf midrib), turning bright scarlet in autumn. *Fruits:* Crimson, fuzzy, in compact clusters to at least 10 cm/4 in. long, on pistillate (female) plants only, colorful in autumn and into winter.

Rhus copallina.

Problems and Maintenance. Diseases and physical damage to the weak wood make this plant relatively short-lived, but this is not a serious problem in large-scale and naturalized plantings where root suckers tend to renew the tops. Maintenance requirements are similar to those of *R. typhina.*

Related Species

Rhus chinensis 6 (Chinese sumac). This plant in time becomes treelike, with creamy white flowers in upright clusters to 25 cm/10 in. long in middle to late summer and orange-red foliage and fruiting clusters in autumn. Useful in Zones 6a–9a.

Rhus vernix 6 (poison sumac). This native of swamps from New England to Florida and westward to Minnesota and Louisiana is as poisonous to the touch as it is handsome, and so it must be avoided rather than planted.

Rhus typhina 6

Staghorn sumac
Deciduous shrub
Anacardiaceae (Cashew Family)

Native Range. Eastern United States and parts of adjacent Canada, Quebec to Georgia and westward to Iowa.

Useful Range. USDA Zones 3b−8a.

Function. Border, specimen, large-scale massing.

Size and Habit

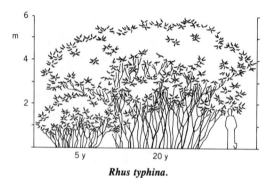

Rhus typhina.

Adaptability

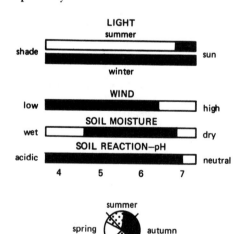

Seasonal Interest. *Flowers:* Greenish in dense, erect, terminal clusters to 20 cm/8 in. long, not very conspicuous because of their color. Dioecious. *Foliage:* Medium green, velvety and hairy when young, pinnately compound with 11−31 leaflets, each up to 10 cm/4 in. long, producing strikingly coarse texture in the landscape and turning to brilliant shades of orange and red in autumn. *Fruits:* Crimson, fuzzy, in erect, club-like clusters to 15 cm/6 in. long on pistillate (female) plants only, colorful from late summer into early winter. *Twigs:* velvety and hairy twigs add mild winter interest. Those bearing the staminate (male) flower clusters after the flowers are gone, resemble velvety antlers, giving the plant its common name.

Rhus typhina, pistillate inflorescence.

Rhus typhina, staminate inflorescence.

Rhus typhina.

Problems and Maintenance. Stem cankers and branch dieback cause this plant to be relatively short-lived. This is usually compensated for in large-scale and naturalized plantings by the tendency to produce new tops by suckering. But *R. typhina*, *R. copallina*, and *R. glabra* as well should be used in extensive situations only if careful maintenance is provided, particularly pruning to remove deadwood and to select some root suckers for renewal and eliminating others.

Cultivars. 'Dissecta' has finely dissected, fernlike leaves and is valued as a specimen for accent in highly architectonic planting situations. It tends to be ineffective when planted with many other plant materials but is striking against wall and window surfaces with gravel mulch.

Related Species

Rhus glabra 6 (smooth sumac). This relative of *R. typhina* ranges even more widely, from Maine to Florida and westward to British Columbia and Texas. It differs little from *R. typhina* in general appearance but has smooth twigs and brighter red fruits. It is useful in much the same ways as *R. typhina* in a slightly larger part of our area: Zones 3a–9a. The cutleaved selection 'Laciniata' gives a similar effect as *R. typhina* 'Dissecta,' but it is less likely to be available in our area and is highly susceptible to mildew in some areas.

Ribes alpinum 5

Alpine currant
Deciduous shrub
Saxifragaceae (Saxifrage Family)

Native Range. Europe.

Useful Range. USDA Zones 3b–7b.

Function. Hedge, massing, border.

Size and Habit

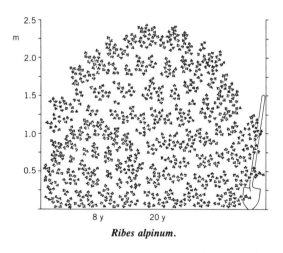

Ribes alpinum.

Adaptability. Even though growth is most compact and suitable for hedging in full sun, the plant will perform relatively well in considerable shade.

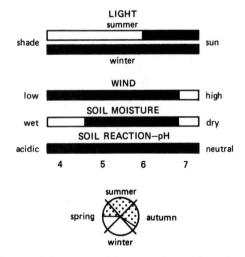

Seasonal Interest. *Flowers:* Greenish yellow, small and not showy, in midspring with the emerging leaves. Dioecious. *Foliage:* Lobed leaves, 2.5–5 cm/1–2 in. long, pale green as they emerge in midspring, turning deep green in summer and falling without color change in autumn. *Fruits:* Scarlet, small, in late summer, on pistillate (female) plants in the presence of staminate plants—an infrequent occurrence since plants in commerce usually are propagated by cuttings and therefore are clonal and of a single sex.

Problems and Maintenance. Several diseases can be minor problems, but *R. alpinum* is much less troubled by disease than most *Ribes* species (currants and gooseberries). The most serious concern when members of this genus are planted is white pine blister rust, for which many currants and gooseberries are alternate hosts and are quarantined from eastern white pine *(Pinus strobus)* habitat areas by federal regulation. *R. alpinum*, even though immune to the disease, is under quarantine and cannot be planted legally in white pine areas. Many of the western and southern parts of our area are outside the range of white pine, and *R. alpinum* does well in such areas having hot dry summers, except that mite infestations are more likely to be severe.

Cultivars. 'Pumilum' (dwarf Alpine currant) is very compact in growth but reaches heights of 1 m/3.3 ft or more in time.

Related Species

Ribes aureum 4 (golden currant).   This western North American counterpart of the clove currant *(R. odoratum)* is so similar that it is interchangeable in landscape use in Zones 3b—7b, and *R. aureum* is also hardy in Zone 3a.

Ribes odoratum 4 (clove currant, buffalo currant).   This species, native to the Great Plains region of the United States from South Dakota to Texas, bears golden yellow flowers with a delicious clove fragrance. The plant is susceptible to premature defoliation by leaf-spot diseases and has minimal landscape character, but it might be included in a mixed shrub border for the spring flowering interest outside white pine areas. Useful in Zones 3b—7b.

Many other species of *Ribes* exist, several of them native to North America, but most have little landscape usefulness in our area.

Robinia hispida 4

Rose acacia
Deciduous shrub
Leguminosae (Legume Family)

Native Range. Southeastern United States.

Useful Range. USDA Zones 4b—9a.

Function. Thickets: naturalizing or massing, specimen (with maintenance).

Size and Habit

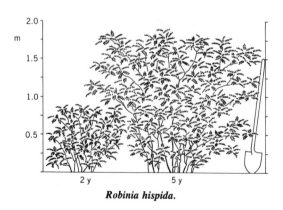

Robinia hispida.

Adaptability

LIGHT
summer

shade ▭ sun

winter

WIND
low ▭ high

SOIL MOISTURE
wet ▭ dry

SOIL REACTION—pH
acidic ▭ neutral

4   5   6   7

summer

spring ⊗ autumn

winter

Seasonal Interest. *Flowers:* Rose to lavender-pink, in showy, pendulous clusters, to 8 cm/3 in. long, in late spring. *Foliage:* pinnately compound leaves with 7—13 leaflets, each to 3.5 cm/1.4 in. long, falling in midautumn without color change. *Fruits:* Bristle-covered pods add minor interest in late summer to early autumn, seldom contain viable seeds. *Twigs and branches:* Young twigs usually are densely bristled like the pods.

Problems and Maintenance. The strong tendency of this shrub to sucker and form thickets makes it an ideal plant for slope stabilization, but it is difficult to keep in bounds in other landscape situations where its use must be accompanied by a careful program to remove unwanted root suckers.

Related Species

Robinia fertilis 4 (bristly locust).   This shrub differs from *R. hispida* in that it has fewer bristles on the reddish brown stems, and smaller flowers. Its bristled seed pods bear abundant crops of seeds. Useful in Zones 5a–9a.

Robinia pseudoacacia 8

Black locust
Deciduous tree
Leguminosae (Legume Family)

Native Range. East-central United States from Pennsylvania to Georgia and westward to Iowa and Oklahoma. Naturalized over most of the rest of our area, as well as in Europe.

Useful Range. USDA Zones 4b–9a and some sites in Zone 4a.

Function. Shade tree, specimen, naturalizing.

Size and Habit

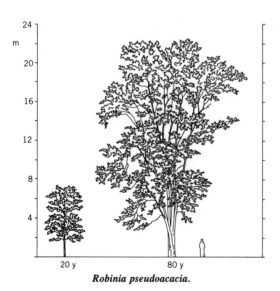

Robinia pseudoacacia.

Adaptability. Grows well in infertile soils because of its ability to assimilate atmospheric nitrogen with the help of bacteria in its roots.

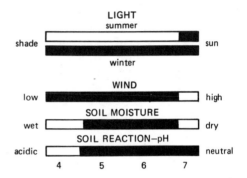

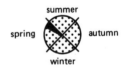

Seasonal Interest. *Flowers:* Creamy white, very fragrant, in pendulous clusters 10–20 cm/4–8 in. long, very late in spring. *Foliage:* Very dark green, compound with rounded leaflets only 2.5–5 cm/1–2 in. long, casting mottled shade and falling in autumn without color change. *Trunk and branches:* Heavy, gray, ropy bark adds mild but distinctive year-round interest.

Problems and Maintenance. Trunk borers are a serious problem that must be controlled by carefully timed spraying to prevent serious and permanent damage, even though infested trees often grow vigorously for some time before becoming seriously weakened. Wood rotting organisms may complicate the situation by invading the borer tunnels and hastening the decline of the tree. A leaf miner insect sometimes disfigures the foliage and the tree produces root suckers, but these are minor problems in comparison with borers.

Varieties and Cultivars. Considerable variety in form exists in R. *pseudoacacia*, from narrow and mastlike, with branches spreading laterally rather abruptly toward the top of the tree, to round-headed. Natural varieties have not been clearly identified. Several individual forms have been selected and given cultivar status, but only 'Umbraculifera' (umbrella black locust) is at all common. This small tree has a densely globose head while young, gradually assuming a more umbrellalike shape with age, and a maximum height of about 5 m/16 ft, and seldom bears flowers.

Related Hybrids and Species

Robinia ×*ambigua* 7 (synonym: R. ×*hybrida*; hybrid locust).   This hybrid (probably R. *viscosa* × R. *pseudoacacia*) is somewhat shorter in stature than R. *pseudoacacia* but not small enough to fit underneath power lines, sometimes reaching heights of 12 m/39 ft. Flowers are similar to the best of R. *pseudoacacia* except that they are rosy pink and showy very late in spring. The most widely used selection is 'Idaho' (= 'Idahoensis'), a popular small tree in the plains and Rocky Mountains in Zones 4b−9a.

Robinia viscosa 7 (clammy locust).   This native of the southern Appalachian Mountains, naturalized elsewhere in the southeastern United States as well, has pink flowers and is usually encountered in landscape use in the form of the hybrid R. ×*ambigua*. It is useful in Zones 4b−9a.

Rosa centifolia 4

Cabbage rose
Deciduous shrub
Rosaceae (Rose Family)

Native Range. Western Asia: eastern Caucasus Mountains.

Useful Range. USDA Zones 5b−9a.

Function. Specimen, border.

Size and Habit

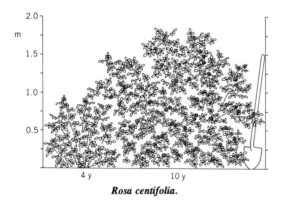

Rosa centifolia.

Adaptability

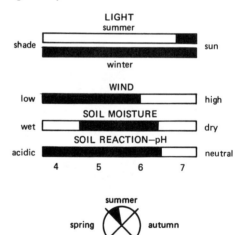

Seasonal Interest. *Flowers:* Fragrant, very double, nodding because of their weight, 4−8 cm/ 1.5−3 in. across, in early summer with little or no rebloom. *Foliage:* Compound, medium green, adding only minor summer interest, falling in autumn with little color change. *Fruits:* Rose hips are borne sparsely and add little interest.

Problems and Maintenance. Roses in general require minimal to considerable maintenance because of their susceptibility to a variety of disease and pest problems, including black spot, mildew, crown gall, cankers, rose chafer, Japanese beetle (within the range of this insect), leaf hoppers, scale insects, mites, and others. Those that are considered to be functional landscape plants require less maintenance than the so-called garden roses that are grown primarily for flowers rather than function. R. *centifolia* and its hybrids have been grown as garden subjects for centuries. For this use they have been superseded by better flowering Hybrid Tea and Floribunda cultivars, their principal usefulness today stemming from their functional value and historical interest. They surpass the modern garden roses functionally, but they do not compare well with some of the other species roses in this respect or in breadth of seasonal interest or freedom from troubles.

Cultivars. There has been a revival of interest in older roses among some specialists in the last decade or two, and hybrids of R. *centifolia* are sometimes available. Selection should be guided by local experience and availability. 'Muscosa' (moss rose) is a distinctive selection from R. *centifolia* with a mossy surfaced receptacle and flower stalk. More than 30 cultivars have been developed from moss parentage, including a few that rebloom after first flowering in early summer. They are mostly available only from specializing nurseries.

Related Species

Rosa ×*alba* 4 (cottage rose). This hybrid group of uncertain origin but believed to have involved R. *canina* and R. *damascena* includes several cultivars with fragrant flowers, usually double and pink, in spite of the implication of the species name, but including a few good white selections such as 'Madame Legras de St. Germain,' with double white flowers. Members of this group are useful in Zones 5a−9a.

Rose canina 5 (dog rose). This native of Europe has been widely used as an understock for other rose cultivars and has some interest and usefulness of its own. It will function as an informal hedge, dense enough for screening under ideal growing conditions, with fragrant, single, pink or white flowers, about 4 cm/1.6 in. across, in early summer and ornamental red fruits later in summer. Useful in Zones 5a−9a and as a somewhat lower shrub (to about 1 m/3.3 ft), owing to winter injury, in Zone 4.

Rosa damascena 4 (damask rose). Like R. *centifolia*, this species originated in Asia Minor and has been cultivated for centuries. Its fragrant, double, pink to red flowers are fully as large as those of R. *centifolia*, and its useful range is similar, Zones 5b−9a, but its overall landscape value is limited. The ancient selection 'Versicolor' (York and Lancaster rose), with flowers varying from white to pink through different degrees of striping and blotching, was designated as a symbol of unity of the red and white rose factions at the end of the War of the Roses in the fifteenth century. The selection 'Semperflorens' (= 'Four Seasons'), unlike other cultivars, reblooms during the summer after the first period of flowering in early summer.

Rosa eglanteria 4 (synonym: R. *rubiginosa*; sweetbrier rose). This European native is widely grown there, functioning much the same as R. *canina* in informal hedges. It is best known for the applelike fragrance of the foliage rather than for its bright pink flowers, which appear in early summer and are followed by colorful, orange-red fruits. Hybrids with pink, copper, red, and yellow flowers exist, mostly useful in Zones 6a−9a.

Rosa gallica 3 (French rose). This longcultivated native of central and southern Europe and western Asia suckers freely, forming thickets. It has limited usefulness as a landscape plant but was an important forerunner of the Hybrid Perpetual roses from which modern garden roses were developed. With single or double, pink to red-purple flowers to 7 cm/2.8 in. across in early summer followed by brick-red fruits, R. *gallica* can be used where its thicket-forming growth is appropriate, in Zones 5a−9a and some cultivars also in Zone 4.

Rosa rubrifolia 4−5 (redleaf rose). This shrub from the mountains of central Europe is valued more for its bluish green foliage overlaid with dark red than for its small, fragrant, rose-pink flowers, which are not borne in large numbers. It is useful for massing or for variety in the shrub border in Zones 2b−8a.

Rose villosa 4 (synonym: R. *pomifera*; apple rose). Another native of Europe and adjacent Asia, R. *pomifera* functions much the same as R. *canina*, with single, pink flowers in early summer followed by unusually large (2.5 cm/1 in. across), red, pear-shaped hips (fruits). The f. *duplex* has semidouble flowers. It is useful in Zones 4b−9a.

Rosa hugonis 5

Father Hugo rose
Deciduous shrub
Rosaceae (Rose Family)

Native Range. Central China.

Useful Range. USDA Zones 4b–8a.

Function. Border, specimen, informal hedge. Not dense enough to make an effective screen.

Size and Habit

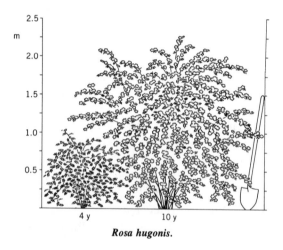

Rosa hugonis.

Adaptability

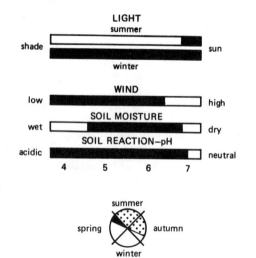

Seasonal Interest. *Flowers:* Single, lightly fragrant, bright butter yellow, to 5 cm/2 in., borne in large numbers on gracefully arching branches in late spring. *Foliage:* Compound, bluish green, and fine-textured because of the small leaflets, only 1–2 cm/0.4–0.8 in. long, falling in midautumn without color change. *Fruits:* Very dark red, only 1.5 cm/0.6 in. across, inconspicuous.

Problems and Maintenance. This species is more trouble-free than most roses but occasionally may need spraying to control insects. Renewal pruning is necessary periodically to maintain good form.

Related Species and Hybrids

Rosa foetida 5 (Austrian brier rose).   This native of western Asia has deep yellow flowers in early summer, to 7 cm/2.8 in. across, with an unpleasant odor, which, along with extreme susceptibility to black spot, has limited the popularity of this otherwise appealing species. Foliage texture is not as fine as that of R. *hugonis*, and the overall size is somewhat greater, so this plant needs plenty of space. The selection 'Bicolor' (= 'Austrian Copper'), with single, bicolored coppery red and yellow flowers, probably is the most popular cultivar, and 'Persiana' (Persian yellow rose), with smaller but double yellow flowers, is another outstanding selection. Both are useful in Zones 3a–8b. R. *foetida* has also been used as the parent of hybrids, one of which is listed below.

Rosa ×*harisonii* 4 (Harison's yellow rose). This hybrid of R. *foetida* × R. *spinosissima* has semidouble, bright yellow flowers, to 5 cm/2 in. across, in late spring to early summer. Its foliage is fine-textured but less so than that of R. *hugonis*, and it is useful in Zones 4a–8a.

Rosa primula 4 (primrose rose).   This central Asian species has pale yellow flowers, to 4 cm/1.6 in. across, well before the end of spring. The aromatic foliage adds another interesting feature in summer. Useful in the same zones as R. *hugonis*.

Rosa spinosissima 3 (synonym: R. *pimpinellifolia*; Scotch rose, Burnett rose).   This low-growing, suckering shrub, to 1 m/3.3 ft, has foliage as fine-textured as that of R. *hugonis* and somewhat smaller flowers, usually 2.5–5 cm/1–2 in.

across, ranging from pink to white or yellow, in late spring. Native to Europe and western Asia, *R. spinosissima* has been widely cultivated in Europe and colonial America in a variety of forms and is variably hardy, generally useful in Zones 5a–8a, some cultivars to Zone 4. Although its cultivars are useful for massing or for seasonal color in shrub borders, they are perhaps less useful today than some of the lower-growing native roses such as *R. arkansana*, *R. carolina*, and *R. nitida* and other low shrubs with more year-round interest.

R. spinosissima var. *altaica* (Altai rose). This is an exceptionally cold-hardy population from the Altai Mountains of central Asia that has been drawn upon for breeding of cold-hardy (to Zone 3) garden roses for the Northern Plains, especially by F. L. Skinner of Dropmore, Manitoba and W. A. Cumming and W. P. Leslie of the Canada Department of Agriculture, Morden, Manitoba.

Modern products of the C.D.A. breeding program include the following.

'Prairie Charm' is a disease-resistant shrub to 1.5 m/5 ft tall with arching stems, pale green foliage, and glowing pink, semidouble flowers borne in large numbers in early summer.

'Prairie Dawn' is similar in size, with upright branching, glossy, dark green foliage and glowing pink double flowers, 5–6 cm/2–2.4 in. across, blooming in early summer and intermittently thereafter.

'Prairie Maid' is a compact selection growing to 1 m/3.3 ft tall with fragrant, double, creamy white flowers in early summer and occasionally thereafter.

'Prairie Youth' is a vigorous selection growing to 2 m/6.6 ft tall with medium dark green foliage and bright salmon pink, semidouble flowers in early summer and intermittently thereafter.

Rosa laevigata 1 and 5

Cherokee rose
Evergreen or semievergreen shrub
Rosaceae (Rose Family)

Native Range. China; naturalized in the southern parts of our area from Florida to Texas.

Useful Range. USDA Zones 8a–9a+.

Function. Large-scale massing or barrier, climbing specimen, naturalizing.

Size and Habit. High-climbing, to 6 m/19 ft or more, or piling up in masses to 2–3 m/7–10 ft tall with a greater spread.

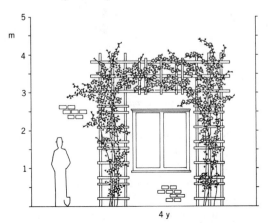

Rosa laevigata.

Adaptability

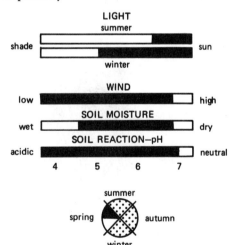

Seasonal Interest. *Flowers:* Fragrant, single, white, to 8 cm/3 in. across, showy in middle to late spring. *Foliage:* Semievergreen to evergreen, deep green and lustrous with medium texture, making an attractive but loose mass. *Fruits:* Orange-red, pear-shaped and bristly, to 4 cm/1.6 in. across, interesting in autumn and much of winter.

Problems and Maintenance. This plant is unusually free of troubles for a rose, but its vigor can be excessive in all but large-scale planting sites.

Allow plenty of room, or pruning maintenance will be excessive.

Cultivars. Red- and pink-flowering selections are occasionally available but do not grow strongly and apparently are in little demand.

Related Species

Rosa bracteata 1 and 5 (Macartney rose).   Like *R. laevigata*, this species originated in China and has become naturalized in the southern states. These two species are similarly wide-scrambling with arching branches, but *R. bracteata* blooms lightly after the first flush of flowering until frost, has finer-textured foliage than *R. laevigata*, and responds better to shearing. This species is useful in Zones 8a−9a+, perhaps in somewhat colder zones as well, but has become a serious weed problem, in parts of the South even more so than *R. multiflora*. The hybrid 'Mermaid,' with delicately buff-yellow flowers to 10 cm/4 in. across, an *R. bracteata* hybrid, is similar in size to *R. bracteata* and a superb plant for large-scale use. It is somewhat more cold-tolerant than *R. bracteata* and *R. laevigata*, useful to Zone 7 and perhaps colder zones as well with protection.

Rosa multiflora 5

Japanese or multiflora rose
Deciduous shrub
Rosaceae (Rose Family)

Native Range. Japan and Korea.

Useful Range. USDA Zones 5b−9a.

Function. Large-scale barrier hedge, specimen, wildlife cover.

Size and Habit

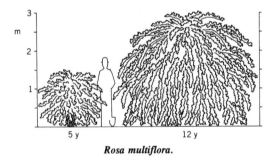

Rosa multiflora.

Adaptability

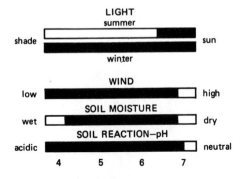

Seasonal Interest. *Flowers:* White, about 2 cm/0.8 in. across, in large clusters, fragrant and very showy in late spring or early summer, but without repeated flowering later in summer. *Foliage:* Lustrous, remaining deep green well into autumn before falling. *Fruits:* Bright red, individually no more than 0.6 cm/0.25 in. across, but borne in large numbers in clusters; colorful from early autumn to midwinter or later.

Rosa multiflora.

Problems and Maintenance. This is one of the most vigorous and trouble-free of all roses. Underestimation of its size and vigor and resulting misuse have given *R. multiflora* a bad reputation. Because of its ultimate height of 4 m/13 ft or more and even greater spread, it should be used *only* in large-scale situations, but given this condition it is a serviceable landscape plant for some areas, fast-growing, functional, and having a substantial range of seasonal interest. Note: legislation has been passed in some states making it illegal to plant this species, since in some areas it has escaped cultivation and has become a serious weed problem. Check with local authorities before specifying this plant.

Cultivars. 'Platyphylla' (seven sisters rose) has single, multicolored flowers, from white to deep rose-purple or pink, fading individually and giving a variety of shades within the same flower cluster. *R. multiflora* also has been an important parent of modern garden rose cultivars, especially the Dwarf Polyantha roses and 'Crimson Rambler.'

Related Species

Rosa roxburghii 5 (chestnut or Roxburgh rose). This Chinese native is like no other shrub rose, with peeling, gray-tan bark that adds year-round interest to the clear, light lavender-pink flowers, to 6 cm/2.4 in. across, that appear in early summer. Two forms are in cultivation. The single-flowered form does not flower very heavily but is vigorous and useful in Zones 6b–9a. The double-flowered form is less vigorous, flowers heavily, and reblooms lightly. It sets few fruits and is essentially seedless, responds well to shearing, and is more tender than the single-flowering form. The fruits are reddish, to 4 cm/1.6 in. across, and very prickly, adding distinctive interest in autumn. Not widely available at present, but useful in Zones 7a–9a.

Rosa setigera 5 (prairie rose). This native of North America, from Ontario to Nebraska and southward to Florida and Texas, requires about as much space as *R. multiflora* but is different in growth habit, with very long canes arching out irregularly or climbing by scrambling where support is available. Although its form can be kept more regular by pruning, it is difficult to contain for long, so it is probably best to reserve this plant for large-scale, informal situations. Flowers, about 5 cm/2 in. across, open rose, fading to pale pink. Flowering is later than that of most roses, in early summer to midsummer, and some clones do not flower well at all. The red fruits, scarcely larger than those of *R. multiflora*, add moderate but unreliable interest in autumn. The foliage is not as handsome during summer as that of *R. multiflora*, but turns reddish orange before falling in autumn. Useful in Zones 4b–9a.

Rosa rugosa 4

Rugosa rose
Deciduous shrub
Rosaceae (Rose Family)

Native Range. Japan, Korea, northern China; naturalized in some localities in the northeastern United States.

Useful Range. USDA Zones 3a–7b with selection of appropriate genetic material.

Function. Massing, specimen, border, informal hedge.

Size and Habit

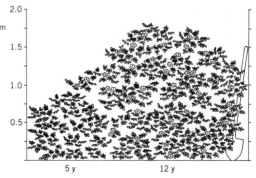

Rosa rugosa.

Adaptability. Grows best in exposed sites with full sun, except in Zone 3. It is not as tolerant of limestone soils as some other roses, but it is notably tolerant of salt, whether at the seashore or near winter-salted walks.

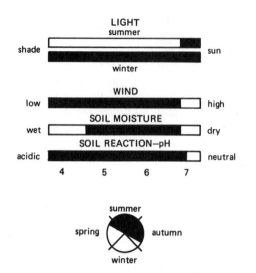

Seasonal Interest. *Flowers:* Rose-pink with a purplish cast to white, fragrant, single or double, to 8 cm/3 in. across, in late spring or early summer and continuing intermittently during the summer. *Foliage:* Deep green, leathery, and wrinkled, producing an outstanding textural effect, turning golden orange in late autumn in some years. *Fruits:* Very large, edible, orange-red hips, to 2.5 cm/1 in. across and showy in late summer and autumn; can be used for making tea and preserves, and are a very rich source of vitamin C (ascorbic acid). *Twigs and branches:* Heavy and very thorny.

Rosa rugosa.

Problems and Maintenance. *R. rugosa* is unusually trouble-free for a rose and usually needs pruning only to remove an occasional borer-infested cane or to give it a little more uniform shape in an informal hedge.

Cultivars and Hybrids. Many selections for cold climates have been made and availability varies locally. A few of the most popular are listed here.

'Agnes' is a hybrid (*R. rugosa* × *R. foetida* 'Persiana') with fragrant, double, pale yellow flowers, to 8 cm/3 in. across, in early summer and excellent glossy foliage. It reaches a height of about 1.5 m/5 ft and is cold-hardy to Zone 4a.

'Amelie Gravereaux' has fragrant, semidouble, rosy red flowers, fading purple, to 8 cm/3 in. across, fairly showy in bloom all summer, and producing long canes. It is cold-hardy to Zone 4b and grows to a height of 1.2 m/4 ft.

'Belle Poitevine' has fragrant, semidouble, purplish pink flowers, to 8 cm/3 in. across, in early summer, and large orange fruits. It is cold-hardy to Zone 3b and reaches a height of about 1.2 m/4 ft.

'F. J. Grootendorst' has double, deep rose-pink flowers, only about 2.5 cm/1 in. across but borne in clusters. It is fairly showy in bloom all summer, cold-hardy to Zone 4b, and reaches a height of about 1.2 m/4 ft.

'Grootendorst Supreme' is similar to 'F. J. Grootendorst' but with double crimson flowers.

'Hansa,' a very popular cultivar in the Northern Plains, is exceptionally cold-hardy, to Zone 3a, with fragrant, double, deep purplish red flowers, about 5 cm/2 in. across, showy all summer, and red fruits. It reaches a height of 1.5 m/5 ft and a greater spread.

'Max Graf' is a trailing hybrid (probably *R. rugosa* × *R. wichuraiana*) to only about 0.5 m/1.6 ft tall, forming a good, large-scale groundcover, useful in Zones 4b–7b. Pinkish white flowers are not fragrant and appear in early summer with little recurrence later.

'Pink Grootendorst' is similar to 'F. J. Grootendorst' but with double, pink flowers.

'Sir Thomas Lipton' has fragrant, semidouble, white flowers, recurring during summer. It is cold-hardy to Zone 3b and reaches a height of about 1.2 m/4 ft.

'Wasagaming' is a complex hybrid involving *R. rugosa*, *R. acicularis*, and a Hybrid Perpetual rose. It grows to nearly 2 m/6.6 ft in height, is cold-hardy to Zone 3a, and its fragrant, double, clear rose flowers open intermittently through the summer.

'Will Alderman' (R. rugosa × R. acicularis) has fragrant, double, lilac-pink flowers in early summer with little or no recurrence, but it is cold-hardy to Zone 3b, and reaches a height of about 1.2 m/4 ft.

Related Species

Rosa acicularis 3 (circumpolar rose, prickly wild rose) and *Rosa arkansana* 3 (Arkansas rose, prairie wild rose). Low growing, very hardy species native to the prairie states and provinces. R. acicularis also grows wild eastward to the maritime provinces, northwestward to Alaska, and southwestward to New Mexico, and R. arkansana eastward to New York and westward to Alberta and Texas. Neither species is in itself much used in landscaping, but both are parents of hardy rose cultivars useful in the Northern Plains. R. acicularis is involved in the parentage of some of the Rugosa Hybrids, and R. arkansana is the dominant parent of the Parkland roses, a recently developed series of hybrids, including the following:

'Adelaide Hoodless' is a vigorous shrub, to 1.2 m/4 ft tall with glossy dark green foliage and faintly fragrant, semidouble, red flowers to 8 cm/3 in. across, blooming continuously through the summer.

'Morden Amorette' is a lower growing plant, less than 0.5 m/1.6 ft tall, with large, double, carmine-rose flowers continuously blooming through summer.

'Morden Ruby' grows vigorously to 1 m/3.3 ft tall, with long-lasting double, ruby-red flowers continuing all summer.

These cultivars suffer some killing back in winter in the Northern Plains extremes of Zone 2 but recover quickly in spring to function well as specimens or for massing or low, informal hedges. They would be expected to perform satisfactorily southward at least to Zone 5, but because of their hardiness, they will find special value in our coldest areas.

Rosa blanda 4 (meadow rose, smooth wild rose, Labrador rose). This native of the northern parts of our area from Newfoundland to Manitoba and southward to Pennsylvania and Missouri is mostly thornless, with red stems and fragrant, single, pink flowers, 5–8 cm/2–3 in. across, in late spring or early summer, and red fruits, about 1 cm/0.4 in. across, in autumn. Its rangy habit and limited flowering season make it of marginal landscape interest, but its extreme cold-hardiness makes it useful for naturalizing in the far northern parts of our area, and there has been some interest in it as a hybrid parent. It is useful in Zones 3a–6b and perhaps colder zones with selection of locally native genetic material.

Rosa virginiana 4

Synonym: *Rosa lucida*
Virginia rose
Deciduous shrub
Rosaceae (Rose Family)

Native Range. Eastern North America: Newfoundland southward to Alabama and westward to Missouri.

Useful Range. USDA Zones 5a–7b, northward to Zone 4 with selection of appropriate genetic material, and southward to Zone 8 in areas having moderate summer temperatures.

Function. Massing, border.

Size and Habit

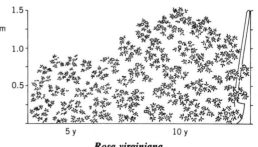

Rosa virginiana.

Adaptability

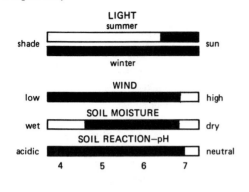

Seasonal Interest. *Flowers:* Light purplish pink, single, to 6 cm/2.4 in. across, moderately showy in early summer. *Foliage:* Deep green, glossy and clean, remaining attractive throughout summer and turning orange-red before falling in autumn. *Fruits:* Bright red, to 1.5 cm/0.6 in. across, ripening in early autumn and remaining colorful well into winter. *Twigs:* Reddish, from early autumn through winter, adding significant interest in combination with the red fruits.

Problems and Maintenance. R. *virginiana* is less subject to disease and insect problems than most roses, and requires little or no maintenance in naturalized settings. When massed in human-made landscapes, renewal pruning will be needed every few years to keep the planting from taking on a ragged look.

Cultivars. 'Alba,' with white flowers, and 'Plena,'

with double purple-pink flowers, add variety but may not be available commercially.

Related Species

Rosa carolina 3 (Carolina rose, American wild rose, pasture rose).   This native of eastern North America from Nova Scotia to Minnesota and southward to Florida and Texas functions as a lower growing version of R. *virginiana* that suckers more freely, forming thickets. Less functional than R. *virginiana* except for covering areas of ground rapidly, and with less handsome foliage, it is still a useful plant for naturalizing and large-scale massing in Zones 5a–8b with selection of locally native genetic material.

Rosa nitida 3 (shining or bristly-hedge rose). This low-growing (no more than 0.5 m/1.6 ft tall) native of northeastern North America (Newfoundland to New England) has very glossy foliage that reddens in autumn and single, bright, rosy red flowers, 5 cm/2 in. across, in early summer. Useful for massing or as a specimen in Zones 4a–6b and perhaps farther south in areas with moderate summer temperatures.

Rosa palustris 4 (swamp rose).   Native to upland as well as swampy areas in eastern North America from Nova Scotia to Minnesota and southward to Florida and Mississippi, this species differs little from R. *virginiana*, with somewhat inferior foliage, but it is to be preferred, when available, for wet soils. It is more likely to be available for preservation in sites being developed than for planting elsewhere, but it can be used in Zones 4b–8b with selection of appropriate genetic material, preferably locally native stock.

Rosa wichuraiana 1 and 2

Memorial rose
Semievergreen climber or groundcover
Rosaceae (Rose Family)

Native Range. Eastern China, Japan, Korea, Taiwan.

Useful Range. USDA Zones 5b–9a.

Function. Large-scale groundcover, cover for highway slopes and other banks. Can also be trained as a climber.

Size and Habit

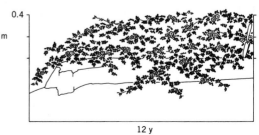

Rosa wichuraiana.

Adaptability

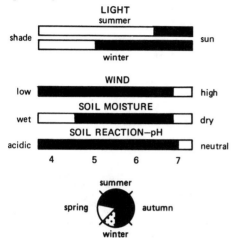

Seasonal Interest. *Flowers:* Fragrant, single, white, 5 cm/2 in. across, in midsummer. *Foliage:* Lustrous to glossy, rich deep green, persisting well into winter or longer with snow cover, making a dense mass quickly. *Fruits:* Red, 1 cm/0.4 in. across, moderately colorful in autumn.

Problems and Maintenance. This species is vigorous and relatively trouble-free, but it occasionally may need protection from mites and insects. When planted in restricted areas, this trailing shrub will need frequent pruning to keep it in bounds. It is best reserved for larger-scale situations.

Hybrids. R. *wichuraiana* has been an important parent in the development of the Rambler and Brownell "Sub-Zero" Hybrid Tea roses and others, including many that are functional as well as decorative. The Ramblers can be used with varying degrees of success as groundcovers or for vertical display on trellises. Selection of cultivars should be based on local experience and current availability, which can change rather quickly. In general, hardiness, plant vigor, and freedom from disease problems are of crucial importance when selecting rose plants for functional application, and decorative aspects are necessarily secondary. Yet there are many opportunities for the creative designer to provide striking beauty in functional plantings.

Related Species

Rosa banksiae 1 (Lady Banks rose). This vigorous, high-climbing rose from China will reach heights of 6 m/19 ft and greater in the Deep South. It is spectacular in late spring, with great masses of more or less fragrant, single or double, creamy white or yellow flowers and fine-textured evergreen foliage. Single-flowered forms probably are not commercially available, but two double-flowered forms are grown. Flowers of the double white form are more fragrant than those of the double yellow form, but both are extremely shade-tolerant and sometimes are encouraged to grow into tree canopies. When trained against walls or buildings, they need wire or trellis support for climbing and can be difficult to keep within bounds. Annual pruning following flowering is necessary, and an additional pruning or two may be necessary during summer, especially when space for its rambling is limited. Useful in Zones 8a−9a+.

Rosa chinensis 3 (China rose). This low shrub with semievergreen foliage and pink flowers is an important parent of the Hybrid Perpetual and Hybrid Tea roses as well as the Polyanthas, Floribundas, and Grandifloras. It was the introduction of R. *chinensis* to existing hybrid lines in Europe in the eighteenth century and R. *odorata* soon afterward, that gave rise to most modern decorative hybrid roses. But the contribution of this species to the development of functional landscape roses—as contrasted with decorative roses—has been minimal except in the Deep South, where the climate is more amenable to hybrids with substantial R. *chinensis* parentage than elsewhere in our area. A few such hybrids are functional landscape plants for informal hedging, massing, and training on vertical surfaces. Selection of cultivars should be based on hardiness, vigor, freedom from disease and, of course, availability.

Rosa moschata 3 (musk rose). This native of southern Europe, noted for the musky fragrance of its flowers, has little value as a landscape plant and is not very cold-hardy, useful in Zones 7a−9a and colder areas only with protection. It is a parent of many of the decorative roses, including the Hybrid Musk roses, some of which are reasonably functional but only slightly more cold-hardy than R. *moschata*.

Rosa odorata 3 (tea rose). This semievergreen, trailing or climbing plant is the key forerunner of Hybrid Tea roses, important more for their decorative than functional effect. Like R. *chinensis*, this species is Chinese in origin, tender north of about Zone 7b, and seldom if ever used in the species form.

Rubus odoratus 5

Flowering raspberry, thimbleberry
Deciduous shrub
Rosaceae (Rose Family)

Native Range. Eastern North America: Nova Scotia to Michigan, south to Georgia.

Useful Range. USDA Zones 4a−7b in areas meeting site requirements (see Adaptability).

Function. Shaded border, naturalizing.

Size and Habit

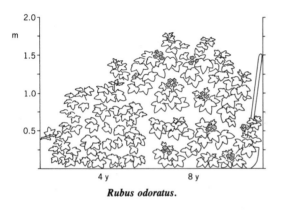

Rubus odoratus.

Adaptability. Planting sites are limited by the need for partial shade, moist (but not wet) soil, and moderate summer temperatures.

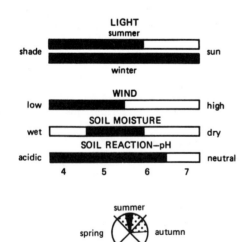

Seasonal Interest. *Flowers:* Fragrant, rose-purple or occasionally whitish, to 5 cm/2 in. across, borne in small clusters from early to midsummer,

not in large numbers but displayed effectively against the coarse foliage. *Foliage:* Medium green, mapleleaf-shaped, 10−20 cm/4−8 in. across, occasionally larger, giving a striking, coarse texture, falling in early autumn with little or no color change. *Fruits:* Flattened red raspberries, borne in small numbers in late summer, inedible.

Rubus odoratus.

Problems and Maintenance. This shrub is trouble-free and requires little or no maintenance in naturalized sites where it performs best.

Related Species

Rubus deliciosus 5 (boulder or Rocky Mountain flowering raspberry). This western relative of *R. odoratus* has white flowers, coarse foliage texture, and arching stems. It is attractive in flower in late spring, and it is of greatest interest in the northwestern parts of our area, useful in Zones 4a−7b.

Rubus hispidus 2 (swamp dewberry, running blackberry). This native of eastern North America from Nova Scotia to Minnesota and south to Georga is a reasonably good groundcover for wet soils, with prickly, trailing stems and glossy, nearly evergreen foliage. The fruits are red, then ripen black, and are very sour. Useful in Zones 4b−7b.

Rubus laciniatus 3 (cutleaf blackberry). This European plant has become naturalized in parts of our area. The trailing to arching stems form a very dense and prickly mass, to 0.5 m/1.6 ft, effective as a groundcover and barrier. The dissected, semievergreen leaves give interesting texture in summer and autumn. Useful in Zones 5a–7b.

Rubus parviflorus 4 (thimbleberry, whiteflowering raspberry). This close relative of R.

odoratus is very similar in landscape effect but has slightly smaller leaves and white flowers. Useful in Zones 4b–7a.

Ruscus aculeatus 3

Butchersbroom
Evergreen shrub
Liliaceae (Lily Family)

Native Range. Europe.

Useful Range. USDA Zones 7b–9a+.

Function. Border, specimen, informal hedge.

Size and Habit

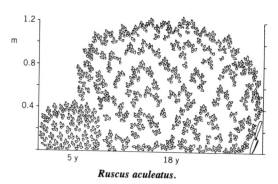

Ruscus aculeatus.

Adaptability. Tolerates full sun to complete shade but performs best with some sun during the growing season. Tolerates wind except in colder areas, where winter wind can cause dehydration.

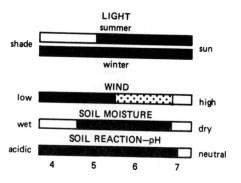

Seasonal Interest. *Flowers:* Inconspicuous, dioecious. *Foliage and stems:* Bristly with small, triangular-pointed cladodes (leaflike protrusions from the stems), year-round. Stems are rigid, forming a good barrier. *Fruits:* Bright red, to 1.5 cm/0.6 in. across, in late autumn and winter on pistillate (female) plants in the presence of staminate (male) plants for pollination. Showy when borne in large numbers, but they seldom are.

Problems and Maintenance. This plant is relatively trouble-free, rarely requiring maintenance of any kind.

Related Species

Danaë racemosa 3 (Alexandrian laurel). This relative of *Ruscus aculeatus* from the Middle East has larger, more leaflike cladodes, to 10 cm/4 in. long, persistent year-round on arching branches arising directly from the ground. This plant is effective for massing, covering small spaces of ground, or for the front of a border. The small white flowers in late spring and orange-red, round fruits, 1–1.5 cm/0.4–0.6 in. across, in autumn give minor seasonal color. Useful in Zones 8a–9a+.

Salix alba 8

White willow
Deciduous tree
Salicaceae (Willow Family)

Native Range. Europe, northern Africa, western to central Asia.

Useful Range. USDA Zones 3a−9a with selection of appropriate genetic material.

Function. Specimen, screen (with pruning).

Size and Habit

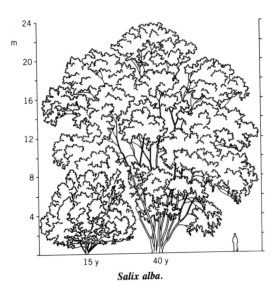

Salix alba.

Adaptability

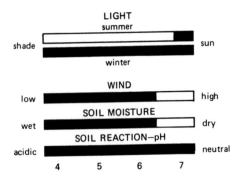

Seasonal Interest. *Flowers:* Yellowish catkins add interest in early spring along with yellow twigs. *Foliage:* Narrow, olive-green leaves, 5−10

cm/2−4 in. long, whitish underneath, fall without color change in midautumn. *Twigs and branches:* Smooth, yellowish bark turns bright yellow in late winter and early spring.

Problems and Maintenance. Willows in general are weak-wooded, prone to a variety of insect and disease problems, and short-lived, especially in warmer climates. They send fast-growing roots into drainage and septic lines, causing serious problems, and therefore they should be planted well away from underground lines unless underground barriers can be constructed, and they should be used in the knowledge that they probably will not be long-lived. Finally, they should be limited to situations where littering by broken twigs and branches can be tolerated. *Salix alba* has all these limitations but is more durable than some other *Salix* species. Its value in landscape use is mostly limited to the varieties listed below.

Varieties. Var. *chermesina* (red-stem willow) has bright red-orange twigs when young and vigorous. This color mostly disappears on established, slower-growing trees, but can be restored by heavy pruning to stimulate new shoot growth. This cultivar is sometimes maintained as a shrub, 1−2 m/3.3−6.6 ft tall, by such pruning, and is used in hedges or borders primarily for the twig color in late winter and early spring.

Var. *sericea* (Siberian white willow) has whitened, silky foliage, giving some of the same effect as *Elaeagnus angustifolia* in the landscape except for its greater size.

Var. *tristis* (golden weeping willow, sometimes also called S. *vitellina* 'Pendula' and Niobe weeping willow), is the most commonly used variety of S. *alba*, and probably the most widely used of the weeping willows because of its bright yellow, pendent branches and cold hardiness, to Zone 4a.

Var. *vitellina* (golden willow) differs from the species type only in having brighter yellow twigs and narrower leaves.

Related Species

Salix exigua 6 (coyote willow).   This small tree is native to much of western North America and useful in the northern and western Central Plains for summer color accent. The form in commerce, at least, has silvery white foliage and a graceful, semipendulous growth habit. It tends to sucker heavily, but this can be eliminated by grafting on nonsuckering rootstocks, which has been done with some plants offered for sale by nurseries in the northwestern extremes of our area. It is useful in Zones 3a−7a with selection of appropriate genetic material.

Salix babylonica 7

Babylon weeping willow
Deciduous tree
Salicaceae (Willow Family)

Native Range. Origin obscure, but cultivated in the Middle East for centuries.

Useful Range. USDA Zones 7a−9a+. May persist for a few years in Zone 6, then be winterkilled to the ground.

Function. Specimen.

Size and Habit

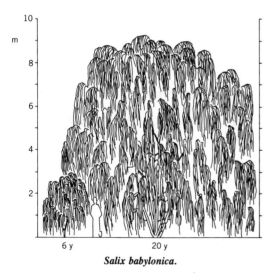

Salix babylonica.

Adaptability

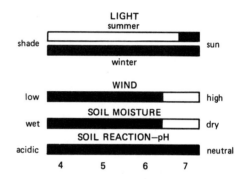

Seasonal Interest. *Flowers:* Delicate green catkins add strong interest to newly emerging foliage in spring. *Foliage:* Pale green and delicate on emergence, then olive green during summer and falling in autumn without color change. Leaves are narrow, only 1−1.5 cm/0.4−0.6 in. wide and 8−15 cm/3−6 in. long, producing a distinctive texture. *Twigs and branches:* Smooth olive to gray-green bark adds minor interest during the leafless season.

Problems and Maintenance. S. *babylonica* has all the limitations of the willows in general (see S. *alba*) and lacks the cold hardiness of most of the other *Salix* species discussed here. Some confusion about its hardiness results from the tendency of some professionals to call all weeping willows by this name. The true S. *babylonica* is a beautiful tree with probably the most strongly pendulous form of all the weeping willows, but it lacks the golden twig color and cold hardiness of S. *alba* var. *tristis.*

Cultivars. 'Aurea' has golden yellow twigs and branches; otherwise it is similar to the species type but is probably not commercially available. 'Crispa' has leaves folded longitudinally and curled into a ring, giving a distinctive texture. It is most useful as a specimen where it can be appreciated at close range.

Related Species

Salix ×*blanda* 7 (Wisconsin weeping willow). This hybrid, probably of *S. babylonica* × *S. fragilis*, is as confused as to identity in commerce as the other weeping willows. True *S.* ×*blanda* resembles *S. babylonica* somewhat but is much less strongly pendulous and probably for this reason seldom available. Useful in Zones 5a−9a when available.

Salix matsudana 7 (Hangkow or Peking willow). This native of northern China resembles *S. babylonica* in foliage and twig color but is not pendulous. It is almost always encountered in the interesting selected form 'Tortuosa' (corkscrew willow), which has spirally twisted twigs and branches and is a popular large shrub or small tree for accent in Zones 5a−9a.

Salix ×*sepulcralis* 8. This little known hybrid of *S. babylonica* × *S. alba* represents a useful compromise between the species types, with greater cold hardiness than *S. babylonica* yet most of that species' growth habit. Winter twigs are as colorful as those of many individuals of *S. alba*, but less so than var. *tristis* or var. *vitellina*. Useful in Zones 5a−9a and probably also Zone 4b.

Salix caprea 5−6

European pussy willow, goat willow
Deciduous shrub or small tree
Salicaceae (Willow Family)

Native Range. Europe and western Asia.

Useful Range. USDA Zones 3b−9a, but fails to attain full size in Zones 3 and 4 because of topkilling in winter.

Function. Specimen, border.

Size and Habit

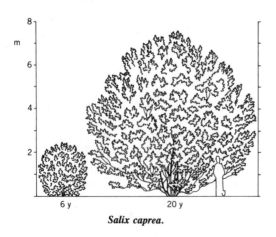

Salix caprea.

Adaptability

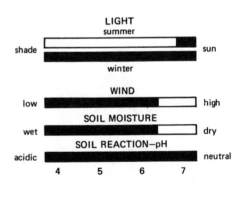

Seasonal Interest. *Flowers:* Dioecious, with silky catkins (pussy willows), to 3.5 cm/1.4 in. long and oval in shape, long before leafing out—one of the first signs of early spring. Staminate (male) catkins turn yellow with pollen to continue the interest for another week or two. *Foliage:* Pale green at emergence, turning very dark green and becoming slightly wrinkled, finally falling in autumn with little or no color change. *Twigs:* Smooth and lustrous, brown in winter with large, smooth, reddish winter buds.

Problems and Maintenance. This species is subject to the problems of willows in general (see *S. alba*), but less so when pruned drastically every year or two to promote vigor and heavy flowering, if the prunings are removed and burned. This reduces overwintering insect populations and inoculum for future disease infections. The problem of roots in drainage lines remains in spite of cultural treatment. Winterkilling of tops occurs in occasional winters in Zones 3 and 4 but is less serious when annual renewal pruning is practiced.

Cultivars. 'Variegata' has variegated, creamy white leaves, adding summer interest, but it is not very widely available.

Related Species

Salix discolor 6 (pussy willow). This is the North American native counterpart of *S. caprea*, growing wild in about the northern half of our area. Its somewhat smaller silky catkins are equally valued for cutting for indoor decoration, and the plant is slightly more cold-hardy, useful in Zones 3a–9a. For maximum early spring display and attractive foliage and growth habit, *S. caprea* is the logical choice, but for long lasting spring display combined with extreme cold-hardiness and, of course, for naturalizing, *S. discolor* is preferred.

Salix sachalinensis 6 (Sakhalin willow). This native of Japan and Sakhalin is represented in landscape use exclusively by the unusual form 'Sekka' (Japanese fantail willow), which has stem tips contorted into fanlike claws by fasciation (fusion) of stems. This form is used exclusively as a specimen for accent, and it is better in formal, architectonic situations than in the middle of a lot of other vegetation. It has significantly showy, silky catkins in early spring on reddish brown stems and is useful in Zones 5a–9a.

Salix pentandra 7

Synonym: *S. laurifolia*
Laurel willow, bay willow
Deciduous tree
Salicaceae (Willow Family)

Native Range. Europe and adjacent Asia.

Useful Range. USDA Zones 3a–9a.

Function. Shade tree, screen, or windbreak.

Size and Habit

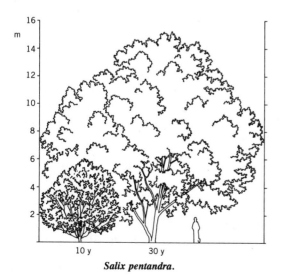

Salix pentandra.

Adaptability

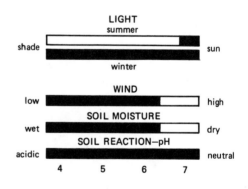

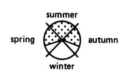

Seasonal Interst. *Flowers:* Golden yellow catkins, 2.5–5 cm/1–2 in. long, add quiet but significant interest in spring. *Foliage:* Leaves are glossy, deep green, and broader than those of most willows, 5–12 cm/2–5 in. long and 2.5–8 cm/1–3 in. wide, making a dense, handsome foliage canopy. Leaves begin to fall in midautumn with little color change.

Problems and Maintenance. *S. pentandra* is subject to the problems of willows in general (see *S. alba*) but is less troubled by insects and diseases than some willows and can function satisfactorily as a handsome shade tree, fast-growing but not long-lived, seldom reaching an age of 40 to 50 years. Some spraying and pruning usually is needed, so this is not a tree for street use or for parks having minimal maintenance budgets.

Related Species

Salix fragilis 8 (brittle willow, crack willow). This large tree, native to Europe and western Asia and naturalized on river banks in the northeastern United States and adjacent Canada, has little to recommend it as a landscape plant other than its tolerance of wet soil and salt. Better willows usually are more widely available, but this species can be used in Zones 3b−9a.

Salix nigra 7 (black willow). This is the native "riverbank" willow in much of our area from New Brunswick to Ontario and southward to Florida and northern Mexico. There is little rationale for planting this species in formal or small-scale landscapes, but it may be planted or a subject for preservation in natural or naturalized sites. Useful in Zones 3b−9a+.

Salix purpurea 5

Purple osier, basket willow
Deciduous shrub
Salicaceae (Willow Family)

Native Range. Europe and North Africa to central Asia and Japan.

Useful Range. USDA Zones 3b−9a.

Function. Hedge (formal or informal), specimen.

Size and Habit

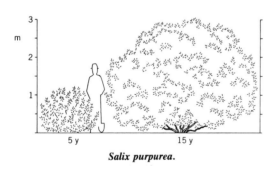

Salix purpurea.

Adaptability. More tolerant of wind than most willows because of its resilient branches, but less tolerant of wet and calcareous soils.

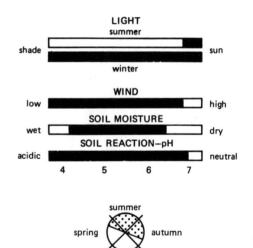

Seasonal Interest. *Flowers*: Catkins are insignificant. *Foliage*: Dull green to blue-green leaves are narrow, 5−10 cm/2−4 in. long, whitened underneath, and fall in autumn without color change. *Twigs and branches*: Slender and resilient, purplish when young, used in basket weaving.

Problems and Maintenance. *S. purpurea* is subject to the problems of willows in general, compounded by slightly different site requirements than most willows. Periodic drastic pruning with removal and burning of prunings may help to control diseases and is useful when maintaining the plant as a compact hedge.

Cultivars. 'Gracilis' (probably = 'Nana;' dwarf arctic willow) is a smaller, slender-twigged form with very narrow, blue-green leaves. This selection is planted in preference to the species type, usually as a formal or informal hedge. Useful in the same zones as the species type and perhaps also in Zone 3a.

Salix repens 2-3

Creeping willow
Deciduous shrub
Salicaceae (Willow Family)

Native Range. Europe and Asia.

Useful Range. USDA Zones 4b-9a and to Zone 3b with snow cover and selection of appropriate genetic material.

Function. Specimen, groundcover, massing.

Size and Habit. Growth habit varies from creeping and mat-forming to ascending.

Salix repens.

Adaptability

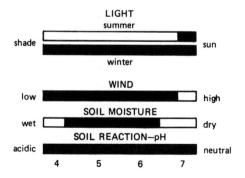

Seasonal Interest. *Foliage:* Gray-green on upper surfaces, densely silky and white on lower surfaces, variable in size from 1.5-3.5 cm/0.6-1.4 in. long and in shape from narrow to elliptical, falling in autumn without color change.

Problems and Maintenance. *S. repens* is subject to the limitations of willows in general (see *S. alba*), but periodic drastic pruning, useful for retaining mass when used as a large-scale groundcover, also helps control diseases by removing infected parts.

Varieties and Cultivars. Var. *argentea* (synonyms: var. *arenaria*, var. *nitida*) is dense, white, and silky or woolly on both upper and lower sides of leaves and preferred for color accent.

Related Species

Salix rosmarinifolia 4 (rosemary-leaved willow). This ascending shrub from central and eastern Europe has linear leaves with a deep green and leathery upper surface and white, silky lower surface. It is useful as a specimen for accent and more effective in architectonic situations than with a variety of plant material, much like *Rhamnus frangula* 'Asplenifolia' in general effect but more useful in wet sites. Useful in Zones 4b-9a.

Salix uva-ursi 2 (bearberry willow). This prostrate, occasionally ascending shrub is small in every respect as compared with the larger willows. It is one of several low-growing *Salix* species found in the subarctic areas of North America and Eurasia. *S. uva-ursi*, native from Labrador to Alaska and southward to a few mountain summits in the northeastern United

States, has lustrous, bright green leaves, 0.5–2.5 cm/0.2–1 in. long, and erect, reddish catkins. It is seldom planted but is an occasional inclusion in an alpine garden. Useful in Zones 1–4b and perhaps milder areas with cool summers as well.

Sambucus canadensis 5

American elderberry
Deciduous shrub
Caprifoliaceae (Honeysuckle Family)

Native Range. Eastern North America: Nova Scotia to Manitoba and southward to Florida and Texas.

Useful Range. USDA Zones 3a–9a.

Function. Specimen, border, screen (with careful maintenance), edible fruits.

after or with the berries in early autumn with little or no color change. *Fruits:* Shiny and purple-black when ripe in late summer, less than 0.5 cm/0.2 in. across but borne in large flattened clusters, often weighing branches down with their collective weight, valued for making preserves and wines.

Size and Habit

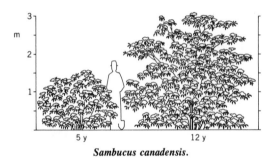

Sambucus canadensis.

Sambucus canadensis.

Adaptability

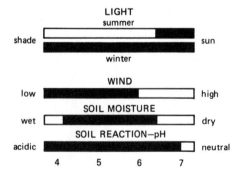

Problems and Maintenance. This shrub is trouble-free but requires pruning to keep it in good form. The long branches are weak and tend to be pulled out of their usual position by the weight of large crops of fruits. Renewal pruning annually or at least biennially is necessary to maintain form and to remove any broken or winter-injured branches.

Cultivars. 'Acutiloba' has dissected foliage. 'Aurea' has golden yellow foliage all summer and red fruits. 'Rubra' has bright red fruits and normal green foliage but probably is not commercially available. 'Adams,' 'Kent,' 'Nova,' and 'York' are among the most popular cultivars selected for heavy fruiting.

Seasonal Interest. *Flowers:* Tiny, creamy white, in large flattened clusters, to 25 cm/10 in. across, very early in summer. *Foliage:* Medium gray-green, compound leaves, serving as a neutral background for the flowers and fruits, falling soon

Related Species

Sambucus nigra 6 (European elderberry). This is the European counterpart of *S. canadensis*, with edible black fruits. It is a rangy plant that tends to go wild in many areas, and is at best no improvement on the native *S. canadensis* as a landscape plant except for the cultivar 'Variegata,' with interesting, white variegated foliage. Useful in Zones 4a−9a.

Sambucus pubens 5 (American red elderberry). This native of much of our area from New Brunswick to Minnesota, southward to Georgia, and westward to Colorado grows wild in partly shaded sites and tolerates more shade in landscape sites than *S. canadensis*. Its yellowish white flowers in late spring and red fruits in midsummer are borne in pyramidal clusters, smaller than those of *S. canadensis*. Best adapted to moist sites, *S. pubens* is useful in Zones 4a−7b.

Sambucus racemosa 5 (European red elderberry). Several superior forms of this European counterpart of *S. pubens* have been selected and are valued for their summer interest in the northern parts of our area. 'Aurea' has yellowish foliage in early summer, later fading to green. 'Dropmore' has finely dissected, fernlike foliage and a dwarf growth habit. 'Laciniata' has coarsely dissected foliage. 'Redman' is compact but eventually large-growing with deeply dissected leaves and showy, bright red fruits. 'Sutherland Golden' has golden foliage. These cultivars are generally useful in Zones 3a−7b. Even though some winter dieback may occur in Zones 3 and 4, the pruning required to maintain form removes any deadwood and recovery is rapid.

Sambucus racemosa 'Sutherland Golden.'

Sambucus pubens.

Santolina chamaecyparissus 3

Synonym: *S. incana*
Lavender cotton
Evergreen shrub or subshrub
Compositae (Composite Family)

Native Range. Southern Europe and North Africa.

Useful Range. USDA Zones 7b−9a+, and as an annual, sometimes surviving winter, in Zones 5b−7a.

Function. Small-scale groundcover, border, formal edging, or low hedge.

Size and Habit

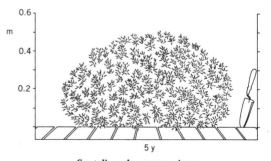

Santolina chamaecyparissus.

Adaptability. Broadly adapted to soils and exposures, but best in full sun in well-drained, even dry, soil.

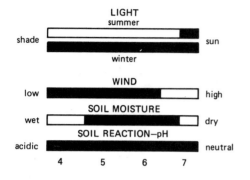

Seasonal Interest. *Flowers:* Bright yellow, in rounded heads, 1–2 cm/0.4–0.8 in. across, in middle to late summer, but do not develop when plants are clipped as a formal edging or hedge. *Foliage:* Small leaves, 1–4 cm/0.4–1.6 in. long and finely divided, comparable in general texture to a juniper, strongly silvery gray with felty hairs, turning duller green from late autumn to midspring, aromatic when crushed.

Santolina chamaecyparissus.

Problems and Maintenance. This plant is unusually free of insect and disease problems but requires frequent to occasional renewal pruning to maintain good form. Replacement of some plants annually may be necessary in Zones 6b–7a, but complete annual replacement is the simplest practice in Zones 5b and 6a. Even in Zones 7–9, plants are not long-lived and may need to be replaced after only a few years.

Related Species

Santolina virens 3 (synonym: *S. viridis;* green lavender cotton). This plant is very similar to *S. chamaecyparissus* in most respects and is useful in the same area, but it has bright to deep green foliage.

Sapium sebiferum 7

Chinese tallow tree
Deciduous tree
Euphorbiaceae (Spurge Family)

Native Range. China, Japan; naturalized in a few areas in the Deep South.

Useful Range. USDA Zones 8b–9a+.

Function. Shade tree for quick effect.

Size and Habit

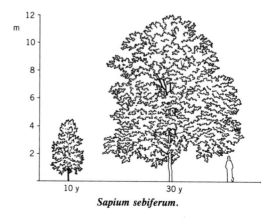

Sapium sebiferum.

Adaptability. Unusually tolerant of widely differing soils.

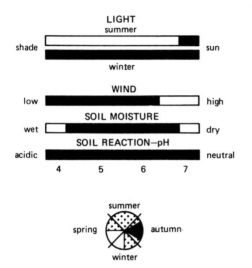

Seasonal Interest. *Flowers:* Very small, yellowish, staminate (male) and pistillate (female) together in catkinlike terminal clusters, to 10 cm/4 in. long, in spring. *Foliage:* Pale to yellowish green, 3−8 cm/1−3 in. long, with long, slender petioles that allow leaf blades to flutter in the wind like those of poplars, turning bright red or yellow before falling in late autumn. *Fruits:* Capsules, to 1.5 cm/0.6 in. across, open to disclose white, waxy coated seeds, usually in clusters of three, which persist well into winter, adding interest after leaf fall.

Problems and Maintenance. This tree is unusually free of insect and disease problems but is usually not long-lived. Flower and fruit litter limit its value as a tree for street or patio planting, for which it is otherwise well suited. Pruning is necessary only for initial shaping and removal of any deadwood, but should be done during the dormant season. When used as a lawn tree, the foliage canopy allows enough light for turf growth underneath, but surface roots can still interfere. A tendency to become naturalized is a problem in a few areas in the Deep South.

Related Species. The following additional members of the Euphorbiaceae (Spurge Family) are not commonly encountered in landscape use in our area but are useful under certain conditions.

Aleurites fordii 6 (tung oil tree). This native of south-central Asia is cultivated primarily for the oil from the seeds, but occasionally it is used as a small shade tree. It is fast growing, with leaves to 12 cm/5 in. long and broad, mostly lobed, turning red-orange before falling in late autumn. Flowers, appearing as the leaves expand in spring, are pale orange to pinkish white in showy clusters, and the smooth, rounded fruits, green at first, turning red and finally almost black, are about the size of small apples, 5−8 cm/2−3 in. across. It is useful as a shade tree in Zones 8b−9a+, but fruit is seldom produced north of Zone 9.

Croton alabamense 5 (Alabama croton). This rangy, thicket-forming shrub, rare in the wild, is even more rarely propagated for landscape use. But with its deep green, rounded leaves, silvery whitened by a mat of fine hairs, it has distinct possibilities for human made landscapes. Not to be confused with the tropical croton of florists, *Codiaeum variegatum*, it is useful in Zones 7b−8b and perhaps elsewhere.

Daphniphyllum macropodum 6. This handsome, large, evergreen shrub from Japan and Korea, variously placed in the Euphorbiaceae or separated as the Daphniphyllaceae, is little known in landscape use in North America. But it has performed well in limited trials in Zone 9a and may be useful in Zone 8 as well. Foliage is dark green, forming a dense mass of lustrous, leathery leaves, each 10−20 cm/4−8 in. long, giving a texture similar to that of *Rhododendron maximum* or *Prunus laurocerasus*, yet distinctive because of the red petioles (leaf stalks) and young twigs. The small, pale green flowers in clusters only about 2.5 cm/1 in. long in late spring and the black fruits, only about 1 cm/0.4 in. long,

Securinega suffruticosa.

add minor additional seasonal interest. The handsome selection 'Variegatum,' with creamy white variegated leaves, probably is not available in North America and has been found in England to be less cold-hardy than the species type.

Securinega suffruticosa 4. This rather ungainly shrub with long, wandlike branches from north-eastern Asia has been planted in the northern parts of our area but is not very useful, versatile, or colorful. Still, its bright green rounded leaves, to 3–6 cm/1.2–2.4 in. long, may add interest to the border. Since it frequently kills to the ground in winter in the areas where is is most likely to be used, Zones 3b–6b, spring pruning is necessary.

Sarcococca ruscifolia 4

Fragrant sarcococca or sweet box
Evergreen shrub
Buxaceae (Boxwood Family)

Native Range. China.

Useful Range. USDA Zones 7b–9a and protected sites in Zone 7a.

Function. Massing, shaded border, or foundation.

Seasonal Interest. *Flowers:* Fragrant, whitish, in small clusters in autumn, not showy but adding seasonal interest. *Foliage:* Evergreen, lustrous, stiff-leathery, sharply pointed, 3–5 cm/1.2–2 in. long, making a handsome, dense mass. *Fruits:* Deep red, rounded, about 0.6 cm/0.25 in. across, in small clusters in autumn and early winter.

Problems and Maintenance. This plant is apparently trouble-free given the proper site, but it is so little used in our area to date that its problems may not yet be fully known. Attention to site requirements, especially shade, is critical.

Related Species

Sarcococca hookerana 4 (Hooker sarcococca or sweet box). This close relative of S. *ruscifolia* differs little but has slightly larger and less sharply

Size and Habit

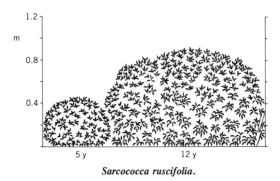

Sarcococca ruscifolia.

Adaptability

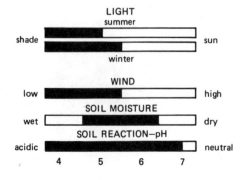

Sarcococca hookerana var. *humilis.*

pointed leaves and black fruits. It is best known for the variety *humilis* (synonym: *S. humilis*; dwarf sarcococca), which seldom exceeds 0.5 m/1.6 ft in height while making a dense mass of foliage. This form has proven useful in the Middle Atlantic and southeastern states as an excellent groundcover where some mass is needed. Its black fruits are less interesting than those of *S. ruscifolia*. It is useful in Zones 6b−9a and sheltered sites in Zone 6a, perhaps also in Zone 5b.

Sassafras albidum 7−8

Synonym: *S. officinale*
Sassafras
Deciduous tree
Lauraceae (Laurel Family)

Native Range. Northeastern United States, southern Ontario, and southward to Florida and Texas.

Useful Range. USDA Zones 5b−9a.

Function. Shade tree, specimen, massing, naturalizing.

Size and Habit

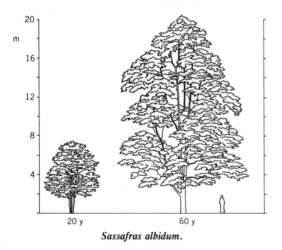

Sassafras albidum.

Adaptability

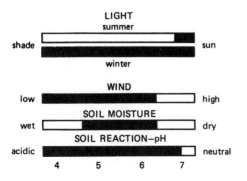

Seasonal Interest. *Flowers:* Small, yellow, in small clusters to 5 cm/2 in. long, before and at the beginning of leaf emergence, mostly dioecious. *Foliage:* Medium green, unlobed, two-lobed (mittenlike), or three-lobed, all three forms commonly found on the same tree, turning brilliant gold, orange, or orange-red in most sites and most years before falling in middle to late autumn. *Fruits:* Blue-black, on pistillate (female) plants, to 1 cm/0.4 in. long, interesting in combination with the bright red stalks and receptacles, which remain colorful for some time after fruits have been taken by birds in early autumn. *Twigs and Branches:* Horizontal branching creates an interesting pattern of greenish twigs, terminated in winter by large dormant buds, from which the next year's flowers will emerge.

Problems and Maintenance. Sassafras is subject to a variety of insect and disease problems. Most are not serious enough to require corrective action, but borers and bagworms can seriously weaken trees if not controlled. Pruning is necessary only for removal of deadwood. This tree produces root suckers, which can result in a thicket, but are easily controlled by mowing when trees are surrounded by turf. Availability is limited by difficulties in propagation and transplanting. Specifying young, container-grown plants will improve chances of successful transplanting.

Saxifraga stolonifera 2

Synonym: *S. sarmentosa*
Strawberry begonia, strawberry geranium
Herbaceous, evergreen or semievergreen
groundcover
Saxifragaceae (Saxifrage Family)

Native Range. Eastern Asia.

Useful Range. USDA Zones 7a−9a+ but fully
evergreen only in Zone 9a+.

Function. Groundcover, specimen.

Size and Habit

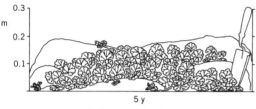

Saxifraga stolonifera.

Adaptability. Useful only in areas that remain
relatively cool in summer, in shade, and with a
fairly reliable supply of moisture.

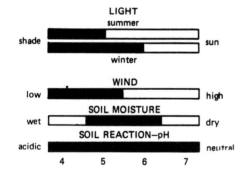

Seasonal Interest. *Flowers:* Small, white, in
loose, upright clusters, 25−50 cm/10−20 in.
tall, in midsummer. *Foliage:* Deep green with
lighter veins, making a dense, fast-growing,
highly decorative mat to 15 cm/6 in. or more
deep. Foliage is the primary landscape feature of
this plant, remaining evergreen or nearly so in
the Deep South. Like strawberry, stolons (run-
ners) are produced, terminating with new
plantlets, enabling this plant to spread rapidly.

Problems and Maintenance. This plant is relatively free of serious problems, but slugs can be
troublesome in the sites where it is at its best.

Related Species

Tiarella cordifolia 2 (foamflower). This
member of the Saxifragaceae is native to the
Appalachian Mountains, southward to Alabama
and northward to Nova Scotia, and makes an
excellent groundcover for shaded or partly shaded
sites with a fairly moist soil. The deep green,
lobed, and toothed leaves, vaguely maple-
shaped, form a mat of interesting texture, and the
delicate white flowers, arranged loosely on erect
racemes to 30 cm/12 in. tall, provide added
interest in midspring. Useful in Zones 5a−7b
and in cool sites in Zone 8.

Sciadopitys verticillata 6−7

Japanese umbrella pine
Evergreen tree
Taxodiaceae (Taxodium Family)

Native Range. Japan.

Useful Range. USDA Zones 6b−7b, protected
sites in Zone 6a, and areas in Zone 8 having
moderate summers.

Function. Specimen, screen (in time).

Size and Habit

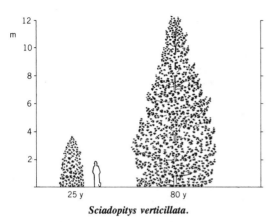

Sciadopitys verticillata.

Adaptability. Protection from full sun and wind in winter is beneficial in Zone 6, especially in the Midwest.

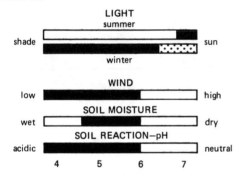

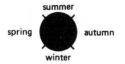

Seasonal Interest. *Foliage:* Large, fleshy needles, to 0.3 cm/0.12 in. thick and 10−12 cm/4−5 in. long, dark green and glossy on upper surface, pale underneath, arranged on the stout stems in whorls of 20 to 30 like spokes radiating from the hub of a wheel, giving a distinctive texture as well as growth habit. *Cones:* To 10−12 cm/4−5 in. long, not borne until trees are relatively old.

Problems and Maintenance. This tree is relatively free of serious problems and requires little or no maintenance in a proper site. The greatest limitation is its very slow growth, making this a plant primarily for the collector of unusual species. But it is handsome and distinctive given time to develop.

Sedum acre 2

Goldmoss stonecrop
Herbaceous, evergreen groundcover
Crassulaceae (Orpine Family)

Native Range. Europe, North Africa, and western Asia.

Useful Range. USDA Zones 4a−9a+.

Function. Groundcover, rock garden.

Size and Habit

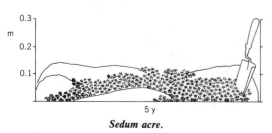

Sedum acre.

Adaptability. Although *Sedum* species are remarkably tolerant of poor, dry soil and other adverse site factors, they must have full sun and very well-drained soil for best results.

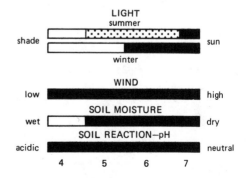

Seasonal Interest. *Flowers:* Bright yellow, making a solid mass of golden yellow in early summer.

Foliage: Bright green year-round but in cold climates becoming dull green from midwinter until new growth begins in spring. Leaves are succulent, vaguely triangular, 0.5 cm/0.2 in. or less long. *Fruits:* Dry capsules are unattractive but can be removed for maximum effect, on a small scale.

Problems and Maintenance. *Sedum* species are unusually trouble-free and require no maintenance except for removal of plants that exceed the limits of the planting. Many *Sedum* species, including *S. acre*, produce unwanted seedlings in nearby areas, but they are easily controlled since they are shallow-rooted. Other species vary in their tendency to be weedy.

Cultivars. 'Aureum,' with bright green, yellow tipped foliage, is not widely available. 'Minor' (= 'Minus') is smaller in all respects, a logical selection for very small areas.

Related Species. Many species of *Sedum* are potentially useful as groundcover plants. A handful of the best and most common are listed here:

Sedum album 2 (white stonecrop).   This native of the Mediterranean region has succulent, teardrop-shaped leaves and white flowers in early summer on stalks 8–20 cm/3–8 in. tall. Useful in Zones 4b–9a+.

Sedum rupestre 2.   This native of western Europe grows a bit taller than *S. acre*, with nearly linear leaves to 1.5 cm/0.6 in. long. Golden

yellow flowers are borne on stalks 15–25 cm/ 6–10 in. tall in late spring and early summer. A dwarf form, 'Minus,' is sometimes available.

Sedum sexangulare 2.   This native of southeastern Europe and adjacent Asia has dark green leaves, 0.6 cm/0.25 in. long, arranged in six longitudinal, spiraled rows. The yellow flowers appear in early summer. Useful in Zones 4b–9a+ but needs to be controlled where space is limited.

Sedum sexangulare.

Sedum spathulifolium 2.   This native of the West Coast has blue-green leaves, averaging nearly 2 cm/0.8 in. long, in rosettes and yellow flowers in late spring. Several selections have been made, including 'Capa Blanca,' a fine, low, spreading form, and 'Purpureum,' with purple leaves.

Sedum spurium 2 (two-row stonecrop).   This mat-forming plant from the Caucasus Mountains has olive to deep green leaves. Its pink flowers open in midsummer and quickly fade to near

Sedum rupestre.

Sedum spurium.

white except in selections such as 'Dragon's Blood' that produce strong red flowers (fading somewhat but remaining red). The foliage also tends to redden in autumn in full sun. Useful in Zones 4b−9a+.

Sempervivum tectorum 2 (hens-and-chickens, house leeks).   This European plant has been long-cultivated in many forms, all with tight rosettes of fleshy leaves that multiply until they fill in all available surface space, making a very effective groundcover for small areas in full sun and well-drained soil, or hardly any soil at all provided they do not remain wet. In addition to the many variants of *S. tectorum*, there are many additional species, although most are not very widely used. One type or another is useful almost anywhere in our area, at least northward to Zone 3b and southward to Zone 9a+.

Euphorbia cyparissias 2 (cypress spurge).   This herbaceous perennial, native to Europe but naturalized in the eastern United States, is included here even though it is in a different family, the Euphorbiaceae, only because its requirements and function are virtually identical with those of the *Sedum* and *Sempervivum* species. It is more vigorous than most of these, presenting more of a weed problem. But it can be controlled and is a most effective groundcover on dry soil. The dull blue-green foliage that first appears is soon followed by the rounded bracts (modified leaves), first yellow and then red-orange, that accompany the flowers in early summer. The top winterkills in most of the useful range and comes back from the ground the next season to a height of about 30 cm/12 in. Useful in Zones 3b−9a+.

Sequoiadendron giganteum 8

Synonyms: *Sequoia gigantea*, *Sequoia wellingtonia*
Giant sequoia, big tree, giant redwood
Evergreen tree
Taxodiaceae (Taxodium Family)

Native Range. California.

Useful Range. USDA Zones 7a−9a+ and maritime and otherwise protected sites in Zone 6b.

Function. Specimen, large-scale screen.

Size and Habit

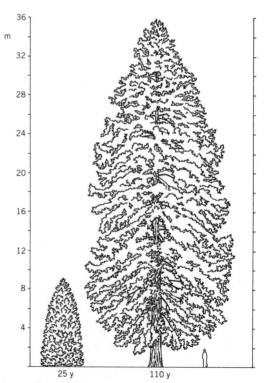

Sequoiadendron giganteum.

Adaptability. Some protection from winter sun and wind is necessary to prevent winter burn, at least in Zone 6.

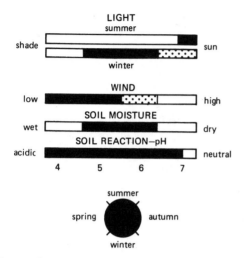

Seasonal Interest. *Foliage:* Evergreen, bluish green to olive-green needles, to 1.8 cm/0.7 in. long, resembling those of *Cryptomeria* in their spiraled arrangement on more-or-less whiplike to plumy branches. *Trunk:* Covered with thick, heavily furrowed red-brown bark.

Problems and Maintenance. A needle blight can be controlled by spraying, and a canker disease that may become troublesome is more difficult to control. The most common problems in experimental plantings in our area have been insufficient atmospheric moisture and winter burn of foliage. Pruning is not necessary.

Cultivars. 'Pendula,' a weeping selection, and 'Pygmaea,' a slow-growing variant, are curiosities and seldom available.

Related Species

Sequoia sempervirens 8 (synonym: *Sequoiadendron sempervirens;* coastal redwood). This tree can exceed *Sequoiadendron giganteum* in height, but it is more slender in growth habit. Native to coastal areas in northern California and even less well adapted to our area than *Sequoiadendron.* If at all useful in our area (and probably not), only in those places with closest to maritime climates in Zones 7a−9a.

Serenoa repens 3−4

Saw palmetto
Evergreen shrub
Palmae (Palm Family)

Native Range. Coastal areas of the southeastern United States: South Carolina to Florida and Texas.

Useful Range. USDA Zones 8b−9a+.

Function. Groundcover, barrier, massing, specimen.

Size and Habit

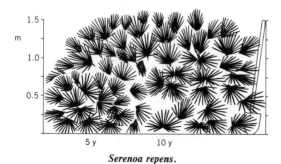

Serenoa repens.

Adaptability. Widely tolerant of soil moisture conditions, but size will vary with moisture supply, from 0.5 m/1.6 ft on dry sites to about 1.0 m/3.3 ft, occasionally 2 m/6.6 ft, on wet sites.

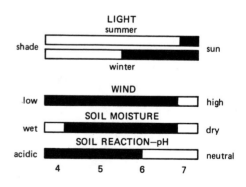

Seasonal Interest. *Flowers:* Fragrant, creamy white, but small, borne sparsely in a loose inflorescence among the leaves, adding minor interest in spring. *Foliage:* Olive to blue-green, evergreen, fanlike leaves 0.5 m/1.6 ft or more across, with saw-toothed margins on leaf stalks.

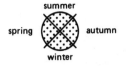

Texture is too coarse for small-scale situations. *Fruits*: Small black fruits add almost negligible interest in late summer and autumn.

Problems and Maintenance. This plant is relatively trouble-free and normally requires no maintenance other than occasional weeding and removal of dead leaves.

Related Species

Sabal minor 3–4 (dwarf palmetto).   This plant is similar in general effect to *Serenoa repens* and native to much the same area of the southeastern

United States from North Carolina to Florida and Texas and northward to southeastern Arkansas. Slightly more cold-hardy than *Serenoa*, *Sabal minor* is useful in Zones 8a–9a+ and in very small size in Zone 7b.

Rhapidophyllum hystrix 3 (needle palm, blue palmetto).   This clump-forming plant is similar in general effect to *Serenoa repens* except for the more distinctly blue-green color and sharp, needlelike leaf sheaths. It grows wild in moist sites from South Carolina to Florida and Mississippi and is useful in both moist and average sites in Zones 8b–9a+ and perhaps also in Zone 8a. The leaf sheaths are a potential hazard to small children, and this should be considered when using this plant.

Shepherdia argentea 6

Buffalo berry, silver buffalo berry
Deciduous shrub
Elaeagnaceae (Oleaster Family)

Native Range. North American plains: Manitoba to Kansas and Nevada.

Useful Range. USDA Zones 2b–6b.

Function. Windbreak, barrier hedge, specimen.

Size and Habit

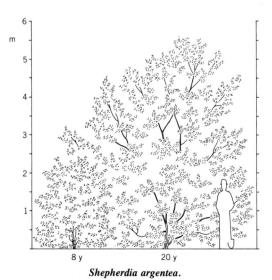

Shepherdia argentea.

Adaptability. Unusually well adapted to dry, alkaline soils. Tolerates infertile soil, in part because of its ability to fix and assimilate atmospheric nitrogren.

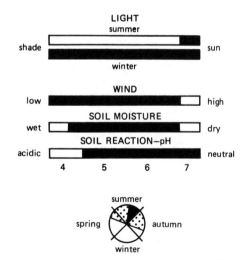

Seasonal Interest. *Flowers*: Small and yellowish, inconspicuous, in midspring. Dioecious. *Foliage*: Fine-textured and silvery like that of the related *Elaeagnus angustifolia*, with narrow leaves 2–6 cm/0.8–2.4 in. long, falling without color change in autumn. *Fruits*: Red to orangered, to 0.6 cm/0.25 in. long, with silver flecks, sour but edible in preserves, on pistillate (female)

plants only, in the presence of staminate (male) plants.

Problems and Maintenance. Leaf-spot and rust diseases are too minor to require control. Root suckers are produced and must eventually be pruned off or dug out if this plant is to be contained within a limited area. Brittle wood makes this plant susceptible to breakage under heavy snow.

Cultivars. 'Xanthocarpa' has yellow fruits.

Related Species

Shepherdia canadensis 5 (russet buffalo berry). This native of a wider range in North America from Newfoundland to Alaska and southward to Ohio, New Mexico, and Oregon is less silvery in

Shepherdia canadensis.

appearance than S. *argentea* and smaller in stature but otherwise similar. Useful in Zones 2b−6b but probably not commercially available.

Skimmia japonica 3

Japanese skimmia
Evergreen shrub
Rutaceae (Rue Family)

Native Range. Japan.

Useful Range. USDA Zones 7b−8b and sheltered sites in Zone 7a. Best in areas having moderate summer temperatures.

Function. Specimen, foundation, border, massing.

Size and Habit

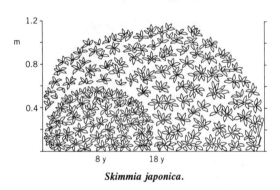

Skimmia japonica.

Adaptability

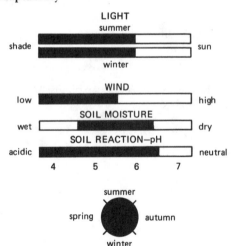

Seasonal Interest. *Flowers:* Small, creamy white, in clusters 5−8 cm/2−3 in. long, borne terminally in middle to late spring. Dioecious. *Foliage:* Evergreen with rich, deep green color and rather coarse texture, the individual leaves 8−12 cm/3−5 in. long. *Fruits:* Bright red berries, 0.8 cm/0.3 in. across, in clusters to 8 cm/3 in. across, on pistillate (female) plants, in the presence of staminate (male) plants for pollination, ripening in autumn and persisting all winter.

Problems and Maintenance. This plant is unusually trouble-free given a proper site with at

Skimmia japonica.

least reasonably moist, organic soil, probably never needing to be pruned.

Cultivars. 'Teufel's Dwarf Female' and 'Teufel's Dwarf Male' are compact selections, similar except for sex, with slightly finer-textured foliage.

Related Species

Skimmia reevesiana 3 (synonym: *S. fortunei*; Reeves skimmia). This Chinese counterpart of *S. japonica* differs from *S. japonica* in being lower-growing, finer-textured, and hermaphroditic (all plants fruiting). Useful in areas with mild summer temperatures in Zones 8a−9a and perhaps also in Zone 7.

Smilax lanceolata 1

Florida or southern smilax, lanceleaf greenbrier
Evergreen vine
Liliaceae (Lily Family)

Native Range. Southeastern and south-central United States, Mexico to Central America.

Useful Range. USDA Zones 7b−9a+.

Function. Specimen, screen (with support and pruning), climbing rapidly by tendrils to heights of 10 m/33 ft.

Size and Habit

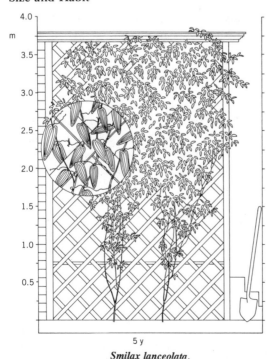

5 y

Smilax lanceolata.

Adaptability. One of the most widely adaptable evergreen vines within its useful range.

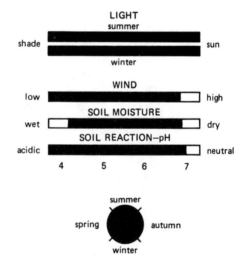

Seasonal Interest. *Flowers:* Pale green to whitish yellow, small and inconspicuous, dioecious. *Foliage:* Evergreen, lustrous, smooth and deep green, arranged rather sparsely on angled, prickly branches, eventually forming a dense mass. Individual leaves 5−8 cm/2−3 in. long and half as wide. *Fruits:* Dark red, 5−8 cm/2−3 in. across, in autumn, not borne in conspicuous numbers.

Problems and Maintenance. This vine is unusually free of insect and disease problems. It can become weedy and rank if not controlled, but control is not very difficult in spite of its tendency to spread by underground stems.

Related Species

Smilax laurifolia 1 (laurel-leaved greenbrier). This plant grows wild in much the same area as the closely related *S. lanceolata* and is often confused with it. The two are roughly equivalent in the landscape, although *S. laurifolia* has black fruits. Useful in Zones 7a−9a+ and perhaps also in Zone 6.

Smilax megalantha 1 (coral greenbrier). This evergreen native of China has very large leaves, to 12 cm/5 in. or more in length, and showy, coral-red fruits, to 2 cm/0.8 in. across. It is useful in Zones 8a−9a+.

Several deciduous *Smilax* species are native to our area but have little landscape value.

Sophora japonica 8

Japanese pagoda tree, Chinese scholar tree
Deciduous tree
Leguminosae (Legume Family)

Native Range. China and Korea.

Useful Range. USDA Zones 6a−9a and Zone 5 with selection of appropriate genetic material.

Function. Shade tree, specimen.

Size and Habit

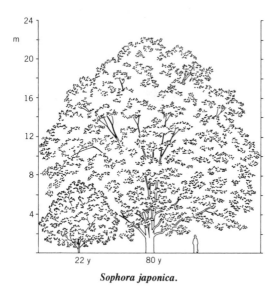

Sophora japonica.

Adaptability

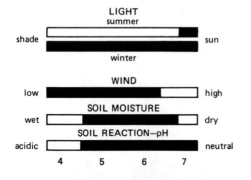

Seasonal Interest. *Flowers:* Pale yellow to creamy white, in loose clusters, 15−30 cm/6−12 in. long, in late summer, striking against the dark green foliage. *Foliage:* Compound, almost as fine-textured as that of *Gleditsia triacanthos*, bright green in early summer, turning dark green as growth ceases in midsummer and flowering begins, falling without color change in late autumn. *Fruits:* Bright yellow-green, lustrous seed pods, 5−8 cm/2−3 in. long, constricted between the seeds to resemble a string of beads, adding significant interest in autumn. *Twigs and Branches:* Smooth, olive-green, adding minor winter interest.

Problems and Maintenance. This tree is relatively trouble-free in Zones 6−9, but affected by twig blight and stem canker diseases, apparently associated with winter injury, in Zone 5. Pruning is seldom necessary except for removal of deadwood.

Cultivars. 'Pendula' is a strongly weeping form, useful only for positive accent but interesting for the form and green twigs. It grows little in height beyond the graft union, usually 1−1.5 m/3.3−5 ft from the ground, reaching 3 m/10 ft only after many years.

'Regent' (Plant Patent No. 2338, 1964) was selected for rapid early growth, flowering at an early age, symmetry, and tolerance of city conditions.

Related Species

Sophora affinis 6 (coralbean). This small tree from Arkansas and eastern Texas is sometimes used in its native habitat and adjacent Louisiana as a small specimen tree with pink tinged white flowers in early summer. Useful in Zones 8b−9a+.

Sophora davidii 5 (synonym: *S. viciifolia*; vetchleaf sophora).   This large shrub from China occasionally is used for its violet flowers, in clusters to 10 cm/4 in. long, in early summer. It is a rather leggy, awkward shrub, but is valued for its ability to grow well in hot, dry situations. Useful in Zones 6a−9a.

Sesbania punicea 5 (synonym: *Daubentonia punicea*; rattle box).   This large, wide-spreading shrub from Argentina has become naturalized in places along the Gulf Coast and occasionally is used as a landscape specimen. It is not very functional, except perhaps as a very small patio tree, but is valued for its hanging clusters of bright orange-red flowers during most of the summer. Seeds become detached and rattle in the angled pods when shaken in autumn and winter, suggesting the common name. Useful in Zone 9a+.

Sorbaria sorbifolia 4

Synonym: *Spiraea sorbifolia*
Ural false spirea
Deciduous shrub
Rosaceae (Rose Family)

Native Range. Northern and eastern Asia.

Useful Range. USDA Zones 3a−8b.

Function. Massing, specimen.

Size and Habit

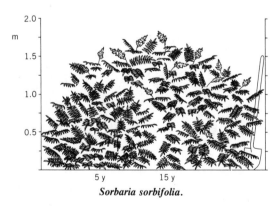

Sorbaria sorbifolia.

Adaptability

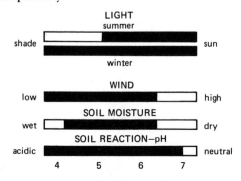

Seasonal Interest. *Flowers:* Small, white, in fuzzy terminal panicles, 15−25 cm/6−10 in. long, showy in early summer to midsummer. *Foliage:* Medium green, compound leaves, to 50 cm/20 in. or more in length, with many sharply toothed leaflets, each 5−10 cm/2−4 in. long, falling in autumn without color change.

Problems and Maintenance. This shrub is relatively trouble-free other than occasional mite infestations and requires little maintenance except pruning for confinement. It spreads rapidly underground and can take over a considerable area if not deliberately limited by root and top pruning. In any case, it is not a plant for small-scale situations. Occasional drastic renewal pruning may be needed to maintain form.

Related Species

Sorbaria aitchisonii 5 (synonym: *Spiraea aitchisonii*; Kashmir false spirea).   This large shrub, to 3 m/10 ft tall, differs from *S. sorbifolia* in its greater stature, larger flower clusters, and reddish, one-year-old stems. It is less likely to spread by suckering, usually remaining a tall, individual shrub, but it is less cold-hardy than *S. sorbifolia*, useful in Zones 6a−8b.

Other species of *Sorbaria* are known in cultivation but seldom if ever available commercially. They offer little variation from the above species except that some of them become much larger, to 5−6 m/16−19 ft tall.

Holodiscus discolor 6 (oceanspray). This close relative of *Sorbaria* from the Pacific Northwest functions as a taller edition of *Sorbaria* without the strong tendency to become weedy, but it is also less cold-hardy. It is useful in Zones 6b−8b and perhaps slightly colder zones, and it is striking with its large flower clusters in early summer to midsummer.

Sorbus alnifolia 8

Korean mountain ash
Deciduous tree
Rosaceae (Rose Family)

Native Range. China, Japan, and Korea.

Useful Range. USDA Zones 4b−7b, perhaps also colder zones with selection of appropriate genetic material.

Function. Specimen, shade tree.

Size and Habit

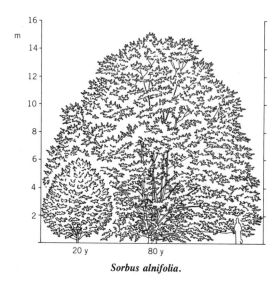

Sorbus alnifolia.

Seasonal Interest. *Flowers:* Small, white, in loose clusters, 5−8 cm/2−3 in. across, effective against the rich green foliage in late spring. *Foliage:* Rich green, turning dark green in late summer, with a crisp texture resembling that of *Alnus*, *Betula*, or *Carpinus*, the simple, toothed leaves, to 5−10 cm/2−4 in. long, turning orange to red before falling in midautumn. *Fruits:* Red-orange berries, to 0.8 cm/0.3 in. across, in loose clusters covering essentially the entire tree, persisting for a time after leaf drop, colorful against the silvery gray twigs and branches. *Trunks and branches:* Smooth, silvery gray bark of large branches resembles that of *Fagus* or *Cladrastis*, adding winter interest.

Sorbus alnifolia.

Adaptability

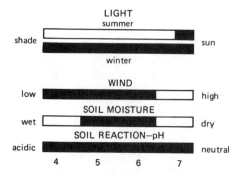

Problems and Maintenance. *S. alnifolia* has a few insect and disease problems like most other members of the Rosaceae, but the most serious pest of *Sorbus* species, borers, does not seem to be a problem with this species, perhaps in part because it is harder-wooded than most other mountain ashes. Unfortunately, *S. alnifolia* appears to be highly susceptible to fire blight, a serious

Sorbus alnifolia.

problem in areas where outbreaks of this disease tend to be severe.

Cultivars. Trees of *S. alnifolia* vary rather widely in form and a few relatively narrow variants have been selected. As yet, named cultivars are not available, but they may be in the future.

Related Species

Sorbus folgneri 6 (Folgner mountain ash). This native of China is smaller in stature than *S. alnifolia*, with leaves white-felted underneath and equally colorful in autumn, with somewhat larger fruits. A graceful, small tree, useful in Zones 6a−7b and perhaps also in Zone 5 but little tried and seldom available.

Sorbus aria 7

Synonym: *Pyrus aria*
White beam mountain ash
Deciduous tree
Rosaceae (Rose Family)

Native Range. Europe.

Useful Range. USDA Zones 6a−7b, probably also Zone 5.

Function. Shade tree, specimen. Used widely as a street tree in Europe but not recommended as such in our area because of the borer problem.

Size and Habit

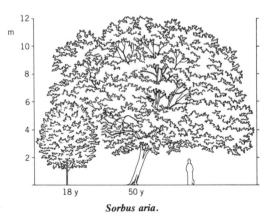

Sorbus aria.

Adaptability

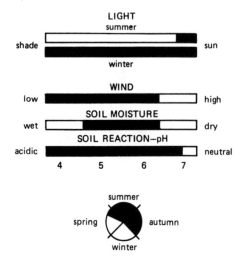

Sorbus aria.

Seasonal Interest. *Flowers:* Small, white, in flattened terminal clusters, 5–8 cm/2–3 in. across, in late spring. *Foliage:* Deep green, the simple, toothed leaves, 5–12 cm/2–5 in. long, covered underneath with white, felty pubescence, giving an interesting bicolored effect in the wind and when viewed from underneath, turning reddish before falling in late autumn. *Fruits:* Bright orange-red, 1.2 cm/0.5 in. across, showy in late summer to early autumn.

Problems and Maintenance. Like most other *Sorbus* species, *S. aria* is subject to a variety of minor insects and diseases and one major problem: borers. Because of this, it should be specified only where an adequate maintenance

program is available, and this rules it out for street plantings in much of our area.

Cultivars. Several selections have been made in Europe, but they are seldom if ever available in our area. The most likely to be found are 'Aurea,' with yellow foliage, and 'Majestica' (= 'Decaisneana'), with larger-than-typical fruits and large leaves, very white underneath.

Sorbus aucuparia 7

Synonym: *Pyrus aucuparia*
European mountain ash
Deciduous tree
Rosaceae (Rose Family)

Native Range. Northern Europe and Asia.

Useful Range. USDA Zones 3b–7b with selection of appropriate genetic material.

Function. Specimen, shade tree.

Size and Habit

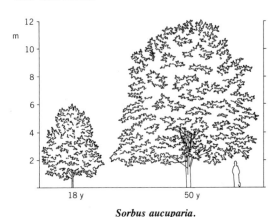

Sorbus aucuparia.

Adaptability

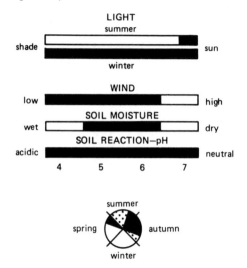

Seasonal Interest.

Seasonal Interest. *Flowers*: Small, white, in large, flattened, terminal clusters, to 8–12 cm/3–5 in. across, in late spring. *Foliage*: Dull green, compound, with about a dozen small, toothed leaflets, giving a rather fine texture, in some years turning reddish before falling in late autumn. *Fruits*: Bright orange to red, individually 0.8 cm/0.3 in. across, in large clusters, very colorful from late summer until middle or late autumn.

Problems and Maintenance. Even though this is the most commonly used species of *Sorbus* in our area, it is no freer of problems than the others mentioned and less so than some. Borers are the big problem, and fire blight also can be destructive in certain geographic areas where outbreaks of this disease frequently are severe. Sun-scald can damage unwrapped trunks of newly planted trees in Zones 3 and 4. *S. aucuparia* and other species (see Related Species and Hybrids) should be used in street planting or other public or large-scale use only where an adequate maintenance program will be followed.

Cultivars. Several variants have been selected. None are common in our area, but a few of those most likely to be encountered are listed here.

'Asplenifolia' (cutleaf European mountain ash) has dissected leaflets and correspondingly finer texture than the species type.

'Fastigiata' (upright European mountain ash) has narrow branching angles and upright growth habit.

'Pendula' (weeping European mountain ash) has pendulous branching and is a curiosity more than a functional tree.

'Xanthocarpa' has orange-yellow fruits.

Related Species and Hybrids

Sorbus americana 7 (synonym: *Pyrus americana*; American mountain ash). This North American counterpart of *S. aucuparia*, growing wild from Newfoundland to Manitoba and southward to high elevations in North Carolina, is very similar to that species in landscape appearance, function, and limitations. There is some evidence that *S. americana* may be slightly less tolerant of hot summers than *S. aucuparia*, but this probably varies within each species. When availability is considered, *S. americana* usually comes off in second place, but it is useful in Zones 2b–6b and farther south at high elevations near or in the natural range.

Sorbus americana.

Sorbus ×*arnoldiana* 7 (Arnold mountain ash). This hybrid of *S. discolor* × *S. aucuparia* is notable for its clear pink fruits, striking in early autumn against the deep green foliage. It is available in very few nurseries but useful in Zones 3b–7b.

Sorbus decora 7 (synonym: *S. americana* var. *decora*; showy mountain ash). This close relative of *S. americana* grows wild in the northern parts of the range of that species and differs in landscape effect only in that its fruits are larger, to 1 cm/0.4 in. across. It is useful in Zones 3a–6b. The selection 'Nana' is compact in growth and narrow in outline, at least in its early years.

Sorbus decora 'Nana.'

Sorbus discolor 7 (snowberry mountain ash). This native of northern China, useful in Zones

3a—7b, is not widely available but distinctive for its snow-white fruits, about the same size as those of *S. aucuparia*.

Sorbus ×*hybrida* 7 (hybrid mountain ash). This vigorous tree with partly lobed, partly compound leaves was originally found in Finland and is considered by some to be a hybrid of *S. aucuparia* × *S. intermedia*, another European species with simple, lobed leaves. Except for their unusual foliage, this and a similar hybrid, *S.* ×*thuringiaca (S. aucuparia* × *S. aria)*, are not very distinctive landscape trees, but one or the other is fairly commonly used in Zones 3b—7b.

Sorbus scopulina 6 (Rocky Mountain mountain ash). This shrubby small tree from western North America is occasionally used as a landscape plant in the western fringes of our area, but usually other species are selected in preference to it east of the Rocky Mountains. Useful in Zones 3a—6b.

Sorbus tianshanica 6 (Turkestan mountain ash). This shrubby tree from central Asia has unusually large flower clusters, and its height of 5 m/16 ft makes it distinctly smaller than the other species listed except for *S. scopulina*. It is useful in Zones 3b—7b but seldom available as yet.

Spiraea ×*billiardii* 4

Billiard spirea
Deciduous shrub
Rosaceae (Rose Family)

Hybrid origin. *S. douglasii* × *S. salicifolia*.

Useful Range. USDA Zones 4a—9a.

Function. Massing, bank cover, border. Quickly forms large thickets, so must be confined in borders.

Size and Habit

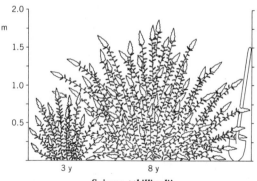

Spiraea ×*billiardii*.

Adaptability. Performs best in open, sunny areas with good air circulation. This species is not as tolerant of calcareous soil as most spireas.

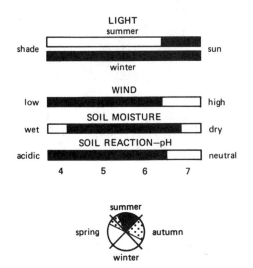

LIGHT
summer
shade | sun
winter

WIND
low | high

SOIL MOISTURE
wet | dry

SOIL REACTION—pH
acidic | neutral
4   5   6   7

summer
spring | autumn
winter

Seasonal Interest. *Flowers:* Bright rose-pink in elongated terminal clusters, 10—20 cm/4—8 in. long, early summer to midsummer and until late summer in some selections. *Foliage:* Medium to light green, whitish gray underneath, arranged sparsely on the long, stiffly arching branches. General appearance is rather coarse.

Problems and Maintenance. Powdery mildew can be troublesome in areas with poor circulation, and aphids frequently disfigure the foliage. Drastic renewal pruning is needed every two to four years to prevent this plant from becoming a tangled mass. This usually is done easily because the stems remain fairly slender, but it constitutes a maintenance expense.

Related Species

Spiraea alba 4 (meadowsweet, meadow spirea). This thicket-forming shrub native to much of the eastern United States is similar in effect to S. ×*billiardii* but has white flowers and is a little more coarse and irregular in growth habit. Useful in Zones 3b—9a.

Spiraea douglasii 5 (Douglas spirea). This native of the Pacific Northwest is a parent of S. ×*billiardii* and very similar in general appearance and function, with deep rose flowers, beginning to open slightly later than those of S. ×*billiardii*. Useful in Zones 3b—8b with selection of appropriate genetic material.

Spiraea latifolia 4 (meadowsweet). This close relative of *S. alba* is similar, with white flowers and thicket-forming habit, but is native to somewhat more northern areas from Newfoundland to the Dakotas. Useful in Zones 3b—9a.

Spiraea menziesii 4 (Menzies spirea). This shrub from the Pacific Northwest is similar to *S. douglasii* except in being somewhat smaller. Useful in Zones 3a—8a with selection of appropriate genetic material.

Spiraea menziesii.

Spiraea tomentosa 3 (hardhack, steeplebush). This common weed of poor pastures in the northern parts of eastern North America seldom exceeds 0.5 m/1.6 ft in height on poor soils and has little value as a landscape species except in natural or naturalized situations, but it can be used for its upright clusters of rosy pink flowers in a shrub border, where it will occasionally reach 1 m/3.3 ft in height in good soil. Useful in Zones 3b—8a.

Spiraea ×*bumalda* 3

Bumalda spirea
Deciduous shrub
Rosaceae (Rose Family)

Hybrid Origin. *S. japonica* × *S. albiflora*.

Useful Range. USDA Zones 4a−9a and parts of Zone 3 with some winter dieback.

Function. Massing, border, foundation.

Size and Habit

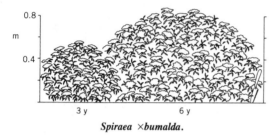

Spiraea ×*bumalda.*

Adaptability

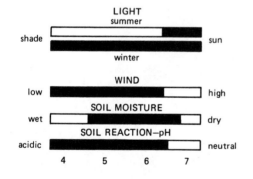

Seasonal Interest. *Flowers:* Bright crimson to rosy pink in flat clusters, to 8−12 cm/3−5 in. across, in early to midsummer and occasionally thereafter. *Foliage:* Leaves emerge purplish or bronze, turning medium green as they expand, with occasional white or pale yellow streaks. They make a fairly compact mass of medium texture, turning orange or crimson in some years before falling.

Spiraea ×*bumalda.*

Problems and Maintenance. This shrub is relatively trouble-free, although several insects occasionally cause minor problems. More sensitive to calcareous (high pH) soils than most spireas, and lime chlorosis occurs on some of the heavier midwestern soils.

Cultivars. 'Anthony Waterer' is probably the oldest cultivar currently in use in North America, and certainly still the most common. With maximum height of about 0.6 m/2 ft, it has flower clusters to 12−15 cm/5−6 in. across under ideal conditions and tends to flower intermittently throughout the summer.

'Crispa' is notable for its deeply cut and twisted leaf margins, giving it significant foliage interest in summer. Otherwise it is similar to 'Anthony Waterer' but slower to develop.

'Froebelii' has dull rose flowers and is somewhat taller than 'Anthony Waterer,' to almost 1 m/3.3 ft.

'Goldflame' has bright gold new foliage, turning green by midsummer.

Related Species

Spiraea albiflora 3 (synonym: *S. japonica* var. *alba*; Japanese white spirea).   This low shrub, usually only to 0.5 m/1.6 ft tall, is very similar to *S.* ×*bumalda* and *S. japonica* except for its white flowers and can be used interchangeably for color contrast in the same zones with the other two species.

Spiraea betulifolia 3.   This white-flowered relative of *S. albiflora* and *S. japonica* from northeastern Asia is not as well known as its hybrid,

'Rosabella,' with pink flowers, developed by F. L. Skinner of Dropmore, Manitoba, and considered a hardier and better replacement for S. ×bumalda 'Anthony Waterer.' Useful in Zones 2b−8a, perhaps farther south as well.

Spiraea bullata 3 (crispleaf spirea).   This distinctive little plant with compact growth and dark green, leathery, crinkled leaves is known only in cultivation, originally in Japan. The rosy pink flowers, in flat clusters similar to those of S. ×bumalda, offer midsummer color, but it is the unusual foliage and compact growth that gives this plant its distinctive usefulness for small-scale border or specimen planting. It is considerably less cold-hardy than most members of this group, useful in Zone 6b−9a+, in sheltered sites in Zones 5b and 6a, and perhaps in colder zones with reliable snow cover.

Spiraea japonica 3 (Japanese spirea).   Native to Japan, this shrub is better known through its hybrid S. ×bumalda than in itself. But the selection 'Atrosanguinea' (Mikado spirea) is well known for its rosy red flowers, brighter than those of the S. ×bumalda cultivars. Otherwise it is very similar to 'Anthony Waterer.' An even more distinctive selection is 'Alpina,' a dwarf, mound-like shrub, only 0.3 m/1 ft tall, with smaller leaves and rose-pink flowers in early summer to midsummer, most useful in rock gardens and other small-scale situations. These cultivars are useful in Zones 5a−9a+ and in colder zones where snow cover is reliable.

Spiraea prunifolia 5

Synonym: S. *prunifolia* 'Plena'
Bridalwreath spirea
Deciduous shrub
Rosaceae (Rose Family)

Native Range. China, Korea, Taiwan.

Useful Range. USDA Zones 5a−9a+.

Function. Border, specimen, informal hedge.

Size and Habit

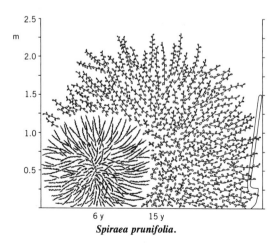

6 y   15 y
Spiraea prunifolia.

Adaptability

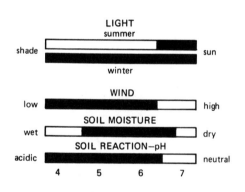

Seasonal Interest. *Flowers:* Pure white, very double, 0.8−1.2 cm/0.3−0.5 in. across, borne in large numbers on the slender, gracefully arching branches in middle to late spring before leaves have expanded. *Foliage:* Deep green, glossy leaves are 2.5−5 cm/1−2 in. long, giving the best landscape interest of any spirea and turning bright orange-red in autumn in most years.

Problems and Maintenance. This shrub is subject to the troubles of spireas in general, but seldom seriously except for aphids, which oc-

Spiraea prunifolia.

casionally disfigure the excellent foliage. Pruning is needed only to remove any deadwood and for renewal of old plants. Shearing should never be

done, since this destroys the gracefulness of the plant.

Forms and Cultivars. 'Plena,' the double-flowered form, is actually the species type, since it was the first form given the name S. *prunifolia,* even though it is a horticultural form. Because of this, it is technically redundant to use the cultivar designation 'Plena,' yet this is the most common way this form is listed by nurseries, and it should cause no confusion.

F. *simpliciflora,* the single-flowered wild type, is seldom encountered in landscape use, nor is it commercially available. The flowers are less showy and not as long-lasting as the double flowers of the species, accounting for the low level of interest in this form.

Spiraea thunbergii 4

Thunberg spirea
Deciduous shrub
Rosaceae (Rose Family)

Native Range. China, Japan.

Useful Range. USDA Zones 4b−9a+.

Function. Border, specimen, informal hedge.

Size and Habit

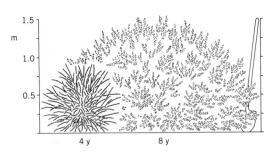

Spiraea thunbergii.

Adaptability

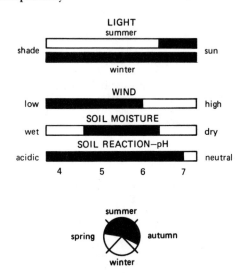

Seasonal Interest. *Flowers:* White, only about 0.8 cm/0.3 in. across but borne in large numbers in loose clusters, showy because they open just as the leaves are beginning to expand in early to midspring. *Foliage:* Bright green, very fine-textured, with narrow leaves averaging about 2.5 cm/1 in. long, giving a loose, billowy appearance to the slender branches and turning yellow-orange in some years before falling in autumn.

Problems and Maintenance. This species is subject to the troubles of spireas in general but is seldom affected seriously except by aphids, which cause leaf curling. Pruning is needed only to remove any deadwood and for renewal of old plants. Shearing destroys the graceful character of this plant and should be avoided. Renewal pruning should be done as described under *S. ×vanhouttei*, Problems and Maintenance.

Related Species

Spiraea ×arguta 4 (garland spirea). This hybrid of *S. thunbergii × S. multiflora* is slightly more cold-hardy than *S. thunbergii* and has medium-green foliage, seldom coloring in autumn, and not as fine-textured as that of *S. thunbergii*. Otherwise the two species are interchangeable in the landscape. Useful at least in Zones 4a–9a. The selection 'Compacta' is more compact in growth habit, remaining below 1.5 m/5 ft in height when grown in full sun and cold-hardy to Zone 3b.

Spiraea ×vanhouttei 4

Vanhoutte spirea, bridalwreath
Deciduous shrub
Rosaceae (Rose Family)

Hybrid origin. *S. cantoniensis × S. trilobata.*

Useful Range. USDA Zones 3b–8b.

Function. Specimen, border, massing, informal hedge.

Size and Habit

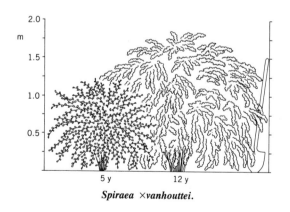

Spiraea ×vanhouttei.

Adaptability

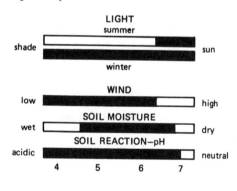

Seasonal Interest. *Flowers:* White, about 0.8 cm/0.3 in. across, in dense flat clusters, to 4 cm/1.6 in. across, showy in late spring against the foliage on gracefully arching branches. *Foliage:* Deep, dull blue-green to dark green, with small leaves that are individually distinctive but not making a very dense or interesting foliage mass, often falling in autumn without color change but occasionally turning a delicate, dull red-orange first.

Problems and Maintenance. There is a long list of insects and diseases that can affect *Spiraea* species, including S. ×*vanhouttei*, but few are commonly troublesome. Aphids frequently disfigure the foliage in summer, and powdery mildew can do the same in later summer with high humidity and poor air circulation, but these problems cause little or no permanent damage. Pruning usually is necessary only for renewal of very old plants or removal of any deadwood and should be avoided when not necessary so as not to interfere with the natural gracefulness of the shrub. When pruning is needed, never use hedge shears but thin by cutting out part (or all in drastic renewal) of the older stems to a few inches from the ground, and then selectively tip prune if necessary to promote fullness. Prune springflowering spireas immediately after flowering so as not to reduce bloom for that year. Summer flowering species that flower on new growth are best pruned in spring before plants have made much new growth. Drastic renewal pruning of any spirea by cutting the entire plant top to the ground should be done in early summer to allow plenty of time for regrowth and acclimation for the following winter.

Cultivars. 'Compacta' has more compact growth and reaches a height of only about 1.5 m/5 ft at maturity but is only occasionally available.

Related Species

Spiraea cantoniensis 5 (synonym: *Spiraea reevesiana*; Reeves spirea). This parent of S. ×*vanhouttei* from China and Japan is used in preference to the hybrid in the Deep South, where it is semievergreen and tolerates extreme heat better. In areas where both species can be grown (Zones 7 and 8), S. *cantoniensis* has a somewhat better growth habit and drops its spent flowers more quickly. It is useful in Zones 7a−9a+, leaving S. ×*vanhouttei* as the preferred species only in Zones 3b−6b, where S. *cantoniensis* is not cold-hardy.

Spiraea nipponica 5 (Nippon spirea). This stiffly upright shrub with outward-arching branches has white flowers against the excellent, dark blue-green foliage in late spring. The variety *tosaensis* (snowmound spirea), more compact than the species, with smaller, denser flower clusters, is useful in Zones 4b−8b.

Spiraea trilobata 4 (threelobe spirea). This cold-hardy parent of S. ×*vanhouttei*, native to northeastern Asia, is not commonly available, nor is it as graceful and showy. But it can function as a smaller version of S. ×*vanhouttei* and in somewhat colder zones. Useful in Zones 2−8a but seldom used except in Zones 3 and 4.

Spiraea veitchii 5

Veitch spirea
Deciduous shrub
Rosaceae (Rose Family)

Native Range. China.

Useful Range. USDA Zones 6a−9a+, possibly also Zone 5.

Function. Specimen, border.

Size and Habit

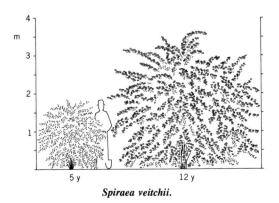

Spiraea veitchii.

Adaptability

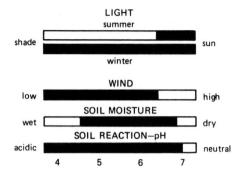

Seasonal Interest. *Flowers:* White, in dense, flattened clusters, 3–6 cm/1.2–2.4 in. across, borne in large numbers on long, gracefully arching branches in early summer. *Foliage:* Medium green, somewhat whitened underneath, falling in autumn with little or no color change.

Problems and Maintenance. This shrub is subject to the troubles of spireas in general (see *S. ×vanhouttei*), most not usually serious. Its greatest limitation may be commercial availability, but *S. henryi* and *S. wilsonii* (see Related Species) can be substituted in some situations when more easily available.

Related Species

Spiraea henryi 5 (Henry spirea). Also native to China, this shrub is not as tall or showy as *S. veitchii*, yet similar in general effect and more cold-hardy. Useful in Zones 4a–8b, perhaps also Zone 3.

Spiraea wilsonii 5 (Wilson spirea). Another Chinese native, this species is similar in flowering effect to *S. veitchii* and intermediate in size and time of flowering between that species and *S. ×vanhouttei*. Useful in Zones 6a–9a.

Staphylea trifolia 6

American bladdernut
Deciduous shrub or small tree
Staphyleaceae (Bladdernut Family)

Native Range. Northeastern United States and adjacent Canada, southward to Georgia and westward to Minnesota.

Useful Range. USDA Zones 4a–7a and sheltered sites in Zone 3b.

Function. Border, specimen, naturalized.

Size and Habit

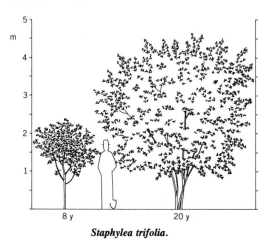

Staphylea trifolia.

Adaptability

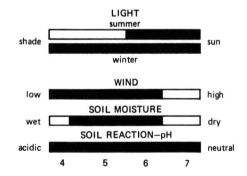

Seasonal Interest. *Flowers:* Creamy or greenish white, lightly fragrant, individually about 0.8 cm/0.3 in. long, in nodding clusters about 4 cm/1.6 in. long, in middle to late spring. *Foliage:* Bright green leaves with three leaflets, arranged sparsely on stiff twigs, falling in midautumn with little or no color change. *Fruits:* Inflated pods, usually 3−4 cm/1.2−1.6 in. long and three-lobed, at first greenish white, ripening light brown.

Staphylea trifolia.

Problems and Maintenance. This species is relatively free of serious problems, although a twig-blight disease occasionally can be troublesome. Availability is very limited, since demand for this plant is restricted to situations where its peculiar fruiting interest and relative freedom from maintenance compensate for its lack of striking seasonal color.

Related Species

Staphylea bumalda 5 (Japanese bladdernut). Except for its size, to 2 m/6.6 ft tall, and slightly more showy and fragrant flowers, this species differs little from *S. trifolia.* Seldom available, but it is useful in Zones 5b−7b, perhaps also in colder zones.

Staphylea colchica 6 (Caucasian bladdernut). The flowers of this shrub are much more showy than those of *S. trifolia,* the leaves mostly have five leaflets, and the inflated fruits are larger, 5−8 cm/2−3 in. long. Less cold-hardy than the American species but useful at least in Zones 6a−8a.

Staphylea holocarpa 6 (Chinese bladdernut). This, the tallest species of *Staphylea,* eventually reaches heights of 8 m/26 ft and can function as a patio tree in Zones 6a−8a. Its flowers are about as showy as those of *S. colchica,* but earlier, before the leaves have expanded, and the var. *rosea,* with pink flowers, is of special interest, although as yet seldom available.

Staphylea pinnata 6 (European bladdernut.) One of the most showy bladdernuts in bloom, with flower clusters 5−12 cm/2−5 in. long. This species has been used in landscape planting in Europe, where it is native, for centuries, but it is seldom available in our area, even though it is useful in Zones 5b−7b.

Stephanandra incisa 4

Cutleaf stephanandra
Deciduous shrub
Rosaceae (Rose Family)

Native Range. Japan and Korea.

Useful Range. USDA Zones 5a−8b.

Function. Border, specimen, massing.

Size and Habit

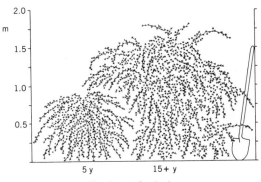

Stephanandra incisa.

Adaptability. Tolerant of considerable shade, but looks best when exposed to some direct sun.

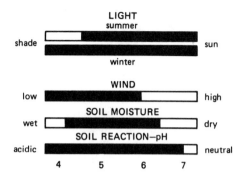

Stephanandra incisa 'Crispa.'

Seasonal Interest. *Flowers:* Pale greenish yellow, individually only about 0.5 cm/0.2 in. across, borne in loose terminal clusters about 2.5–5 cm/1–2 in. across, adding some interest in late spring or early summer. *Foliage:* Lobed, fine-textured, and bright green, loosely spaced on the slender, red, arching and zigzag branches, turning reddish before falling in autumn on branches exposed to full sun.

Stephanandra incisa 'Crispa.'

Problems and Maintenance. This shrub is seldom seriously troubled by insects and diseases, but twigs winterkill to varying degrees in the North, making at least minimal pruning a necessity. Pruning should be done selectively, removing deadwood and thinning old plants lightly. Shearing destroys the character of the plant and should be avoided.

Cultivars. 'Crispa' is much more compact in growth habit with strongly arching branches, not usually exceeding a height of 1 m/3.3 ft when planted in full sun. More useful for massing or as a tall groundcover than the species type.

Related Species

Stephanandra tanakae 4 (Tanaka stephanandra). This Japanese shrub has larger leaves, more vigorous and coarser growth habit, and usually more brightly colored autumn foliage: yellow, orange, or scarlet. It is rarely used or available, and its useful range is not accurately known but includes at least Zones 6a–8b.

Neillia sinensis 4 (Chinese neillia). This gracefully arching shrub appears intermediate in growth habit and foliage character between its close relatives, *Physocarpus* and *Stephanandra*, but with character of its own in its bright green, lightly incised leaves, zigzag stems, and small, nodding pink flowers in late spring or early summer. Seldom available commercially but useful in Zones 6a–8b and possibly Zone 5 as well, with site requirements similar to *Stephanandra*. Several other *Neillia* species are included in institutional collections, but these are even rarer than *N. sinensis* at present.

Stewartia ovata 6

Mountain stewartia
Deciduous shrub or small tree
Theaceae (Tea Family)

Native Range. Southern Appalachian Mountains: Kentucky to Georgia.

Useful Range. USDA Zones 7a–8b, perhaps also sheltered sites in Zone 6b.

Function. Specimen, border, patio tree.

Size and Habit

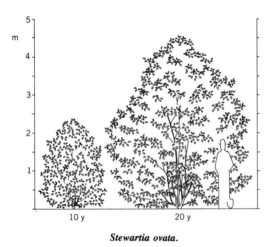

Stewartia ovata.

Adaptability. Partial shade from summer sun is desirable for best performance and flowering, especially in areas having hot summers. Requires unusually good soil drainage.

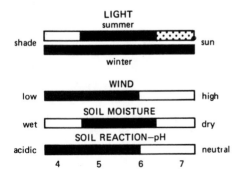

Seasonal Interest. *Flowers:* White with yellow stamens in the center, 5–8 cm/2–3 in. across, resembling single white camellias, borne singly along the stems and opening a few at a time from

middle to late summer. *Foliage:* Light green and rather coarse, serving as an effective background for the showy flowers but not very interesting in itself until autumn, when in some years it turns orange or scarlet before falling in midautumn. *Trunk and branches:* Brownish gray bark is finely fissured and rough, sometimes exposing the green inner bark but lacking the smooth, sculpted, multicolored and flaking character of the oriental stewartias.

Stewartia ovata.

Problems and Maintenance. This plant has been relatively trouble-free to date, but limited use may not yet have given full opportunity for evaluation of disease problems. Its greatest limitation at present other than limited availability is difficulty in transplanting. Best results can be obtained by specifying container-grown plants in small sizes, although skilled contractors can move most trees when given flexibility as to season.

Forms. F. *grandiflora* (showy mountain stewartia) is definitely more showy in flower than the species type, with larger flowers, to 8–10 cm/3–4 in. across, having purple stamens. Some flowers have a few extra petals. Useful in Zones 6a–8b.

Related Species

Stewartia malacodendron 6 (synonym: *S. virginica*; Virginia stewartia, silky camellia).   Native to the southeastern states, this small, shrubby tree is as showy in flower as *S. ovata* f. *grandiflora*, similarly with white flowers and purple stamens, a little earlier in summer than those of *S. ovata*. The flaking, bicolored, brown and tan bark is about as interesting as that of *S. pseudocamellia*. Its useful range is more southerly: Zones 7b−9a.

Stewartia pseudocamellia 7

Japanese stewartia
Deciduous tree
Theaceae (Tea Family)

Native Range. Japan.

Useful Range. USDA Zones 6a−8b.

Function. Specimen tree, massing.

Size and Habit

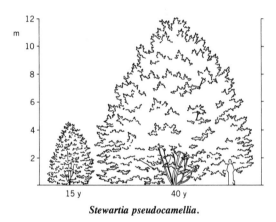

Stewartia pseudocamellia.

Adaptability. Partial shade from summer sun is desirable for best performance and flowering, especially in areas having hot summers. Requires unusually good soil drainage.

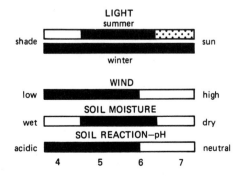

Seasonal Interest. *Flowers:* White, with yellow-orange stamens in the center, 5−6 cm/2−2.4 in. across, resembling single white camellias, opening a few at a time from middle to late summer. *Foliage:* Rich green and of medium texture, serving as an effective background for the flowers and turning deep red-purple before falling in autumn. *Trunk and branches:* Smooth bark gives a molded or sculpted look to trunk and branches, the reddish brown outer bark peeling away in irregularly rounded flakes to expose lighter brown underneath, giving a striking, multicolored pattern, effective in all seasons.

Problems and Maintenance. This tree is relatively trouble-free but difficult to transplant in any but small sizes. Specify container-grown material for best results. It is not widely available, but may be more so as it becomes better known.

Cultivars. 'Korean Splendor' (see Related Species).

Related Species

Stewartia koreana 7 (Korean stewartia). Plants carried under this name are generally similar to those of *S. pseudocamellia* except that they bear larger flowers that open over a longer time period in summer and have more colorful autumn foliage: golden to red-orange. There is considerable doubt as to the validity of this species. Specialists have variously classified Korean stewartia as a species, as *S. pseudocamellia* var. *koreana*, and most recently as *S. pseudocamellia* 'Korean Splendor.' Under whatever name, it is increasing in popularity and availability and is useful in Zones 6a−8b and perhaps also Zone 5.

Stewartia monadelpha 7 (Hime-Syara stewartia). This close relative of *S. pseudocamellia*

Stewartia koreana (S. pseudocamellia 'Korean Splendor').

and S. *sinensis* has smaller flowers than either, to 2.5–3.5 cm/1–1.4 in. across, and smooth, reddish brown bark that gives it outstanding winter interest. It is less likely to be available than S. *pseudocamellia* but is nevertheless useful in Zones 6a–8b.

Stewartia sinensis 6 (Chinese stewartia). Slightly shorter than either S. *monadelpha* or S. *pseudocamellia*, with more cupped flowers, about 5 cm/2 in. across, and reddish brown, flaking bark, this small tree seems to have become more popular in Europe than in North America. It is seldom available but potentially useful in Zones 6b–8b.

Stewartia koreana (S. pseudocamellia 'Korean Splendor').

Styrax japonicus 6

Japanese snowbell
Deciduous tree
Styracaceae (Styrax Family)

Native Range. China, Japan.

Useful Range. USDA Zones 6b–8b, sheltered sites in Zone 6a, and areas in Zone 9a having moderate summers.

Function. Specimen, patio tree (where lateral space is available).

Size and Habit

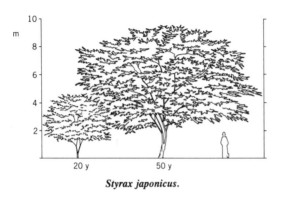

Styrax japonicus.

Adaptability

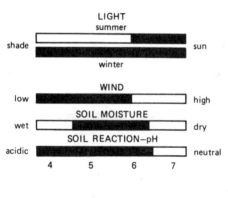

Seasonal Interest. *Flowers:* White, slightly fragrant, vaguely bell-shaped but with spreading petals, to 2 cm/0.8 in. across in small clusters to 5 cm/2 in. long, gracefully pendulous below the branches. *Foliage:* Deep green and lustrous, 3–8 cm/1–3 in. long and half as wide, giving a rather fine texture and forming a canopy above the branches, not covering the flowers hanging be-

low, turning yellow or dull red in some years. *Fruit:* Dry, rounded capsules dangling beneath the branches are distinctive but not conspicuous. *Trunk and branches:* Bark is dark gray and fairly smooth; sometimes trunks and main limbs are sinewy.

Styrax japonicus.

Styrax japonicus.

Problems and Maintenance. *S. japonicus* is usually trouble-free and requires little maintenance. Light pruning may help establish the tree's growth habit but is neither necessary nor desirable thereafter except to remove any deadwood.

Related Species

Styrax americanus 5 (American snowbell). This large shrub is native to the southeastern United States from Virginia to Florida and Louisiana. Occasionally it is used in human-made landscapes in Zones 6b−9a but is more likely to be encountered as a subject for preservation or naturalization in and near its native habitat. Its flowering interest is similar to that of S. *japonicus*.

Styrax grandifolius 6 (bigleaf snowbell). This large shrub or small tree, native to the southeast-

ern United States from Virginia to Florida, has fragrant flowers. Like S. *americanus*, it is more likely to be available for preservation than for planting, but it is useful for either, when available, in Zones 7b−9a.

Styrax obassia 6 (fragrant snowbell). This large shrub or small tree from Japan has the largest leaves of any *Styrax* species mentioned here, to as much as 20 cm/8 in. long and frequently 10 cm/4 in. or more across. In fact, the heavy foliage partly obscures the fragrant flowers, in pendulous racemes 10−20 cm/4−8 in. long, which otherwise would be at least as showy as those of S. *japonicus*. Nevertheless, this is a handsome, small tree, more upright in growth habit than S. *japonicus*, and useful in Zones 6b−8b.

Symphoricarpos ×*chenaultii* 3

Chenault coralberry
Deciduous shrub
Caprifoliaceae (Honeysuckle Family)

Hybrid Origin. Probably S. *microphyllus* × S. *orbiculatus*.

Useful Range. USDA Zones 5a−8b.

Function. Border, massing, large-scale ground-cover.

Size and Habit

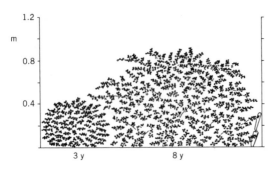

Symphoricarpos ×*chenaultii*.

Adaptability

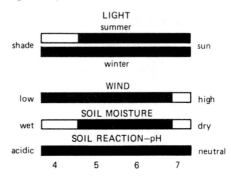

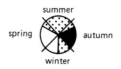

Seasonal Interest. *Flowers:* Pink, small, and inconspicuous, in midsummer. *Foliage:* Dull green, fine textured, not distinctive except in the selection 'Hancock' (see Cultivars), turning dull yellow briefly in some years before falling in early to middle autumn. *Fruits:* Berrylike, coral-red, 0.6 cm/0.25 in. across, some whitened on the side away from the sun, in terminal clusters to 4 cm/1.6 in. long, showy in autumn and persistent well into winter.

Problems and Maintenance. Several diseases occasionally may infect foliage, fruits, and stems, requiring the removal of infected material and protection with fungicidal sprays. Drastic renewal pruning, needed every few years to keep this plant in good condition, furnishes an opportunity to remove and burn any infected parts along with the rest of the tops. Protective sprays can be applied at this time if symptoms of disease have been observed.

Cultivars. 'Hancock' is an outstanding dwarf selection, reaching heights of a little over 0.5 m/1.6 ft tall with much more handsome foliage than average for the species. An excellent, large-scale groundcover, slightly less cold-hardy than the Zone 5a limit given for S. ×chenaultii generally, but at least to Zone 5b.

Related Species

Symphoricarpos albus 3 (synonym: *S. racemosus*; eastern snowberry). This low shrub, native to much of northeastern North America, has whitish fruits in middle to late summer but is seldom planted, in deference to the larger and more showy *S. rivularis* (synonym: *S. albus* var. *laevigatus*). It is useful in Zones 3b−6b.

Symphoricarpos orbiculatus 3 (coralberry; Indian currant). This parent of *S. ×chenaultii*, native to much of eastern North America from New York to South Dakota and southward to Florida and Mexico, is predictably variable in response to climate. With selection of appropriate (nearby origin) genetic material, it is a useful, large-scale groundcover with coral-red fruits, about 0.5 cm/0.2 in. across, in autumn and early winter in Zones 3b−9a, but it is most useful in Zones 3b−6b.

Symphoricarpos rivularis 4 (synonym: *S. albus* var. *laevigatus*; western snowberry). This native of western North America is the common snowberry used in eastern North America. With inconspicuous pink flowers in early summer, blue-green foliage, and showy white fruits to 1 cm/0.4 in. or more across in autumn, this shrub is useful for mass planting or for color interest in the shrub border, in Zones 4a−7a.

Symplocos paniculata 6

Asiatic sweetleaf, sapphireberry
Deciduous shrub
Symplocaceae (Sweetleaf Family)

Native Range. China, Himalayas, Japan, Korea.

Useful Range. USDA Zones 6a−8b.

Function. Screen, specimen, large border.

Size and Habit

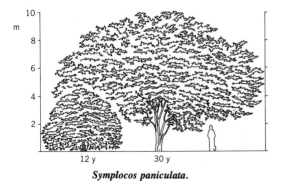

Symplocos paniculata.

Adaptability

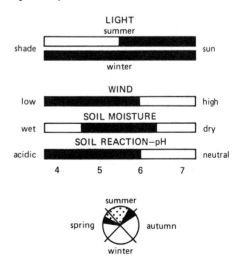

Seasonal Interest. *Flowers:* Fragrant, creamy white, to only 1 cm/0.4 in. across, in panicles 4−8 cm/1.6−3 in. long, fairly showy in middle to late May. *Foliage:* Bright green and crisp-appearing in early summer, turning dull green and coarse-appearing later, falling with little other color change in midautumn. *Fruits:* Bright blue, individually 0.8 cm/0.3 in. across, borne in large numbers and showy, but usually taken rather quickly by birds.

Symplocos paniculata.

Problems and Maintenance. Minor leaf-spot diseases and insect infestations are seldom

serious enough to require control. Pruning is needed only for removal of any deadwood or for gradual renewal of old plants.

Related Species

Symplocos tinctoria 6 (common sweetleaf, horse sugar). This seldom-planted native of the southeastern United States from Delaware to Florida and Louisiana is of interest primarily as a subject for preservation in natural and naturalized landscapes. It forms a large shrub or small tree with semievergreen foliage, almost fully evergreen in the Deep South. Its primary landscape interest lies in its yellow flowers, borne in clusters to 5 cm/2 in. across before the new leaves emerge in midspring. Fruits are not conspicuous, and the plant form is loose and not highly functional. Useful in Zones 7b−9a+.

Syringa ×*chinensis* 6

Synonym: *S. rothomagensis*
Chinese lilac
Deciduous shrub
Oleaceae (Olive Family)

Hybrid Origin. *S. laciniata* × *S. vulgaris.*

Useful Range. USDA Zones 4a−8a.

Function. Specimen, border, screen, informal hedge.

Size and Habit

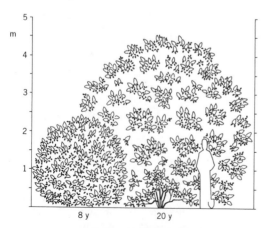

Syringa ×*chinensis.*

Adaptability

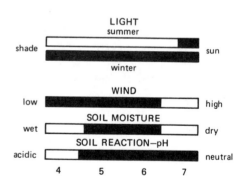

Seasonal Interest. *Flowers:* Lavender to red-purple, in rather loose, mostly erect panicles, 10−20 cm/4−8 in. long, larger in some selections under ideal conditions, very showy in late spring. *Foliage:* Medium to bright green, similar to those of *S. vulgaris* but only about 6 cm/2.5 in. long and 2 cm/0.8 in. wide, making a dense mass effective for screening but otherwise not adding distinctive interest, falling in autumn without color change.

Problems and Maintenance. Several diseases and insects can be troublesome, including borers, leaf miners, scale insects, and leaf and twig blights. Powdery mildew is a perennial problem in some areas where it disfigures the foliage in late summer but does little permanent damage. Pruning is necessary for renewal of older plants. Since this species does not sucker freely, it is easier to maintain in form than its parent, *S. vulgaris*. Most lilacs are not low-maintenance plants.

Cultivars. 'Alba' has white flowers. 'Saugeana' (= 'Red Rothomagensis,' = 'Rubra') has reddish lilac flowers and flowers unusually freely. Many other variants exist, most as yet unnamed. Further selection and naming of desirable variants can be expected.

Related Species

Syringa laciniata 4 (synonym: *S.* ×*persica* var. *laciniata*; cutleaf lilac).   This graceful, fountainlike shrub has strongly arching branches and fine foliage texture brought about by the deeply dissected leaves. It makes an interesting addition to the shrub border because of its distinctive foliage effect and pale lavender flowers and is useful in Zones 5a−9a.

Syringa ×*persica* 4 (Persian lilac).   This hybrid of *S. afghanica* × *S. laciniata* is as graceful as *S. laciniata* although not cutleaved, with foliage of finer texture than that of *S.* ×*chinensis*. Most plants sold under the name "Persian lilac" probably are actually *S.* ×*chinensis*. True *S.* ×*persica* is neither tall enough nor dense enough to serve as a visual screen. Mostly with lavender to rosy lavender flowers, but the selection 'Alba' has pure white flowers. Useful in Zones 4b−8b.

Syringa meyeri 4

Synonyms: *S. microphylla* 'Minor,' *S. palibiniana*
Meyer lilac
Deciduous shrub
Oleaceae (Olive Family)

Native Range. Northern China.

Useful Range. USDA Zones 4a−7b.

Function. Specimen, border, foundation.

Size and Habit

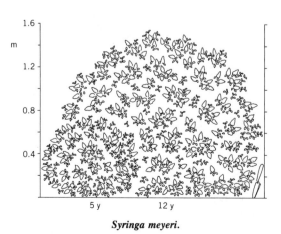

Syringa meyeri.

Adaptability

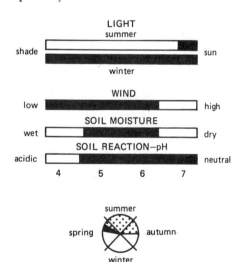

Seasonal Interest. *Flowers:* Pale purple flowers with little fragrance in erect panicles to 8 cm/3 in. long in late spring, beginning when plants are no more than 30 cm/12 in. tall. *Foliage:* Rich green, lustrous, compact, and neatly textured, the leaves 2.5−4 cm/1−1.6 in. long with wavy margins, falling in autumn with little color change.

Problems and Maintenance. Several diseases and insects can be troublesome (see *Syringa* ×*chinensis*) but are not often serious problems. Pruning is seldom needed for any purpose, making this one of the most maintenance-free of all lilacs.

Related Species

Syringa microphylla 4 (littleleaf lilac). This Chinese species has leaves as small as those of its close relative *S. meyeri*, but its foliage texture is less interesting, and *S. microphylla* does not flower as well as a young plant. The selection 'Superba' is outstanding: a vigorous plant approaching screening height with deep pink flowers barely earlier than those of *S. meyeri*. Useful in Zones 5a−7b.

Syringa patula 5 (synonyms: *S. palibiniana*, *S. velutina*; Korean lilac). This shrub from China and Korea has dark green, pubescent foliage of medium texture with leaves to 10 cm/4 in. long and pale purple flowers in panicles to 12 cm/5 in. long. The selection 'Miss Kim' is compact and dense with unusually handsome foliage, turning dull red-purple in autumn, and eventually becomes nearly as tall as the species type. Useful in Zones 3a−7b.

Syringa pubescens 4. This Chinese shrub is intermediate in size, foliage, flowers, and landscape effect between *S. meyeri* and *S. patula*, but with conspicuously fragrant flowers. Useful in Zones 4a−7b.

Syringa reticulata 6−7

Synonym: *S. amurensis* var. *japonica*
Japanese tree lilac
Deciduous tree
Oleaceae (Olive Family)

Native Range. Japan, Manchuria, northern China.

Useful Range. USDA Zones 3a−7b with selection of appropriate genetic material.

Function. Small street tree (in cool climates), patio tree, border.

Size and Habit

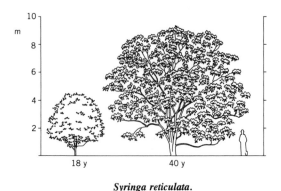

Syringa reticulata.

Adaptability

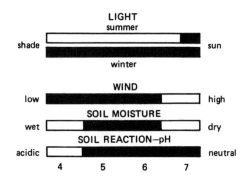

Seasonal Interest. *Flowers:* Creamy white in loose pyramidal clusters, 15−30 cm/6−12 in. long, with odor resembling that of *Ligustrum* flowers, early in summer but after flowering of *S. villosa* and its related species. *Foliage:* Dark green leaves, 8−15 cm/3−6 in. long and broadly heart-shaped like those of *S. vulgaris*, giving a rather coarse texture and sometimes turning dull yellow before falling in early to middle autumn. *Fruits:* Capsules, 1−2 cm/0.4−0.8 in. long, in loose clusters, turning yellowish in late summer.

Trunk and branches: Bark is purplish brown and somewhat cherrylike with prominent horizontal lenticels, adding quiet winter interest.

Problems and Maintenance. This species is subject to the troubles of lilacs in general, especially borers and scale insects, and especially in warmer climates. Relatively trouble-free in Zones 3b−5b and areas of Zones 6 and 7 having mild summers. Pruning is needed only for initial training when it is used as a tree and for removing any deadwood. As with *S. vulgaris,* flowering tends to be in alternate years unless spent flower clusters are removed to prevent fruit and seed set, which competes with flower bud initiation for the following year.

Varieties and Cultivars

Var. mandshurica (synonym: *S. amurensis*; Amur lilac, Manchurian tree lilac). This shrubby small tree, to 6 m/20 ft tall, is the northern variant from China and Manchuria. It is more cold-hardy than the Japanese species type, probably at least to Zone 2b, but less useful as a tree where both forms are hardy.

Few cultivars have been selected because of difficulties in vegetative propagation, but a superior form for use as a small street tree, 'Ivory Silk,' has been selected in Canada.

Related Species

Syringa pekinensis 6 (Peking lilac). This large, rangy shrub or small tree has flowering interest similar to that of *S. reticulata* but usually is less showy. It is more irregular in form, with much

Syringa pekinensis.

narrower leaves, and usually remains below 5 m/16 ft in height, yet old trees in good soil at the Morton Arboretum near Chicago have become much larger. Bark of certain trees is strongly curling, amber in color, adding winter interest. Selection and propagation of superior types seems warranted. Useful in Zones 4a−7a, perhaps also Zone 3, but seldom available.

Syringa villosa 5

Late lilac
Deciduous shrub
Oleaceae (Olive Family)

Native Range. Northern China.

Useful Range. USDA Zones 3a−7b.

Function. Screen, specimen, border.

Size and Habit

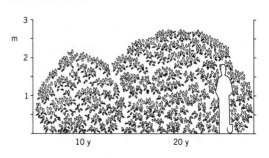

Syringa villosa.

Adaptability

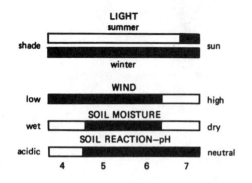

Seasonal Interest. *Flowers:* Barely fragrant, pale rosy purple to white, in dense, erect panicles, 8–15 cm/3–6 in. long, very late in spring after *S. vulgaris* has finished flowering. *Foliage:* Dark green, paler underneath, with leaves to 15 cm/6

Syringa villosa.

in. long, making a rather coarse but dense mass, sometimes turning dull yellow before falling in midautumn.

Problems and Maintenance. This species is subject to most of the problems of lilacs in general (see *S. ×chinensis*). Scale insects are especially troublesome in this species and its close relatives (see Related Species and Hybrids, below). Little pruning is necessary, since the normal form of this plant is dense and it does not sucker.

Cultivars. Few if any selections have been made directly from *S. villosa*, but this species frequently has been a parent of hybrid selections (see Related Species and Hybrids).

Related Species and Hybrids

Syringa ×henryi 5 (Henry lilac).   This hybrid of *S. villosa × S. josikaea*, similar to the parent species, is represented in commerce by the selection 'Lutece' with rosy violet flowers.

Syringa ×josiflexa 5.   This group of hybrids of *S. reflexa × S. josikaea* includes several cultivars developed by the Canada Department of Agriculture at Ottawa and at Morden, Manitoba. One of the finest products of this cross is 'Miss Canada,' an *S. ×josiflexa × S. ×prestoniae* hybrid with outstanding, rosy pink flowers, probably the best of all pink late lilacs. Useful in Zones 3a–7b, perhaps also Zone 2.

Syringa josikaea 5 (Hungarian lilac).   This native of southeastern Europe is similar in general effect to *S. villosa* except that it is more upright and leggy in growth habit and less functional as a result. Useful in Zones 2b–7b.

Syringa ×prestoniae 5 (Preston hybrid lilacs). This group of hybrids of *S. reflexa × S. villosa* was developed by the Canada Department of Agriculture at about the same time as the *S. ×josiflexa* group. There are many of these cultivars and their open-pollinated progeny, and a considerable number of cultivars are commercially available in the northern plains of Canada and the adjacent United States. They are similar to *S. villosa* but with a variety of flower colors. Most are fast-growing, vigorous shrubs, useful in Zones 2b–7b.

Syringa reflexa 5 (nodding lilac).   This Chinese species, flowering with the rest of the late lilac

Syringa ×*swegiflexa*.

group, is unusual for its long and narrow, nodding to pendulous panicles of pink flowers. Even though distinctive and useful in Zones 5a–7b, it is not often commercially available. 'Alba' has white flowers.

Syringa ×*swegiflexa* 5.   This hybrid of *S. reflexa* × *S. sweginzowii* combines the nodding flowering character of *S. reflexa* and some of the fragrance and airy gracefulness of *S. sweginzowii* and is useful in Zones 5b–7b but is not widely available.

Syringa sweginzowii 5.   This graceful, open shrub from northwest China has smaller leaves than most of the late-flowering lilacs yet not as small as those of *S. meyeri* or *S. microphylla*, and has fragrant, rosy lilac flowers in showy clusters to 20 cm/8 in. long. It is useful in Zones 5b–7b, but available only from nurseries specializing in unusual lilacs.

Syringa vulgaris 6

Common and French hybrid lilacs
Deciduous shrub
Oleaceae (Olive Family)

Native Range. Southeastern Europe; naturalized in many parts of the Northern Hemisphere, including much of North America.

Useful Range. USDA Zones 3b–7b, some selections in Zone 3a.

Function. Border, specimen, informal hedge, screen (with attention to pruning).

Size and Habit

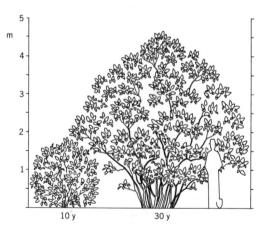

Syringa vulgaris.

Adaptability

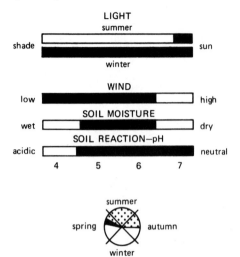

Seasonal Interest. *Flowers:* Highly fragrant, lavender, pink, purple, bluish, white, and many intermediate colors, in more or less erect clusters 10–20cm/4–8 in. long, very showy in late spring. *Foliage:* Bright green, smooth, and distinctively heart-shaped, giving a medium texture, falling in autumn with little or no color change.

Problems and Maintenance. Several insects and diseases can be troublesome (see *Syringa ×chinensis*). Powdery mildew disfigures the foliage annually in areas that are typically warm and humid in late summer. Borers and scale insects may do permanent damage if not controlled. For best flowering, dried up flower clusters should be removed promptly to prevent seed development, which competes with initiation of flower buds for the next year. Failure to do this results in full flowering only in alternate years in some cultivars. Suckers form freely on most cultivars and a decision must be made as to whether they are to be removed annually. This practice is common where hybrid lilacs are being grown primarily as showy specimens, but it may be neither necessary nor desirable when lilacs are being used for large-scale visual screening, since

the suckers may contribute to basal fullness of the foliage mass. Otherwise careful renewal pruning is necessary to prevent "legginess."

Cultivars. Several hundred, perhaps a thousand, cultivars of *S. vulgaris* have been selected. Many of the earlier ones were developed in France, leading to the use of the name "French Hybrids" to refer to this group. But many cultivars have originated in other European countries, Canada, the United States, and the Soviet Union. The Lilac Survey Committee of the American Association of Botanical Gardens and Arboreta in 1968 published a list of 100 "recommended" *S. vulgaris* cultivars and hybrids, still a fairly unwieldy group. Most cultivars differ more in flower characteristics (color, size, doubleness) than in functionality, so no listing will be provided here. In any case, selection must be guided by availability of cultivars at a specific time and place. For purely functional purposes, there are many better choices than *S. vulgaris* and its hybrids (e.g., *S. ×chinensis*).

Related Species

Syringa ×hyacinthiflora 6. This group of hybrids of *S. oblata* × *S. vulgaris* has become very popular in colder parts of Canada because of outstanding cold-hardiness, early flowering, and, in a few cases, autumn foliage color. The more than 40 cultivars that have been selected are often lumped with the French Hybrids of *S. vulgaris*. Most are better known in Canada than in the United States and are useful in Zones 3b–7b.

Syringa oblata 5 (early lilac). This close relative of *S. vulgaris* from China and Korea is best known in the form of var. *dilatata* (synonym: *S. dilatata*; Korean early lilac), which has pink-lilac flowers a week or so earlier than those of *S. vulgaris* and reddish purple autumn foliage color reminiscent of that of *Fraxinus americana*, but not as colorful as the best cultivars of that species. Useful in Zones 4a–7b.

Tamarix ramosissima 5

Synonyms: *T. odessana, T. pentandra*
Five-stamen or Odessa tamarisk
Deciduous shrub
Tamaricaceae (Tamarisk Family)

Native Range. Southeastern Europe to central Asia.

Useful Range. USDA Zones 4a−9a+ with selection of appropriate genetic material. Some forms are less cold-hardy.

Function. Specimen, border.

Size and Habit. Ultimate height is variable, from 2 m/6.6 ft to more than 5 m/16 ft if left unpruned, but when pruned to retain good form, height will seldom exceed 3−4 m/10−13 ft.

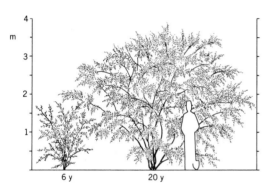

Tamarix ramosissima.

Adaptability. Relatively salt-tolerant at seashore or near salted walks.

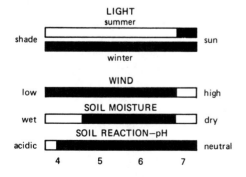

Seasonal Interest. *Flowers:* Light to rosy pink, very small but borne in large, fluffy clusters, highly showy in midsummer and continuing

with less color until late summer. *Foliage:* Bright to bluish green, very fine-textured with tiny, scalelike leaves, turning duller or yellowish before falling in autumn.

Problems and Maintenance. Stem cankers occasionally can be troublesome and can be controlled by removing and destroying infected branches. Drastic renewal pruning is necessary every few years to retain good landscape form and to keep in useful size. Burning of pruned tops will reduce future disease problems by removing inoculum.

Cultivars. 'Cheyenne Red' has unusually bright rosy pink flowers. 'Pink Cascade' has blue-green foliage and outstanding flowering interest. 'Rubra' is a cultivar name that has been applied to at least two clones under two synonymous species names. The one listed as *T. odessana* 'Rubra' is smaller in stature than that listed as *T. pentandra* 'Rubra,' but both have bright rosy pink flowers. 'Summer Glow' is similar if not identical to the selection that is also listed as *T. pentandra* 'Rubra.'

Related Species

Tamarix hispida 4 (Kashgar tamarisk). This central Asian species is distinctive for its silvery blue-green, silky foliage and somewhat later flowering, in late summer. Useful in Zones 5a−9a+ and perhaps sheltered sites in Zone 4.

Tamarix parviflora 5 (small-flowered tamarisk). This southern European species differs from the other *Tamarix* species listed in that it flowers in spring from flower buds initiated the previous summer. Because of this, winterkilling of tops in extreme winters in Zones 5 and 6 can eliminate most of the potential flowering interest for a year afterward. This also means that pruning should be carried out after flowering, in contrast to other *Tamarix* species, which are best pruned earlier in spring. Useful in Zones 5b−9a+ and sheltered sites in Zone 5a.

Taxodium distichum 8

Bald cypress
Deciduous tree
Taxodiaceae (Taxodium Family)

Native Range. Southeastern United States and northward to Delaware and Indiana in coastal areas and river basins.

Useful Range. USDA Zones 5a–9a+, perhaps also Zone 4 with selection of appropriate genetic material.

Function. Specimen, massing, naturalizing, street tree in some areas.

Size and Habit

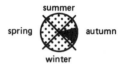

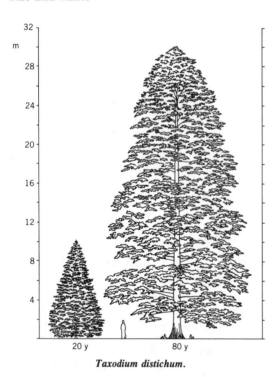

Taxodium distichum.

Adaptability

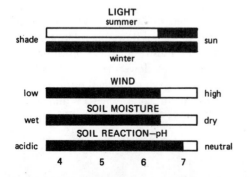

Seasonal Interest. *Foliage:* Deciduous, flattened, soft, needlelike, giving fine, billowy texture, light green in spring, soft green in summer, and turning a warm russet brown before falling in late autumn. *Trunk and branches:* Lower branches are borne horizontally on a strong, straight, tapered central trunk. Bark texture adds winter interest along with buttressing of the bases of older trunks and upward-protruding "knees," especially in wet sites.

Taxodium distichum.

Problems and Maintenance. Twig blight and wood-rot diseases occasionally can be problems in weakened trees, but ordinarily *T. distichum* is free of any major problems that would limit its use. Its broad adaptability from the swamps of its native habitat to soils of average moisture content does not extend to very dry soils, where it can be damaged by drought, setting the stage for other problems. Pruning is not needed except to remove any deadwood, but when necessary it should be carried out after the leaves emerge so that deadwood can be seen clearly.

Varieties and Cultivars. Var. *nutans* (synonym: *T. ascendens;* pond cypress). This variant, limited in the wild to the Gulf Coast portion of the range and northward to Virginia, has smaller, scalelike leaves, giving the foliage a more stringy texture and the tree a narrower outline, useful for vertical accent. Useful in Zones 6a–9a+ and probably at least parts of Zone 5.

'Pendens' has drooping or semipendulous branches.

The following cultivars were selected in the 1970s by Mr. Earl Cully of Jacksonville, Illinois. They are adaptable northward at least to Zone 5b, and some probably to Zone 4. 'Monarch of Illinois'·(Plant Patent No. 3547, 1974), has an unusually wide-spreading form, suitable for large-scale lawn or park use. 'Prairie Sentinel' (Plant Patent No. 3548, 1974), a selection from var. *nutans*, has a characteristically very narrow form and is well adapted to fairly dry soils. 'Shawnee Brave' (Plant Patent No. 3551, 1974) is a narrow selection of the typical *T. distichum*, but not as narrow as 'Prairie Sentinel,' with height typically only about four times its spread.

Taxus cuspidata 4—6

Japanese yew
Evergreen tree or shrub
Taxaceae (Yew Family)

Native Range. Japan, Korea, Manchuria.

Useful Range. USDA Zones 4b—7b.

Function. Screen, hedge, foundation, specimen, border.

Size and Habit. 'Capitata' (left), 'Densa' (right front), and 'Thayerae' (right rear) are illustrated.

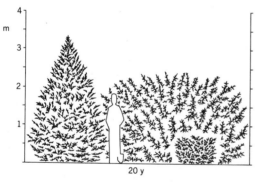

Taxus cuspidata cvs. 'Capitata' (left), 'Densa' (right front), and 'Thayerae' (right rear).

Adaptability. Tolerant of a wide range of sun or shade in most situations, but light shade is necessary for best results in areas having hot, dry summers, and protection from full sun and wind in winter is desirable in Zone 5 to prevent drying of foliage. Newly planted yews are notoriously sensitive to poorly drained soil (often caused by planting too deeply), but well established plants are slightly more tolerant of wet soils.

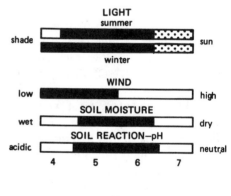

Seasonal Interest. *Flowers:* Dioecious and inconspicuous. The staminate (male) flowers discharge pollen in large quantities in late spring. *Foliage:* Rich, deep green, making a dense mass very effective in screening. Needles are flattened and more succulent than those of most other needle evergreens, clustered thickly on lighter green twigs. Those of the better cultivars retain their color well in winter and persist for several years. *Fruits:* Scarlet, round, and fleshy arils, 1.2 cm/0.5 in. across, on pistillate (female) plants, enclosing the black seeds. Interesting and sometimes conspicuous in quantity, but secondary in interest to the foliage.

Problems and Maintenance. The most common problems of yews result from unfavorable site conditions, especially poor soil drainage. The best solution to such problems is prevention, either by improving drainage during site construction or by selecting alternate species. In addition, diseases can occasionally be troublesome, but insect and mite problems are more common, the most serious being black vine weevil. Instructions for control of this and other insects can be obtained from state, provincial, or county extension service offices.

Most parts of the yew plant are poisonous to warm-blooded animals. Most cases of death by poisoning have resulted from livestock eating hedge clippings, which apparently become more toxic as they dry following removal from the plant. The red aril (fleshy part of the fruit) is not poisonous but the black seed within is highly toxic.

Cultivars. Over the years, many selections have been made, named, and introduced. In 1942 a major comparison of cultivars of *Taxus* was begun by Professor L. C. Chadwick, The Ohio State University, at the Ohio Agricultural Research and Development Center at Wooster. The few cultivars that follow are among those considered the best for that region by Professor Chadwick, but the descriptions are mine.

'Capitata' is the upright, pyramidal form of *T. cuspidata* and, in fact, the species type as it is known in the wild. Selections of spreading growth habit have mostly if not entirely originated by rooting of cuttings from lower branches of tree-form yews. Technically the species type of yew, most commonly propagated by seed and somewhat variable, should not receive cultivar status, but this is how it is listed commercially.

'Densa,' a pistillate (fruiting) clone, is one of the finest low, slow-growing selections, but it is difficult to locate commercially. Specimens in Boston had not exceeded 1.5 m/5 ft in height and twice that spread in 45 years of growth, and this cultivar can be relied on to remain small for years, requiring little or no pruning. 'Densa' should never be confused with 'Densiformis,' a very different selection (see *Taxus* ×*media*, Cultivars).

'Nana' (also incorrectly called 'Brevifolia'), usually referred to as "dwarf Japanese yew" is actually somewhat faster growing than 'Densa,' yet slower and more compact and "blocky" in

form than the species type. It is popular and usually readily available.

'Thayerae' is an excellent, low-growing, pistillate (fruiting) selection with unusually attractive foliage. It is faster growing than either 'Densa' or 'Nana,' yet compact and remaining relatively low for years.

Many other cultivars are commercially available. Some are probably as good as these for specific situations. As with all plants, attention should be given to local availability and experience.

Related Species and Hybrids

Taxus canadensis 3–4 (Canada yew).   This loosely spreading native of northeastern North America grows wild in Zones 3a–6b, yet has winter hardiness problems in cultivation in exposed sites throughout much of this range. It should be protected from full sun in both summer and winter in most areas. Usually cultivars of *T. cuspidata* will outperform this species in landscape use, but it has value for naturalizing.

Taxus floridana 5 (Florida yew).   This native of northern Florida generally resembles *T. cuspidata* except for its sparseness and very narrow needles. Its landscape value comes from its tolerance of more southern climates than the other yews. It is useful, primarily for naturalizing or as an object of preservation, in Zones 8 and 9, but seldom if ever is available for planting.

Taxus ×*hunnewelliana* 5 (Hunnewell yew). This hybrid of *T. cuspidata* × *T. canadensis* is intermediate in form and foliage between the parents. It has a spreading habit and intermediate growth rate and turns reddish brown in winter, an objectionable color to some. Useful in Zones 4a–7a but should be protected from full sun and wind in winter in Zone 4.

Cephalotaxus fortunei 5 (Chinese or Fortune plum-yew).   This native of China is closely related to *Taxus* in the family Cephalotaxaceae, but has green to purplish fruits, 2.5 cm/1 in. across, and larger needles. It functions much as a loose-growing, spreading yew, usually at least as wide as tall, with rich green foliage. It is useful in Zones 7b–9a+, but only in those coastal areas that have mild summer temperatures, which eliminates it as a landscape plant from most of our area.

Cephalotaxus harringtonia 4 (Japanese plum-yew). This somewhat slower-growing counterpart of *C. fortunei* is similar in its effect and limitations except that it is useful in somewhat colder areas in Zones 6a–9a+.

Torreya nucifera 5–7 (Japanese torreya). This close relative of *Taxus* becomes a full-size tree in its native Japan, but seldom is seen as more than a tall shrub in our area. Its sharp-pointed needles are easily distinguished from the superficially similar, blunter ones of *Cephalotaxus* and have a citruslike aroma when crushed. This plant is not widely used, but it is a useful evergreen shrub or small tree in Zones 6b–9a+ and sheltered spots in Zone 6a.

Torreya taxifolia 5 (Florida torreya, stinking cedar). This shrubby plant is seldom planted except near its natural range in northern and central Florida, but it is available for naturalizing and preservation there.

Taxus ×*media* 4–6

Anglo-Japanese or intermediate yew
Evergreen shrub
Taxaceae (Yew Family)

Hybrid Origin. *T. cuspidata* × *T. baccata*.

Useful Range. USDA Zones 5a–7b, and areas in Zone 8 having mild summers.

Function. Hedge, screen, foundation, specimen, border.

Size and Habit. 'Hicksii' (left), 'Wardii' (center), and 'Brownii' (right rear) are illustrated.

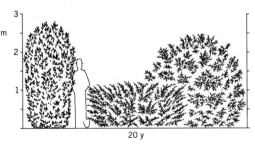

Taxus ×*media* cvs. 'Hicksii' (left), 'Wardii' (center), and 'Brownii' (right rear).

Adaptability. Partial shade in summer is beneficial in the South and Midwest. Protection from winter sun and wind is desirable for best results in Zone 5. Poorly drained soils are troublesome in new plantings, especially when planted too deeply, but established plants are slightly more tolerant of wet soils.

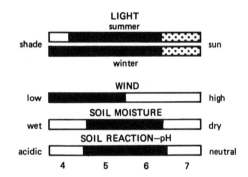

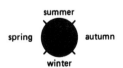

Seasonal Interest. *Flowers:* Dioecious and inconspicuous. Staminate (male) flowers discharge pollen in large quantities in late spring. *Foliage:* Rich, deep green, making a dense mass that is very effective in screening. Flattened needles, more succulent than those of most other needle evergreens, are tightly clustered on the lighter green twigs. Those of the better cultivars retain their color well into winter. *Fruits:* Scarlet, round, and fleshy, 1.2 cm/0.5 in. across, on pistillate (female) plants, enclosing the black seeds. Interesting and conspicuous in quantity but secondary in interest to the foliage.

Problems and Maintenance. The most common problems of yews result from unfavorable site conditions, but diseases and insects also can be troublesome (see *T. cuspidata*, Problems and Maintenance). Most parts of yew plants are poisonous to warm-blooded animals (see *T. cuspidata*, Problems and Maintenance).

Cultivars. The following cultivars are included among those considered the best by Professor L. C. Chadwick at Ohio State University (see *T. cuspidata*, Cultivars).

'Brownii' (Brown yew) is an excellent, broad-pyramidal, staminate (nonfruiting) form with dark green foliage, eventually growing above eye level and spreading to about 1.5 times that distance. Unusually cold-hardy (to Zone 4b), 'Brownii' is classified by some experts as a cultivar of *T. cuspidata*.

'Chadwick' is an excellent, low, wide-spreading, pistillate (fruiting) selection remaining below 1.5 m/5 ft in height for many years.

'Densiformis' is a fast-growing yet compact selection, similar to 'Brownii' in general outline and considerably faster-growing but less cold-hardy (to Zone 5b and protected sites in Zone 5a), with inferior winter color.

'Halloriana' (Halloran yew) is an excellent, compact, broad-spreading, pistillate (fruiting) selection with unusually heavy, dark green foliage, cold-hardy to Zone 5b, eventually attaining a height of 3 m/10 ft or more and a spread twice this distance if left unpruned.

'Hatfieldii' (Hatfield yew) is a staminate (non-fruiting) selection, symmetrically columnar when young, then spreading to a broad-pyramidal form with age. One of the most handsome of this type, but not among the most cold-hardy, useful northward only to Zone 6a and protected sites in Zone 5b.

'Hicksii' (Hicks yew) is a pistillate (fruiting) form with columnar habit and greater cold hardiness than 'Hatfieldii,' useful in Zone 5b and protected sites in Zone 5a.

'Stovekenii' (Stoveken yew) is a vigorous, fast-growing staminate (nonfruiting) selection with broad-columnar form. In tests in Burlington, Vermont, it has proved faster-growing

and more cold-hardy than either 'Hatfieldii' or 'Hicksii,' at least to Zone 5a, and has retained its columnar form better. Long overlooked by the landscape industry, this cultivar promises to become more widely popular and available as its qualities become better known.

'Wardii,' like 'Thayerae,' is a fruiting selection that remains compact and low, but it spreads horizontally rather quickly, becoming even broader than 'Thayerae.'

Many other good cultivars are commercially available. As with other landscape plants, rely on local experience and availability.

Related Species

Taxus baccata 3–6 (English yew).   Although this species from Europe and adjacent Africa and Asia can attain heights of more than 15 m/50 ft in cool climates in its native habitat, seldom does it reach half that height in our area. Since it is less cold-hardy than *T. canadensis*, *T. cuspidata*, or its hybrid *T. ×media* without gaining correspondingly in heat tolerance, it is generally less useful in our area than these, typically only in Zones 6b–7b and those parts of Zone 8a with mild summers, with exceptions noted below. A few cultivars are of interest in our area, and are listed here:

Taxus baccata.

'Dovastoniana' is a vigorous selection with semiweeping branches that has reached massive proportions in the climate of Newport, Rhode Island, ideally suited to yews, and has performed well in Zone 6a at the Ohio Agricultural Research and Development Center at Wooster.

'Fastigiata' (= 'Hibernica,' = 'Stricta'; Irish yew) is the strikingly columnar form so commonly seen in old churchyards in the British Isles. It appears to be somewhat more cold-hardy than many plants of *T. baccata*, performing fairly well in Cave Hill Cemetery, Louisville, Kentucky in Zone 6b, or perhaps effectively 7a because of the microclimatic effect of the surrounding city.

'Repandens' is a low, broad-spreading form with feathery, dark green foliage not exceeding a height of 1 m/3.3 ft for 10−20 years while spreading to 2−3 times that distance. Unpruned plants under good conditions can reach heights of 2 m/6.6 ft but can easily be kept below eye level by pruning when desired. One of the most cold-hardy of all *T. baccata* selections, north-

Taxus baccata 'Repandens.'

ward to Zone 6a and in sheltered sites in Zone 5b.

Ternstroemia gymnanthera 6

Synonyms: *T. japonica, Cleyera japonica*
Japanese ternstroemia
Evergreen shrub or small tree
Theaceae (Tea Family)

Native Range. Japan to Malaysia and India.

Useful Range. USDA Zones 8a−9a+, perhaps also Zone 7b.

Function. Specimen shrub or small tree, screen.

Size and Habit

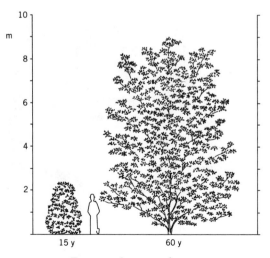

Ternstroemia gymnanthera.

Adaptability. Very intolerant of poorly drained soils.

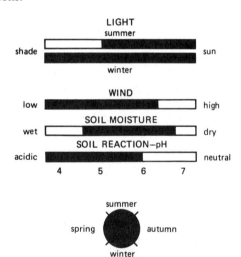

Seasonal Interest. *Flowers:* Whitish yellow and fragrant, about 1.5 cm/0.6 in. across, in late spring. *Foliage:* Handsome, evergreen, lustrous, and leathery, leaves to 15 cm/6 in. long and one third as wide, dark green and turning deep wine red in winter. *Fruits:* Round to elongated, to 2 cm/0.8 in. long, turning from green to yellow as they ripen in early autumn but not giving major landscape interest.

Problems and Maintenance. This plant is relatively trouble-free, except for a minor leaf-spot

Ternstroemia gymnanthera.

disease, if given a good site. Occasional pruning may be needed to maintain density of the lower part of the plant for screening or for size control in small-scale situations. Usually it is sold as *Cleyera japonica*, the name for another plant (see Related Species).

Related Species

Cleyera japonica 5 (synonyms: *C. ochnacea*, *Eurya ochnacea*; Japanese cleyera).   Like the closely related *Ternstroemia*, this plant is native to eastern Asia. The two are similar enough to have become thoroughly confused in the landscape industry. They differ in that the leaves of *Cleyera* are not clustered toward the twig tips like those of *Ternstroemia* but are evenly spaced along the stem, and in other botanical details. Except for the size difference and the fact that *Cleyera* is more spreading in its branching habit and bears red fruits eventually turning black, they can be considered to be roughly equivalent as landscape plants.

Eurya japonica 4−5 (Japanese eurya).   This close relative of *Ternstroemia*, also from eastern Asia, has handsome evergreen leaves, only to 6 cm/2.4 in. long, dark green and rounded or notched at the ends, turning wine red in winter sun. Its greenish white flowers and black fruits are inconspicuous. It is useful in the same zones as *Ternstroemia* but less often commercially available.

Eurya emarginata 3−4.   This evergreen shrub, also from eastern Asia, is smaller and looser in habit than *E. japonica* and is seldom seen other than in the form of var. *microphylla*, which bears leaves only 1 cm/0.4 in. long and wide and has distinctive branching reminiscent of the her-ringbone pattern of *Cotoneaster horizontalis*. The useful range of this plant is not well known because it has been used so little, but it includes at least Zones 8b−9a+.

Eurya emarginata.

Eurya emarginata var. *microphylla.*

Cleyera japonica.

Teucrium chamaedrys 2

Germander
Evergreen groundcover
Labiatae (Mint Family)

Native Range. Europe and southwestern Asia.

Useful Range. USDA Zones 6a–8a, areas in Zone 8b and 9a having moderate summers, and perhaps colder zones in sites with reliable snow cover.

Function. Groundcover, front of border, low hedge.

Size and Habit

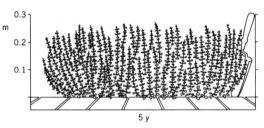

Teucrium chamaedrys.

Adaptability

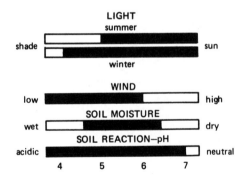

Seasonal Interest. *Flowers:* Rosy purple, individually to 1.5 cm/0.6 in. across, in fairly showy upright spikes in late summer. *Foliage:* Deep green, glossy, semievergreen leaves, less than 2.5 cm/1 in. long and narrow, form an elegantly fine-textured foliage mass that eventually deteriorates in middle and late winter except under constant snow cover.

Teucrium chamaedrys.

Problems and Maintenance. The few diseases and insects that can be troublesome are seldom seriously so, and this plant requires little maintenance other than an occasional shearing in spring to control height and for renewal and removal of deadwood.

Cultivars. 'Prostratum' is lower growing than the species type, to no more than 20 cm/8 in. tall, otherwise little different from the species type.

Thuja occidentalis 3–7

American or eastern arborvitae, eastern white cedar
Evergreen tree or shrub
Cupressaceae (Cypress Family)

Native Range. Northeastern North America: Nova Scotia to Manitoba and southward to North Carolina and Illinois.

Useful Range. USDA Zones 3a–7b with selection of appropriate genetic material.

Function. Screen, hedge, massing, specimen.

Size and Habit

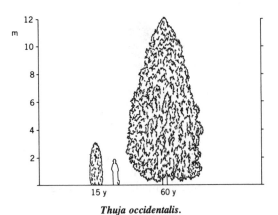

Thuja occidentalis.

Adaptability. Protection from full winter sun in Zones 3 and 4 reduces foliage scorch.

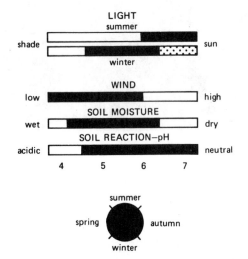

Seasonal Interest. *Foliage:* Evergreen, dark green and lustrous to dull blue-green or golden, with scalelike, mature foliage (except in an occasional dwarf cultivar). *Cones:* Small, greenish, turning brown as they ripen, providing little interest.

Problems and Maintenance. This plant is subject to several diseases and insect pests. A few of them such as bagworms, mites, scale insects, and leaf miners require control when infestations occur. Pruning is rarely necessary except for hedges and for repairing winter damage. Cultivars lacking strong leading trunks are prone to damage from heavy snow and ice, and scorch of foliage from fast freezing caused by intermittent bright sun and shadow can be disfiguring in Zones 3 and 4.

Cultivars. Many cultivars have been selected for growth rate and habit, foliage color and texture, and special characteristics. A few of the most commonly used are listed here.

'Douglasii Pyramidalis' is a tall-growing columnar selection with rich green, frondlike foliage giving unusually interesting texture, and cold-hardy to Zone 3b.

'Ellwangerana' is a dwarf, broad-pyramidal form with light green, mostly juvenile (soft, needlelike) foliage, cold-hardy to Zone 5a but experiencing occasional winterburn in Zone 5.

'Ellwangerana Aurea' is similar to 'Ellwangerana' except that it has golden foliage where exposed to full sun and bronzes in winter.

'Ericoides' and 'Hetz Junior' are dwarf forms with juvenile foliage, soft green in summer and bronzing in winter, cold-hardy to Zone 4b but experiencing occasional winterburn in Zones 4 and 5.

'Globosa' and 'Woodwardii' are moderately slow-growing, globose forms, rather difficult to use in many landscape situations because of their formality, and cold-hardy to Zone 4a.

'Hetz Midget' and 'Pumila' (also called 'Little Gem') are dwarf, globose forms with normal mature (scalelike) foliage, very dense and growing only a few inches annually, cold-hardy at least to Zone 4a.

'Hetz Wintergreen' is narrow and spirelike, with good winter color, hardy at least to Zone 4a.

'Lutea' is tall-growing and narrow-pyramidal with yellow foliage, especially bright in spring and early summer, cold-hardy to Zone 3b.

'Nigra' is similar to the species type, but with dark green foliage, cold-hardy at least to Zone 4a.

'Ohlendorffii' is a distinctive, slow-growing form with two types of leaves: juvenile and needlelike in the center and scalelike on mostly unbranched whiplike branches, useful as a specimen for accent in highly architectonic situations, somewhat more tender than other cultivars of this species but cold-hardy to at least Zone 5b.

'Techny' is a tall, vigorous, pyramidal form with dark green foliage, one of the best selections for screening, cold-hardy at least to Zone 4a.

'Wareana' (= 'Robusta') has large, scalelike, dull blue-green leaves, making a heavy mass of foliage. It is very effective as a screen but takes longer than some other cultivars to reach screening size. It is more drought-resistant than most other cultivars and is cold-hardy to Zone 3b.

Related Species

Thuja koraiensis 5 (Korean arborvitae).   This broad- to upright-pyramidal shrub or small tree is little known in landscape use in our area and probably is not commercially available, but it has looked promising in test plantings. The broad, scalelike leaves are similar to those of *T. occidentalis* except that they are distinctly white-marked on the undersides of branches. Probably useful in Zones 5a−7b and perhaps more widely with selection of appropriate genetic material.

Thuja orientalis 4−7 (synonym: *Biota orientalis*; Oriental arborvitae).   This native of China and Korea has recently been reclassified by some experts as *Platycladus orientalis*. In its colorful forms it is all-too-common in landscape use in our area. The tree form is symmetrical and somewhat more open because of its small, scalelike leaves and slender branches often turned vertically. The color variants are even more formally symmetrical, the twisted branches arranged densely and forming strikingly vertical planes. Frequently sold as low-cost plants in garden centers, they are too positive for most landscape situations and often are killed or severely damaged in winter in many areas where they are sold. Useful in Zones 6b−8b, but frequently offered for sale in areas as cold as Zone 5a. Many cultivars have been selected. A few of the most common are listed here.

'Aurea Nana' (= 'Berckmans') is a semidwarf, ovoid form, seldom exceeding 1.5 m/5 ft in height, with yellow-green foliage that turns brownish in winter.

'Bakeri' is compact and pyramidal in form, becoming larger than 'Aurea Nana' and unusually well adapted to the hot dry summers of the Middle South (Zones 7a−8b).

'Bonita' is semidwarf and broadly pyramidal in form with lustrous, light green, golden tipped foliage.

'Elegantissima' is compact and narrowly pyramidal, eventually to 3−4 m/10−13 ft or more in height, with foliage golden tipped in spring, greenish yellow in summer, and reddish brown in winter.

Thuja plicata 7−8 (giant arborvitae, western red cedar).   This native of the Pacific Northwest from Montana to Alaska and northern California is a huge timber tree in its native habitat and may reach 20−30 m/66−98 ft with time in our area, but it also makes an excellent screening shrub, more trouble-free in some areas than *T. occidentalis*. It would be expected that there is considerable variation in climatic adaptability in this species, with trees of far-inland origin being more adaptable to our colder zones, but more investigation of this is needed. One form of *T. plicata*, apparently 'Elegantissima,' is proving useful in full exposure in central Indiana (Zone 5b) and in colder areas (to Zone 4a) in Vermont. 'Elegantissima' has golden-yellow branch tips in early summer and a tendency to bronze in full winter sun. 'Atrovirens,' a full-scale tree form, has unusually deep green foliage color, holding well in winter, but its limits of cold hardiness are not well known. With selection of appropriate genetic material, the useful range of *T. plicata* should extend at least through Zones 4a−7b.

Thuja plicata.

Thuja standishii 6−7 (Japanese arborvitae). This spreading pyramidal tree is more graceful than other arborvitae species. Its foliage remains green in winter but is no better than that of the best selections of *T. occidentalis* and *T. plicata*. Leaves are white-marked underneath, much like those of *T. koraiensis*. Useful in Zones 6a−7b and perhaps also Zones 5 and 8.

Thujopsis dolobrata 5 (false or Hiba arborvitae). This native of Japan is adapted only to small portions of our area where mild, moist climates enable it to perform well. It functions as a loose-growing, shrubby tree, probably to no more than 4−5 m/13−16 ft under our best conditions, with glossy, bright green leaves similar to those of *Thuja* but larger and white-marked underneath. Useful in Zones 6b−9a. 'Nana' is slower-growing, remaining small.

Tilia americana 8

Basswood, American linden
Deciduous tree
Tiliaceae (Linden Family)

Native Range. Northeastern and central United States and adjacent Canada: New Brunswick westward to North Dakota and southward to Virginia and northeastern Texas.

Useful Range. USDA Zones 3a−8a and areas with mild summers southward to Zone 9a.

Function. Shade or avenue tree, naturalizing.

Size and Habit

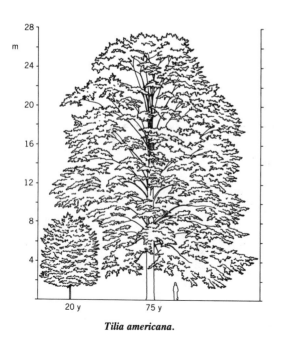

Tilia americana.

Adaptability

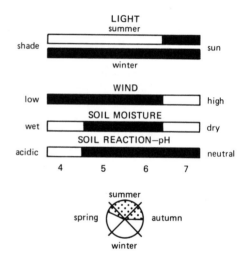

Seasonal Interest. *Flowers*: Highly fragrant and attractive to bees, light yellow, individually 1.5 cm/0.6 in. across, in loose, drooping clusters attached to large, pale greenish yellow, leaflike bracts, conspicuous in early summer. *Foliage*: Coarse, medium green, with broad, heart-shaped leaves 10−20 cm/4−8 in. long, turning dull green or occasionally yellowish before falling in midautumn. *Fruits*: Whitish yellow, round, nut-like, 0.5−0.8 cm/0.2−0.3 in. across, interesting in late summer.

Problems and Maintenance. Mites and a variety of insects including aphids, beetles, borers, leaf miners, and scale insects are potentially troublesome. For fully adequate performance, a spray program eventually will be needed. Lindens are also susceptible to several diseases, usually not serious but occasionally requiring corrective

Tilia americana.

treatment. Pruning is necessary only for early training and removal of deadwood and basal sprouts. *T. americana* has a strong tendency to produce basal sprouts and is coarser in appearance than many other *Tilia* species but finds special value in naturalized plantings.

Cultivars. 'Fastigiata' has narrower branching and more narrowly pyramidal form than the species type but is seldom available.

Tilia cordata 8

Littleleaf linden
Deciduous tree
Tiliaceae (Linden Family)

Native Range. Europe.

Useful Range. USDA Zones 3b−8a and areas with mild summers southward to Zone 9a.

Function. Shade or street tree.

Size and Habit

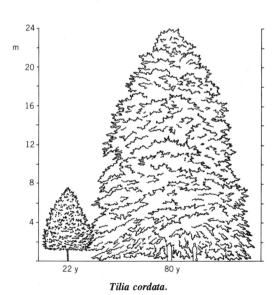

Tilia cordata.

Adaptability. *T. cordata* and other European lindens (see Related Species) are well adapted to urban planting.

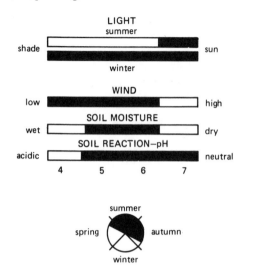

LIGHT
summer
shade — sun
winter

WIND
low — high
SOIL MOISTURE
wet — dry
SOIL REACTION—pH
acidic — neutral
4   5   6   7

summer
spring — autumn
winter

Seasonal Interest. *Flowers:* Highly fragrant and attractive to bees, light yellow, individually small but borne in loose, drooping clusters attached to large, pale greenish yellow, leaflike bracts, contrasting with the deep green leaves in early summer. *Foliage:* Medium to deep green, light green underneath, only 3–6 cm/1.2–2.4 in. long, producing a dense canopy of neat texture, falling after midautumn with little color change. *Fruits:* Whitish yellow, round, nutlike, 0.5–0.8 cm/0.2–0.3 in. across, interesting in late summer.

Tilia cordata.

Problems and Maintenance. Even though *T. cordata* can be troubled by a wide range of insects and diseases, it is less likely to be than some other

lindens and frequently goes essentially trouble-free for years in urban plantings away from other lindens. Pruning is needed only for early training and removal of any deadwood, and basal sprouting is minimal in this species.

Cultivars. 'Chancellor' (Plant Patent No. 2712, 1967) has been selected for use as a street tree, with compact, narrowly pyramidal form, straight central trunk, and sturdy branching that resists storm damage. It is said to be unusually drought-resistant. Its ultimate value in comparison with other cultivars will be better known after another decade of use.

'Glenleven' is faster-growing and more symmetrical than most seedling trees of *T. cordata*, with larger leaves and a very straight trunk. It is popular in southern Canada.

'Greenspire' is a symmetrical, narrowly oval to pyramidal selection that has been used widely in street plantings in much of our area. It is one of the first selections of *T. cordata* in the United States and the standard against which other cultivars must be compared in determining their value as street trees.

'Morden' is compact, pyramidal, and symmetrical in form and is usually cold-hardy to Zone 3a, giving it special value in the Northern Plains.

'Rancho' is upright in form and vigorous, with small leaves. It has not received as wide an acceptance as 'Greenspire' and consequently has been less fully evaluated at present, but some observers consider it superior.

Several cultivars have been introduced more recently, and there has not been time for full evaluation. They should be watched during the next decade or so as they become more widely used.

Related Species and Hybrids

Tilia dasystyla 8 (Caucasian linden). This native of southwestern Europe and adjacent Asia with rather coarse foliage is little used and seldom if ever available but is known through its parentage of the following hybrid.

Tilia ×euchlora 8 (Crimean linden). In spite of the common name, a hybrid, probably of *T. cordata* × *T. dasystyla*, this tree is valued for street and lawn planting, where it grows somewhat faster than *T. cordata*. The selection 'Redmond,' usually assigned to *T. ×euchlora* but by some to *T. americana,* is especially valued for its dark green, leathery foliage, early flowering, and drought-resistance in the western parts of our area from eastern Texas to southern Minnesota. Useful in Zones 4b–8a and perhaps also Zone 4a.

Tilia ×europaea 8 (common or hybrid European linden). This hybrid of *T. cordata* × *T. platyphyllos* is very widely planted in Europe but usually considered inferior to the parents in our area because of its tendency to sprout at the base very heavily. Nevertheless, it is a useful street or lawn tree where maintenance is available in Zones 3b–8a. The selection 'Pallida' has large leaves, very pale underneath.

Tilia mongolica 6–7 (Mongolian linden). The chief advantages of this species from northern China and Mongolia are its hardiness and small size, usually 6–10 m/20–33 ft in height or even less in dry sites. Its leaves are nearly as small as those of *T. cordata,* triangular and birchlike in outline, and its bark is rough and flaking. Even though this tree is not yet widely available, it may become so as it is better known, because it is a useful small tree in Zones 3a–6a.

Tilia platyphyllos 8 (bigleaf linden). In spite of its common name, the leaves of this European native are considerably smaller than those of *T. americana* with only a moderately coarse texture. This is a serviceable tree valued in the northern states and adjacent Canada. It develops basal sprouts but not nearly in the same numbers as *T. ×europaea.* Useful in Zones 3b–8a.

Tilia tomentosa 8

Silver linden
Deciduous tree
Tiliaceae (Linden Family)

Native Range. Southeastern Europe and adjacent Asia.

Useful Range. USDA Zones 5a–8a and areas with mild summers southward to Zone 9a.

Function. Shade or avenue tree.

Size and Habit

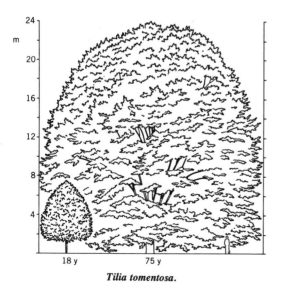

Tilia tomentosa.

Adaptability. Full foliage interest is seen best in sites exposed to at least minimal breezes.

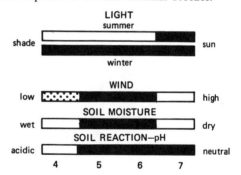

Seasonal Interest. *Flowers:* Highly fragrant, attractive but according to some sources injurious to bees, light yellow, borne in clusters attached to pale greenish yellow, leaflike bracts. *Foliage:* Deep green, strikingly whitened underneath with silky hairs, 5–10 cm/2–4 in. long, giving medium texture and a bicolored effect when the leaves are turned over by the wind. *Fruits:* Whitish yellow, round, nutlike, 0.5–0.8 cm/ 0.2–0.3 in. across, interesting in late summer in clusters with the attached leafy bracts.

Tilia tomentosa.

Problems and Maintenance. This tree is troubled occasionally by a wide range of disease and insect problems that affect lindens in general (see *T. americana*, Problems and Maintenance), but less seriously so than some species. The white tomentum that is so attractive in clean air can become grayed by solid air pollution until it is unattractive by late summer in some areas. Recovery from transplanting is slower than with most *Tilia* species, and trees may need to remain staked longer, for up to three years in some cases,

or until considerable new top growth has occurred.

Related Species

Tilia heterophylla 8 (white or beetree basswood). This native of the eastern United States from West Virginia to Indiana and southward to northern Florida and Alabama has leaves intermediate in size between those of *T. americana* and *T. tomentosa*, with a thick mat of white or brownish hairs underneath. It has some of the foliage interest of *T. tomentosa* but without its symmetry and neat texture. Seldom available commercially, it is useful in preservation or for naturalizing in Zones 6a–9b and perhaps in colder zones as well.

Tilia petiolaris 8 (pendent silver linden). This graceful tree, perhaps native to southeastern Europe and adjacent Asia, resembles *T. tomentosa* except for its more or less pendulous growth habit. Since its branches often reach the ground and removal of lower branches would destroy its form, this tree is limited to large-scale situations in Zones 6a–9a and possibly somewhat colder zones as well.

Trachelospermum asiaticum 1 and 2

Synonym: *Rhynchospermum asiaticum*
Yellow star jasmine
Evergreen vine or groundcover
Apocynaceae (Dogbane Family)

Native Range. Japan, Korea.

Useful Range. USDA Zones 8a–9a+ and sheltered sites in Zone 7 as a groundcover.

Function. Groundcover, specimen vine, or screen (with support), climbing by twining to heights of 3–5 m/10–16 ft.

Size and Habit

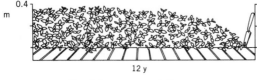

Trachelospermum asiaticum.

Adaptability. Grows best in light shade in parts of our area with very hot summers.

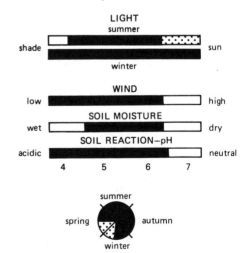

Seasonal Interest. *Flowers:* Fragrant, yellowish white, in loose terminal clusters, but they do not develop in significant numbers in groundcover use. *Foliage:* Evergreen, leathery, pointed leaves are 2.5−5 cm/1−2 in. long, borne on wiry stems, the overall effect as a groundcover similar to that of the related *Vinca minor.* Foliage turns dark red-purple in winter from Zone 8a northward. By late winter, foliage may be less attractive, but new growth in spring covers the old foliage.

Trachelospermum asiaticum.

Problems and Maintenance. Scale insects, white fly, and mites can be troublesome occasionally and require spraying. This can be done after shearing off the tops of groundcover plantings in spring, a practice which, if done every third year or so, keeps the groundcover low and neat in appearance.

Related Species

Trachelospermum jasminoides 1 and 2 (synonym: *Rhynchospermum jasminoides;* Confederate jasmine, Chinese star jasmine). This evergreen vine from China is popular in the far southern parts of our area, used primarily as a specimen or screening vine, climbing to heights of 3−6 m/10−20 ft, although it is effective as a groundcover as well. It has heavier and larger leaves than *T. asiaticum,* 5−8 cm/2−3 in. long, light green as they first emerge, then turning deep green, and waxy looking, very fragrant white flowers resembling small pinwheels because of the way the petals are twisted. Useful in Zone 9a+ and perhaps some sheltered areas in Zone 8.

Periploca graeca 1 (Grecian silkvine). This deciduous, high-twining climber, a member of the Milkweed Family from southeastern Europe and adjacent Asia, is effective as a visual screen (with support) to heights of 8−10 m/26−33 ft from late spring until very late autumn, since its foliage persists and remains dark green until nearly winter. Neither the unpleasant smelling flowers nor the fruits provide significant landscape interest, but for a dense foliage mass for screening, this climber is one of the best. It can be rampant and weedy if not controlled, but it is useful in Zones 6a−8a in relatively dry sites in full sun.

Trachycarpus fortunei 6

Synonyms: *T. excelsus, Chamaerops excelsa, C. fortunei*
Windmill palm
Evergreen tree
Palmae (Palm Family)

Native Range. Burma, China.

Useful Range. USDA Zones 8b−9a+.

Function. Street tree, specimen.

Size and Habit

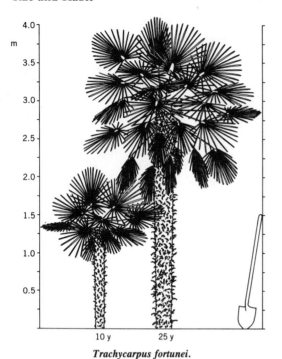

Trachycarpus fortunei.

Adaptability. Relatively tolerant of salt in seashore sites.

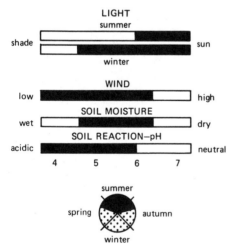

Seasonal Interest. *Flowers:* Small, yellow, among the leaves in hanging clusters, to 0.5 m/1.6 ft long in late spring and continuing during summer. *Foliage:* Dark green, fanlike, with segments radiating nearly in a complete circle, sometimes to 1 m/3.3 ft across, the leaflets turning duller

and drooping with age but persisting year-round. *Fruits:* Bluish, more-or-less rounded, individually about 1 cm/0.4 in. across, fairly conspicuous, in large clusters. *Trunks:* Slender, very straight, covered with a conspicuous "fabric" of hairlike black fiber from old leaf sheaths.

Problems and Maintenance. The most serious pest problem is scale insects, which at some point will need to be controlled with carefully timed sprays. Pruning is necessary only to remove dead leaves that otherwise would be unsightly.

Related Species

Butia capitata 6 (synonyms: *Butia australis,* sometimes sold as *Cocos australis;* Brazilian butia palm).   This native of Brazil and other parts of South America makes a good small specimen tree, 4–6 m/13–20 ft tall, for Zone 9a and sheltered sites in Zone 8b. Its bluish, pinnately compound leaves, 1–1.5 m/3.3–5 ft long, are ascending at the base but arch gracefully back downward, giving a distinctive form. The flowers, red or yellow, are borne in dense clusters within very large orange bracts, to 1 m/3.3 ft long and nearly as wide, in spring and summer. Fruits are edible, datelike, yellowish, about 2.5 cm/1 in. long, borne in huge clusters. Trunks are very wide, especially toward the base, roughened with persistent leaf bases.

Phoenix canariensis 7 (Canary Island date palm).   This native of the Canary Islands reaches heights of 15 m/50 ft and greater on fertile soils in Zone 9b, where it is used as an avenue tree. It functions as a smaller tree for specimen use, in the mildest parts of Zone 9a but occasionally suffers winter damage. It has long, pinnately compound leaves, ascending when young but later becoming pendulous, and a massive, light brown trunk, commonly 0.5 m/1.6 ft and greater in diameter. Since the leaves commonly reach 3 m/10 ft in length, young plants occupy a large area of ground until such time as the trunk has become tall enough to lift remaining leaves about head level. This palm is dioecious but seldom sets fruit in our area. Dead leaves and inflorescences must be removed by pruning, or they give the tree a ragged appearance.

Tsuga canadensis 3−8

Canada hemlock
Evergreen tree or shrub
Pinaceae (Pine Family)

Native Range. Eastern North America from Nova Scotia to Minnesota and Illinois and southward in the Appalachian Mountains to northern Alabama.

Useful Range. USDA Zones 3a−8a with selection of appropriate genetic material; best in areas with cool summers.

Function. Screen, specimen, one of the finest of all evergreens for formal or informal hedges.

Size and Habit

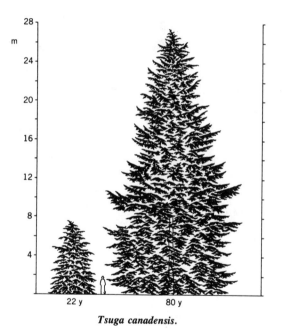

Tsuga canadensis.

Adaptability. Windswept sites and dry soils should be avoided, since the foliage, especially of newly planted trees, is very susceptible to desiccation in winter and during dry periods in summer. Light shade during summer is beneficial in the South and Midwest.

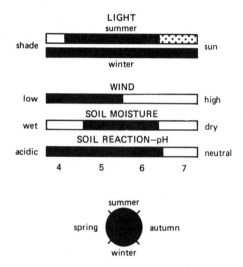

Seasonal Interest. *Foliage:* Evergreen, individual needles flattened, light green when new, then lustrous dark green and whitened on the lower surfaces, the longest only 1.7 cm/0.7 in. long, arranged mostly in a plane on twigs, giving a flat, feathery appearance to the branches. *Cones:* Light brown, 1.5−2 cm/0.6−0.8 in. long, frequently borne in large numbers, adding quiet but significant interest at close range.

Problems and Maintenance. Hemlocks are subject to a wide variety of insect and disease problems, but most are rarely serious. Probably the most common problem other than foliage drying in improper sites or hot summers is mite infestations, and even this can be minimized by selecting cool, moist sites. Yet in some areas occasional spraying will be needed.

Cultivars. Many variants selected from the wild have been given cultivar names. In an intensive study at Cornell University in the 1930s, John C. Swartley reduced all the variants then known into 20 classes distinct enough to justify cultivar names, showing that there had been much duplication in naming variants. Considerable confusion in names still exists, and the best way to obtain a specific form is to hand-select plants in a nursery. A few of the currently most common cultivars are listed here:

'Brandley' is slow-growing and densely but asymmetrically pyramidal with outstanding dark green color, reaching a height of at least 1 m/3.3 ft after about 20 years.

'Cole' (= 'Cole's Prostrate') is a fully prostrate selection, not exceeding 20 cm/8 in. high for many years, but spreading widely, eventually to a meter or two, 3.3–6.6 ft, useful in rock gardens but outgrows small spaces in time.

'Nana' is irregularly semidwarf, growing somewhat more slowly than 'Brandley' and remaining below 1 m/3.3 ft for many years.

'Pendula' (= 'Sargentii;' Sargent weeping hemlock) is a weeping form with contorted branches. It is one of the most striking specimen evergreens, but it is not particularly functional. Old specimens have reached heights of 2 m/6.6 ft and greater while spreading to more than twice that distance. This form shows a strong tendency to reproduce fairly true from seeds.

Tsuga canadensis 'Pendula.'

'Pomfret' is densely pyramidal in form and slow-growing, yet eventually becomes large enough for a low-maintenance screen where time is no object or to function as a specimen or foundation plant while young.

Related Species

Tsuga caroliniana 8 (Carolina hemlock). This native of the southern Appalachian Mountains from Virginia to Georgia differs from *T. canadensis* in having more open, less feathery branching habit, needles radiating irregularly from the twigs, and more interesting cones, opening widely when mature. Reputedly more tolerant of city conditions than *T. canadensis*, this tree makes an equally effective hedge or screen. Useful in Zones 5b–7b, areas with cool summers in Zone 8a, and perhaps sheltered sites in Zone 5a.

Tsuga caroliniana.

Tsuga diversifolia 6–7 (Japanese hemlock). This compact, low-growing tree from Japan has unusually striking foliage with short needles radiating in all directions from the twigs and showing the whitened undersides to good advantage. Useful as a small, often shrubby tree that will not exceed 10 m/33 ft for many years in our area, even though it can grow much larger in Japan. Useful in Zones 5b–7b, areas with cool summers in Zone 8a, and perhaps also in Zone 5a, but as yet seldom commercially available.

Ulmus americana 8

American elm, white elm
Deciduous tree
Ulmaceae (Elm Family)

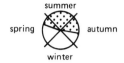

Native Range. Eastern North America: New-foundland to Alberta and southward to Florida and Texas.

Useful Range. USDA Zones 2b−9a+.

Function. Shade or avenue tree, specimen. One of the most effective of all trees for a high canopy of shade.

Size and Habit

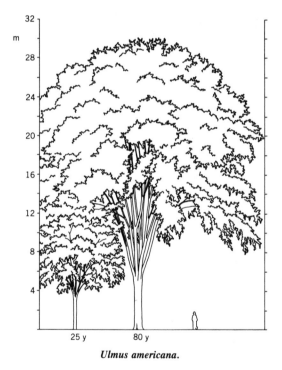

Ulmus americana.

Adaptability

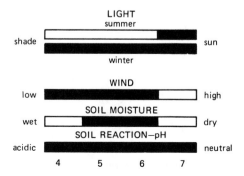

Seasonal Interest. *Flowers:* Very small but open-ing in large numbers before the leaves unfold, giving the tree a misty, pale yellow color. *Foliage:* Deep green and lustrous leaves, 8−15 cm/3−6 in. long, turn golden yellow before falling in autumn in some years and locations, especially in the northeastern and north-central parts of our area. *Fruits:* Small and inconspicuous, mostly concealed by the foliage.

Problems and Maintenance. The most serious problems of this and most other *Ulmus* species are Dutch elm disease and phloem necrosis. These diseases, individually or sometimes to-gether, have all but eliminated *U. americana* from many areas of the northeastern and north-central states, and they continue to move into new areas. The spread has been arrested, at least temporarily, in some urban and suburban areas, through a careful program of sanitation, pruning, and spraying to control the elm leaf beetle, which is responsible for the spread of the fungus that causes Dutch elm disease. The cost of Dutch elm disease, whether in removal of infected trees or in preventive programs, is substantial, and further planting of *U. americana* and other susceptible elms in some areas probably is unwise until more effective control of these diseases is possible.

Concern over the possible demise of this useful and sometimes majestic tree has brought eulogies, and it is often forgotten that the Ameri-can elm was displaying other unfortunate qual-ities long before the appearance of Dutch elm disease. It is troubled by a wide range of lesser diseases and insects and seldom can be counted on, even in the absence of Dutch elm disease, to perform well without maintenance. It forms large buttress roots that cause serious problems when planted close to sidewalks, and it is susceptible to storm breakage, but not as much as its notori-ously softwooded relative, the Siberian elm (*U. pumila*).

Considerable interest in landscape substitutes for the American elm has arisen as the serious-ness of Dutch elm disease has become apparent, and several candidates have been nominated for this role, including certain maples (*Acer* species), hackberries (*Celtis* species), ashes (*Fraxinus* species), honeylocust (*Gleditsia triacanthos*), Japanese zelkova (*Zelkova serrata*), and other elms. How effective these are in filling the role is discussed under the individual species.

Cultivars. 'Augustine' is narrowly vase-shaped, nearly columnar, dense and fast growing, a good form for use in smaller spaces than those required for the species type. Other cultivars of *U. americana* have been introduced but are seldom if ever available. None of these selections show resistance to Dutch elm disease.

Related Species

Ulmus alata 7 (winged elm, wahoo elm).   This small tree, usually 10–15 m/33–49 ft tall, is native to the southeastern states from Virginia to Illinois and southward to Florida and Texas. It is seldom available in nurseries, but collected trees are sometimes available in the natural range, and it is worth preserving in development, even though it is susceptible to Dutch elm disease. The winged twigs provide easy identification but add little landscape interest. Useful in Zones 6b–9a.

Ulmus carpinifolia 8 (smooth-leaved elm). This native of Europe and adjacent Africa and Asia has been cultivated for a long time and many distinctive forms have been selected and named. The selection 'Christine Buisman' is a full-size tree growing to at least 20 m/66 ft tall, selected in Holland and found to be resistant to Dutch elm disease by scientists at the U.S. Department of Agriculture. Unfortunately, it is very different in form and landscape effect from *U. americana* and cannot be considered seriously as a landscape substitute for that species. 'Koopmanii' is compact and oval in form, usually remaining well below 10 m/33 ft for many years, and 'Umbraculifera' (globe elm) is similar but more globose in outline. *Ulmus carpinifolia* and its cultivars are generally useful in Zones 5b–9a.

Ulmus davidiana 8 (David elm).   This large tree from northeastern Asia is known in our area only in the form of var. *japonica* (synonym: *U. japonica*; Japanese elm) from Japan, which has been examined closely in recent years as a possible source of resistance to Dutch elm disease.

Ulmus carpinifolia.

Otherwise it offers little more than *U. carpinifolia* and *U. procera* in landscape use. It is potentially useful in Zones 3b–9a, if disease-resistant forms should be found, but is seldom available at present.

Ulmus glabra 8 (Scotch or Wych elm).   This native of Europe and adjacent Africa and Asia, like *U. carpinifolia*, has long been cultivated, and many cultivars have been selected. This species has not been very widely used in our area, and since it is susceptible to Dutch elm disease and many lesser pests as well, it probably will not find much use in the future. Useful in Zones 4b–9a.

Ulmus ×*hollandica* 8 (Holland elm).   This group of hybrids of *U. glabra* × *U. carpinifolia* shows great vigor, and it is hoped that more resistant forms such as 'Bea Schwartz' can be derived from this cross. But members of this group have not shown form similar enough to that of *U. americana* to be considered substitutes in form for that species. Useful in Zones 5a–9a and perhaps also colder zones.

Ulmus laevis 8 (Russian elm, European white elm). This native of central Europe to western Asia is a large tree similar to *U. americana*. It has been planted only experimentally in our area with no evidence to date of significant resistance to Dutch elm disease. It probably is not available commercially, although potentially useful in Zones 5a–9a and perhaps also colder zones.

Ulmus procera 8 (synonym: *U. campestris*; English elm). This large tree from Europe is widely planted there and in the United States, especially in cities, where it seems unusually well adapted. Even though it is not considered highly resistant to Dutch elm disease, many plantings have thus far escaped and remain in good condition, but the form of this tree does not resemble that of *U. americana*, so it cannot be considered a landscape substitute for that species. Useful in Zones 6a–9a.

Ulmus rubra 8 (synonym: *U. fulva*; red or slippery elm). This American native has a range only slightly less extensive than that of *U. americana* and differs primarily in its coarser texture and less striking form. Since it has not demonstrated high resistance to Dutch elm disease and is otherwise considered somewhat inferior in the landscape industry, it seldom is available, but it is potentially useful in Zones 4b–9a.

Ulmus thomasii 8 (rock elm). This native of northeastern North America from Quebec to Nebraska and southward to Tennessee has poor growth habit for use as a shade tree and is seldom if ever planted. It may be worth preserving in development in some sites in Zones 4b–7b.

Ulmus ×*vegeta* 8 (Huntingdon or Chichester elm). This typically large hybrid (*U. carpinifolia* × *U. glabra*) is best known in our area for the strikingly pendulous selection 'Camperdownii' (Camperdown elm), usually seen grafted on a standard (trunk) about 1.5 m/5 ft tall. This plant is useful in Zones 4b–9a, but only as a specimen for accent. It is susceptible to Dutch elm disease.

Ulmus ×*vegeta* 'Camperdownii.'

Ulmus ×*vegeta* 'Camperdownii.'

Ulmus parvifolia 7–8

Chinese elm
Deciduous or semievergreen tree
Ulmaceae (Elm Family)

Native Range. China, Japan, Korea.

Useful Range. USDA Zones 5b–9a and sheltered areas in Zone 5a.

Function. Shade tree, specimen.

Size and Habit

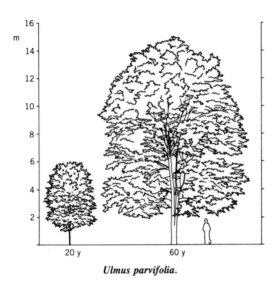

Ulmus parvifolia.

Adaptability

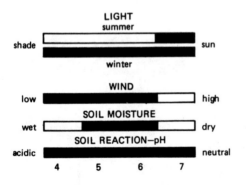

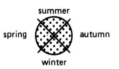

Seasonal Interest. *Flowers:* Small and inconspicuous, opening in late summer. *Foliage:* Leathery, deep green leaves are small and tidy, 2.5−5 cm/1−2 in. long, remaining green until late autumn in the North, then turning purplish briefly before falling, but persisting and remaining green well into winter in Zone 9a. *Fruits:* Bright green, waferlike, individually about 1 cm/0.4 in. long, in clusters in early autumn, adding minor autumn interest. *Trunk and branches:* Bark of young trunks and main branches of some trees peels off in rounded patches, tan and brown, in much the same way as that of *Platanus occidentalis* except that the patches are much smaller and the mottled effect produced is finer-textured and more refined in appearance.

Problems and Maintenance. This species is resistant (although not immune) to Dutch elm disease and not as seriously affected by other disease and insect problems (such as leaf beetles) as some of the other elms, but it still needs maintenance to keep it in good condition. It is somewhat prone to breakage by ice and wind, but no more so than *U. americana* and considerably less so than *U. pumila* (see Related Species). Pruning is needed for initial training and for removing any dead or damaged branches thereafter.

Varieties and Cultivars. Plants listed as var. *sempervirens* probably do not constitute a varietal group and may differ little from plants listed only as the species. Yet there is a great amount of variation in this species that could be exploited for selection of outstanding cultivars. This would be especially valuable for selection of outstanding bark character as well as disease resistance, fast growth, and cold-hardiness.

Related Species

Ulmus crassifolia 7−8 (cedar elm).   This small to large tree, generally similar to *U. parvifolia* but native from Mississippi to Texas and Mexico, is an important landscape tree in the southwestern corner of our area, which coincides with the eastern part of its natural range. On good sites in this area (Zones 7b−9a), it will reach heights of 20−25 m/66−82 ft in time, although its form may be quite variable. It is often seen more in the 10−15 m/33−49 ft size range. Like *U. parvifolia*, it flowers in late summer, is less troubled by leaf beetles and other problems than most elms, and seems to have some resistance to Dutch elm disease. Some trees have winged twigs reminiscent of those of *U. alata*. Most trees used in the past have been collected from the wild, but there is increasing interest in nursery production, so availability may increase.

Ulmus pumila 7−8 (Siberian elm).   This native of eastern Siberia and northern China to Central Asia unfortunately is often called Chinese elm, confusing it with the much superior, true Chinese elm, *U. parvifolia*. *U. pumila* has its place in the western extremities of our area on the dry plains, where its cold- and drought-hardiness enables it to succeed where few other trees can. However, it is commonly planted in much of the rest of our area where many better alternatives are available. Its good qualities are high resistance to Dutch elm disease and fast growth. Its liabilities are that it is softwooded and storm prone, extremely susceptible to leaf beetles, which can nearly defoliate trees by midsummer, and tends to give rise to many weed seedlings. Moreover, it has hardly any seasonal interest. Yet from Manitoba through the Dakotas, Nebraska, Kansas, and Oklahoma to Texas and westward it is admittedly a useful tree, and several cultivars of

superior form and foliage have been selected, including 'Coolshade' and 'Dropmore.' Useful, with selection of appropriate genetic material, in Zones 2b–9a.

In 1973, a hybrid of *U. pumila*, probably by *U. davidiana* var. *japonica*, was selected at the University of Wisconsin from seed sent from Hokkaido University, Sapporo, Japan, and named 'Sapporo Autumn Gold.' This cultivar apparently resembles *U. americana* in many respects but shows resistance to Dutch elm disease. It could become an important landscape tree if its early promise is borne out in future performance.

Vaccinium angustifolium 2–3

Lowbush blueberry
Deciduous groundcover
Ericaceae (Heath Family)

Native Range. Northeastern North America: Newfoundland to Saskatchewan and south to Illinois and Virginia.

Useful Range. USDA Zones 2a–6b with selection of appropriate genetic material.

Function. Groundcover, especially for naturalizing, edible fruits.

Size and Habit

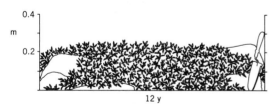

12 y

Vaccinium angustifolium.

Adaptability. Once the requirement for acidic, well-drained soil has been met, this is one of the most widely adaptable groundcovers to sun or shade and to dry soil.

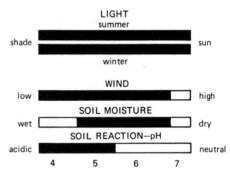

Seasonal Interest. *Flowers:* Greenish white, bell-shaped, less than 0.8 cm/0.3 in. long and not very conspicuous. *Foliage:* Lustrous, bright green, 0.8–3.5 cm/0.3–1.4 in. long, making an irregular, rather fine-textured mass, turning bright scarlet before falling in late autumn. *Fruits:* Small, edible blueberries, ripening in late summer, adding only slight additional landscape interest.

Problems and Maintenance. This plant is subject to several insect and disease problems, but they are rarely serious enough to require spraying. Yellowing of young foliage, caused by iron deficiency, is common in soils that are not sufficiently acidic, this is, not below about pH 5.5. Renewal pruning by mowing or burning (seldom feasible in landscape situations) will keep this plant a low, vigorous groundcover.

Varieties and Cultivars. Var. *laevifolium* occurs in the southern parts of the natural range, overlapping with the range of the species type. The variety grows taller than the species type, to 0.6 m/2 ft, and has larger leaves, 1.5−3.5 cm/ 0.6−1.4 in. long, and may not be fully cold-hardy in Zones 2 and 3. Var. *laevifolium* is the form of *V. angustifolium* that exists in large stands at low elevations in Maine, and its fruits are harvested commercially.

'Leucocarpum' has white berries but is seldom used or commercially available.

Vaccinium corymbosum 5

Highbush blueberry
Deciduous shrub
Ericaceae (Heath Family)

Native Range. Eastern North America: Maine to Minnesota and southward to Florida and Louisiana on suitable soils.

Useful Range. USDA Zones 4b−9a with selection of appropriate genetic material.

Function. Border, specimen, screen, naturalizing, edible fruits.

Adaptability. Tolerant of shade in landscape use but requires close to full sun for best fruit production.

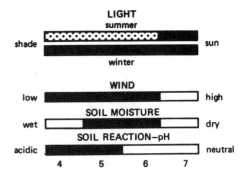

Size and Habit

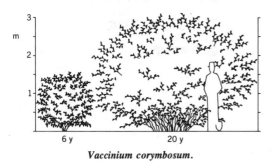

Vaccinium corymbosum.

Seasonal Interest. *Flowers:* White or pinkish, bell-shaped, mostly less than 1 cm/0.4 in. long, adding minor landscape interest along with the unfolding leaves in late spring. *Foliage:* Lustrous, bright to deep green, 3−8 cm/1.2−3 in. long, making a rather open to fairly dense mass, turning orange and scarlet, and falling in late autumn. *Fruits:* Medium to large, edible blueberries, to 1 cm/0.4 in. or larger in cultivars, ripening from middle to late summer. *Twigs and branches:* Twigs of vigorous plants turn red in winter, adding significant landscape interest.

Problems and Maintenance. Several insects and diseases can be troublesome, and spraying is sometimes necessary, even in landscape plant-

Vaccinium corymbosum.

ings. A careful spray program should be followed when fruit production is the primary reason for growing this shrub. Details can be obtained from county and state or provincial extension service offices. Iron chlorosis (leaf yellowing) is common in soils that are not sufficiently acidic. When soil acidification is not feasible and chlorosis is not extreme, it may be corrected by the use of chelated iron and/or foliage sprays. This information also is available from extension service offices. Regular pruning as carried out in commercial fruit production reduces the number of branches to increase fruit size, whereas pruning for use as a visual screen does just the opposite. For dual-purpose use, pruning should be limited to any that is necessary to increase fullness for screening. Even though the berries may be smaller than commercial blueberries, their total production will be considerable. Since the fullness required for effective screening can be obtained only in vigorously growing plants, this function is only attainable in sites where soil conditions are close to ideal.

Cultivars. Many cultivars have been developed for berry production. Recommended cultivars vary regionally, and information for specific areas can be obtained from extension service offices. Relative effectiveness of fruiting cultivars for landscape use has not been completely determined; suggestions probably can be obtained from local blueberry growers and extension specialists.

Related Species

Vaccinium arboreum 6 (tree huckleberry, sparkleberry, farkleberry). This tall shrub or small tree grows to 6−8 m/20−26 ft tall under ideal conditions in the southern parts of its natural range, which extends from Virginia and southern Illinois southward to Florida and Texas. Its small evergreen leaves, 2.5−5 cm/1−2 in. long, form a foliage mass a little sparse for effective screening unless thickened by pruning, but the plant's principal landscape usefulness is for naturalizing (or preservation) or as a small, multiple-stemmed tree with handsomely "molded" trunks and branches covered with close cinnamon-brown bark. Seldom used or available, but a landscape plant worthy of greater attention in Zones 7a−9a+ with selection of appropriate genetic material. Its fruits are not edible.

Vaccinium ashei 4−6 (rabbiteye blueberry). This variable species, native to the southeastern states, is an important parent of fruiting cultivars for the Deep South because of its low winter-chilling requirement. It is grown more in the form of such cultivars than as the wild type. Most cultivars grow to less than 2 m/6.6 ft in height. Their small, often rosy pink flowers are somewhat more showy in spring than those of V. *corymbosum*, and their foliage is not greatly different except that it is semievergreen, usually turning scarlet before falling in early winter. Useful in Zones 8a−9a+.

Vaccinium vitis-idaea 2

Cowberry, mountain cranberry, lingonberry
Evergreen groundcover
Ericaceae (Heath Family)

Native Range. Circumpolar: northern Asia, Europe, and North America as far south as Massachusetts and British Columbia.

Useful Range. USDA Zones 2−6b with selection of appropriate genetic material (see Varieties), possibly also Zone 7.

Function. Small-scale groundcover, specimen, rock garden.

Size and Habit

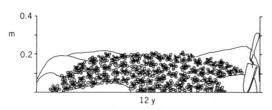

Vaccinium vitis-idaea.

Adaptability

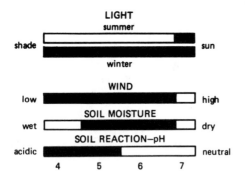

Seasonal Interest. *Flowers:* White to pinkish, only 0.6 cm/0.25 in. long but adding significant interest at close range, where this plant is most effective, in late spring and early summer. *Foliage:* Evergreen and leathery, dark green and lustrous, the convex leaf surfaces enhancing the luster, only 1–3 cm/0.4–1.2 in. long, producing an elegantly fine-textured mass. *Fruits:* deep red, to 1 cm/0.4 in. across, conspicuous in late summer and early autumn when borne in significant numbers.

Problems and Maintenance. This plant is relatively trouble-free when growing in a good soil and site. It never needs pruning other than to remove any dead stems.

Varieties. Var. *majus* (cowberry) is the Eurasian and lowland form of the species, growing to heights of 30 cm/12 in. with leaves as much as 3 cm/1.2 in. long. Not as cold-hardy as var. *minus*, but useful at least in Zones 5b–6b, perhaps also colder zones and areas with mild summers in Zone 7, and more vigorous and useful in southern zones than var. *minus*.

Var. *minus* (mountain cranberry, lingonberry) is the arctic form of the species, growing southward in our area to high elevations in New England. It is extremely cold-hardy but poorly adapted to areas having hot, dry summers. This variety probably should be limited in landscape use to Zones 2–4 and areas in Zones 5–6 having mild summers. It is slow-growing, useful only in small-scale situations, where it is one of the finest evergreen groundcovers, its lustrous, convex leaves, no more than 1 cm/0.4 in. long, forming a dense mat 10–20 cm/4–8 in. thick.

Vaccinium vitis-idaea var. *minus*.

Related Species

Gaylussacia brachycera 2 (box huckleberry). This blueberry relative, native to the central Appalachian mountains from Pennsylvania to Tennessee, is an effective evergreen groundcover for acidic soils, 30–50 cm/12–20 in. high, with dark green leaves about the same size as those of V. *vitis-idaea* var. *majus*. Useful in Zones 6a–7a, perhaps farther south as well, but not widely available.

Viburnum ×burkwoodii 5

Burkwood viburnum
Semievergreen shrub
Caprifoliaceae (Honeysuckle Family)

Hybrid Origin. V. *carlesii* × V. *utile*.

Useful Range. USDA Zones 5b—8b, perhaps also Zone 9a.

Function. Border, specimen. Tall but not dense enough to function as a screen.

Size and Habit

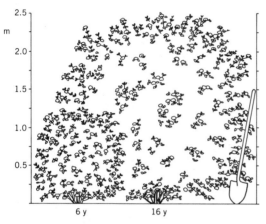

Viburnum ×burkwoodii.

Adaptability

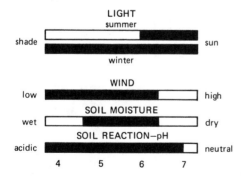

Seasonal Interest. *Flowers:* Fragrant (clovelike), pink in bud, opening white, in rounded clusters (cymes) about 6 cm/2.4 in. across as the foliage is unfolding in midspring. *Foliage:* Lustrous, dark green leaves, 3—8 cm/1.2—3 in. long, semievergreen, turning yellowish to wine-red before falling in early winter. *Fruits:* Red berries ripen black in early autumn but seldom are borne in large numbers.

Problems and Maintenance. Several diseases and insects can be troublesome occasionally, but not enough to justify a regular program of control. V. ×*burkwoodii* usually is sold on its own roots, since it can be propagated easily by cuttings, avoiding the rootstock problems that grafted plants are subject to (see V. *carlesii,* Problems and Maintenance).

Cultivars. 'Chenault' differs very little from the species type but is slightly more compact in growth habit and is said to be slightly less cold-hardy, but the difference in hardiness, if any, is very small.

'Mohawk' is a hybrid of V. ×*burkwoodii* back-crossed with V. *carlesii* at the U.S. National Arboretum. It differs from V. ×*burkwoodii* in having slightly larger leaves and deeper pink buds that are colorful for several weeks before the flowers open. It is highly resistant to leafspot and powdery mildew diseases and has the same useful range as V. ×*burkwoodii*.

Related Species

Viburnum utile 4 (Honan viburnum). This parent of V. ×*burkwoodii* differs from the hybrid in being lower and more open in growth habit, with smaller but fully evergreen leaves. Even though the glossy, dark green foliage is very beautiful, the plant is less functional because of its sparseness and lesser cold-hardiness. It is useful in Zones 7b—9a+ and perhaps also in Zone 7a.

Viburnum carlesii 4

Korean spice viburnum
Deciduous shrub
Caprifoliaceae (Honeysuckle Family)

Native Range. Korea.

Useful Range. USDA Zones 4b−8a.

Function. Specimen, border, foundation.

Size and Habit

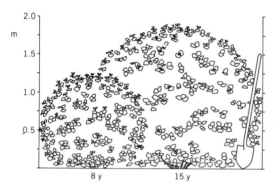

8 y   15 y

Adaptability

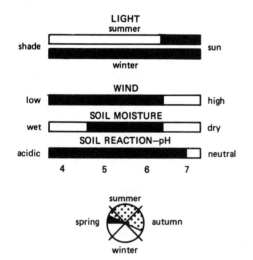

Seasonal Interest. *Flowers:* Very fragrant (clovelike), pink in bud, opening white, in rounded clusters (cymes) 5−8 cm/2−3 in. across with the unfolding foliage in midspring. *Foliage:* Gray-green, slightly lustrous to velvety, 5−10 cm/2−4 in. long and nearly as broad, turning dull reddish in some years before falling in autumn. *Fruits:* Rounded, elongated to 1 cm/0.4 in., dull red in late summer, ripening black in early autumn but seldom showy.

Problems and Maintenance. Several diseases and insects can be troublesome occasionally, but seldom are serious enough to justify control. In the past, V. *carlesii* was grafted on V. *lantana*, which, because of its greater vigor, often would overgrow the V. *carlesii* until the entire plant would appear to have been transformed into V. *lantana*. Modern cutting propagation techniques have been more successful with this species, and seedlings and cutting-grown plants on their own roots are usually available.

Cultivars. 'Compactum' is more compact in habit and remains below 1.5 m/5 ft for a fairly long time. Otherwise it is similar to the species.

Viburnum carlesii 'Compactum.'

Viburnum carlesii 'Compactum.'

Related Species and Hybrids

Viburnum bitchiuense 5 (Bitchiu viburnum). This Japanese native is taller and looser in growth habit than V. *carlesii*, with more slender stems and fragrant but somewhat smaller flower clusters. Seldom available commercially except when it is involved in the hybrid V. ×*juddii*, but useful in Zones 4b−8a.

Viburnum ×*carlcephalum* 5 (fragrant snowball). This hybrid of V. *carlesii* × V. *macrocephalum* combines the large, dense flower clusters of V. *macrocephalum*, to 12 cm/5 in., with the fragrance and cold hardiness of V. *carlesii*. It is a larger shrub, functioning fairly well as a visual screen, unlike most of the related species, useful in Zones 5a−8b. The selection 'Cayuga,' released by the U.S. National Arboretum, is a hybrid of V. *carlesii* back-crossed with V. ×*carlcephalum*, intermediate in stature between the parents, about 2 m/6.6 ft tall, and more resistant to leaf-spot and powdery mildew diseases than V. *carlesii*. Flower clusters are smaller than those of V. ×*carlcephalum*, but are borne in great numbers, and it is useful in the same area as the parents.

Viburnum ×*juddii* 5 (Judd viburnum). This hybrid of V. *carlesii* × V. *bitchiuense* is intermediate between the parents, tall enough for visual screening but not sufficiently dense, the fragrant flowers in slightly smaller clusters than those of V. *carlesii*. It has more slender twigs and more open habit than V. *carlesii*, and is useful in Zones 4b−8a. In some areas it has been less troubled by leaf-spot disease than V. *carlesii*.

Viburnum macrocephalum 5 (Chinese snowball). This tall shrub from China is notable for its enlarged sterile flowers, more than 2.5 cm/1 in. across, in very large, dense, rounded clusters, 8−15 cm/3−6 in. across, and semievergreen foliage. This "snowball" form, f. *macrocephalum* (= 'Sterile'), is the species type, since the species name was first applied to this garden form. The wild type, f. *keteleerii*, has enlarged, sterile flowers only around the margin of the inflorescence and is seldom available. Both can function as visual screens only with careful pruning, since they are rather open in habit. Useful in Zones 6b−8b.

Viburnum dentatum 6

Synonyms: V. *pubescens*, V. *recognitum*
Arrowwood
Deciduous shrub
Caprifoliaceae (Honeysuckle Family)

Native Range. Eastern North America: New Brunswick to Minnesota, southward to Georgia.

Useful Range. USDA Zones 4a−9a with selection of appropriate genetic material (see Varieties).

Function. Border, screen, naturalizing.

Size and Habit

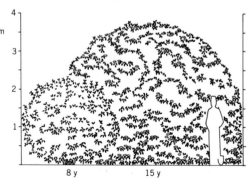

Viburnum dentatum.

Adaptability

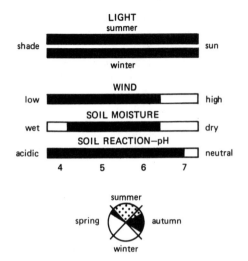

Seasonal Interest. *Flowers:* Creamy white, individually only 0.6 cm/0.25 in. across, in flattened clusters to 8 cm/3 in. across, conspicuous in late spring. *Foliage:* Dark green, usually lustrous, coarsely toothed and with prominent veins, making a handsome neutral mass, then turning bright red in some sites before falling in late autumn. *Fruits:* Blue-black, only 0.6 cm/0.25 in. across, in flattened clusters, adding mild landscape interest in early autumn.

Problems and Maintenance. This is one of the most trouble-free of the viburnums, requiring little maintenance other than spraying to control occasional insect outbreaks. Pruning may be necessary occasionally for thinning and renewal because of the tendency to produce large numbers of basal shoots, but not in naturalized plantings.

Varieties. Var. *scabrellum* (synonym: V. *scabrellum*; rough arrowwood) occurs naturally in the southeastern United States to Florida and Texas and extends the useful range of the species southward. Var. *pubescens* (synonym: V. *pubescens*; downy arrowwood) has been described as including forms with downy leaves and branches, but its status as a taxonomic unit is at best confused.

Related Species

Viburnum acerifolium 4 (mapleleaf viburnum, dockmackie). This shrub with leaves of the same general shape as V. *trilobum* is of landscape

interest for its ability to tolerate rather dense shade. In fact it does not grow well in full sun. Seasonal interest is minimal with small clusters of yellow-white flowers in late spring and purplish autumn foliage. It is native in much of eastern North America from New Brunswick to Manitoba and southward to North Carolina and is useful in Zones 3b–9a.

Viburnum acerifolium.

Viburnum acerifolium.

Viburnum bracteatum 5 (bracted arrowwood). This close relative of V. *dentatum*, native to Georgia, has large leaves, 5–12 cm/2–5 in. long, and conspicuous bracts below the flower clusters. It probably is not commercially available but is worthy of preservation in its native habitat and a satisfactory substitute for V. *dentatum*, at least in Zones 6a–9a.

Viburnum molle 5 (Kentucky arrowwood). This native of the midwestern United States from Indiana and Kentucky to Missouri differs from V. *dentatum* in its light-colored, flaking bark and is an equivalent landscape plant useful near its native range, at least in Zones 5a–9a.

Viburnum rafinesquianum 4 (Rafinesque arrow-wood). This shrub is native to a wide area of eastern North America from Quebec to Manitoba and southward to Georgia and Illinois. It differs little from V. *dentatum* except that it does not grow as tall, reaching heights of about 2 m/6.6 ft and making it a questionable choice for screening. Useful in Zones 3b–8a.

Viburnum dilatatum 5

Linden viburnum
Deciduous shrub
Caprifoliaceae (Honeysuckle Family)

Native Range. Japan.

Useful Range. USDA Zones 5b–8b.

Function. Border, screen, specimen.

Size and Habit

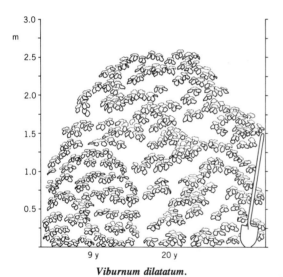

Viburnum dilatatum.

Adaptability

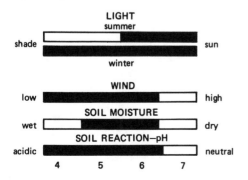

Seasonal Interest. *Flowers:* White, small but numerous, in flattened clusters 8–12 cm/3–5 in. across, showy in late spring with sporadic flowering continuing in late summer in some years. *Foliage:* Medium to deep green, usually lustrous, irregularly toothed and varying greatly in shape on the same plant, from nearly round and lindenlike to elongated and troughlike, especially on vigorous shoots, generally 5–12 cm/2–5 in. long, making a neutral and irregular but dense foliage mass, usually turning deep reddish before falling in middle to late autumn. *Fruits:* Bright red, individually only 0.8 cm/0.3 in. across but borne in clusters to 12 cm/5 in. across, showy for a long period in early through middle autumn.

Viburnum dilatatum.

Problems and Maintenance. This species is relatively trouble-free most of the time, although several insects occasionally can cause damage. Borers, the most serious, may need to be controlled. Pruning usually is not necessary except to remove any dead or weak branches or to control size if planted in too small an area.

Cultivars. 'Catskill' is a U.S. National Arboretum introduction, selected for compact, wide-spreading growth habit and small leaves that color well in autumn. The original plant did not exceed 1.5 m/5 ft in height in 12 years but spread to about 2.5 m/8 ft. The rounded leaves turn yellow, orange, and red in autumn and the dark red fruits remain colorful into winter.

'Iroquois,' another U.S. National Arboretum introduction, was selected for its unusually large, leathery leaves, heavy flowering, large fruits, dense, globose growth habit, and colorful foliage in autumn. This is an outstanding selection for use as a visual screen, reaching heights of 2.5 m/8 ft while spreading to about 3 m/10 ft.

'Oneida,' still another U.S. National Arboretum introduction, actually is a hybrid of V. *dilatatum* × V. *lobophyllum*, a closely related species from China. After flowering heavily in late spring, it continues to bloom intermittently during summer, and the relatively fine-textured foliage makes a lovely display as it turns yellow and orange-red in autumn. Both flowering and fruiting are consistent and impressive.

'Xanthocarpum' is an older selection with clear yellow fruits, effective in early autumn against the foliage, which is still dark green until midautumn.

Related Species

Viburnum setigerum 5 (synonym: V. *theiferum*; tea viburnum). This distinctive, open, vase-shaped shrub from China is one of the most impressive of all viburnums in fruit, with bright orange-red berries, 0.8 cm/0.3 in., in clusters to 5 cm/2 in. across from early through middle autumn. The starkly vase-shaped form of this plant limits its usefulness, and it is most effective

Viburnum setigerum.

planted in the rear of the shrub border so that its leggy base is covered by other plants while its branches arch out bearing the display of fruits. The small white flowers are among the latest to open of all the viburnums, in very late spring, and the distinctively arrowhead-shaped leaves usually undergo little or no color change before falling in late autumn. Useful in Zones 6a–8b and in some years in Zone 5b, but occasionally winterkilling to the ground there.

Viburnum wrightii 5 (Wright viburnum). Some specialists believe that this is the finest of all viburnums for autumn color, with crimson foliage and brilliant scarlet fruits. The better clones are at least equal to V. *dilatatum* and V. *setigerum*. Many plants sold as V. *wrightii* turn out to be V. *dilatatum*, but some nurseries are careful to offer the true V. *wrightii*, which differs from V. *dilatatum* in having glabrous (nonhairy) stems and leaves and deeper red autumn foliage color. Not all clones are equally impressive in fruiting display, but the best are spectacular over a long period in autumn. Useful in Zones 6a–8b and with mixed success in Zone 5b as well.

Viburnum farreri 5

Synonym: V. *fragrans*
Fragrant viburnum
Deciduous shrub
Caprifoliaceae (Honeysuckle Family)

Native Range. Northern China.

Useful Range. USDA Zones 5a–8a.

Function. Border, specimen, screen.

Size and Habit

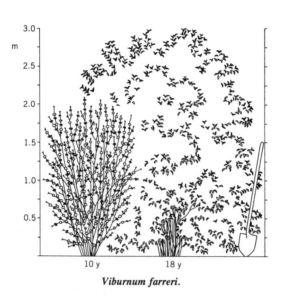

Viburnum farreri.

Adaptability

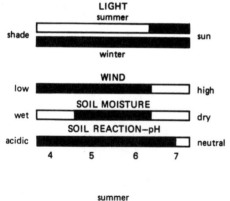

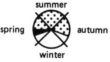

Seasonal Interest. *Flowers:* Highly fragrant, pink or white, in clusters 2.5—5 cm/1—2 in. across, small but effective because they precede the foliage in early spring, a few opening in late autumn in some sites and some years. *Foliage:* Medium green, the leaves, 5—7 cm/2—2.8 in. long and rather narrow, with red petioles on the pink-flowered species type, making a fairly dense, irregular mass of medium texture, turning reddish before falling in midautumn.

Problems and Maintenance. This shrub usually is trouble-free, although insect problems occasionally can develop. Annual pruning may be necessary to maintain fullness of form for use as a screen, but removal of deadwood and thinning every second or third year should be sufficient otherwise. Prune as soon as possible after flowering. Flower buds often open during warm periods in late winter, then are killed when freezing temperatures return. In warm, moist weather, flowers sometimes open partly or fully in autumn, to be frozen soon afterward by normal freezes or left more susceptible to winter cold. This plant is most effective in flower year after year where temperature fluctuations are modulated by closeness to bodies of water.

Cultivars. 'Album' has pure white flowers and green leaf petioles. 'Nanum' is dwarf in growth habit, remaining below 0.5 m/1.6 ft for several years and probably not exceeding 1.0 m/3.3 ft after many years.

Related Species

Viburnum ×bodnantense 5 (Bodnant viburnum). This hybrid of V. *farreri* × V. *grandiflorum* functions as a large, vigorous, and more floriferous version of V. *farreri*, with larger clusters of pink flowers, opening from late autumn to very early spring. Useful in Zones 7a—9a+ and in protected sites in Zone 6b, but the flowers are subject to winterkilling in some years in Zones 6b and 7. It is known in our area only in the form of the excellent selection 'Dawn,' although other selections may eventually become available.

Viburnum grandiflorum 5. This Himalayan shrub is not known in landscape use in our area and may not be adapted climatically, but it is stiffly upright in form and bears masses of rosy pink flowers in late winter or early spring. It probably is useful only in Zones 8 and 9, if at all in our area. The selection 'Snow White,' greatly appreciated in the climate of England, has white flowers.

Viburnum lantana 6

Wayfaring tree
Deciduous shrub
Caprifoliaceae (Honeysuckle Family)

Native Range. Europe and western Asia.

Useful Range. USDA Zones 4a−7b, some selections to Zone 3b.

Function. Border, screen, hedge, massing, specimen.

Size and Habit

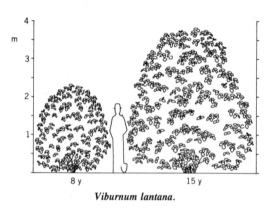

Viburnum lantana.

Adaptability. This is more tolerant of dry soils than most viburnums.

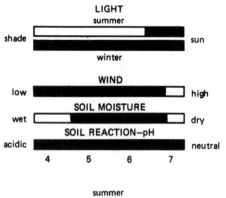

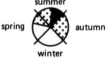

Seasonal Interest. *Flowers:* White, small but in nearly flat clusters 5−10 cm/2−4 in. across, fairly showy in late spring. *Foliage:* Dark gray-green leaves have a wrinkled, leathery appearance, 5−12 cm/2−5 in. long and nearly as broad, with whitish, scurfy pubescence underneath, remaining dark green or turning dull reddish before falling in late autumn. *Fruits:* Berries turn from green to red to blue-black, sometimes with all stages of ripeness appearing in the same cluster, colorful in late summer, then drying and persisting, raisinlike, until taken by birds in early to late autumn.

Viburnum lantana.

Problems and Maintenance. This is one of the most trouble-free of all viburnums, only occasionally troubled by a leaf spot disease and chewing insects. It tends to grow suckers from the root system but not in such great numbers that it is a problem in most landscape situations.

Cultivars. 'Aureum' has golden young foliage, turning to dull yellowish green as the season progresses, and grows vigorously, although perhaps not as rapidly as the species type or the following cultivar. 'Mohican' is a vigorous but compact U.S. National Arboretum selection with a dense growth habit, resistance to leaf-spot disease, and unusually long-lasting fruits that remain in the red stage for several weeks.

Related Species

Viburnum alnifolium 5 (synonym: *V. lantanoides*; hobblebush). This native of northeastern North America from New Brunswick to northern Michigan and southward in the Appalachian Mountains to North Carolina must be planted in at least partly shaded, moist sites to grow well. Its form is rather leggy and open, but in natural areas it makes a fine display in open woodlands in middle to late spring with its showy flowers, the outermost sterile and nearly 2.5 cm/1 in. across, borne in flat clusters 8−12 cm/3−5 in. across. The rounded leaves, 10−20 cm/4−8 in. long, provide interestingly coarse texture and turn deep red in autumn. Fruiting interest is similar to that of V. *lantana*. Useful primarily for naturalizing in Zones 3b−6b in areas having relatively cool summers.

Viburnum burejaeticum 5 (Manchurian viburnum). This uncommon species, perhaps not yet available commercially, has performed well in Minnesota and Manitoba, where it functions in much the same way as V. *lantana* but has smaller leaves, 4−10 cm/1.6−4 in. long and half as broad, and smaller but abundant flower clusters in middle to late spring. Fruits are similar in seasonal effect to those of V. *lantana* but are borne in smaller clusters. One of the most distinctive features of this species is the speed with which it starts growth in spring, often producing 10−15 cm/4−6 in. of stem growth before some other species have fully opened buds. Useful in Zones 3b−6b and perhaps also Zone 7.

Viburnum odoratissimum 5−6

Sweet viburnum
Evergreen shrub
Caprifoliaceae (Honeysuckle Family)

Native Range. Japan to the Himalayas.

Useful Range. USDA Zone 9a+ and sheltered sites in Zone 8.

Function. Screen, border, specimen, small patio tree.

Size and Habit

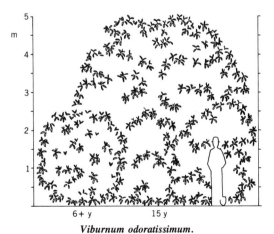

6+ y   15 y

Viburnum odoratissimum.

Adaptability. Protection from full winter sun and wind is necessary in Zone 8 to reduce leaf scorch.

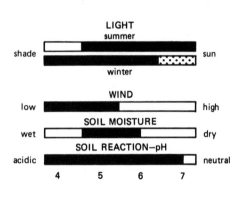

Seasonal Interest. *Flowers:* Fragrant, white, in pyramidal clusters to 10 cm/4 in. high and nearly as wide, in midspring. *Foliage:* Evergreen, bright green, lustrous to glossy, elliptical, to 15 cm/6 in. long, giving an outstanding, year-round, coarse textural effect. *Fruits:* Red, then ripening black in late summer.

Problems and Maintenance. In the colder parts of the useful range (Zone 8), winterscorch of foliage is the most common problem, but other problems such as scale insects occasionally require corrective measures. As with all evergreen viburnums, selection of site to minimize exposure to wind is essential for best results. Pruning is needed only to repair damage or restrain growth where space is inadequate.

Varieties and Cultivars. Var. *awabuki* (synonym: V. *awabuki* and sometimes incorrectly called V. *japonicum,* the correct name for another plant—see Related Species). This so-called leatherleaf form of V. *odoratissimum* has unusually large and glossy leaves. 'Nanum' is a dwarf shrub, remaining below 1 m/3.3 ft in height. It seldom is commercially available.

Related Species

Viburnum japonicum 4−5 (synonym: V. *macrophyllum;* Japanese viburnum). This native of Japan is frequently confused with V. *odoratissimum.* It differs from that species primarily in its lower stature, usually under 2−3 m/6.6−10 ft, and foliage that is lustrous but not as glossy as that of V. *odoratissimum* var. *awabuki.* V. *japonicum* has been credited with greater cold hardiness than V. *odoratissimum,* but this may not be a safe assumption when the confusion between the two is taken into account. Useful at least in Zone 9a+.

Viburnum opulus 5

European cranberrybush
Deciduous shrub
Caprifoliaceae (Honeysuckle Family)

Native Range. Europe, northern Asia, and northern Africa.

Useful Range. USDA Zones 3b−8b.

Function. Border, screen, specimen.

Size and Habit

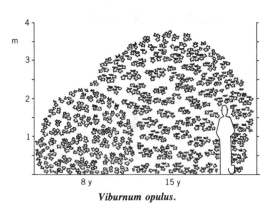

Viburnum opulus.

Adaptability

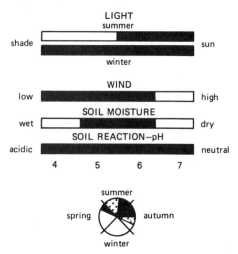

Seasonal Interest. *Flowers:* White, the fertile flowers small, surrounded by a ring of sterile flowers, each nearly 2 cm/0.8 in. across, in flattened clusters, 8−10 cm/3−4 in. across, or a globose cluster entirely of showy sterile flowers in 'Roseum' (see Cultivars). In either case, showy against the new foliage in late spring. *Foliage:* Deep green leaves are maplelike in outline, 5−12 cm/2−5 in. long and nearly as broad, providing distinctive texture and remaining green until they fall in middle to late autumn. *Fruits:* Scarlet when ripe, to 1 cm/0.4 in. across, in showy clusters about 8 cm/3 in. across, effective in late summer and until midautumn.

Viburnum opulus.

Problems and Maintenance. This shrub has few troubles, but frequently is infested with aphids, especially the form 'Roseum' (see Cultivars). Gradual renewal pruning, removing about one third of the oldest branches each year, is necessary with older plants to maintain fullness, but little other maintenance is needed.

Cultivars. 'Aureum' has dull yellowish foliage, is not very attractive, and lacks vigor.

'Compactum' is compact in form, remaining below 1.5 m/5 ft for several years, and flowers and fruits well. This is an attractive and useful selection but slightly less cold-hardy than the species type. Useful northward to Zone 4a.

'Nanum' is a dwarf, remaining below 0.5 m/1.6 ft for several years and below 1 m/3.3 ft for many years. It does not bear appreciable numbers of flowers or fruits, but its foliage texture gives it much character. Unfortunately, a leaf-spot disease disfigures the foliage in some areas. Useful northward to Zone 4a.

'Notcutt' is slightly more vigorous than the species type with somewhat larger fruits but is not significantly different for most landscape usage.

'Roseum' (synonym: 'Sterile'; European snowball) has globose clusters of all-sterile flowers. Lack of fruiting interest and high susceptibility to aphids, which disfigure the foliage, greatly limit the usefulness of this form.

'Xanthocarpum' differs from the species type in that its fruits remain clear yellow as they ripen, effective against the dark green foliage.

Related Species

Viburnum sargentii 5 (Sargent cranberrybush). This species from northeastern Asia is very similar to V. *opulus*, in fact, it has been included in that species by some specialists, as V. *opulus* var. *sargentii*. It differs in minute details and has been reported by some observers to be less cold-hardy than V. *opulus*, but there is disagreement about this. In any case it is useful in Zones 4a–8b, and at least certain selections are fully hardy in Zone 3b as well. The selection 'Flavum' has golden yellow fruits, slightly more showy than those of V. *opulus* 'Xanthocarpum.' Two selections have been made at the U.S. National Arboretum: 'Onondaga' has fine-textured, dark red new foliage that maintains a tinge of red-purple when mature and a compact growth habit, remaining below 2 m/6.6 ft for many years; 'Susquehanna,' on the other hand, is extremely vigorous, with very heavy, corky branches and leathery leaves giving a coarse texture and making a very large, upright mound, quickly reaching heights of at least 3 m/10 ft with an equal spread.

Viburnum opulus 'Nanum.'

Viburnum sargentii 'Susquehanna.'

Viburnum trilobum 5 (synonym: V. *americanum*; American cranberrybush). This northern North American species is very similar to V. *opulus*, treated by some specialists as a subpopulation of that species: V. *opulus* var. *americanum*. By whatever classification, it differs from European cranberrybush in three ways. It may be slightly more cold-hardy, at least to Zone 2b; its foliage frequently develops rather attractive reddish fall coloration; and its fruits are useful for making preserves if one does not object to the musky odor of the cooking berries. Several cultivars have been selected: 'Andrews,' 'Hahs,' and 'Wentworth' fruit more heavily than average for the species, but their availability is limited. 'Compactum' is more widely available, compact in growth habit, not exceeding 2 m/6.6 ft for many years, and is distinctly upright in its branching but susceptible to deformation by heavy snow. 'Garry Pink' has slightly pink-tinged flowers but is not widely available. 'Phillips' was selected at the University of New Hampshire for its fruit quality and has been described as being entirely free of the musky flavor and odor that are common in the species type, making jellies equal in flavor and color to red currant. It may not be commercially available yet.

Viburnum plicatum 5

Synonym: V. *tomentosum*
Japanese snowball, doublefile viburnum
Deciduous shrub
Caprifoliaceae (Honeysuckle Family)

Native Range. China and Japan.

Useful Range. USDA Zones 5b−8a with selection of appropriate cultivars (see Forms and Cultivars) and relatively cool, moist sites in Zone 8b.

Function. Border, specimen, screen (with careful pruning).

Size and Habit. F. *tomentosum* is illustrated.

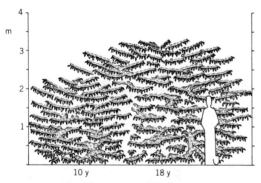

Viburnum plicatum f. *tomentosum*.

Adaptability. This is one of the least drought-tolerant of the viburnums.

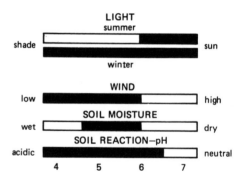

Seasonal Interest. *Flowers:* White; in f. *tomentosum* a central cluster of small, fertile flowers is surrounded by a ring of sterile flowers, each about 3 cm/1.2 in. across. The resulting flattened clusters, 5−10 cm/2−4 in. across, are borne in leaf axils in conspicuous double rows, hence the name doublefile viburnum; in f. *plicatum*, sterile florets are crowded into globose clusters 5−8 cm/2−3 in. across. *Foliage:* Medium to deep green toothed leaves, 5−10 cm/2−4 in. long, are covered with brownish, scurfy pubescence, the prominent veins providing strong textural interest, and turn velvety dull red in autumn. *Fruits:* Borne only on plants of f. *tomentosum* and its cultivars; red for a few weeks in late summer before turning blue-black, when they are usually taken quickly by birds; small but effective in flat clusters, especially in the red stage, when they accentuate the horizontal branching.

Problems and Maintenance. This shrub is relatively trouble-free most of the time except for its sensitivity to summer drought, but several insects occasionally can be troublesome. Borers are the worst offenders and must be controlled promptly to prevent serious damage. Pruning is seldom necessary and should be minimized so as not to detract from the gracefully horizontal branching habit, but gradual renewal of old plants by removing a few of the oldest branches annually helps to maintain the plant's character and prevent it from becoming excessively leggy.

Forms and Cultivars. F. *plicatum* (synonym: V. *tomentosum* var. *sterile*; Japanese snowball) is the species type, that is, the form to which the species name was first correctly applied. With its snowball-type flower clusters hanging somewhat unevenly because of their weight, this form lacks the strong horizontally layered growth habit of f. *tomentosum* and has no fruiting interest since all flowers are sterile. It is significantly less cold-hardy than f. *tomentosum*, useful in Zones 6a–8a, but may be injured in unusually severe winters in Zone 6. The cultivar 'Grandiflorum,' with larger flowers and clusters, is less cold-hardy, probably only to Zone 6b or 7a.

Viburnum plicatum f. *plicatum*.

F. *tomentosum* (synonym: V. *tomentosum*; doublefile viburnum) is the wild form of the species, with mostly fertile flowers, which logic would lead us to consider as the species type, except for the application of the rule of priority in naming plants. Several superior or distinctive cultivars have been selected and introduced, including the following.

'Lanarth' is compact in form, even more strikingly horizontally layered than ordinary f. *tomentosum*, with light green foliage. As yet it is seldom commercially available in the United States, but it is available in Canada.

Viburnum plicatum 'Lanarth.'

'Mariesii' has larger clusters of flowers and fruits and slightly greater vigor than ordinary f. *tomentosum* and is gaining rapidly in popularity.

'Roseum' has pale pink flowers, deeper in some locations and years and nearly white in others, but the plant is not vigorous or as cold-hardy as ordinary f. *tomentosum*, only to Zone 6a. It is seldom available.

Viburnum prunifolium 6

Black haw
Deciduous shrub or small tree
Caprifoliaceae (Honeysuckle Family)

Native Range. Eastern United States, Connecticut to Wisconsin and southward to Florida and Texas.

Useful Range. USDA Zones 3b−9a.

Function. Border, screen, small specimen tree (with some training).

Size and Habit

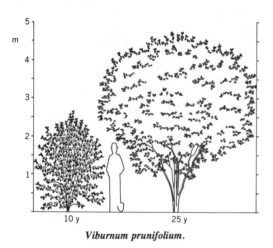

Viburnum prunifolium.

Adaptability

Viburnum prunifolium.

Seasonal Interest. *Flowers:* White, small but numerous, in clusters 5−10 cm/2−4 in. across, usually fairly showy in late spring. *Foliage:* Medium to dark green, lustrous and somewhat leathery, finely toothed, 3−8 cm/1.2−3 in. long, turning deep purple to scarlet before falling

in middle to late autumn. *Fruits:* Pale green to yellow-green in late summer, ripening blue-black in early to middle autumn, about 1 cm/0.4 in. long, adding interest to the colorful autumn foliage.

Viburnum prunifolium.

Problems and Maintenance. This plant is usually fairly trouble-free but occasionally subject to insect problems. Scale insects and borers can be serious enough to require control measures. Pruning is seldom necessary except to remove deadwood unless this plant is to be used as a small tree, in which case initial training and the removal of an occasional sucker shoot is needed.

Viburnum prunifolium trained as a tree.

Cultivars. Much variation exists in this species, and a few superior clones have been selected, but none are yet generally available.

Related Species

Viburnum cassinoides 4 (withe-rod, Appalachian tea). This native of northeastern North America from Newfoundland to Manitoba and southward to high elevations in North Carolina functions as a smaller, shrubby counterpart of V. *prunifolium*, with more slender, willowy branches. It flowers later than V. *prunifolium*, in early to middle summer, and has comparable autumn foliage and fruiting interest. It is more tolerant of wet soil but less tolerant of calcareous soil than most viburnums and is useful in Zones 3b−6b with selection of appropriate genetic material, and areas with mild summers in Zone 7.

Viburnum lentago.

Viburnum cassinoides.

Viburnum lentago 6 (nannyberry). This large shrub, occasionally more than 8 m/26 ft tall, is generally similar to V. *prunifolium* and sometimes confused with it, but it can be recognized easily by its wavy margined leaf petioles, more arching branches, and greater tendency to form root suckers than V. *prunifolium*. Because of this suckering habit it is less practical for training into tree form, even though it grows tall enough in time. It is also much more susceptible to powdery mildew than V. *prunifolium*. Naturally wide-ranging, from Hudson Bay southward to Georgia and Mississippi, V. *lentago* is useful in Zones 2−7b with selection of appropriate genetic material.

Viburnum nudum 5 (smooth withe-rod). This is the southern counterpart of V. *cassinoides*, native from Connecticut to Kentucky and southward to Florida and Louisiana. Generally similar in appearance to V. *cassinoides* except larger in stature, flowers, and foliage. Useful in Zones 6a−9a+, perhaps some sites in Zone 5.

Viburnum rufidulum 6 (southern black haw). The southern counterpart of V. *prunifolium*, this very large shrub, sometimes to more than 8 m/26 ft tall and wide-spreading, resembles V. *prunifolium* except in having larger, broader, and more leathery leaves, larger flower clusters, and a more irregular, spreading growth habit. Native from Virginia to southern Illinois and southward to Florida and Texas, V. *rufidulum* is useful in Zones 5a−9a+ with selection of appropriate genetic material.

Viburnum rufidulum.

Viburnum rhytidophyllum 5

Leatherleaf viburnum
Evergreen shrub
Caprifoliaceae (Honeysuckle Family)

Native Range. Central and Western China.

Useful Range. USDA Zones 6b–8a, protected sites in Zone 6a, and areas with mild summers in Zone 8b.

Function. Border, specimen.

Size and Habit

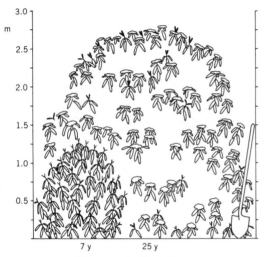

Viburnum rhytidophyllum.

Seasonal Interest. *Flowers:* Creamy-white, small but numerous in flattened clusters, 10–20 cm/4–8 in. across, showy with the handsome foliage in late spring. *Foliage:* Evergreen in Zones 7 and 8, wrinkled and leathery leaves, 8–18 cm/3–7 in. long and 3–5 cm/1.2–2 in. wide, lustrous and dark green on the upper surface, with a heavy layer of felty pubescence turning the lower surface whitish or rusty brown. *Fruits:* Red, ripening black, 0.8 cm/0.3 in. across in clusters 10–15 cm/4–6 in. across, effective in late summer and into early autumn.

Viburnum rhytidophyllum.

Adaptability. Protection from full sun in summer is beneficial in the South and Midwest. Protection from full sun and wind in winter reduces leaf scorch, a serious problem in the colder parts of the useful range.

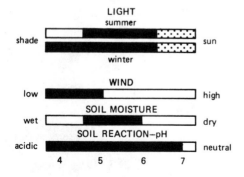

Problems and Maintenance. Winter leaf scorch is the most common problem, making the plant less than fully evergreen in some winters in Zone 6. Borers and scale insects occasionally may require corrective action. Nothing is more important to the success of this plant than careful selection of planting sites to minimize exposure to wind.

Cultivars. Little attention has been given to selection of superior forms of this species, but considerable variation may exist in China that has not yet been seen in North America. One selection for flowers that are pink in bud, 'Roseum, also is somewhat slower-growing but probably not presently commercially available.

Related Species and Hybrids

Viburnum buddleifolium 4 (buddleia viburnum).   This deciduous native of China has soft-tomentose leaves similar to those of V. ×*rhytidophylloides* and can function as a lower version of that species in landscape use, but it is seldom seen in commerce. Useful, when available, in Zone 6a–8a.

Viburnum ×*rhytidocarpum* 5.   This hybrid of V. *rhytidophyllum* × V. *buddleifolium* is similar in general effect to V. ×*rhytidophylloides* and may be confused with that species in commerce. It is useful in Zones 6a–8a.

Viburnum ×*rhytidophylloides* 5 (lantanaphyllum or hybrid leatherleaf viburnum).   This hybrid of V. *rhytidophyllum* × V. *lantana* has come into wide use in the Midwest. Even though it is not fully evergreen, it holds its foliage throughout autumn and until the first severe cold of winter, until then having much of the character of V. *rhytidophyllum*. But it is more cold-hardy and more vigorous, at least in the central states, than

V. *rhytidophyllum* and more effective for screening during the growing season. Useful in Zones 5b–8a and possibly areas of Zone 8b with mild winters. The selection 'Willowwood' is outstanding in form, flowering, and fruiting, with substantial flowering in early autumn as well as spring. 'Alleghany,' a more recent introduction by the U.S. National Arboretum, also shows promise.

Viburnum ×*rhytidophylloides* 'Willowwood.'

Viburnum sieboldii 6

Siebold viburnum
Deciduous shrub
Caprifoliaceae (Honeysuckle Family)

Native Range. Japan.

Useful Range. USDA Zones 5b–8a.

Function. Specimen, screen, border.

Size and Habit

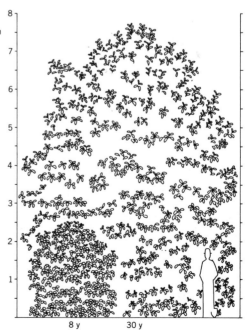

Viburnum sieboldii.

Adaptability

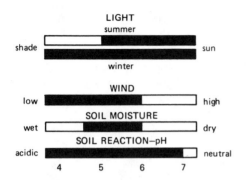

Viburnum sieboldii.

Seasonal Interest. *Flowers:* Creamy white, small but borne in rounded clusters to 10 cm/4 in. across in late spring. *Foliage:* Bright to deep green leaves, 6–12 cm/2.5–5 in. long, are lustrous and leathery, giving much of the character of large-leaved evergreen species such as V. *odoratissimum* in summer and early autumn but falling before the onset of winter. *Fruits:* Berries turn red, then blue-black, in middle to late summer, then dropping or taken by birds. The red stalks persist into autumn.

Problems and Maintenance. This is one of the most trouble-free of the viburnums, but insects sometimes can be a minor problem. Pruning is seldom if ever needed except for renewal of old plants. The outstanding foliage gives off a musky "green pepper" odor when crushed, a feature apparently objectionable to a few people.

Cultivars. Considering the variation that exists in this species and its value as a landscape plant, there has been very little selection of superior forms. But one such form, 'Seneca,' has been selected at the U.S. National Arboretum for its heavy flowering and especially for its fruits, which persist for as long as three months in the red stage, providing outstanding landscape interest in summer and early autumn.

Viburnum suspensum 4–5

Sandankwa viburnum
Evergreen shrub
Caprifoliaceae (Honeysuckle Family)

Native Range. Islands of southern Japan.

Useful Range. USDA Zones 8b–9a+.

Function. Specimen, border, foundation, hedge, screen (with maximum vigor in Zone 9a+).

Size and Habit

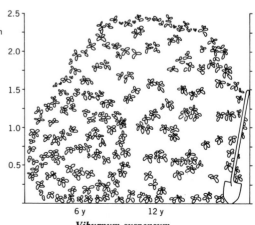

Viburnum suspensum.

Adaptability. Performs best with light shade during summer and benefits from protection from full sun and wind in winter, especially at the northern edge of its useful range.

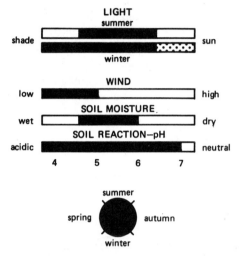

Viburnum suspensum.

pale to bright green, lustrous and rather leathery, 5–10 cm/2–4 in. long, making a dense mass. *Fruits:* Small, in small clusters, inconspicuous until they ripen bright red in early autumn.

Problems and Maintenance. Winter injury at the limits of its useful range is the only serious problem of this excellent shrub. Pruning is needed only to repair any winter damage or when training as a hedge.

Seasonal Interest. *Flowers:* Somewhat fragrant, white or pink-tinted, in dense clusters to 4 cm/1.6 in. across in early summer. *Foliage:* Evergreen,

Viburnum tinus 5

Laurestinus viburnum
Evergreen shrub
Caprifoliaceae (Honeysuckle Family)

Native Range. Mediterranean Region.

Useful Range. USDA Zones 8a–9a with proper cultural treatment (see Problems and Maintenance).

Function. Screen, border, hedge, specimen, foundation.

Size and Habit

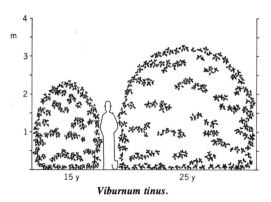

Viburnum tinus.

Adaptability

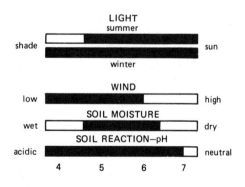

Seasonal Interest. *Flowers:* White or pinkish, slightly fragrant, in clusters 5–8 cm/2–3 in. across in early spring, or winter in mildest areas. *Foliage:* Evergreen, dark green, and finer-textured than other evergreen viburnums, the leaves mostly under 8 cm/3 in. long. Larger leaves are a sign of excessive vigor (see Problems and Maintenance). *Fruits:* Dark blue, ripening black in late summer, fairly conspicuous, in small clusters.

Problems and Maintenance. This versatile shrub is relatively free of problems and requires little maintenance, but it can be troubled by mites. Its most persistent problem is failure to harden sufficiently to withstand the first hard freezes of autumn because of excessive vigor. To avoid this, late summer irrigation, fertilization, and pruning should be avoided. Pruning is seldom needed, except when this shrub is used as a hedge. Then a single shearing in early summer is sufficient, and informal hedges will not need to be pruned more than once every few years. Planting in full sun and perfectly drained soil will also reduce the likelihood of late-season growth.

Cultivars. 'Compactum' and 'Eve Price' are dense and slow-growing with leaves smaller than the species type, making them ideal for smaller hedges but less useful for screening because of the time required to reach functional size. 'Eve Price' also has pink flowers but is not widely available.

'Lucidum' has larger leaves and flower clusters than the species type, and is more tender, useful in Zones 8b−9a+.

'Variegatum' has yellow variegated foliage but is seldom if ever available. It is useful, when it

can be found, in Zones 8b−9a+ and is best shaded from full sun.

Related Species

Viburnum davidii 3 (David viburnum). This excellent evergreen viburnum from China remains below 1 m/3.3 ft in height after many years, forming a low, broad mound. Its deeply creased leaves, mostly 8−12 cm/3−5 in. long and elliptical, give elegant textural accent in all seasons, and its clusters of white flowers in early summer are followed by bright blue fruits in late summer through autumn, at least on some plants. This shrub has been little used in our area but should be useful in Zones 7b−9a in sites protected from both summer and winter extremes and with a reliable moisture supply.

Viburnum davidii.

Vinca minor 2

Myrtle, common periwinkle
Evergreen groundcover
Apocynaceae (Dogbane Family)

Native Range. Europe and western Asia.

Useful Range. USDA Zones 4b−7b, perhaps also Zone 8 in areas with moderate summers.

Function. Groundcover.

Size and Habit

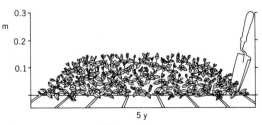

Vinca minor.

Adaptability. Performance is improved by protection from winter sun and wind in Zones 4 and 5 and from full summer sun in the Midwest and South.

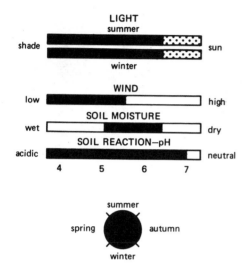

Seasonal Interest. *Flowers:* Blue, purple, or white, in early spring, handsome against the dark green foliage. *Foliage:* Evergreen, lustrous and leathery, deep green, neatly textured, the leaves elliptical, 2–4 cm/0.8–1.6 in. long, making a dense mass.

Vinca minor.

Problems and Maintenance. Except for one problem, a stem-dieback disease, V. *minor* is usually free of problems and requires little or no maintenance once established. Establishment may be slow, however, and a mulch to conserve moisture and control weed growth during this period may make the difference between success

and failure. The stem-dieback disease is troublesome in dense masses of established plants, usually during prolonged wet periods. Avoiding excessive vigor and thinning thick masses slightly (strange as that seems for a ground cover) to allow better air circulation during damp spells may help to prevent infections.

Cultivars. 'Alba' has pure white flowers and is less vigorous than most other forms.

'Argenteo-variegata' has white variegated foliage and less vigor than most other selections. It is rare and probably not commercially available. Plants with white variegated foliage are also sold as 'Variegata,' so the color of variegation may sometimes need to be specified.

'Atropurpurea' has deep purple flowers.

'Azurea' has pale blue flowers but is seldom available commercially.

'Bowlesii' (= 'Bowles Variety') is a popular selection with large numbers of deep blue flowers. It tends to grow in dense clumps and is best planted at closer spacing than other selections (i.e., 0.5 m/20 in. or closer).

'Flore Pleno' (= 'Multiplex'), with double, purple flowers, is not widely available.

'Variegata' (= 'Aureo-variegata') has yellow variegated foliage and is more likely to be available than 'Argenteo-variegata.' When white variegated plants are available, they are sometimes called simply 'Variegata,' causing some confusion.

Vinca minor 'Argenteo-variegata.'

Related Species

Vinca major 2 (bigleaf periwinkle). This more vigorous but less cold-hardy relative of V. *minor* from southern Europe is useful in Zones 8a−9a+ but may suffer occasional winter injury in Zone 8a. It completely replaces V. *minor* in the South. Although it is less tidy and fine textured than V. *minor*, it is faster-growing and easier to establish and can be supplemented with *Trachelospermum asiaticum* when finer texture is desired in the Deep South. The selection 'Variegata' has leaves with creamy white margins. It is used as a summer annual in the North and occasionally as a groundcover in Zone 9a+.

Vinca major 'Variegata.'

Vinca major.

Viola sororia 2

Synonyms: V. *papilionacea*, V. *priceana*
Common or wooly blue violet
Herbaceous groundcover
Violaceae (Violet Family)

Native Range. Eastern North America.

Useful Range. USDA Zones 3b−8a.

Function. Groundcover, naturalizing.

Size and Habit

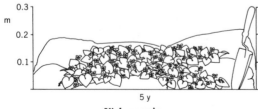

Viola sororia.

Adaptability. Other species of V*iola* differ in site requirements (see Related Species).

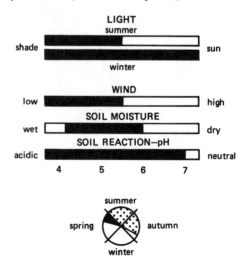

Seasonal Interest. *Flowers:* Small but showy, usually deep rich blue, but light, grayish blue, or white in some forms, in middle to late spring. *Foliage:* Deep, rich green, broad, making an attractive, dense mass. Leaves die at the onset of winter and new leaves appear in midspring.

Problems and Maintenance. Once established in a site with ample moisture and protection from full sun, maintenance is practically nil, but this plant can become invasive in some areas. It is probably not available from the usual commercial sources but may be available from existing wild or naturalized stands.

Varieties. The nonhairy form of V. *sororia* sometimes is called V. *papilionacea*. It does not differ in landscape character from the species type. Another form, the confederate violet, is sometimes called V. *priceana*. Its flowers are two-toned: whitish with blue-violet veining. Many other local variations exist but are not important from a landscape viewpoint.

Related Species. More than 50 species of *Viola* are cultivated as landscape or garden plants in North America. Most perform best in partial shade and moist soil, but some are at their best in full sun and sandy soil, and some require wet sites. Several are potentially effective groundcovers, at least in local areas. Since few are available from the usual commercial sources, the best approach may be to use native species that are known to perform well in the locality in question. An exception to this is *Viola odorata* (sweet or garden violet) and its forms. This native of Europe and the Mediterranean Region has long been cultivated in gardens and as a florist crop. Its blue-purple flowers are fragrant, and double-flowered forms exist, but primarily for florist use. It is useful in Zones 6a−9a+.

Vitis coignetiae 1

Gloryvine
Deciduous vine
Vitaceae (Grape Family)

Native Range. Japan.

Useful Range. USDA Zones 5b−9a.

Function. Specimen, shade, or screen (with support). Grows extremely rapidly, scrambling over ground or climbing by tendrils to heights of 15 m/49 ft or more.

Size and Habit

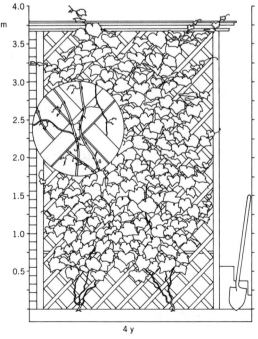

Vitis coignetiae.

Adaptability

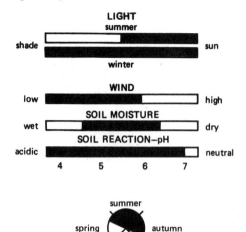

Seasonal Interest. *Flowers:* Small and inconspicuous in early summer. *Foliage:* Leaves, up to 25 cm/10 in. across, are barely lobed, dull and roughened with prominent veins, make an impressive, coarse foliage mass, and turn bright red before falling in autumn. *Fruits:* Purplish black, 0.8 cm/0.3 in. across, not edible, ripening in early autumn.

Vitis coignetiae.

Problems and Maintenance. This vine is relatively trouble-free, although mildew and chewing insects, including Japanese beetles, occasionally may disfigure the foliage. Pruning will be needed in all but very large-scale situations, since the growth rate of this vine is exceeded only by *Pueraria lobata.* It should be avoided when space is limited. Grapes in general are rather coarse vines, useful only in highly informal or naturalized settings or where they are also desired for their fruit. V. *coignetiae* probably has more

seasonal interest than any other species but lacks edible fruit.

Related Species

Vitis amurensis 1 (Amur grape). This native of Manchuria and adjacent Siberia is somewhat less vigorous and more cold-hardy than its Japanese counterpart, V. *coignetiae.* Even though its foliage is not as handsome in summer and a more subdued red-purple in autumn, this vine is a reasonably effective substitute for V. *coignetiae* in Zones 5a–8a, perhaps also Zone 4, but it is seldom commercially available.

Vitis labrusca 1 (fox grape). This native of the northeastern United States and southward to Georgia grows vigorously, making a dense, handsome foliage mass useful for screening on fence support and overhead enclosure of arbors and similar structures. It is the primary parent of most of the commercial grape cultivars used in northeastern North America, and itself has edible fruit that is made into preserves. Useful in Zones 5a–7b but available mostly as commercial fruiting cultivars that function much the same as this species.

Vitis riparia 1 (frost or riverbank grape). This high-climbing grape, native from the Canadian Maritime Provinces to Manitoba and Texas, climbs well up into tall trees in the wild. It can be used for screening (with support) but is not as effective as V. *labrusca,* where that species can be grown. The advantage of V. *riparia* is its cold hardiness, and it is useful in Zones 3b–6b but available only by propagating from the wild.

Vitis rotundifolia 1 (Muscadine or scuppernong grape). This vigorous, high-climbing native of the southeastern and south-central United States and Mexico is of greatest value for its fruits, useful for preserves and other processed products, but it may also be planted as dual-purpose landscape plants (such as for supported screens) in Zones 7b–9a. Unlike other grapes, this species and its cultivars tend to be dioecious (flowers of only one sex on an individual plant), so an occasional staminate (male) plant should be included for pollination unless newer cultivars, bearing staminate as well as pistillate flowers, are used. In any case, when grapes are being grown for their fruit, cultural instructions can be obtained from local, state, or provincial extension service offices.

Waldsteinia fragarioides 2

Barren strawberry
Herbaceous groundcover
Rosaceae (Rose Family)

Native Range. Northeastern and central United States and adjacent Canada: New Brunswick to Minnesota and southward to Georgia and Missouri.

Useful Range. USDA Zones 4a−7b.

Function. Groundcover.

Size and Habit

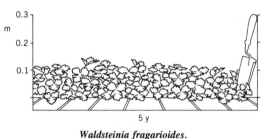

Waldsteinia fragarioides.

Adaptability

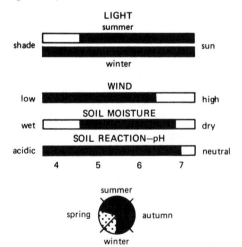

Seasonal Interest. *Flowers:* Bright yellow, about 1.2 cm/0.5 in. across, in fairly showy clusters in late spring. *Foliage:* Deep green and lustrous, similar to that of strawberries, evergreen and bronzing in winter but becoming dull in late winter and early spring. *Fruits:* Small and borne in small numbers with little landscape significance.

Problems and Maintenance. This groundcover is usually trouble-free and requires little or no

Waldsteinia fragarioides.

maintenance once established. In good sites it forms a thick mat, resisting weed encroachment.

Related Species

Duchesnea indica 2 (Indian strawberry, mockstrawberry). This native of India, naturalized in the eastern United States, is similar in general effect to *Waldsteinia*, with small yellow flowers and strawberrylike foliage and fruits. The leaves are not as completely evergreen as those of *Waldsteinia* but remain handsome and lustrous into early winter. Useful in Zones 5b−9a+ and northward at least to Zone 5a, perhaps also Zone 4 in areas having reliable snow cover.

Fragaria ×*ananassa* 2 (cultivated strawberry). This hybrid group involving *F. chiloensis*, the beach strawberry that grows wild on the western coasts of the Americas from Alaska to southern Chile, and *F. virginiana* (see below) can be used as an effective groundcover with the added advantage of the edible fruit. Specific maintenance requirements for good fruiting can be obtained from local and state or provincial extension offices. Unlike *Waldsteinia*, strawberries are not evergreen, but they are adaptable to much of our area in Zones 5a−8a and colder areas where snow cover is reliable.

Fragaria virginiana 2 (Virginia or wild strawberry). This native of much of eastern North America from Newfoundland to Georgia and westward to Alberta and Oklahoma is useful as a natural or naturalized groundcover, although it is not as vigorous or aggressive as the other species mentioned here. The fruits are delicious but so small that picking them can be tedious. Useful in Zones 3a−7b.

Weigela florida 5

Synonym: W. *rosea*
Old-fashioned weigela
Deciduous shrub
Caprifoliaceae (Honeysuckle Family)

Native Range. Northern China and Korea.

Useful Range. USDA Zones 5a−9a, marginally hardy in Zone 4b.

Function. Border, specimen, screen (taller selections in Zones 6−9a).

Size and Habit

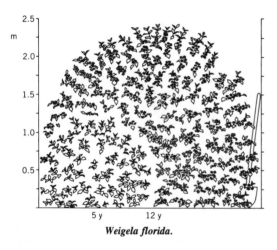

Weigela florida.

Adaptability

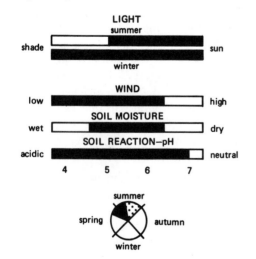

Seasonal Interest. *Flowers:* Rosy pink to deep rosy red or white, funnel-shaped, about 3 cm/1.2 in. long, borne singly or in small clusters in late spring or early summer, continuing spasmodically through the summer in some cultivars. *Foliage:* Medium green leaves, 5−10 cm/2−4 in. long, give medium texture and no autumn interest, falling without color change.

Problems and Maintenance. Pest problems are few and minor, and little maintenance is required. Gradual thinning every year or two is required to maintain good form. In Zones 4b−6a, and perhaps farther south, plants may be killed back severely in occasional winters and will need corrective pruning.

Varieties, Cultivars, and Hybrids. Var. *venusta*, from Korea, has smaller leaves and lower stature (1.5−2 m/5−6.6 ft) than the species type and rosy flowers. It generally is considered to be somewhat more cold-hardy than the species but is not as widely used in cold climates as some of the cultivars listed.

Many cultivars of *Weigela* have been named. Most are hybrids of W. *florida*, with W. *floribunda*, W. *praecox*, and probably other species as well. In most cases, parentage is unknown or at best confused. Most of the large, pink-flowering selections are not superior to W. *florida* as landscape plants, so only a few of the more distinctive cultivars are listed here:

'Alba,' 'Bristol Snowflake,' and 'Candida' bear white flowers. Of these, only 'Bristol Snowflake' is commonly available. This selection has light green foliage and compact growth, somewhat slower growing and lower at maturity than 'Bristol Ruby.'

'Bristol Ruby' and 'Vanicekii' (= 'Newport Red') have bright red flowers and a tendency to bear a few flowers intermittently after the principal burst of bloom in late spring and early summer, these from flower buds initiated in the same season. These are among the most cold-hardy *Weigela* cultivars, excepting 'Centennial' and 'Dropmore Pink,' and even when they are severely damaged in hard winters, they sometimes return to light flowering during the following summer. They begin to flower freely when less than 1 m/3.3 ft tall and remain below 2 m/6.6 ft in height for many years.

'Centennial,' an introduction by the Canada Department of Agriculture Research Station at Morden, Manitoba in the Canadian Centennial

Year of 1967, is distinctive for its unusual cold-hardiness, to Zone 3b, and has rosy red flowers and compact growth, reaching heights of 2.5 m/8 ft.

'Dropmore Pink' is an unusually cold-hardy selection made by the late F. L. Skinner of Dropmore, Manitoba. It has mauve-pink flowers and is comparable to 'Centennial' in cold-hardiness.

'Eva Rathke' has deep red flowers, somewhat less showy than those of 'Bristol Ruby' and 'Vanicekii,' and a weaker tendency toward late summer flowering. It also grows somewhat taller than those cultivars.

'Foliis Purpuriis' has purplish foliage in early summer, turning green later, and pink flowers. Its best feature is its low stature, remaining below 1.5 m/5 ft for many years.

'Pink Princess' is compact, remaining under 1.5 m/5 ft, and has bright pink flowers and purple-edged leaves.

'Variegata' is a name apparently applied to at least two clones with either creamy white or yellow margins. Both are useful color variants in Zones 5a–7a, perhaps also some sites in Zone 4.

Related Species

Weigela floribunda 5 (crimson weigela).   This Japanese shrub differs little from W. *florida* except that its deeper reddish brown flowers are usually less showy. It is somewhat less cold-hardy than W. *florida*, useful in Zones 6a–9a, and less likely to be commercially available.

Weigela middendorffiana 4 (yellow or Middendorff weigela).   This native of northern China, Manchuria, and Japan, has greenish yellow flowers and good form. At least in its northern native forms it is unusually cold-hardy, probably useful in Zones 4a–7a, but it does not perform well in hot, dry summers. This rare species probably is not commercially available, although plants of *Diervilla* have been sold under this name. True W. *middendorffiana* holds promise for northern climates and might well be reintroduced.

Weigela praecox 4 (early weigela).   This native of Korea is similar to W. *florida* but flowers as much as two weeks earlier and does not become as tall. It is useful in the same range as W. *florida* and perhaps slightly colder zones as well.

Wisteria floribunda 1

Japanese wisteria
Deciduous vine
Leguminosae (Pea Family)

Native Range. Japan.

Useful Range. USDA Zones 5b–9a+.

Function. Specimen, screen (with support). Grows rapidly, once established, climbing by twining to heights of 8–10 m/26–33 ft or greater.

Size and Habit

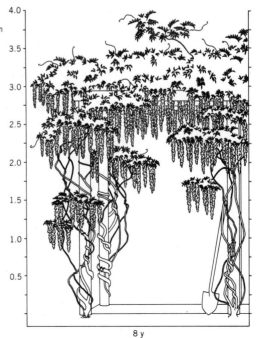

8 y

Wisteria floribunda.

Adaptability

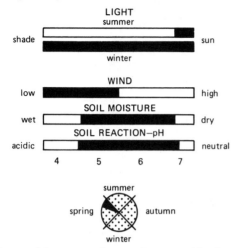

Seasonal Interest. *Flowers:* Fragrant, bluish violet to reddish violet, pink, or white, individually about 2 cm/0.8 in. long, borne in large numbers in pendent clusters 20–50 cm/8–20 in. long, longer in some cultivars, in late spring, sometimes continuing with shorter clusters into summer. *Foliage:* Rich green, compound leaves form a dense mass, remaining green until middle to late autumn, when they fall without color change. *Trunks:* Old specimens frequently develop picturesquely sinuous trunks with smooth gray bark, adding interest at close range.

Problems and Maintenance. Relatively trouble-free, wisteria vines require little maintenance once they are established and flowering well. But establishment is sometimes difficult, and pot-grown plants should be specified to minimize difficulty in transplanting. Established plants of many cultivars often do not flower for another five to ten years or even longer. Methods most commonly used to promote earlier flowering include root pruning and withholding irrigation and fertilization, except with phosphate fertilizers, but the results seem to be uncertain at best. Seedling plants may require longer to flower well than cultivars, since the latter in most cases have been selected for relatively early flowering and sometimes have been grafted onto seedling rootstocks, the scions coming from parent plants of flowering age. In the colder parts of the useful range, flower buds may be killed in some winters, greatly reducing landscape value. Wisterias in general may succeed in establishment and growth in colder areas than indicated, but may flower so seldom that they have little landscape value.

Cultivars. 'Alba' has white flowers with moderate fragrance and flower clusters of medium length.

'Longissima' has long clusters of fragrant violet flowers.

'Longissima Alba' is similar to 'Longissima' except that its flowers are white.

'Macrobotrys' (synonym: *W. multijuga*) has violet flowers with excellent fragrance in unusually long clusters, occasionally approaching 1 m/39 in., but more typically averaging no more than 0.5 m/20 in. long.

'Praecox' (synonyms: 'Issai,' *W. multijuga* var. *praecox*) has moderately fragrant violet flowers in clusters of medium length. It is reputed to come into flower at an early age, but it is unclear at this time whether this is true throughout our area.

'Rosea' has highly fragrant, rose-pink flowers in clusters of medium length.

'Royal Purple' has deep violet flowers, only moderately fragrant, but in clusters sometimes approaching 0.5 m/20 in. long.

Several Japanese cultivars have been introduced into North America during the last half century. Many have received limited trial in eastern North America and few are commercially available in our area, but some may prove superior, especially in precocity of flowering, to some of those listed here.

Related Species and Hybrids

Wisteria frutescens 1 (American wisteria). This native of the southeastern United States from Virginia to Florida and Texas is useful for naturalizing but is not as effective for accent as the Asian species because its flower clusters are mostly less than 10 cm/4 in. long and are borne intermittently during the summer. Useful in Zones 7b–9a+.

Wisteria macrostachya 1 (Kentucky wisteria). Like *W. frutescens*, this species flowers after the foliage is well developed in early summer, but its violet flowers are borne in clusters as large as those of *W. sinensis*, and so it is showy, extending the season of bloom for wisterias by two to four weeks or more. Native from Kentucky and Tennessee to southern Illinois, Missouri, and Texas, this plant is useful in Zones 5a–9a.

Wisteria sinensis 1 (Chinese wisteria). Perhaps the most common wisteria in landscape plantings in our area, this Chinese species differs from *W.*

floribunda in several respects. It has a narrower range of flower color: violet to blue-violet and white. Its flowers tend to be borne in smaller clusters, mostly 15–30 cm/6–12 in. long and more dense than those of most *W. floribunda* cultivars. Moreover, *W. sinensis* is somewhat less cold-hardy than *W. floribunda*, useful in Zones 6a–9a+. A few of the more common cultivars are listed here.

'Alba' has white flowers. Otherwise, it is similar to the species type.

'Jako' has highly fragrant white flowers in relatively long clusters and is generally regarded as superior to 'Alba' for landscape effect.

'Sierra Madre' has fragrant, blue-violet flowers, borne in large numbers.

Wisteria venusta 1 (silky wisteria).   This close relative of *W. sinensis* has fragrant white flowers in the forms in which it has been most cultivated. The selection 'Plena' has double white flowers, and 'Violacea' has lavender-violet flowers. This species differs little from *W. sinensis* in landscape use in Zones 6a–9a+.

Xanthorhiza simplicissima 2

Synonym: X. *apiifolia*
Yellowroot
Deciduous groundcover
Ranunculaceae (Buttercup Family)

Native Range. Eastern United States: New York to Alabama and Florida.

Useful Range. USDA Zones 5b–9a+.

Function. Massing, groundcover.

Size and Habit

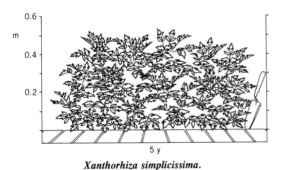

Xanthorhiza simplicissima.

Adaptability

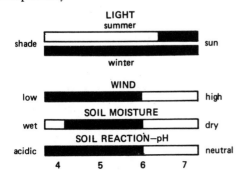

Seasonal Interest. *Flowers:* Tiny, brownish crimson, borne in large numbers in loose clusters, lending a reddish cast to the plant in middle to late spring before new leaves unfold. *Foliage:* Compound, medium-green leaves give medium-fine texture similar to that of *Aegopodium podagraria* and turn dull yellow-orange before falling in autumn.

Xanthorhiza simplicissima.

Problems and Maintenance. Relatively trouble-free, given the required site conditions, *Xanthorhiza* makes such a dense foliage mass once established that weed growth is minimal. Since it spreads vigorously, it can become a weed itself unless restrained by buildings, pavement or steel edging.

Yucca smalliana 3

Synonym: Often sold as Y. *filamentosa*
Adam's needle
Evergreen shrub or groundcover
Agavaceae (Agave Family)

Native Range. Southeastern United States: South Carolina to Florida and Mississippi, naturalized farther northward.

Useful Range. USDA Zones 5b−9a and protected sites in Zone 5a.

Function. Specimen or massing, especially in situations where architectural and paving materials predominate.

Size and Habit

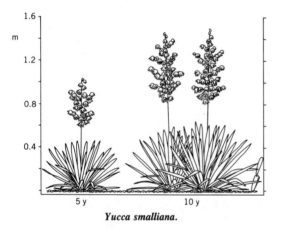

Yucca smalliana.

Adaptability

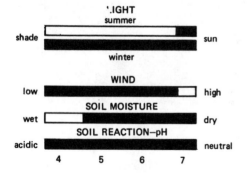

Seasonal Interest. *Flowers:* Creamy white, 5−8 cm/2−3 in. across, nodding, borne in large, upright clusters, often 1 m/3.3 ft tall, giving

striking landscape accent in early summer. *Foliage:* Evergreen, stiff, gray-green, swordlike leaves, to 0.6 m/2 ft long and 5 cm/2 in. wide with curly fibers on the margins, forming a rosette with little or no stem growth in height. *Fruits:* Seed pods, about 5 cm/2 in. long, add little landscape interest and become untidy in appearance.

Problems and Maintenance. This plant is relatively trouble-free and requires little maintenance other than weed control and removal of dead leaves and flowerstalks. Stone or sand mulches are effective for weed control and visually compatible with the character of this plant. The leaves are sufficiently sharp-pointed to be dangerous in areas frequented by small children. The fruiting stalks become untidy and are best removed following flowering.

Related Species

Yucca aloifolia 4−5 (Spanish bayonet, aloe yucca). Unlike the other *Yucca* species mentioned here, this native of the Deep South and Mexico makes considerable stem growth, forming trunks 2−4 m/6.6−13 ft tall, or taller south of our area. Foliage and flowering interest is not greatly different from that of Y. *smalliana*, although the leaves are even sharper-pointed than those of Y. *smalliana*, and so are potentially dangerous in some situations. Useful in Zones 8a−9a+ for positive accent. The selection 'Marginata' has yellow leaf margins.

Yucca filamentosa 3 (spoonleaf yucca). Most plants offered for sale as Y. *filamentosa* are really Y. *smalliana*. Nevertheless, there is a true Y. *filamentosa*, native to much the same area, with longer leaves, but it is seldom commercially available. Useful in Zones 6a−9a+ and probably also Zone 5b.

Yucca flaccida 3 (weakleaf yucca). This plant is similar to Y. *smalliana*, native to about the same area, and often substituted in landscape use, but its leaves are less rigid, the outer ones bending back to the ground. Useful in Zones 5b−9a+. The selection 'Ivory Tower' has unusually large flower clusters, to 1.5 m/5 ft tall, with erect flowers, and is superior for accent at flowering time in early summer.

Yucca glauca 3 (Great Plains yucca, soapweed).   This native of western North America from South Dakota to New Mexico has strongly

Yucca glauca.

bluish leaves, about as long as those of *Y. smalliana* but only about 1 cm/0.4 in. wide. It is useful as a specimen in Zones 4b−7b but not as appropriate for large-scale massing as other *Yucca* species.

Yucca gloriosa 4−5 (Spanish dagger, moundlily yucca).   Like *Y. aloifolia*, this species is native to the southeastern states and makes considerable stem growth, sometimes reaching heights of 2−4 m/6.6−13 ft but often multiple-trunked and remaining lower. Useful for accent and massing in Zones 8a−9a+, some forms northward into Zone 7.

Agave americana 4 (century plant).   This native of Mexico is useful for accent in dry sites in Zone 9a+ and makes a striking specimen with succulent gray leaves 1 m/3.3 ft and more in length and up to 25 cm/10 in. wide. Plants grow in rosette form, sometimes for many years without flowering. When flowering does occur it is most dramatic, since the inflorescence towers far over the vegetative plant. Following flowering the original plant dies and usually is replaced by one or more sucker shoots.

Zelkova serrata 8

Japanese zelkova
Deciduous tree
Ulmaceae (Elm Family)

Native Range. Japan.

Useful Range.   USDA Zones 6a−9a, perhaps also Zone 5b with selection of most cold-hardy genetic material.

Function. Shade tree.

Size and Habit

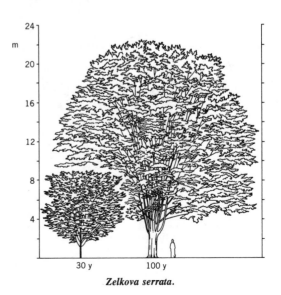

Zelkova serrata.

Adaptability

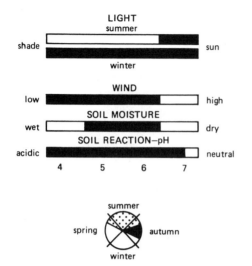

Seasonal Interest. *Foliage:* Pale green on emergence, turning a rich, deep green in summer, then russet-yellow before falling in autumn. *Trunk and branches:* Bark on large trees peels off in patches to expose the orange-brown inner bark.

Zelkova serrata.

Problems and Maintenance. Usually free of serious problems, this elm relative has been found resistant (although apparently not immune) to Dutch elm disease and has been recommended as a substitute for the American elm in some areas. When considering it for this role, it is important to remember the differences in cold hardiness, ultimate size, and growth rate between the two species.

Cultivars. 'Village Green' (Plant Patent No. 2337, 1964), has been selected for its symmetrical, upright growth habit, relatively rapid growth, resistance to insects and diseases, and cold hardiness. Its foliage turns reddish in autumn. Although it is still too early to predict the exact limits of its cold hardiness, it appears that it may be useful at least in Zones 5b–9a.

Related Species

Zelkova carpinifolia 8 (Caucasian zelkova). This large, graceful tree from the Caucasus makes a majestic shade tree in Europe. It is similar to Z. *serrata* in ultimate size and habit and seems fully as likely a substitute for the form of American elm, but is somewhat less cold-hardy, useful in Zones 7a–9a and perhaps also Zone 6b with selection of the most cold-hardy material. Older trees have peeling bark at least as colorful as that of Z. *serrata.*

Zelkova sinica 7 (Chinese zelkova). This tree has attracted interest in the Midwest because of its presumed cold hardiness, but it probably is little more cold-hardy than the hardiest material of Z. *serrata.* Since it also lacks the elegant form of Z. *serrata,* it probably is of little interest as a substitute for the American elm, even though it may be a useful landscape tree in Zones 6a–9a and perhaps parts of Zone 5b as well.

Hemiptelea davidii 6 (David hemiptelea). This shrubby small tree from northeastern Asia, if it should become available commercially, would be useful in Zones 5a–8a at least, as a small specimen tree or hedge plant. Its foliage is similar to that of some of the small-leaved elms, but it has little other landscape interest.

Ziziphus jujuba 6

Common jujube, Chinese date
Deciduous shrub or small tree
Rhamnaceae (Buckthorn Family)

Native Range. Southeastern Europe through Asia to China; naturalized in some parts of the southeastern United States.

Useful Range. USDA Zones 6b−9a+.

Function. Small specimen tree, edible fruits.

Size and Habit

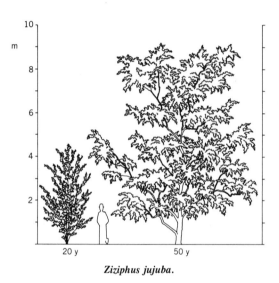

Ziziphus jujuba.

Adaptability. This tree is unusually widely tolerant of soil conditions, including alkaline soils, but not tolerant of wet soils.

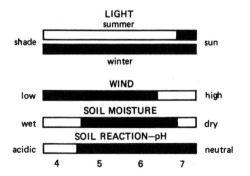

Seasonal Interest. *Flowers:* Greenish yellow, very small and not showy, before the leaves in mid-spring. *Foliage:* Olive-green leaves, mostly not

more than 5 cm/2 in. long and only half as wide, sparsely arranged on the spiny branches. *Fruits:* Dull green, then red, and ripening very dark red-brown in late summer, up to 2.5 cm/1 in. long, resembling dates, edible as preserves or dried.

Ziziphus jujuba.

Problems and Maintenance. This plant is essentially trouble-free and requires little or no maintenance. Pruning is seldom necessary other than for initial training.

Varieties and Cultivars. Var. *inermis* is free of spines, an important consideration when the fruits are to be harvested. Several cultivars have been selected for outstanding fruit production, especially in Asia, but these are seldom commercially available in our area. In fact the species type often is not easy to locate.

Related Species. The following additional members of the Rhamnaceae are not commonly encountered in landscape use but could become more important than they are at present.

Hovenia dulcis 7 (Japanese raisin tree). This native of China (cultivated widely in Japan) is a graceful, trouble-free, small to medium-size tree, useful in Zones 6b−7b and perhaps warmer zones as well. The flowers, opening during summer, are not showy, but the reddish stalks are interesting and allegedly edible. The fruits are

Hovenia dulcis.

Paliurus spina-christi.

not colorful but come to resemble raisins as they ripen in early autumn.

Paliurus spina-christi 6 (synonym: *P. aculeatus*; Christ thorn, Jerusalem thorn).   This exceedingly spiny large shrub or small tree from southern Europe and Asia has bright green leaves, about 2.5 cm/1 in. long, too loosely arranged to be effective for screening, but the thorns and dense growth make it a good choice for a barrier hedge. The small, greenish yellow flowers are fairly showy when they appear in large numbers in late spring along with the expanding leaves. It is useful in Zones 7b−9a+.

LISTS OF PLANTS BY CATEGORIES

A. Vines, Climbers (Size Group 1)

Actinidia spp.
Akebia spp.
Ampelopsis spp.
Antigonon leptopus
Aristolochia durior
Bignonia capreolata
Campsis spp.
Celastrus spp.
Clematis spp. (most)
Clytostoma callistegioides
Cocculus carolinus
Decumaria barbara
Euonymus fortunei (part)
Ficus pumila

Gelsemium sempervirens
Hedera spp.
Hydrangea anomala
Jasminum spp. (part)
Kadsura japonica
Lonicera spp. (part)
Macfadyena unguis-cati
Menispermum canadense
Parthenocissus spp.
Passiflora spp.
Periploca graeca
Pieris phillyreifolia
Pileostegia viburnoides
Polygonum aubertii

Pueraria lobata
Rosa banksiae
Rosa bracteata
Rosa laevigata
Rosa wichuraiana
Schisandra spp.
Schizophragma hydrangeoides
Smilax spp.
Trachelospermum spp.
Tripterygium regelii
Vitis spp.
Wisteria spp.

B. Ground covers to 0.5 m tall (Size Group 2)

Aegopodium podagraria
Ajuga spp.
Akebia spp.
Andromeda polifolia
Arctostaphylos uva-ursi
Ardisia japonica
Arundinaria pygmaea
Asarum spp.
Bruckenthalia spiculifolia
Calluna vulgaris
Cassiope tetragona
Cassiope umbellata
Celastrus spp.
Comptonia peregrina
Convallaria majalis
Corema conradii
Cornus canadensis
Coronilla varia
Cotoneaster adpressus
Cotoneaster dammeri
Cytisus spp. (part)
Daphne alpina
Daphne cneorum
Decumaria barbara
Empetrum spp.
Epigaea repens

Epimedium spp.
Erica spp. (most)
Euonymus fortunei (part)
Euonymus obovata
Euphorbia cyparissias
Fragaria spp.
Galax urceolata
Galium spp.
Gaultheria hispidula
Gaultheria procumbens
Gaylussacia brachycera
Gelsemium sempervirens
Genista spp. (part)
Hedera spp.
Helianthemum nummularium
Hosta spp. (part)
Hydrangea anomala
Hypericum buckleyi
Hypericum calycinum
Iberis spp.
Juniperus chinensis (part)
Juniperus communis (part)
Juniperus conferta
Juniperus horizontalis
Juniperus sabina (part)
Juniperus squamata (part)

Lamiastrum galeobdolon
Lamium maculatum
Ledum spp. (part)
Leiophyllum buxifolium
Liriope spp.
Loiseleuria procumbens
Lonicera spp. (part)
Lotus corniculatus
Mahonia repens
Menispermum canadense
Mitchella repens
Nepeta mussinii
Ophiopogon japonicus
Pachysandra spp.
Parthenocissus spp. (most)
Passiflora caerulea
Paxistima canbyi
Phlox spp.
Pileostegia viburnoides
Podophyllum peltatum
Potentilla spp. (part)
Rhododendron lapponicum
Rosa wichuraiana
Rubus hispidus
Salix repens
Salix uva-ursi

Saxifraga stolonifera
Schizophragma hydrangeoides
Sedum spp. (most)
Sempervivum tectorum
Shortia galacifolia

Teucrium chamaedrys
Tiarella cordifolia
Trachelospermum spp.
Vaccinium spp. (part)
Vinca spp.

Viola spp.
Waldsteinia fragarioides
Xanthorhiza simplicissima

C. Dwarf Shrubs and Tall Ground covers, 0.5 – 1 m tall (Size Group 3)

Amorpha canescens
Amorpha nana
Ardisia spp. (part)
Aronia melanocarpa (part)
Artemisia spp. (part)
Arundinaria spp. (part)
Aspidistra elatior
Berberis candidula
Berberis verruculosa
Buxus microphylla
Caragana aurantiaca
Caragana pygmaea
Caryopteris spp. (part)
Ceanothus spp. (part)
Chaenomeles japonica
Chamaecyparis cvs. (part)
Chamaedaphne calyculata
Cistus spp. (part)
Cornus hessei
Cotoneaster spp. (part)
Cycas revoluta
Cyrtomium falcatum
Cytisus spp. (part)
Daboecia cantabrica
Danaë racemosa
Daphne spp. (part)
Deutzia gracilis
Diervilla lonicera
Elsholtzia stauntonii
Erica spp. (part)

Escallonia virgata
Euonymus nana
Eurya emarginata (part)
Fothergilla spp. (part)
Fuchsia magellanica (part)
Gaultheria shallon
Genista spp. (part)
Hemerocallis spp.
Hosta spp. (part)
Hydrangea arborescens
Hydrangea macrophylla
Hypericum spp. (part)
Ilex crenata (part)
Ilex rugosa
Indigofera spp.
Jasminum spp. (part)
Juniperus spp. (part)
Kalmia spp. (part)
Lavandula angustifolia
Ledum spp. (part)
Leptodermis oblonga
Lespedeza cuneata
Lonicera pileata
Lonicera spinosa
×Mahoberberis aquicandidula
Mahonia spp. (part)
Paxistima myrsinites
Pernettya mucronata
Picea abies cvs. (part)
Pieris phillyreifolia

Polygonum cuspidatum (part)
Potentilla spp. (part)
Prunus besseyi
Prunus pumila
Pueraria lobata
Raphiolepis indica
Rhapidophyllum hystrix
Rhododendron spp. (part)
Rosa spp. (part)
Rubus laciniatus
Ruscus aculeatus
Sabal minor
Salix repens
Santolina spp.
Sasa veitchii
Serenoa repens
Skimmia spp.
Spiraea spp. (part)
Symphoricarpos spp. (part)
Taxus cvs. (part)
Thuja occidentalis cvs. (part)
Trifolium incarnatum
Tsuga canadensis cvs. (part)
Vaccinium angustifolium
  (part)
Viburnum davidii
Yucca spp.
Zamia floridana

D. Small Shrubs, 1 – 2 m tall (Size Group 4)

Deciduous and Semievergreen

Abelia ×grandiflora (part)
Abeliophyllum distichum
Amelanchier spp. (part)
Aronia melanocarpa (part)
Artemisia abrotanum
Berberis spp. (part)
Buddleia davidii
Callicarpa spp.
Calycanthus spp.

Caragana brevifolia
Caryopteris incana
Chaenomeles spp. (part)
Clerodendrum bungei
Corylopsis spp. (part)
Cotoneaster spp. (part)
Cytisus spp. (part)
Daphne spp. (part)
Deutzia spp. (part)

Diervilla spp. (part)
Dirca palustris
Edgeworthia papyrifera
Enkianthus perulatus
Forsythia spp. (part)
Fothergilla monticola
Fuchsia magellanica
Genista cinerea
Halimodendron halodendron

Hydrangea quercifolia
Hypericum hookeranum
Itea spp. (part)
Jasminum spp. (part)
Kerria japonica
Leycesteria formosa
Ligustrum obtusifolium (part)
Ligustrum vulgare (part)
Lindera melissifolia
Lonicera spp. (part)
Myrica spp. (part)
Neillia sinensis
Neviusia alabamensis
Paeonia spp. (part)
Philadelphus spp. (part)

Physocarpus opulifolius (part)
Polygonum cuspidatum (part)
Prinsepia uniflora
Prunus glandulosa
Prunus japonica
Prunus maritima
Prunus tenella
Pyracantha coccinea (part)
Rhamnus pallasii
Rhodotypos scandens
Rhus aromatica (part)
Rhus trilobata (part)
Ribes spp. (part)
Robinia spp. (part)
Rosa spp. (part)

Salix rosmarinifolia
Securinega suffruticosa
Sorbaria sorbifolia
Spiraea spp. (part)
Stephanandra spp. (part)
Symphoricarpos rivularis
Syringa spp. (part)
Tamarix hispida
Tripetaleia paniculata
Vaccinium spp. (part)
Viburnum spp. (part)
Vitex spp. (part)
Weigela spp. (part)

Evergreen

Agave americana
Ardisia spp. (part)
Berberis spp. (part)
Buxus spp. (part)
Cephalotaxus harringtonia
Ceratiola ericoides
Chamaecyparis cvs. (part)
Chamaedaphne calyculata
Cistus spp. (part)
Cycas revoluta
Daphne spp. (part)
Escallonia ×langleyensis
Euonymus fortunei (part)
Eurya spp. (part)
×Fatshedera lizei

Fatsia japonica
Gardenia jasminoides
Itea spp. (part)
Jasminum spp. (part)
Juniperus spp. (part)
Leucothoë spp. (part)
Lyonia spp.
×Mahoberberis spp. (part)
Mahonia spp. (part)
Myrtus communis
Nandina domestica
Osmanthus delavayi
Picea abies cvs. (part)
Pieris spp. (part)
Pinus aristata (part)

Pinus mugo (part)
Pinus pumila (part)
Prunus laurocerasus (part)
Raphiolepis spp. (part)
Rhododendron spp. (part)
Sabal minor (part)
Sarcococca spp.
Sasa palmata
Serenoa repens (part)
Taxus spp. and cvs. (part)
Thuja spp. and cvs. (part)
Tsuga canadensis cvs. (part)
Vaccinium spp. (part)
Yucca spp. (part)
Zenobia pulverulenta

E. Medium Shrubs, 2–4 m tall (Size Group 5)

Deciduous and Semievergreen

Abelia ×grandiflora (part)
Acanthopanax sieboldianus
Adina rubella
Aesculus parviflora
Aesculus splendens
Amelanchier spp. (part)
Aronia spp. (part)
Artemisia tridentata
Baccharis halimifolia
Berberis spp. (part)
Buddleia alternifolia
Calycanthus spp. (part)
Caragana spp. (part)
Cassia corymbosa

Cephalanthus occidentalis
Chimonanthus praecox
Clerodendrum trichotomum
Clethra alnifolia
Cliftonia monophylla
Colutea arborescens
Cornus spp. (part)
Corylopsis spp. (part)
Corylus spp. (part)
Cotoneaster spp. (part)
Crataegus chrysocarpa
Deutzia spp. (part)
Disanthus cercidifolius
Elaeagnus spp. (part)

Elliottia racemosa
Enkianthus campanulatus
Euonymus spp. (part)
Exochorda macrantha
Ficus carica
Fontanesia spp. (part)
Forestiera acuminata
Forsythia spp. (part)
Fothergilla major
Hamamelis vernalis
Hibiscus syriacus
Hydrangea quercifolia (part)
Ilex verticillata
Itea virginica

Jasminum nudiflorum
Juniperus spp. (part)
Kolkwitzia amabilis
Leitneria floridana
Lespedeza spp. (part)
*Leucophyllum frutescens
Leucothoë racemosa
Ligustrum spp. (part)
Lindera benzoin
Lonicera spp. (part)
Lycium halimifolium
Magnolia spp. (part)
Malus spp. (part)
Myrica pensylvanica
Myrtus communis
*Nearly evergreen

Nemopanthus mucronatus
Orixa japonica
Philadelphus spp. (part)
Physocarpus opulifolius
Polygonum cuspidatum
Prinsepia sinensis
Prunus spp. (part)
Pyracantha spp. (part)
Rhododendron spp. (part)
Rhus aromatica (part)
Rhus trilobata (part)
Ribes alpinum
Rosa spp. (part)
Rubus spp. (part)
Salix spp. (part)
Sambucus spp. (part)

Sesbania punicea
Shepherdia canadensis
Sophora davidii
Sorbaria aitchisonii
Spartium junceum
Spiraea spp. (part)
Stachyurus praecox
Staphylea bumalda
Styrax americanus
Syringa spp. (part)
Tamarix spp. (part)
Tripterygium regelii
Vaccinium spp. (part)
Viburnum spp. (part)
Vitex spp. (part)
Weigela spp. (part)

Evergreen

Arctostaphylos manzanita
Aucuba japonica
Bambusa glaucescens
Callistemon citrinus
Cephalotaxus fortunei
Chamaecyparis cvs. (part)
Choisya ternata
Cistus ×cyprius
Cleyera japonica
Croton alabamense
Elaeagnus spp. (part)
Escallonia spp. (part)
Euonymus japonica
Eurya japonica
Fatsia japonica

Ilex spp. (part)
Illicium spp. (part)
Kalmia latifolia
Leucothoë populifolia
Ligustrum spp. (part)
Loropetalum chinense
Mahonia spp. (part)
Michelia figo
Nandina domestica
Osmanthus spp. (part)
Phillyrea decora
Photinia glabra
Picea abies cvs. (part)
Pieris spp. (part)
Pinus aristata

Pinus mugo
Pinus pumila
Pittosporum tobira
Podocarpus macrophyllus
   (part)
Prunus spp. (part)
Rhododendron spp. (part)
Rosa spp. (part)
Taxus spp. and cvs. (part)
Thuja spp. (part)
Thujopsis dolobrata
Torreya spp. (part)
Tsuga canadensis (part)
Viburnum spp. (part)
Yucca spp. (part)

F. Large Shrubs and Small Trees, 4–8 m tall (Size Group 6)

Deciduous and Semievergreen

Acer spp. (part)
Aesculus pavia
Albizia julibrissin
Aleurites fordii
Alnus spp. (part)
Amelanchier spp. (part)
Amorpha fruticosa
Aralia spp.
Asimina triloba
Betula populifolia
Bumelia lanuginosa
Caragana arborescens
Castanea pumila

Cedrela sinensis
Cercis spp.
Chionanthus spp.
Clerodendrum trichotomum
Clethra spp. (part)
Cornus spp. (part)
Corylus maxima
Cotinus coggygria
Cotoneaster spp. (part)
Crataegus spp. (most)
Cydonia spp.
Cyrilla racemiflora
Cytisus battandieri

Davidia involucrata
Elaeagnus angustifolia
Elliottia racemosa
Enkianthus campanulatus
Euonymus spp. (part)
Evodia daniellii
Exochorda spp. (part)
Ficus carica
Firmiana simplex
Forestiera acuminata
Franklinia alatamaha
Fraxinus spp. (part)
Hamamelis spp. (most)

Hemiptelea davidii
Hippophaë rhamnoides
Holodiscus discolor
Hovenia dulcis
Hydrangea paniculata
Ilex decidua
Laburnum spp.
Lagerstroemia indica
Leitneria floridana
Ligustrum vulgare
Lindera obtusiloba
Lonicera maackii
Magnolia spp. (part)
Malus spp. and cvs. (most)
Melia azedarach
Paliurus spina-christi

Parkinsonia aculeata
Parrotia persica
Parrotiopsis jacquemontiana
Philadelphus purpurascens
Photinia villosa
Picrasma quassioides
Pinckneya pubens
Poncirus trifoliata
Populus spp. (part)
Prunus spp. (part)
Ptelea trifoliata
Pterostyrax corymbosus
Punica granatum
Rhamnus spp. (most)
Rhus spp. (part)
Salix spp. (part)

Sambucus nigra
Shepherdia argentea
Sophora affinis
Sorbus spp. (part)
Staphylea spp. (most)
Stewartia spp. (part)
Styrax spp. (most)
Symplocos spp.
Syringa spp. (part)
Tilia mongolica
Vaccinium spp. (part)
Viburnum spp. (part)
Vitex negundo
Xanthoceras sorbifolium
Zanthoxylum spp.
Ziziphus jujuba

Evergreen

Arundinaria simonii
Bambusa glaucescens
Butia capitata
Callistemon citrinus
Camellia spp.
Chamaecyparis cvs. (part)
Daphniphyllum macropodum
Eriobotrya spp.
Eucalyptus spp. (part)
Feijoa sellowiana
Hibiscus rosa-sinensis
Ilex spp. (part)

Illicium anisatum
Juniperus spp. (part)
Laurus nobilis
Ligustrum spp. (part)
Myrica cerifera
Nerium oleander
Osmanthus spp. (part)
Persea spp. (part)
Photinia spp. (part)
Phyllostachys spp. (part)
Picea abies cvs. (part)
Pinus spp. (part)

Podocarpus macrophyllus
Prunus spp. (part)
Pyracantha spp. (part)
Rhododendron spp. (part)
Sciadopitys verticillata
Taxus spp. (part)
Ternstroemia gymnanthera
Thuja spp. (part)
Torreya nucifera
Trachycarpus fortunei
Tsuga spp. and cvs. (part)

G. Medium Trees, 8–16 m tall (Size Group 7)

Deciduous and Semievergreen

Acer spp. (part)
Aesculus glabra
Ailanthus altissima
Alnus spp. (most)
Amelanchier arborea
Aralia spp.
Asimina triloba
Betula spp. (part)
Broussonetia papyrifera
Carpinus spp.
Castanea spp. (part)
Catalpa spp. (part)
Cedrela sinensis
Celtis bungeana
Cercis canadensis
Cladrastis lutea

Cornus spp. (part)
Corylus colurna
Cotinus obovatus
Crataegus spp. (part)
Davidia involucrata
Diospyros spp.
Eucommia ulmoides
Evodia hupehensis
Firmiana simplex
Fraxinus spp. (part)
Halesia spp. (part)
Idesia polycarpa
Juglans ailanthifolia
Koelreuteria spp.
Maackia spp.
Maclura pomifera

Magnolia spp. (part)
Malus spp. (part)
Morus spp.
Ostrya virginiana
Oxydendrum arboreum
Parrotia persica
Paulownia tomentosa
Phellodendron amurense
Populus spp. (part)
Prunus spp. (part)
Pterostyrax hispidus
Pyrus spp.
Quercus spp. (part)
Robinia spp. (part)
Salix spp. (part)
Sapindus drummondii

Sapium sebiferum
Sassafras albidum
Sorbus spp. (part)

Stewartia spp. (part)
Syringa reticulata
Ulmus spp. (part)

Zelkova sinica

Evergreen

Abies koreana
Calocedrus decurrens
Cedrus spp.
Chamaecyparis spp. (part)
Cinnamomum camphora
Cupressus spp. (most)
Eucalyptus spp. (part)
Gordonia lasianthus

Ilex spp. (part)
Juniperus spp. (part)
Myrica cerifera
Persea palustris
Phoenix canariensis
Phyllostachys bambusoides
Picea mariana
Pinus spp. (part)

Podocarpus macrophyllus
Prunus caroliniana
Rhododendron arboreum
Sciadopitys verticillata
Thuja spp, (part)
Torreya nucifera
Tsuga spp. (part)
Umbellularia californica

H. Large Trees, 16 m and taller (Size Group 8)

Deciduous and Semievergreen

Acer spp. (part)
Aesculus spp. (part)
Ailanthus altissima
Betula spp. (part)
Carya spp.
Castanea spp. (part)
Catalpa speciosa
Celtis spp. (most)
Cercidiphyllum japonicum
Cladrastis platycarpa
Cornus coreana
Corylus colurna
Fagus spp.
Fraxinus spp. (part)
Ginkgo biloba
Gleditsia triacanthos

Gymnocladus dioica
Halesia monticola
Juglans spp.
Juniperus virginiana
Kalopanax pictus
Keteleeria spp.
Larix spp.
Liquidambar spp.
Liriodendron spp.
Magnolia spp. (part)
Metasequoia glyptostroboides
Morus spp.
Nyssa spp.
Ostrya virginiana
Oxydendrum arboreum
Phellodendron spp.

Pistacia chinensis
Platanus spp.
Populus spp. (part)
Prunus spp. (few)
Pseudolarix kaempferi
Pterocarya spp.
Quercus spp. (part)
Robinia pseudoacacia
Salix spp. (part)
Sassafras albidum
Sophora japonica
Sorbus alnifolia
Taxodium distichum
Tilia spp. (most)
Ulmus spp. (most)
Zelkova spp. (most)

Evergreen

Abies spp. (most)
Araucaria spp.
Chamaecyparis spp. (part)
Cryptomeria japonica
Cunninghamia lanceolata
×Cupressocyparis leylandii

Cupressus macrocarpa
Picea spp. (most)
Pinus spp. (part)
Pseudotsuga menziesii
Quercus virginiana
Sequoia sempervirens

Sequoiadendron giganteum
Taiwania cryptomerioides
Thuja plicata
Tsuga spp. (part)
Umbellularia californica

I. Small- to Medium-scale Screens: Shrubs and Vines

Deciduous and Semievergreen

Acanthopanax sieboldianus 5
Acer ginnala 6
Actinidia spp. 1
Aesculus parviflora 5

Akebia spp. 1
Ampelopsis spp. 1
Aristolochia durior 1
Calycanthus fertilis 5

Campsis spp. 1
Celastrus spp. 1
Chimonanthus praecox 5
Clematis maximowicziana 1

Clematis montana 1
Clematis vitalba 1
Clerodendrum trichotomum
    5–6
Clethra alnifolia 5
Cornus alba 5
Cornus amomum 5
Cornus mas 6
Cornus racemosa 5
Cornus sanguinea 5
Cornus sericea 5
Corylopsis glabrescens 5
Corylopsis sinensis 5
Cotoneaster acutifolius 5
Cotoneaster frigidus 6
Cotoneaster henryanus 5
Cotoneaster lacteus 5
Cotoneaster lucidus 5
Cotoneaster multiflorus 5
Cotoneaster racemiflorus 5
Cotoneaster salicifolius 5
Cotoneaster ×watereri 6
Deutzia scabra 5
Elaeagnus multiflora 5
Elaeagnus umbellata 5
Enkianthus campanulatus 5–6
Euonymus alata 5
Euonymus kiautschovica 5
Exochorda spp. 5–6
Fontanesia spp. 5
Forsythia ×intermedia 5
Forsythia suspensa 4–5
Fothergilla major 5
Franklinia alatamaha 6
Hamamelis vernalis 5
Hydrangea quercifolia 4–5
Leucothoë racemosa 5
Ligustrum ×ibolium 5

Ligustrum ovalifolium 5
Ligustrum sinense 5
Ligustrum vulgare 5–6
Lonicera alpigena 5
Lonicera ×amoena 5
Lonicera ×bella 5
Lonicera fragrantissima 5
Lonicera korolkowii 5
Lonicera ×purpusii 5
Lonicera tatarica 5
Lonicera ×xylosteoides 5
Lonicera xylosteum 5
Menispermum canadense 1
Myrica pensylvanica 4–5
Orixa japonica 5
Parthenocissus quinquefolia 1
Philadelphus coronarius 5
Philadelphus inodorus 5
Philadelphus purpurascens
    5–6
Philadelphus schrenkii 5
Philadelphus ×splendens 5
Polygonum aubertii 1
Prinsepia sinensis 5
Prunus tomentosa 5
Pueraria lobata 1
Punica granatum 6
Rhamnus davurica 6
Rhododendron vaseyi 5
Rosa multiflora 5
Rosa setigera 5
Sambucus spp. 5–6
Schisandra spp. 1
Shepherdia spp. 5–6
Sorbaria aitchisonii 5
Symplocos paniculata 6
Syringa ×chinensis 6
Syringa ×henryi 5

Syringa ×hyacinthiflora 6
Syringa ×josiflexa 5
Syringa josikaea 5
Syringa oblata 5
Syringa patula 5
Syringa ×prestoniae 5
Syringa reflexa 5
Syringa ×swegiflexa 5
Syringa villosa 5
Syringa vulgaris 6
Vaccinium corymbosum 5
Viburnum ×bodnantense 5
Viburnum bracteatum 5
Viburnum burejaeticum 5
Viburnum ×burkwoodii 5
Viburnum ×carlcephalum 5
Viburnum dentatum 6
Viburnum dilatatum 5
Viburnum farreri 5
Viburnum lantana 6
Viburnum lentago 6
Viburnum molle 5
Viburnum nudum 5
Viburnum opulus 5
Viburnum plicatum 5
Viburnum prunifolium 6
Viburnum ×rhytidocarpum 5
Viburnum ×rhytidophylloides 5
Viburnum rufidulum 6
Viburnum sargentii 5
Viburnum sieboldii 6
Viburnum trilobum5
Viburnum wrightii 5
Vitis spp. 1
Wisteria spp. 1

Evergreen

Arctostaphylos manzanita 5
Arundinaria simonii 6
Aucuba japonica 5
Bambusa glaucescens 5–6
Bignonia capreolata 1
Callistemon citrinus 5–6
Camellia sasanqua 6
Chamaecyparis spp. and cvs.
    5–6
Clematis armandii 1
Elaeagnus ×ebbingei 5

Elaeagnus macrophylla 5
Elaeagnus pungens 5
Euonymus japonica 5
Ilex aquifolium 6
Ilex ×aquipernyi 6
Ilex bioritensis 6
Ilex cassine 6
Ilex ciliospinosa 6
Ilex cornuta 5–6
Ilex glabra 6
Ilex sugerokii 5

Illicium spp. 5–6
Kadsura japonica 1
Kalmia latifolia 5
Leucothoë populifolia 5
Ligustrum japonicum 5–6
Loropetalum chinense 5
Michelia figo 5
Myrica cerifera 6
Nerium oleander 6
Osmanthus spp. 5–6
Passiflora caerulea 1

Phillyrea decora 5
Photinia spp. 5—6
Pieris forrestii 5
Pinus cembra 6—8
Pittosporum tobira 5
Podocarpus macrophyllus 5—7
Prunus caroliniana 6—7
Prunus laurocerasus 4—6
Pyracantha koidzumii 5
Quercus acuta 7

Quercus glauca 7
Rhododendron arboreum 7
Rhododendron catawbiense 5
Rhododendron decorum 6
Rhododendron fortunei 5
Rhododendron maximum 6
Rhododendron smirnowii 5
Sciadopitys verticillata 6—7
Taxus spp. and cvs. 5—6
Ternstroemia gymnanthera 6

Thuja spp. and cvs. 5—6
Thujopsis dolobrata 5
Torreya spp. 5—7
Tsuga canadensis cvs. 5—6
Viburnum japonicum 5
Viburnum odoratissimum 5—6
Viburnum rhytidophyllum 5
Viburnum tinus 5

J. Large-scale Screens and Windbreaks: Large Shrubs and Trees

Deciduous and Semievergreen

Acer campestre 7
Alnus spp. 6—7
Caragana arborescens 6
Carpinus betulus 7
Crataegus crus-galli 7
Crataegus laevigata 6
Crataegus ×lavallei 6
Crataegus phaenopyrum 6
Crataegus viridis 7
Elaeagnus angustifolia 6

Euonymus europaea 6
Euonymus hamiltoniana 6
Euonymus latifolia 6
Euonymus sachalinensis 6
Hamamelis virginiana 6
Ilex decidua 6
Maclura pomifera 7
Metasequoia glyptostroboides 8
Populus alba 8
Populus ×berolinensis 7—8

Populus ×canadensis 8
Populus nigra 8
Populus simonii 7
Prunus padus 7
Quercus robur 7—8
Salix alba 8
Salix pentandra 8
Syringa reticulata 6—7
Taxodium distichum 8

Evergreen

Abies spp. 7—8
Araucaria spp. 8
Calocedrus decurrens 7
Cedrus libani 8
Chamaecyparis spp. 6—8
Cinnamomum camphora 7
Cryptomeria japonica 8
Cunninghamia lanceolata 8
×Cupressocyparis leylandii 8
Cupressus spp. 7—8
Daphniphyllum macropodum 6
Eucalyptus spp. 6—7

Feijoa sellowiana 6
Ilex ×altaclarensis 7
Ilex ×attenuata 6
Ilex cornuta 5—6
Ilex integra 6
Ilex ×koehneana 7
Ilex latifolia 6
Ilex opaca 7
Ilex pedunculosa 6
Juniperus chinensis 6—7
Juniperus scopulorum 7
Juniperus virginiana 6—8

Keteleeria spp. 8
Ligustrum lucidum 6
Phyllostachys spp. 6—7
Picea spp. 7—8
Pinus spp. 7—8 (most)
Prunus caroliniana 6—7
Pseudotsuga menziesii 8
Quercus ilex 7
Sequoia sempervirens 8
Sequoiadendron giganteum 8
Thuja spp. 7—8
Tsuga spp. 6—8

K. Street and Avenue Trees

Small

Acer buergeranum 6
Acer ginnala 6
Acer mandshuricum 6
Acer tataricum 6
Acer truncatum 6
Cercis canadensis 6—7
Cornus florida 6—7

Cornus mas 6
Crataegus aprica 6
Crataegus laevigata 6
Crataegus ×lavallei 6
Crataegus marshallii 6
Crataegus nitida 6
Crataegus phaenopyrum 6

Crataegus ×prunifolia 6
Fraxinus cuspidata 6
Fraxinus mariesii 6
Ligustrum japonicum 5—6
Malus tschonoskii 6
Pinus thunbergiana 6—7
Prunus caroliniana 6—7

Prunus serrulata 6
Prunus subhirtella 6

Syringa reticulata 6−7
Tilia mongolica 6

Viburnum prunifolium 6
Viburnum rudifulum 6

Medium

Acer campestre 7
Acer maximowicziana 7
Acer mono 7
Carpinus betulus 7
Carpinus caroliniana 7
Carpinus cordata 7
Carpinus japonica 7
Celtis bungeana 7
Cinnamomum camphora 7
Crataegus crus-galli 7

Crataegus viridis 7
Eucommia ulmoides 7
Fraxinus biltmoreana 7
Fraxinus ornus 7
Fraxinus texensis 7
Fraxinus velutina 7
Halesia carolina 7
Halesia diptera 7
Koelreuteria spp. 7
Morus spp. 7−8

Ostrya virginiana 7−8
Pinus densiflora 7−8
Pinus virginiana 7
Prunus sargentii 7−8
Pyrus calleryana 7
Quercus mongolica 7−8
Sapindus drummondii 7
Ulmus alata 7
Ulmus crassifolia 7−8
Zelkova sinica 7

Large

Acer platanoides 8
Acer pseudoplatanus 8
Acer rubrum 8
Acer saccharum 8
Celtis laevigata 8
Celtis occidentalis 8
Cercidiphyllum japonicum 8
Fraxinus americana 8
Fraxinus pennsylvanica 8
Fraxinus quadrangulata 8
Ginkgo biloba 8
Gleditsia triacanthos 8
Halesia monticola 8
Liquidambar spp. 8
Liriodendron spp. 8
Magnolia grandiflora 8
Phellodendron spp. 7−8

Pinus armandii 8
Pinus elliottii 8
Pinus flexilis 8
Pinus koraiensis 8
Pinus nigra 8
Pinus strobus 8
Pinus taeda 8
Pinus wallichiana 8
Platanus spp. 8
Pterocarya spp. 8
Quercus cerris 8
Quercus coccinea 8
Quercus ellipsoidalis 8
Quercus falcata 8
Quercus imbricaria 8
Quercus macrocarpa 8
Quercus michauxii 8

Quercus muehlenbergii 8
Quercus nigra 8
Quercus palustris 8
Quercus phellos 8
Quercus prinus 8
Quercus rubra 8
Quercus shumardii 8
Quercus virginiana 8
Sophora japonica 8
Tilia spp. 8
Ulmus americana 8
Ulmus carpinifolia 8
Ulmus procera 8
Ulmus ×vegeta 8
Zelkova carpinifolia 8
Zelkova serrata 8

L. Plants for Cold Climates

Adapted to Hardiness Zone 3b or Colder

Abies balsamea 8
Abies veitchii 8
Acer ginnala 6
Acer negundo 7
Acer rubrum 8
Acer saccharinum 8
Acer spicatum 6
Aegopodium podagraria 2
Aesculus glabra 7
Ajuga spp. 2
Alnus incana 6−7
Alnus rugosa 6

Amelanchier arborea 6−7
Amelanchier ×grandiflora 6
Amorpha spp. 3−6
Ampelopsis spp. 1
Andromeda polifolia 2
Arctostaphylos uva-ursi 2
Aronia melanocarpa 3−4
Artemisia abrotanum 4
Betula alleghaniensis 7−8
Betula papyrifera 8
Betula pendula 7−8
Caragana spp. 3−6

Carpinus caroliniana 7
Caryopteris mongholica 3
Cassiope tetragona 2
Ceanothus americanus 3
Celastrus scandens 1&2
Celtis occidentalis 8
Chamaedaphne calyculata
  3−4
Chimaphila umbellata 2
Clematis macropetala 1
Clematis occidentalis 1
Clematis tangutica 1

Clematis virginiana 1
Convallaria majalis 2
Cornus alba 5
Cornus canadensis 2
Cornus purpusii 5
Cornus racemosa 5
Cornus rugosa 5
Cornus sericea 5
Coronilla varia 2
Corylus americana 5
Corylus cornuta 5
Cotoneaster acutifolius 5
Cotoneaster lucidus 5
Cotoneaster racemiflorus 5
Crataegus chrysocarpa 5
Crataegus crus-galli 7
Crataegus mollis 6
Crataegus ×mordenensis 6
Crataegus pinnatifida 6
Crataegus ×prunifolia 6
Crataegus punctata 6
Daphne giraldii 3
Daphne mezereum 3
Diervilla lonicera 3
Elaeagnus angustifolia 6
Elaeagnus commutata 5
Empetrum spp. 2
Epigaea repens 2
Epimedium spp. 2
Euonymus atropurpurea 6
Euonymus nana 3
Euphorbia cyparissias 2
Fragaria virginiana 2
Fraxinus americana 8
Fraxinus nigra 8
Fraxinus pennsylvanica 8
Gaultheria procumbens 2
Genista sagittalis 3
Genista tinctoria 3
Halimodendron halodendron 4
Hemerocallis spp. 3
Hippophaë rhamnoides 6
Hosta spp. 2−3
Juniperus communis 2−6
Juniperus horizontalis 2
Juniperus sabina 2−5
Juniperus scopulorum 7
Juniperus virginiana 3−8
Kalmia angustifolia 3
Kalmia poliifolia 3
Larix laricina 8

Ledum spp. 2−3
Loiseleuria procumbens 2
Lonicera caerulea 4
Lonicera maackii 6
Lonicera spinosa 3
Lonicera tatarica 5
Lonicera ×xylosteoides 5
Lonicera xylosteum 5
Lotus corniculatus 2
Malus ×adstringens 7
Malus baccata 7
Malus pumila 7
Malus ×purpurea 6
Malus ×robusta 6
Myrica gale 4
Ostrya virginiana 7−8
Parthenocissus inserta 1&2
Parthenocissus quinquefolia
   1&2
Philadelphus lewisii 4−5
Philadelphus schrenkii 5
Phlox subulata 2
Physocarpus opulifolius 4−5
Picea abies 3−8
Picea engelmanii 8
Picea glauca 8
Picea mariana 7−8
Picea pungens 8
Picea rubens 8
Pinus banksiana 8
Pinus cembra 6−8
Pinus mugo 4−6
Pinus resinosa 8
Pinus sibirica 8
Pinus strobus 8
Pinus sylvestris 7−8
Populus angustifolia 7
Populus balsamifera 8
Populus ×berolinensis 7−8
Populus ×canadensis 8
Populus deltoides 8
Populus nigra 8
Populus simonii 7
Populus tremula 6−8
Populus tremuloides 6−8
Populus trichocarpa 8
Potentilla davurica 3
Potentilla ×friedrichsenii 3
Potentilla fruticosa 3−4
Potentilla grandiflora 3
Potentilla parviflora 3

Potentilla tridentata 2
Prinsepia sinensis 5
Prunus besseyi 3
Prunus ×cistena 5
Prunus japonica 4
Prunus maackii 7
Prunus nigra 5−6
Prunus padus 7
Prunus pensylvanica 7
Prunus pumila 4
Prunus serotina 8
Prunus tenella 4
Prunus tomentosa 5
Prunus virginiana 6
Pseudotsuga menziesii 8
Pyrus ussuriensis 7
Quercus bicolor 8
Quercus ellipsoidalis 8
Quercus macrocarpa 8
Quercus mongolica 7−8
Quercus rubra 8
Rhamnus cathartica 6
Rhamnus davurica 6
Rhamnus pallasii 4
Rhododendron canadense 6
Rhododendron lapponicum 2
Rhododendron prinophyllum
   5
Rhus aromatica 4−5
Rhus glabra 6
Rhus trilobata 4−5
Rhus typhina 6
Ribes spp. 4−5
Rosa acicularis 3
Rosa arkansana 3
Rosa blanda 4
Rosa foetida 5
Rosa rubrifolia 4−5
Rosa rugosa 4
Salix alba 8
Salix caprea 5−6
Salix discolor 6
Salix exigua 6
Salix fragilis 7
Salix nigra 7
Salix pentandra 8
Salix purpurea 5
Salix repens 2−3
Salix uva-ursi 2
Sambucus racemosa 5
Securinega suffruticosa 4

Sempervivum tectorum 2
Shepherdia spp. 5−6
Sorbaria sorbifolia 4
Sorbus americana 7
Sorbus ×arnoldiana 7
Sorbus aucuparia 7
Sorbus decora 7
Sorbus discolor 7
Sorbus ×hybrida 7
Sorbus scopulina 6
Sorbus ×thuringiaca 7
Sorbus tianshanica 6
Spiraea alba 4
Spiraea ×arguta 4
Spiraea betulifolia 3
Spiraea douglasii 5
Spiraea latifolia 4
Spiraea menziesii 4
Spiraea tomentosa 3
Spiraea trilobata 4

Spiraea ×vanhouttei 4
Staphylea trifolia 6
Symphoricarpos albus 3
Symphoricarpos orbiculatus 3
Syringa ×henryi 5
Syringa ×hyacinthiflora 6
Syringa ×josiflexa 5
Syringa ×josikaea 5
Syringa meyeri 4
Syringa microphylla 4
Syringa patula 5
Syringa ×prestoniae 5
Syringa pubescens 4
Syringa reticulata 6−7
Syringa villosa 5
Syringa vulgaris 6
Taxus canadensis 3−4
Thuja occidentalis 3−7
Tilia americana 8
Tilia cordata 8

Tilia ×europaea 8
Tilia mongolica 6−7
Tilia platyphyllos 8
Ulmus americana 8
Ulmus pumila 7−8
Vaccinium angustifolium 2−3
Vaccinium vitis-idaea 2
Viburnum acerifolium 4
Viburnum alnifolium 5
Viburnum burejaeticum 5
Viburnum cassinoides 4
Viburnum lantana 6
Viburnum lentago 6
Viburnum opulus 5
Viburnum prunifolium 6
Viburnum rafinesquianum 4
Viburnum trilobum 5
Viola sororia 2
Vitis riparia 1

Adapted to Hardiness Zone 4b, but not Zone 3b

Abeliophyllum distichum 4
Abies concolor 8
Abies koreana 7
Acanthopanax sieboldianus 5
Acer mandshuricum 6
Acer pensylvanicum 7
Acer platanoides 8
Acer tataricum 6
Acer truncatum 6
Actinidia arguta 1
Actinidia kolomikta 1
Actinidia polygama 1
Aesculus hippocastanum 8
Akebia spp. 1&2
Alnus glutinosa 7
Amelanchier alnifolia 4−5
Amelanchier florida 4−6
Amelanchier laevis 6
Amelanchier spicata 3−4
Amelanchier stolonifera 4
Aralia elata 6−7
Aristolochia durior 1
Aronia arbutifolia 5
Aronia prunifolia 5
Asarum canadense 2
Baccharis halimifolia 5
Berberis thunbergii 4
Berberis vulgaris 5

Betula lenta 7−8
Betula nigra 8
Betula populifolia 6−7
Buddleia alternifolia 5
Calycanthus spp. 4−5
Campsis radicans 1
Carya cordiformis 8
Caryopteris ×clandonensis 3
Catalpa spp. 7−8
Ceanothus ovatus 3
Cephalanthus occidentalis 5
Chaenomeles japonica 3
Chaenomeles speciosa 4
Cladrastis lutea 7
Clematis apiifolia 1
Clematis ×jackmanii 1
Clematis ×jouiniana 1
Clematis maximowicziana 1
Clematis texensis 1
Clematis vitalba 1
Clethra alnifolia 5
Comptonia peregrina 2
Cornus alternifolia 6
Cornus amomum 5
Cornus drummondii 5−6
Cornus sanguinea 5
Corylus avellana 5
Cotoneaster multiflorus 5

Crataegus ×lavallei 6
Crataegus nitida 6
Crataegus phaenopyrum 6
Crataegus succulenta 6
Daphne ×burkwoodii 3
Daphe cneorum 2
Deutzia parviflora 4
Diervilla rivularis 4
Diervilla sessilifolia 4
Dirca palustris 4
Euonymus alata 5
Euonymus bungeana 6
Euonymus europaea 6
Euonymus fortunei 1&2
Euonymus hamiltoniana 6
Euonymus obovata 2
Fagus grandifolia 8
Fontanesia fortunei 5
Fraxinus excelsior 8
Fraxinus holotricha 7
Fraxinus quadrangulata 8
Gaultheria hispidula 2
Gleditsia triacanthos 8
Gymnocladus dioicus 8
Hamamelis virginiana 6
Hydrangea arborescens 3
Hydrangea paniculata 6
Hypericum kalmianum 3

Hypericum prolificum 3
Ilex laevigata 5
Ilex rugosa 3
Ilex verticillata 5
Juglans cinerea 8
Juniperus 2—7
Kerria japonica 4
Larix decidua 8
Larix kaempferi 8
Ligustrum amurense 5
Ligustrum obtusifolium 4—5
Ligustrum vulgare 4—6
Lonicera ×amoena 5
Lonicera ×bella 5
Lonicera ×brownii 1&2
Lonicera ×heckrottii 1&2
Lonicera hirsuta 1&2
Lonicera sempervirens 1&2
Maackia amurensis 7
Magnolia acuminata 8
Magnolia tripetala 7
Malus ×arnoldiana 6
Malus floribunda 6
Malus hupehensis 6
Malus ioensis 6
Malus ×magdeburgensis 6
Malus ×micromalus 6
Malus ×prunifolia 6
Malus sargentii 5
Malus sieboldii 6
Malus toringoides 6
Malus tschonoskii 6
Mitchella repens 2
Morus spp. 7—8
Myrica pensylvanica 4—5
Nemopanthus mucronatus 5
Parthenocissus tricuspidata 1
Paxistima canbyi 2
Phellodendron spp. 7—8
Philadelphus coronarius 5
Philadelphus ×lemoinei 4
   (most)
Philadelphus ×virginalis 4—5
   (most)
Phlox divaricata 2
Picea omorika 8

Pinus albicaulis 6
Pinus aristata 4—6
Pinus flexilis 8
Pinus koraiensis 8
Pinus nigra 8
Pinus pumila 4—5
Pinus rigida 7—8
Podophyllum peltatum 2
Polygonum spp. 1&3—5
Populus alba 8
Populus grandidentata 6—7
Populus maximowiczii 8
Potentilla cinerea 2
Potentilla crantzii 2
Prinsepia uniflora 4
Prunus americana 5
Prunus cerasifera 6
Prunus glandulosa 4
Prunus maritima 4
Prunus triloba 5—6
Ptelea trifoliata 6
Quercus alba 8
Quercus velutina 8
Rhamnus frangula 6
Rhododendron catawbiense 5
Rhododendron japonicum 4
Rhododendron maximum 6
Rhododendron micranthum 5
Rhododendron viscosum 5
Rhus copallina 6
Robinia ×ambigua 7
Robinia hispida 4
Robinia pseudoacacia 8
Robinia viscosa 5
Rosa canina 5
Rosa ×harisonii 4
Rosa hugonis 5
Rosa nitida 3
Rosa palustris 4
Rosa primula 4
Rosa setigera 5
Rosa villosa 4
Rubus deliciosus 5
Rubus hispidus 2
Rubus odoratus 5
Salix repens 2—3

Salix rosmarinifolia 4
Salix ×sepulcralis 8
Sambucus canadensis 5
Sambucus nigra 6
Sambucus pubens 5
Sedum spp. 2
Sorbus alnifolia 8
Spiraea albiflora 4
Spiraea ×billiardii 4
Spiraea ×bumalda 3
Spiraea henryi 5
Spiraea nipponica 5
Spiraea thunbergii 4
Symphoricarpos rivularis 4
Syringa ×chinensis 6
Syringa oblata 5
Syringa pekinensis 6
Syringa ×persica 4
Syringa reflexa 5
Syringa ×swegiflexa 5
Taxus cuspidata 4—6
Taxus ×hunnewelliana 5
Thuja plicata 7—8
Tilia dasystyla 8
Tilia ×euchlora 8
Tsuga canadensis 3—8
Ulmus glabra 8
Ulmus rubra 8
Ulmus thomasii 8
Ulmus ×vegeta 8
Vaccinium corymbosum 5
Viburnum bitchiuense 5
Viburnum ×carlcephalum 5
Viburnum carlesii 4
Viburnum dentatum 6
Viburnum ×juddii 5
Viburnum lantana 6
Viburnum sargentii 5
Vinca minor 2
Waldsteinia fragarioides 2
Weigela florida 5
Weigela middendorffiana 4
Weigela praecox 4
Yucca glauca 3
Zanthoxylum americanum 6

M. Plants for Warm Climates

Adapted to Hardiness Zone 9a or Warmer

Abelia ×grandiflora 4−5
Abies firma 8
Acer barbatum 7
Acer davidii 7
Acer grosseri 6
Acer palmatum 6
Acer rubrum 8
Acer saccharinum 8
Actinidia chinensis 1
Adina rubella 5
Aegopodium podagraria 2
Aesculus parviflora 5
Aesculus pavia 6
Aesculus splendens 5
Agave americana 4
Ailanthus altissima 7−8
Ajuga spp. 2
Akebia spp. 1&2
Albizia julibrissin 6
Aleurites fordii 6
Alnus rugosa 6
Amorpha spp. 3−6
Ampelopsis spp. 1
Antigonon leptopus 1
Aralia spp. 6−7
Araucaria spp. 8
Arctostaphylos manzanita 5
Ardisia spp. 2−4
Aronia arbutifolia 5
Aronia prunifolia 5
Artemisia schmidtiana 2
Arundinaria spp. 2−6
Aspidistra elatior 3
Aucuba japonica 5
Baccharis halimifolia 5
Bambusa glaucescens 5−6
Berberis candidula 3
Berberis ×chenaultii 4
Berberis gagnepainii 4
Berberis julianae 4
Berberis ×mentorensis 4
Berberis panlanensis 4
Berberis sargentiana 4
Berberis thunbergii 4
Berberis verruculosa 3
Berberis vulgaris 5
Berberis wisleyensis 4

Betula nigra 8
Bignonia capreolata 1
Broussonetia papyrifera 7
Bumelia lanuginosa 6
Butia capitata 6
Buxus spp. 3−4
Callicarpa americana 4
Callistemon citrinus 5−6
Calocedrus decurrens 7
Calycanthus spp. 4−5
Camellia spp. 6
Campsis spp. 1
Carya glabra 8
Carya illinoinensis 8
Carya tomentosa 8
Caryopteris incana 4
Cassia corymbosa 5
Castanea pumila 6
Catalpa spp. 7−8
Cedrela sinensis 6−7
Cedrus spp. 7
Celtis bungeana 7
Celtis laevigata 8
Cephalanthus occidentalis 5
Cephalotaxus spp. 4−5
Ceratiola ericoides 4
Cercidiphyllum japonicum 8
Cercis spp. 6−7
Chaenomeles spp. 3−4
Chamaecyparis thyoides 5−7
Chimonanthus praecox 5
Chionanthus spp. 6
Choisya ternata 5
Cinnamomum camphora 7
Cistus spp. 3−5
Clematis apiifolia 1
Clematis armandii 1
Clematis delavayi 1
Clematis flammula 1
Clematis ×jouiniana 1
Clematis maximowicziana 1
Clematis vitalba 1
Clethra spp. 5−6
Cleyera japonica 5
Cliftonia monophylla 5
Clytostoma callistegioides 1
Cocculus carolinus 1

Colutea arborescens 5
Cornus amomum 5
Cornus florida 6−7
Cornus stricta 5
Coronilla varia 2
Corylopsis spp. 4−5
Cotoneaster congestus 3
Cotoneaster conspicuus 3
Cotoneaster dammeri 2
Cotoneaster henryanus 5
Cotoneaster lacteus 5
Cotoneaster microphyllus 3
Cotoneaster pannosus 4
Cotoneaster salicifolius 5
Cotoneaster ×watereri 6
Crataegus aprica 6
Crataegus marshallii 6
Crataegus viridis 7
Cryptomeria japonica 8
Cunninghamia lanceolata 8
×Cupressocyparis leylandii 8
Cupressus spp. 7−8
Cycas revoluta 3−4
Cydonia sinensis 6
Cyrilla racemiflora 6
Cyrtomium falcatum 3
Cytisus spp. 2−4,6
Daphne collina 3
Daphne genkwa 3
Daphniphyllum macropodum 6
Decumaria barbara 1&2
Diospyros spp. 7
Disanthus cercidifolius 5
Duchesnea indica 2
Edgeworthia papyrifera 4
Elaeagnus ×ebbingei 5
Elaeagnus macrophylla 5
Elaeagnus multiflora 5
Elaeagnus pungens 5
Elaeagnus umbellata 5
Elliottia racemosa 5−6
Eriobotrya spp. 6
Escallonia spp. 3−6
Eucalyptus spp. 6−7
Euonymus americana 5
Euonymus japonica 5

Euonymus kiautschovica 5
Euphorbia cyparissias 2
Eurya spp. 3−5
Exochorda spp. 5−6
Fagus spp. 8
×Fatshedera lizei 4
Fatsia japonica 4−5
Feijoa sellowiana 6
Ficus carica 5−6
Ficus pumila 1
Firmiana simplex 6−7
Fontanesia phillyreoides 5
Forestiera acuminata 5−6
Fothergilla spp. 3−5
Fraxinus americana 8
Fraxinus biltmoreana 7
Fraxinus caroliniana 7
Fraxinus cuspidata 6
Fraxinus mariesii 6
Fraxinus pennsylvanica 8
Fraxinus texensis 7
Fraxinus tomentosa 8
Fraxinus velutina 7
Fuchsia magellanica 3−4
Galium odoratum 2
Gardenia jasminoides 4
Gelsemium sempervirens 1&2
Genista cinerea 3−4
Genista hispanica 2
Gleditsia triacanthos 8
Gordonia lasianthus 7
Halesia carolina 7
Halesia diptera 7
Hamamelis ×intermedia 6
Hamamelis japonica 6
Hamamelis mollis 6
Hamamelis vernalis 5
Hamamelis virginiana 6
Hedera canariensis 1&2
Hedera colchica 1&2
Hedera helix 1&2
Helianthemum nummularium
    2
Hemerocallis spp. 3
Hibiscus rosa-sinensis 6
Hibiscus syriacus 5
Hosta spp. 2−3
Hydrangea arborescens 3
Hydrangea macrophylla 3
Hydrangea quercifolia 4−5
Hypericum beanii 3

Hypericum calycinum 2
Hypericum forrestii 3
Hypericum frondosum 3
Hypericum hookeranum 4
Hypericum kouytchense 3
Hypericum ×moseranum 3
Hypericum patulum 3
Iberis gibraltarica 3
Iberis pruitii 2
Iberis saxatilis 2
Idesia polycarpa 7
Ilex spp. 3−6
Illicium spp. 5−6
Indigofera divaricata 3
Itea spp. 4−5
Jasminum spp. 1&3−5
Juglans nigra 8
Juniperus chinensis 2−7
Juniperus conferta 2
Juniperus horizontalis 2
Juniperus virginiana 3−8
Kadsura japonica 1
Kalmia latifolia 5
Kerria japonica 4
Keteleeria spp. 8
Koelreuteria spp. 7
Lagerstroemia indica 6
Lamiastrum galeobdolon 2
Laurus nobilis 6
Leitneria floridana 5−6
Leptodermis oblonga 3
Lespedeza cuneata 3
Leucophyllum frutescens 5
Leucothoë spp. 4−5
Leycesteria formosa 4
Ligustrum japonicum 5−6
Ligustrum lucidum 6
Ligustrum ovalifolium 5
Ligustrum quihoui 5
Ligustrum sinense 5
Lindera spp. 4−6
Liquidambar spp. 8
Liriodendron spp. 8
Liriope spp. 2
Lonicera ×brownii 1&2
Lonicera etrusca 1&2
Lonicera flava 1&2
Lonicera fragrantissima 5
Lonicera henryi 1&2
Lonicera ×heckrottii 1&2
Lonicera hildebrandiana 1&2

Lonicera hirsuta 1&2
Lonicera japonica 1&2
Lonicera nitida 4
Lonicera periclymenum 1&2
Lonicera pileata 3
Lonicera ×purpusii 5
Lonicera sempervirens 1&2
Lonicera standishii 4
Lonicera ×tellmanniana 1&2
Lonicera tragophylla 1&2
Loropetalum chinense 5
Lotus corniculatus 2
Lycium halimifolium 5
Lyonia spp. 4
Macfadyena unguis-cati 1
Maclura pomifera 7
Magnolia fraseri 7
Magnolia grandiflora 8
Magnolia heptapeta 7
Magnolia hypoleuca 7−8
Magnolia ×kewensis 7
Magnolia kobus 7
Magnolia ×loebneri 6−7
Magnolia macrophylla 7
Magnolia ×proctoriana 6
Magnolia quinquepeta 5
Magnolia salicifolia 7
Magnolia sieboldii 6
Magnolia ×soulangiana 7
Magnolia sprengeri 7
Magnolia stellata 5
Magnolia ×thompsoniana 7
Magnolia tripetala 7
Magnolia virginiana 6−7
Magnolia ×wieseneri 6
×Mahoberberis spp. 3−4
Mahonia spp. 3−5
Malus angustifolia 6
Malus florentina 5
Melia azedarach 6
Menispermum canadense 1&2
Metasequoia glyptostroboides 8
Michelia figo 5
Mitchella repens 2
Morus spp. 7−8
Myrica cerifera 6−7
Myrica pensylvanica 4−5
Myrtus communis 4−5
Nandina domestica 4−5
Nepeta mussinii 2
Nerium oleander 6

Nyssa spp. 8
Ophiopogon japonicus 2
Orixa japonica 5
Osmanthus spp. 4−6
Ostrya virginiana 7−8
Oxydendrum arboreum 7−8
Paliurus spina-christi 6
Parkinsonia aculeata 6
Parrotia persica 6−7
Parrotiopsis jacquemontiana 6
Parthenocissus henryana 1&2
Parthenocissus inserta 1&2
Parthenocissus quinquefolia
   1&2
Passiflora spp. 1&2
Paulownia tomentosa 7
Pernettya mucronata 3
Persea spp. 6−7
Philadelphus inodorus 5
Phillyrea decora 5
Phoenix canariensis 7
Photinia ×fraseri 6
Photinia glabra 5
Photinia serrulata 6
Phyllostachys spp. 6−7
Picrasma quassioides 6
Pieris forrestii 5
Pieris japonica 4−5
Pieris phillyreifolia 1&3
Pileostegia viburnoides 1&2
Pinckneya pubens 6
Pinus armandii 8
Pinus bungeana 6−7
Pinus echinata 8
Pinus elliottii 8
Pinus glabra 8
Pinus halepensis 7
Pinus palustris 8
Pinus parviflora 7−8
Pinus peuce 7
Pinus pinaster 7−8
Pinus taeda 8
Pinus thunbergiana 6−7
Pinus virginiana 7
Pinus wallichiana 8
Pistacia chinensis 8
Pittosporum tobira 5
Platanus spp. 8
Podocarpus macrophyllus 5−7
Podophyllum peltatum 2
Polygonum cuspidatum 3−5

Poncirus trifoliata 6
Populus alba 8
Populus ×berolinensis 7−8
Populus ×canadensis 8
Populus deltoides 8
Populus nigra 8
Prunus angustifolia 5
Prunus armeniaca 7
Prunus ×blireiana 6
Prunus campanulata 6
Prunus caroliana 6−7
Prunus cerasifera 6
Prunus dulcis 6
Prunus glandulosa 4
Prunus laurocerasus 4−6
Prunus lusitanica 5−6
Prunus mexicana 6
Prunus mume 6−7
Prunus persica 6
Prunus salicina 6−7
Prunus sargentii 7−8
Prunus serotina 8
Prunus triloba 5−6
Prunus yedoensis 6
Ptelea trifoliata 6
Pterocarya spp. 8
Pterostyrax spp. 6−7
Pueraria lobata 1&3
Punica granatum 6
Pyracantha spp. 4−6
Pyrus calleryana 7
Quercus acuta 7
Quercus acutissima 7
Quercus alba 8
Quercus cerris 8
Quercus coccinea 8
Quercus falcata 8
Quercus glauca 7
Quercus ilex 7
Quercus imbricaria 8
Quercus laurifolia 8
Quercus lyrata 8
Quercus macrocarpa 8
Quercus marilandica 7
Quercus michauxii 8
Quercus nigra 8
Quercus phellos 7−8
Quercus prinus 8
Quercus robur 7−8
Quercus shumardii 8
Quercus stellata 7−8

Quercus suber 7
Quercus variabilis 8
Quercus velutina 8
Quercus virginiana 7
Raphiolepis spp. 3−4
Rhamnus caroliniana 6
Rhapidophyllum hystrix 3
Rhododendron arborescens 5
Rhododendron atlanticum 3
Rhododendron austrinum 5
Rhododendron canescens 5
Rhododendron chapmanii 4
Rhododendron fortunei 5
Rhododendron griffithianum 6
Rhododendron indicum 4
Rhododendron kaempferi 5
Rhododendron kiusianum 3
Rhododendron molle 4
Rhododendron mucronatum 4
Rhododendron obtusum 3
Rhododendron prunifolium 5
Rhododendron serrulatum 3
Rhododendron simsii 5
Rhododendron viscosum 5
Rhus spp. 4−6 (most)
Robinia spp. 4&7−8
Rohdea japonica 3
Rosa ×alba 4
Rosa banksiae 1
Rosa bracteata 1&5
Rosa canina 5
Rosa centifolia 4
Rosa chinensis 3
Rosa damascena 4
Rosa eglanteria 4
Rosa gallica 3
Rosa laevigata 1&5
Rosa moschata 3
Rosa multiflora 5
Rosa odorata 3
Rosa roxburghii 5
Rosa setigera 5
Rosa villosa 4
Rosa wichuraiana 1&2
Ruscus aculeatus 3
Sabal minor 3−4
Salix spp. 2−8 (most)
Sambucus canadensis 5
Sambucus nigra 6
Santolina spp. 3
Sapindus drummondii 7

Sapium sebiferum 7
Sarcococca spp. 4
Sasa veitchii 3
Sassafras albidum 7−8
Saxifraga stolonifera 2
Schisandra spp. 1
Sedum spp. 2
Sempervivum tectorum 2
Sequoia sempervirens 8
Sequoiadendron giganteum 8
Serenoa repens 3−4
Sesbania punicea 5
Skimmia reevesiana 3
Smilax spp. 1
Sophora spp. 5−8
Spartium junceum 5
Spiraea alba 4
Spiraea albiflora 3
Spiraea ×billiardii 4
Spiraea bullata 3
Spiraea ×bumalda 3
Spiraea cantoniensis 5
Spiraea japonica 3
Spiraea latifolia 4
Spiraea prunifolia 5
Spiraea thunbergii 4
Spiraea veitchii 5
Spiraea wilsonii 5
Stachyurus praecox 5

Stewartia malacodendron 6
Styrax americanus 5
Styrax grandifolius 6
Symplocos tinctoria 6
Syringa laciniata 4
Taiwania cryptomerioides 8
Tamarix spp. 4−5
Taxodium distichum 8
Taxus floridana 5
Ternstroemia gymnanthera 6
Teucrium chamaedrys 2
Thujopsis dolobrata 5
Tilia heterophylla 8
Tilia petiolaris 8
Tilia tomentosa 8
Torreya spp. 5−7
Trachelospermum spp. 1&2
Trachycarpus fortunei 6
Trifolium incarnatum 3
Tripetaleia paniculata 4
Ulmus spp. 7−8 (most)
Umbellularia californica 7−8
Vaccinium arboreum 6
Vaccinium ashei 4−6
Vaccinium corymbosum 5
Viburnum ×bodnantense 5
Viburnum bracteatum 5
Viburnum ×burkwoodii 5
Viburnum davidii 3

Viburnum dentatum 6
Viburnum grandiflorum 5
Viburnum japonicum 5
Viburnum molle 5
Viburnum nudum 5
Viburnum odoratissimum 5−6
Viburnum prunifolium 6
Viburnum rufidulum 6
Viburnum suspensum 4
Viburnum tinus 5
Viburnum utile 4
Vinca major 2
Viola odorata 2
Vitex spp. 4−6
Vitis coignetiae 1
Vitis rotundifolia 1
Weigela floribunda 5
Weigela florida 5
Weigela praecox 4
Wisteria spp. 1
Xanthoceras sorbifolium 6
Xanthorhiza simplicissima 2
Yucca spp. 3−5 (most)
Zamia floridana 3
Zanthoxylum spp. 6
Zelkova spp. 7−8
Zenobia pulverulenta 4
Ziziphus jujuba 6

Adapted to Hardiness Zone 8a, but not Zone 9a

Abies cephalonica 8
Abies pinsapo 8
Acer buergeranum 6
Acer campestre 7
Acer circinatum 6
Acer diabolicum 6
Acer japonicum 6
Acer negundo 7
Acer rufinerve 7
Actinidia arguta 1
Actinidia kolomikta 1
Actinidia polygama 1
Aesculus ×carnea 8
Aesculus glabra 7
Aesculus hippocastanum 8
Aesculus octandra 8
Alnus glutinosa 7
Amelanchier alnifolia 4−5
Amelanchier arborea 6−7
Amelanchier florida 4−6

Amelanchier ×grandiflora 6
Amelanchier laevis 6
Amelanchier spicata 3−4
Amelanchier stolonifera 4
Artemisia spp. 3−5
Asarum spp. 2
Asimina triloba 6−7
Berberis buxifolia 5
Berberis gilgiana 4
Berberis koreana 4
Betula albo-sinensis 8
Callicarpa dichotoma 4
Callicarpa japonica 4
Carpinus cordata 7
Carpinus japonica 7
Carya cordiformis 8
Carya laciniosa 8
Carya ovata 8
Caryopteris ×clandonensis 3
Celastrus spp. 1&2

Celtis occidentalis 8
Chamaecyparis lawsoniana
  3−7
Chamaecyparis obtusa 3−7
Chamaecyparis pisifera 3−8
Cladrastis lutea 7
Clematis alpina 1
Clematis drummondii 1
Clematis florida 1
Clematis lanuginosa 1
Clematis ×lawsoniana 1
Clematis montana 1
Clematis patens 1
Clematis texensis 1
Clematis viorna 1
Clerodendrum spp. 4−6
Comptonia peregrina 2
Cornus alba 5
Cornus controversa 7
Cornus coreana 7−8

Cornus drummondii 5-6
Cornus hessei 3
Cornus mas 6
Cornus officinalis 6
Cornus purpusii 5
Cornus sanguinea 5
Cornus sericea 5
Corylus americana 5
Corylus avellana 5
Corylus colurna 7-8
Corylus cornuta 5
Corylus maxima 6
Cotoneaster adpressus 2
Cotoneaster apiculatus 3
Cotoneaster dielsianus 4
Cotoneaster franchetii 5
Cotoneaster frigidus 6
Cotoneaster horizontalis 3
Crataegus nitida 6
Crataegus phaenopyrum 6
Croton alabamense 5
Daphne ×mantensiana 3
Daphne odora 4
Davidia involucrata 6-7
Deutzia spp. 3-5
Diervilla rivularis 4
Diervilla sessilifolia 4
Dirca palustris 4
Enkianthus spp. 4-6
Epigaea repens 2
Erica cinerea 2
Erica ×darleyensis 2
Erica mediterranea 3
Eucommia ulmoides 7
Euonymus alata 5
Evodia spp. 6-7
Fontanesia fortunei 5
Forsythia ×intermedia 5
Forsythia suspensa 4-5
Forsythia viridissima 5
Fragaria ×ananassa 2
Fraxinus bungeana 6
Fraxinus excelsior 8
Fraxinus holotricha 7
Fraxinus ornus 7
Fraxinus quadrangulata 8
Galax urceolata 2
Genista pilosa 2
Genista sagittalis 3
Genista tinctoria 3
Ginkgo biloba 8
Halesia monticola 8

Hemiptelea davidii 6
Holodiscus discolor 6
Hydrangea anomala 1&2
Hydrangea paniculata 6
Hypericum buckleyi 2
Hypericum kalmianum 3
Hypericum prolificum 3
Indigofera incarnata 3
Juglans ailanthifolia 7
Juniperus communis 2-6
Juniperus rigida 6
Juniperus sabina 2-5
Juniperus squamata 2-5
Kalopanax pictus 8
Kolkwitzia amabilis 5
Lavandula angustifolia 3
Leiophyllum buxifolium 2
Lespedeza cyrtobotrya 5
Lespedeza japonica 5
Lespedeza thunbergii 5
Ligustrum amurense 5
Ligustrum ×ibolium 5
Ligustrum obtusifolium 4-5
Ligustrum ×vicaryi 5
Ligustrum vulgare 4-6
Lonicera alpigena 5
Lonicera ×amoena 5
Lonicera ×bella 5
Lonicera korolkowii 5
Lonicera maackii 6
Lonicera morrowii 4
Lonicera spinosa 3
Lonicera syringantha 5
Lonicera tatarica 5
Lonicera ×xylosteoides 5
Lonicera xylosteum 5
Magnolia acuminata 8
Magnolia ×brooklynensis 7
Malus ×arnoldiana 6
Malus ×atrosanguinea 6
Malus ×dawsoniana 6
Malus florentina 5
Malus floribunda 6
Malus halliana 5
Malus hupehensis 6
Malus sargentii 5
Malus ×scheideckeri 6
Malus sieboldii 6
Malus spectabilis 6
Malus toringoides 6
Malus tschonoskii 6
Myrica gale 4

Neillia sinensis 4
Neviusia alabamensis 4
Orixa japonica 5
Parthenocissus tricuspidata 1
Paxistima myrsinites 3
Periploca graeca 1
Philadelphus purpurascens
   5-6
Philadelphus ×splendens 5
Philadelphus ×virginalis 4-5
Phlox spp. 2
Photinia villosa 6
Picea asperata 8
Picea omorika 8
Picea orientalis 8
Pieris floribunda 4
Pinus contorta 6-8
Pinus edulis 7
Pinus jeffreyi 8
Pinus lambertiana 8
Pinus nigra 8
Pinus ponderosa 8
Pinus sylvestris 7-8
Polygonum aubertii 1
Potentilla davurica 3
Potentilla ×friedrichsenii 3
Potentilla fruticosa 3-4
Potentilla grandiflora 3
Potentilla parviflora 3
Potentilla tridentata 2
Prunus avium 6-8
Prunus cerasus 6-7
Prunus ×cistena 5
Prunus domestica 6-7
Prunus nipponica 6
Prunus serrula 6
Prunus serrulata 6
Prunus subhirtella 6
Prunus yedoensis 6
Pseudolarix kaempferi 8
Quercus bicolor 8
Quercus muehlenbergii 8
Quercus palustris 8
Rhamnus frangula 6
Rhododendron arboreum 7
Rhododendron bakeri 3-5
Rhododendron calendulaceum
   5
Rhododendron flammeum 5
Rhododendron japonicum 4
Rhododendron ×kosteranum 4
Rhododendron ×laetevirens 4

Rhododendron luteum 5
Rhododendron minus 5—6
Rhododendron
    periclymenoides 4
Rhododendron ponticum 5
Rhododendron
    schlippenbachii 5
Rhododendron vaseyi 5
Rhododendron yakusimanum
    3
Rhododendron yedoense 4
Rhodotypos scandens 4
Rhus typhina 6
Rosa carolina 3
Rosa foetida 5
Rosa ×harisonii 4
Rosa hugonis 5
Rosa palustris 4
Rosa primula 4
Rosa rubrifolia 4—5
Rosa spinosissima 3
Sasa palmata 4
Sciadopitys verticillata 6—7
Shortia galacifolia 2
Skimmia japonica 3
Sorbaria spp. 4—5

Spiraea betulifolia 3
Spiraea douglasii 5
Spiraea henryi 5
Spiraea menziesii 4
Spiraea nipponica 5
Spiraea tomentosa 3
Spiraea trilobata 4
Spiraea ×vanhouttei 4
Staphylea colchica 6
Staphylea holocarpa 6
Stephanandra spp. 4
Stewartia spp. 6—7 (most)
Styrax japonicus 6
Styrax obassia 6
Symplocos paniculata 6
Syringa ×chinensis 6
Syringa ×persica 4
Taxus baccata 3—6
Taxus ×media 4—6
Thuja orientalis 4—7
Tiarella cordifolia 2
Tilia americana 8
Tilia cordata 8
Tilia dasystyla 8
Tilia ×euchlora 8
Tilia ×europaea 8

Tilia mongolica 6—7
Tilia platyphyllos 8
Tripterygium regelii 1&5
Tsuga spp. 3—8
Viburnum buddleifolium 4
Viburnum ×carlcephalum 5
Viburnum carlesii 4
Viburnum dilatatum 5
Viburnum farreri 5
Viburnum ×juddii 5
Viburnum macrocephalum 5
Viburnum opulus 5
Viburnum plicatum 5
Viburnum rafinesquianum 4
Viburnum ×rhytidocarpum 5
Viburnum ×rhytidophylloides
    5
Viburnum rhytidophyllum 5
Viburnum sargentii 5
Viburnum setigerum 5
Viburnum sieboldii 6
Viburnum trilobum 5
Viburnum wrightii 5
Vinca minor 2
Viola sororia 2
Vitis amurensis 1

N. Plants that Require Full Sun in Summer, in at Least Parts of Their Useful Ranges

Abies lasiocarpa 8
Aesculus glabra 7
Ailanthus altissima 7—8
Albizia julibrissin 6
Aleurites fordii 6
Amorpha spp. 3&6
Antigonon leptopus 1
Baccharis halimifolia 5
Bumelia lanuginosa 6
Callistemon citrinus 5—6
Caragana spp. 3—6
Carya spp. 8
Caryopteris spp. 3—4
Castanea spp. 6—8
Ceanothus spp. 3
Celtis spp. 7—8
Ceratiola ericoides 4
Cinnamomum camphora 7
Cistus spp. 3—5
Colutea arborescens 5
Corema conradii 2

Coronilla varia 2
Corylus spp. 5—8
Cotoneaster spp. 2—6 (most)
Crataegus spp. 5—7 (most)
Cytisus spp. 2—4&6
Elaeagnus spp. 5—6
    (deciduous spp.)
Empetrum spp. 2
Eucalyptus spp. 6—7
Euphorbia cyparissias 2
Fraxinus pennsylvanica 8
Fraxinus texensis 7
Fraxinus velutina 7
Genista spp. 2—4
Ginkgo biloba 8
Gleditsia triacanthos 8
Gymnocladus dioica 8
Helianthemum nummularium
    2
Hippophaë rhamnoides 6
Idesia polycarpa 7

Indigofera incarnata 3
Indigofera kirilowii 3
Juniperus spp. 2—7 (most)
Lagerstroemia indica 6
Laurus nobilis 6
Ledum spp. 2—3
Leiophyllum buxifolium 2
Leucophyllum frutescens 5
Loiseleuria procumbens 2
Lotus corniculatus 2
Lycium halimifolium 5
Maackia spp. 7
Macfadyena unguis-cati 1
Malus angustifolia 6
Malus coronaria 6
Malus glaucescens 5
Malux ×heterophylla 6
Malus ioensis 6
Malus platycarpa 6
Malus ×soulardii 6
Melia azedarach 6

Myrtus communis 4−5
Nerium oleander 6
Paliurus spina-christi 6
Parkinsonia aculeata 6
Passiflora spp. 1&2
Persea spp. 6−7
Phellodendron spp. 7−8
Picea asperata 8
Picea engelmannii 8
Picea glauca 8
Picea mariana 8
Picea omorika 8
Picea orientalis 8
Picea rubens 8
Picrasma quassioides 6
Pinus albicaulis 6
Pinus aristata 4−6
Pinus banksiana 8
Pinus bungeana 6−7
Pinus cembra 6−8
Pinus contorta 6−8
Pinus echinata 8
Pinus edulis 7
Pinus elliottii 8

Pinus flexilis 8
Pinus halepensis 7
Pinus jeffreyi 8
Pinus palustris 8
Pinus pinaster 7−8
Pinus ponderosa 8
Pinus sibirica 8
Pinus sylvestris 8
Pinus taeda 8
Pinus virginiana 7
Populus spp. 6−8
Potentilla spp. 2−4
Prunus spp. 3−8 (deciduous spp.)
Ptelea trifoliata 6
Pterocarya spp. 8
Pterostyrax spp. 6−7
Punica granatum 6
Pyrus spp. 7
Quercus spp. 7−8
Rhus spp. 4−6 (most)
Robinia ×ambigua 7
Robinia pseudoacacia 8
Robinia viscosa 7

Rosa spp. 3−5 (deciduous spp.)
Sabal minor 3−4
Salix spp. 2−8
Santolina spp. 3
Sapium sebiferum 7
Sassafras albidum 7−8
Sciadopitys verticillata 6−7
Securinega suffruticosa 4
Sequoiadendron giganteum 8
Serenoa repens 3−4
Sesbania punicea 5
Shepherdia spp. 5−6
Sophora spp. 5−8
Sorbus spp. 6−8
Stachyurus praecox 5
Syringa spp. 4−7
Tamarix spp. 4−5
Trifolium incarnatum 3
Umbellularia californica 7−8
Vaccinium vitis-idaea 2
Wisteria spp. 1
Yucca spp. 3−5
Ziziphus jujuba 6

O. Plants that Require Shade in Summer, in at Least Parts of Their Useful Ranges

Abies homolepis 8
Acer davidii 7
Acer grosseri 6
Acer pensylvanicum 7
Acer spicatum 6
Ajuga spp. 2
Ardisia spp. 2−4
Asarum spp. 2
Aspidistra elatior 3
Berberis spp. 3−5 (evergreen spp.)
Cephalotaxus spp. 4−5
Chimaphila umbellata 2
Chimonanthus praecox 5
Clematis alpina 1
Clematis armandii 1
Clematis delavayi 1
Clematis florida 1
Clematis lanuginosa 1
Clematis ×lawsoniana 1
Clematis macropetala 1
Clematis montana 1
Clematis occidentalis 1

Clematis patens 1
Clematis viticella 1
Convallaria majalis 2
Cornus alternifolia 6
Cornus florida 6−7
Cornus nuttallii 6
Cyrtomium falcatum 3
Daphne spp. 3−4 (evergreen spp.)
Epigaea repens 2
Epimedium spp. 2
Euonymus japonica 5
×Fatshedera lizei 4
Fatsia japonica 4−5
Galax urceolata 2
Galium odoratum 2
Gardenia jasminoides 4
Gaultheria spp. 1&2−3
Hamamelis virginiana 6
Hosta spp. 2−3
Ilex ×altaclarensis 7
Ilex aquifolium 6
Ilex ×aquipernyi 6

Ilex crenata 3−5
Ilex fargesii 6
Ilex integra 6
Ilex ×koehneana 7
Ilex latifolia 6
Ilex sugerokii 5
Ilex yunnanensis 5
Indigofera divaricata 3
Itea spp. 4−5
Leucothoë spp. 4−5
Lindera spp. 4−6
Loropetalum chinense 5
Mitchella repens 2
Pachysandra spp. 2
Paeonia spp. 4
Paxistima spp. 2−3
Pernettya mucronata 3
Pileostegia viburnoides 1&2
Podocarpus macrophyllus 5−7
Podophyllum peltatum 2
Rhododendron arboreum 7
Rhododendron austrinum 5
Rhododendron bakeri 3−5

Rhododendron brachycarpum 5
Rhododendron calendulaceum 5
Rhododendron carolinianum 4
Rhododendron catawbiense 5
Rhododendron caucasicum 3
Rhododendron chapmanii 4
Rhododendron dauricum 4
Rhododendron decorum 6
Rhododendron degronianum 4
Rhododendron flammeum 5
Rhododendron fortunei 5
Rhododendron ×gandavense 5
Rhododendron griffithianum 6
Rhododendron indicum 4
Rhododendron kaempferi 5

Rhododendron keiskei 5
Rhododendron kiusianum 3
Rhododendron ×laetevirens 4
Rhododendron luteum 5
Rhododendron maximum 6
Rhododendron minus 5−6
Rhododendron mucronatum 4
Rhododendron mucronulatum 4
Rhododendron obtusum 3
Rhododendron ponticum 5
Rhododendron prunifolium 5
Rhododendron pulchrum 4
Rhododendron simsii 5
Rhododendron smirnowii 5
Rhododendron yakusimanum 3
Rhododendron yedoense 4

Rubus odoratus 5
Sarcococca spp. 4
Saxifraga stolonifera 2
Shortia galacifolia 2
Skimmia spp. 3
Stewartia spp. 6−7
Taxus spp. 3−6
Tiarella cordifolia 2
Torreya spp. 5−7
Trachelospermum spp. 1&2
Tsuga spp. 3−8
Vinca spp. 2
Viola spp. 2

P. Plants that Require Shade in Winter, in at Least Parts of Their Useful Ranges

Arctostaphylos spp. 2&5
Ardisia spp. 2−4
Asarum spp. 2
Aspidistra elatior 3
Berberis spp. 3−5 (evergreen spp.)
Bruckenthalia spiculifolia 2
Buxus spp. 3−4
Calluna vulgaris 2
Camellia spp. 6
Cephalotaxus spp. 4−5
Chamaecyparis lawsoniana 3−7
Chimaphila umbellata 2
Cyrtomium falcatum 3
Daboecia cantabrica 3
Daphne spp. 3−4 (evergreen spp.)
Epigaea repens 2
Erica spp. 2−3
Euonymus fortunei 1&2−4
×Fatshedera lizei 4
Fatsia japonica 4−5
Galax urceolata 2
Gaylussacia brachycera 2
Hedera spp. 1&2
Ilex ×altaclarensis 7
Ilex aquifolium 6
Ilex ×aquipernyi 6

Ilex fargesii 6
Ilex integra 6
Ilex ×koehneana 7
Ilex latifolia 6
Ilex ×meserveae 4
Ilex opaca 6
Ilex pedunculosa 6
Ilex rugosa 3
Kalmia latifolia 5
Lamiastrum galeobdolon 2
Lamium maculatum 2
Leucothoë spp. 4−5 (evergreen spp.)
Loropetalum chinense 5
×Mahoberberis spp. 3−4
Mahonia spp. 3−5 (most)
Pachysandra spp. 2
Paeonia spp. 4
Paxistima spp. 2−3
Pieris spp. 1&3−5
Pileostegia viburnoides 1&2
Podocarpus macrophyllus 5−7
Rhododendron arboreum 7
Rhododendron brachycarpum 5
Rhododendron carolinianum 4
Rhododendron catawbiense 5
Rhododendron caucasicum 3
Rhododendron chapmanii 4

Rhododendron decorum 6
Rhododendron degronianum 4
Rhododendron fastigiatum 2
Rhododendron ferrugineum 3
Rhododendron fortunei 5
Rhododendron griffithianum 6
Rhododendron hirsutum 3
Rhododendron impeditum 3
Rhododendron indicum 4
Rhododendron kaempferi 5
Rhododendron keiskei 3−5
Rhododendron kiusianum 3
Rhododendron ×laetevirens 4
Rhododendron lapponicum 2
Rhododendron maximum 6
Rhododendron micranthum 5
Rhododendron minus 5−6
Rhododendron mucronatum 4
Rhododendron obtusum 3
Rhododendron ponticum 5
Rhododendron pulchrum 4
Rhododendron russatum 3
Rhododendron scintillans 3
Rhododendron simsii 5
Rhododendron smirnowii 5
Rhododendron yakusimanum 3
Sarcococca spp. 4
Saxifraga stolonifera 2

Sciadopitys verticillata 6−7
Sequoia sempervirens 8
Sequoiadendron giganteum 8
Shortia galacifolia 2
Skimmia spp. 3
Taxus spp. 3−6

Thuja spp. 3−8
Thujopsis dolobrata 5
Tiarella cordifolia 2
Torreya spp. 5−7
Viburnum davidii 3
Viburnum japonicum 5

Viburnum odoratissimum 5−6
Viburnum rhytidophyllum 5
Viburnum suspensum 4
Vinca spp. 2

Q. Plants that Tolerate Full Shade in Summer in at Least Parts of Their Useful Ranges

Acanthopanax sieboldianus 5
Acer circinatum 6
Actinidia arguta 1
Akebia spp. 1&2
Arundinaria spp. 2−3&6
Asarum spp. 2
Asimina triloba 6−7
Aspidistra elatior 3
Bambusa glaucescens 5−6
Celastrus spp. 1&2
Cephalotaxus spp. 4−5
Cornus amomum 5
Cornus drummondii 5−6
Cornus mas 6
Cornus officinalis 6
Cornus purpusii 5
Cyrtomium falcatum 3
Daphne spp. 3−4 (evergreen spp.)
Daphniphyllum macropodum 6
Decumaria barbara 1&2
Epimedium spp. 2

Euonymus fortunei 1&2−4
Euonymus obovata 2
×Fatshedera lizei 4
Fatsia japonica 4−5
Ficus spp. 1&5−6
Galax urceolata 2
Gaylussacia brachycera 2
Hamamelis virginiana 6
Hydrangea anomala 1&2
Hydrangea quercifolia 4−5
Liriope spp. 2
Lonicera henryi 1&2
Lonicera japonica 1&2
Loropetalum chinense 5
Menispermum canadense 1&2
Nepeta mussinii 2
Ophiopogon japonicus 2
Pachysandra spp. 2
Parthenocissus spp. 1&2
Phyllostachys spp. 6−7
Pileostegia viburnoides 1&2
Podocarpus macrophyllus 5−7
Podophyllum peltatum 2

Sarcococca spp. 4
Sasa spp. 3−4
Saxifraga stolonifera 2
Schizophragma hydrangeoides 1&2
Shortia galacifolia 2
Skimmia spp. 3
Smilax spp. 1
Taxus spp. 3−6
Tiarella cordifolia 2
Torreya spp. 5−7
Trachelospermum spp. 1&2
Tsuga spp. 3−8
Vaccinium spp. 2−6 (most)
Viburnum acerifolium 4
Viburnum alnifolium 5
Viburnum bracteatum 5
Viburnum dentatum 6
Viburnum molle 5
Viburnum rafinesquianum 4
Vinca spp. 2
Viola spp. 2

R. Plants that Tolerate Strong Winds, in at Least Parts of Their Useful Ranges

Abies concolor 8
Abies koreana 7
Abies lasiocarpa 8
Acanthopanax sieboldianus 5
Acer ginnala 6
Acer mandshuricum 6
Acer maximowiczianum 7
Acer negundo 8
Aegopodium podagraria 2
Aesculus glabra 7
Amorpha spp. 3&6
Antigonon leptopus 1
Artemisia spp. 3−5

Bumelia lanuginosa 6
Callistemon citrinus 5−6
Caragana spp. 3−6
Cassiope tetragona 2
Castanea spp. 6−8
Catalpa spp. 7−8
Ceanothus spp. 3
Celtis spp. 7−8
Cephalanthus occidentalis 5
Ceratiola ericoides 4
Cercis spp. 6−7
Chaenomeles spp. 3−4
Cinnamomum camphora 7

Cistus spp. 3−5
Clematis tangutica 1
Clematis texensis 1
Comptonia peregrina 2
Corema conradii 2
Cornus alba 5
Cornus alternifolia 6
Cornus hessei 3
Cornus racemosa 5
Cornus rugosa 5
Cornus sanguinea 5
Cornus sericea 5
Cornus stricta 5

Coronilla varia 2
Corylus spp. 5−8
Cotoneaster acutifolius 5
Cotoneaster apiculatus 3
Cotoneaster divaricatus 4
Cotoneaster lucidus 5
Crataegus spp. 5−7 (most)
Cydonia spp. 6
Diervilla spp. 3−4
Dirca palustris 4
Elaeagnus spp. 5−6
Empetrum spp. 2
Escallonia spp. 3−6
Eucalyptus spp. 6−7
Eucommia ulmoides 7
Euonymus alata 5
Euonymus atropurpurea 6
Euonymus europaea 6
Euonymus hamiltoniana 6
Euonymus latifolia 6
Euonymus nana 3
Euonymus phellomana 6
Euonymus sachalinensis 6
Euphorbia cyparissias 2
Fontanesia fortunei 5
Fraxinus pennsylvanica 8
Fraxinus texensis 7
Fraxinus velutina 7
Genista spp. 2−4
Ginkgo biloba 8
Gleditsia triacanthos 8
Gymnocladus dioica 8
Helianthemum nummularium
   2
Hippophaë rhamnoides 6
Indigofera incarnata 3
Indigofera kirilowii 3
Juniperus spp. 2−7
Kalmia poliifolia 3
Larix spp. 8
Ledum spp. 2−3
Leiophyllum buxifolium 2
Lespedeza spp. 3&5
Leucophyllum frutescens 5
Ligustrum amurense 5
Ligustrum quihoui 5
Ligustrum vulgare 4−6
Loiseleuria procumbens 2
Lonicera nitida 4
Lonicera pileata 3

Lotus corniculatus 2
Lycium halimifolium 5
Maclura pomifera 7
Morus spp. 7−8
Myrica spp. 4−7
Myrtus communis 4−5
Nerium oleander 6
Parkinsonia aculeata 6
Persea spp. 6−7
Picea abies 3−8
Picea engelmannii 8
Picea glauca 8
Picea mariana 7−8
Picea pungens 8
Picea rubens 8
Pinus albicaulis 6
Pinus aristata 4−6
Pinus banksiana 8
Pinus bungeana 6−7
Pinus cembra 6−8
Pinus contorta 6−8
Pinus echinata 8
Pinus edulis 7
Pinus flexilis 8
Pinus halepensis 7
Pinus jeffreyi 8
Pinus mugo 4−6
Pinus nigra 8
Pinus pinaster 7−8
Pinus ponderosa 8
Pinus resinosa 8
Pinus rigida 7−8
Pinus sibirica 8
Pinus sylvestris 8
Pinus taeda 8
Pinus uncinata 7−8
Pinus virginiana 7
Pittosporum tobira 5
Polygonum spp. 1&3−5
Populus spp. 6−8 (most)
Potentilla spp. 2−4
Prinsepia spp. 4−5
Prunus alleghaniensis 5
Prunus americana 5
Prunus angustifolia 5
Prunus besseyi 3
Prunus ×cistena 5
Prunus japonica 4
Prunus maritima 4
Prunus mexicana 6

Prunus nigra 5−6
Prunus pensylvanica 7
Prunus pumila 4
Prunus tomentosa 5
Pseudotsuga menziesii 8
Ptelea trifoliata 6
Pueraria lobata 1&3
Pyrus spp. 7
Quercus alba 8
Quercus bicolor 8
Quercus macrocarpa 8
Quercus mongolica 7−8
Quercus muehlenbergii 8
Quercus stellata 7−8
Raphiolepis spp. 3−4
Rhus aromatica 4−5
Ribes spp. 4−5
Robinia ×ambigua 7
Robinia pseudoacacia 8
Robinia viscosa 7
Rosa bracteata 1&5
Rosa carolina 3
Rosa laevigata 1&5
Rosa multiflora 5
Rosa nitida 3
Rosa odorata 3
Rosa palustris 4
Rosa roxburghii 5
Rosa rugosa 4
Rosa setigera 5
Rosa virginiana 4
Rosa wichuraiana 1&2
Sabal minor 3−4
Salix exigua 6
Salix purpurea 5
Salix repens 2−3
Salix rosmarinifolia 4
Salix uva-ursi 2
Sedum spp. 2
Sempervivum tectorum 2
Serenoa repens 3−4
Shepherdia spp. 5−6
Smilax spp. 1
Symphoricarpos spp. 3−4
Tamarix spp. 4−5
Trifolium incarnatum 3
Umbellularia californica 7−8
Vaccinium spp. 2−6 (most)
Viburnum lantana 6
Yucca spp. 3−5

S. Plants that Tolerate Little Wind, in at Least Parts of Their Useful Ranges

Acer circinatum 6
Acer davidii 7
Acer grosseri 6
Acer japonicum 6
Acer palmatum 6
Arctostaphylos spp. 2&5
Ardisia spp. 2−4
Aristolochia durior 1
Arundinaria spp. 2−3&6
Asarum spp. 2
Asimina triloba 6−7
Aspidistra elatior 3
Aucuba japonica 5
Bambusa glaucescens 5−6
Berberis spp. 3−5 (evergreen
    spp.)
Buxus spp. 3−4
Calocedrus decurrens 7
Camellia spp. 6
Cephalotaxus spp. 4−5
Chamaecyparis lawsoniana
    3−7
Chimaphila umbellata 2
Clerodendrum spp. 4−6
Cornus florida 6−7
Cornus kousa 6
Corylopsis spp. 4−5
Cotoneaster frigidus 6
Cotoneaster lacteus 5
Cotoneaster salicifolius 5
Cotoneaster ×watereri 6
Cryptomeria japonica 8
Cyrtomium falcatum 3
Cytisus spp. 2−4&6
Danaë racemosa 3
Daphne spp. 3−4 (evergreen
    spp.)
Daphniphyllum macropodum
    6

Davidia involucrata 6−7
Decumaria barbara 1&2
Epigaea repens 2
Epimedium spp. 2
×Fatshedera lizei 4
Fatsia japonica 4−5
Ficus spp. 1&5−6
Firmiana simplex 6−7
Franklinia alatamaha 6
Fuchsia magellanica 3−4
Galax urceolata 2
Hemerocallis spp. 3
Hibiscus spp. 5−6
Hosta spp. 2−3
Hydrangea spp. 3−6 (most)
Ilex spp. 3−7 (most evergreen
    spp.)
Laburnum spp. 6
Leucothoë spp. 4−5
Magnolia acuminata 8
Magnolia fraseri 7
Magnolia hypoleuca 7−8
Magnolia macrophylla 7
Magnolia sieboldii 6
Magnolia tripetala 7
×Mahoberberis spp. 3−4
Mahonia spp. 3−5
Oxydendrum arboreum 7−8
Pachysandra spp. 2
Paeonia spp. 4
Pieris spp. 1&3−5
Pinus wallichiana 8
Podocarpus macrophyllus 5−7
Podophyllum peltatum 2
Rhododendron spp. 3−7
    (most)
Rubus odoratus 5
Ruscus aculeatus 3
Sarcococca spp. 4

Sasa spp. 3−4
Saxifraga stolonifera 2
Schizophragma hydrangeoides
    1&2
Sciadopitys verticillata 6−7
Sequoia sempervirens 8
Sequoiadendron giganteum 8
Shortia galacifolia 2
Skimmia spp. 3
Stephanandra spp. 4
Stewartia spp. 6−7
Symplocos spp. 6
Taiwania cryptomerioides 8
Taxus spp. 3−6
Teucrium chamaedrys 2
Thuja spp. 3−8
Thujopsis dolobrata 5
Tiarella cordifolia 2
Torreya spp. 5−7
Tsuga spp. 3−8
Viburnum acerifolium 4
Viburnum alnifolium 5
Viburnum davidii 3
Viburnum japonicum 5
Viburnum odoratissimum 5−6
Viburnum plicatum 5
Viburnum rhytidophyllum 5
Viburnum sieboldii 6
Viburnum suspensum 4
Viburnum tinus 5
Viburnum utile 4
Vinca spp. 2
Viola spp. 2
Vitis spp. 1
Wisteria spp. 1
Xanthorhiza simplicissima 2

T. Plants that Tolerate Wet Soil

Acer pensylvanicum 7
Acer rubrum 8
Acer saccharinum 8
Aegopodium podagraria 2
Aleurites fordii 6

Alnus spp. 6−7
Arundinaria spp. 2−3&6
Asimina triloba 6−7
Aspidistra elatior 3
Bambusa glaucescens 5−6

Betula nigra 8
Bignonia capreolata 1
Calocedrus decurrens 7
Calycanthus spp. 4−5
Campsis spp. 1

Carya illinoinensis 8
Catalpa spp. 7—8
Celastrus spp. 1&2
Cephalanthus occidentalis 5
Chaenomeles spp. 3—4
Chamaecyparis spp. 3—8
Chimonanthus praecox 5
Chionanthus spp. 6
Clethra spp. 5—6
Cliftonia monophylla 5
Cocculus carolina 1
Convallaria majalis 2
Cornus alba 5
Cornus sericea 5
Cryptomeria japonica 8
Cydonia spp. 6
Cyrilla racemiflora 6
Cyrtomium falcatum 3
Decumaria barbara 1&2
Diospyros spp. 7
Dirca palustris 4
Forsythia spp. 4—5 (most)
Fothergilla spp. 3—5
Fraxinus americana 8
Fraxinus biltmoreana 7
Fraxinus caroliniana 7
Fraxinus nigra 8
Fraxinus quadrangulata 8
Fraxinus tomentosa 8
Fuchsia magellanica 3—4
Hemerocallis spp. 3
Hibiscus spp. 5—6
Holodiscus discolor 6
Hydrangea spp. 1&2—6

Ilex spp. 3—7
Illicium spp. 5—6
Indigofera spp. 3
Itea spp. 4—5
Jasminum floridum 4
Jasminum mesneyi 4
Kalmia angustifolia 3
Kalmia poliifolia 3
Kerria japonica 4
Kolkwitzia amabilis 5
Larix spp. 8
Ledum spp. 2—3
Leitneria floridana 5—6
Lespedeza spp. 3&5
Ligustrum spp. 4—6
Lindera spp. 4—6
Liquidambar spp. 8
Liriope spp. 2
Lonicera spp. 1&2—6
Maclura pomifera 7
Magnolia spp. 5—8
Menispermum canadense 1&2
Metasequoia glyptostroboides 8
Neillia sinensis 4
Nyssa spp. 8
Osmanthus spp. 4—6
Phyllostachys spp. 6—7
Physocarpus opulifolius 4—5
Platanus spp. 8
Populus spp. 6—8 (most)
Potentilla spp. 2—4 (most)
Quercus bicolor 8
Quercus ellipsoidalis 8
Quercus lyrata 8

Quercus nigra 8
Quercus palustris 8
Quercus phellos 7—8
Quercus virginiana 7
Rhododendron atlanticum 3
Rhododendron canadense 3
Rhododendron serrulatum 6
Rhododendron vaseyi 5
Rhododendron viscosum 5
Rosa carolina 3
Rosa multiflora 5
Rosa palustris 4
Rubus hispidus 4
Sabal minor 3—4
Salix spp. 2—8
Sambucus spp. 5—6
Sapium sebiferum 7
Sasa spp. 3—4
Shepherdia spp. 5—6
Smilax spp. 1
Sorbaria spp. 4—5
Staphylea spp. 6
Stephanandra spp. 4
Taiwania cryptomerioides 8
Taxodium distichum 8
Thuja spp. 3—8
Thujopsis dolobrata 5
Viburnum bracteatum 5
Viburnum cassinoides 4
Viburnum dentatum 6
Viburnum lentago 6
Viburnum molle 5
Viola spp. 2
Xanthorhiza simplicissima 2

U. Plants that Tolerate Dry Soil

Acanthopanax sieboldianus 5
Acer ginnala 6
Acer maximowicziana 7
Acer negundo 7
Acer saccharinum 8
Acer tataricum 6
Aegopodium podagraria 2
Aesculus glabra 7
Agave americana 4
Ailanthus altissima 7—8
Albizia julibrissin 6
Amorpha spp. 3&6
Antigonon leptopus 1
Arctostaphylos uva-ursi 2

Artemisia spp. 3—5
Asimina triloba 6—7
Baccharis halimifolia 5
Berberis gilgiana 4
Berberis koreana 4
Berberis ×mentorensis 4
Berberis vulgaris 5
Bignonia capreolata 1
Callistemon citrinus 5—6
Campsis spp. 1
Caragana spp. 3—6
Caryopteris spp. 3—4
Castanea spp. 6—8
Catalpa spp. 7—8

Ceanothus spp. 3
Cedrela sinensis 6—7
Celastrus spp. 1&2
Celtis spp. 7—8
Cercis spp. 6—7
Chaenomeles spp. 3—4
Choisya ternata 5
Cinnamomum camphora 7
Cistus spp. 3—5
Cladrastis spp. 7—8
Clematis tangutica 1
Clematis texensis 1
Clerodendrum spp. 4—6
Cleyera japonica 5

Comptonia peregrina 2
Cornus racemosa 5
Coronilla varia 2
Corylus spp. 5—8
Cotinus spp. 6—7
Cotoneaster spp. 2—6 (most)
Crataegus spp. 5—7
Cydonia spp. 6
Cyrilla racemiflora 6
Cytisus spp. 2—6
Diervilla spp. 3—4
Elaeagnus spp. 5—6
Elsholtzia stauntonii 3
Escallonia spp. 3—6
Eucalyptus spp. 6—7
Eucommia ulmoides 7
Euphorbia cyparissias 2
Eurya spp. 3—5
Evodia spp. 6—7
Fagus sylvatica 8
Ficus spp. 1&5—6
Fontanesia spp. 5
Galium spp. 2
Genista spp. 2—4
Ginkgo biloba 8
Gleditsia triacanthos 8
Gymnocladus dioica 8
Helianthemum nummularium
  2
Hippophaë rhamnoides 6
Hypericum kalmianum 3
Hypericum prolificum 3
Indigofera spp. 3
Jasminum spp. 1&3—5
Juglans spp. 7—8
Juniperus spp. 2—8
Koelreuteria spp. 7
Kolkwitzia amabilis 5
Laurus nobilis 6
Lavandula angustifolia 3
Ledum spp. 2—3
Leiophyllum buxifolium 2
Lespedeza spp. 3&5
Leucophyllum frutescens 5

Liriope spp. 2
Lonicera spp. 1&2—6
Lotus corniculatus 2
Lycium halimifolium 5
Maackia spp. 7
Maclura pomifera 7
Melia azedarach 6
Morus spp. 7—8
Myrica spp. 4—7
Myrtus communis 4—5
Paliurus spina-christi 6
Parkinsonia aculeata 6
Passiflora spp. 1&2
Persea spp. 6—7
Phellodendron spp. 7—8
Photinia spp. 5—6
Physocarpus opulifolius 4—5
Picea engelmannii 8
Picea pungens 8
Picrasma quassioides 6
Pinus spp. 4—8 (most)
Pistacia chinensis 8
Pittosporum tobira 5
Polygonum spp. 1&3—5
Poncirus trifoliata 6
Populus angustifolia 7
Populus balsamifera 8
Populus trichocarpa 8
Prinsepia spp. 4—5
Prunus alleghaniensis 5
Prunus americana 5
Prunus angustifolia 5
Prunus besseyi 3
Prunus ×blireiana 6
Prunus cerasifera 6
Prunus ×cistena 5
Prunus glandulosa 4
Prunus japonica 4
Prunus maritima 4
Prunus mexicana 6
Prunus nigra 5—6
Prunus pensylvanica 7
Prunus pumila 4
Prunus tenella 4

Prunus tomentosa 5
Prunus triloba 5—6
Ptelea trifoliata 6
Pueraria lobata 1&3
Punica granatum 6
Pyracantha spp. 4—6
Pyrus spp. 7
Quercus macrocarpa 8
Quercus mongolica 7—8
Quercus muehlenbergii 8
Quercus prinus 8
Quercus stellata 7—8
Quercus velutina 8
Raphiolepis spp. 3—4
Rhus spp. 4—6
Ribes spp. 4—5
Robinia spp. 4&7—8
Rosa spp. 1&2—5 (most)
Ruscus aculeatus 3
Sabal minor 3—4
Santolina spp. 3
Sapindus drummondii 7
Sapium sebiferum 7
Sedum spp. 2
Sempervivum tectorum 2
Serenoa repens 3—4
Sesbania punicea 5
Shepherdia spp. 5—6
Smilax spp. 1
Sophora spp. 5—6&8
Spiraea spp. 3—5
Symphoricarpos spp. 3—4
Tamarix spp. 4—5
Ternstroemia gymnanthera 6
Trifolium incarnatum 3
Umbellularia californica 7—8
Vaccinium spp. 2—6 (most)
Waldsteinia fragarioides 2
Wisteria spp. 1
Xanthoceras sorbifolium 6
Yucca spp. 3—5
Zanthoxylum spp. 6
Ziziphus jujuba 6

V. Plants that Require Distinctly Acidic Soil (pH 6.0 or Lower)

Andromeda polifolia 2
Arctostaphylos spp. 2,5
Calluna vulgaris 2
Cassiope tetragona 2

Chamaedaphne calyculata
  3—4
Chimaphila umbellata 2
Ceratiola ericoides 4

Clethra spp. 5—6
Cleyera japonica 5
Cliftonia monophylla 5
Comptonia peregrina 2

Corema conradii 2
Cornus canadensis 2
Corylopsis spp. 4−5
Cryptomeria japonica 8
Cunninghamia lanceolata 8
Cyrilla racemiflora 6
Cyrtomium falcatum 3
Daboecia cantabrica 3
Elliottia racemosa 5−6
Elsholtzia stauntonii 3
Empetrum spp. 2
Enkianthus spp. 4−6
Epigaea repens 2
Erica spp. 2−3
Eurya spp. 3−5
Firmiana simplex 6−7
Fothergilla spp. 3−5
Franklinia alatamaha 6
Galax urceolata 2
Galium odoratum 2
Gardenia jasminoides 4
Gaultheria spp. 2−3

Gaylussacia brachycera 2
Gordonia lasianthus 7
Hydrangea macrophylla 3
  (blue)
Idesia polycarpa 7
Ilex spp. 3−7 (most)
Kalmia spp. 3,5
Ledum spp. 2−3
Leiophyllum buxifolium 2
Leitneria floridana 5−6
Leucothoë spp. 4−5
Loiseleuria procumbens 2
Loropetalum chinense 5
Lyonia spp. 4
Michelia figo 5
Mitchella repens 2
Nyssa spp. 8
Oxydendrum arboreum 7−8
Pachysandra spp. 2
Pernettya mucronata 3
Phoenix canariensis 7
Pieris spp. 1&3−5

Pinus elliottii 8
Pinus palustris 8
Potentilla tridentata 2
Pseudolarix kaempferi 8
Quercus coccinea 8
Quercus palustris 8
Quercus phellos 8
Rhododendron spp. 2−7
Sabal minor 3−4
Sciadopitys verticillata 6−7
Serenoa repens 3−4
Shortia galacifolia 2
Stachyurus praecox 5
Stewartia spp. 6−7
Symplocos spp. 6
Taiwania cryptomerioides 8
Ternstroemia gymnanthera 6
Trachycarpus fortunei 6
Tripetaleia paniculata 4
Vaccinium spp. 2−6
Xanthorhiza simplicissima 2
Zenobia pulverulenta 4

W. Plants that Tolerate Neutral or Alkaline Soil (pH 7.0 or Higher)

Abeliophyllum distichum 4
Abies concolor 8
Abies lasiocarpa 8
Abies procera 8
Acanthopanax sieboldianus 5
Acer spp. 5−8 (most)
Actinidia spp. 1
Aesculus glabra 7
Agave americana 4
Ailanthus altissima 7−8
Akebia spp. 1&2
Albizia julibrissin 6
Aleurites fordii 6
Alnus spp. 6−7
Amelanchier spp. 3−7
Amorpha spp. 3&6
Ampelopsis spp. 1
Antigonon leptopus 1
Aralia spp. 6−7
Aristolochia durior 1
Artemisia spp. 3−5
Arundinaria spp. 2−3&6
Asimina triloba 6−7
Baccharis halimifolia 5
Bambusa glaucescens 5−6
Berberis spp. 3−5 (most)

Bignonia capreolata 1
Callistemon citrinus 5−6
Campsis spp. 1
Caragana spp. 3−6
Carya spp. 8
Caryopteris spp. 3−4
Cassia corymbosa 5
Castanea spp. 6−8
Catalpa spp. 7−8
Ceanothus spp. 3
Cedrela sinensis 6−7
Celtis spp. 7−8
Cephalanthus occidentalis 5
Cercidiphyllum japonicum 8
Cercis spp. 6−7
Chaenomeles spp. 3−4
Chionanthus spp. 6
Choisya ternata 5
Cinnamomum camphora 7
Cistus spp. 3−5
Cladrastis spp. 7−8
Clematis spp. 1
Cocculus carolinus 1
Colutea arborescens 5
Cornus spp. 3−7 (most)
Coronilla varia 2

Corylus spp. 5−8
Cotoneaster spp. 2−6
Crataegus spp. 5−7
Cytisus spp. 2−6
Daphne spp. 2−4
Decumaria barbara 1&2
Diervilla spp. 3−4
Diospyros spp. 7 ·
Dirca palustris 4
Edgeworthia papyrifera 4
Elaeagnus spp. 5−6
Escallonia spp. 3−6
Eucalyptus spp. 6−7
Eucommia ulmoides 7
Euonymus spp. 1&2−6
Euphorbia cyparissias 2
Evodia spp. 6−7
Exochorda spp. 5−6
Feijoa sellowiana 6
Ficus spp. 1&5−6
Fontanesia spp. 5
Forestiera acuminata 5−6
Forsythia spp. 4−5
Fraxinus spp. 6−8
Genista spp. 2−4
Ginkgo biloba 8

Gleditsia triacanthos 8
Gymnocladus dioica 8
Halimodendron halodendron 4
Hamamelis vernalis 5
Hamamelis virginiana 6
Hedera spp. 1&2
Helianthemum nummularium 2
Hemiptelea davidii 6
Hippophaë rhamnoides 6
Holodiscus discolor 6
Hosta spp. 2–3
Hovenia dulcis 6
Hydrangea spp. 1&2–6 (most)
Iberis spp. 2
Indigofera spp. 3
Juglans spp. 7–8
Juniperus spp. 2–8
Kerria japonica 4
Koelreuteria spp. 7
Kolkwitzia amabilis 5
Laburnum spp. 6
Lagerstroemia indica 6
Lamiastrum galeobdolon 2
Lamium maculatum 2
Laurus nobilis 6
Lavandula angustifolia 3
Leptodermis oblonga 3
Lespedeza spp. 3&5
Leucophyllum frutescens 5
Leycesteria formosa 4
Ligustrum spp. 4–6
  (deciduous spp.)
Lindera spp. 4–6
Liriodendron spp. 8
Liriope spp. 2
Lonicera spp. 1&2–6
Lotus corniculatus 2
Lycium halimifolium 5
Maackia spp. 7
Maclura pomifera 7
Magnolia spp. 5–8
×Mahoberberis spp. 3–4
Mahonia spp. 2–5
Malus spp. 5–7
Melia azedarach 6
Menispermum canadense 1&2
Metasequoia glyptostroboides 8
Morus spp. 7–8
Myrtus communis 4–5
Neillia sinensis 4

Nerium oleander 6
Orixa japonica 5
Osmanthus spp. 4–6
Ostrya virginiana 7–8
Paliurus spina-christi 6
Parkinsonia aculeata 6
Parthenocissus spp. 1&2
Passiflora spp. 1&2
Paulownia tomentosa 7
Paxistima spp. 2–3
Persea spp. 6–7
Phellodendron spp. 7–8
Philadelphus spp. 4–5
Phlox spp. 2
Photinia spp. 5–6
Phyllostachys spp. 6–7
Physocarpus opulifolius 4–5
Picea spp. 3–8
Picrasma quassioides 6
Pinus spp. 4–8 (most)
Pistacia chinensis 8
Pittosporum tobira 5
Platanus spp. 8
Podocarpus macrophyllus 5–7
Polygonum spp. 1&3–5
Poncirus trifoliata 6
Populus spp. 6–8
Potentilla spp. 2–4 (most)
Prinsepia spp. 4–5
Prunus spp. 4–8
Pseudotsuga menziesii 8
  (some)
Ptelea trifoliata 6
Pterocarya spp. 8
Pterostyrax spp. 6–7
Pueraria lobata 1&3
Punica granatum 6
Pyracantha spp. 4–6
Pyrus spp. 7
Quercus spp. 7–8 (most)
Raphiolepis spp. 3–4
Rhamnus spp. 4&6
Rhodotypos scandens 4
Rhus spp. 4–6
Ribes spp. 4–5
Robinia spp. 4&7–8
Rosa spp. 1&2–5 (most)
Ruscus aculeatus 3
Salix spp. 2–8
Sambucus spp. 5–6
Santolina spp. 3

Sapindus drummondii 7
Sapium sebiferum 7
Sarcococca spp. 4
Sasa spp. 3–4
Sassafras albidum 7–8
Saxifraga stolonifera 2
Securinega suffruticosa 4
Sedum spp. 2
Sempervivum tectorum 2
Sequoia sempervirens 8
Sequoiadendron giganteum 8
Sesbania punicea 5
Shepherdia spp. 5–6
Smilax spp. 1
Sophora spp. 5–6&8
Sorbaria spp. 4–5
Sorbus spp. 6–8
Spiraea ×arguta 4
Spiraea cantoniensis 5
Spiraea henryi 5
Spiraea nipponica 5
Spiraea thunbergii 4
Spiraea trilobata 4
Spiraea ×vanhouttei 4
Spiraea veitchii 5
Spiraea wilsonii 5
Staphylea spp. 6
Stephanandra spp. 4
Symphoricarpos spp. 3–4
Syringa spp. 4–7
Tamarix spp. 4–5
Taxodium spp. 8
Teucrium chamaedrys 2
Thuja spp. 3–8
Tiarella cordifolia 2
Tilia spp. 6–8
Trifolium incarnatum 3
Ulmus spp. 7–8
Umbellularia californica 7–8
Viburnum spp. 3–6
Vinca spp. 2
Viola spp. 2
Vitis spp. 1
Waldsteinia fragarioides 2
Weigela spp. 4–5
Wisteria spp. 1
Xanthoceras sorbifolium 6
Yucca spp. 3–5
Zanthoxylum spp. 6
Zelkova spp. 7–8
Ziziphus jujuba 6

X. Plants that Tolerate Salt (Seaside or Roadside)

Acer ginnala 6
Acer negundo 7
Acer platanoides 8
Acer pseudoplatanus 8
Aesculus spp. 5—8
Agave americana 4
Ailanthus altissima 7—8
Amelanchier spp. 3—7
Antigonon leptopus 1
Araucaria spp. 8
Arctostaphylos spp. 2&5
Aronia spp. 3—5
Artemisia spp. 3—5
Arundinaria spp. 2—3&6
Baccharis halimifolia 5
Bambusa glaucescens 5—6
Bignonia capreolata 1
Bumelia lanuginosa 6
Buxus harlandii 4
Buxus microphylla 3
Callistemon citrinus 5—6
Calluna vulgaris 2
Celastrus spp. 1&2
Celtis spp. 7—8
Chamaecyparis spp. 3—8
Cinnamomum camphora 7
Cistus spp. 3—5
Clematis maximowicziana 1
Clematis vitalba 1
Cocculus carolinus 1
Coronilla varia 2
Comptonia peregrina 2
Cotoneaster spp. 2—6
Crataegus spp. 5—7 (some)
Cryptomeria japonica 8
×Cupressocyparis leylandii 8
Cupressus spp. 7—8
Cycas revoluta 3—4
Cytisus spp. 2—6
Daboecia cantabrica 3
Elaeagnus spp. 5—6
Empetrum spp. 2
Erica spp. 2—3
Eriobotrya spp. 6
Escallonia spp. 3—6
Eucalyptus spp. 6—7
Eurya spp. 3—5
×Fatshedera lizei 4
Fatsia japonica 4—5

Feijoa sellowiana 6
Ficus spp. 1&5—6
Galium odoratum 2
Gardenia jasminoides 4
Gelsemium sempervirens 1&2
Halimodendron halodendron 4
Hedera spp. 1&2
Hemerocallis spp. 3
Hibiscus spp. 5—6
Hippophaë rhamnoides 6
Hydrangea spp. 1&2—6
Hypericum spp. 2—4
Iberis spp. 2
Ilex ×attenuata 6
Ilex cassine 6
Ilex crenata 3—5
Ilex glabra 6
Ilex opaca 7
Ilex vomitoria 6
Illicium spp. 5—6
Jasminum spp. 1&3—5
Juniperus spp. 2—8 (most)
Lavandula angustifolia 3
Leiophyllum buxifolium 2
Lespedeza spp. 3&5
Leucophyllum frutescens 5
Ligustrum spp 4—6
Liquidambar spp. 8
Liriope spp. 2
Lonicera spp. 1&2—6 (most)
Lotus corniculatus 2
Lycium halimifolium 5
Lyonia spp. 4
Magnolia grandiflora 8
Magnolia virginiana 6—7
Michelia figo 5
Morus spp 7—8
Myrica spp. 4—7
Myrtus communis 4—5
Nerium oleander 6
Nyssa spp. 8
Ophiopogon japonicus 2
Parkinsonia aculeata 6
Passiflora spp. 1&2
Pernettya mucronata 3
Phoenix canariensis 7
Photinia spp. 5—6
Picea pungens 8
Pinus contorta 6—8

Pinus echinata 8
Pinus elliottii 8
Pinus halepensis 7
Pinus mugo 4—6
Pinus nigra 8
Pinus palustris 8
Pinus pinaster 7—8
Pinus rigida 7—8
Pinus sylvestris 6—7
Pinus thunbergiana 6—7
Pittosporum tobira 5
Platanus spp. 8
Podocarpus macrophyllus 5—7
Potentilla spp. 2—4
Prunus caroliniana 6—7
Prunus maritima 4
Prunus serotina 8
Punica granatum 6
Pyracantha spp. 4—6
Quercus ilex 7
Quercus marilandica 7
Quercus nigra 8
Quercus virginiana 7
Raphiolepis spp. 3—4
Rhamnus spp. 4&6
Rhapidophyllum hystrix 3
Rhus spp. 4—6
Robinia spp. 4&7—8
Rosa spp. 1&2—5 (most)
Ruscus aculeatus 3
Sabal minor 3—4
Salix repens 2—3
Salix rosmarinifolia 4
Sambucus spp. 5—6
Sapium sebiferum 7
Schizophragma hydrangeoides
   1&2
Sciadopitys verticillata 6—7
Sedum spp. 2
Sempervivum tectorum 2
Serenoa repens 3—4
Sesbania punicea 5
Shepherdia spp. 5—6
Smilax spp. 1
Spiraea spp. 3—5
Syringa spp. 4—7
Taiwania cryptomerioides 8
Tamarix spp. 4—5
Taxodium distichum 8

Taxus spp. 3–6
Ternstroemia gymnanthera 6
Ulmus crassifolia 7–8
Ulmus parvifolia 7–8
Ulmus pumila 7–8
Umbellularia californica 7–8

Vaccinium spp. 2–6
Viburnum cassinoides 4
Viburnum dentatum 6
Viburnum japonicum 5
Viburnum odoratissimum 5–6
Viburnum suspensum 4

Viburnum tinus 5
Vinca major 2
Viola spp. 2
Vitex spp. 4–6
Yucca spp. 3–5
Zamia floridana 3

INDEX OF PLANT NAMES